U.S. Department of
Homeland Security

United States
Coast Guard

LIGHT LIST

Volume IV

GULF OF MEXICO

Econfina River, Florida to the Rio Grande, Texas

This Light List contains a list of lights, sound
signals, buoys, daybeacons, and other aids to navigation.

IMPORTANT
**THIS LIGHT LIST SHOULD BE CORRECTED
EACH WEEK FROM THE LOCAL NOTICES TO MARINERS
OR NOTICES TO MARINERS AS APPROPRIATE.**

2018

COMDTPUB P16502.4

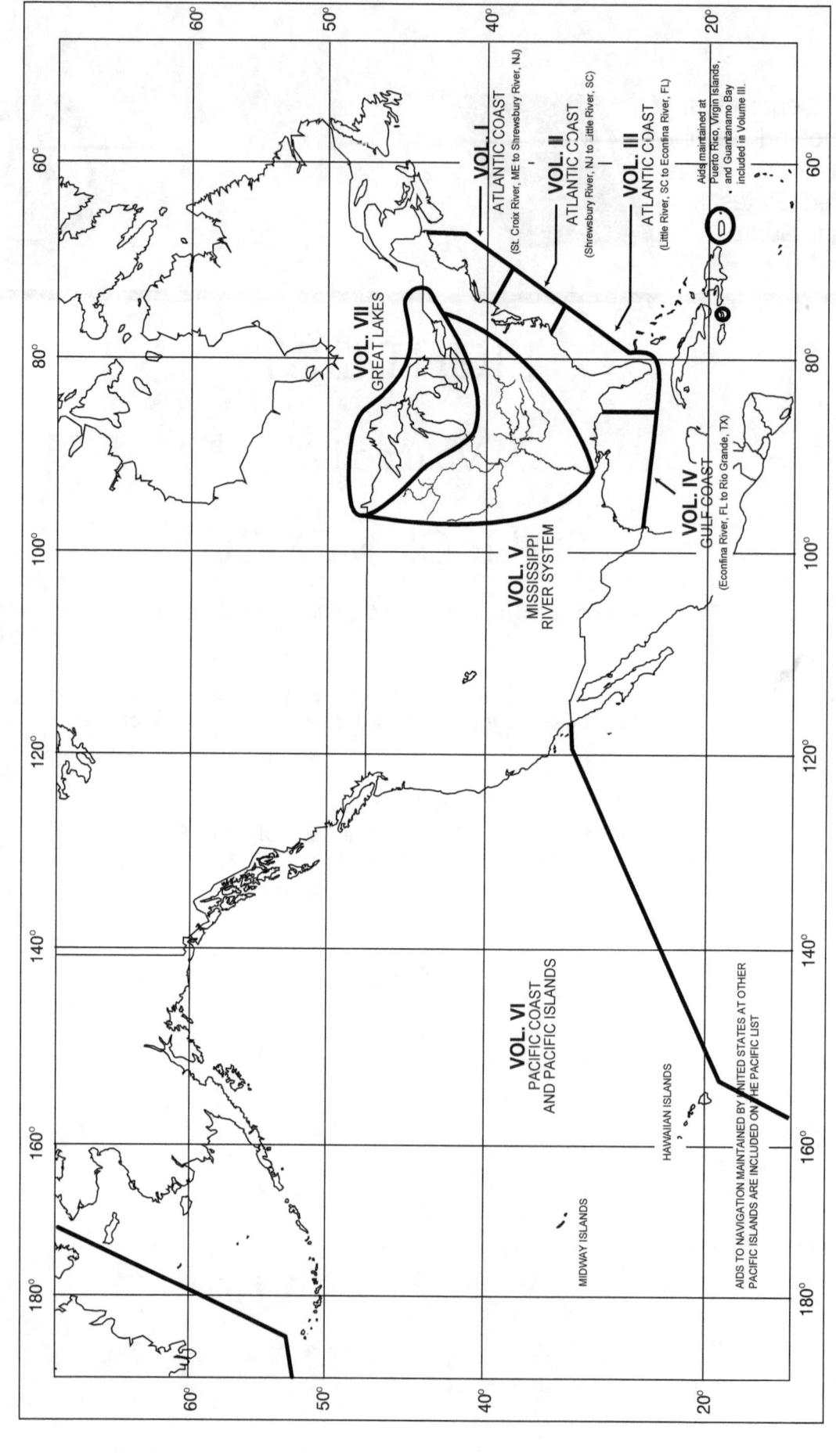

LUMINOUS RANGE DIAGRAM

The nominal range given in this Light List is the maximum distance a given light can be seen when the meteorological visibility is 10 nautical miles. If the existing visibility is less than 10 NM, the range at which the light can be seen will be reduced below its nominal range. And, if the visibility is greater than 10 NM, the light can be seen at greater distances. The distance at which a light may be expected to be seen in the prevailing visibility is called its luminous range.

This diagram enables the mariner to determine the approximate luminous range of a light when the nominal range and the prevailing meteorological visibility are known. The diagram is entered from the bottom border using the nominal range listed in column 6 of this book. The intersection of the nominal range with the appropriate visibility curve (or, more often, a point between two curves) yields, by moving horizontally to the left border, the luminous range.

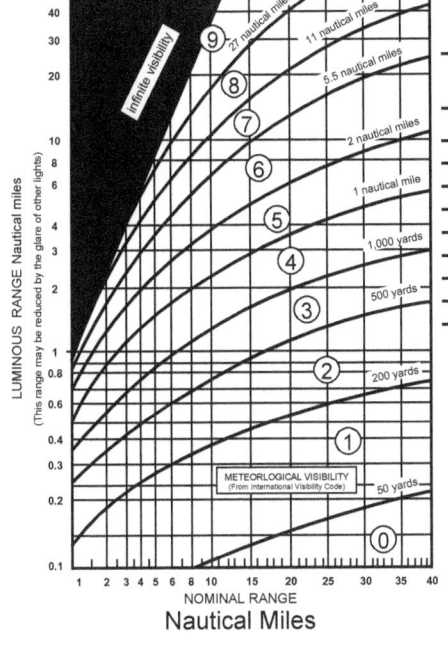
Nautical Miles

METEOROLOGICAL VISIBILITY
(From International Visibility Code)

Code	Metric	Nautical (approximate)
0	less than 50 meters	less than 50 yards
1	50-200 meters	50-200 yards
2	200-500 meters	200-500 yards
3	500-1,000 meters	500-1,000 yards
4	1-2 kilometers	1,000-2,000 yards
5	2-4 kilometers	1-2 nautical miles
6	4-10 kilometers	2-5.5 nautical miles
7	10-20 kilometers	5.5-11 nautical miles
8	20-50 kilometers	11-27 nautical miles
9	greater than 50 km	greater than 27 nm

CAUTION
When using this diagram it must be remembered that:
1. The ranges obtained are approximate.
2. The transparency of the atmosphere may vary between observer and light.
3. Glare from background lighting will reduce the range that lights are sighted.
4. The rolling motion of a vessel and/or of a lighted aid may reduce the distance that lights can be detected or identified.

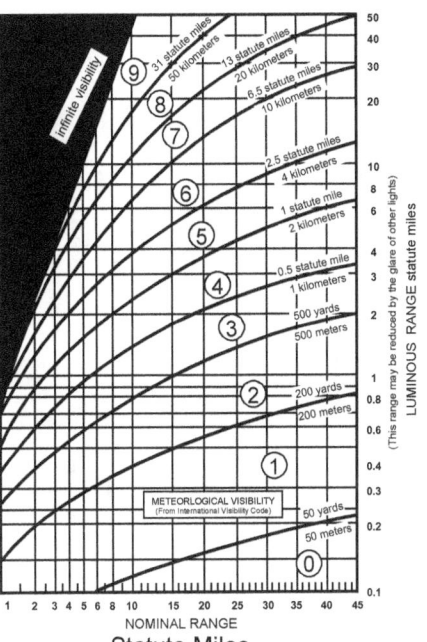
Statute Miles

GEOGRAPHIC RANGE TABLE

The following table gives the approximate geographic range of visibility for an object which may be seen by an observer at sea level. It is necessary to add to the distance for the height of any object the distance corresponding to the height of the observer's eye above sea level.

Height Feet / Meters	Distance Nautical Miles (NM)	Height Feet / Meters	Distance Nautical Miles (NM)	Height Feet / Meters	Distance Nautical Miles (NM)
5/1.5	2.6	70/21.3	9.8	250/76.2	18.5
10/3.1	3.7	75/22.9	10.1	300/91.4	20.3
15/4.6	4.5	80/24.4	10.5	350/106.7	21.9
20/6.1	5.2	85/25.9	10.8	400/121.9	23.4
25/7.6	5.9	90/27.4	11.1	450/137.2	24.8
30/9.1	6.4	95/29.0	11.4	500/152.4	26.2
35/10.7	6.9	100/30.5	11.7	550/167.6	27.4
40/12.2	7.4	110/33.5	12.3	600/182.9	28.7
45/13.7	7.8	120/36.6	12.8	650/198.1	29.8
50/15.2	8.3	130/39.6	13.3	700/213.4	31.0
55/16.8	8.7	140/42.7	13.8	800/243.8	33.1
60/18.3	9.1	150/45.7	14.3	900/274.3	35.1
65/19.8	9.4	200/61.0	16.5	1000/304.8	37.0

Example: Determine the geographic visibility of an object, with a height above water of 65 feet, for an observer with a height of eye of 35 feet.

Enter above table;
Height of object 65 feet= 9.4 NM
Height of observer 35 feet= 6.9 NM
Computed geographic visibility= 16.3 NM

This Page Intentionally Left Blank

TABLE OF CONTENTS

Light List Regions .... Inside Front Cover

U.S. DGPS Sites i

USCG Contact Information ii

Preface vi

Introduction vii

SEACOAST
    Florida 1
    Alabama 2
    Mississippi 3
    Louisiana 4
    Texas 9

BAYS, RIVERS, AND HARBORS
    Pensacola Bay 38
    Mobile Bay 50
    Pascagoula Harbor 68
    Lake Pontchartrain 96
    Mississippi River 103
    Timbalier Bay 154
    Vermilion Bay 177
    Sabine Pass 195
    Galveston Bay 207
    Matagorda Bay 233
    Corpus Christi Bay 243
    Intracoastal Waterway, Florida - Pensacola Bay 282
    Intracoastal Waterway, Louisiana – New Orleans 295
    Intracoastal Waterway, Louisiana – Morgan City 300
    Intracoastal Waterway, Texas – Sabine Neches Canal 304
    Intracoastal Waterway, Texas – Carlos Bay 321
    Intracoastal Waterway, Texas – Laguna Madre 340

INDEX .... Index 1

CROSS REFERENCE .... Cross Reference 1

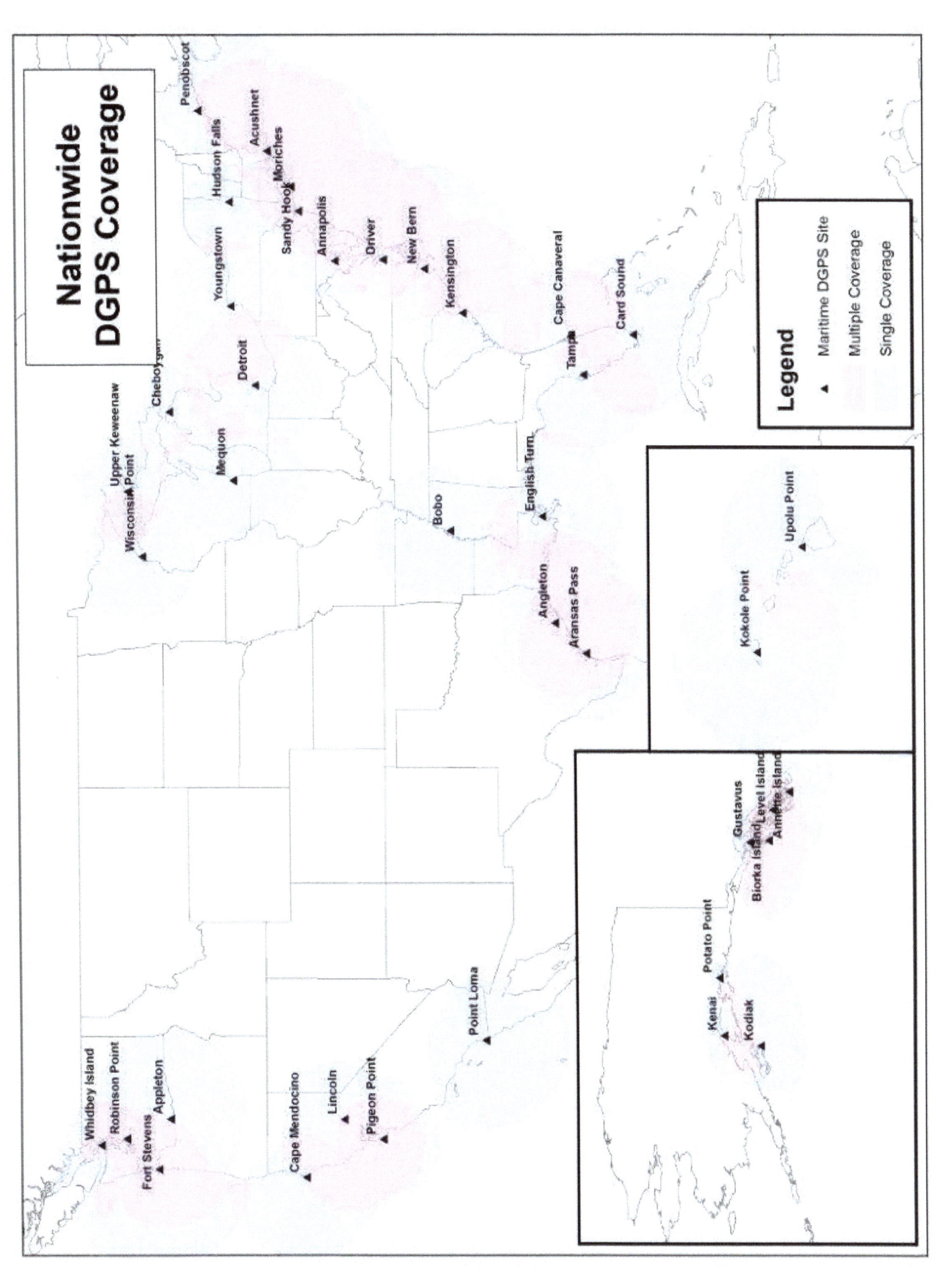

COAST GUARD DISTRICT COMMANDERS

DISTRICT	ADDRESS	WATERS OF JURISDICTION
FIRST	408 Atlantic Avenue Boston, MA 02110-3350 Tel: (617) 223-8351 http://www.uscg.mil/d1	Maine, New Hampshire, Massachusetts, Vermont (Lake Champlain), Rhode Island, Connecticut, New York, to Shrewsbury River, New Jersey.
FIFTH	Federal Building 431 Crawford Street Portsmouth, VA 23704-5004 Tel: (757) 398-6486 (757) 398-6552 http://www.uscg.mil/d5	Shrewsbury River, New Jersey to Delaware, Maryland, Virginia, District of Columbia, and North Carolina.
SEVENTH	Brickell Plaza Federal Building 909 SE 1st Avenue; Rm:406 Miami, FL 33131-3050 Tel: (305) 415-6752 (305) 415-6800 http://www.uscg.mil/d7	South Carolina, Georgia, Florida to 83°50'W, and Puerto Rico and adjacent islands of the United States.
EIGHTH	Hale Boggs Federal Building 500 Poydras Street New Orleans, LA 70130-3310 Tel: (504) 671-2327 (504) 671-2137 http:www.uscg.mil/d8	Florida westward from 83°50'W, Alabama, Mississippi, Louisiana, Texas, the Mississippi River System except that portion of the Illinois River north of Joliet, Illinois.
NINTH	1240 East 9th Street Cleveland, OH 44199-2060 Tel: (216) 902-6060 (216) 902-6117 http://www.uscg.mil/d9	Great Lakes and St. Lawrence River above St. Regis River.
ELEVENTH	Coast Guard Island Building 50-2 Alameda, CA 94501-5100 Tel: (510) 437-2975 http://www.uscg.mil/d11	California, Nevada, Utah, Arizona.
THIRTEENTH	Federal Building 915 Second Avenue 35th Floor, Rm 3510 Seattle, WA 98174-1067 Tel: (206) 220-7270 (206) 220-7004 http://www.uscg.mil/d13	Oregon, Washington, Idaho, and Montana.
FOURTEENTH	Prince Kalanianaole Federal Bldg. 300 Ala Moana Blvd 9th Floor, Room 9-220 Honolulu, HI 96850-4982 Tel: (808) 535-3409 (808) 535-3414 http://www.uscg.mil/d14	Hawaiian, American Samoa, Marshall, Marianas, and Caroline Islands.
SEVENTEENTH	PO Box 25517 Juneau, AK 99802-5517 Tel: (907) 463-2029 (907) 463-2269 http://www.uscg.mil/d17	Alaska.

U. S. COAST GUARD EIGHTH DISTRICT UNIT LISTING
AIDS TO NAVIGATION TEAMS

ANT CORPUS CHRISTI
1201 East Navigation Blvd
Corpus Christi, TX 78402
Tel: (361) 844-6521

ANT DULAC
241 Coast Guard Rd
Dulac, LA 70353 Tel:
(985) 563-4473

ANT GALVESTON
3000 Fort Point Rd
Galveston, TX 77553
Tel: (409) 766-5654

ANT GULFPORT
991 23rd Rd. Ave
Gulfport, MS 39501
Tel: (228) 575-9173

ANT MOBILE
1500 15th St.
Mobile, AL 36615
Tel: (251) 441-6244

ANT MORGAN CITY
800 Youngs Rd Suite 100
Morgan City, LA 70380
Tel: (985) 384-7000

ANT NEW ORLEANS
1790 Saturn Rd.
New Orleans, LA 70129
Tel: (504) 253-4834

ANT PANAMA CITY
1700 Thomas Drive
Panama City, FL 32408-5804
Tel: (850) 234-8139

ANT PENSACOLA
21 Slemmer Ave.
Pensacola, FL 32508-7851
Tel: (850) 455-2354

ANT PORT O'CONNOR
PO Box 98
Port O'Connor, TX 77982
Tel: (361) 983-4313

ANT SABINE
7034 S. First St.
Sabine Pass, TX 77655
Tel: (409) 971-2111

ANT SOUTH PADRE
1 Wallace Reed Road South
Padre Island, TX 78597
Tel: (956) 364-7433

ANT VENICE
436 Coast Guard Rd
Venice, LA 70091
Tel: (504) 534-7650

BUOY TENDERS

USCGC AXE (WLIC-75310)
800 Youngs Road
Morgan City, LA 70380
Tel: (985) 385-0037

USCGC BARBARA MABRITY (WLM-559)
1500 15th St.
Mobile, AL 36615
Tel: (251) 441-6275

USCGC CLAMP (WLIC-75306)
1 Ferry Rd
Galveston, TX 77550
Tel: (409) 766-4779

USCGC CYPRESS (WLB-210)
211 South Ave. Bldg 38 Suite C
Pensacola, FL 32508
Tel: (850) 452-9044

USCGC HATCHET (WLIC-75309)
1 Ferry Road
Galveston, TX 77550
Tel: (409) 766-4776

USCGC HARRY CLAIBORNE (WLM-561)
1 Ferry Rd
Galveston, TX 77550
Tel: (409) 766-4771

USCGC MALLET (WLIC-75304)
1201 East Navigation Blvd
Corpus Christi, TX 78402-1911
Tel: (361) 844-6531

USCGC PAMLICO (WLIC-800)
1790 Saturn St.
New Orleans, LA 70129
Tel: (504) 253-2420

USCGC SAGINAW (WLIC-803)
1500 15th St.
Mobile, AL 36615
Tel: (251) 441-5197

USCG NAVIGATION CENTER
Navigation Information Service (NIS)

The U.S. Coast Guard Navigation Center (NAVCEN) is the official government source of information for civil users of the Global Positioning System (GPS). The Navigation Information Service (NIS) is available 24 hours a day, seven days a week, for all Radio Navigation and maritime related needs via phone, fax or e-mail. The NIS provides users the ability to access real time or archived GPS, NDGPS, DGPS, and LNM information at http://www.navcen.uscg.gov, as well as subscribe to an automated list service which enables users to receive GPS status messages and Notice to NAVSTAR User (NANU) messages via direct Internet e-mail.

The NAVCEN also disseminates GPS and DGPS safety advisory broadcast messages through USCG broadcast stations utilizing VHF-FM voice, HF-SSB voice, and NAVTEX broadcasts. The broadcasts provide the GPS and DGPS user in the marine environment with the current status of the navigation systems, as well as any planned/unplanned system outages that could affect GPS and DGPS navigational accuracy.

To comment on any of these services or ask questions about the service offered, contact the NAVCEN at:

Commanding Officer
U.S. Coast Guard NAVCEN (NIS)
MS 7310
7323 Telegraph Road
Alexandria, VA 20598-7310
Phone: (703) 313-5900
FAX: (703) 313-5920
Internet: http://www.navcen.uscg.gov

This Light List is corrected through:

Eighth Coast Guard District Local Notice to Mariners **No. 01/18**

and through National Geospatial-Intelligence Agency (NGA) Notice to Mariners **No. 01/18**

The 2018 edition supersedes the 2017 edition.

RECORD OF CORRECTIONS

YEAR 2018

1.........	2.........	3.........	4.........	5.........
6.........	7.........	8.........	9.........	10.........
11.........	12.........	13.........	14.........	15.........
16.........	17.........	18.........	19.........	20.........
21.........	22.........	23.........	24.........	25.........
26.........	27.........	28.........	29.........	30.........
31.........	32.........	33.........	34.........	35.........
36.........	37.........	38.........	39.........	40.........
41.........	42.........	43.........	44.........	45.........
46.........	47.........	48.........	49.........	50.........
51.........	52.........			

YEAR 2019

1.........	2.........	3.........	4.........	5.........
6.........	7.........	8.........	9.........	10.........
11.........	12.........	13.........	14.........	15.........
16.........	17.........	18.........	19.........	20.........
21.........	22.........	23.........	24.........	25.........
26.........	27.........	28.........	29.........	30.........
31.........	32.........	33.........	34.........	35.........
36.........	37.........	38.........	39.........	40.........
41.........	42.........	43.........	44.........	45.........
46.........	47.........	48.........	49.........	50.........
51.........	52.........			

PREFACE

Lights and other marine aids to navigation, maintained by or under authority of the U.S. Coast Guard and located on waters used by general navigation, are described in the Light List. This volume includes aids located in Econfina River, Florida to Rio Grande, Texas.

Included are all Coast Guard aids to navigation used for general navigation such as lights, sound signals, buoys, daybeacons, and other aids to navigation. Not included are some buoys having no lateral significance, such as special purpose, anchorage, fish net, and dredging.

Aids to Navigation Link: http://www.uscgboating.org

CAUTION: Mariners attempting to pass a buoy close aboard risk collision with a yawing buoy or with the obstruction, which the buoy marks. Mariners must not rely on buoys alone for determining their positions due to factors limiting buoy reliability.

PRIVATE AIDS TO NAVIGATION

Included: Class I aids to navigation on marine structures or other works which the owners are legally obligated to establish, maintain, and operate as prescribed by the Coast Guard.

Included: Class II aids to navigation exclusive of Class I, located in waters used by general navigation.

Not included: Class III aids to navigation exclusive of Class I and Class II, located in waters not ordinarily used by general navigation.

Reporting Private Aids to Navigation Discrepancies D8:
http://www.atlanticarea.uscg.mil/District-8/District-Divisions/Waterways/PATON/

LIGHT LIST AVAILABILITY

This Light List is published annually and is intended to furnish more complete information concerning aids to navigation than can be conveniently shown on charts. This Light List is not intended to be used in place of charts or Coast Pilots. Charts should be consulted for the location of all aids to navigation. It may be dangerous to use aids to navigation without reference to charts.

This list is corrected to the date of the notices to mariners shown on the title page. Changes to aids to navigation during the year are advertised in U.S. Coast Guard Local Notices to Mariners and National Geospatial-Intelligence Agency (NGA) Notices to Mariners. Important changes to aids to navigation are also broadcast through Coast Guard or Naval radio stations and NAVTEX. Mariners should keep their Light Lists, charts and other nautical publications corrected from these notices and should consult all notices issued after the date of publication of this Light List.

The electronic version of this publication is updated monthly and is available at.
http://www.navcen.uscg.gov/index.php?pageName=lightLists

A weekly- updated electronic copy of this publication is also available at:
http://www.navcen.uscg.gov/index.php?pageName=lightListWeeklyUpdates

IMPORTANT: A summary of corrections for this publication, which includes corrections from the dates shown on the title page to the date of availability, is advertised in the Local Notice to Mariners and the Notice to Mariners. These corrections must be applied in order to bring the Light List up-to-date. Additionally, this publication should be corrected weekly from the Local Notices to Mariners or the Notices to Mariners, as appropriate.

Mariners and others are requested to bring any apparent errors or omissions in these lists to the attention of:

or

Commander (dpw)
Eighth Coast Guard District
500 Poydras Street
New Orleans, LA 70130-3396
D8marineinfo@uscg.mil

USCG Navigation Center
Charting Branch
MS 7310
7323 Telegraph Road
Alexandria, VA 20598-7310
Email: TIS-PF-NISWS@USCG.MIL

INTRODUCTION

Light List Arrangement

In the context of the Light List, aids to navigation on the coasts are arranged in geographic order clockwise from north to south along to Atlantic coast, east to west along the Gulf of Mexico, and south to north along the Pacific coast. On the Great Lakes, aids to navigation are arranged from east to west and from south to north, except on Lake Michigan, which is arranged from north to south. Seacoast aids to navigation are listed first, followed by entrance and harbor aids to navigation, arranged from seaward to the head of navigation.

Names of aids to navigation are printed as follows to help distinguish at a glance the type of aid to navigation.

> **Seacoast/Lake coast Lights and Secondary Lights**
> **RACONS**
> **Sound Signals**
> RIVER, HARBOR, OTHER LIGHTS, AND VIRTUAL AIS
> *Lighted Buoys*
> Daybeacons, Unlighted Buoys, and Virtual Automatic Identification System (V-AIS) ATON

Light List numbers are assigned to all Federal aids to navigation and many private aids to navigation for reference in the Light List. Aids to navigation are numbered by fives in accordance with their order of appearance in each volume of the Light List. Other numbers and decimal fractions are assigned where newly established aids to navigation are listed between previously numbered aids to navigation. The Light Lists are renumbered periodically to assign whole numbers to all aids to navigation.

International numbers are assigned to certain aids to navigation in cooperation with the International Hydrographic Organization. They consist of an alphabetic character followed by three or four numeric characters. A cross reference listing appears after the index.

Description of Columns

Column (1): Light List Number.

Column (2): Name and location of the aid to navigation.
Note: A dash (-) is used to indicate the bold heading is part of the name of the aid to navigation. When reporting discrepancies or making references to such an aid to navigation in correspondence, the full name of the aid including the geographic heading, should be given.

Bearings are in degrees true, read clockwise from 000° through 359°.

Bearings on range lines are given in degrees and tenths or hundredths where applicable.

(C) indicates Canadian aid to navigation.

Column (3): Geographic position of the aid to navigation in latitude and longitude.

Column (4): Light characteristic for lighted aids to navigation.

Column (5): Height above water from the focal plane of the fixed light to mean high water, listed in feet.

For Volume 7 (Great Lakes), height above water from the focal plane of the fixed light to low water datum, listed in feet and meters.

Column (6): Nominal range of lighted aids to navigation, in nautical miles, listed by color for sector and passing lights. Not listed for ranges, directional lights, or private aids to navigation.

Column (7): The structural characteristic of the aid to navigation, including: dayboard (if any), description of fixed structure, color and type of buoy, height of structure above ground for major lights.

Column (8): Aid remarks, sound signal characteristics, including: VHF-FM channel if remotely activated, RACON characteristic, light sector arc of visibility, radar reflector, emergency lights, seasonal remarks, and private aid to navigation identification. AIS specific information may include its unique Maritime Mobile Service Identity (MMSI), the MMSI(s) of its source AIS transmission, and the application identifier of any Application Specific Messages (ASM) it may also be transmitting.

U.S. Coast Guard Light List Distribution

U.S. regulations require that most commercial vessels maintain on board a currently corrected, copy or pertinent extract, of the U.S. Coast Guard Light Lists which are available for free and are updated weekly on the Coast Guard Navigation Center's website at https://www.navcen.uscg.gov/?pageName=BulletinSubscription. Commercially printed versions are also available, but the Coast Guard does not attest to their veracity or sanction such publications.

CHARTS & PUBLICATIONS

Nautical Charts & Publications
Nautical charts covering the coastal waters of the United States and its territories are published by the National Ocean Service (NOS). Up-to-date paper copies of NOS charts are available from NOS Certified Agents. A list of agents can be found at:
https://www.nauticalcharts.noaa.gov/charts/noaa-raster-charts.html#paper-nautical-charts.
NOS also produces Raster Navigational Charts (RNC) and Electronic Navigational Charts (ENC). RNCs can be found at https://www.nauticalcharts.noaa.gov/charts/noaa-raster-charts.html#rnc-charts.
ENCs can be found at
https://www.nauticalcharts.noaa.gov/charts/noaa-enc.html.

Inland Electronic Navigational Charts (IENC) and chart books are published by the U.S. Army Corps of Engineers and are available online at http://www.agc.army.mil/Missions/Echarts.aspx. Tide Tables and Tidal Current Tables are no longer printed or distributed by NOS. NOS Tide and Tidal Current predictions are available online at
http://tidesandcurrents.noaa.gov/tide_predictions.html. Commercially printed versions, using data provided by NOS, are also available. These products may be obtained from local stores that carry marine publications.

Notices to Mariners

Broadcast Notices to Mariners are made by the Coast Guard through Coast Guard radio stations. These notices, which are broadcast on VHF-FM, NAVTEX, and other maritime frequencies, are warnings that contain important navigational safety information. Included are reports of discrepancies and changes to aids to navigation, the positions of ice and derelicts, and other important hydrographic information.

Radio stations broadcasting Notices to Mariners are listed in the National Ocean Service United States Coast Pilot and in the National Geospatial-Intelligence Agency publication Radio Navigational Aids (Publication No. 117). VHF-FM voice broadcast times can be found online at http://www.nws.noaa.gov/om/marine/vhfvoice.htm.

Local Notices to Mariners (U.S. regional coverage) are another means which the Coast Guard disseminates navigational information for the United States, its territories, and possessions. A Local Notice to Mariners is issued by each Coast Guard district and is used to report changes and discrepancies to aids to navigation maintained by and under the authority of the Coast Guard. The Local Notice to Mariners also contain chart and Light List corrections, proposed aids to navigation projects open for public comment, ongoing waterway projects, bridge regulation changes, marine event information, and other concerns pertinent to the mariner.

Local Notices to Mariners are essential to all navigators for the purposes of keeping charts, Light Lists, Coast Pilots, and other nautical publications up-to-date. These notices are published weekly and can be found online at http://www.navcen.uscg.gov/index.php?pageName=lnmMain. Mariners may register with the Coast Guard Navigation Center to receive automatic notifications via email when new editions of the Local Notice to Mariners are available. Register at http://www.navcen.uscg.gov/?pageName=listServerForm. Vessels operating in ports and waterways in several districts will have to obtain the Local Notice to Mariners for each district.

Notice to Mariners are prepared jointly by the National Geospatial-Intelligence Agency (NGA), the U.S. Coast Guard, and the National Ocean Service, and are published weekly by the NGA. The weekly Notice to Mariners advises mariners of important matters affecting navigational safety including new hydrographic discoveries, changes to aids to navigation, and foreign marine information. Also included are corrections to Light Lists, Coast Pilots, and Sailing Directions. This notice is intended for mariners and others who have a need for information related to oceangoing operations. Because it is intended for use by oceangoing vessels, many corrections that affect small craft navigation and associated waters are not included. Information concerning small craft is contained in the Coast Guard Local Notice to Mariners only. The weekly Notices to Marines may be found online at http://msi.nga.mil/NGAPortal/MSI.portal.

ATON DISCREPANCIES

The Coast Guard does not keep the tens of thousands of aids to navigation comprising the U.S. Aids to Navigation System under simultaneous and continuous observation. Mariners should realize that it is impossible to maintain every aid to navigation operating properly and on its assigned position at all times. Therefore, for the safety of all mariners, anyone who discovers an aid to navigation that is either off station or exhibiting characteristics other than those listed in

the Light Lists should promptly notify the nearest Coast Guard unit. Radio messages should be prefixed "COAST GUARD" and transmitted on VHF-FM channel 16 or directly to one of the U.S. Government radio stations listed in Chapter 3, Section 300L, Radio Navigation Aids (Publication No. 117). In addition to notifying the nearest Coast Guard unit by radio, a discrepant aid to navigation can be reported online at
http://www.navcen.uscg.gov/?pageName=atonOutageReport.

U.S. AIDS TO NAVIGATION SYSTEM

GENERAL

The navigable waters of the United States are marked to assist navigation using the U.S. Aids to Navigation System, a system consistent with the International Association of Marine Aids to Navigation and Lighthouse Authorities (IALA) Maritime Buoyage System. The IALA Maritime Buoyage System is followed by most of the world's maritime nations and improves maritime safety by encouraging conformity in buoyage systems worldwide. IALA buoyage is divided into two regions made up of Region A and Region B. All navigable waters of the United States follow IALA Region B, except U.S. possessions west of the International Date Line and south of 10° north latitude, which follow Region A. Lateral aids to navigation in Region A vary from those located within Region B. Non-lateral aids to navigation in Region A are the same as those used in Region B. Appropriate nautical charts and publications should be consulted to determine whether the Region A or Region B marking schemes are in effect for a given area.

Aids to navigation are developed, established, operated, and maintained by the U.S. Coast Guard to accomplish the following:

1. Assist navigators in determining their position,
2. Assist the navigator in determining a safe course,
3. Warn the navigator of dangers and obstructions,
4. Promote the safe and economic movement of commercial vessel traffic, and
5. Promote the safe and efficient movement of military vessel traffic, and cargo of strategic military importance.

The U.S. Aids to Navigation System is designed for use with nautical charts. Nautical charts portray the physical features of the marine environment, which include: soundings, landmarks, hazards to navigation, and aids to navigation. To best understand the purpose of a specific aid to navigation, mariners should consult the associated nautical chart, which illustrates the relationship of the aid to navigation to channel limits, obstructions, hazards to navigation, and to the aids to navigation system as a whole. Seasonal aids to navigation are placed into service, withdrawn, or changed at specified times of the year. The dates shown in the Light Lists are approximate and may vary due to adverse weather or other conditions. These aids will be changed on Electronic Navigational Charts (ENC) based on Light List dates and electronic navigation system settings.

Mariners should maintain and consult suitable publications and navigation equipment depending on the vessel's requirements. This shipboard navigation equipment is separate from the aids to navigation system, but is often essential to its use.

The U.S. Aids to Navigation System is primarily a lateral system, which employs a simple arrangement of colors, shapes, numbers, and light characteristics to mark the limits of navigable routes. This lateral system is supplemented with non-lateral aids to navigation where appropriate.

Federal aids to navigation consist of Coast Guard operated aids to navigation. The Coast Guard establishes, maintains, and operates a system of aids to navigation consisting of visual, audible, and electronic signals designed to assist the prudent mariner in the process of navigation.

The U.S. Aids to Navigation System contains the following subsystems:

1. **Intracoastal Waterway**: The aids to navigation marking the Intracoastal Waterway are arranged geographically from north to south on the Atlantic Coast and generally east to west on the coast of the Gulf of Mexico. Red lights (if so equipped), even numbers, and red buoys or triangle shaped daymarks are located on the southbound/westbound starboard waterway boundary. Green lights (if so equipped), odd numbers, and green buoys or square shaped daymarks are on the southbound/westbound port waterway boundary.

2. **Western Rivers**: The Western Rivers System is employed on the Mississippi River System, in addition to the Tennessee-Tombigbee Waterway and the Alabama, Atchafalaya, and Apalachicola-Chattahoochee-Flint River Systems. The Western Rivers System consists of the following characteristics:

    a. Buoys are not numbered.
    b. Numbers on beacons do not have lateral significance, but rather indicate mileage from a fixed point (normally the river mouth).
    c. Diamond shaped non-lateral dayboards, red and white or green and white as appropriate, are used to indicate where the river channel crosses from one bank to the other.
    d. Lights on green aids to navigation show a single-flash characteristic, which may be green or white.
    e. Lights on red aids to navigation show a group-flash characteristic, which may be red or white.
    f. Isolated danger marks are not used.

3. **Bridge Markings**: Bridges across navigable waters are marked with red, green and/or white lights for nighttime navigation. Red lights mark piers and other parts of the bridge. Red lights are also placed on drawbridges to show when they are in the closed position. Green lights are placed on drawbridges to show when they are in the open position. The location of these lights will vary according to the bridge structure. Green lights are also used to mark the centerline of navigable channels through fixed bridges. If there are two or more channels through the bridge, the preferred channel is also marked by three white lights in a vertical line above the green light.

    Red and green retro-reflective panels may be used to mark bridge piers and may also be used on bridges not required to display lights. Lateral red and green lights and dayboards may mark main channels through bridges. Adjacent piers are marked with fixed yellow lights when the main channel is marked with lateral aids to navigation.

Centerlines of channels through fixed bridges may be marked with a safe water mark and an occulting white light when lateral marks are used to mark main channels. The centerline of the navigable channel through the draw span of floating bridges may be marked with a special mark. The mark will be a yellow diamond with yellow retro-reflective panels and may exhibit a yellow light that displays a Morse code "B" (a long flash followed by three short flashes). AIS-ATON and RACONs may be placed on the bridge structure to mark the centerline of the navigable channel through the bridge.

Vertical clearance gauges may be installed to enhance navigation safety. The gauges are located on the right channel pier or pier protective structure facing approaching vessels. Clearance gauges indicate the vertical distance between "low steel" of the bridge channel span (in the closed to navigation position for drawbridges) and the level of the water, measured to the bottom of the foot marks, read from top to bottom.

Drawbridges equipped with radiotelephones display a blue and white sign which indicates what VHF radiotelephone channels should be used to request bridge openings.

Private aids to navigation include aids to navigation that are either operated by private persons and organizations, or that are operated by states. Private aids to navigation are classified into three categories:

1. **Class I**: Aids to navigation on marine structures or other works which the owners are legally obligated to establish, maintain, and operate as prescribed by the U.S. Coast Guard.
2. **Class II:** Aids to navigation that, exclusive of Class I aids, are located in waters used by general navigation.
3. **Class III:** Aids to navigation that, exclusive of Class I and Class II aids, are located in waters not ordinarily used by general navigation.

Authorization for the establishment of a Class II or Class III private aid to navigation by the U.S. Coast Guard imposes no legal obligation that the aid actually be established and operated. It only specifies the location and operational characteristics of the aid for which the authorization was requested. Once the aid is established, however, the owner is legally obligated to maintain it in good working order and properly painted.

Lights and sound signals on oil wells or other offshore structures in navigable waters are private aids to navigation and are generally not listed in the Light List unless they are equipped with a RACON. Where space allows, the structures are shown on the appropriate nautical charts. Information concerning the location and characteristics of those structures which display lights and sound signals not located in obstruction areas are published in Local and/or weekly Notices to Mariners.

In general, during the nighttime, a series of white lights are displayed extending from the platform to the top of the derrick when drilling operations are in progress. At other times, structures are usually marked with one or more quick flashing white, red, or yellow lights, visible for at least one nautical mile during clear weather. Obstructions, which are a part of the appurtenances to the main structure, such as mooring piles, anchors, and mooring buoys, etc., are not normally lighted. In addition, some structures are equipped with a sound signal that produces a single two-second blast every 20 seconds.

BUOYS, BEACONS, AND AIS-ATON

The primary components of the U.S. Aids to Navigation System are buoys, beacons, and AIS-ATON.

Buoys are floating aids to navigation used extensively throughout U.S. waters. They are moored to sinkers by varying lengths of chain and may shift due to sea conditions and other causes. Buoys may also be carried away, capsized, or sunk. Prudent mariners will not rely solely on any single aid to navigation, particularly floating aids.

Buoy positions represented on nautical charts are approximate position only, due to the practical limitations of positioning and maintaining buoys and their sinkers in precise geographical locations. The position of buoys and beacons are indicated with a circle on the chart. The center of the symbol corresponds with the position of the aid.

Positions of Federal aids to navigation are verified during periodic maintenance visits. Between visits, environmental conditions, including atmospheric and sea conditions, seabed slope and composition, may shift buoys off their charted positions. Buoys may also be dragged off station, sunk, or capsized by a collision with a vessel.

Beacons are aids to navigation which are permanently fixed to the earth's surface. They range from large lighthouses to small single-pile structures and may be located on land or in the water. Lighted beacons are called lights; unlighted beacons are called daybeacons. Lighthouses are placed on shore or on marine sites and most often do not indicate lateral significance. Lighthouses with no lateral significance exhibit a white light.

Beacons exhibit a daymark. For small structures, these are colored geometric shapes that make an aid to navigation readily visible and easily identifiable against background conditions. Generally, the daymark conveys to the mariner, during daylight hours, the same significance as the aid's light or reflector does at night. The daymark of towers, however, consists of the structure itself. As a result, these daymarks do not infer lateral significance.

Ranges are non-lateral aids to navigation composed of two beacons, which when the structures appear to be in line, assist the mariner in maintaining a safe course. The appropriate nautical chart must be consulted when using ranges to determine whether the range marks the centerline of the navigable channel and also what section of the range may be safely traversed. Ranges typically display rectangular dayboards of various colors and are generally, but not always lighted. Ranges may display lights during daylight and at night. When lighted, ranges may display lights of any color.

Vessels should not pass fixed aids to navigation close aboard due to the danger of collision with rip-rap or structure foundations, or with the obstruction or danger being marked.

Aids to Navigation (ATON) may be enhanced by the use of an automatic identification system (AIS). AIS is a maritime navigation safety communications protocol standardized by the International Telecommunication Union and adopted by the International Maritime Organization for the broadcast or exchange of navigation information between vessels, aircraft, and shore

stations. AIS ATON can autonomously and at fixed intervals broadcast the name, position, dimensions, type, characteristics, and status from or concerning an aid to navigation.
AIS ATON can be either real (physically fitted to an aid to navigation), synthetic (physically fitted somewhere other than to an aid to navigation) or virtual (physically nonexistent, but capable of being portrayed on AIS-capable displays).

Note: Physical AIS ATON can actively monitor and report the health and position status of its host; while Synthetic AIS ATON broadcasted from ashore (i.e. NAIS) can be used to electronically augment the range or portrayal (i.e., on radar and ECDIS) of an existing aid to navigation.

Although all existing AIS mobile devices can receive AIS ATON Reports and ASM messages, they may not readily appear on an AIS Minimal Keyboard Display or other shipboard navigational display systems (i.e., radar, ECDIS, ECS), which would require software updates to make these systems compliant with international navigation presentation standards (i.e., IEC 62288 (Ed. 2), IHO S-52 (Ed. 4.4.0)).

AIS ATON can also be used to broadcast both laterally (*e.g.,* Port Hand Mark) and non-laterally significant marine safety information (*e.g.,* environmental data, tidal information, and navigation warnings).

Note: AIS ATON stations broadcast their presence, identity (9-digit Marine Mobile Service Identity (MMSI) number), position, type, and status at least every three minutes or less via an AIS (ITU-R M.1371) message 21–AIS ATON Report. In addition to its AIS ATON Report, AIS ATON can broadcast significant marine safety information via Application Specific Messages (ASM), which are customized messages that can be used to broadcast additional aid information or other marine safety information (i.e., environmental conditions, wind speed and direction, tidal/current data, bridge air clearances, area notices, etc. They are identified by their: AIS message number (i.e. 6, 8, 25 or 26), Designated Area Code (DAC), Function Identifier (FI), and Version Number, e.g. U.S. Geographic Notice message: Msg# = 8, DAC = 367, FI = 22, Version = 2, and, denoted as 8/367.22.2.

TYPES OF SIGNALS

Lighted aids to navigation are, for the most part, equipped with daylight controls which automatically cause the light to operate during darkness and to be extinguished during daylight. These devices are not of equal sensitivity; therefore, all lights do not come on or go off at the same time. Mariners should ensure correct identification of aids to navigation during twilight periods when some lighted aids to navigation are lit while others are not.

The lighting apparatus is serviced at periodic intervals to assure reliable operation, but there is always the possibility of a light being extinguished or operating improperly.
The condition of the atmosphere has a considerable effect upon the distance at which lights can be seen. Sometimes lights are obscured by fog, haze, dust, smoke, or precipitation which may be present at the light, or between the light and the observer, and which is possibly unknown by the observer. Atmospheric refraction may cause a light to be seen farther than under ordinary circumstances.

A light of low intensity will be easily obscured by unfavorable conditions of the atmosphere and little dependence can be placed on it being seen. For this reason, the intensity of a light should always be considered when expecting to sight it in reduced visibility. Haze and distance may reduce the apparent duration of the flash of a light. In some atmospheric conditions, white lights may have a reddish hue. Lights placed at high elevations are more frequently obscured by clouds, mist, and fog than those lights located at or near sea level.

In regions where ice conditions prevail in the winter, the lantern panes of lights may become covered with ice or snow, which will greatly reduce the visibility of the lights and may also cause colored lights to appear white.

The increasing use of brilliant shore lights for advertising, illuminating bridges, and other purposes, may cause marine navigational lights, particularly those in densely inhabited areas, to be outshone and difficult to distinguish from the background lighting. Mariners are requested to report such cases in order that steps may be taken to improve the conditions.

The "loom" (glow) of a powerful light is often seen beyond the limit of visibility of the actual rays of the light. The loom may sometimes appear sufficiently sharp enough to obtain a bearing. At short distances, some flashing lights may show a faint continuous light between flashes.

The distance of an observer from a light cannot be estimated by its apparent intensity. Always check the characteristics of lights in order to avoid mistaking powerful lights, visible in the distance, for nearby lights (such as those on lighted buoys) showing similar characteristics of low intensity. If lights are not sighted within a reasonable time after prediction, a dangerous situation may exist, requiring prompt resolution or action in order to ensure the safety of the vessel.

The apparent characteristic of a complex light may change with the distance of the observer. For example, a light which actually displays a characteristic of fixed white varied by flashes of alternating white and red (the rhythms having a decreasing range of visibility in the order: flashing white, flashing red, fixed white) may, when first sighted in clear weather, show as a simple flashing white light. As the vessel draws nearer, the red flash will become visible and the characteristics will appear as alternating flashing white and red. Later, the fixed white light will be seen between the flashes and the true characteristic of the light will finally be recognized as fixed white, alternating flashing white and red (F W Al WR).

If a vessel has considerable vertical motion due to pitching in heavy seas, a light sighted on the horizon may alternatively appear and disappear. This may lead the unwary to assign a false characteristic and hence, to error in its identification. The true characteristic will be evident after the distance has been sufficiently decreased or by increasing the height of eye of the observer.

Similarly, the effect of wave motion on lighted buoys may produce the appearance of incorrect light phase characteristics when certain flashes occur, but are not viewed by the mariner. In addition, buoy motion can reduce the distance at which buoy lights are detected.

Sectors of colored glass are placed in the lanterns of some lights in order to produce a system of light sectors of different colors. In general, red sectors are used to mark shoals or to warn the mariner of other obstructions to navigation or of nearby land. Such lights provide approximate bearing information, since observers may note the change of color as they cross the boundary between sectors. These boundaries are indicated in the Light List (Col. 8) and by dotted lines on charts. These bearings, as all bearings referring to lights, are given in true degrees from 000° to 359°, as observed from a vessel toward the light.

Altering course on the changing sectors of a light or using the boundaries between light sectors to determine the bearing for any purpose is not recommended. Be guided instead by the correct compass bearing to the light and do not rely on being able to accurately observe the point at which the color changes. This is difficult to determine because the edges of a colored sector cannot be cut off sharply. On either side of the line of demarcation between white, red, or green sectors, there is always a small arc of uncertain color. Moreover, when haze or smoke is present in the intervening atmosphere, a white sector might have a reddish hue.

The area in which a light can be observed is normally an arc with the light as the center and the range of visibility as the radius. However, on some bearings, the range may be reduced by obstructions. In such cases, the obstructed arc might differ with height of eye and distance. When adjoining land cuts off a light and the arc of visibility is given, the bearing on which the light disappears may vary with the distance of the vessel from which observed and with the height of eye. When the light is cut off by a sloping hill or point of land, the light may be seen over a wider arc by a vessel farther away than by one closer to the light.

The arc drawn on charts around a light is not intended to give information as to the distance at which it can be seen. The arc indicates the bearings between which the variation of visibility or obstruction of the light occurs.

Only aids to navigation with green or red lights have lateral significance and exhibit either flashing, quick flashing, group flashing, occulting, or isophase light rhythms. When proceeding in the conventional direction of buoyage, the mariner in IALA Region B, may see the following lighted aids to navigation:

Green lights on aids to navigation mark port sides of channels and locations of wrecks or obstructions that must be passed by keeping these lighted aids to navigation on the port hand of a vessel. Green lights are also used on preferred channel marks where the preferred channel is to starboard (i.e., aid to navigation left to port when proceeding in the conventional direction of buoyage). Red lights on aids to navigation mark starboard sides of channels and locations of wrecks or obstructions that must be passed by keeping these lighted aids to navigation on the starboard hand of a vessel. Red lights are also used on preferred channel marks where the preferred channel is to port (i.e., aid to navigation left to starboard when proceeding in the conventional direction of buoyage).

White and yellow lights have no lateral significance. The shapes, colors, letters, and light rhythms may determine the purpose of aids to navigation exhibiting white or yellow lights.

Most aids to navigation are fitted with retro reflective material to increase their visibility in darkness. Colored reflective material is used on aids to navigation that, if lighted, will display lights of the same color.

Preferred channel marks exhibit a composite group-flashing light rhythm of two flashes followed by a single flash.

Safe water marks exhibit a white Morse code "A" rhythm (a short flash followed by a long flash).

Isolated danger marks exhibit a white flashing (2) rhythm (two flashes repeated regularly).

Special marks exhibit yellow lights and exhibit a flashing or fixed rhythm.

Information and regulatory marks exhibit a white light with any light rhythm except quick flashing, flashing (2) and Morse code "A."

For situations where lights require a distinct cautionary significance, as at sharp turns, sudden channel constrictions, wrecks, or obstructions, a quick flashing light rhythm will be used.

Shapes are used to provide easy identification on certain unlighted buoys and daybeards on beacons. These shapes are laterally significant only when associated with laterally significant colors.

In IALA Region B, cylindrical buoys (referred to as "can buoys") and square daybeards mark the port side of a channel when proceeding from seaward. These aids to navigation are associated with solid green or green and red-banded marks where the topmost band is green.
Conical buoys (referred to as "nun buoys") and triangular daybeards mark the starboard side of the channel when proceeding from seaward. These aids to navigation are associated with solid red or red and green-banded marks where the topmost band is red.

Unless fitted with topmarks; lighted, sound, pillar, and spar buoys have no shape significance. Their numbers, colors, and light characteristics convey their meanings.

Daybeards throughout the U.S. Aids to Navigation System are described using standard designations that describe the appearance of each dayboard. A brief explanation of the designations and of the purpose of each type of dayboard in the system is given below, followed by a verbal description of the appearance of each dayboard type.

Designations:

1. First Letter – Shape or Purpose

    C: Crossing (Western Rivers only) diamond-shaped, used to indicate the points at which the channel crosses the river.

    J: Junction (square or triangle) used to mark (preferred channel) junctions or bifurcations in the channel, or wrecks or obstructions which may be passed on either side; color of top band has lateral significance for the preferred channel.

    K: Range (rectangular) when both the front and rear range daybeards are aligned on the same bearing, the observer is on the azimuth of the range, usually used to mark the center of the channel.

    M: Safe Water (octagonal) used to mark the fairway or middle of the channel.

    N: No lateral significance (diamond or rectangular) used for special purpose, warning, distance, or location markers.

    S: Square used to mark the port side of channels when proceeding from seaward.

    T: Triangle used to mark the starboard side of channels when proceeding from seaward.

2. Second Letter – Key Color

B – Black   G – Green   R – Red   W – White   Y – Yellow

3. Third Letter – Color of Center Stripe (Range Dayboards Only)

4. Additional Information after a (-)

-I: Intracoastal Waterway; a yellow reflective horizontal band on a dayboard; indicates the aid to navigation marks the Intracoastal Waterway.

-SY: Intracoastal Waterway; a yellow reflective square on a dayboard; indicates the aid to navigation is a port hand mark for vessels traversing the Intracoastal Waterway. May appear on a triangular daymark where the Intracoastal Waterway coincides with a waterway having opposite conventional direction of buoyage.

-TY: Intracoastal Waterway; a yellow reflective triangle on a dayboard; indicates the aid to navigation is a starboard hand mark for vessels traversing the Intracoastal Waterway. May appear on a square daymark where the Intracoastal Waterway coincides with a waterway having opposite conventional direction of buoyage.

Descriptions:

CNG: Diamond-shaped dayboard divided into four diamond-shaped colored sectors with the sectors at the side corners white and the sectors at the top and bottom corners green, with green reflective diamonds at the top and bottom corners and white reflective diamonds in the side corners (Western Rivers only).

CNR: Diamond-shaped dayboard divided into four diamond-shaped colored sectors with the sectors at the side corners white and the sectors at the top and bottom corners red, with red reflective diamonds at the top and bottom corners and white reflective diamonds in the side corners (Western Rivers only).

JG: Dayboard bearing horizontal bands of green and red, green band topmost, with corresponding reflective borders.

JG-I: Square dayboard bearing horizontal bands of green and red, green band topmost, with corresponding reflective borders and a yellow reflective horizontal band.

JG-SY: Square dayboard bearing horizontal bands of green and red, green band topmost, with corresponding reflective borders and a yellow reflective square.

JG-TY: Square dayboard bearing horizontal bands of green and red, green band topmost, with corresponding reflective borders and a yellow reflective triangle.

JR: Dayboard bearing horizontal bands of red and green, red band topmost, with corresponding reflective borders.

JR-I: Triangular dayboard bearing horizontal bands of red and green, red band topmost, with corresponding reflective borders and a yellow reflective horizontal band.

JR-SY: Triangular dayboard bearing horizontal bands of red and green, red band topmost, with corresponding reflective borders and a yellow reflective square.

JR-TY: Triangular dayboard bearing horizontal bands of red and green, red band topmost, with corresponding reflective borders and a yellow reflective triangle.

KBG: Rectangular black dayboard bearing a central green stripe.

KBG-I: Rectangular black dayboard bearing a central green stripe and a yellow reflective horizontal band.

KBR: Rectangular black dayboard bearing a central red stripe.

KBR-I: Rectangular black dayboard bearing a central red stripe and a yellow reflective horizontal band.

KBW: Rectangular black dayboard bearing a central white stripe.

KBW-I: Rectangular black dayboard bearing a central white stripe and a yellow reflective horizontal band.

KGB: Rectangular green dayboard bearing a central black stripe.

KGB-I: Rectangular green dayboard bearing a central black stripe and a yellow reflective horizontal band.

KGR: Rectangular green dayboard bearing a central red stripe.

KGR-I: Rectangular green dayboard bearing a central red stripe and a yellow reflective horizontal band.

KGW: Rectangular green dayboard bearing a central white stripe.

KGW-I: Rectangular green dayboard bearing a central white stripe and a yellow reflective horizontal band.

KRB: Rectangular red dayboard bearing a central black stripe.

KRB-I: Rectangular red dayboard bearing a central black stripe and a yellow reflective horizontal band.

KRG: Rectangular red dayboard bearing a central green stripe.

KRG-I: Rectangular red dayboard bearing a central green stripe and a yellow reflective horizontal band.

KRW: Rectangular red dayboard bearing a central white stripe.

KRW-I: Rectangular red dayboard bearing a central white stripe and a yellow reflective horizontal band.

KWB: Rectangular white dayboard bearing a central black stripe.

KWB-I: Rectangular white dayboard bearing a central black stripe and a yellow reflective horizontal band.

KWG: Rectangular white dayboard bearing a central green stripe.

KWG-I: Rectangular white dayboard bearing a central green stripe and a yellow reflective horizontal band.

KWR: Rectangular white dayboard bearing a central red stripe.

KWR-I: Rectangular white dayboard bearing a central red stripe and a yellow reflective horizontal band.

MR: Octagonal dayboard bearing stripes of white and red, with a white reflective border.

MR-I: Octagonal dayboard bearing stripes of white and red, with a white reflective border and a yellow reflective horizontal band.

NB: Diamond-shaped dayboard divided into four diamond-shaped colored sectors with the sectors at the side corners white and the sectors at the top and bottom corners black, with a white reflective border.

ND: Rectangular white mileage marker with black numerals indicating the mile number (Western Rivers only).

NG: Diamond-shaped dayboard divided into four diamond-shaped colored sectors with the sectors at the side corners white and the sectors at the top and bottom corners green, with a white reflective border.

NL: Rectangular white location marker with an orange reflective border and black letters indicating the location.

NR: Diamond-shaped dayboard divided into four diamond-shaped colored sectors with the sectors at the side corners white and the sectors at the top and bottom corners red, with a white reflective border.

NW: Diamond-shaped white dayboard with an orange reflective border and black letters describing the information or regulatory nature of the mark.

NY: Diamond-shaped yellow dayboard with yellow reflective border.

SG: Square green dayboard with a green reflective border.

SG-I: Square green dayboard with a green reflective border and a yellow reflective horizontal band.

SG-SY: Square green dayboard with a green reflective border and a yellow reflective square.

SG-TY: Square green dayboard with a green reflective border and a yellow reflective triangle.

SR: Square red dayboard with a red reflective border. (IALA Region "A")

TG: Triangular green dayboard with a green reflective border. (IALA Region "A")

TR: Triangular red dayboard with a red reflective border.

TR-I: Triangular red dayboard with a red reflective border and a yellow reflective horizontal band.

TR-SY: Triangular red dayboard with a red reflective border and a yellow reflective square.

TR-TY: Triangular red dayboard with a red reflective border and a yellow reflective triangle. These abbreviated descriptions are used in column (7) and may also be found on the illustrations of the U.S. Aids to Navigation System.

Numbers are used to provide easy identification of aids to navigation. In IALA Region B, all solid red and solid green aids are numbered, with the exception of buoys located on the Western Rivers. Red aids to navigation have even numbers and green aids to navigation have odd numbers. The numbers for each increase from seaward when proceeding in the conventional direction of buoyage. Numbers are kept in approximate sequence on both sides of the channel by omitting numbers where necessary.

Letters may be used to augment numbers when lateral aids to navigation are added to channels with previously completed numerical sequences. Letters will increase in alphabetical order from seaward, proceeding in the conventional direction of buoyage and are added to numbers as suffixes. Letters are not used for buoys on the Western Rivers.
No other aids to navigation are numbered. Preferred channel, safe water, isolated danger, special marks, and information and regulatory aids to navigation may be lettered, but not numbered.

Sound signal is a generic term used to describe aids to navigation that produce an audible signal designed to assist the mariner in periods of reduced visibility. These aids to navigation can be activated by several means (e.g., manually, remotely, or fog detector). The Coast Guard is replacing many fog detectors with mariner radio activated sound signals (MRASS). To activate, mariners key their VHF-FM radio a designated number of times on a designated VHF-FM channel. The sound signal is activated for a period of 15, 30, 45, or 60 minutes after which the activated assistance automatically turns off. In cases where a fog detector is in use, there may be a delay in the automatic activation of the signal. Additionally, fog detectors may not be capable of detecting patchy fog conditions.

Sound signals are distinguished by their tone and phase characteristics. The devices producing the sound, e.g., diaphones, diaphragm horns, sirens, whistles, bells, or gongs determine tones.

Phase characteristics are defined by the signal's sound pattern, i.e., the number of blasts and silent periods per minute and their durations. Sound signals sounded from fixed structures generally produce a specific number of blasts and silent periods each minute when operating. Sound signals installed on buoys are generally activated by the motion of the sea and therefore do not emit a regular signal characteristic. It is common, in fact, for a buoy to produce no sound signal when seas are calm.

The characteristic of a sound signal is listed in column (8) of the Light List. If the sound signal is remotely activated, column (8) will contain the VHF-FM channel and number of times the VHF-FM radio should be keyed. All waterway users equipped with a VHF-FM radio may activate the sound signal, but they are not required to do so. Unless it is specifically stated that a sound signal "Operates continuously," or the signal is a bell, gong, or whistle on a buoy, it can be assumed that the sound signal only operates during times of fog, reduced visibility, or adverse weather.

Caution: Mariners should not rely on sound signals to determine their position. Distance cannot be accurately determined by sound intensity. Occasionally, sound signals may not be heard in areas close to their location. Signals may not sound in cases where fog exists close to, but not at, the location of the sound signal.

Radar Beacons (RACONS) are radar transponders that when triggered by an X-band radar produce a coded response from its location, which is portrayed radially as a series of dots and dashes on the triggering radar. Although RACONS may be used on both laterally significant and non-laterally significant aids to navigation, their signal should just be used for identification purposes only.

RACONS have a typical output of 600 milliwatts and are considered a short range aid to navigation. Reception varies from a nominal range of 6 to 8 nautical miles when mounted on a buoy to as much as 17 nautical miles for a RACON mounted on a fixed structure. It must be understood that these nominal ranges are dependent upon many factors.

The beginning of the RACON presentation occurs about 50 yards beyond the RACON position and will persist for a number of revolutions of the radar antenna (depending on its rotation rate). Distance to the RACON can be measured to the point at which the RACON flash begins, but the figure obtained will be greater than the vessel's distance from the RACON. This is due to the slight response delay in the RACON apparatus.

Radar operators may notice some broadening or spoking of the RACON presentation when their vessel approaches closely to the source of the RACON. This effect can be minimized by adjusting the IF gain or sweep gain control of the radar. If desired, the RACON presentation can be virtually eliminated by operation of the FTC (fast time constant) controls of the radar.

Radar Reflectors are special fixtures, incorporated into both lighted and unlighted aids to navigation, to enhance the reflection of radar energy. These fixtures help radar-equipped vessels to detect buoys and beacons, which are so equipped. However, they do not positively identify a radar target as an aid to navigation.

NAVIGATION SERVICES

GLOBAL POSITIONING SYSTEM (GPS), DIFFERENTIAL GPS (DGPS), AND NATION-WIDE AUTOMATIC IDENTIFICATION SYSTEM (NAIS)

Global Positioning System (GPS) is a satellite based navigation system, operated and controlled by the Department of Defense (DOD) under U.S. Air Force management, which provides precise, worldwide, three-dimensional navigation capabilities. The system was originally designed for military application; however, it is now available to all and used almost ubiquitously. The United States is committed to maintaining the availability of at least 24 operational GPS satellites, in six precise orbital planes, each of which complete a circular 10,900 nautical mile orbit of the earth once every 12 hours. Ideally, a minimum of four satellites will be visible from any position on the earth and will provide positions with a global horizontal accuracy within 3 meters, 95% percent of the time. Whenever possible, advance notice of when GPS satellites should not be used will be provided by the DOD and made available by the U.S. Coast Guard through GPS status messages.

The Navigation Center coordinates and manages the Civil GPS Service Interface Committee (CGSIC), which comprises members from U.S. and international private, government, and industry user groups. The CGSIC is the recognized worldwide forum for effective interaction between all civil GPS users and the U.S. GPS authorities.

At least three satellites are required for a two-dimensional solution, however, GPS does not provide integrity information and mariners should exercise extreme caution when using GPS in restricted waterways.

Differential GPS (DGPS) is an augmentation to the GPS signals. Each site corrects for small variations in the signals from each satellite that is in view at that time. Satellite signals can vary due to small changes in the satellite's circuitry and orbit and from changes caused by local weather conditions. Satellite corrections are transmitted to users via radio signals in the medium frequency band (285-325 kHz) previously used for marine radiobeacons. DGPS corrections and integrity information are transmitted using Minimum Shift Keying (MSK) modulation. The modulation data rate is usually 100 or 200 bits per second (bps), but can also be 50 bps. The range of DGPS transmissions is from 40 to 300 nautical miles.

DGPS was the first Federal radionavigation system capable of providing the 10-meter navigation service required for the Harbor Entrance and Approach phase of maritime navigation. DGPS provides integrity messages for signals from the GPS satellites, as well as DGPS position corrections, and typically provides position accuracy of 1-3 meters.

Each DGPS site has two reference stations (which calculate the differential corrections), two integrity monitors (which ensure the differential corrections are accurate), a transmitter, and equipment to communicate status information to and receive commands from the control station. Each transmitter and reference station has a unique identification number that permits users to determine which site/equipment is providing their differential corrections. As distance from the transmitting site increases, the small error in the differential corrections increases. The best accuracy is achieved when using the DGPS site closest to the user.

Information regarding the location of DGPS transmitters is given on the map labeled U.S. DGPS Sites & Identification Numbers on page i. Users can access additional information and DGPS statuses, submit questions, and provide comments via the Navigation Information Service's website or by calling the Coast Guard Navigation Center DGPS watchstander at (703) 313-5902.

Navigation Information Service (NIS): The Coast Guard is the government interface for civil users of GPS and has established a Navigation Information Service (NIS) to meet the information needs of the civil user. The NIS is a Coast Guard entity that is manned 24 hours a day, 7 days a week, and is located at the Navigation Center (NAVCEN) in Alexandria, VA. It provides data broadcasts and on-line computer-based information services which are available 24 hours a day. The information provided includes present or future satellite outages, constellation changes, user instructions and tutorials, lists of service and receiver provides/users, and other GPS and DGPS related information.

Navigation Center Internet Service (www) website also offers an e-mail subscription service for GPS status messages, Notice Advisory to NAVSTAR Users (NANU) messages, Local Notice to Mariners, and Coast Guard Light List.

The NAVCEN disseminates GPS and DGPS safety advisory broadcast messages through USCG broadcast stations utilizing VHF-FM voice, HF-SSB voice, and NAVTEX broadcasts. The broadcasts provide the GPS and DGPS user in the marine environment with the current status of the navigation systems, as well as any planned/unplanned system outages that could affect GPS and DGPS navigational accuracy.

Nationwide Automatic Identification System (NAIS) consists of approximately 200 VHF receiver sites located throughout the coastal continental United States, inland rivers, Alaska, Hawaii, Puerto Rico, and Guam. NAIS couples AIS technology with a comprehensive network infrastructure to achieve ship-to-shore and shore-to-ship data transmission throughout the navigable waters of the United States. The system enables AIS-equipped vessels to receive important marine information such as safety and security messages, weather alerts, and electronic aids to navigation.

NAIS is designed to collect safety and security data from AIS-equipped vessels in navigable waters of the United States and share that data with Coast Guard operators and other government and port partners. The primary goal of NAIS is to increase situational awareness through data dissemination via a network infrastructure, particularly focusing on improving maritime security, marine and navigational safety, search and rescue, and environmental protection services. Collected AIS data improves the safety of vessels and ports through collision avoidance and the safety of the nation through detection, identification, and classification of vessels. NAIS broadcasts navigation enhancing safety related messages such as Synthetic AIS ATON Reports and Application Specific Messages.

For more information see:
- AIS messages at www.navcen.uscg.gov/?pageName=AISMessages,
- IMO Safety of Navigation Circular 289 and 290 regarding ASM's at www.navcen.uscg.gov/?pageName=AISReferences,
- IALA AIS ASM Catalog at www.e-navigation.nl/asm, and
- USCG Special Notice 14-02 regarding eATON at www.navcen.uscg.gov/?pageName=AISFAQ#21.

To comment on any of these services or ask questions about the service offered, contact the NAVCEN at:

Commanding Officer
U.S. Coast Guard Navigation Center
7323 Telegraph Road STOP 7310
Alexandria, VA 20598-7310
Phone: (703) 313-5900
Internet: https://www.navcen.uscg.gov

ABBREVIATIONS

Various abbreviations are utilized in Broadcast Notices to Mariners, Local Notices to Mariners, on charts, and in the Light Lists. Refer to the following list.

Light Characteristics

Alternating	AL
Characteristic	CHAR
Composite Group-Flashing	FL (2+1)
Composite Group-Occulting	OC (2+1)
Continuous Quick-Flashing	Q
Eclipse	EC
Fixed and Flashing	FFL
Fixed	F
Group-Flashing	FL (3)
Group-Occulting	OC (2)
Interrupted Quick-Flashing	IQ
Isophase	ISO
Morse Code	MO (A)
Occulting	OC
Single-Flashing	FL

Sound Signal Characteristics

Blast	BL
Every	EV
Seconds	S
Silent	SI

Colors*

Black	B
Blue	BU
Green	G
Orange	OR
Red	R
White	W
Yellow	Y

*NOTE: Color refers to characteristics of aids to navigation only.

Aids to Navigation

Aeronautical Radiobeacon	AERO RBN
Automatic Identification System	AIS
Daybeacon	DBN
Destroyed	DESTR
Differential GPS	DGPS
Discontinued	DISCONTD
Established	ESTAB
Exposed Location Buoy	ELB
Extinguished	EXT
Fog Signal Station	FOG SIG
Light List Number	LLNR
Light	LT
Lighted Bell Buoy	LBB
Lighted Buoy	LB
Lighted Gong Buoy	LGB
Lighted Horn Buoy	LHB
Lighted Whistle Buoy	LWB
Mariner Radio Activated Sound Signal	MRASS
Ocean Data Acquisition System	ODAS
Privately Maintained	PRIV MAINTD
Radar Reflector	RA REF
Radar Responder Beacon	RACON
Remote Radio Activated Sound Signal	RRASS
Single Point Mooring Buoy	SPM
Sound Signal	SS
Temporarily Replaced by Lighted Buoy	TRLB
Temporarily Replaced by Unlighted Buoy	TRUB
Topmark	TMK
Virtual AIS Aid to Navigation	V-AIS
Whistle	WHIS

Organizations

Commander, Coast Guard District	CCGD (#)
Coast Guard	CG
Corps of Engineers	USACE
National Geospatial-Intelligence Agency	NGA
National Ocean Service	NOS
National Weather Service	NWS

Vessels

Aircraft	A/C
Fishing Vessel	F/V
Liquefied Natural Gas Carrier	LNG
Motor Vessel (includes Steam Ship, Container Ship, Cargo Vessel, Tanker etc)	M/V
Pleasure Craft	P/C
Research Vessel	R/V
Sailing Vessel	S/V

Compass Directions

North	N

South	S	Explosive Anchorage	EXPLOS ANCH
East	E	Fathom(s)	FM(S)
West	W	Foot/Feet	FT
Northeast	NE	Harbor	HBR
Northwest	NW	Height	HT
Southeast	SE	Hertz	HZ
Southwest	SW	Horizontal Clearance	HOR CL
		Hour	HR
Months		International Regulations for Preventing Collisions at Sea	COLREGS
January	JAN		
February	FEB	Kilohertz	KHZ
March	MAR	Kilometer	KM
April	APR	Knot(s)	KT(S)
May	MAY	Minute (time, geo, pos)	MIN
June	JUN	Megahertz	MHZ
July	JUL	Moderate	MOD
August	AUG	Mountain, Mount	MT
September	SEP	Nautical Mile(s)	NM
October	OCT	Notice to Mariners	NTM
November	NOV	Obstruction	OBSTR
December	DEC	Occasion/Occasionally	OCCASION
		Operating Area	OPAREA
Days of the Week		Pacific	PAC
Monday	MON	Point(s)	PT(S)
Tuesday	TUE	Position	POS
Wednesday	WED	Position Approximate	PA
Thursday	THU	Pressure	PRES
Friday	FRI	Private, Privately	PRIV
Saturday	SAT	Prohibited	PROHIB
Sunday	SUN	Publication	PUB
		Range	RGE
Various		Reported	REP
Anchorage	ANCH	Restricted	RESTR
Anchorage Prohibited	ANCH PROHIB	River	RIV
Approximate	APPROX	Rock	RK
Atlantic	ATL	Saint	ST
Authorized	AUTH	Second (time, geo, pos)	SEC
Average	AVG	Signal Station	SIG STA
Bearing	BRG	Station	STA
Breakwater	BKW	Statute Mile(s)	SM
Broadcast Notice to Mariners	BNM	Storm Signal Station	S SIG STA
Canadian Aid	(C)	Temporary	TEMP
Captain of the Port	COTP	Thunderstorm	TSTORM
Channel	CHAN	Through	THRU
Code of Federal Regulations	CFR	True	T
Continue	CONT	Uncovers, Dries	UNCOV
Degrees (temp, geo, pos)	DEG	Universal Coordinate Time	UTC
Diameter	DIA	Urgent Marine Information Broadcast	UMIB
Edition	ED	Velocity	VEL
Effect/Effective	EFF	Vertical Clearance	VERT CL
Entrance	ENTR	Vessel Traffic Service	VTS

Visibility	VIS	Missouri	MO
Yard(s)	YD	Mississippi	MS
Warning	WARN	Mexico	MX
Weather	WX	Michigan	MI
Wreck	WK	Minnesota	MN
		Montana	MT
Countries and States		Nebraska	NE
Alabama	AL	Nevada	NV
Alaska	AK	New Hampshire	NH
American Samoa	AS	New Jersey	NJ
Arizona	AZ	New Mexico	NM
Arkansas	AR	New York	NY
California	CA	North Carolina	NC
Canada	CN	North Dakota	ND
Colorado	CO	Northern Marianas	MP
Connecticut	CT	Ohio	OH
Delaware	DE	Oklahoma	OK
District of Columbia	DC	Oregon	OR
Florida	FL	Pennsylvania	PA
Georgia	GA	Puerto Rico	PR
Guam	GU	Rhode Island	RI
Hawaii	HI	South Carolina	SC
Idaho	ID	South Dakota	SD
Illinois	IL	Tennessee	TN
Indiana	IN	Texas	TX
Iowa	IA	United States	US
Kansas	KS	Utah	UT
Kentucky	KY	Vermont	VT
Louisiana	LA	Virgin Islands	VI
Maine	ME	Washington	WA
Maryland	MD	West Virginia	WV
Marshall Islands	MH	Wisconsin	WI
Massachusetts	MA	Wyoming	WY

GLOSSARY OF AIDS TO NAVIGATION TERMS

Adrift: Afloat and unattached in any way to the shore or seabed.

Aid to Navigation: Any device external to a vessel or aircraft specifically intended to assist navigators in determining their position or safe course, or to warn them of dangers or obstructions to navigation.

Alternating Lights: A rhythmic light showing light of alternating colors.

Arc of Visibility: The portion of the horizon over which a lighted aid to navigation is visible from seaward.

Articulated Beacon: A beacon-like buoyant structure, tethered directly to the seabed and having no watch circle. Called articulated light or articulated daybeacon, as appropriate.

Assigned Position: The latitude and longitude position for an aid to navigation.

Beacon: A lighted or unlighted fixed aid to navigation attached directly to the earth's surface. (Lights and daybeacons both constitute beacons.

Bearing: The horizontal direction of a line of sight between two objects on the surface of the earth.

Bell: A sound signal producing bell tones by means of a hammer actuated by electricity on fixed aids and by sea motion on buoys.

Bifurcation: The point where a channel divides when proceeding from seaward. The place where two tributaries meet.

Broadcast Notice to Mariners: A radio broadcast designed to provide important marine information.

Buoy: A floating object of defined shape and color, which is anchored at a given position and serves as an aid to navigation.

Characteristic: The audible, visual, or electronic signal displayed by an aid to navigation to assist in the identification of an aid to navigation. Characteristic refers to lights, sound signals, RACONS, and daybeacons.

Commissioned: The action of placing a previously discontinued aid to navigation back in service.

Composite Group Flashing Light: A group flashing light in which the flashes are combined in successive groups of different numbers of flashes.

Composite Group-Occulting Light: A light similar to a group occulting light except that the successive groups in a period have different numbers of eclipses.

Conventional Direction of Buoyage: Some reference direction for defining the lateral and numbering significance of an aid system. In U.S. waters, the direction of flood current provides the most common indication. For coastal marking, the conventional direction of buoyage is southerly along the East coast, northerly and westerly along the Gulf coast and northerly along the West coast.

Daybeacon: An unlighted fixed structure which is equipped with a dayboard for daytime identification.

Dayboard: The daytime identifier of an aid to navigation presenting one of several standard shapes (square, triangle, rectangle) and colors (red, green, white, orange, yellow, or black).

Daymark: The daytime identifier of an aid to navigation. (See column 7 of the Light List)

Diaphone: A sound signal which produces sound by means of a slotted piston moved back and forth by compressed air. A "two-tone" diaphone produces two sequential tones with a second tone of lower pitch.

Directional Light: A light illuminating a sector or very narrow angle and intended to mark a direction to be followed.

Discontinued: To remove from operation (permanently of temporarily) a previously authorized aid to navigation.

Discrepancy: Failure of an aid to navigation to maintain its position or function as prescribed in the Light List.

Discrepancy Buoy: An easily transportable buoy used to temporarily replace an aid to navigation not watching properly.

Dolphin: A minor aid to navigation structure consisting of a number of piles driven into the seabed or riverbed in a circular pattern and drawn together with rope.

Eclipse: An interval of darkness between appearances of a light.

Emergency Light: A light of reduced intensity displayed by certain aids to navigation when the main light is extinguished.

Establish: To place an authorized aid to navigation in operation for the first time.

Extinguished: A lighted aid to navigation which fails to show a light characteristic.

Fixed Light: A light showing continuously and steady, as opposed to a rhythmic light. (Do not confuse with "fixed" as used to differentiate from "floating".)

Flash: A relatively brief appearance of a light, in comparison with the longest interval of darkness in the same characteristic.

Flash tube: An electronically controlled high-intensity discharge lamp with a very brief flash duration.

Flashing Light: A light in which the total duration of the light in each period is clearly shorter than the total duration of the darkness and in which the flashed of light are all of equal duration. (Commonly used for a single-flashing light which exhibits only single flashes which are repeated at regular intervals.)

Floating Aid to Navigation: A buoy, secured in its assigned position by a mooring.

Fog Detector: An electronic devise used to automatically determine conditions of visibility which warrant the activation of a sound signal or additional light signals.

Fog Signal: See sound signal.

Geographic Range: The greatest distance the curvature of the earth permits an object of a given height to be seen from a particular height of eye without regard to luminous intensity or visibility conditions.

Global Positioning System (GPS): A satellite based radio-navigation system providing continuous worldwide coverage. It provides navigation, position, and timing information to air, marine, and land users.

Gong: A wave actuated sound signal on buoys which uses a group of saucer-shaped bells to produce different tones.

Group Flashing Light: A flashing light in which a group of flashes, specified in number, is regularly repeated.

Group Occulting Light: An occulting light in which a group of eclipses, specified in number, regularly repeated.

Horn: A sound signal which uses electricity or compressed air to vibrate a disc diaphragm.

Inoperative: Sound signal or electronic aid to navigation out of service due to a malfunction.

Interrupted Quick Flash: A quick flashing light in which the rapid alternations are interrupted at regular intervals by eclipses of long duration.

Isolated Danger Mark: A mark erected on, or moored above or very near, an isolated danger which has navigable water all around it.

Isophase Light: A rhythmic light in which all durations of light and darkness are equal.

Junction: The point where a channel divides when proceeding seaward. The place where a distributary departs from the main stream.

Lateral System: A system of aids to navigation in which characteristics of buoys and beacons indicate the sides of a channel or route relative to a Conventional Direction of Buoyage (usually upstream).

Light: The signal emitted by a lighted aid to navigation. The illuminating apparatus used to emit the light signal. A lighted aid to navigation on a fixed structure.

Light Sector: The arc over which a light is visible, described in degrees true, as observed from seaward towards the light. May be used to define distinctive color difference of two adjoining sectors, or an obscured sector.

Lighted Ice Buoy (LIB): A lighted buoy without a sound signal, and designed to withstand the forces of shifting and flowing ice. Used to replace a conventional buoy when that aid to navigation is endangered by ice.

Lighthouse: A lighted beacon of major importance.

Local Notice to Mariners: A written document issued by each U.S. Coast Guard district to disseminate important information affecting aids to navigation, dredging, marine construction, special marine activities, and bridge construction on waterways within that district.

Luminous Range: The greatest distance a light can be expected to be seen given its nominal range and the prevailing meteorological visibility.

Mark: A visual aid to navigation. Often called navigational mark, including floating marks (buoys) and fixed marks (beacons).

Meteorological Visibility: The greatest distance at which a black object of suitable dimension could be seen and recognized against the horizon sky by day, or in case of night observations, could be seen and recognized if the general illumination were raised to the daylight level.

Mileage Number: A number assigned to aids to navigation which gives the distance in sailing miles along the river from a reference point to the aid to navigation. The number is used principally in the Mississippi River System.

Nominal Range: The maximum distance a light can be seen in clear weather (meteorological visibility of 10 nautical miles). Listed for all lighted aids to navigation except range lights, directional lights, and private aids to navigation.

Occulting Light: A light in which the total duration of light in each period is clearly longer than the total duration of the darkness and in which the intervals of darkness (occultations) are all of equal duration. Commonly used for single occulting light which exhibits only single occultations which are repeated at regular intervals.

Ocean Data Acquisition System (ODAS): Certain very large buoys in deep water for the collection of oceanographic and meteorological information. All ODAS buoys are yellow in color and display a yellow light.

Off Shore Tower: Monitored light stations built on exposed marine sites to replace lightships.

Off Station: A floating aid to navigation that is not on its assigned position.

Passing Light: A low intensity light which may be mounted on the structure of another light to enable the mariner to keep the latter light in sight when passing out of its beam during transit.

Period: The interval of time between the commencement of two identical successive cycles of the characteristic of the light or sound signal.

Pile: A long, heavy steel, concrete or timber driven into the seabed or riverbed to serve as a support for an aid to navigation.

Port Hand Mark: A buoy or beacon which is left to the port hand when proceeding in the "Conventional Direction of Buoyage".

Preferred Channel Mark: A lateral mark indicating a channel junction or bifurcation, or a wreck or other obstruction which after consulting a chart, may be passed on either side.

Primary Aid to Navigation: An aid to navigation established for the purpose of making landfalls and coastwise passages from headland to headland.

Quick Light: A light exhibiting very rapid regular alternations of light and darkness, normally 60 flashes per minute.

RACON: A radar beacon which produces a coded response or radar paint, when triggered by a radar signal.

Radar: An electronic system designed to transmit radio signals and receive reflected images of those signals from a "target" in order to determine the bearing and distance to the "target".

Radar Reflector: A special fixture fitted to or incorporated into the design of certain aids to navigation to enhance their ability to reflect radar energy. In general, these fixtures will materially improve the aid to navigation for use by vessels with radar.

Range: A line formed by the extension of a line connecting two charted points.

Range lights: Two lights associated to form a range which often, but not necessarily, indicates the channel centerline. The front range light is the lower of the two, and nearer to the mariner using the range. The rear light is higher and further from the mariner.

Rebuilt: A fixed aid to navigation, previously destroyed, which has been restored as an aid to navigation.

Regulatory Marks: A white and orange aid to navigation with no lateral significance. Used to indicate a special meaning to the mariner, such as danger, restricted operations, or exclusion area.

Relighted: An extinguished aid to navigation returned to its advertised light characteristics.

Replaced: An aid to navigation previously off station, adrift, or missing, restored by another aid to navigation of the same type and characteristics.

Replaced (temporarily): An aid to navigation previously off station, adrift, or missing restored by another aid to navigation of a different type and/or characteristic.

Reset: A floating aid to navigation previously off station, adrift or missing, returned to its assigned position (station).

Rhythmic Light: A light showing intermittently with a regular periodicity.

Sector: See light sector.

Setting a Buoy: The act of placing a buoy on assigned position in the water.

Siren: A sound signal which uses electricity or compressed air to actuate either a disc or a cup shaped rotor.

Skeleton Tower: A tower, usually of steel, constructed of heavy corner members and various horizontal and diagonal bracing members.

Sound Signal: A device which transmits sound, intended to provide information to mariners during periods of restricted visibility and foul weather.

Starboard Hand Mark: A buoy or beacon which is right to the starboard hand when proceeding in the Conventional Direction of Buoyage.

Topmark: One or more relatively small objects of characteristic shape and color placed on aid to identify its purpose.

Traffic Separation Scheme: Shipping corridors marked by buoys which separate incoming from outgoing vessels. Improperly called SEA LANES.

Watching Properly: An aid to navigation on its assigned position exhibiting the advertised characteristics in all respects.

Whistle: A wave actuated sound signal on buoys which produces sound by emitting compressed air through a circumferential slot into a cylindrical bell chamber.

Winter Marker: An unlighted buoy without a sound signal, used to replace a conventional buoy when an aid to navigation is endangered by ice.

Winter Light: A light which is maintained during those winter months when the regular light is extinguished. It is of lower candlepower than the regular light, but usually the same characteristic.

Withdrawn: The discontinuance of an aid to navigation or equipment on an aid to navigation during severe ice conditions or for the winter season.

CHARACTERISTICS OF LIGHTS

Illustration	Type Description	Abbreviation

1.
F
A light showing continuously and steadily.

Abbreviation: FIXED.

2. OCCULTING.
A light in which the total duration of light in a period is longer than the total duration of darkness and the intervals of darkness (eclipses) are usually of equal duration

2.1 Single-occulting.
An occulting light in which an eclipse is regularly repeated.

Abbreviation: Oc

2.2 Group-occulting.
An occulting light in which a group of eclipses, specified in numbers, is regularly repeated.

Abbreviation: Oc (2)

2.3 Composite group-occulting.
A light, similar to a group-occulting light, except that successive groups in a period have different numbers of eclipses.

Abbreviation: Oc (2+1)

3. ISOPHASE.
A light in which all durations of light and darkness are equal.

Abbreviation: Iso

4. FLASHING.
A light in which the total duration of light in a period is shorter than the total duration of darkness and the appearances of light (flashes) are usually of equal duration.

4.1 Single-flashing.
A flashing light in which a flash is regularly repeated (frequency not exceeding 30 flashes per minute).

Abbreviation: Fl

4.2 Group-flashing.
A flashing light in which a group of flashes, specified in number, is regularly repeated.

Abbreviation: Fl (2)

4.3 Composite group-flashing.
A light similar to a group flashing light except that successive groups in the period have different numbers of

Abbreviation: Fl (2+1)

5. QUICK.
A light in which flashes are produced at a rate of 60 flashes per minute.

5.1 Continuous quick.
A quick light in which a flash is regularly repeated.

Abbreviation: Q

5.2 Interrupted quick.
A quick light in which the sequence of flashes is interrupted by regularly repeated eclipses of constant and long duration.

Abbreviation: I Q

6. MORSE CODE.
A light in which appearances of light of two clearly different durations (dots and dashes) are grouped to represent a character or characters in the Morse code.

Abbreviation: Mo (A)

7. FIXED AND FLASHING.
A light in which a fixed light is combined with a flashing light of higher luminous intensity.

Abbreviation: F Fl

8. ALTERNATING.
A light showing different colors alternately

Abbreviation: Al RW

This Page Intentionally Left Blank

Light List corrected through LNM week: 01/18

(1) No.	(2) Name and Location	(3) Position	(4) Characteristic	(5) Height	(6) Range	(7) Structure	(8) Remarks
	GULF COAST (Florida) - Eighth District						
	APALACHEE BAY (Chart 11405)						
5	Ochlockonee Shoals Lighted Buoy 24	29-51-27.465N 084-10-18.999W	Fl R 4s		4		Red.
10 1490	ST MARKS LIGHT	30-04-25.725N 084-10-46.689W	Oc W 4s	80		White conical tower.	Light obscured from 106° to 246°.
15	South Shoal Lighted Buoy 26	29-47-57.166N 084-20-41.718W	Fl R 6s		4		Red.
	TAMPA BAY TO CAPE SAN BLAS (Chart 11400)						
	U.S. Air Force Instrumentation Tower						
20	- LIGHT SMI	29-04-54.000N 084-19-12.000W	Q W	100		On pile.	Maintained by U.S. Air Force. HORN: 1 blast ev 20s (2s bl). Private aid.
25	- LIGHT N6	29-24-54.000N 084-20-42.000W	Q W	120		On pile.	Maintained by U.S. Air Force. HORN: 1 blast ev 20s (2s bl). Private aid.
30	- LIGHT N7	29-39-54.000N 084-22-12.000W	Q W	120		On pile.	Maintained by U.S. Air Force. HORN: 1 blast ev 20s (2s bl). Private aid.
35	- LIGHT N5	29-17-54.000N 084-36-42.000W	Q W	120		On pile.	Maintained by U.S. Air Force. HORN: 1 blast ev 20s (2s bl). Private aid.
40	- LIGHT N3	29-32-18.000N 084-37-00.000W	Q W	120		On pile.	Maintained by U.S. Air Force. HORN: 1 blast ev 20s (2s bl). Private aid.
45	- LIGHT N4	29-24-42.000N 084-51-24.000W	Q W	160		On pile.	Maintained by U.S. Air Force. HORN: 1 blast ev 20s (2s bl). Private aid.
	APALACHEE BAY (Chart 11405)						
50 2515	CROOKED RIVER LIGHT	29-49-38.100N 084-42-02.600W	Fl (2)W 15s	115		Square skeleton tower. Lower half white, upper half red.	Private aid.
55 2520	Carrabelle Channel Lighted Buoy 2	29-44-32.767N 084-39-12.146W	Fl R 4s		4		Red.
60	USF Marine Lighted Buoy	28-49-00.875N 084-50-00.446W	Fl Y 4s				Yellow. Private aid.
65 2820	St George Island West Jetty Lighted Buoy 1	29-36-09.878N 084-57-13.271W	Fl G 2.5s		4		Green.
70 2825	St George Island East Jetty Lighted Buoy 2	29-36-10.278N 084-57-09.471W	Fl R 2.5s		4		Red.
	APALACHICOLA BAY TO CAPE SAN BLAS (Chart 11401)						
75	ST. GEORGE LIGHTHOUSE	29-39-46.580N 084-51-46.330W	Fl W 6s	76		White conical tower.	Visible 244° to 061°. Non-operational May 1 to October 31 annually. Private aid.
80	NOAA Lighted Buoy 42056	19-52-27.000N 085-03-33.000W	Fl (4)Y 20s		4	Yellow disc buoy with mast.	Aid maintained by National Oceanic and Atmospheric Administration.
85	Cape San Blas Shoal Inner Buoy 1	29-37-26.700N 085-19-43.320W				Green can.	
90	Cape San Blas Shoal Inner Buoy 3	29-38-20.754N 085-22-35.701W				Green can.	
	ST. JOSEPH AND ST. ANDREW BAYS (Chart 11389)						
95 3030	**St Joseph Bay Light & Entrance A Range Rear Light** 2924 yards, 61.9° from front light.	29-55-05.668N 085-22-49.794W	Iso W 6s	78	13	KRW on skeleton tower. 78	
100	Bay County Midway II Artificial Reef Lighted Buoy	30-01-18.000N 085-42-13.260W	Fl Y 2.5s			Yellow.	SIGN: MIDWAY II/RED SEA TUG REEF-BAY COUNTY FL. Private aid.

Light List corrected through LNM week: 01/18

(1) No.	(2) Name and Location	(3) Position	(4) Characteristic	(5) Height	(6) Range	(7) Structure	(8) Remarks
		GULF COAST (Florida) - Eighth District					
	ST. JOSEPH AND ST. ANDREW BAYS (Chart 11389)						
	St Andrew Bay						
105 3335	- Entrance Lighted Buoy SA	30-05-29.735N 085-46-25.752W	Mo (A) W		6	Red and white stripes with red spherical topmark.	AIS MMSI: 993682022
	ST. JOSEPH AND ST. ANDREW BAYS (Chart 11389)						
115	NOAA Lighted Buoy 42039	28-47-17.565N 086-00-30.589W	Fl (4)Y 20s			Yellow disc buoy with mast.	Aid maintained by National Oceanic and Atmospheric Administration.
	CHOCTAWATCHEE BAY (Chart 11388)						
120	Old Pass Lagoon Intake Lighted Buoy	30-22-06.000N 086-29-01.000W	Fl R 2.5s			White with orange bands.	Private aid.
125 4535	Choctawhatchee Bay Entrance Lighted Buoy CB	30-22-14.568N 086-30-55.952W	Mo (A) W		5	Red and white stripes with red spherical topmark.	
	CAPE ST. GEORGE TO MISSISSIPPI PASSES (Chart 11360)						
135	Continental Shelf Oceanographic Lighted Buoy Marks subsea installation.	29-55-24.000N 087-13-06.000W	Fl Y 4s			Yellow.	Private aid.
138	NOAA Lighted Data Buoy 42012	30-03-50.964N 087-33-05.197W	Fl (4)Y 20s			Yellow disc buoy with mast.	Aid maintained by National Oceanic and Atmospheric Administration.
	PENSACOLA BAY AND APPROACHES (Chart 11382)						
140 4715	**Pensacola Light**	30-20-46.045N 087-18-29.109W	Fl W 20s	191	27	Conical brick tower, lower third white, upper two thirds black. 191	White light visible from 222° to 090°. Aircraft warning light shows F R from 090° to 222°.
145 4695	Pensacola Bay Entrance Lighted Buoy 1	30-16-15.724N 087-17-32.898W	Fl G 2.5s		4	Green.	
150 4700	Pensacola Bay Entrance Lighted Buoy 2	30-16-16.749N 087-17-23.505W	Fl R 2.5s		4	Red.	
		GULF COAST (Alabama) - Eighth District					
	PENSACOLA BAY AND APPROACHES (Chart 11382)						
160	**TEXACO-VK-786A-A RACON**	29-13-44.410N 087-46-51.480W				On Texaco platform.	RACON: C (-.-.) BAND: S,X SIGN: Texaco-VK-786A-A. Private aid.
163	NOAA Scientific Monitoring Buoy Z	29-16-06.000N 087-45-30.000W	Fl Y 2.5s				AIS - 993689001 Private aid.
165 5885	Perdido Pass Entrance Lighted Buoy PP	30-15-30.728N 087-33-24.333W	Mo (A) W		6	Red and white stripes with red spherical topmark.	AIS MMSI: 993682023
175	**COX-104-03 RACON**	30-05-39.780N 087-52-59.463W	Q W			On freestanding caisson.	RACON: C (-.-.) BAND: S, X SIGN: COX-104-03 Private aid.
	MOBILE BAY (Chart 11376)						
180 6095	**Mobile Point Light**	30-13-41.487N 088-01-26.531W	Fl W 10s	125	14	On skeleton tower. 125	
185 6075	Mobile Entrance Lighted Buoy M	30-07-30.961N 088-04-07.197W	Mo (A) W		6	Red and white stripes with red spherical topmark.	
190	W&T Offshore Mooring Buoy	30-10-45.240N 088-04-55.500W				White with blue band.	Private aid.
195	Geological Survey Research Lighted Buoys (2)	29-57-07.000N 088-10-46.000W	Fl Y 4s			Yellow.	Maintained by U.S. Geological Survey. Private aid.
	CAPE ST. GEORGE TO MISSISSIPPI PASSES (Chart 11360)						
215	Seneca-111-1 Lighted Buoy	29-55-33.921N 088-03-19.036W	Fl W 2.5s			White with orange Bands.	Private aid.
225	Conoco-Phillips Lighted Oceanographic Buoy	30-05-25.200N 088-12-42.000W	Fl Y 2.5s			Yellow.	Private aid.

Light List corrected through LNM week: 01/18

(1) No.	(2) Name and Location	(3) Position	(4) Characteristic	(5) Height	(6) Range	(7) Structure	(8) Remarks
		GULF COAST (Alabama) - Eighth District					
	CAPE ST. GEORGE TO MISSISSIPPI PASSES (Chart 11360)						
230	Tana-117-05 (Lighted Buoy)	29-25-00.027N 088-23-16.394W	Fl W 2.5s			White with orange bands.	Sign: MAGNUM HUNTER-MP-232-1. Private aid.
245	NOAA Lighted Buoy 42040 (ODAS)	29-12-30.280N 088-13-32.462W	Fl (4)Y 20s			Yellow disc buoy with mast.	Aid maintained by National Oceanic and Atmospheric Administration.
250	Magnum Hunter 102-1 Lighted Buoy Marks Subsea installation.	29-18-51.810N 088-13-30.700W	Q R			Red.	SIGN: MAGNUM HUNTER-MP-263-1. Private aid.
255	Texas A&M Research Lighted Buoy D	29-21-06.000N 088-15-54.000W	Fl W 4s			White with orange bands.	Private aid.
260	**CHEVRON-116-2 (RACON)**	28-20-29.527N 088-15-56.472W				On Chevron Platform Blind Faith	RACON: B (-...) BAND: S, X SIGN: CHEVRON-MC-650 BLIND FAITH. Private aid.
262	**BP NAKIKA MC-474-A RACON**	28-31-14.500N 088-17-19.800W				On BP Nakika TLP platform.	RACON: U (.. _) BAND S, X SIGN: BP-MC-474-A Private aid.
265	Tana-117-02 (Lighted Buoy) Marks subsea installation.	29-32-48.429N 088-16-31.387W	Fl W 2.5s			White with orange bands.	SIGN: MAGNUM HUNTER-MP-187-1. Private aid.
270	Tana-117-01 (Lighted Buoy) Marks subsea installation.	29-32-47.852N 088-21-57.025W	Fl W 2.5s			White with orange bands.	SIGN: MAGNUM HUNTER-MP-185-1. Private aid.
280	Tana-117-30 (Lighted Buoy) Marks subsea installation.	29-25-48.748N 088-25-34.714W	Fl W 2.5s			White with orange bands.	SIGN: TEC-MP-233-1. Private aid.
285	**BP EXPLORATION-MC-778-A RACON**	28-11-26.205N 088-29-44.318W		160		On BP-MC-778-Thunderhorse platform.	RACON: Y (-.--) BAND: S,X SIGN: THUNDERHORSE. Private aid. Private aid.
290	**COX-104-04 RACON**	30-05-04.000N 088-29-47.000W	Q W			On Cox platform A.	RACON: Q (--.-) BAND: S, X SIGN: COX-104-04 Private aid.
295	Energy Resource-200-1 Lighted Buoy	29-25-08.710N 088-29-34.910W	Fl W 2.5s			White with orange bands.	SIGN: ENERGY RESOURCE-MP-234-1 Private aid.
		GULF COAST (Mississippi) - Eighth District					
	MISSISSIPPI SOUND AND APPROACHES (Chart 11373)						
305	Noble Energy Lighted Mooring Buoy A	29-13-15.229N 088-33-40.596W	Q W			White with blue band.	Private aid.
307	**ENERGY XXI-MP-61-D RACON**	29-19-33.840N 088-52-37.390W				On Energy XXI platform D.	BAND: S,X SIGN:EXXI-MP-61-D. Private aid.
310 7850	Horn Island Pass Lighted Buoy HI	30-08-30.049N 088-34-40.125W	Mo (A) W		5	Red and white stripes with red spherical topmark.	
312	Apache-101-40 (Lighted Buoy)	29-16-07.436N 088-38-04.048W	Fl W 2.5s			White with orange band.	SIGN: Apache-MP-295-1 Private aid.
315	Usm Research Lighted Buoy A	30-02-32.930N 088-38-50.330W	Fl Y 4s			Yellow.	Private aid.
320	Dog Keys Pass Lighted Buoy 1	30-12-55.723N 088-47-27.089W	Fl G 4s		4	Green.	
325	Dog Key Pass Reef Lighted Buoy J	30-12-19.260N 088-49-51.600W	Fl Y 2.5s			Yellow.	Private aid.
330	U.S.G.S. SHIP ISLAND MONITORING PLATFORM LIGHT	30-15-27.000N 088-52-15.000W	Fl Y 2.5s	37			Maintained by U.S. Geological Survey. Private aid.

Light List corrected through LNM week: 01/18

(1) No.	(2) Name and Location	(3) Position	(4) Characteristic	(5) Height	(6) Range	(7) Structure	(8) Remarks
	GULF COAST (Mississippi) - Eighth District						
	MISSISSIPPI SOUND AND APPROACHES (Chart 11373)						
335 0680	SHIP ISLAND LIGHT	30-12-45.414N 088-57-58.736W	Fl W 6s	82	6	Skeleton tower on block. On same structure as Ship Channel Upper Reach Outbound Range Rear Light.	
340 9575	*Gulfport Ship Channel Lighted Buoy GP*	30-07-09.931N 088-52-39.881W	Mo (A) W		4	Red and white stripes with red spherical topmark.	
	GULF COAST (Louisiana) - Eighth District						
	CAPE ST. GEORGE TO MISSISSIPPI PASSES (Chart 11360)						
345	MS-AL AQUACULTURE RESEARCH CAGE LIGHT	29-58-38.940N 088-36-17.870W	Fl Y 4s			On research cage.	Private aid.
350	*Mobil-194-6 Lighted Horn Buoy* Marks subsea installation.	29-35-05.000N 088-40-58.000W	Q R			Red.	SIGN: MO-MP-99-1. HORN: 1 blast ev 20s (2s bl). Private aid.
355	**BENNU-102-1 RACON**	28-02-00.610N 089-06-02.200W				On ATP Titan Spar.	RACON: A (. -) BAND: S, X SIGN: ATP TITAN-MC-941-A. Private aid.
	MISSISSIPPI RIVER DELTA (Chart 11361)						
365	*Harvey Ward Wreck Buoy*	29-10-00.420N 088-53-00.850W				White with orange bands.	Private aid.
370	*Energy XXI-102-10 (Lighted Horn Buoy)*	29-14-20.408N 088-52-59.480W	Q G			Green.	Private aid.
375	*Pass A Loutre North Pass Lighted Buoy 2*	29-14-16.794N 088-57-28.149W	Fl R 6s		4	Red.	
380	*Pass A Loutre Lighted Buoy 4*	29-09-53.802N 088-56-32.145W	Fl R 2.5s		4	Red.	
385	*Ocean Energy Lighted Mooring Buoy A*	29-07-02.000N 088-51-30.000W	Q W			White with blue bands.	Private aid.
387	*Taylor Energy Lighted Buoy A*	28-56-12.619N 088-58-10.303W	Fl Y 2.5s			Marks subsea containment system.	TAYLOR ENERGY-MC-20 Private aid.
390	*Ocean Energy-102-2 Buoy*	28-59-19.222N 089-04-54.359W				White with orange bands.	SIGN: OE-SP-32-1. Private aid.
395	*Ocean Energy-102-1 Lighted Horn Buoy* Marks subsea installation.	28-59-17.194N 089-04-56.752W	Q R			Red.	SIGN: OE-SP-32-1. Private aid.
400	CAT ISLAND REEF LIGHT K	30-12-07.380N 089-04-52.080W	Fl Y 2.5s			NY on pile.	Private aid.
420 12740	**Southwest Pass Entrance Light**	28-54-21.376N 089-25-43.025W	Fl W 10s	122 85	12	Tower on white dwelling on piles.	RACON: K (- . -) Emergency light of reduced intensity: Fl W 10s.
425.01	**COX-105-1 RACON**	28-50-01.000N 089-27-10.000W	Q W			On platform A.	RACON: T (-) BAND: S, X SIGN: Cox-105-1 Private aid.
430 12680	*Southwest Pass Entrance Lighted Buoy SW*	28-52-39.100N 089-25-55.000W	Mo (A) W		5	Red and white stripes with red spherical topmark.	
435	*Walter-110-6 Lighted Buoy* Marks Subsea Installation.	28-49-47.390N 089-31-35.304W	Fl W 2.5s			White with orange bands.	SIGN: WALTER-WD-107-1. Private aid.
440	*Walter-110-8 Lighted Buoy*	28-52-37.156N 089-32-08.610W	Fl W 2.5s			White with orange bands.	SIGN: WALTER-WD-107-6 Private aid.
445	*Tarpon-101-1 Lighted Buoy*	28-47-49.141N 089-33-29.983W	Fl W 2.5s			White with orange bands.	SIGN: TARPON-WD-112-1. Private aid.
450	*Furgo Geoscience Lighted Buoy* Marks suction piles.	28-59-49.916N 089-31-41.942W	Q R			Red.	Private aid.
455	**SHELL-138-13 RACON**	28-39-42.360N 089-33-04.600W	Q W			On Shell-WD-143-platform 1.	RACON: G (- - .) BAND: S,X SIGN: SH-WD-143-1. Private aid.

Light List corrected through LNM week: 01/18

(1) No.	(2) Name and Location	(3) Position	(4) Characteristic	(5) Height	(6) Range	(7) Structure	(8) Remarks
	GULF COAST (Louisiana) - Eighth District						
	BARATARIA BAY AND APPROACHES (Chart 11358)						
470	Louisiana State University Oceanographic Lighted Buoy A	30-23-03.420N 086-45-47.820W	Fl Y 4s			Yellow.	Private aid.
480	Fr-La-27 Lighted Tension Buoy A	29-11-36.660N 089-52-59.340W	Fl Y 2.5s			Yellow buoy.	SIGN: FR-LA-27-A. Private aid.
485	Fr-La-27 Lighted Tension Buoy B	29-11-42.133N 089-53-29.609W	Fl Y 2.5s			Yellow buoy.	SIGN: FR-LA-27-B. Private aid.
490	Fr-La-27 Lighted Tension Buoy C	29-11-12.817N 089-53-54.707W	Fl Y 2.5s			Yellow buoy.	SIGN: FR-LA-27-C. Private aid.
495	Fr-La-27 Lighted Tension Buoy D	29-10-56.680N 089-53-20.080W	Fl Y 2.5s			Yellow buoy.	SIGN: FR-LA-27-D. Private aid.
500	Fr-La-27 Lighted Tension Buoy E	29-11-02.620N 089-52-47.590W	Fl Y 2.5s			Yellow buoy.	SIGN: FR-LA-27-E. Private aid.
	LOOP DEEPWATER PORT (Chart 11359)						
505	LOOP PUMPING PLATFORM LIGHT-100-5	28-53-06.000N 090-01-30.000W	Fl W 10s	213		On platform.	RACON: O (- - -) Platform additionally lighted by (9) Q W lights. HORN (2): 1 blast (2s bl) in unison every 20s. Private aid.
510	Loop Fairway Lighted Horn Buoy 1	28-48-36.000N 089-55-00.000W	Fl G 6s			Green.	Private aid.
515	Apache-122-3 Lighted Buoy	28-41-08.290N 089-57-33.280W	Fl W 2.5s			White with orange bands.	SIGN: APACHE-GI-82-A Private aid.
520	Loop Fairway Lighted Buoy 2	28-50-18.000N 089-53-54.000W	Fl R 6s			Red.	Private aid.
525	Loop Fairway Lighted Buoy 3	28-50-09.000N 090-02-24.000W	Fl G 6s			Green.	Private aid.
530	Loop Fairway Lighted Buoy 4	28-54-52.000N 089-57-00.000W	Fl R 6s			Red.	Private aid.
535	Loop Spm Lighted Mooring Buoy 102	28-53-18.000N 089-59-59.000W	Q W			White deck with yellow sides.	Private aid.
540	Loop Lighted Mooring Buoy 103	28-52-16.000N 090-00-18.000W	Q W			White deck with yellow sides.	Private aid.
545	LOOP SPM LIGHTED MOORING BUOY 104	28-51-45.000N 090-01-24.000W	Q W			White deck with yellow sides.	Private aid.
550	Loop Lighted Mooring Buoy Vm-1	28-53-43.000N 090-01-26.000W	Fl W 4s			White.	Private aid.
555	Loop Lighted Mooring Buoy Vm-2	28-53-23.000N 090-01-58.000W	Fl W 4s			White.	Private aid.
560	Loop Lighted Mooring Buoy Vm-3	28-53-41.000N 090-03-26.000W	Fl W 4s			White.	Private aid.
565	Loop Anchorage Lighted Buoy L-B	28-52-06.000N 089-52-42.000W	Fl Y 6s			Yellow.	Private aid.
570	Loop Anchorage Lighted Buoy L-A	28-54-06.000N 089-56-36.000W	Fl Y 6s			Yellow.	Private aid.
	BARATARIA BAY AND APPROACHES (Chart 11358)						
580	LOOP 100-7 LIGHT	29-06-00.000N 090-06-48.000W	Fl W 4s			On pile.	SIGN: LOOP-GI-25-B. HORN: 1 blast ev 20s (2s bl). Private aid.
585	LOOP 100-6 LIGHT	29-06-06.000N 090-06-54.000W	Fl W 4s			On pile.	SIGN: LOOP-GI-25-A. Private aid.
590	Walter-115-3 Lighted Buoy	28-25-47.672N 090-08-05.142W	Fl W 2.5s			White with orange bands.	SIGN: WOG-GI-101-1. Private aid.
	LOOP DEEPWATER PORT (Chart 11359)						
600	Shell Flare Pipe Buoy 153-15	28-58-30.000N 090-10-36.000W				White with orange bands.	Marks subsea installation. SIGN: SH-ST-26-BUOY. Private aid.
605	Helis-106-4 Lighted Buoy Marks Subsea Installation.	28-26-35.377N 090-11-04.550W	Fl W 2.5s			White with orange bands.	SIGN: HELIS-ST-209-1. Private aid.
610	Walter-116-3 Lighted Buoy	28-16-47.769N 090-14-21.460W	Fl W 2.5s			White with orange bands.	SIGN: WALTER-ST-260-2. Private aid.
	MISSISSIPPI RIVER TO GALVESTON (Chart 11340)						
615 16970	Belle Pass Entrance Lighted Buoy 2	29-04-15.965N 090-13-40.336W	Q R		4	Red.	

(1) No.	(2) Name and Location	(3) Position	(4) Characteristic	(5) Height	(6) Range	(7) Structure	(8) Remarks
	GULF COAST (Louisiana) - Eighth District						
	MISSISSIPPI RIVER TO GALVESTON (Chart 11340)						
620	**NORTHSTAR-SP-86-C RACON**	28-43-05.951N 089-23-35.127W				On Platform C.	RACON: M (- -) BAND: S, X SIGN: Northstar-SP-86-C. Private aid.
625	**BP EXPLORATION-GC-787-A (RACON)**	27-11-43.641N 090-01-37.150W		94		On BP-GC-787 Atlantis platform.	RACON: X (- . . -) BAND: X SIGN: ATLANTIS Private aid.
626	**BP MAD DOG GC-782-A RACON**	27-11-18.000N 090-16-07.000W				On BP spar Mad Dog platform.	RACON: Z (_ _ . .) BAND: S, X SIGN: BP-GC-782-A Private aid.
627	*BP Exploration Lighted Scientific Data Buoy A*	27-12-24.370N 090-16-57.660W	Fl Y 4s			Yellow.	SIGN: BP-GC-782. Private aid.
630	*Agip-103-1 Lighted Buoy* Marks subsea installation.	28-25-38.000N 090-05-24.000W	Q W			White with orange bands.	Private aid.
635	*Hunt-114-6 Lighted Buoy*	28-32-43.904N 090-09-01.644W	Fl W 2.5s			White with orange bands.	SIGN: HUNT-ST-155-1. Private aid.
640	*University of Southern Mississippi Special Lighted Buoy A*	28-52-02.040N 090-28-45.300W	Fl Y 2.5s			Marks scientific monitoring location.	Private aid.
645	*Remington-105-1 Lighted Buoy* Marks Subsea Installation.	28-33-36.595N 090-19-26.174W	Q W			White with orange bands.	SIGN: ROG-ST-159-1. Private aid.
650	*Hunt-114-4 Lighted Buoy* Marks subsea installation.	28-20-27.220N 090-22-05.192W	Fl W 2.5s			White with orange bands.	Private aid.
655	*Fugro Metocean Lighted Buoy*	26-41-28.445N 090-27-27.822W	Fl Y 2.5s			Yellow.	SIGN: FUGRO-WR-294 Private aid.
	GULF OF MEXICO (Chart 411)						
659	*SBM Stones Special Lighted Buoy*	26-25-38.740N 090-48-45.350W	Fl Y 2.5s				Marks subsurface turret buoy. Buoy not present when FPSO is onsite. Private aid.
660	*Petrobras BW Pioneer Lighted Buoy*	26-41-46.250N 090-30-30.160W	Fl Y 2.5s			Yellow.	Marks subsurface turret buoy. Buoy not present when FPSO is onsite. Private aid.
662	**CHEVRON-218-1 RACON**	26-14-51.000N 091-15-32.000W				On Chevron (Jack St. Malo) WR-718-B structure.	BAND: S, X RACON: U (. . _) Private aid.
	MISSISSIPPI RIVER TO GALVESTON (Chart 11340)						
665	*NS-Hamilton Oceanographic Lighted Buoy*	27-46-11.470N 090-31-14.560W	Fl Y 4s			Yellow.	Private aid.
670	*Ns-Hamilton Oceanographic Buoy*	27-46-01.000N 090-31-14.860W				Yellow.	Private aid.
675	*Walter-116-2 Lighted Buoy*	28-21-26.804N 090-32-41.802W	Fl W 2.5s			White with orange Bands.	SIGN: WALTER-ST239-2 Private aid.
680 17680	*Cat Island Pass Lighted Buoy CI*	29-00-12.927N 090-33-54.912W	Mo (A) W		5	Red and white stripes with red spherical topmark.	
685	*Trunkline-103-1 Lighted Buoy* Marks subsea installation.	28-47-16.000N 090-36-30.000W	Q R			Red.	SIGN: TGC-ST-72-T-21. Private aid.
690	*Probe-102-1 Lighted Buoy* Marks subsea installation.	28-26-18.764N 090-41-18.069W	Fl W 2.5s			White with orange bands.	SIGN: EP-ST-214. Private aid.
695	*Shell Lighted Mooring Buoy A*	28-09-29.000N 090-43-23.000W	Q W			White with blue bands.	Private aid.
707	*Fugro Lighted Scientific Monitoring Buoy*	26-24-15.420N 090-47-32.160W	Fl Y 2.5s			Provides real-time environmental reports to FPSO SBM Stone Turritella.	Private aid.
712	*Whistler Energy West Lighted Mooring Buoy*	27-56-37.005N 091-01-50.576W	Fl W 2.5s				Private aid.
712.01	*Whistler Energy East Lighted Mooring Buoy*	27-56-36.846N 091-01-39.428W	Fl W 2.5s				Private aid.

Light List corrected through LNM week: 01/18

(1) No.	(2) Name and Location	(3) Position	(4) Characteristic	(5) Height	(6) Range	(7) Structure	(8) Remarks
	**GULF COAST (Louisiana) - Eighth District**							

(1) No.	(2) Name and Location	(3) Position	(4) Characteristic	(5) Height	(6) Range	(7) Structure	(8) Remarks
	MISSISSIPPI RIVER TO GALVESTON (Chart 11340)						
715	*Kerr Mc Gee-111-8 Lighted Buoy)* Marks subsea installation.	28-30-09.000N 091-03-16.000W	Q W			Red.	SIGN: KM-SS-218-7. HORN: 1 blast ev 20s (2s bl). Private aid.
720	*Ankor Energy-100-6 (Lighted Buoy)* Marks subsea location.	28-15-33.470N 091-03-39.110W	Fl W 2.5s			White with orange bands.	Private aid.
725	*Chevron-196-39 Lighted Buoy* Marks subsea installaion.	28-40-01.000N 091-04-50.000W	Q R			Red.	SIGN: CH-SS-170-1. Private aid.
730	SHIP SHOAL OBSTRUCTION LIGHTS	28-54-52.328N 091-04-16.080W	Q W		4	Brown skeleton structure on piles. (Abandoned Lighthouse.)	Shows 2 Quick Flashing White Obstruction lights, displayed at a height of 17 feet from perimeter of lower platform.
735	*Century Offshore-106-2 Lighted Horn Buoy* Marks subsea installation.	28-44-09.000N 091-14-29.000W	Q R			Red.	SIGN: COMC-SS-150-9& 10. HORN: 1 blast ev 20s (2s bl). Private aid.
740	*Dominion-102-2 Lighted Buoy* Marks subsea installation.	28-21-58.900N 091-15-49.900W	Q W			White with orange bands.	SIGN: DEP-SS-249-6. Private aid.
745	Ship Shoal Buoy WR2 Marks remains of platform SS-199A.	28-34-34.000N 091-17-23.000W				Red nun.	Private aid.
760	*Remington-102-4 Lighted Buoy* Marks subsea installation.	28-17-49.431N 091-25-08.075W	Fl W 2.5s			White with orange bands.	SIGN: Remington-EI-302-3. Private aid.
765	*Ridgelake-103-1 Lighted Buoy*	28-18-30.294N 091-26-37.902W	Q W			White with orange bands.	SIGN: RIDGELAKE-EI-303. Private aid.
770	FOREST-112-23 LIGHTED BUOY Marks subsea installation.	28-10-46.670N 091-28-57.460W	Q G			Green.	SIGN: FOC-EI-342-A. Private aid.
775	*Apache-102-77 Lighted Buoy* Marks Subsea Installation.	28-24-13.206N 091-29-02.086W	Fl W 2.5s			White with orange bands.	SIGN: APACHE-EI-282-1. Private aid.
776	*BP Exploration-124-1 Lighted Buoy*	29-01-36.345N 091-31-36.855W	Fl W 2.5s			Marks submerged platform obstruction.	Private aid.
777	*Energy Resource-107-16 Lighted Buoy*	28-19-52.398N 091-32-30.277W	Fl W 2.5s			White with orange bands.	SIGN: TARPON-EI-305-1 Private aid.
780	NEWFIELD 102-23 LIGHTED BUOY Marks subsea installation.	28-40-13.000N 091-35-46.000W	Q W			White with orange bands.	SIGN: NFE-EL-206-B. Private aid.
805	*Walter-114-10 Lighted Buoy*	28-34-58.783N 091-47-20.670W	Fl W 2.5s			White with orange bands.	Private aid.
809	MERIT ENERGY OBSTRUCTION LIGHTS (4)	29-14-19.110N 091-52-52.390W	Q W			Marks 4 concrete obstructions.	Private aid.
810	*Talos-109-1 Lighted Buoy*	28-26-35.528N 091-56-03.894W	Fl W 2.5s			White with orange bands.	SIGN: TALOS-SMI-108-8. Private aid.
815	MCMORAN-SMI-224 MOORING FACILITY LIGHTS(8)	29-23-01.800N 091-57-26.900W	Q W	9		On pile.	Private aid.
825	*Remington-300-6 Lighted Buoy* REMINGTON-300-6 Lighted Buoy Marks Subsea Installation.	28-23-18.444N 092-03-46.363W	Fl W 2.5s			White with orange bands.	SIGN: ROG-SMI-116-1. Private aid.
835	MCMORAN-SMI-217-226 MOORING FACILITY LIGHTS(8)	29-26-19.900N 092-02-26.000W	Q W	9		On pile.	Private aid.
840	MCMORAN-SMI-212-228 MOORING FACILITY LIGHTS(10)	29-28-30.400N 092-02-55.900W	Q W	9		On pile.	Private aid.
845	MCMORAN-SMI-212-NORTH MOORING FACILITY LIGHTS(16)	29-29-19.200N 092-03-25.800W	Q W			On pile.	Private aid.
850	MCMORAN SOUTH MARSH ISLAND WELL 6 MOORING FACILITY LIGHTS (10)	29-28-48.000N 091-52-40.800W	Q W			On pile.	Private aid.
855	Tiger Shoal Buoy 2	29-19-24.716N 092-09-29.815W				Red nun.	

Light List corrected through LNM week: 01/18

(1) No.	(2) Name and Location	(3) Position	(4) Characteristic	(5) Height	(6) Range	(7) Structure	(8) Remarks
	GULF COAST (Louisiana) - Eighth District						

MISSISSIPPI RIVER TO GALVESTON (Chart 11340)

(1) No.	(2) Name and Location	(3) Position	(4) Characteristic	(5) Height	(6) Range	(7) Structure	(8) Remarks
860	El Paso-106-5 Lighted Buoy EL PASO-106-5 Lighted Buoy Marks Subsea Installation.	28-26-42.366N 092-16-04.464W	Fl W 4s			White with orange bands.	SIGN: EPP-VE-274-B. Private aid.
865	Energy Resource-103-12 Lighted Buoy Marks subsea installation.	28-34-23.159N 092-14-55.454W	Fl W 2.5s			White with orange bands.	SIGN: ENERGY RESOURCE-VR-249-1 Private aid.
870	Energy XXI-101-10 Lighted Buoy Marks subsea installation	28-30-30.073N 092-21-08.353W	Fl W 2.5s			White with orange bands.	Sign: ENERGY XXI-EI-256. Private aid.
875	Remington-104-3 Lighted Buoy	29-00-32.636N 092-23-17.846W	Q R			Red.	SIGN: REMINGTON-VE-136-1. Private aid.
880	Energy Resource-103-17 Lighted Buoy	28-09-57.930N 092-29-09.690W	Fl W 2.5s			White with orange bands.	SIGN: ENERGY RESOURCE-VR-348-1. Private aid.
882	Tana-109-2 (Lighted Buoy)	28-24-53.220N 092-29-02.200W	Fl W 2.5s			White with orange bands.	SIGN: TANA-VE-284-1. Private aid.
890	Mcmoran-130-13 Lighted Buoy Marks subsea installation.	28-55-52.400N 092-34-37.500W	Q R			Red.	SIGN: MOXY-VR-160-1. Private aid.
895	Texas A&M Current Meter Lighted Buoy P	29-10-00.000N 092-44-00.250W	Fl Y 4s			Yellow.	Maintained by Texas A&M. Private aid.
900	Transworld-102-10 Lighted Buoy Marks subsea installation.	28-56-49.018N 092-45-06.259W	Q G			Green.	SIGN: TEPI-EC-160-1. Private aid.
905	Tarpon-105-2 Lighted Buoy Marks subsea location.	28-28-11.517N 092-49-47.329W	Fl W 2.5s			White with orange bands.	Private aid.
920	**FIELDWOOD-100-13 (RACON)**	28-09-50.6592 092-51-44.8452				On Fieldwood Energy platform A.	RACON: G (- - .) BAND: S, X SIGN: FE-EC-332-A. Private aid.
930	**NOVUS-EC-318-B RACON**	28-13-07.960N 092-55-31.197W				On Novus Platform.	RACON: T (-) BAND: S, X SIGN: NOVUS-EC-318-B. Private aid.
932	Rooster-104-2 (Lighted Buoy)	28-31-29.310N 092-57-01.920W	Fl W 2.5s			White with orange bands.	ROOSTER-EC-246. Private aid.
943	Nippon-102-10 (Lighted Buoy)	28-21-12.631N 093-01-24.898W	Q G			Marks subsea obstruction.	SIGN: NIPPON-WC-533-A. Private aid.
945	Remington-250-11 Lighted Buoy	28-37-10.859N 093-01-21.972W	Fl W 2.5s			White and orange bands.	SIGN: REMINGTON-WC-457-1. Private aid.
957	Nippon-102-5 Lighted Buoy	28-21-05.696N 093-02-50.150W	Q R			Red	Marks subsea installation. SIGN:NIPPON-WC-534-A Private aid.
980	Helis-122-7 Lighted Buoy Marks subsea installation.	28-06-34.370N 093-11-46.240W	Fl W 2.5s			White with orange bands.	Private aid.
986	McMoran-999-10 (Lighted Buoy)	27-58-18.400N 093-12-13.100W	Fl W 2.5s			White with orange bands.	Private aid.
988	McMoran-999-11 (Lighted Buoy)	27-56-44.022N 093-12-06.102W	Fl W 2.5s			White with orange bands.	Private aid.
990	Gryphon-104-1 Lighted Buoy Marks subsea installation.	28-29-05.468N 093-16-19.634W	Q R			Red.	SIGN: GRAPHON-WC-489-1. Private aid.
995	**ENERGY XXI-112-3**	29-37-38.440N 093-18-11.500W				On El Paso platform 1.	RACON: C (- . - .) BAND: S, X SIGN: EL PASO-WC-62-1 Private aid.
998	Arena Offshore-108-7 (Lighted Buoy)	28-16-14.951N 093-20-29.660W	Fl W 2.5s			White with orange bands.	SIGN: ARENA-WC-564-1 Private aid.
1000	**TEXACO-GB-189-A RACON**	27-46-43.000N 093-18-34.000W				On Texaco platform A.	RACON: X (- . . -) BAND: S, X SIGN: TEXACO-GB-189-A. Private aid.
1005	Remington-250-14 Lighted Buoy Marks subsea installation.	29-24-34.562N 093-18-58.779W	Q R			Red.	SIGN: REMINGTON-WC-170-8. Private aid.

Light List corrected through LNM week: 01/18

(1) No.	(2) Name and Location	(3) Position	(4) Characteristic	(5) Height	(6) Range	(7) Structure	(8) Remarks
	GULF COAST (Louisiana) - Eighth District						
	MISSISSIPPI RIVER TO GALVESTON (Chart 11340)						
1010 21195	Calcasieu Channel Lighted Buoy CC	29-20-00.870N 093-13-17.564W	Mo (A) W		4	Red and white stripes with red spherical topmark.	
1015	Tarpon-100-2 Lighted Buoy Marks subsea installation.	28-03-02.454N 093-19-09.682W	Fl W 2.5s			White with orange bands.	SIGN: TARPON-WC-616-6&7. Private aid.
1020	**PISCES-WC-96-A RACON**	29-33-36.386N 093-25-53.867W		92		On Pisces Energy platform.	RACON: M (- -) Band: S, X SIGN: Pisces-WC-96-A Private aid.
1025	Eighteen Ft Shoal Lighted Buoy 3	29-30-36.846N 093-27-24.574W	Fl G 2.5s		5	Green.	
1030 20700	Mermentau Channel Entrance Lighted Buoy 2	29-42-04.047N 093-00-34.389W	Fl (2)R 5s		4	Red.	
1040	Dept. of Energy Brine Diffuser Lighted Buoy F	29-40-16.000N 093-28-09.000W	Fl Y 4s			Yellow.	Private aid.
1045	D.O.E. Brine Diffuser Lighted Gong Buoy G	29-39-52.000N 093-28-35.000W	Fl Y 4s			Yellow.	Private aid.
1055	Oryx-110-3 Lighted Buoy Marks subsea installation.	28-47-28.000N 093-35-34.000W	Q R			Red.	SIGN: SUN-WC-398-1. Ra ref. Private aid.
1060	TEXAS A&M CURRENT METER LIGHTED BUOY V	27-54-01.090N 093-37-15.610W	Fl Y 4s			Yellow.	Private aid.
1065	Seneca-120-2 Lighted Buoy Marks subsea installation.	28-04-44.120N 093-38-46.260W	Fl W 2.5s			White with orange bands.	SIGN : SENACA-HI-345-1. Private aid.
1070	Tarpon-103-1 Lighted Buoy Marks subsea installation.	28-14-02.298N 093-35-11.711W	Fl W 2.5s			White with orange bands.	SIGN: TARPON-HI-308-001. Private aid.
1075	Texas A&M Lighted Current Meter Buoy R	29-38-01.000N 093-38-30.000W	Fl Y 4s			Yellow.	Maintained by Texas A&M. Private aid.
1085 22300	Sabine Bank Channel Lighted Buoy SB	29-25-00.846N 093-40-00.586W	Mo (A) W		6	Red and white stripes with red spherical topmark.	
1090	Kerr Mc Gee-138-1 Lighted Buoy Marks subsea installation.	27-44-53.846N 093-43-18.429W	Fl Y 4s			Yellow.	SIGN: KM-GB-224-5. Private aid.
1095	SABINE BANK LIGHT	29-28-21.678N 093-43-21.264W	Q W	30	5	Red conical tower on cylindrical caisson.	Shows 2 quick flashing obstruction lights.
1100	Tarpon-103-2 Lighted Buoy	28-07-47.131N 093-44-41.360W	Fl W 2.5s			White and orange bands.	SIGN: TARPON-HI-366-001. Private aid.
1105 22440	**Sabine Pass East Jetty Light**	29-38-40.574N 093-49-21.938W	Iso W 2s	42	8	Cylindrical tower on piles. 25	
1110	Garden Banks Lighted Buoy E	27-54-34.260N 093-35-50.400W	Fl Y 4s			Yellow.	Private aid.
1115	Garden Banks Lighted Buoy W	27-52-35.100N 093-48-52.000W	Fl Y 4s			Yellow.	Private aid.
1120	Garden Banks Lighted Buoy S	28-09-55.080N 093-17-46.080W	Fl Y 4s			Yellow.	Private aid.
	GULF OF MEXICO (Chart 411)						
1122	NOAA Lighted Data Buoy 42055	22-12-10.000N 094-00-01.000W	Fl (4)Y 20s		4	Yellow disc buoy with mast.	Aid maintained by National Oceanic and Atmospheric Administration.
	GULF COAST (Texas) - Eighth District						
	MISSISSIPPI RIVER TO GALVESTON (Chart 11340)						
1130	Energy Resource-106-12 Lighted Buoy Marks subsea installation.	28-02-41.220N 094-00-33.280W	Fl W 2.5s			White with orange bands.	SIGN: Energy Resource-HI-545-2. Private aid.
1135	Texas A&M Lighted Buoy N	27-53-24.000N 094-02-12.000W	Fl Y 4s			Yellow.	Private aid.
1145	Energy Resource-106-11 Lighted Buoy	28-19-23.823N 094-03-13.837W	Fl W 2.5s			White with orange bands.	SIGN: Energy Resource-HI-466-1. Private aid.

Light List corrected through LNM week: 01/18

(1) No.	(2) Name and Location	(3) Position	(4) Characteristic	(5) Height	(6) Range	(7) Structure	(8) Remarks
			GULF COAST (Texas) - Eighth District				
	MISSISSIPPI RIVER TO GALVESTON (Chart 11340)						
1165	*Texas A&M Crnt Metr Lighted Buoy F*	28-50-30.000N 094-14-30.000W	Fl Y 4s			Yellow.	Ra ref. Private aid.
1170	*Mobil-213-3 Lighted Horn Buoy* *Marks Subsea Installation.*	28-50-11.000N 094-15-37.000W	Q R			Red.	SIGN: MO-HI-A68-2. HORN: 1 blast ev 20s (2s bl). Private aid.
1180	*Walter-112-6 Lighted Buoy* *Marks subsea installation.*	28-02-40.502N 094-14-16.588W	Fl W 2.5s			White with orange bands.	SIGN: WOG-HI-540-1. Private aid.
1185	*Texas Fishing Reef FR-TX-53 Lighted Buoy*	28-26-38.430N 094-17-06.160W	Fl Y 2.5s			Yellow.	SIGN: FR-TX-53. Private aid.
1190	**TEXACO-195-9 (RACON)**	28-00-42.529N 094-21-19.216W				On Texaco platform.	RACON: C (-.-.) CHAR: C (-•-•) BAND: S,X SIGN: CHEVRON-HI-555-A Private aid.
1195	**EXXON-HI-176-B RACON**	29-10-32.000N 094-22-14.000W		63		On Exxon platform B.	RACON: N (-.) BAND: S, X Private aid.
1200	*NOAA Lighted Data Buoy 42035*	29-13-54.000N 094-24-46.000W	Fl (4)Y 20s		3	Yellow disc buoy with mast.	Aid maintained by National Oceanic and Atmospheric Administration.
1205	*Galveston Entrance Precaution Area Wreck Lighted Buoy B*	29-06-34.808N 094-24-05.236W	Fl (2)W 5s		5	Black with red band.	Marks submerged wreck.
1210 23660	*Galveston Bay Entrance Lighted Buoy GA*	29-09-28.867N 094-25-53.670W	Mo (A) W		6	Red and white stripes with red spherical topmark.	
1215 23665	*Galveston Bay Entrance Traffic Lane Lighted Buoy A*	29-10-47.784N 094-27-35.533W	Fl Y 2.5s		5	Yellow.	
1220 23670	*Galveston Bay Entrance Traffic Lane Lighted Buoy C*	29-12-06.639N 094-29-17.469W	Fl Y 4s		6	Yellow.	
1225 23675	*Galveston Bay Entrance Traffic Lane Lighted Buoy E*	29-13-25.498N 094-30-59.436W	Fl Y 6s		5	Yellow.	
1230 23680	*Galveston Bay Entrance Lighted Buoy GB*	29-14-44.348N 094-32-41.467W	Mo (A) W		5	Red and white stripes with red spherical topmark.	AIS MMSI: 993682024
1241 23686	*Fieldwood-123-3 Lighted Buoy* *Marks subsea installation.*	29-13-31.445N 094-34-40.878W	Q R				Private aid.
1245	*Eaglescliff Wreck Lighted Buoy WR4* *185 yards, 140° from wreck.*	29-21-44.922N 094-39-21.328W	Q R		3	Red.	
1250	**FOREST-HI-A20-A RACON**	29-03-42.000N 094-16-06.000W				On Forest Oil platform A.	RACON: O (---) BAND: S, X SIGN: FOC-HI-A20-A. Private aid.
1255	**EXXON-GA-209-A RACON**	29-07-49.000N 094-32-48.000W		55		On Exxon platform A.	RACON: M (--) BAND: S, X SIGN: EXXON-GA-209-A. Private aid.
1260	*Galveston Safety Wreck Lighted Buoy WR 4*	28-58-24.900N 094-39-49.500W	Q R		3	Red.	Marks submerged wreck.
1265	*Texas Artificial Fishing Reef Lighted Buoy Fr-Tx-25* *Marks old platforms.*	29-08-34.431N 094-40-50.069W	Fl Y 6s			Yellow.	SIGN: FR-TX-25. Private aid.
1270	*Texas Artificial Fishing Reef Lighted Buoy*	28-53-31.670N 094-41-44.710W	Fl Y 6s			Yellow.	SIGN: FR-TX-41. Private aid.
1275	*Texas Artificial Fishing Reef Lighted Buoy*	28-52-04.976N 094-41-55.484W	Fl Y 6s			Yellow.	SIGN: FR-TX-42. Private aid.
1280	*Walter-101-16 Lighted Buoy* *Marks subsea installation.*	28-02-04.440N 094-45-32.721W	Q R			Red.	SIGN: WALTER-GA-A-192-1 Private aid.
1285	*NOAA Lighted Data Buoy 42019*	27-54-47.790N 095-21-10.116W	Fl (4)Y 20s		3	Yellow disc buoy with mast.	Aid maintained by National Oceanic and Atmospheric Administration.

Light List corrected through LNM week: 01/18

(1) No.	(2) Name and Location	(3) Position	(4) Characteristic	(5) Height	(6) Range	(7) Structure	(8) Remarks
	GULF COAST (Texas) - Eighth District						
	MISSISSIPPI RIVER TO GALVESTON (Chart 11340)						
1290	Texas A & M Lighted Oceanographic Buoy C Marks subsea installation.	28-48-39.400N 094-45-35.900W	Fl Y 4s			Yellow.	Private aid.
1300	Texas A & M Lighted Oceanographic Buoy B Marks subsea installation.	28-58-53.900N 094-53-58.800W	Fl Y 4s			Yellow.	Private aid.
1305	**SEAGULL-GA-330-A RACON**	28-47-16.000N 095-03-40.000W				On free standing caisson.	RACON: K (- . -) BAND: S, X SIGN: SEEP-GA-330-A. Private aid.
1310	PEREGRINE-102-1 Lighted Buoy Marks subsea installation.	28-09-37.740N 094-44-23.110W	Fl W 2.5s			White with orange bands.	SIGN: PEREGRINE-GA-A155-1. Private aid.
	GALVESTON TO RIO GRANDE (Chart 11300)						
1315 26905	Freeport Entrance Lighted Buoy FP	28-52-36.699N 095-14-08.815W	Mo (A) W		5	Red and white stripes with red spherical topmark.	AIS MMSI: 993682025
1320	George Vancvr Fish Reef Buoy Marks sunken liberty ship.	28-47-34.817N 095-20-52.052W				Yellow.	Private aid.
	MISSISSIPPI RIVER TO GALVESTON (Chart 11340)						
1322	MATAGORDA COUNTY PIER LIGHT	28-45-44.000N 095-37-42.560W	Fl W 2.5s			Marks outermost pier structure.	Private aid.
	GALVESTON TO RIO GRANDE (Chart 11300)						
1325	Pioneer-103-1 Lighted Horn Buoy Marks subsea installation.	28-36-52.709N 095-21-56.137W	Q R			Red.	SIGN: PIONEER-BR-397-1. Horn: 1 BLAST EV 20S(2S BL) Private aid.
1330	Brazos Area Wreck Lighted Buoy WR2	28-43-33.733N 095-32-37.286W	Q R		3	Red.	
1335	Mariner-101-3 Lighted Buoy	28-07-12.517N 095-39-12.146W	Fl W 2.5s			White with orange bands.	SIGN: MARINER-BR-24-1 Private aid.
1337	Texas Artificial Fish Reef FR-TX-54 Lighted Buoy	28-07-38.500N 095-42-56.550W	Fl Y 2.5s			Yellow spar buoy.	Private aid.
	MISSISSIPPI RIVER TO GALVESTON (Chart 11340)						
1340	Texas Parks and Wildlife Special Lighted Buoy FR-TX-55	28-03-24.700N 095-52-24.340W	Fl Y 2.5s			Marks artificial reef.	Private aid.
	GALVESTON TO RIO GRANDE (Chart 11300)						
1345	Pioneer-102-1 Lighted Buoy	28-23-17.909N 095-53-29.726W	Q R			Red.	Private aid.
1350	Texas A&M Current Meter Lighted Buoy W	28-21-00.000N 096-00-00.000W	Fl Y 4s			Yellow.	Private aid.
1355	Anadarko-120-1 Lighted Buoy	26-04-10.389N 096-00-00.137W	Fl W 2.5s				Private aid.
1357	Texas A&M Lighted Oceanographic Buoy X	27-03-57.730N 096-20-17.760W	Fl Y 2.5s				Private aid.
1360 27105	Enron-106-17 Lighted Buoy Marks subsea installation.	28-11-10.000N 096-23-07.000W	Q R			Red.	SIGN: ENRON MI BLK 586 RA REF. Private aid.
1365 27100	Matagorda Ship Channel Approach Lighted Buoy MSC	28-12-01.026N 096-05-12.882W	Mo (A) W		5	Red and white stripes with red spherical topmark.	
1375 27045	COLORADO RIVER WEST JETTY ENTRANCE LIGHT 1	28-35-27.975N 095-59-03.871W	Fl G 2.5s	17	4	SG on pile with platform.	
1377 27047	COLORADO RIVER EAST JETTY ENTRANCE OBSTRUCTION LIGHT	28-35-25.974N 095-58-48.871W	Q W	20	4	NB on platform.	
1380 27050	COLORADO RIVER EAST JETTY ENTRANCE LIGHT 2	28-35-27.720N 095-58-57.498W	Fl R 2.5s	17	4	TR on skeleton tower.	
1385 27110	**Matagorda Ship Channel Entrance Light**	28-25-18.466N 096-19-05.915W	Fl W 10s	64	5	On same structure as Matagorda Ship Channel Range B Rear Light.	Obscured from 257° to 040°.
1392 27117	Matagorda Ship Channel Entrance Lighted Buoy MB	28-23-01.012N 096-17-00.897W	Mo (A) W		6	Red and white stripes with red spherical topmark.	

11

Light List corrected through LNM week: 01/18

(1) No.	(2) Name and Location	(3) Position	(4) Characteristic	(5) Height	(6) Range	(7) Structure	(8) Remarks
		GULF COAST (Texas) - Eighth District					
	GALVESTON TO RIO GRANDE (Chart 11300)						
1395	MATAGORDA LIGHT HOUSE	28-20-12.000N 096-25-24.000W	Fl W 2.5s	90		Black conical tower.	Private aid.
1400	Texas A&M Lighted Buoy K	26-13-00.000N 096-30-00.000W	Fl Y 4s			Yellow.	Private aid.
1405	NOAA Lighted Data Buoy 42020	26-58-06.601N 096-41-36.894W	Fl (4)Y 20s		3	Yellow disc buoy with mast.	Aid maintained by National Oceanic and Atmospheric Administration.
1410	Texas A & M Oceangraphic Lighted Buoy H	27-52-01.200N 096-32-36.060W	Fl Y 4s			Yellow.	Private aid.
1415	Texas Fishing Reef-Fr-Tx-50 Lighted Buoy	26-11-11.228N 096-51-20.508W	Fl Y 2.5s			Yellow spar buoy.	Private aid.
1420	Shoreline Ten Wreck Lighted Buoy WR2	28-04-48.080N 096-42-56.425W	Q R		3	Red.	
1425	Denbury-101-1 Lighted Buoy Marks subsea installation.	27-11-10.639N 096-48-19.903W	Q R			Red.	SIGN: DENBURY- NP I-A9-1&2. Private aid.
1430 28135	Aransas Pass Entrance Lighted Buoy AP	27-47-34.122N 096-57-22.143W	Mo (A) W		6	Red and white stripes with red spherical topmark.	AIS MMSI: 993682026
1432	Texas Fishing Reef FR-TX-52 Lighted Buoy	27-38-47.040N 097-00-26.640W	Fl Y 2.5s			Yellow spar.	Private aid.
1440	Texas A & M Lighted Oceanographic Buoy J	26-11-30.000N 097-03-00.000W	Fl Y 4s			Yellow.	Private aid.
1445	FR-TX-58 Special Lighted Buoy	26-16-32.705N 097-02-19.838W	Fl Y 2.5s			Marks artificial reef.	Private aid.
1450 29455	Brazos Santiago Pass Entrance Lighted Buoy BS	26-03-55.982N 097-06-34.990W	Mo (A) W		5	Red and white stripes with red spherical topmark.	
1455	Texas Fishing Reef Lighted Buoy-Fr-Tx-51	26-31-32.100N 097-09-12.922W	Fl Y 2.5s			Yellow spar.	Private aid.
		GULF OF MEXICO (Central Part) - Eighth District					
	GULF OF MEXICO (Chart 411)						
1460	NOAA Lighted Data Buoy 42003 (ODAS)	26-00-25.000N 085-38-54.000W	Fl (4)Y 20s		3	Yellow disc buoy with mast.	Aid maintained by National Oceanic and Atmospheric Administration.
1462	NOAA Lighted Data Buoy 42S13-SCP01	26-00-25.000N 085-44-24.000W	Fl (4)Y 20s		3	Yellow.	Aid maintained by National Oceanic and Atmospheric Administration.
1463	NOAA Lighted Data Buoy 42S23-SCP03	25-55-48.000N 085-42-00.000W	Fl (4)Y 20s		3	Yellow.	Aid maintained by National Oceanic and Atmospheric Administration.
1465	NOAA Lighted Buoy 42001 (ODAS)	25-54-00.000N 089-40-00.000W	Fl (4)Y 20s		3	Yellow disc buoy with mast.	Aid maintained by National Oceanic and Atmospheric Administration.
1468	NOAA Data Buoy 42409	25-51-05.000N 089-15-05.000W				Yellow DART buoy.	Aid maintained by National Oceanic and Atmospheric Administration.
1470	NOAA Lighted Data Buoy 42002	26-04-31.445N 093-46-01.301W	Fl (4)Y 20s		5	Yellow disc buoy with mast.	Aid maintained by National Oceanic and Atmospheric Administration.
		FLORIDA - Eighth District					
	APALACHEE BAY (Chart 11405) Apalachee Bay						
1475	ECONFINA RIVER LIGHT	30-02-05.000N 083-55-35.000W	Fl W 4s			On pile.	Private aid.
1480	GAMBLE POINT LIGHT	30-04-38.600N 083-59-22.400W	Q W			On pile.	Private aid.

Light List corrected through LNM week: 01/18

(1) No.	(2) Name and Location	(3) Position	(4) Characteristic	(5) Height	(6) Range	(7) Structure	(8) Remarks
		FLORIDA - Eighth District					
	ST. MARKS RIVER AND APPROACHES (Chart 11406)						
	St Marks River						
1485	- OBSTRUCTION LIGHT	30-02-27.162N 084-10-37.224W	Q W	17	4		
1490 10	ST MARKS LIGHT 4,002 yards, 356° from front light.	30-04-25.725N 084-10-46.689W	Oc W 4s	80		White conical tower.	Light obscured from 106° to 246°. Higher intensity on rangeline.
1500	- *Lighted Buoy 1*	30-01-30.926N 084-10-34.793W	Fl G 4s		4	Green.	
1505	- Buoy 2	30-01-31.823N 084-10-30.992W				Red nun.	
1510	- Buoy 2A	30-01-54.197N 084-10-32.584W				Red nun.	
1515	- Buoy 3	30-01-54.634N 084-10-37.102W				Green can.	
1520	- Buoy 3A	30-02-17.552N 084-10-37.679W				Green can.	
1525	- Buoy 4	30-02-17.248N 084-10-34.370W				Red nun.	
1530	- Buoy 5	30-03-00.086N 084-10-59.854W				Green can.	
1535	- Buoy 4A	30-03-01.260N 084-10-56.719W				Red nun.	
1540	- LIGHT 7	30-03-44.980N 084-11-23.436W	Fl G 4s	17	4	SG on pile.	Ra ref.
1545	- Buoy 6	30-03-43.775N 084-11-19.360W				Red nun.	
1550	- Buoy 8	30-04-06.207N 084-11-22.607W				Red nun.	
1555	- Buoy 9	30-04-16.934N 084-11-28.151W				Green can.	
1560	- LIGHT 10	30-04-18.445N 084-11-22.190W	Fl R 4s	17	3	TR on pile.	Ra ref.
1565	- LIGHT 11	30-04-35.809N 084-11-17.441W	Fl G 4s	16	4	SG on dolphin.	
1570	- Buoy 12	30-04-36.743N 084-11-14.811W				Red nun.	
1575	- Buoy 13	30-04-40.743N 084-11-17.611W				Green can.	
1580	- LIGHT 14	30-04-48.836N 084-11-16.678W	Fl R 4s	17	4	TR on pile.	Ra ref.
1585	- Buoy 15	30-04-49.943N 084-11-21.611W				Green can.	
1590	- Buoy 16	30-04-56.201N 084-11-26.334W				Red nun.	
1595	- Buoy 16A	30-05-04.291N 084-11-35.971W				Red nun.	
1600	- LIGHT 17	30-05-05.419N 084-11-40.600W	Fl G 4s	17	4	SG on pile.	Ra ref.
1605	- Buoy 17A	30-05-15.084N 084-11-40.568W				Green can.	
1610	- Buoy 18	30-05-09.042N 084-11-38.212W				Red nun.	
1615	- Buoy 19	30-05-18.442N 084-11-41.212W				Green can.	
1620	- Buoy 20	30-05-26.242N 084-11-39.436W				Red nun.	
1625	- Buoy 22	30-05-37.632N 084-11-38.829W				Red nun.	
1630	- Buoy 23	30-05-37.487N 084-11-41.147W				Green can.	
1635	- Buoy 25	30-05-45.641N 084-11-41.412W				Green can.	
1640	- LIGHT 26	30-05-50.738N 084-11-40.139W	Q R	17	4	TR on pile.	Ra ref.

Light List corrected through LNM week: 01/18

(1) No.	(2) Name and Location	(3) Position	(4) Characteristic	(5) Height	(6) Range	(7) Structure	(8) Remarks
		FLORIDA - Eighth District					
	ST. MARKS RIVER AND APPROACHES (Chart 11406)						
	St Marks River						
1645	- Buoy 27	30-05-54.470N 084-11-44.660W				Green can.	
1650	- Buoy 28	30-06-04.288N 084-11-48.656W				Red nun.	
1655	- Buoy 27A	30-06-05.705N 084-11-52.393W				Green can.	
1660	- LIGHT 29	30-06-15.742N 084-11-59.605W	Fl G 4s	17	4	SG on pile.	Ra ref.
1665	- Buoy 30	30-06-18.915N 084-11-58.095W				Red nun.	
1670	- Buoy 32	30-06-26.155N 084-12-02.582W				Red nun.	
1675	- Buoy 33	30-06-33.173N 084-12-07.429W				Green can.	
1680	- LIGHT 34	30-06-37.345N 084-12-06.921W	Fl R 2.5s	17	4	TR on pile.	Ra ref.
1685	- Buoy 35	30-06-39.334N 084-12-11.094W				Green can.	
1690	- Buoy 36	30-06-49.432N 084-12-13.557W				Red nun.	
1695	- LIGHT 37	30-06-48.308N 084-12-18.233W	Fl G 4s	17	4	SG on pile.	Ra ref.
1700	- Buoy 37A	30-06-55.335N 084-12-13.572W				Green can.	
1705	- Buoy 39	30-07-03.740N 084-12-08.615W				Green can.	
1710	- LIGHT 40	30-07-06.779N 084-12-04.868W	Fl R 4s	17	4	TR on pile.	Ra ref.
1715	- Buoy 41	30-07-13.241N 084-12-04.554W				Green can.	
1720	- Buoy 42	30-07-18.105N 084-12-01.156W				Red nun.	
1725	- Buoy 43	30-07-27.390N 084-12-00.047W				Green can.	
1730	- LIGHT 44	30-07-30.814N 084-11-56.979W	Q R	17	4	TR on pile.	Ra ref.
1735	- Buoy 45	30-07-34.181N 084-12-00.649W				Green can.	
1740	- Buoy 45A	30-07-36.329N 084-12-01.401W				Green can.	
1745	- Buoy 46	30-07-39.274N 084-12-00.200W				Red nun.	
1750	- Buoy 47	30-07-46.539N 084-12-07.915W				Green can.	
1755	- LIGHT 48	30-07-48.009N 084-12-05.257W	Fl R 4s	17	3	TR on pile.	
1760	- Buoy 50	30-07-54.357N 084-12-12.368W				Red nun.	
1765	- Day beacon 51	30-07-55.704N 084-12-18.173W				SG on pile.	
1770	- Buoy 52	30-08-01.201N 084-12-17.005W				Red nun.	
1775	- Buoy 53	30-08-03.096N 084-12-21.486W				Green can.	
1780	- Day beacon 54	30-08-08.880N 084-12-22.715W				TR on pile.	
1785	- LIGHT 55	30-08-11.514N 084-12-27.862W	Fl G 2.5s	17	4	SG on pile.	Ra ref.
1790	- Buoy 56	30-08-15.738N 084-12-24.616W				Red nun.	
1795	- Buoy 57	30-08-22.538N 084-12-28.116W				Green can.	
1800	- Buoy 58	30-08-25.557N 084-12-26.631W				Red nun.	

(1) No.	(2) Name and Location	(3) Position	(4) Characteristic	(5) Height	(6) Range	(7) Structure	(8) Remarks
			FLORIDA - Eighth District				
	ST. MARKS RIVER AND APPROACHES (Chart 11406)						
	St Marks River						
1805	- Buoy 59	30-08-39.240N 084-12-32.881W				Green can.	
1810	- Buoy 60	30-08-40.861N 084-12-31.335W				Red nun.	
1815	- Day beacon 62	30-08-51.973N 084-12-38.711W				TR on pile.	
1820	- LIGHT 63	30-08-53.941N 084-12-42.436W	Fl G 4s	17	4	SG on pile.	Ra ref.
1825	- Buoy 64	30-08-56.337N 084-12-38.217W				Red nun.	
	APALACHEE BAY (Chart 11405)						
	Apalachee Bay						
1830	SHELL POINT LIGHT	30-02-21.007N 084-17-40.584W	Fl W 6s	17	5	NG on pile.	
1835	SHELL POINT MARINA LIGHT 2	30-03-04.000N 084-16-54.000W	Q R	12		TR on dolphin.	Private aid.
	Shell Point Channel						
1840	- Day beacon 1	30-02-50.000N 084-17-11.000W				SG on pile.	Private aid.
1845	- Day beacon 2	30-03-03.000N 084-17-06.000W				TR on pile.	Private aid.
1850	- Day beacon 3	30-03-03.000N 084-17-12.000W				SG on pile.	Private aid.
1855	- Day beacon 4	30-03-12.000N 084-17-11.000W				TR on pile.	Private aid.
1860	- Day beacon 5	30-03-08.000N 084-17-15.000W				SG on pile.	Private aid.
1865	- Day beacon 6	30-03-11.000N 084-17-08.000W				TR on pile.	Private aid.
1870	- Day beacon 7	30-03-13.000N 084-17-19.000W				SG on pile.	Private aid.
1875	- Day beacon 8	30-03-15.000N 084-17-12.000W				TR on pile.	Private aid.
1880	- Day beacon 9	30-03-20.000N 084-17-30.000W				SG on pile.	Private aid.
1885	- Day beacon 10	30-03-20.000N 084-17-18.000W				TR on pile.	Private aid.
1890	- Day beacon 11	30-03-28.000N 084-17-15.000W				SG on pile.	Private aid.
1895	- Day beacon 12	30-03-24.000N 084-17-12.000W				TR on pile.	Private aid.
1900	- Day beacon 13	30-03-30.000N 084-17-11.000W				SG on pile.	Private aid.
1905	- Day beacon 14	30-03-30.000N 084-17-06.000W				TR on pile.	Private aid.
1910	- Day beacon 15	30-03-34.000N 084-17-06.000W				SG on pile.	Private aid.
1915	- Day beacon 16	30-03-36.000N 084-17-02.000W				TR on pile.	Private aid.
	Junction Channel						
1920	- Day beacon 1	30-03-21.000N 084-17-35.000W				SG on pile.	Private aid.
1925	- Day beacon 2	30-03-26.000N 084-17-37.000W				TR on pile.	Private aid.
1930	- Day beacon 3	30-03-17.000N 084-17-45.000W				SG on pile.	Private aid.
1935	- Day beacon 4	30-03-21.000N 084-17-51.000W				TR on pile.	Private aid.
1940	- Day beacon 5	30-03-09.000N 084-17-56.000W				SG on pile.	Private aid.
1945	- Day beacon 6	30-03-15.000N 084-18-00.000W				TR on pile.	Private aid.
1950	- Day beacon 7	30-03-05.000N 084-18-06.000W				SG on pile.	Private aid.

Light List corrected through LNM week: 01/18

(1) No.	(2) Name and Location	(3) Position	(4) Characteristic	(5) Height	(6) Range	(7) Structure	(8) Remarks
		FLORIDA - Eighth District					
	APALACHEE BAY (Chart 11405)						
	Apalachee Bay						
	Oyster Bay Channel						
1955	- Day beacon 1	30-03-50.000N 084-18-21.000W				SG on pile.	Private aid.
1960	- Day beacon 2	30-03-48.000N 084-18-16.000W				TR on pile.	Private aid.
1965	- Day beacon 3	30-03-56.000N 084-18-24.000W				SG on pile.	Private aid.
1970	- Day beacon 4	30-03-55.000N 084-18-16.000W				TR on pile.	Private aid.
	Spring Creek Channel						
1975	- Day beacon 1	30-02-30.000N 084-18-08.000W				SG on pile.	Private aid.
1980	- Day beacon 2	30-02-37.000N 084-18-00.000W				TR on pile.	Private aid.
1985	- Day beacon 3	30-02-37.000N 084-18-22.000W				SG on pile.	Private aid.
1990	- Day beacon 4	30-02-42.000N 084-18-12.000W				TR on pile.	Private aid.
1995	- Day beacon 5	30-02-54.000N 084-18-21.000W				SG on pile.	Private aid.
2000	- Day beacon 6	30-02-55.000N 084-18-20.000W				TR on pile.	Private aid.
2005	- Day beacon 7	30-03-01.000N 084-18-19.000W				SG on pile.	Private aid.
2010	- Day beacon 8	30-03-02.000N 084-18-14.000W				TR on pile.	Private aid.
2015	- Day beacon 9	30-03-06.000N 084-18-24.000W				SG on pile.	Private aid.
2020	- Day beacon 10	30-03-10.000N 084-18-17.000W				TR on pile.	Private aid.
2025	- Day beacon 11	30-03-12.000N 084-18-24.000W				SG on pile.	Private aid.
2030	- Day beacon 12	30-03-14.000N 084-18-20.000W				TR on pile.	Private aid.
2035	- Day beacon 13	30-03-15.000N 084-18-28.000W				SG on pile.	Private aid.
2040	- Day beacon 14	30-03-18.000N 084-18-22.000W				TR on pile.	Private aid.
2045	- Day beacon 15	30-03-20.000N 084-18-30.000W				SG on pile.	Private aid.
2050	- Day beacon 16	30-03-24.000N 084-18-28.000W				TR on pile	Private aid.
2055	- Day beacon 17	30-03-24.000N 084-18-37.000W				SG on pile.	Private aid.
2060	- Day beacon 18	30-03-25.000N 084-18-36.000W				TR on pile.	Private aid.
2065	- Day beacon 19	30-03-24.000N 084-18-47.000W				SG on pile.	Private aid.
2070	- Day beacon 20	30-03-26.000N 084-18-41.000W				TR on pile.	Private aid.
2075	- Day beacon 21	30-03-35.000N 084-18-43.000W				SG on pile.	Private aid.
2080	- Day beacon 22	30-03-33.000N 084-18-37.000W				TR on pile.	Private aid.
2085	- Day beacon 23	30-03-38.000N 084-18-37.000W				SG on pile.	Private aid.
2090	- Day beacon 24	30-03-38.000N 084-18-33.000W				TR on pile.	Private aid.
2095	- Day beacon 25	30-03-50.000N 084-18-42.000W				SG on pile.	Private aid.
2100	- Day beacon 26	30-03-54.000N 084-18-37.000W				TR on pile.	Private aid.
2105	- Day beacon 27	30-03-48.000N 084-19-00.000W				SG on pile.	Private aid.

Light List corrected through LNM week: 01/18

(1) No.	(2) Name and Location	(3) Position	(4) Characteristic	(5) Height	(6) Range	(7) Structure	(8) Remarks
	FLORIDA - Eighth District						
	APALACHEE BAY (Chart 11405)						
	Apalachee Bay						
	Spring Creek Channel						
2110	- Day beacon 28	30-03-54.000N 084-18-55.000W				TR on pile.	Private aid.
2115	- Day beacon 29	30-03-55.000N 084-19-13.000W				SG on pile.	Private aid.
2120	- Day beacon 30	30-03-59.000N 084-19-07.000W				TR on pile.	Private aid.
2125	- Day beacon 31	30-04-05.000N 084-19-27.000W				SG on pile.	Private aid.
2130	- Day beacon 32	30-04-11.000N 084-19-22.000W				TR on pile.	Private aid.
2135	- Day beacon 33	30-04-18.000N 084-19-22.000W				SG on pile.	Private aid.
2140	- Day beacon 34	30-04-19.000N 084-19-18.000W				TR on pile.	Private aid.
2145	- Day beacon 35	30-04-20.000N 084-19-35.000W				SG on pile.	Private aid.
2150	- Day beacon 36	30-04-24.000N 084-19-30.000W				TR on pile.	Private aid.
2155	- Day beacon 38	30-04-25.000N 084-19-38.000W				TR on pile.	Private aid.
	Panacea Channel						
2160	- Day beacon 2	30-00-23.739N 084-18-42.938W				TR on pile.	
2165	- LIGHT 3	30-00-14.139N 084-20-10.120W	Fl G 4s	17	5	SG on dolphin.	
2170	- Day beacon 4	30-00-16.408N 084-20-09.974W				TR on pile.	
2175	- Day beacon 5	30-00-15.483N 084-20-22.524W				SG on pile.	Ra ref.
2180	- Day beacon 7	30-00-16.590N 084-20-36.535W				SG on pile.	
2185	- LIGHT 8	30-00-19.235N 084-20-39.302W	Fl R 2.5s	15	3	TR on dolphin.	
2190	- Buoy 9	30-00-16.663N 084-20-41.706W				Green can.	
2195	- Day beacon 10	30-00-03.574N 084-21-19.328W				TR on pile.	
2200	- LIGHT 11	30-00-01.657N 084-21-21.777W	Q G	16	3	SG on dolphin.	
2205	- Day beacon 12	30-00-05.490N 084-21-26.249W				TR on pile.	
2210	- Day beacon 14	30-00-09.242N 084-21-35.709W				TR on pile.	
2215	- Day beacon 14A	30-00-14.115N 084-21-41.290W				TR on pile.	
2220	- LIGHT 15	30-00-09.334N 084-21-39.709W	Fl G 2.5s	16	3	SG on dolphin.	
2225	- Buoy 15A	30-00-14.533N 084-21-44.548W				Green can.	
2230	- LIGHT 18	30-00-37.221N 084-21-57.850W	Fl R 2.5s	16	3	TR on pile.	Ra ref.
2235	- Day beacon 19	30-00-37.581N 084-22-00.078W				SG on pile.	
2240	- Day beacon 19A	30-00-44.227N 084-22-13.054W				SG on pile.	
2245	- Day beacon 21	30-00-46.573N 084-22-19.135W				SG on pile.	
2250	- Day beacon 22	30-00-55.730N 084-22-34.243W				TR on pile.	
2255	- LIGHT 23	30-00-55.281N 084-22-36.834W	Fl G 2.5s	17	3	SG on dolphin.	
2260	- Buoy 24	30-00-58.252N 084-22-36.585W				Red nun.	

(1) No.	(2) Name and Location	(3) Position	(4) Characteristic	(5) Height	(6) Range	(7) Structure	(8) Remarks
		FLORIDA - Eighth District					
	APALACHEE BAY (Chart 11405)						
	Apalachee Bay						
	Panacea Channel						
2265	- Buoy 25	30-01-10.851N 084-22-44.781W				Green can.	
2270	- LIGHT 26	30-01-16.800N 084-22-45.640W	Q R	16	3	TR on dolphin.	
2275	- Day beacon 27	30-01-15.551N 084-22-48.911W				SG on pile.	
2280	- Day beacon 28	30-01-18.970N 084-22-56.922W				TR on pile.	
2285	- Day beacon 29	30-01-17.274N 084-22-59.006W				SG on pile.	
2287	WEI SPECIAL LIGHT A	30-01-59.940N 084-21-21.420W	Fl Y 2.5s			Marks aquaculture perimeter.	Private aid.
2287.01	WEI SPECIAL LIGHT B	30-02-06.660N 084-21-19.740W	Fl Y 2.5s			Marks aquaculture perimeter.	Private aid.
2287.02	WEI SPECIAL LIGHT C	30-02-06.660N 084-21-23.340W	Fl Y 2.5s			Marks aquaculture perimeter.	Private aid.
2287.03	WEI SPECIAL LIGHT D	30-01-59.940N 084-21-24.900W	Fl Y 2.5s			Marks aquaculture perimeter.	Private aid.
2287.04	FLORIDA DEPARTMENT OF AGRICULTURE OYSTER BAY SPECIAL LIGHT A	30-02-43.080N 084-20-02.039W	Fl Y 2.5s			Marks perimeter of aquaculture farm.	Private aid.
2287.05	FLORIDA DEPARTMENT OF AGRICULTURE OYSTER BAY SPECIAL LIGHT B	30-02-45.275N 084-19-59.520W	Fl Y 2.5s			Marks perimeter of aquaculture farm.	Private aid.
2287.06	FLORIDA DEPARTMENT OF AGRICULTURE OYSTER BAY SPECIAL LIGHT C	30-03-01.835N 084-20-09.960W	Fl Y 2.5s			Marks perimeter of aquaculture farm.	Private aid.
2287.07	FLORIDA DEPARTMENT OF AGRICULTURE OYSTER BAY SPECIAL LIGHT D	30-03-16.307N 084-20-09.960W	Fl Y 2.5s			Marks perimeter of aquaculture farm.	Private aid.
2287.08	FLORIDA DEPARTMENT OF AGRICULTURE OYSTER BAY SPECIAL LIGHT E	30-03-25.920N 084-20-09.960W	Fl Y 2.5s			Marks perimeter of aquaculture farm.	Private aid.
2287.09	FLORIDA DEPARTMENT OF AGRICULTURE OYSTER BAY SPECIAL LIGHT F	30-03-25.883N 084-20-22.919W	Fl Y 2.5s			Marks perimeter of aquaculture farm.	Private aid.
2287.11	FLORIDA DEPARTMENT OF AGRICULTURE OYSTER BAY SPECIAL LIGHT G	30-03-16.272N 084-20-24.719W	Fl Y 2.5s			Marks perimeter of aquaculture farm.	Private aid.
2287.12	FLORIDA DEPARTMENT OF AGRICULTURE OYSTER BAY SPECIAL LIGHT H	30-03-02.052N 084-20-18.959W	Fl Y 2.5s			Marks perimeter of aquaculture farm.	Private aid.
2287.13	FLORIDA DEPARTMENT OF AGRICULTURE EARL AND LEWIS SPECIAL LIGHT A	30-01-40.018N 084-21-28.501W	Fl Y 2.5s			Marks perimeter of aquaculture farm.	Private aid.
2287.14	FLORIDA DEPARTMENT OF AGRICULTURE EARL AND LEWIS SPECIAL LIGHT B	30-01-42.059N 084-21-25.740W	Fl Y 2.5s			Marks perimeter of aquaculture farm.	Private aid.
2287.15	FLORIDA DEPARTMENT OF AGRICULTURE EARL AND LEWIS SPECIAL LIGHT C	30-01-44.759N 084-21-25.318W				Marks perimeter of aquaculture farm.	Private aid.
2287.16	FLORIDA DEPARTMENT OF AGRICULTURE EARL AND LEWIS SPECIAL LIGHT D	30-01-44.759N 084-21-28.800W	Fl Y 2.5s			Marks perimeter of aquaculture farm.	Private aid.
2287.17	FLORIDA DEPARTMENT OF AGRICULTURE EARL AND LEWIS SPECIAL LIGHT E	30-01-40.018N 084-21-32.219W	Fl Y 2.5s			Marks perimeter of aquaculture farm.	Private aid.
2287.18	FLORIDA DEPARTMENT OF AGRICULTURE WAKULLA OYSTER FARMS SPECIAL LIGHT A	30-01-51.319N 084-21-21.639W	Fl Y 2.5s			Marks perimeter of aquaculture farm.	Private aid.
2287.19	FLORIDA DEPARTMENT OF AGRICULTURE WAKULLA OYSTER FARMS SPECIAL LIGHT B	30-01-59.541N 084-21-19.630W	Fl Y 2.5s			Marks perimeter of aquaculture farm.	Private aid.

Light List corrected through LNM week: 01/18

(1) No.	(2) Name and Location	(3) Position	(4) Characteristic	(5) Height	(6) Range	(7) Structure	(8) Remarks
			FLORIDA - Eighth District				
	APALACHEE BAY (Chart 11405)						
	Apalachee Bay						
	Panacea Channel						
2287.21	FLORIDA DEPARTMENT OF AGRICULTURE WAKULLA OYSTER FARMS SPECIAL LIGHT C	30-01-59.739N 084-21-22.409W	Fl Y 2.5s			Marks perimeter of aquaculture farm.	Private aid.
2287.22	FLORIDA DEPARTMENT OF AGRICULTURE WAKULLA OYSTER FARMS SPECIAL LIGHT D	30-01-51.744N 084-21-24.728W	Fl Y 2.5s			Marks perimeter of aquaculture farm.	Private aid.
2287.23	FLORIDA DEPARTMENT OF AGRICULTURE SKIPPER BAY OYSTER FARM SPECIAL LIGHT A	30-02-11.520N 084-21-39.680W	Fl Y 2.5s			Marks aquaculture farm perimeter.	Private aid.
2287.24	FLORIDA DEPARTMENT OF AGRICULTURE SKIPPER BAY OYSTER FARM SPECIAL LIGHT B	30-02-11.760N 084-21-29.520W	Fl Y 2.5s			Marks aquaculture farm perimeter.	Private aid.
2287.25	FLORIDA DEPARTMENT OF AGRICULTURE SKIPPER BAY OYSTER FARM SPECIAL LIGHT C	30-02-16.580N 084-21-29.520W	Fl Y 2.5s			Marks aquaculture farm perimeter.	Private aid.
2287.26	FLORIDA DEPARTMENT OF AGRICULTURE SKIPPER BAY OYSTER FARM SPECIAL LIGHT D	30-02-22.550N 084-21-33.480W	Fl Y 2.5s			Marks aquaculture farm perimeter.	Private aid.
2287.27	FLORIDA DEPARTMENT OF AGRICULTURE SKIPPER BAY OYSTER FARM SPECIAL LIGHT E	30-02-29.140N 084-21-32.610W	Fl Y 2.5s			Marks aquaculture farm perimeter.	Private aid.
2287.28	FLORIDA DEPARTMENT OF AGRICULTURE SKIPPER BAY OYSTER FARM SPECIAL LIGHT F	30-02-34.140N 084-21-27.720W	Fl Y 2.5s			Marks aquaculture farm perimeter.	Private aid.
2287.29	FLORIDA DEPARTMENT OF AGRICULTURE SKIPPER BAY OYSTER FARM SPECIAL LIGHT G	30-02-39.550N 084-21-25.200W	Fl Y 2.5s			Marks aquaculture farm perimeter.	Private aid.
2287.31	FLORIDA DEPARTMENT OF AGRICULTURE SKIPPER BAY OYSTER FARM SPECIAL LIGHT H	30-02-40.230N 084-21-29.520W	Fl Y 2.5s			Marks aquaculture farm perimeter.	Private aid.
2287.32	FLORIDA DEPARTMENT OF AGRICULTURE SKIPPER BAY OYSTER FARM SPECIAL LIGHT I	30-02-33.480N 084-21-34.660W	Fl Y 2.5s			Marks aquaculture farm perimeter.	Private aid.
2287.33	FLORIDA DEPARTMENT OF AGRICULTURE SKIPPER BAY OYSTER FARM SPECIAL LIGHT J	30-02-29.000N 084-21-37.730W	Fl Y 2.5s			Marks aquaculture farm perimeter.	Private aid.
2287.34	FLORIDA DEPARTMENT OF AGRICULTURE SKIPPER BAY OYSTER FARM SPECIAL LIGHT K	30-02-23.710N 084-21-38.420W	Fl Y 2.5s			Marks aquaculture farm perimeter.	Private aid.
2287.35	FLORIDA DEPARTMENT OF AGRICULTURE SKIPPER BAY OYSTER FARM SPECIAL LIGHT L	30-02-16.550N 084-21-39.600W	Fl Y 2.5s			Marks aquaculture farm perimeter.	Private aid.
	APALACHEE BAY (Chart 11405)						
2290	OCHLOCKONEE BAY ENTRANCE LIGHT OB	29-56-02.787N 084-18-04.613W	Fl G 4s	17	4	SG on dolphin.	
2295	*Apalachee Bay Lighted Buoy 4*	29-58-48.000N 084-13-08.187W	Fl R 4s		4	Red.	
2300	APALACHEE BAY LIGHT 2	29-56-01.997N 084-15-44.932W	Fl R 4s	17	3	TR on pile.	
2305	LIGHT HOUSE POINT LH	29-52-26.043N 084-19-33.210W	Fl G 6s	17	5	SG on pile.	Ra ref.

Light List corrected through LNM week: 01/18

(1) No.	(2) Name and Location	(3) Position	(4) Characteristic	(5) Height	(6) Range	(7) Structure	(8) Remarks
		FLORIDA - Eighth District					
	APALACHEE BAY (Chart 11405)						
	Alligator Harbor						
2310	- ENTRANCE LIGHT 2	29-55-15.800N 084-27-07.000W	Fl R 2.5s	10		On dolphin.	Private aid.
2315	- Day beacon 4	29-55-23.300N 084-27-03.500W				TR on pile.	Private aid.
2320	- Day beacon 6	29-55-26.900N 084-27-02.300W				TR on pile.	Private aid.
2325	- Day beacon 8	29-55-29.000N 084-26-58.800W				TR on pile.	Private aid.
2328	FLORIDA DEPARTMENT OF AGRICULTURE SPECIAL LIGHT A	29-55-00.031N 084-24-11.798W	Fl Y 2.5s			Marks aquaculture perimeter.	Private aid.
2328.01	FLORIDA DEPARTMENT OF AGRICULTURE SPECIAL LIGHT B	29-55-07.852N 084-24-09.466W	Fl Y 2.5s			Marks aquaculture perimeter.	Private aid.
2328.02	FLORIDA DEPARTMENT OF AGRICULTURE SPECIAL LIGHT C	29-55-10.932N 084-24-23.047W	Fl Y 2.5s			Marks aquaculture perimeter.	Private aid.
2328.03	FLORIDA DEPARTMENT OF AGRICULTURE SPECIAL LIGHT D	29-55-13.025N 084-24-32.287W	Fl Y 2.5s			Marks aquaculture perimeter.	Private aid.
2328.04	FLORIDA DEPARTMENT OF AGRICULTURE SPECIAL LIGHT E	29-55-15.119N 084-24-41.524W	Fl Y 2.5s			Marks aquaculture perimeter.	Private aid.
2328.05	FLORIDA DEPARTMENT OF AGRICULTURE SPECIAL LIGHT F	29-55-17.998N 084-24-54.226W	Fl Y 2.5s			Marks aquaculture perimeter.	Private aid.
2328.06	FLORIDA DEPARTMENT OF AGRICULTURE SPECIAL LIGHT K	29-55-10.196N 084-24-56.549W	Fl Y 2.5s			Marks aquaculture perimeter.	Private aid.
2328.07	FLORIDA DEPARTMENT OF AGRICULTURE SPECIAL LIGHT L	29-55-07.639N 084-24-45.295W	Fl Y 2.5s			Marks aquaculture perimeter.	Private aid.
2328.08	FLORIDA DEPARTMENT OF AGRICULTURE SPECIAL LIGHT M	29-55-05.285N 084-24-34.884W	Fl Y 2.5s			Marks aquaculture perimeter.	Private aid.
2328.09	FLORIDA DEPARTMENT OF AGRICULTURE SPECIAL LIGHT N	29-55-02.861N 084-24-24.226W	Fl Y 2.5s			Marks aquaculture perimeter.	Private aid.
2328.11	FLORIDA DEPARTMENT OF AGRICULTURE SPECIAL LIGHT J	29-55-10.460N 084-24-59.051W	Fl Y 2.5s			Marks aquaculture perimeter.	Private aid.
2328.12	FLORIDA DEPARTMENT OF AGRICULTURE SPECIAL LIGHT G	29-55-18.394N 084-24-57.381W	Fl Y 2.5s			Marks aquaculture perimeter.	Private aid.
2328.13	FLORIDA DEPARTMENT OF AGRICULTURE SPECIAL LIGHT H	29-55-19.655N 084-25-05.319W	Fl Y 2.5s			Marks aquaculture perimeter.	Private aid.
2328.14	FLORIDA DEPARTMENT OF AGRICULTURE SPECIAL LIGHT I	29-55-11.719N 084-25-06.981W	Fl Y 2.5s			Marks aquaculture perimeter.	Private aid.
2330	- Day beacon 10	29-55-28.400N 084-26-55.400W				TR on pile.	Private aid.
2335	- Day beacon 12	29-55-27.000N 084-26-53.000W				TR on pile.	Private aid.
2340	- Day beacon 14	29-55-23.000N 084-26-48.700W				TR on pile.	Private aid.
2345	- Day beacon 16	29-55-17.600N 084-26-44.500W				TR on pile.	Private aid.
2350	- Day beacon 18	29-55-06.600N 084-26-34.600W				TR on pile.	Private aid.
2355	- Day beacon 20	29-54-58.600N 084-26-27.000W				TR on pile.	Private aid.
2360	- Day beacon 22	29-54-51.800N 084-26-18.500W				TR on pile.	Private aid.
2365	- Day beacon 24	29-54-43.100N 084-26-08.500W				TR on pile.	Private aid.

Light List corrected through LNM week: 01/18

(1) No.	(2) Name and Location	(3) Position	(4) Characteristic	(5) Height	(6) Range	(7) Structure	(8) Remarks
	APALACHEE BAY (Chart 11405)						
	Alligator Harbor						
2370	- Day beacon 26	29-54-35.900N 084-25-54.000W				TR on pile.	Private aid.
2375	- Day beacon 28	29-54-29.200N 084-25-40.100W				TR on pile.	Private aid.
2380	- Day beacon 30	29-54-28.000N 084-25-35.400W				TR on pile.	Private aid.
2385	- Day beacon 31	29-54-29.300N 084-25-34.500W				SG on pile.	Private aid.
2390	- Day beacon 32	29-54-25.600N 084-25-26.700W				TR on pile.	Private aid.
2395	- Day beacon 33	29-54-27.000N 084-25-26.200W				SG on pile.	Private aid.
2400	- Day beacon 34	29-54-23.000N 084-25-18.200W				TR on pile.	Private aid.
2405	- Day beacon 35	29-54-25.100N 084-25-18.000W				SG on pile.	Private aid.
2410	- Day beacon 36	29-54-25.000N 084-25-00.100W				TR on pile.	Private aid.
2415	- Day beacon 37	29-54-26.000N 084-25-09.300W				SG on pile.	Private aid.
2420	- Day beacon 39	29-54-26.900N 084-25-07.200W				SG on pile.	Private aid.
2425	- Marina Junction Day beacon A	29-54-26.900N 084-25-07.300W				JR on pile.	Private aid.
	St. George Sound						
2430	DOG ISLAND REEF EAST LIGHT 1	29-52-15.023N 084-26-41.797W	Fl G 2.5s	17	5	SG on pile.	
2435	Dog Island Reef Wrk Buoy WR1	29-48-29.451N 084-26-47.881W				Green can.	
	Turkey Point						
2440	- Day beacon 2	29-52-30.000N 084-30-18.000W				TR on pile.	Private aid.
2445	- Day beacon 4	29-53-24.000N 084-30-30.000W				TR on pile.	Private aid.
2450	- Day beacon 6	29-53-44.000N 084-30-33.000W				TR on pile.	Private aid.
2455	- Day beacon 8	29-54-06.000N 084-30-36.000W				TR on pile.	Private aid.
2460	- Day beacon 10	29-54-18.000N 084-30-36.000W				TR on pile.	Private aid.
2465	- Day beacon 12	29-54-34.000N 084-30-38.000W				TR on pile.	Private aid.
2470	- Day beacon 14	29-54-48.000N 084-30-40.000W				TR on pile.	Private aid.
	St. George Sound						
2480	DOG ISLAND LIGHT 3	29-51-29.943N 084-31-30.028W	Fl G 4s	20	5	SG on pile.	
	CARRABELLE TO APALACHICOLA (Chart 11404)						
2485	DOG ISLAND LIGHT 5	29-51-05.981N 084-33-47.134W	Fl G 2.5s	17	4	SG on dolphin.	Ra ref.
2490	DOG ISLAND LIGHT 7	29-50-10.014N 084-35-16.919W	Fl G 4s	17	5	SG on pile.	
2495	DOG ISLAND LIGHT 8	29-48-47.995N 084-37-06.989W	Fl R 6s	17	5	TR on pile.	Ra ref.
2500	St. George Sound North Spoil Day beacon	29-49-32.172N 084-39-06.871W				NG on pile.	
2505	St. George Sound Middle Spoil Day beacon	29-48-57.460N 084-39-22.915W				NR on pile.	
2510	St. George Sound South Spoil Day beacon	29-48-13.770N 084-39-43.891W				NR on pile.	Ra ref.
2515 50	CROOKED RIVER LIGHT	29-49-38.100N 084-42-02.600W	Fl (2)W 15s	115		Square skeleton tower. Lower half white, upper half red.	Private aid.

FLORIDA - Eighth District

CARRABELLE TO APALACHICOLA (Chart 11404)

Carrabelle Channel

(1) No.	(2) Name and Location	(3) Position	(4) Characteristic	(5) Height	(6) Range	(7) Structure	(8) Remarks
2520 55	- Lighted Buoy 2	29-44-32.767N 084-39-12.146W	Fl R 4s		4	Red.	
2525	- Buoy 3	29-44-59.766N 084-39-27.647W				Green can.	
2530	- Lighted Buoy 5	29-45-42.515N 084-39-41.086W	Fl G 4s		3	Green.	
2535	- Buoy 7	29-45-59.765N 084-40-02.539W				Green can.	
2540	- Buoy 9	29-46-38.061N 084-40-35.004W				Green can.	
2545	- Lighted Buoy 10	29-46-41.346N 084-40-28.881W	Fl R 2.5s		3	Red.	
2550	- Lighted Buoy 12	29-47-04.762N 084-40-39.695W	Fl R 4s		3	Red.	
2555	- Lighted Buoy 13	29-47-49.967N 084-40-20.940W	Fl G 2.5s		3	Green.	
2560	- INNER LEADING LIGHT	29-49-47.889N 084-39-17.448W	Q W	19			Visible all around; higher intensity on heading 023.1°.
2570	- LIGHT 15	29-48-36.125N 084-39-53.849W	Fl G 4s	17	4	SG on dolphin.	Ra ref.
2575	- Buoy 17	29-49-04.933N 084-39-39.953W				Green can.	
2580	- South Spit Day beacon	29-49-39.083N 084-39-34.172W				NG on pile.	
2585	- Buoy 18	29-49-28.791N 084-39-24.298W				Red nun.	
2590	Carrabelle River Day beacon	29-49-18.426N 084-39-54.661W				NG on pile.	

Carrabelle River

(1) No.	(2) Name and Location	(3) Position	(4) Characteristic	(5) Height	(6) Range	(7) Structure	(8) Remarks
2595	- LIGHT 1	29-49-46.223N 084-39-22.393W	Q G	17	3	SG on pile.	Ra ref.
2600	- LIGHT 2	29-50-03.033N 084-39-32.007W	Fl R 4s	17	3		
2605	- Day beacon 3	29-50-01.049N 084-39-34.022W				SG on pile.	Ra ref.
2610	- Day beacon 4	29-50-15.038N 084-39-41.927W				TR on pile.	
2615	- LIGHT 5	29-50-14.921N 084-39-45.087W	Fl G 4s	17	3		
2620	- Lighted Buoy 6	29-50-26.806N 084-39-51.101W	Q R		3	Red.	
2625	- Day beacon 7	29-50-39.875N 084-39-57.135W				SG on pile.	Ra ref.
2630	- Day beacon 9	29-51-00.833N 084-39-58.741W				SG on pile.	
2635	- Day beacon 11	29-51-03.965N 084-40-01.850W				SG on pile.	
2640	- Day beacon 13	29-51-05.567N 084-40-05.504W				SG on pile.	
2645	- Day beacon 15	29-51-06.873N 084-40-11.364W				SG on pile.	Ra ref.
2650	- Day beacon 17	29-51-06.544N 084-40-17.655W				SG on pile.	
2655	- Day beacon 18	29-51-00.024N 084-40-25.235W				TR on pile.	
2660	- Day beacon 19	29-50-57.500N 084-40-26.039W				SG on pile.	
2665.01	- Buoy 21	29-50-57.481N 084-40-44.419W				Green can.	
2670.01	- Buoy 22	29-51-00.974N 084-40-47.706W				Red nun.	

Light List corrected through LNM week: 01/18

(1) No.	(2) Name and Location	(3) Position	(4) Characteristic	(5) Height	(6) Range	(7) Structure	(8) Remarks
	FLORIDA - Eighth District						
	CARRABELLE TO APALACHICOLA (Chart 11404)						
	Carrabelle River						
2670.02	- Buoy 21A	29-51-03.123N 084-40-52.834W				Green can.	
2675.01	- Buoy 23	29-51-04.832N 084-40-57.268W				Green can.	
2680.01	- Buoy 25	29-51-03.271N 084-41-09.862W				Green can.	
2685.01	- Buoy 26	29-51-04.471N 084-41-13.192W				Red nun.	
2690.01	- Buoy 28	29-51-05.633N 084-41-16.950W				Red nun.	
2695.01	- Buoy 30	29-51-07.391N 084-41-20.806W				Red nun.	
2700.01	- Buoy 32	29-51-12.280N 084-41-23.235W				Red nun.	
2705.01	- Buoy 34	29-51-16.958N 084-41-22.955W				Red nun.	
2710	- Buoy 36	29-51-19.251N 084-41-21.655W				Red nun.	
2715.01	- Buoy 38	29-51-21.591N 084-41-18.421W				Red nun.	
2720.01	- Buoy 40	29-51-23.708N 084-41-14.641W				Red nun.	
2725.01	- Buoy 42	29-51-24.701N 084-41-11.514W				Red nun.	
2730.01	- Buoy 43	29-51-26.519N 084-41-09.233W				Green can.	
2735.01	- Buoy 44	29-51-24.578N 084-41-07.124W				Red nun.	
2740.01	- Buoy 45	29-51-24.467N 084-41-00.224W				Green can.	
2745.01	- Buoy 46	29-51-22.520N 084-40-57.951W				Red nun.	
2750.01	- Buoy 47	29-51-24.368N 084-40-50.691W				Green can.	
2755	- Buoy 49	29-51-24.718N 084-40-44.461W				Green can.	
2760.01	- Buoy 51	29-51-26.323N 084-40-39.664W				Green can.	
2765	- Buoy 53	29-51-27.732N 084-40-37.049W				Green can.	
2770.01	- Buoy 54	29-51-28.196N 084-40-33.940W				Red nun.	
2775.01	- Buoy 55	29-51-30.416N 084-40-34.270W				Green can.	
2780.01	- Buoy 56	29-51-38.784N 084-40-27.205W				Red nun.	
2785.01	- Buoy 57	29-51-39.309N 084-40-28.746W				Green can.	
2790.01	- Buoy 59	29-51-52.105N 084-40-26.270W				Green can.	
2795.01	- Buoy 61	29-51-55.294N 084-40-27.789W				Green can.	
2800	- Buoy 63	29-51-57.562N 084-40-29.371W				Green can.	
2805.01	- Buoy 65	29-51-59.946N 084-40-37.181W				Green can.	
2810.01	- Buoy 67	29-51-59.645N 084-40-41.795W				Green can.	
2815.01	- Buoy 68	29-51-59.604N 084-40-45.233W				Red nun.	
	APALACHICOLA BAY TO LAKE WIMICO (Chart 11402)						
	St George Island						
2820 65	- West Jetty Lighted Buoy 1	29-36-09.878N 084-57-13.271W	Fl G 2.5s		4	Green.	

Light List corrected through LNM week: 01/18

(1) No.	(2) Name and Location	(3) Position	(4) Characteristic	(5) Height	(6) Range	(7) Structure	(8) Remarks
		FLORIDA - Eighth District					
	APALACHICOLA BAY TO LAKE WIMICO (Chart 11402)						
	St George Island						
2825 70	- *East Jetty Lighted Buoy 2*	29-36-10.278N 084-57-09.471W	Fl R 2.5s		4	Red.	
2840	- *LIGHTED BUOY 3*	29-37-07.222N 084-57-44.027W	Fl G 2.5s		3	Green can.	
2842	- *LIGHTED BUOY 5*	29-37-19.710N 084-57-50.007W	Fl G 4s		3	Green can.	
2845	- *LIGHTED BUOY 4*	29-37-07.408N 084-57-42.223W	Fl R 2.5s		3	Red nun.	
2846	- *LIGHTED BUOY 6*	29-37-20.193N 084-57-48.114W	Fl R 4s		3	Red nun.	
2850	APALACHICOLA BAY WRECK LIGHT	29-39-20.143N 084-59-51.901W	Fl W 2.5s	17	5	NW on pile.	Ra ref.
	Apalachicola Bay						
	Two Mile Channel						
2855	- LIGHT 1	29-41-31.757N 085-00-45.332W	Fl G 2.5s	17	3	SG on pile.	Ra ref.
2860	- Buoy 2	29-41-45.891N 085-00-43.642W				Red nun.	
2865	- Buoy 3	29-42-02.187N 085-00-46.012W				Green can.	
2870	- Buoy 4	29-42-14.440N 085-00-44.482W				Red nun.	
2875	- Buoy 5	29-42-29.310N 085-00-46.781W				Green can.	
2880	- Buoy 7	29-42-42.163N 085-00-47.105W				Green can.	
2885	- Buoy 8	29-42-42.666N 085-00-45.307W				Red nun.	
2890	- Buoy 9	29-42-44.264N 085-00-48.508W				Green can.	
2895	- Day beacon 10	29-42-44.218N 085-00-43.366W				TR on pile.	Ra ref.
2900	- West End Day beacon 11	29-42-44.094N 085-01-01.951W				SG on pile.	
2905	- West End Day beacon 13	29-42-43.688N 085-01-16.772W				SG on pile.	
2910	- East End Day beacon 12	29-42-45.079N 085-00-28.268W				TR on pile.	Ra ref.
2915	- East End Day beacon 14	29-42-44.982N 085-00-15.445W				TR on pile.	Ra ref.
2920	- East End Buoy 16	29-42-45.156N 085-00-01.007W				Red nun.	
2925	- East End Day beacon 17	29-42-46.883N 084-59-50.652W				SG on pile.	NW also on pile worded CAUTION MANATEE
2930	- East End Buoy 18	29-42-51.040N 084-59-33.111W				Red nun.	
2935	- East End Day beacon 19	29-42-57.481N 084-59-19.902W				SG on pile.	Ra ref.
2940	- East End Day beacon 20	29-43-04.035N 084-59-04.906W				TR on pile.	Ra ref.
2945 30395	- JUNCTION LIGHT TM	29-43-12.327N 084-58-49.464W	Fl (2+1)G 6s	17	3	JG-SY on pile.	Ra ref.
2945.01	APALACHICOLA RIVER						From Mile 5.9 to Mile 106, the river is marked with numerous unlisted day beacons and unlighted buoys which are perodically relocaed to meet minor changing conditions.

Light List corrected through LNM week: 01/18

(1) No.	(2) Name and Location	(3) Position	(4) Characteristic	(5) Height	(6) Range	(7) Structure	(8) Remarks
			FLORIDA - Eighth District				
	APALACHICOLA BAY TO LAKE WIMICO (Chart 11402)						
	Apalachicola Bay						
	Two Mile Channel						
2945.02	FLINT RIVER						From Mile 1.0 to Mile 26.6, the river is marked with numerous unlisted day beacons and unlighted buoys which are periodaclly relocated to meet minor changing conditions.
2945.03	CHATTAHOOCHEE RIVER						From Mile 1.0 to Mile 165.0, the river is marked with numerous unlisted day beacons and unlighted buoys which are periodaclly relocated to meet minor changing conditions.
	West Pass						
2950	- LIGHT	29-37-56.708N 085-05-50.250W	Fl W 2.5s	17	5	NB on dolphin.	
2955	- Day beacon 8	29-37-18.775N 085-04-35.683W				TR on pile.	
2960	- LIGHT 10	29-36-32.438N 085-03-12.685W	Fl R 4s	17	3	TR on pile.	Ra ref.
2965	- LIGHT 12	29-36-18.547N 085-02-03.529W	Fl R 4s	17	5	TR on dolphin.	
	Presnells Channel						
2970	- Buoy 1	29-45-00.000N 085-18-50.000W				Green can.	Private aid.
2975	- Buoy 2	29-44-55.000N 085-18-51.000W				Red nun.	Private aid.
2980	- Buoy 3	29-44-56.000N 085-18-38.000W				Green can.	Private aid.
2985	- Buoy 4	29-44-54.000N 085-18-37.000W				Red nun.	Private aid.
2990	- Buoy 5	29-44-54.000N 085-18-24.000W				Green can.	Private aid.
2995	- Buoy 6	29-44-52.000N 085-18-22.000W				Red nun.	Private aid.
3000	Port St. Joe City Marina Channel Buoy 1	29-48-30.000N 085-18-24.000W				Green can.	Private aid.
3005	Port St. Joe City Marina Channel Buoy 2	29-48-16.000N 085-18-31.000W				Red nun.	Private aid.
3010	ST JOSEPH STATE PARK ENTRANCE LIGHT 1	29-45-52.560N 085-24-07.980W	Fl G 2.5s	6		SG on pile.	Private aid.
3015	ST JOSEPH STATE PARK ENTRANCE LIGHT 2	29-45-53.520N 085-24-11.280W	Fl R 2.5s	6		TR on pile.	Private aid.
	LAKE WIMICO TO EAST BAY (Chart 11393)						
	St Joseph Bay Entrance						
3020	- Lighted Buoy 2	29-52-14.267N 085-28-53.928W	Fl (2)R 5s		4	Red.	
3023	Port St. Joe Lighted Mooring Buoy	29-48-32.580N 085-30-22.340W	Fl W 2.5s			White with blue band.	Private aid.
3025	- A RANGE FRONT LIGHT	29-54-24.743N 085-24-17.714W	Q W	30		KRW on piles.	Visible all around; higher intensity on rangeline.
3030 95	**St Joseph Bay Light & Entrance A Range Rear Light** 2924 yards, 61.9° from front light.	29-55-05.668N 085-22-49.794W	Iso W 6s	78	13	KRW on skeleton tower. 78	
3035	- Lighted Buoy 3	29-52-33.346N 085-28-27.376W	Fl G 4s		4	Green.	
3040	- Buoy 4	29-52-47.068N 085-27-43.096W				Red nun.	
3045	- Buoy 5	29-53-08.437N 085-27-07.866W				Green can.	

(1) No.	(2) Name and Location	(3) Position	(4) Characteristic	(5) Height	(6) Range	(7) Structure	(8) Remarks
		FLORIDA - Eighth District					
	LAKE WIMICO TO EAST BAY (Chart 11393)						
	St Joseph Bay Entrance						
3050	- Lighted Buoy 6	29-53-20.009N 085-26-32.109W	Fl R 2.5s		3	Red.	
3055	- Lighted Buoy 8	29-53-39.245N 085-25-48.716W	Q R		3	Red.	
3060	- RANGE B & D FRONT LIGHT	29-53-44.049N 085-23-03.893W	Q R	29		KRW on pile.	Visible all around; higher intensity on rangeline.
3065	- RANGE B REAR LIGHT 1,432 yards, 089.3° from front light.	29-53-44.682N 085-22-15.101W	Iso R 6s	53		KRW on pile.	Visible on rangeline only.
3070	- RANGE B REAR LIGHT PASSING LIGHT	29-53-44.682N 085-22-15.101W	Fl W 4s	15	4	On same structure as St. Joseph Bay Entrance Range B Rear Light.	
3075	- Lighted Buoy 10	29-53-40.518N 085-24-15.666W	Fl R 2.5s		3	Red.	
3080	- C RANGE FRONT LIGHT	29-52-54.705N 085-22-31.397W	Fl W 2.5s	28		KRW on pile.	Visible all around, higher intensity on rangeline.
3085	- C RANGE REAR LIGHT 1,562 yards, 118.2° from front light.	29-52-32.802N 085-21-44.469W	Iso W 6s	52		KRW on pile.	Visible 4° each side of rangeline.
3090	- C RANGE REAR PASSING LIGHT	29-52-32.802N 085-21-44.469W	Fl W 2.5s	15	4	On same structure as St. Joseph Bay Entrance Range C Rear Light.	
3095	- Lighted Buoy 12	29-53-12.181N 085-23-14.696W	Q R		3	Red.	
3100	- Lighted Buoy 14	29-52-58.146N 085-23-04.443W	Fl R 2.5s		3	Red.	
3105	- RANGE D REAR LIGHT 1,235 yards, 358.3° from front light.	29-54-20.696N 085-23-05.140W	Iso R 6s	55		KRW on pile.	Visible on rangeline only. Range DOES NOT mark the channel centerline.
3110	- RANGE D REAR LIGHT PASSING LIGHT	29-54-20.696N 085-23-05.140W	Fl W 4s	15	4	On same structure as St. Joseph Bay Entrance Range D Light.	
3115	- Lighted Buoy 16	29-52-40.104N 085-22-58.210W	Fl R 2.5s		4	Red.	
3120	- Lighted Buoy 17 75 feet outside channel limit.	29-52-17.831N 085-22-48.413W	Fl G 4s		4	Green.	
3125	- Buoy 18	29-51-34.748N 085-23-01.812W				Red nun.	
	Port St Joe North Channel						
3130	- Lighted Buoy 19	29-50-42.750N 085-22-47.712W	Q G		4	Green.	
3135	- Lighted Buoy 21	29-50-09.645N 085-21-25.343W	Fl G 2.5s		4	Green.	
3140	- Buoy 22	29-49-52.138N 085-20-51.330W				Red nun.	
3145	- Lighted Buoy 24	29-49-38.542N 085-20-14.120W	Fl R 2.5s		3	Red.	
3150	- Buoy 26	29-49-26.243N 085-19-41.914W				Red nun.	
3155	- Buoy 27	29-49-17.751N 085-19-06.084W				Green can.	
3160	- Lighted Buoy 28	29-49-12.079N 085-19-03.357W	Fl R 4s		3	Red.	
3165	PORT ST JOE TURNING BASIN LIGHT 30	29-48-54.749N 085-18-55.488W	Fl R 6s	17	4	TR on pile.	

Light List corrected through LNM week: 01/18

(1) No.	(2) Name and Location	(3) Position	(4) Characteristic	(5) Height	(6) Range	(7) Structure	(8) Remarks
	FLORIDA - Eighth District						
	APALACHICOLA BAY TO LAKE WIMICO (Chart 11402)						
	West Pass						
	Presnells Channel						
3170	PORT ST JOE MARINA ENTRANCE LIGHT 2	29-48-48.280N 085-18-38.240W	Fl R 2.5s	7		TR on pile.	Private aid.
3175	PORT ST JOE MARINA ENTRANCE LIGHT 1	29-48-49.330N 085-18-38.490W	Fl G 2.5s	7		SG on pile.	Private aid.
	LAKE WIMICO TO EAST BAY (Chart 11393)						
	Port St Joe North Channel						
	Gulf County Canal						
3180	- Spoil Dump Buoy 2	29-49-32.875N 085-19-18.725W				Red nun.	
3185	- Buoy 3	29-49-45.344N 085-19-12.815W				Green can.	
3190	- *Entrance Lighted Buoy 4*	29-49-43.438N 085-19-13.047W	Fl R 2.5s		3	Red.	
3195	- Buoy 5	29-49-49.502N 085-19-03.450W				Green can.	
3200	- Entrance Buoy 6 50 feet outside channel limit.	29-49-48.165N 085-19-02.194W				Red nun.	
3205	- Buoy 7	29-49-53.009N 085-18-55.351W				Green can.	
3210	- Buoy 8	29-49-51.432N 085-18-54.359W				Red nun.	
	Windmark Beach						
3215	- East Channel Daybeacon 1	29-50-44.187N 085-20-03.566W				SG on pile.	Private aid.
3220	- East Channel Daybeacon 2	29-50-43.978N 085-20-02.559W				TR on pile.	Private aid.
3225	- East Channel Daybeacon 3	29-50-45.420N 085-20-03.329W				SG on pile.	Private aid.
3230	- East Channel Daybeacon 4	29-50-46.213N 085-20-02.417W				TR on pile.	Private aid.
3235	- Middle Channel Daybeacon 1	29-50-52.748N 085-20-12.554W				SG on pile.	Private aid.
3240	- Middle Channel Daybeacon 2	29-50-52.015N 085-20-12.125W				TR on pile.	Private aid.
3245	- Middle Channel Daybeacon 3	29-50-54.027N 085-20-10.554W				SG on pile.	Private aid.
3250	- Middle Channel Daybeacon 4	29-50-53.603N 085-20-10.204W				TR on pile.	Private aid.
3255	- West Channel Daybeacon 1	29-50-58.915N 085-20-16.939W				SG on pile.	Private aid.
3260	- West Channel Daybeacon 2	29-50-58.413N 085-20-16.513W				TR on pile.	Private aid.
	Mexico Beach Canal Entrance						
3265	- LIGHT 1	29-56-55.440N 085-25-49.200W	Fl G 6s	10		SG on pile.	Private aid.
3270	- LIGHT 2	29-56-55.200N 085-25-48.200W	Fl R 6s	10		TR on pile.	Private aid.
3285	- LIGHT 5	29-56-59.040N 085-25-49.320W	Fl G 6s	10		SG on pile.	Private aid.
3290	- LIGHT 6	29-56-59.460N 085-25-48.420W	Fl R 6s	10		TR on pile.	Private aid.
	ST. ANDREW BAY (Chart 11391)						
	St Andrew Bay Entrance						
3335 105	- *Lighted Buoy SA*	30-05-29.735N 085-46-25.752W	Mo (A) W		6	Red and white stripes with red spherical topmark.	AIS MMSI: 993682022
3340	ST ANDREW BAY A RANGE FRONT LIGHT	30-08-45.701N 085-41-34.203W	Fl W 2.5s	25		KRW on skeleton tower on piles	Lighted throughout 24 hours. Visible all around, higher intensity on range line.

Light List corrected through LNM week: 01/18

(1) No.	(2) Name and Location	(3) Position	(4) Characteristic	(5) Height	(6) Range	(7) Structure	(8) Remarks
		FLORIDA - Eighth District					
	ST. ANDREW BAY (Chart 11391)						
	St Andrew Bay Entrance						
3345	ST ANDREW BAY A RANGE REAR LIGHT 2,319 yards, 052.6° from front light.	30-09-27.753N 085-40-31.227W	Iso W 6s	65		KRW on skeleton tower on piles.	Lighted throughout 24 hours.
3350	- Lighted Buoy 1 75 feet outside channel limit.	30-06-36.316N 085-44-53.457W	Fl G 4s		4	Green.	
3355	- Lighted Buoy 2 75 feet outside channel limit.	30-06-31.645N 085-44-49.258W	Fl R 4s		3	Red.	
3360	- Lighted Buoy 3	30-06-53.463N 085-44-27.374W	Fl G 2.5s		4	Green.	
3365	- Lighted Buoy 4	30-06-49.158N 085-44-23.557W	Fl R 2.5s		3	Red.	
3370	- Lighted Buoy 6	30-07-15.503N 085-43-44.719W	Fl R 4s		3	Red.	
3375	- Lighted Buoy 8 75 feet outside channel limit.	30-07-27.528N 085-43-27.169W	Fl R 2.5s		3	Red.	
3378	ST. ANDREWS STATE PARK DANGER BREAKWATER LIGHT	30-07-32.520N 085-43-50.880W	Fl W 2.5s			Marks breakwater structure.	Private aid.
3378.01	ST. ANDREWS STATE PARK DANGER BREAKWATER LIGHT	30-07-33.960N 085-43-47.640W	Fl W 2.5s			Marks breakwater structure.	Private aid.
3378.02	ST. ANDREWS STATE PARK DANGER BREAKWATER LIGHT	30-07-35.040N 085-43-44.760W	Fl W 2.5s			Marks breakwater structure.	Private aid.
3378.03	ST. ANDREWS STATE PARK DANGER BREAKWATER LIGHT	30-07-36.810N 085-43-40.240W	Fl W 2.5s			Marks breakwater structure.	Private aid.
3380	- Lighted Buoy 9 75 feet outside channel limit.	30-07-42.682N 085-43-14.518W	Fl G 4s		4	Green.	
3385	- Lighted Buoy 10	30-07-36.731N 085-43-13.947W	Fl R 4s		3	Red.	
3390	- Lighted Buoy 11	30-07-57.123N 085-42-50.816W	Fl G 2.5s		3	Green	
3395	- Lighted Buoy 12 75 feet outside channel limit.	30-07-53.852N 085-42-47.976W	Fl R 2.5s		3	Red.	
3400	ST ANDREW BAY B RANGE FRONT LIGHT	30-08-03.060N 085-42-53.982W	Iso W 2s	25		KRW on tower on piles.	Ra ref. Visible all around, higher intensity on rangeline.
3405	ST ANDREW BAY B RANGE REAR LIGHT 1,217 yards, 251.6° from front light.	30-07-51.398N 085-43-34.801W	Iso W 6s	50		KRW on tower on piles.	Ra ref. Visible only on the rangeline.
3410	- Lighted Buoy 13	30-08-12.119N 085-42-28.218W	Fl G 4s		4	Green.	
3415	- Lighted Buoy 14	30-08-08.590N 085-42-25.082W	Fl R 4s		3	Red.	
3420	- Lighted Buoy 15	30-08-20.320N 085-42-03.060W	Fl G 2.5s		4	Green.	
3425	- Lighted Buoy 16	30-08-15.950N 085-42-01.360W	Fl R 2.5s		3	Red.	
3430	- Lighted Buoy 15A	30-08-38.119N 085-41-05.019W	Q G		4	Green.	
	St Andrew Bay						
3435 31120	- Junction Lighted Buoy	30-08-59.377N 085-40-47.122W	Fl (2+1)G 6s		4	Green can with red band and yellow triangle.	
3440	MASSALINA BAYOU ENTRANCE LIGHT 2	30-08-57.027N 085-39-44.040W	Fl R 2.5s	17	3	TR on pile.	Ra ref.
3445 31115	- Lighted Buoy 17	30-08-39.784N 085-39-57.886W	Q G		3	Green with yellow triangle.	

Light List corrected through LNM week: 01/18

(1) No.	(2) Name and Location	(3) Position	(4) Characteristic	(5) Height	(6) Range	(7) Structure	(8) Remarks
	FLORIDA - Eighth District						
	ST. ANDREW BAY (Chart 11391)						
	St Andrew Bay						
3450 31110	- LIGHT 18	30-08-34.642N 085-40-03.209W	Q R	17	3	TR-SY on pile.	
3455 31105	- *Lighted Buoy 19*	30-08-33.926N 085-39-32.985W	Fl G 2.5s		3	Green can with yellow triangle.	
3460 31100	- *Lighted Buoy 20*	30-08-19.803N 085-39-28.989W	Fl R 2.5s		3	Red with yellow square.	
3465 31095	- *Lighted Buoy 21*	30-08-01.827N 085-39-04.210W	Q G		4	Green with yellow triangle.	
3470 31090	- LIGHT 24	30-07-34.818N 085-38-32.747W	Fl R 4s	17	3	TR-SY on pile.	Ra ref.
3475 31085	- Coast Guard Mooring Buoy	30-07-27.548N 085-38-12.044W					For use by USCG only.
3480 31080	- *Lighted Buoy 25*	30-07-53.179N 085-37-53.445W	Fl G 2.5s		3	Green with yellow triangle.	
3485 31075	- LIGHT 28	30-07-39.529N 085-37-16.435W	Q R	17	3	TR-SY on pile.	Ra ref.
	Gulf Power Electrical Tower						
3490 31055	- DANGER LIGHT	30-07-49.570N 085-36-56.350W	Fl W 2.5s			NW on power line structure worded: DANGER OVERHEAD POWER LINE.	Private aid.
3495 31060	- DANGER LIGHTS(2)	30-07-44.890N 085-36-59.460W	Fl W 2.5s			NW on power line structure worded: DANGER OVERHEAD POWER LINE.	Private aid.
3500 31065	- DANGER LIGHTS (2)	30-07-38.920N 085-37-07.290W	Fl W 2.5s			NW on power line structure worded: DANGER OVERHEAD POWER LINE.	Private aid.
3505 31070	- DANGER LIGHT	30-07-33.790N 085-37-14.010W	Fl W 2.5s			NW on power line structure worded: DANGER OVERHEAD POWER LINE.	Private aid.
3510	Gainer Bayou Channel Day beacon 1	30-16-21.520N 085-37-31.690W				SG on pile.	Private aid.
3515	Gainer Bayou Channel Day beacon 2	30-16-21.550N 085-37-31.010W				TR on pile.	Private aid.
3520	Gainer Bayou Channel Day beacon 3	30-16-23.590N 085-37-31.820W				SG on pile.	Private aid.
3525	Gainer Bayou Channel Day beacon 4	30-16-23.380N 085-37-31.120W				TR on pile.	Private aid.
3530	Gainer Bayou Channel Day beacon 5	30-16-28.400N 085-37-27.080W				SG on pile.	Private aid.
3535	Gainer Bayou Channel Day beacon 6	30-16-28.220N 085-37-26.360W				TR on pile.	Private aid.
3540	Gainer Bayou Channel Day beacon 7	30-16-30.160N 085-37-27.330W				SG on pile.	Private aid.
3545	Gainer Bayou Channel Day beacon 8	30-16-30.240N 085-37-26.650W				TR on pile.	Private aid.
	St Andrew Bay						
3550 31050	- LIGHT 29	30-07-22.535N 085-36-41.759W	Fl G 2.5s	17	3	SG-TY on pile.	Ra ref.
3555 31125	- *West Lighted Buoy 3*	30-09-03.503N 085-41-16.512W	Q G		3	Green with yellow square.	
3560 31130	- *West Lighted Buoy 5*	30-09-16.301N 085-41-52.343W	Fl G 4s		4	Green with yellow square.	
3565	Buena Vista Day beacon	30-09-42.727N 085-41-35.744W				NW on pile worded DANGER.	Ra ref.
3570 31135	- *West Lighted Buoy 6*	30-09-29.544N 085-42-20.582W	Fl R 2.5s		3	Red with yellow triangle.	

Light List corrected through LNM week: 01/18

(1) No.	(2) Name and Location	(3) Position	(4) Characteristic	(5) Height	(6) Range	(7) Structure	(8) Remarks
	**FLORIDA - Eighth District**						
	ST. ANDREW BAY (Chart 11391)						
	St Andrew Bay						
3575 31140	- West Lighted Buoy 8	30-09-40.432N 085-42-36.298W	Fl R 4s		3	Red with yellow triangle.	
3580 31145	- West Lighted Buoy 9	30-09-50.184N 085-42-49.581W	Fl G 2.5s		4	Green with yellow square.	
3585 31150	- West Lighted Buoy 10	30-10-09.875N 085-43-00.709W	Fl R 4s		3	Red with yellow triangle.	
3590 31155	- West Lighted Buoy 11	30-09-57.727N 085-43-14.747W	Fl G 4s		4	Green with yellow square.	
3595 31160	- West Lighted Buoy 13	30-10-19.783N 085-43-29.111W	Fl G 2.5s		4	Green with yellow triangle.	
3600 31165	- WEST LIGHT 14	30-10-34.903N 085-44-10.493W	Fl R 4s	17	3	TR-TY on pile.	Ra ref.
	Navy Dive School						
3605	- Buoy A	30-09-55.000N 085-44-15.000W				Yellow sphere.	U.S. Navy maintained. Private aid.
3610	- Buoy B	30-09-56.000N 085-43-57.000W				Yellow sphere.	U.S. Navy maintained. Private aid.
3615	- Buoy C	30-09-56.600N 085-43-43.000W				Yellow sphere.	U.S. Navy maintained. Private aid.
3620	- Buoy D	30-09-57.000N 085-43-24.000W				Yellow sphere.	U.S. Navy maintained. Private aid.
	Section Base Magazine Area						
3625	- Day beacon 1	30-09-54.806N 085-44-17.943W				SG on pile.	Ra ref.
3630	- Day beacon 2	30-09-59.456N 085-44-20.049W				TR on pile.	Ra ref.
3635	- Day beacon 3	30-09-54.188N 085-44-29.259W				SG on pile.	Ra ref.
3640	- Day beacon 4	30-09-56.402N 085-44-28.305W				TR on pile.	Ra ref.
3645	- Day beacon 6	30-09-56.744N 085-44-30.219W				TR on pile.	Ra ref.
	Section Base Channel						
3650	- RANGE FRONT LIGHT	30-10-11.740N 085-45-21.011W	Q G	25		KRW on skeleton tower.	Visible only on the rangeline.
3655	- RANGE REAR LIGHT 161 yards, 239.9° from front light.	30-10-09.254N 085-45-25.904W	Oc G 4s	36		KRW on skeleton tower on block.	Visible only on the rangeline.
3660	- LIGHT 1	30-10-27.551N 085-44-47.090W	Fl G 4s	17	4	SG on pile.	Ra ref.
3665	- LIGHT 2	30-10-29.428N 085-44-49.751W	Fl R 4s	17	3	TR on pile.	Ra ref.
3670	- LIGHT 3	30-10-18.372N 085-45-02.985W	Fl G 2.5s	17	3	SG on pile.	Ra ref.
3675	- LIGHT 4	30-10-23.289N 085-45-02.584W	Fl R 2.5s	17	3	TR on pile.	Ra ref.
	Sulphur Point						
3680 31170	- Buoy 1	30-10-55.897N 085-44-35.144W				Green can with yellow square.	
3685 31175	- Buoy 2	30-10-56.024N 085-44-27.033W				Red nun with yellow triangle.	
3690 31180	- Buoy 3	30-11-05.534N 085-44-34.567W				Green can with yellow square.	
3695 31185	- Buoy 4	30-11-03.488N 085-44-27.084W				Red nun with yellow triangle.	
3700	GULF POWER COMPANY STRUCTURE LIGHT A	30-11-22.500N 085-44-20.500W	Q W	30		On skeleton tower.	Private aid.
3705	GULF POWER COMPANY STRUCTURE LIGHT B	30-11-23.000N 085-44-38.500W	Q W	30		On skeleton tower.	Private aid.

Light List corrected through LNM week: 01/18

(1) No.	(2) Name and Location	(3) Position	(4) Characteristic	(5) Height	(6) Range	(7) Structure	(8) Remarks
		FLORIDA - Eighth District					
	ST. ANDREW BAY (Chart 11391)						
	St Andrew Bay						
	Sulphur Point						
3710 31190	- Buoy 5	30-11-27.511N 085-44-32.740W				Green can with yellow square.	
3715 31195	- Buoy 6	30-11-26.748N 085-44-26.234W				Red nun with yellow triangle.	
3720 31200	- Buoy 7	30-11-36.130N 085-44-33.364W				Green can with yellow square.	
3725 31205	- Buoy 8	30-11-35.615N 085-44-23.871W				Red nun with yellow triangle.	
	Woodlawn Bayou Channel						
3730	- Day beacon 1	30-11-32.340N 085-44-58.500W				SG on pile.	Private aid.
3735	- Day beacon 2	30-11-33.480N 085-44-58.260W				TR on pile.	Private aid.
3740	- Day beacon 3	30-11-32.820N 085-45-00.780W				SG on pile.	Private aid.
3745	- Day beacon 4	30-11-33.720N 085-45-00.660W				TR on pile.	Private aid.
3750	- Day beacon 5	30-11-33.240N 085-45-04.200W				SG on pile.	Private aid.
3755	- Day beacon 6	30-11-34.020N 085-45-03.720W				TR on pile.	Private aid.
3760	- Day beacon 7	30-11-33.660N 085-45-06.900W				SG on pile.	Private aid.
3765	- Day beacon 8	30-11-34.440N 085-45-06.720W				TR on pile.	Private aid.
3770	- Day beacon 9	30-11-34.200N 085-45-08.460W				SG on pile.	Private aid.
3775	- Day beacon 10	30-11-34.560N 085-45-07.860W				TR on pile.	Private aid.
	Harbor Towne Channel						
3780	- Day beacon 1	30-11-55.260N 085-44-43.380W				SG on pile.	Private aid.
3785	- Day beacon 2	30-11-55.800N 085-44-42.720W				TR on pile.	Private aid.
3790	- Day beacon 3	30-11-56.700N 085-44-45.300W				SG on pile.	Private aid.
3795	- Day beacon 4	30-11-57.120N 085-44-44.760W				TR on pile.	Private aid.
3800	- Day beacon 5	30-11-57.688N 085-44-47.226W				SG on pile.	Private aid.
3805	- Day beacon 6	30-11-58.320N 085-44-46.620W				TR on pile.	Private aid.
3810	- Day beacon 7	30-11-58.832N 085-44-48.770W				SG on pile.	Private aid.
3815	- Day beacon 8	30-11-59.520N 085-44-48.840W				TR on pile.	Private aid.
	Posten Bayou Channel						
3820	- Day beacon 1	30-11-42.000N 085-43-20.160W				SG on pile.	Private aid.
3825	- Day beacon 2	30-11-41.220N 085-43-20.400W				TR on pile.	Private aid.
3830	- Day beacon 3	30-11-41.880N 085-43-16.200W				SG on pile.	Private aid.
3835	- Day beacon 4	30-11-41.280N 085-43-16.560W				TR on pile.	Private aid.
3840	- Day beacon 5	30-11-41.700N 085-43-08.400W				SG on pile.	Private aid.
3845	- Day beacon 6	30-11-41.280N 085-43-08.160W				TR on pile.	Private aid.
3850	- Day beacon 7	30-11-35.760N 085-43-00.840W				SG on pile.	Private aid.
3855	- Day beacon 8	30-11-39.120N 085-43-05.880W				TR on pile.	Private aid.

Light List corrected through LNM week: 01/18

(1) No.	(2) Name and Location	(3) Position	(4) Characteristic	(5) Height	(6) Range	(7) Structure	(8) Remarks
		FLORIDA - Eighth District					
	ST. ANDREW BAY (Chart 11391)						
	St Andrew Bay						
	Posten Bayou Channel						
3860	- Day beacon 9	30-11-33.840N 085-43-00.720W				SG on pile.	Private aid.
3865	- Day beacon 10	30-11-35.880N 085-43-01.320W				TR on pile.	Private aid.
3870	- Day beacon 11	30-11-31.920N 085-43-00.480W				SG on pile.	Private aid.
3875	- Day beacon 12	30-11-33.990N 085-43-01.080W				TR on pile.	Private aid.
	Pretty Bayou Channel						
3880	- North Day beacon 1	30-12-06.900N 085-42-32.580W				SG on pile.	Private aid.
3885	- North Day beacon 2	30-12-05.940N 085-42-32.940W				TR on pile.	Private aid.
3890	- North Day beacon 3	30-12-06.840N 085-42-30.240W				SG on pile.	Private aid.
3895	- North Day beacon 4	30-12-05.700N 085-42-30.540W				TR on pile.	Private aid.
3900	- North Day beacon 5	30-12-06.600N 085-42-28.440W				SG on pile.	Private aid.
3905	- North Day beacon 6	30-12-05.640N 085-42-28.620W				TR on pile.	Private aid.
3910	- North Day beacon 7	30-12-06.960N 085-42-26.340W				SG on pile.	Private aid.
3915	- North Day beacon 8	30-12-05.760N 085-42-26.580W				TR on pile.	Private aid.
3920	- North Day beacon 9	30-12-06.780N 085-42-22.260W				SG on pile.	Private aid.
3925	- North Day beacon 10	30-12-05.700N 085-42-24.840W				TR on pile.	Private aid.
3930	- North Day beacon 11	30-12-06.480N 085-42-22.260W				SG on pile.	Private aid.
3935	- North Day beacon 12	30-12-05.820N 085-42-22.560W				TR on pile.	Private aid.
3940	- South Day beacon 1	30-11-53.090N 085-42-18.480W				SG on pile.	Private aid.
3945	- South Day beacon 2	30-11-53.580N 085-42-18.360W				TR on pile.	Private aid.
3950	- South Day beacon 3	30-11-53.390N 085-42-20.710W				SG on pile.	Private aid.
3955	- South Day beacon 4	30-11-53.640N 085-42-21.590W				TR on pile.	Private aid.
3960	- South Day beacon 5	30-11-51.910N 085-42-23.120W				SG on pile.	Private aid.
	EAST BAY TO WEST BAY (Chart 11390)						
	North Bay Channel						
3965	- Day beacon 2	30-12-57.000N 085-42-08.000W				TR on pile.	Private aid.
3970	- Day beacon 4	30-12-54.000N 085-42-04.000W				TR on pile.	Private aid.
3975	- Day beacon 6	30-12-51.000N 085-42-02.000W				TR on pile.	Private aid.
3980	- Day beacon 8	30-12-48.000N 085-41-59.000W				TR on pile.	Private aid.
3985	- Day beacon 10	30-12-46.000N 085-41-57.000W				TR on pile.	Private aid.
	Robinson Bayou						
3990	- Day beacon 1	30-12-49.070N 085-42-12.720W				SG on pile.	Private aid.
3995	- Day beacon 2	30-12-47.940N 085-42-15.600W				TR on pile.	Private aid.
4000	- Day beacon 3	30-12-48.070N 085-42-07.090W				SG on pile.	Private aid.
4010	- Day beacon 5	30-12-45.720N 085-42-02.410W				SG on pile.	Private aid.

Light List corrected through LNM week: 01/18

(1) No.	(2) Name and Location	(3) Position	(4) Characteristic	(5) Height	(6) Range	(7) Structure	(8) Remarks
	FLORIDA - Eighth District						
	EAST BAY TO WEST BAY (Chart 11390)						
	Robinson Bayou						
4015	- Day beacon 4	30-12-43.770N 085-42-04.180W				TR on pile.	Private aid.
4020	- Day beacon 7	30-12-40.900N 085-41-59.550W				SG on pile.	Private aid.
4025	- Day beacon 6	30-12-40.240N 085-42-02.480W				TR on pile.	Private aid.
	Goose Bayou Channel						
4030	- Day beacon 1	30-13-35.730N 085-41-24.660W				SG on pile.	Private aid.
4035	- Day beacon 2	30-13-32.280N 085-41-34.140W				TR on pile.	Private aid.
4040	- Day beacon 3	30-13-30.600N 085-41-21.780W				SG on pile.	Private aid.
4045	- Day beacon 4	30-13-27.600N 085-41-28.920W				TR on pile.	Private aid.
4050	- Day beacon 5	30-13-23.940N 085-41-19.980W				SG on pile.	Private aid.
4055	- Day beacon 6	30-13-21.420N 085-41-25.200W				TR on pile.	Private aid.
4060	- Day beacon 8	30-13-18.360N 085-41-17.340W				TR on pile.	Private aid.
4065	- Day beacon 9	30-13-22.620N 085-41-08.880W				SG on pile.	Private aid.
4070	- Day beacon 10	30-13-16.080N 085-41-09.240W				TR on pile.	Private aid.
4075	- Day beacon 11	30-13-22.860N 085-41-04.560W				SG on pile.	Private aid.
4080	- Day beacon 12	30-13-19.140N 085-41-02.940W				TR on pile.	Private aid.
	Upper Goose Bayou Channel						
4085	- Day beacon 1	30-14-29.100N 085-40-55.020W				SG on pile.	Private aid.
4090	- Day beacon 2	30-14-25.740N 085-41-03.780W				TR on pile.	Private aid.
4095	- Day beacon 3	30-14-20.760N 085-40-45.780W				SG on pile.	Private aid.
4100	- Day beacon 4	30-14-20.820N 085-40-54.600W				TR on pile.	Private aid.
4105	- Day beacon 5	30-14-14.820N 085-40-39.120W				SG on pile.	Private aid.
4110	- Day beacon 6	30-14-11.160N 085-40-40.920W				TR on pile.	Private aid.
4115	- Day beacon 7	30-14-09.180N 085-40-32.760W				SG on pile.	Private aid.
4120	- Day beacon 8	30-14-07.380N 085-40-35.460W				TR on pile.	Private aid.
4125	- Day beacon 9	30-14-06.780N 085-40-31.920W				SG on pile.	Private aid.
	North Bay						
4130	- Day beacon 1	30-13-37.317N 085-43-11.442W				SG on pile.	
4135	- LIGHT 3	30-13-37.489N 085-42-27.723W	Fl G 6s	17	4	SG on pile.	
4145	- Day beacon 4	30-14-18.554N 085-41-33.008W				TR on pile.	
4150	- LIGHT 5	30-14-43.367N 085-41-30.853W	Fl G 4s	17	4	SG on pile.	
4155	- LIGHT 6	30-15-02.095N 085-41-01.888W	Fl R 4s	17	3	TR on pile.	
	Beatty Bayou Channel						
4160	- Day beacon 1	30-15-17.013N 085-37-11.708W				SG on pile.	Private aid.
4165	- Day beacon 2	30-15-17.057N 085-37-12.272W				TR on pile.	Private aid.

Light List corrected through LNM week: 01/18

(1) No.	(2) Name and Location	(3) Position	(4) Characteristic	(5) Height	(6) Range	(7) Structure	(8) Remarks
		FLORIDA - Eighth District					
	EAST BAY TO WEST BAY (Chart 11390)						
	North Bay						
	Beatty Bayou Channel						
4170	- Day beacon 3	30-15-14.650N 085-37-11.985W				SG on pile.	Private aid.
4175	- Day beacon 4	30-15-14.742N 085-37-12.544W				TR on pile.	Private aid.
4180	- Day beacon 5	30-15-11.925N 085-37-12.520W				SG on pile.	Private aid.
4185	- Day beacon 6	30-15-11.991N 085-37-13.102W				TR on pile.	Private aid.
	Fannin Bayou						
4190	- Day beacon 1	30-16-11.121N 085-39-26.188W				SG on pile.	
4195.01	- Buoy 2	30-16-08.971N 085-39-18.814W				Red nun.	
4200.01	- Buoy 3	30-16-17.162N 085-39-13.654W				Green can.	
	Fannin Bayou Channel A						
4210	- Day beacon 4	30-16-29.000N 085-39-00.000W				TR on pile.	Private aid.
4215	- Day beacon 5	30-16-39.000N 085-38-50.000W				SG on pile.	Private aid.
4220	- Day beacon 6	30-16-37.000N 085-38-46.000W				TR on pile.	Private aid.
4225	- Day beacon 7	30-16-40.000N 085-38-36.000W				SG on pile.	Private aid.
4230	- Day beacon 8	30-16-42.000N 085-38-34.000W				TR on pile.	Private aid.
4235	- Day beacon 9	30-16-51.000N 085-38-36.000W				SG on pile.	Private aid.
4240	- Day beacon 10	30-16-51.000N 085-38-31.000W				TR on pile.	Private aid.
4245	- Day beacon 11	30-16-53.000N 085-38-26.000W				SG on pile.	Private aid.
4250	- Day beacon 12	30-16-52.000N 085-38-25.000W				TR on pile.	Private aid.
4255	- Day beacon 13	30-16-54.000N 085-38-23.000W				SG on pile.	Private aid.
4260	- Day beacon 14	30-17-00.000N 085-38-25.000W				TR on pile.	Private aid.
4265	Fannin Bayou Channel Junction Day beacon A	30-16-33.000N 085-38-59.000W				JG on pile.	Private aid.
4270	Fannin Bayou Channel Junction Day beacon B	30-16-51.000N 085-39-00.000W				JG on pile.	Private aid.
	North Bay						
4275	Fannin Bayou Channel C Day beacon 1	30-16-53.000N 085-39-12.000W				SG on pile.	Private aid.
4280	Fannin Bayou Channel C Day beacon 2	30-16-56.000N 085-39-23.000W				TR on pile.	Private aid.
	Fannin Bayou Channel B						
4285	- Day beacon 1	30-16-56.000N 085-38-52.000W				SG on pile.	Private aid.
4290	- Day beacon 3	30-17-06.000N 085-38-49.000W				SG on pile.	Private aid.
4295	- Day beacon 5	30-17-11.000N 085-38-49.000W				SG on pile.	Private aid.
4300	- Day beacon 6	30-17-14.000N 085-38-55.000W				TR on pile.	Private aid.
	ST. ANDREW BAY (Chart 11391)						
	Grand Lagoon Channel						
4305	- LIGHT 2	30-07-52.644N 085-43-13.299W	Q R	17	3	TR on pile.	Ra ref.
4310	- LIGHT 3	30-07-57.811N 085-43-39.451W	Fl G 2.5s	17	3	SG on pile.	

Light List corrected through LNM week: 01/18

(1) No.	(2) Name and Location	(3) Position	(4) Characteristic	(5) Height	(6) Range	(7) Structure	(8) Remarks
	FLORIDA - Eighth District						
	ST. ANDREW BAY (Chart 11391)						
	Grand Lagoon Channel						
4315	- LIGHT 4	30-08-17.730N 085-43-57.748W	Fl R 2.5s	17	3	TR on pile.	Ra ref.
4320	- Day beacon 6	30-08-26.703N 085-44-03.751W				TR on pile.	
4325	- LIGHT 5	30-08-25.188N 085-44-05.109W	Fl G 4s	17	4	SG on pile.	Ra ref.
4330	- Day beacon 7	30-08-32.987N 085-44-18.052W				SG on pile.	Ra ref.
4335	- Day beacon 8	30-08-36.878N 085-44-20.334W				TR on pile.	
4340	- JUNCTION LIGHT A	30-08-42.241N 085-44-30.658W	Fl (2+1)G 6s	17	3	JG on pile.	
4345	- Day beacon 9	30-08-46.602N 085-44-35.532W				SG on pile.	
4350	- Day beacon 11	30-08-51.175N 085-44-49.780W				SG on pile.	
	Treasure Island Marina Channel						
4355	- Day beacon 2	30-08-43.700N 085-44-42.009W				TR on pile.	
4360	- Day beacon 3	30-08-42.035N 085-44-39.963W				SG on pile.	
4365	- Day beacon 4	30-08-44.729N 085-44-51.850W				TR on pile.	
	West Grand Lagoon Channel						
4370	- Day beacon 1	30-08-51.600N 085-44-55.200W				SG on pile.	Private aid.
4375	- Day beacon 2	30-08-55.800N 085-44-54.600W				TR on pile.	Private aid.
4380	- Day beacon 2A	30-09-01.850N 085-45-00.060W				TR on pile.	Private aid.
4385	- Day beacon 3A	30-09-01.140N 085-45-00.480W				SG on pile.	Private aid.
4390	- Day beacon 3	30-08-55.200N 085-44-55.200W				SG on pile.	Private aid.
4395	- Day beacon 4	30-09-01.200N 085-45-04.800W				TR on pile.	Private aid.
4400	- Day beacon 5	30-09-01.000N 085-45-02.000W				SG on pile.	Private aid.
4405	- Day beacon 6	30-09-04.980N 085-45-13.080W				TR on pile.	Private aid.
4410	- Day beacon 7	30-09-04.020N 085-45-13.080W				SG on pile.	Private aid.
4415	- Day beacon 8	30-09-09.420N 085-45-22.260W				TR on pile.	Private aid.
4420	- Day beacon 9	30-09-08.640N 085-45-22.940W				SG on pile.	Private aid.
4425	- Day beacon 10	30-09-19.260N 085-45-36.540W				TR on pile.	Private aid.
4430	- Day beacon 11	30-09-18.420N 085-45-37.140W				SG on pile.	Private aid.
4435	- Day beacon 12	30-09-28.800N 085-45-48.680W				TR on pile.	Private aid.
4440	- Day beacon 13	30-09-27.900N 085-45-48.980W				SG on pile.	Private aid.
4445	- Day beacon 14	30-09-30.060N 085-45-55.200W				TR on pile.	Private aid.
4450	- Day beacon 15	30-09-30.480N 085-45-56.280W				SG on pile.	Private aid.
4455	- Day beacon 16	30-09-34.440N 085-46-04.340W				TR on pile.	Private aid.
4460	- Day beacon 17	30-09-33.360N 085-46-04.580W				SG on pile.	Private aid.
4465	- Day beacon 18	30-09-43.920N 085-46-21.020W				TR on pile.	Private aid.

Light List corrected through LNM week: 01/18

(1) No.	(2) Name and Location	(3) Position	(4) Characteristic	(5) Height	(6) Range	(7) Structure	(8) Remarks
		FLORIDA - Eighth District					
	ST. ANDREW BAY (Chart 11391)						
	West Grand Lagoon Channel						
4470	- Day beacon 19	30-09-42.720N 085-46-21.860W				SG on pile.	Private aid.
4475	- Day beacon 21	30-09-49.080N 085-46-33.440W				SG on pile.	Private aid.
4480	- Day beacon 22	30-09-50.880N 085-46-37.520W				TR on pile.	Private aid.
4485	- Day beacon 24	30-09-52.020N 085-46-43.100W				TR on pile.	Private aid.
4490	- Day beacon 26	30-09-53.760N 085-46-45.740W				TR on pile.	Private aid.
4495	- Day beacon 27	30-09-56.820N 085-46-51.240W				SG on pile.	Private aid.
4505	- Day beacon 28	30-10-07.820N 085-47-11.080W				TR on pile.	Private aid.
4510	- Day beacon 29	30-10-07.610N 085-47-11.320W				SG on pile.	Private aid.
4515	- Day beacon 30	30-10-10.560N 085-47-14.380W				TR on pile.	Private aid.
4520	- Day beacon 31	30-10-10.340N 085-47-14.600W				SG on pile.	Private aid.
4525	- Day beacon 32	30-10-12.590N 085-47-16.680W				TR on pile.	Private aid.
4530	- Day beacon 33	30-10-12.390N 085-47-16.930W				SG on pile.	Private aid.
	WEST BAY TO SANTA ROSA SOUND (Chart 11385)						
	Choctawhatchee Bay						
	Positions of buoys frequently shifted with changing conditions.						
4535 125	- Entrance Lighted Buoy CB	30-22-14.568N 086-30-55.952W	Mo (A) W		5	Red and white stripes with red spherical topmark.	
4540	- Entrance Buoy 1	30-22-30.043N 086-30-50.448W				Green can.	
4545	- Entrance Buoy 2	30-22-30.000N 086-30-46.044W				Red nun.	
4550	- ENTRANCE LIGHT 3	30-22-51.145N 086-30-37.527W	Q G	30	3	SG on skeleton tower on pile.	
4555	- ENTRANCE LIGHT 4	30-22-51.433N 086-30-27.256W	Q R	30	3	TR on skeleton tower on pile.	
4560	- Entrance Buoy 5A	30-23-09.936N 086-30-32.453W				Green can.	
4565	- Entrance Buoy 7	30-23-14.951N 086-30-42.308W				Green can.	
4570	- Entrance Lighted Buoy 8	30-23-24.474N 086-30-45.391W	Fl R 2.5s		3	Red nun.	
4575	- Entrance Buoy 9	30-23-21.217N 086-30-49.284W				Green can.	
4578	CITY OF DESTIN DANGER LIGHT	30-23-26.522N 086-30-39.156W	Fl W 2.5s			Marks breakwater.	Private aid.
4578.01	CITY OF DESTIN DANGER LIGHT	30-23-28.514N 086-30-42.092W	Fl W 2.5s			Marks breakwater.	Private aid.
4578.02	CITY OF DESTIN DANGER LIGHT	30-23-30.756N 086-30-45.344W	Fl W 2.5s			Marks breakwater.	Private aid.
4578.03	CITY OF DESTIN DANGER LIGHT	30-23-32.679N 086-30-46.635W	Fl W 2.5s			Marks breakwater.	Private aid.
4578.04	CITY OF DESTIN DANGER LIGHT	30-23-34.702N 086-30-51.791W	Fl W 2.5s			Marks breakwater.	Private aid.
4578.05	CITY OF DESTIN DANGER LIGHT	30-23-37.049N 086-30-52.343W	Fl W 2.5s			Marks breakwater.	Private aid.
4578.06	CITY OF DESTIN DANGER LIGHT	30-23-36.072N 086-30-47.622W	Fl W 2.5s			Marks breakwater.	Private aid.
4580	- Entrance Buoy 10	30-23-31.847N 086-30-51.195W				Red nun.	
4585	- Entrance Buoy 11	30-23-27.817N 086-30-55.885W				green can.	Ra ref.

(1) No.	(2) Name and Location	(3) Position	(4) Characteristic	(5) Height	(6) Range	(7) Structure	(8) Remarks
	FLORIDA - Eighth District						
	WEST BAY TO SANTA ROSA SOUND (Chart 11385)						
	Choctawhatchee Bay						
	Old East Pass Harbor Channel						
4590	- Buoy 2	30-23-33.091N 086-30-37.981W				Red nun.	
4595	- Day beacon 3	30-23-33.096N 086-30-35.582W				SG on pile.	Ra ref.
4600	- Buoy 4	30-23-31.240N 086-30-31.492W				Red nun.	
4605	- Day beacon 6	30-23-31.541N 086-30-28.180W				TR on pile.	
4610	- Lighted Buoy 8	30-23-30.097N 086-30-22.394W	Fl R 4s		3	Red nun.	
4615	- LIGHT 13	30-23-22.165N 086-29-28.923W	Fl G 4s	17	4	SG on pile.	Ra ref.
4620	- LIGHT 14	30-23-21.939N 086-29-18.075W	Fl R 2.5s	17	3	TR on pile.	Ra ref.
4625	- LIGHT 15	30-23-22.094N 086-29-15.642W	Fl G 2.5s	17	3	SG on pile.	Ra ref.
4630	- LIGHT 16	30-23-18.861N 086-29-13.125W	Fl R 4s	17	3	TR on pile.	Ra ref.
4635	Old East Pass East Danger Day beacon	30-23-28.534N 086-30-26.342W				NW on pile worded DANGER SHOAL.	
4640	- Day beacon 18	30-23-13.876N 086-29-10.292W				TR on pile.	
4645	Old East Pass West Danger Day beacon	30-23-30.388N 086-30-30.410W				NW on pile worded DANGER SHOAL.	
4650	OKALOOSA COUNTY FISHING PIER LIGHTS	30-23-30.000N 086-35-36.000W				Fishing pier.	Private aid.
	U. S. Coast Guard Base						
4655	- Day beacon 2	30-23-38.351N 086-31-06.292W				TR on pile.	Ra ref.
4656	- Buoy G	30-23-35.389N 086-31-25.928W				White with orange bands.	Restricted Access Area.
4656.01	- Buoy H	30-23-35.793N 086-31-27.412W				White with orange bands.	Restricted Access Area.
4657	- Buoy F	30-23-35.029N 086-31-34.440W				White with orange bands.	Restricted Access Area.
4657.01	- Buoy E	30-23-34.316N 086-31-32.774W				White with orange bands.	Restricted Access Area.
4657.02	- Buoy D	30-23-34.125N 086-31-30.283W				White with orange bands.	Restricted Access Area.
4659	- Buoy 6	30-23-36.339N 086-31-26.131W				Red nun.	
4660	- Day beacon 4	30-23-33.322N 086-31-17.402W				TR on pile.	
4662	Okaloosa County Crab Island Exclusion Buoys (32)	30-23-38.160N 096-31-25.140W				Marks boat Exclusion Area.	Private aid.
4663	- Buoy 8	30-23-38.125N 086-31-29.741W				Red nun.	
4663.01	- Buoy 7	30-23-36.768N 086-31-31.117W				Green can.	
4664	- Buoy C	30-23-31.844N 086-31-29.644W				White with orange bands.	Restricted Access Area.
4665	- Day beacon A	30-23-32.567N 086-31-27.054W				NW on pile worded Restricted Area.	Maintain 100ft from shoreline, do not impede access to Coast Guard Station, 33 CFR 334.746.
4667	- Buoy B	30-23-31.014N 086-31-29.941W				White with orange bands.	Restricted Access Area.
4668	- Buoy 5	30-23-34.647N 086-31-27.217W				Green can.	

(1) No.	(2) Name and Location	(3) Position	(4) Characteristic	(5) Height	(6) Range	(7) Structure	(8) Remarks
		FLORIDA - Eighth District					

WEST BAY TO SANTA ROSA SOUND (Chart 11385)
Choctawhatchee Bay
Positions of buoys frequently shifted with changing conditions.

(1) No.	(2) Name and Location	(3) Position	(4) Characteristic	(5) Height	(6) Range	(7) Structure	(8) Remarks
4670	- Entrance Day beacon 13	30-24-05.557N 086-30-58.585W				SG on pile.	Ra ref.
4675	- Entrance Day beacon 14	30-24-05.900N 086-30-54.311W				TR on pile.	Ra ref.
4680	- Entrance Day beacon 15	30-24-16.469N 086-31-10.873W					
4685	- ENTRANCE LIGHT 16	30-24-26.643N 086-31-08.830W	Fl R 2.5s	17	4	TR on pile.	Ra ref.
4690	- ENTRANCE LIGHT 17	30-24-25.821N 086-31-18.354W	Fl G 2.5s	17	4		Ra ref.

PENSACOLA BAY ENTRANCE (Chart 11384)
Pensacola Bay

(1) No.	(2) Name and Location	(3) Position	(4) Characteristic	(5) Height	(6) Range	(7) Structure	(8) Remarks
4695 145	- Entrance Lighted Buoy 1	30-16-15.724N 087-17-32.898W	Fl G 2.5s		4	Green.	
4700 150	- Entrance Lighted Buoy 2	30-16-16.749N 087-17-23.505W	Fl R 2.5s		4	Red.	
4705	CAUCUS CHANNEL RANGE FRONT LIGHT	30-19-33.932N 087-18-44.157W	Q G	26		KRW on skeleton tower on piles.	Higher intensity on range line.
4710	CAUCUS CHANNEL RANGE REAR LIGHT 1,408 yards, 341.4° from front light.	30-20-15.183N 087-19-00.131W	Iso G 6s	67		KRW on skeleton tower.	Visible 2° each side of rangeline.
4715 140	**Pensacola Light**	30-20-46.045N 087-18-29.109W	Fl W 20s	191	27	Conical brick tower, lower third white, upper two thirds black. 191	White light visible from 222° to 090°. Aircraft warning light shows F R from 090° to 222°.
4720	- Entrance Lighted Buoy 3	30-17-20.923N 087-17-57.399W	Fl G 6s		4	Green.	
4725	- Entrance Lighted Buoy 4	30-17-21.923N 087-17-48.100W	Fl R 6s		4	Red.	
4730	Massachusetts Wreck Lighted Buoy WR2	30-17-43.400N 087-18-44.216W	Q R		3	Red.	
4735	- Entrance Lighted Buoy 5	30-18-02.099N 087-18-12.890W	Fl G 4s		4	Green.	
4740	- Entrance Lighted Buoy 6	30-18-03.988N 087-18-04.083W	Fl R 4s		3	Red.	
4745	- Entrance Buoy 7	30-18-37.535N 087-18-26.756W				Green can.	
4750	- Entrance Lighted Buoy 8	30-18-42.521N 087-18-18.001W	Q R		3	Red.	
4755	- Entrance Lighted Buoy 9	30-18-55.486N 087-18-32.471W	Q G		4	Green.	
4760	Caucas Channel East Side Dredging Range Front Day beacon					Orange diamond day mark on pile.	Range marks edge of channel for dredging purposes. F W light will be exhibited during dredging operations. Maintained by U.S. Army Corps of Engineers. Aid maintained by U.S. Army Corps of Engineers.
4765	Caucas Channel East Side Dredging Range Rear Day beacon					Orange diamond day mark on pile.	F W light will be exhibited during dredging operations. Maintained by U.S. Army Corps of Engineers. Aid maintained by U.S. Army Corps of Engineers.

Light List corrected through LNM week: 01/18

(1) No.	(2) Name and Location	(3) Position	(4) Characteristic	(5) Height	(6) Range	(7) Structure	(8) Remarks
			FLORIDA - Eighth District				
	PENSACOLA BAY ENTRANCE (Chart 11384)						
	Pensacola Bay						
4770	Caucas Channel West Side Dredging Range Front Day beacon					Orange diamond day mark on pile.	Range marks edge of channel for dredging purposes. F W light wil be exhibited during dredging operations. Maintained by U.S. Army Corps of Engineers.
							Aid maintained by U.S. Army Corps of Engineers.
4775	Caucus Channel West Side Dredging Range Rear Day beacon					Orange diamond day mark on pile.	F W light will be exhibited during dredging operations. Maintained by U.S. Army Corps of Engineers.
							Aid maintained by U.S. Army Corps of Engineers.
4780	FORT BARRANCAS RANGE FRONT LIGHT	30-20-34.723N 087-18-29.135W	Fl G 2.5s	30		KRW on skeleton tower on piles.	Visible only on the rangeline.
4785	FORT BARRANCAS RANGE REAR LIGHT 350 yards, 000° from front light.	30-20-45.258N 087-18-29.109W	F G	54		KRW on skeleton tower.	Visible only on the rangeline.
4790	Barrancas Cut East Side Dredging Range Front Day beacon					Orange diamond day mark on pile.	Range marks edge of channel for dredging purposes. F W light will be exhibited during dredging operations. Maintained by U.S. Army Corps of Engineers.
							Aid maintained by U.S. Army Corps of Engineers.
4795	Barrancas Cut East Side Dredging Range Rear Day beacon					Orange diamond day mark on pile.	F W light will be exhibited during dredging operations. Maintained by U.S. Army Corps of Engineers.
							Aid maintained by U.S. Army Corps of Engineers.
4800	Barrancas Cut West Side Dredging Range Front Day beacon					Orange diamond day mark on pile.	Range marks edge of channel for dredging purposes. F W light will be exhibited during dredging operations. Maintained by U.S. Army Corps of Engineers.
							Aid maintained by U.S. Army Corps of Engineers.
4805	Barrancas Cut West Side Dredging Range Rear Day beacon					Orange diamond day mark on pile.	F W light will be exhibited during dredging operations. Maintained by U.S. Army Corps of Engineers.
							Aid maintained by U.S. Army Corps of Engineers.
4810	- Entrance Buoy 10	30-19-15.748N 087-18-24.237W				Red nun.	
4815	- Entrance Lighted Buoy 11	30-19-16.220N 087-18-34.102W	Fl G 4s		4	Green.	
4820	- Entrance Lighted Buoy 12	30-19-41.907N 087-18-27.003W	Fl (2)R 5s		3	Red.	
4830	- Entrance Lighted Buoy 13	30-19-52.719N 087-18-34.902W	Fl G 6s		4	Green.	
4835	- Lighted Buoy 14	30-19-56.278N 087-18-19.191W	Fl R 2.5s		3	Red.	
4840 33085	- Lighted Buoy 15	30-20-15.224N 087-18-07.464W	Fl G 2.5s		4	Green with yellow triangle.	

(1) No.	(2) Name and Location	(3) Position	(4) Characteristic	(5) Height	(6) Range	(7) Structure	(8) Remarks
			FLORIDA - Eighth District				
	PENSACOLA BAY ENTRANCE (Chart 11384)						
	Pensacola Bay						
4845 33080	- Lighted Buoy 16	30-19-55.719N 087-17-39.900W	Q R		3	Red with yellow square.	
4850 33060	- NAVY RANGE FRONT LIGHT	30-20-04.514N 087-18-58.739W	Fl G 2.5s	34		KRW on skeleton tower on piles.	Visible all around; higher intensity 1.5° each side of range line.
4855 33065	- NAVY RANGE REAR LIGHT 300 yards, 273.5° from front light.	30-20-05.059N 087-19-09.065W	Iso G 6s	58		KRW on skeleton tower.	Visible only on the rangeline.
4860	PENSACOLA COAST GUARD JETTY LIGHT 1	30-20-37.718N 087-17-23.900W	Fl G 6s	10	4	SG on skeleton tower.	
4865	PENSACOLA COAST GUARD JETTY LIGHT 2	30-20-37.718N 087-17-21.900W	Fl R 6s	10	4	TR on skeleton tower.	
4870 33075	- Lighted Buoy 17	30-20-01.719N 087-16-55.899W	Fl G 4s		4	Green with yellow triangle.	
	Pensacola Navy Homeport Channel						
4875	- Buoy 1	30-20-10.121N 087-16-33.552W				Green can.	
4880	- Buoy 3	30-20-28.297N 087-16-12.138W				Green can.	
4885	- Lighted Buoy 4	30-20-23.737N 087-16-01.523W	Fl R 2.5s		3	Red.	
4890	- Buoy 6	30-20-26.977N 087-15-43.040W				Red nun.	
4895	- Buoy 7	30-20-47.995N 087-15-46.258W				Green can.	
4900	- Buoy 8	30-20-42.844N 087-15-34.898W				Red nun.	
	Pensacola Bay						
4905 33070	- Lighted Buoy 18	30-19-53.498N 087-16-41.945W	Fl R 4s		3	Red with yellow square.	
4910	- Obstruction Day beacon	30-20-36.410N 087-16-14.296W				NW on pile worded DANGER SUBMERGED SEAWALL.	
4915 33055	- Lighted Buoy 20	30-19-48.719N 087-15-17.895W	Q R		3	Red with yellow square.	
	PENSACOLA BAY (Chart 11383)						
	Pensacola Bay						
4918	FDOT PENSACOLA BAY BRIDGE LOCATION FOUR WEST MOORING LIGHTS (4)	30-22-36.560N 087-10-49.460W	Fl W 2.5s			Marks four mooring piling locations.	Private aid.
4920	- CHANNEL RANGE FRONT LIGHT	30-24-25.593N 087-11-35.542W	Fl W 2.5s	18		On skeleton tower on piles.	DAY: Visible 2° each side of rangeline. NIGHT: Visible all around, higher intensity 2° each side of rangeline.
4925	- CHANNEL RANGE REAR LIGHT 1,931 yards, 032.6° from front light.	30-25-13.930N 087-10-59.921W	Iso G 6s (NIGHT) Iso W 6s (DAY)	74 72		On skeleton tower on piles.	Visible 2° each side of rangeline.
4930	- Lighted Buoy 21	30-20-30.718N 087-14-31.893W	Fl G 2.5s		4	Green.	
4935	- Lighted Buoy 22	30-20-27.719N 087-14-26.894W	Fl R 2.5s		3	Red.	
4940	- Navy Marker Lighted Buoy 1	30-21-03.933N 087-15-27.278W	Fl G 4s		4	Green.	
4945	- Lighted Buoy 23	30-21-17.165N 087-13-58.459W	Fl G 4s		4	Green.	
4950	- Buoy 24	30-21-14.717N 087-13-52.893W				Red nun.	
4955	- Lighted Buoy 25	30-21-59.230N 087-13-27.479W	Fl G 2.5s		3	Green.	

Light List corrected through LNM week: 01/18

(1) No.	(2) Name and Location	(3) Position	(4) Characteristic	(5) Height	(6) Range	(7) Structure	(8) Remarks
	FLORIDA - Eighth District						
	PENSACOLA BAY (Chart 11383)						
	Pensacola Bay						
4960	FAIR POINT LIGHT 2	30-21-57.110N 087-12-48.812W	Fl R 6s	17	4	TR on pile.	Ra ref.
4965	- Buoy 26	30-21-57.316N 087-13-21.392W				Red nun.	
4970	- Lighted Buoy 27	30-22-43.215N 087-12-54.092W	Q G		3	Green.	
4975	- Buoy 28	30-22-45.737N 087-12-46.561W				Red nun.	
4980	- EAST CHANNEL OUTER RANGE FRONT LIGHT	30-22-23.058N 087-12-14.063W	Q W	20		KRW on skeleton tower on piles.	Visible all around; higher intensity on rangeline.
4985	- EAST CHANNEL OUTER RANGE REAR LIGHT 574 feet, 169° from front light.	30-22-00.765N 087-12-08.922W	Iso W 6s	40		KRW on skeleton tower on piles.	Visible all around; higher intensity on rangeline.
4990	- EAST CHANNEL INNER RANGE FRONT LIGHT	30-24-10.694N 087-12-38.156W	Q G	52		KRW on skelaton tower on building.	Visible all around.
4995	- EAST CHANNEL INNER RANGE REAR LIGHT 207 yards, 348.6° from front light.	30-24-16.722N 087-12-39.556W	Oc G 4s	69		KRW on skeleton tower.	Visible all around.
5000	- Lighted Buoy 29	30-23-12.715N 087-12-32.392W	Q G		3	Green.	
5005	- Lighted Buoy 30 75 feet outside channel limit.	30-23-16.715N 087-12-22.891W	Q R		2	Red nun.	
5010	- Lighted Buoy 31	30-23-45.784N 087-12-34.186W	Fl G 2.5s		4	Green.	
5015	- Lighted Buoy 32 75 feet outside channel limit.	30-23-47.314N 087-12-29.892W	Fl R 2.5s		2	Red nun.	
5020	Pensacola Marine Terminal Buoy PMT1	30-23-45.620N 087-13-03.568W				Green can.	
5025	Pensacola Marine Terminal Lighted Buoy PMT2	30-23-55.214N 087-12-48.493W	Fl R 4s		4	Red.	
5030	- Obstruction Day beacon A	30-24-01.768N 087-13-21.274W				NG on pile.	Ra ref.
5035	- WRECK LIGHT WR2	30-23-57.030N 087-13-17.291W	Q R	17	3	TR on pile.	
5040	- Channel Day beacon 1	30-22-25.000N 087-10-45.000W				SG on pile.	Private aid.
5045	- Channel Day beacon 2	30-22-24.000N 087-10-48.000W				TR on pile.	Private aid.
5050	- Channel Day beacon 3	30-22-18.000N 087-10-42.000W				SG on pile.	Private aid.
5055	- Channel Day beacon 4	30-22-17.000N 087-10-46.000W				TR on pile.	Private aid.
5060	- Channel Day beacon 5	30-22-11.000N 087-10-40.000W				SG on pile.	Private aid.
5065	- Channel Day beacon 6	30-22-10.000N 087-10-43.000W				TR on pile.	Private aid.
	PENSACOLA BAY ENTRANCE (Chart 11384)						
	Pensacola Bay						
	Bayou Texar						
5070	- LIGHT 2	30-24-50.713N 087-11-21.010W	Fl R 2.5s	17	3	TR on pile.	
5075	- JETTY LIGHT	30-25-06.000N 087-11-29.000W	Fl R 4s	7		On jetty.	Private aid.
5080	- Day beacon 4	30-24-57.384N 087-11-27.262W				TR on pile.	
5085	- Day beacon 5	30-25-03.806N 087-11-31.301W				SG on pile.	
5090	- Day beacon 6	30-25-06.342N 087-11-32.058W				TR on pile.	Ra ref.

(1) No.	(2) Name and Location	(3) Position	(4) Characteristic	(5) Height	(6) Range	(7) Structure	(8) Remarks
		FLORIDA - Eighth District					
	PENSACOLA BAY ENTRANCE (Chart 11384)						
	Pensacola Bay						
	Bayou Texar						
5095	- Day beacon 1A	30-25-16.460N 087-11-35.403W				SG on pile.	Private aid.
5100	- Day beacon 2A	30-25-15.858N 087-11-34.183W				TR on pile.	Private aid.
5105	- Day beacon 3A	30-25-18.743N 087-11-30.862W				SG on pile.	Private aid.
5110	- Day beacon 4A	30-25-17.752N 087-11-31.924W				TR on pile.	Private aid.
5115	- Day beacon 5A	30-25-18.535N 087-11-27.127W				SG on pile.	Private aid.
5120	- Day beacon 6A	30-25-17.119N 087-11-26.120W				TR on pile.	Private aid.
5125	- Day beacon 7A	30-25-17.927N 087-11-23.189W				SG on pile.	Private aid.
5130	- Day beacon 8A	30-25-17.174N 087-11-20.467W				TR on pile.	Private aid.
5135	- Day beacon 9A	30-25-18.706N 087-11-19.684W				SG on pile.	Private aid.
5140	- Day beacon 10A	30-25-19.183N 087-11-16.457W				TR on pile.	Private aid.
5145	- Day beacon 11A	30-25-20.786N 087-11-16.798W				SG on pile.	Private aid.
5150	- Day beacon 12A	30-25-24.161N 087-11-15.156W				TR on pile.	Private aid.
5155	- Day beacon 13A	30-25-25.799N 087-11-16.242W				SG on pile.	Private aid.
5160	- Day beacon 14A	30-25-29.291N 087-11-14.384W				TR on pile.	Private aid.
5165	- Day beacon 15A	30-25-29.218N 087-11-15.799W				SG on pile.	Private aid.
	PENSACOLA BAY (Chart 11383)						
	Pensacola Bay						
5170	Florida Department of Environmental Protection Danger Buoy	30-24-59.470N 087-11-41.930W				White with orange bands and diamond worded: DANGER ROCKS.	Private aid.
5175	Florida Department of Environmental Protection Danger Buoy	30-24-59.470N 087-11-45.970W				White with orange bands and diamond worded: DANGER ROCKS.	Private aid.
5180	Florida Department of Environmental Protection Danger Buoy	30-24-58.820N 087-11-50.190W				White with orange bands and diamond worded: DANGER ROCKS.	Private aid.
5185	Florida Department of Environmental Protection Danger Buoy	30-24-55.430N 087-11-53.320W				White with orange bands and diamond worded: DANGER ROCKS.	Private aid.
5190	Florida Department of Environmental Protection Danger Buoy	30-24-48.900N 087-11-55.980W				White with orange bands and diamond worded: DANGER ROCKS.	Private aid.
5195	Florida Department of Environmental Protection Danger Buoy	30-24-50.190N 087-11-58.180W				White with orange bands and diamond worded: DANGER ROCKS.	Private aid.
5200	Florida Department of Environmental Protection Danger Buoy	30-24-45.690N 087-11-59.010W				White with orange bands and diamond worded: DANGER ROCKS.	Private aid.
5205	Florida Department of Environmental Protection Danger Buoy	30-24-43.300N 087-12-01.680W				White with orange bands and diamond worded: DANGER ROCKS.	Private aid.

Light List corrected through LNM week: 01/18

(1) No.	(2) Name and Location	(3) Position	(4) Characteristic	(5) Height	(6) Range	(7) Structure	(8) Remarks
			FLORIDA - Eighth District				
	PENSACOLA BAY (Chart 11383)						
	Pensacola Bay						
5210	Florida Department of Environmental Protection Danger Buoy	30-24-43.030N 087-12-02.230W				White with orange bands and diamond worded: DANGER ROCKS.	Private aid.
5215	Florida Department of Environmental Protection Danger Buoy	30-24-39.810N 087-12-03.420W				White with orange bands and diamond worded: DANGER ROCKS.	Private aid.
5220	Florida Department of Environmental Protection Danger Buoy	30-24-38.250N 087-12-05.170W				White with orange bands and diamond worded: DANGER ROCKS.	Private aid.
5225	Florida Department of Environmental Protection Danger Buoy	30-24-39.900N 087-12-07.370W				White with orange bands and diamond worded: DANGER ROCKS.	Private aid.
5230	- Bridge Approach Lighted Buoy 7	30-23-51.595N 087-10-30.026W	Fl G 2.5s		4	Green.	
5235	- Bridge Approach Buoy 8	30-23-46.811N 087-10-29.034W				Red nun.	
5240	- Bridge Approach Buoy 5	30-23-46.232N 087-10-47.066W				Green can.	
5245	- Bridge Approach Buoy 6	30-23-42.866N 087-10-46.728W				Red nun.	
5250	- Bridge Approach Buoy 3	30-23-37.209N 087-11-24.291W				Green can.	
5255	- Bridge Approach Buoy 4	30-23-33.855N 087-11-22.971W				Red nun.	
5260	- Bridge Approach Buoy 1	30-23-33.811N 087-11-38.932W				Green can.	
5265	- Bridge Approach Buoy 2	30-23-28.900N 087-11-36.483W				Red nun.	
5270	DEADMANS ISLAND BREAKWATER DANGER LIGHT	30-22-10.912N 087-11-08.363W	Fl W 2.5s			NW on pile WORDED: DANGER BREAKWATER.	Private aid.
5275	DEADMANS ISLAND BREAKWATER DANGER LIGHT	30-22-10.490N 087-11-12.189W	Fl W 2.5s			NW on pile WORDED: DANGER BREAKWATER.	Private aid.
5280	DEADMANS ISLAND BREAKWATER DANGER LIGHT	30-22-09.712N 087-11-17.188W	Fl W 2.5s			NW on pile WORDED: DANGER BREAKWATER.	Private aid.
5285	Deadmans Island Breakwater Danger Daybeacon	30-22-07.062N 087-11-16.788W				NW on pile WORDED: DANGER BREAKWATER.	Private aid.
5290	DEADMANS ISLAND BREAKWATER DANGER LIGHT	30-22-05.193N 087-11-15.801W	Fl W 2.5s			NW on pile WORDED: DANGER BREAKWATER.	Private aid.
	Bayou Chico						
5295	- LIGHT 2	30-23-31.830N 087-13-44.062W	Fl R 2.5s	17	3	TR on pile.	
5300	- Daybeacon 4	30-23-36.173N 087-13-51.149W				TR on pile.	
5305	- LIGHT 5	30-23-35.485N 087-13-57.025W	Fl G 4s	17	4	SG on pile.	Ra ref.
5310	- Daybeacon 6	30-23-46.914N 087-14-06.895W				TR on pile.	Ra ref.
5315	- Daybeacon 7	30-23-48.038N 087-14-12.544W				SG on pile.	
5320	- Buoy 8	30-23-49.319N 087-14-10.798W				Red nun.	
5325	- LIGHT 10	30-23-56.080N 087-14-20.359W	Fl R 4s	20	3	TR on pile.	

Light List corrected through LNM week: 01/18

(1) No.	(2) Name and Location	(3) Position	(4) Characteristic	(5) Height	(6) Range	(7) Structure	(8) Remarks
			FLORIDA - Eighth District				
	PENSACOLA BAY (Chart 11383)						
	Pensacola Bay						
	Bayou Chico						
5330	CHICO MARINA LIGHT	30-23-57.543N 087-14-33.733W	Fl G 2.5s			On pile.	Private aid.
5335	- Buoy 11	30-24-12.126N 087-15-03.888W				Green can.	
5340	- Day beacon 13	30-24-18.213N 087-15-14.897W				SG on pile.	
5345	- Day beacon 15	30-24-16.800N 087-15-21.085W				SG on pile.	
5350	- Day beacon 17	30-24-21.332N 087-15-28.450W				SG on pile.	
5355	- West Channel Day beacon 2	30-24-20.460N 087-15-28.080W				TR on pile.	Private aid.
5360	- West Channel Day beacon 1	30-24-19.680N 087-15-26.940W				SG on pile.	Private aid.
5365	- West Channel Day beacon 4	30-24-16.980N 087-15-33.900W				TR on pile.	Private aid.
5370	- West Channel Day beacon 3	30-24-15.300N 087-15-35.760W				SG on pile.	Private aid.
5375	Harbor View Marina Entrance Day beacon 1	30-24-00.100N 087-15-00.000W				SG on pile.	Private aid.
5380	Harbor View Marina Entrance Day beacon 2	30-24-00.100N 087-15-00.000W				TR on pile.	Private aid.
5385	- South Channel Day beacon 1	30-24-08.000N 087-15-02.000W				SG on pile.	Private aid.
5390	- South Channel Day beacon 2	30-24-10.000N 087-15-01.000W				TR on pile.	Private aid.
5395	- South Channel Day beacon 3	30-24-06.000N 087-15-08.000W				SG on pile.	Private aid.
5400	- South Channel Day beacon 4	30-24-09.000N 087-15-05.000W				TR on pile.	Private aid.
5405	- South Channel Day beacon 5	30-24-14.000N 087-15-19.000W				SG on pile.	Private aid.
5410	- South Channel Shoal Day beacons (2)	30-24-13.000N 087-15-15.000W				NW on pile worded DANGER SHOAL.	Private aid.
	Bayou Grande						
5415	- ENTRANCE LIGHT 1	30-22-23.000N 087-15-40.000W	Fl G 4s		8	SG on pile.	Private aid.
5420	- Day beacon 2	30-22-27.000N 087-15-39.000W				TR on pile.	Private aid.
5425	- Buoy 2A	30-22-27.000N 087-15-43.000W				Red nun.	Private aid.
5430	- Day beacon 3	30-22-23.000N 087-15-43.000W				SG on pile.	Private aid.
5435	- Day beacon 4	30-22-27.000N 087-15-51.000W				TR on pile.	Private aid.
5440	- Day beacon 5	30-22-25.000N 087-16-00.000W				SG on pile.	Private aid.
5445	- Day beacon 6	30-22-27.000N 087-16-00.000W				TR on pile.	Private aid.
5450	- Day beacon 7	30-22-18.000N 087-16-06.000W				SG on pile.	Private aid.
5455	- Day beacon 8	30-22-20.000N 087-16-06.000W				TR on pile.	Private aid.
5460	- Day beacon 9	30-22-18.000N 087-16-09.000W				SG on pile.	Private aid.
5465	- Day beacon 10	30-22-20.000N 087-16-13.000W				TR on pile.	Private aid.
5470	- Day beacon 11	30-22-13.000N 087-16-09.000W				SG on pile.	Private aid.
5475	- Day beacon 12	30-22-13.000N 087-16-12.000W				TR on pile.	Private aid.

FLORIDA - Eighth District

WEST BAY TO SANTA ROSA SOUND (Chart 11385)

Garcon Point

(1) No.	(2) Name and Location	(3) Position	(4) Characteristic	(5) Height	(6) Range	(7) Structure	(8) Remarks
5478	FDOA PENSACOLA BAY OYSTER COMPANY EAST BAY SPECIAL LIGHT A	30-26-17.800N 087-05-17.800W	Fl Y 2.5s			Marks perimeter of aquaculture farm.	Private aid.
5478.01	FDOA PENSACOLA BAY OYSTER COMPANY EAST BAY SPECIAL LIGHT B	30-26-17.590N 087-05-14.610W	Fl Y 2.5s			Marks perimeter of aquaculture farm.	Private aid.
5478.02	FDOA PENSACOLA BAY OYSTER COMPANY EAST BAY SPECIAL LIGHT C	30-26-25.400N 087-05-08.400W	Fl Y 2.5s			Marks perimeter of aquaculture farm.	Private aid.
5478.03	FDOA PENSACOLA BAY OYSTER COMPANY EAST BAY SPECIAL LIGHT D	30-26-25.500N 087-05-11.600W	Fl Y 2.5s			Marks perimeter of aquaculture farm.	Private aid.

Blackwater Channel

(1) No.	(2) Name and Location	(3) Position	(4) Characteristic	(5) Height	(6) Range	(7) Structure	(8) Remarks
5480	- APPROACH LIGHT 3	30-25-38.956N 087-03-15.302W	Fl G 4s	17	4	SG on pile.	
5485	- Day beacon 4	30-26-10.810N 087-02-48.920W				TR on pile.	Ra ref.
5490	- Day beacon 6	30-26-45.898N 087-02-41.720W				TR on pile.	
5495	- Day beacon 8	30-27-27.040N 087-02-33.320W				TR on pile.	Ra ref.
5500	- Day beacon 10	30-28-05.128N 087-02-25.406W				TR on pile.	Ra ref.
5505	- Day beacon 12	30-28-38.938N 087-02-18.374W				TR on pile.	
5510	- Day beacon 14	30-29-15.640N 087-02-10.766W				TR on pile.	
5515	- Day beacon 16	30-29-42.766N 087-02-04.724W				TR on pile.	
5520	- Day beacon 18	30-30-27.274N 087-01-55.112W				TR on pile.	Ra ref.
5525	- Day beacon 20	30-31-14.068N 087-01-44.698W				TR on pile.	
5530	- LIGHT 21	30-31-20.717N 087-01-46.357W	Q G	17	4	SG on pile.	Ra ref.
5535	- Day beacon 22	30-31-36.241N 087-01-31.262W				TR on pile.	
5540	- Day beacon 24	30-32-10.425N 087-01-06.902W				TR on pile.	
5545	- Day beacon 26	30-32-39.832N 087-00-46.094W				TR on pile.	
5550	- Day beacon 28	30-33-18.895N 087-00-19.978W				TR on pile.	
5555	- LIGHT 30	30-33-58.037N 086-59-54.902W	Fl R 4s	17	3	TR on dolphin.	
5560	- Buoy 31	30-34-07.390N 086-59-58.200W				Green can.	
5565	- Day beacon 32	30-34-28.957N 087-00-13.348W				TR on pile.	
5570	- Buoy 32A	30-34-35.435N 087-00-24.233W				Red nun.	
5575	- LIGHT 33	30-34-51.263N 087-00-45.031W	Fl G 4s	17	4	SG on pile.	Ra ref.
5580	- Day beacon 34	30-34-57.358N 087-00-44.060W				TR on pile.	
5585	- Buoy 35	30-35-18.063N 087-00-50.225W				Green can.	
5590	- Day beacon 36	30-35-24.519N 087-00-48.368W				TR on pile.	
5595	- Day beacon 37	30-35-33.109N 087-00-54.847W				SG on pile.	
5600	- Day beacon 38	30-35-53.520N 087-01-00.060W				TR on pile.	

Light List corrected through LNM week: 01/18

(1) No.	(2) Name and Location	(3) Position	(4) Characteristic	(5) Height	(6) Range	(7) Structure	(8) Remarks
		FLORIDA - Eighth District					
	WEST BAY TO SANTA ROSA SOUND (Chart 11385)						
	Blackwater Channel						
5605	- Buoy 39	30-35-51.427N 087-01-01.650W				Green can.	
5610	- Day beacon 41	30-36-08.761N 087-01-25.118W				SG on pile.	
5615	- Day beacon 42	30-36-21.126N 087-01-39.211W				TR on pile.	
5620	- Day beacon 43	30-36-24.696N 087-01-53.876W				SG on pile.	Ra ref.
	Polynesian Isle Channel						
5635	- Day beacon 1	30-24-13.380N 087-05-38.820W				SG on pile.	Private aid.
5640	- LIGHT 2	30-24-12.360N 087-05-40.380W				TR on pile.	Private aid.
5645	- Day beacon 4	30-24-05.760N 087-05-35.460W				TR on pile.	Private aid.
5650	- Day beacon 6	30-24-00.000N 087-05-29.880W				TR on pile.	Private aid.
5655	- Day beacon 8	30-23-54.660N 087-05-24.240W				TR on pile.	Private aid.
5660	- Day beacon 9	30-23-56.400N 087-05-18.600W				SG on pile.	Private aid.
	SANTA ROSA SOUND TO DAUPHIN ISLAND (Chart 11378)						
	Escambia Bay						
5665	- LIGHT 2	30-28-00.355N 087-07-19.294W	Fl R 6s	17	5	TR on pile.	
5670	- WRECK LIGHT WR3	30-28-37.441N 087-07-47.061W	Q G	17	3	SG on pile.	Marks submerged wreck.
5675	- Day beacon 4	30-28-38.671N 087-07-34.945W				TR on pile.	Ra ref.
5680	- LIGHT 7	30-29-18.238N 087-08-02.690W	Fl G 2.5s	17	3	SG on pile.	
5685	- Day beacon 9	30-29-58.889N 087-08-21.375W				SG on pile.	Ra ref.
5690	- Day beacon 10	30-30-00.322N 087-08-17.492W				TR on pile.	Ra ref.
5695	- Day beacon 11	30-30-36.845N 087-08-42.220W				SG on pile.	
5700	- Buoy 12	30-30-53.579N 087-08-47.634W				Red nun.	
5705	Tidewater Skanska Lighted Mooring Buoy A	30-31-05.000N 087-08-30.000W	Fl W 4s			White with blue band.	Private aid.
5710	Tidewater Skanska Lighted Mooring Buoy B	30-31-12.000N 087-08-12.000W	Fl W 4s			White with blue band.	Private aid.
5715	Tidewater Skanska Lighted Mooring Buoy C	30-30-58.000N 087-09-20.000W	Fl W 4s			White with blue band.	Private aid.
5720	Tidewater Skanska Lighted Mooring Buoy D	30-30-45.000N 087-09-38.000W	Fl W 4s			White with blue band.	Private aid.
5725	Tidewater Skanska Lighted Mooring Buoy E	30-30-48.000N 087-09-00.000W	Q W			White with blue band.	Private aid.
5730	Tidewater Skanska Lighted Mooring Buoy F	30-30-41.000N 087-08-57.000W	Q W			White with blue band.	Private aid.
5735	Tidewater Skanska Lighted Mooring Buoy G	30-30-53.000N 087-08-38.000W	Q W			White with blue band.	Private aid.
5740	Tidewater Skanska Lighted Mooring Buoy H	30-30-56.000N 087-08-24.000W	Fl W 4s			White with blue band.	Private aid.
	Santa Rosa County Channel						
5745	- Day beacon 1	30-31-45.770N 087-07-52.290W				SG on pile.	Private aid.
5750	- Day beacon 2	30-31-45.770N 087-07-51.890W					Private aid.
5755	- Day beacon 3	30-31-51.200N 087-07-51.960W				SG on pile.	Private aid.
5760	- Day beacon 4	30-31-51.170N 087-07-51.530W				TR on pile.	Private aid.

Light List corrected through LNM week: 01/18

(1) No.	(2) Name and Location	(3) Position	(4) Characteristic	(5) Height	(6) Range	(7) Structure	(8) Remarks
			FLORIDA - Eighth District				
	SANTA ROSA SOUND TO DAUPHIN ISLAND (Chart 11378)						
	Escambia Bay						
	Santa Rosa County Channel						
5765	- Day beacon 5	30-31-52.210N 087-07-51.530W				SG on pile.	Private aid.
5770	- Day beacon 6	30-31-51.960N 087-07-51.200W				TR on pile.	Private aid.
5775	- Day beacon 7	30-31-53.870N 087-07-49.730W				SG on pile.	Private aid.
5780	- Day beacon 8	30-31-53.620N 087-07-49.440W				TR on pile.	Private aid.
	Escambia Bay						
5785	- Day beacon 13	30-31-31.759N 087-09-10.476W				SG on pile.	
5790	- Day beacon 14	30-31-33.262N 087-09-08.306W				TR on pile.	
5795	- Day beacon 15	30-32-06.785N 087-09-33.359W				SG on pile.	Ra ref.
5800	- Day beacon 16	30-32-10.310N 087-09-31.279W				TR on pile.	Ra ref.
5805	- Buoy 17	30-32-21.480N 087-09-42.599W				Green can.	
5810	- LIGHT 18	30-32-25.082N 087-09-40.586W	Q R	17	3	TR on pile.	Ra ref.
5815	- Buoy 19	30-32-27.980N 087-09-56.088W				Green can.	
5818	FDOA PENSACOLA BAY OYSTER COMPANY ESCAMBIA BAY SPECIAL LIGHT A	30-26-17.000N 087-10-10.700W	Fl Y 2.5s			Marks perimeter of aquaculture farm.	Private aid.
5818.01	FDOA PENSACOLA BAY OYSTER COMPANY ESCAMBIA BAY SPECIAL LIGHT	30-26-24.300N 087-10-09.100W	Fl Y 2.5s			Marks perimeter of aquaculture farm.	Private aid.
5818.02	FDOA PENSACOLA BAY OYSTER COMPANY ESCAMBIA BAY SPECIAL LIGHT C	30-26-24.900N 087-10-12.800W	Fl Y 2.5s			Marks perimeter of aquaculture farm.	Private aid.
5818.03	FDOA PENSACOLA BAY OYSTER COMPANY ESCAMBIA BAY SPECIAL LIGHT D	30-26-17.600N 087-10-14.300W	Fl Y 2.5s			Marks perimeter of aquaculture farm.	Private aid.
5820	- Buoy 19A	30-32-29.963N 087-10-03.614W				Green can.	
5825	- Buoy 20	30-32-29.129N 087-09-54.326W				Red nun.	
5830	- Day beacon 21	30-32-30.936N 087-10-10.573W				SG on pile.	Ra ref.
	Escambia River						
5835	- Buoy 21A	30-32-39.108N 087-10-40.043W				Green can.	
5840	- Buoy 22	30-32-32.817N 087-10-08.725W				Red nun.	
5845	- Buoy 25	30-33-08.174N 087-12-02.438W				Green can.	
5850	- Buoy 26	30-34-23.712N 087-13-25.122W				Red nun.	
5855	- Buoy 27	30-34-29.232N 087-13-28.272W				Green can.	
5860	- Buoy 28	30-34-30.210N 087-13-26.262W					
5862	- Buoy 28A	30-34-34.524N 087-13-26.352W				Red nun.	
5865	- Buoy 29	30-34-35.946N 087-13-28.536W				Green can.	

Light List corrected through LNM week: 01/18

(1) No.	(2) Name and Location	(3) Position	(4) Characteristic	(5) Height	(6) Range	(7) Structure	(8) Remarks
	FLORIDA - Eighth District						
	SANTA ROSA SOUND TO DAUPHIN ISLAND (Chart 11378)						
	Escambia Bay						
5870	- PIPELINE LIGHT A	30-33-12.000N 087-09-06.000W	Fl Y 2.5s	10		NW on pile.	Private aid.
5875	- PIPELINE LIGHT B	30-33-24.000N 087-08-59.000W	Fl Y 2.5s	10		NW on pile.	Private aid.
5880	- PIPELINE LIGHT C	30-33-38.000N 087-08-54.000W	Fl Y 2.5s	10		NW on pile.	Private aid.
	ALABAMA - Eighth District						
	PENSACOLA BAY AND APPROACHES (Chart 11382)						
	Perdido Pass						
5885 165	- *Entrance Lighted Buoy PP*	30-15-30.728N 087-33-24.333W	Mo (A) W		6	Red and white stripes with red spherical topmark.	AIS MMSI: 993682023
	GULF COAST (Louisiana) - Eighth District						
	SANTA ROSA SOUND TO DAUPHIN ISLAND (Chart 11378)						
	Perdido Pass						
5890	- LIGHT 1	30-16-11.213N 087-33-29.018W	Q G	17	3	SG on steel pile.	
5895	- LIGHT 2	30-16-10.622N 087-33-24.291W	Q R	17	3	TR on pile.	
5900	- Buoy 4	30-16-13.918N 087-33-25.938W				Red nun.	Relocated frequently to mark shoaling.
5905	- *Lighted Buoy 6*	30-16-25.798N 087-33-23.393W	Fl R 2.5s		3	Red.	
5910	- Buoy 7	30-16-26.062N 087-33-29.067W				Green can.	
5915	- Buoy 8	30-16-45.299N 087-33-10.479W				Red nun.	
5920	- Buoy 9	30-16-46.924N 087-33-14.009W				Green can.	
5925	- Buoy 10	30-16-55.458N 087-33-12.237W				Red nun.	
5930	- Buoy 11	30-16-54.986N 087-33-15.293W				Green can.	
5935	- LIGHT 12	30-17-09.865N 087-33-11.836W	Fl R 4s	17	3	TR on pile.	Ra ref.
	ALABAMA - Eighth District						
	SANTA ROSA SOUND TO DAUPHIN ISLAND (Chart 11378)						
	Bayou St John						
5940.01	- Buoy 1	30-16-46.235N 087-33-01.839W				Green can.	
5945	- Day beacon 2	30-16-49.619N 087-32-49.537W				TR on pile.	Ra ref.
5950	- Day beacon 3	30-16-55.926N 087-32-38.792W				SG on pile.	
5955	- Day beacon 4	30-16-54.311N 087-32-38.174W				TR on pile.	
5960	- Day beacon 5	30-16-59.521N 087-32-29.761W				SG on pile.	
5965	- Day beacon 6	30-16-57.826N 087-32-29.583W				TR on pile.	Ra ref.
5970	- Day beacon 7	30-17-07.982N 087-32-05.313W				SG on pile.	
5975	- Day beacon 8	30-17-05.406N 087-32-04.978W				TR on pile.	
5980	- Day beacon 9	30-17-08.712N 087-31-54.145W				SG on pile.	Ra ref.
5985	- Day beacon 11	30-17-11.205N 087-31-49.681W				SG on pile.	Ra ref.
5990	- Day beacon 12	30-17-22.452N 087-31-37.890W				TR on pile.	
5993	ALABAMA DCNR BAYOU ST. JOHN DANGER LIGHTS (8)	30-17-38.240N 087-31-52.370W	Fl W 2.5s			Marks submerged fishing reef.	Private aid.

Light List corrected through LNM week: 01/18

ALABAMA - Eighth District

SANTA ROSA SOUND TO DAUPHIN ISLAND (Chart 11378)

Bayou St John

(1) No.	(2) Name and Location	(3) Position	(4) Characteristic	(5) Height	(6) Range	(7) Structure	(8) Remarks
5995	ONO ISLAND JETTY LIGHT WEST	30-17-28.920N 087-31-06.180W	Fl R 2.5s			On jetty.	Private aid.
6000	- Day beacon 13	30-17-36.492N 087-31-05.227W				SG on pile.	Ra ref.
6005	- Day beacon 15	30-17-46.827N 087-30-33.780W				SG on pile.	
6010	ONO ISLAND JETTY LIGHT EAST	30-17-45.120N 087-30-28.440W	Fl R 2.5s			On jetty.	Private aid.
6015	- Day beacon 17	30-17-59.046N 087-30-30.238W				SG on pile.	Ra ref.
6020	- LIGHT 18	30-17-58.601N 087-30-24.335W	Q R	17	3	TR on pile.	
6025	Soldier Creek Entrance Day beacon 1	30-20-36.000N 087-29-34.000W				SG on pile.	Private aid.
6025.01	Soldier Creek Day beacon 2	30-20-42.000N 087-29-38.000W				Marks starboard side channel.	Private aid.
6025.02	Soldier Creek Day beacon 3	30-20-42.000N 087-29-39.000W				Marks port side channel.	Private aid.
6025.03	Soldier Creek Day beacon 4	30-20-45.000N 087-29-40.000W				Marks starboard side channel.	Private aid.
6025.04	*Soldier Creek Daybeacon 5*	30-20-44.000N 087-29-40.000W				Marks port side channel.	Private aid.
6025.05	Soldier Creek Day beacon 6	30-20-48.000N 087-29-42.000W				Marks starboard side channel.	Private aid.
6025.06	Soldier Creek Day beacon 7	30-20-46.000N 087-29-41.000W				Marks port side channel.	Private aid.
6025.07	Soldier Creek Day beacon 8	30-20-49.000N 087-29-42.000W				Marks starboard side channel.	Private aid.
6025.08	Soldier Creek Day beacon 9	30-20-48.000N 087-29-43.000W				Marks port side channel.	Private aid.
6025.09	Soldier Creek Day beacon 11	30-20-50.000N 087-29-42.000W				Marks port side channel.	Private aid.
6027	ALABAMA DCNR DANGER LIGHT	30-19-19.550N 087-30-40.400W	Fl W 2.5s			Marks submerged fishing reef.	Private aid.
6027.01	ALABAMA DCNR DANGER LIGHT	30-19-19.510N 087-30-43.480W	Fl W 2.5s			Marks submerged fishing reef.	Private aid.
6027.02	ALABAMA DCNR DANGER LIGHT	30-19-26.310N 087-30-43.190W	Fl W 2.5s			Marks submerged fishing reef.	Private aid.
6027.03	ALABAMA DCNR DANGER LIGHT	30-19-26.130N 087-30-40.080W	Fl W 2.5s			Marks submerged fishing reef.	Private aid.
6028	ALABAMA MARINE RESOURCES DIVISION DANGER LIGHT	30-20-04.080N 087-30-00.030W	Fl W 2.5s			Marks perimeter of fishing reef.	Private aid.
6028.01	ALABAMA MARINE RESOURCES DIVISION DANGER LIGHT	30-20-04.080N 087-29-54.390W	Fl W 2.5s			Marks perimeter of fishing reef.	Private aid.
6028.02	ALABAMA MARINE RESOURCES DIVISION DANGER LIGHT	30-20-04.080N 087-29-49.120W	Fl R 2.5s			Marks perimeter of fishing reef.	Private aid.
6028.03	ALABAMA MARINE RESOURCES DIVISION DANGER LIGHT	30-19-57.430N 087-30-00.030W	Fl W 2.5s			Marks perimeter of fishing reef.	Private aid.
6028.04	ALABAMA MARINE RESOURCES DIVISION DANGER LIGHT	30-19-57.430N 087-29-54.390W	Fl W 2.5s			Marks perimeter of fishing reef.	Private aid.
6028.05	ALABAMA MARINE RESOURCES DIVISION DANGER LIGHT	30-19-57.430N 087-29-49.120W	Fl W 2.5s			Marks perimeter of fishing reef.	Private aid.

Bayou Garcon

(1) No.	(2) Name and Location	(3) Position	(4) Characteristic	(5) Height	(6) Range	(7) Structure	(8) Remarks
6030	- Day beacon 1	30-19-15.110N 087-26-54.890W				SG on pile.	Private aid.
6035	- Day beacon 2	30-19-15.830N 087-26-47.930W				TR on pile.	Private aid.
6040	- Day beacon 3	30-19-18.140N 087-26-44.070W				SG on pile.	Private aid.

Light List corrected through LNM week: 01/18

(1) No.	(2) Name and Location	(3) Position	(4) Characteristic	(5) Height	(6) Range	(7) Structure	(8) Remarks
			ALABAMA - Eighth District				
	SANTA ROSA SOUND TO DAUPHIN ISLAND (Chart 11378)						
	Bayou Garcon						
6045	- Day beacon 4	30-19-18.880N 087-26-38.730W				TR on pile.	Private aid.
6050	- Day beacon 5	30-19-21.640N 087-26-32.830W				SG on pile.	Private aid.
	MOBILE BAY (Chart 11376)						
	Navy Cove Harbor Channel						
6055	- Day beacon 1	30-14-15.000N 087-58-28.800W				SG on pile.	Private aid.
6060	- Day beacon 2	30-14-15.000N 087-58-30.000W				TR on pile.	Private aid.
6065	- Day beacon 3	30-14-08.400N 087-58-28.800W				SG on pile.	Private aid.
6070	- Day beacon 4	30-14-08.400N 087-58-30.000W				TR on pile.	Private aid.
6072	WILSON AQUACULTURE SPECIAL LIGHTS (4)	30-13-58.000N 087-58-45.000W	Fl Y 2.5s			Marks perimeter of aquaculture farm.	Private aid.
	Mobile Bay						
6075 185	Mobile Entrance Lighted Buoy M	30-07-30.961N 088-04-07.197W	Mo (A) W		6	Red and white stripes with red spherical topmark.	
6080	MOBILE CHANNEL A RANGE FRONT LIGHT	30-12-18.010N 088-02-02.801W	F R (NIGHT) F W (DAY)	16 19		On same structure as Mobile Channel A Range Front Light.	
6085	MOBILE POINT RANGE FRONT PASSING LIGHT	30-12-18.010N 088-02-02.801W	Fl R 6s	21	4	On same structure as Mobile Point Range Front Light.	
6090	MOBILE CHANNEL A RANGE REAR LIGHT 3,004 yards, 020.7° from front light.	30-13-41.487N 088-01-26.531W	F R (NIGHT) F W (DAY)	80 77		On same structure and 47 feet below Mobile Point Light.	
6095 180	**Mobile Point Light**	30-13-41.487N 088-01-26.531W	Fl W 10s	125	14	On skeleton tower. 125	
	Mobile Bar						
6100	- Lighted Buoy 1	30-08-28.739N 088-03-47.992W	Fl (2)G 5s		3	Green.	
6105	- Lighted Buoy 2	30-08-25.345N 088-03-37.763W	Fl (2)R 5s		3	Red.	
6110	- Lighted Buoy 3 140 feet outside channel limit.	30-08-53.627N 088-03-36.806W	Fl G 2.5s		3	Green.	
6115	- Lighted Buoy 4 109 feet outside channel limit.	30-08-50.618N 088-03-27.780W	Fl R 2.5s		3	Red.	
6120	- Lighted Buoy 5	30-09-25.981N 088-03-22.578W	Q G		3	Green.	
6125	- Lighted Buoy 6	30-09-23.238N 088-03-14.291W	Fl R 4s		3	Red.	
6130	- Lighted Buoy 7	30-09-54.238N 088-03-11.692W	Fl G 2.5s		4	Green.	
6135	- Lighted Buoy 8	30-09-51.138N 088-03-02.491W	Q R		3	Red.	
6140	- Lighted Buoy 9	30-10-21.247N 088-03-03.404W	Q G		3	Green.	
6145	- Lighted Buoy 10	30-10-20.437N 088-02-54.691W	Fl R 2.5s		3	Red.	
6150	- Lighted Buoy 11	30-11-01.337N 088-02-55.092W	Fl G 4s		3	Green.	
6155	- Lighted Buoy 12	30-10-59.937N 088-02-44.291W	Fl R 4s		3	Red.	
6160	- Lighted Buoy 13	30-12-00.786N 088-02-37.066W	Fl G 2.5s		3	Green.	
6165	- Lighted Buoy 14	30-11-59.335N 088-02-28.691W	Fl R 2.5s		3	Red.	

Light List corrected through LNM week: 01/18

(1) No.	(2) Name and Location	(3) Position	(4) Characteristic	(5) Height	(6) Range	(7) Structure	(8) Remarks
			ALABAMA - Eighth District				
	MOBILE BAY (Chart 11376)						
	Mobile Bay						
	Mobile Bar						
6170	- Lighted Buoy 15	30-12-51.235N 088-02-23.992W	Fl G 4s		3	Green.	
6175	- Lighted Buoy 16	30-12-48.989N 088-02-15.326W	Fl R 4s		3	Red.	
6180	MOBILE CHANNEL B RANGE FRONT LIGHT	30-15-26.263N 088-02-28.533W	Q G	29		KRW on skeleton tower on piles.	Visible 2° each side of range line.
6185	MOBILE CHANNEL B RANGE FRONT LIGHT PASSING LIGHT	30-15-26.274N 088-02-28.526W	Q W	15	5	On same structure as Mobile Channel B Range Front Light.	Obscured on range line, visible elswhere.
6190	MOBILE CHANNEL B RANGE REAR LIGHT 611 yards, 350.3° from front light.	30-15-44.152N 088-02-32.047W	Iso G 6s	50		KRW on skeleton tower on piles.	Visible 2° each side of range line.
6195	MOBILE CHANNEL B RANGE REAR LIGHT PASSING LIGHT	30-15-44.150N 088-02-32.029W	Fl W 4s	17	5	On same structure as Mobile Channel B Range Rear Light.	Obscured on range line, visible elsewhere.
6200	Mobile Point Buoy T	30-13-48.246N 088-01-35.995W				Yellow can.	
6205	FORT MORGAN WRECK LIGHT WR2	30-14-00.016N 088-01-13.576W	Q R	17	4	TR on pile.	
6210	Fort Morgan Wreck Lighted Buoy WR2A	30-13-57.510N 088-01-15.872W	Q R		3	Red.	Buoy is set on the west side of wreck. Mariners should use extreme caution when transiting in the vicinity of the buoy and avoid the area by a wide margin.
6215	Fort Morgan Danger Wreck Daybeacon	30-13-59.760N 088-01-15.120W				NW on pile worded DANGER SUBMERGED WRECK.	MARKS PERIMETER OF SUKEN BARGE. Private aid.
6220	- Lighted Buoy 17	30-13-27.034N 088-02-14.892W	Q G		3	Green.	
6225	- Lighted Buoy 18	30-13-37.327N 088-02-01.681W	Q R		3	Red.	
6230	- Lighted Buoy 19	30-14-17.679N 088-02-19.509W	Fl G 2.5s		3	Green.	
6235	- Lighted Buoy 20	30-14-20.234N 088-02-10.392W	Fl R 2.5s		3	Red.	
	Mobile Channel						
6240	- C RANGE FRONT LIGHT	30-14-06.263N 088-02-29.932W	Fl W 2.5s (NIGHT) Fl W 2.5s (DAY)	19 21		Platform on pile.	DAY: Visible on range line only. NIGHT: Visible all around, higher intensity on range line.
6245	- C RANGE REAR LIGHT 2,340 yards, 187.1° from front light.	30-12-57.304N 088-02-39.844W	Oc W 4s (NIGHT) Oc W 4s (DAY)	87 85		Skeleton tower on piles.	
6250	- C RANGE REAR LIGHT PASSING LIGHT	30-12-57.140N 088-02-39.350W	Fl W 4s	23	6	On same structure as Mobile Channel C Range Rear Light.	
	Mobile Channel						
6255	- Lighted Buoy 21	30-14-52.946N 088-02-27.568W	Q G		3	Green.	
6260	- Lighted Buoy 22	30-15-09.044N 088-02-16.711W	Q R		3	Red.	
6265	- Lighted Buoy 23	30-15-46.530N 088-02-18.791W	Fl G 2.5s		3	Green.	
6270	- Lighted Buoy 24	30-15-44.531N 088-02-11.792W	Fl R 2.5s		3	Red.	

Light List corrected through LNM week: 01/18

(1) No.	(2) Name and Location	(3) Position	(4) Characteristic	(5) Height	(6) Range	(7) Structure	(8) Remarks
		ALABAMA - Eighth District					
	MOBILE BAY (Chart 11376)						
	Mobile Channel						
6275 33960	- Lighted Buoy 25	30-16-27.229N 088-02-13.491W	Fl G 4s		3	Green with yellow triangle.	
6280 33955	- Lighted Buoy 26	30-16-25.007N 088-02-06.029W	Fl (2)R 5s		3	Red with yellow triangle.	
6285	- Lighted Buoy 27	30-17-24.227N 088-02-06.091W	Fl G 2.5s		3	Green.	
6290	- Lighted Buoy 28	30-17-25.768N 088-01-57.071W	Fl R 2.5s		3	Red.	
6295	- LIGHT 29 300 feet outside channel limit.	30-18-25.065N 088-01-58.492W	Fl G 4s	17	4	SG on pile.	Ra ref.
6300	- LIGHT 30 300 feet outside channel limit.	30-18-23.839N 088-01-47.172W	Fl R 4s	17	4	TR on pile.	Ra ref.
6305	- LIGHT 31 300 feet outside channel limit.	30-19-20.896N 088-01-50.463W	Fl G 6s	17	4	SG on pile.	Ra ref.
6310	- LIGHT 32 300 feet outside channel limit.	30-19-19.671N 088-01-39.141W	Oc R 4s	17	4	TR on piles.	Ra ref.
6315	- LIGHT 33 300 feet outside channel limit.	30-20-17.197N 088-01-42.273W	Fl G 4s	17	4	SG on pile.	Ra ref.
6320	- LIGHT 34 300 feet outside channel limit.	30-20-16.293N 088-01-30.992W	Fl R 2.5s	17	3	TR on dolphin.	Ra ref.
6325	- LIGHT 36 300 feet outside channel limit.	30-20-36.534N 088-01-28.079W	Fl (2)R 5s	17	4	TR on dolphin.	Ra ref.
6330	- LIGHT 37 300 feet outside channel limit.	30-21-36.817N 088-01-30.903W	Fl G 4s	17	4	SG on pile.	Ra ref.
6335	- LIGHT 38 300 feet outside channel limit.	30-21-35.599N 088-01-18.887W	Fl R 4s	17	4	TR on piles.	Ra ref.
6340	- LIGHT 39 300 feet outside channel limit.	30-22-43.828N 088-01-21.256W	Fl G 6s	17	4	SG on pile.	Ra ref.
6345	ADCNR Mobile Bay West Oyster Reef Boat Exclusion Day beacon	30-25-22.140N 088-05-52.920W				NW on pile. BOAT EXCLUSION AREA.	Maintained by Alabama Department of Conservation and Natural Resources. Private aid.
6350	ADCNR Mobile Bay West Oyster Reef Boat Exclusion Day beacon	30-25-04.800N 088-05-53.940W				NW on pile. BOAT EXCLUSION AREA.	Maintained by Alabama Department of Conservation and Natural Resources. Private aid.
6355	ADCNR Mobile Bay West Oyster Reef Boat Exclusion Day beacon	30-24-47.700N 088-05-55.860W				NW on pile. BOAT EXCLUSION AREA.	Maintained by Alabama Department of Conservation and Natural Resources. Private aid.
6360	ADCNR Mobile Bay West Oyster Reef Boat Exclusion Day beacon	30-24-30.540N 088-05-57.600W				NW on pile. BOAT EXCLUSION AREA.	Maintained by Alabama Department of Conservation and Natural Resources. Private aid.
6365	ADCNR Mobile Bay West Oyster Reef Boat Exclusion Day beacon	30-24-13.440N 088-06-00.360W				NW on pile. BOAT EXCLUSION AREA.	Maintained by Alabama Department of Conservation and Natural Resources. Private aid.
6370	ADCNR Mobile Bay West Oyster Reef Boat Exclusion Day beacon	30-23-56.340N 088-06-02.700W				NW on pile. BOAT EXCLUSION AREA.	Maintained by Alabama Department of Conservation and Natural Resources. Private aid.
6375	ADCNR Mobile Bay West Oyster Reef Boat Exclusion Day beacon	30-23-39.120N 088-06-02.880W				NW on pile. BOAT EXCLUSION AREA.	Maintained by Alabama Department of Conservation and Natural Resources. Private aid.

Light List corrected through LNM week: 01/18

(1) No.	(2) Name and Location	(3) Position	(4) Characteristic	(5) Height	(6) Range	(7) Structure	(8) Remarks
	ALABAMA - Eighth District						
	MOBILE BAY (Chart 11376)						
	Mobile Channel						
6380	ADCNR Mobile Bay West Oyster Reef Boat Exclusion Day beacon	30-23-21.900N 088-06-02.520W				NW on pile. BOAT EXCLUSION AREA.	Maintained by Alabama Department of Conservation and Natural Resources. Private aid.
6385	ADCNR Mobile Bay West Oyster Reef Boat Exclusion Day beacon	30-25-21.900N 088-05-34.860W				NW on pile. BOAT EXCLUSION AREA.	Maintained by Alabama Department of Conservation and Natural Resources. Private aid.
6390	ADCNR Mobile Bay West Oyster Reef Boat Exclusion Day beacon	30-25-04.560N 088-05-31.080W				NW on pile. BOAT EXCLUSION AREA.	Maintained by Alabama Department of Conservation and Natural Resources. Private aid.
6395	ADCNR Mobile Bay West Oyster Reef Boat Exclusion Day beacon	30-24-47.100N 088-05-28.860W				NW on pile. BOAT EXCLUSION AREA.	Maintained by Alabama Department of Conservation and Natural Resources. Private aid.
6400	ADCNR Mobile Bay West Oyster Reef Boat Exclusion Day beacon	30-24-29.640N 088-05-26.820W				NW on pile. BOAT EXCLUSION AREA.	Maintained by Alabama Department of Conservation and Natural Resources. Private aid.
6405	ADCNR Mobile Bay West Oyster Reef Boat Exclusion Day beacon	30-24-12.180N 088-05-24.720W				NW on pile. BOAT EXCLUSION AREA.	Maintained by Alabama Department of Conservation and Natural Resources. Private aid.
6410	ADCNR Mobile Bay West Oyster Reef Boat Exclusion Day beacon	30-23-54.780N 088-05-26.820W				NW on pile. BOAT EXCLUSION AREA.	Maintained by Alabama Department of Conservation and Natural Resources. Private aid.
6415	ADCNR Mobile Bay West Oyster Reef Boat Exclusion Day beacon	30-23-37.440N 088-05-30.000W				NW on pile. BOAT EXCLUSION AREA.	Maintained by Alabama Department of Conservation and Natural Resources. Private aid.
6420	ADCNR Mobile Bay West Oyster Reef Boat Exclusion Day beacon	30-23-20.100N 088-05-33.180W				NW on pile. BOAT EXCLUSION AREA.	Maintained by Alabama Department of Conservation and Natural Resources. Private aid.
6425	ADCNR Mobile Bay West Oyster Reef Boat Exclusion Day beacon	30-23-02.760N 088-05-36.360W				NW on pile. BOAT EXCLUSION AREA.	Maintained by Alabama Department of Conservation and Natural Resources. Private aid.
6430	- *Lighted Buoy 40* 300 feet outside channel limit.	30-22-42.601N 088-01-09.926W	Fl R 6s		4	Red.	
6435	- LIGHT 41 300 feet outside channel limit.	30-23-34.650N 088-01-14.295W	Fl G 4s	17	4	SG on pile.	Ra ref.
6440	- *Lighted Buoy 42* 300 feet outside channel limit.	30-23-33.365N 088-01-02.614W	Fl R 4s		4	Red.	
6445	- LIGHT 43 300 feet outside channel limit.	30-24-35.835N 088-01-05.120W	Fl G 2.5s	17	4	SG on pile.	Ra ref.
6450	- LIGHT 44 300 feet outside channel limit.	30-24-34.608N 088-00-53.789W	Fl R 2.5s	17	4	TR on pile.	Ra ref.
6455	- E RANGE FRONT LIGHT	30-25-42.638N 088-00-41.857W	Q R	25		KRW on skeleton tower on piles.	Visible 3° each side of range line.
6460	- E RANGE FRONT PASSING LIGHT	30-25-42.632N 088-00-41.863W	Q W	12	5	On same structure as Mobile Channel E Range Front Light.	
6465	- E RANGE REAR LIGHT 2,103 yards, 174.5 from front light.	30-24-40.480N 088-00-34.904W	Oc R 4s	67		KRW on skeleton tower on piles.	Visible 3° each side of range line.

(1) No.	(2) Name and Location	(3) Position	(4) Characteristic	(5) Height	(6) Range	(7) Structure	(8) Remarks
	**ALABAMA - Eighth District**						

MOBILE BAY (Chart 11376)
Mobile Channel

(1) No.	(2) Name and Location	(3) Position	(4) Characteristic	(5) Height	(6) Range	(7) Structure	(8) Remarks
6470	- E RANGE REAR PASSING LIGHT	30-24-40.763N 088-00-34.947W	Fl W 4s	12	5	On same structure as Mobile Channel E Range Rear Light.	
6475	- LIGHT 45 250 feet outside channel limit.	30-25-45.145N 088-00-55.132W	Q G	17	3	SG on piles.	Ra ref.
6480	- Lighted Buoy 46 250 feet outside channel limit.	30-25-44.329N 088-00-44.989W	Q R		3	Red.	
6485	- Lighted Buoy 47 300 feet outside channel limit.	30-26-14.872N 088-00-54.804W	Fl G 2.5s		4	Green.	
6490.01	MOBILE BAY LIGHT	30-26-14.721N 088-00-40.443W	Fl R 6s			Lighthouse on piles.	Private aid.
6495	- D RANGE FRONT LIGHT	30-26-24.109N 088-00-43.760W	Q W	26		KGR on skeleton tower on piles.	Visible all around; higher intensity 1.5° each side of range line.
6500	- D RANGE REAR LIGHT 2,199 yards, 007.1 from front light.	30-27-28.641N 088-00-34.446W	Oc W 4s	63		KGR on skeleton tower on piles.	Visible 2° each side of range line.
6505	- D RANGE REAR LIGHT PASSING LIGHT	30-27-28.642N 088-00-34.453W	Fl W 4s	12	3	On same structure as Mobile Channel D Range Rear Light.	
6510	- LIGHT 49 200 feet outside channel limit.	30-26-44.214N 088-00-54.446W	Q G	17	4	SG on pile.	Ra ref.
6515	- LIGHT 50 200 feet outside channel limit.	30-26-44.658N 088-00-44.541W	Q R	17	4	TR on pile.	Ra ref.
6520	- LIGHT 51 200 feet outside channel limit.	30-27-52.264N 088-01-00.946W	Fl G 2.5s	17	4	SG on piles.	Ra ref.
6525	- Lighted Buoy 52 200 feet outside channel limit.	30-27-53.028N 088-00-51.847W	Fl R 2.5s		4	Red.	
6530	- Lighted Buoy 54	30-28-37.352N 088-00-56.393W	Fl R 4s		4	Red.	
6535 7350	THEODORE SHIP CHANNEL LIGHT 1 350 feet outside channel limit.	30-28-38.703N 088-01-08.485W	Q G	17	3	SG on pile.	Ra ref.
6540	Theodore Ship Channel Buoy 1A	30-28-38.405N 088-01-07.900W				Green can.	
6545 7355	THEODORE SHIP CHANNEL JUNCTION LIGHT T	30-28-58.365N 088-01-11.700W	Fl (2+1)G 6s	17	4	JG on pile.	Ra ref.
6550	- Lighted Buoy 55 200 feet outside channel limit.	30-29-22.305N 088-01-10.486W	Fl G 4s		4	Green.	
6555	- LIGHT 57 200 feet outside channel limit.	30-30-16.091N 088-01-17.050W	Fl G 6s	17	4	SG on pile.	Ra ref.
6560	- LIGHT 58 200 feet outside channel limit.	30-30-16.856N 088-01-07.947W	Fl R 6s	17	4	TR on pile.	Ra ref.
6565	- Lighted Buoy 59	30-31-20.460N 088-01-24.512W	Oc G 4s		4	Green.	
6570	- LIGHT 60 200 feet outside channel limit.	30-31-20.874N 088-01-14.929W	Oc R 4s	17	4	TR on pile.	Ra ref.
6575	- LIGHT 63 200 feet outside channel limit.	30-32-20.465N 088-01-30.989W	Fl G 4s	17	4	SG on pile.	Ra ref.

(1) No.	(2) Name and Location	(3) Position	(4) Characteristic	(5) Height	(6) Range	(7) Structure	(8) Remarks
			ALABAMA - Eighth District				
	MOBILE BAY (Chart 11376)						
	Mobile Channel						
6580	- LIGHT 64 200 feet outside channel limit.	30-32-21.230N 088-01-21.884W	Fl R 4s	17	3	TR on pile.	Ra ref.
6585	- LIGHT 65 200 feet outside channel limit.	30-33-17.671N 088-01-37.405W	Fl G 4s	17	4	SG on pile.	Ra ref.
6590	- LIGHT 66 200 feet outside channel limit.	30-33-18.436N 088-01-28.298W	Fl R 4s	17	4	TR on pile.	Ra ref.
6595	- LIGHT 67 200 feet outside channel limit.	30-34-26.640N 088-01-45.135W	Fl G 6s	17	4	SG on pile.	Ra ref.
6600	- LIGHT 68 200 feet outside channel limit.	30-34-27.129N 088-01-36.002W	Fl R 6s	17	4	TR on pile.	Ra ref.
6605	- LIGHT 69 200 feet outside channel limit.	30-35-23.812N 088-01-51.558W	Fl G 4s	17	4	SG on piles.	Ra ref.
6610	- LIGHT 70 200 feet outside channel limit.	30-35-24.577N 088-01-42.448W	Fl R 4s	17	5	TR on pile.	Ra ref.
6615	- LIGHT 71 200 feet outside channel limit.	30-36-20.604N 088-01-57.934W	Fl G 2.5s	17	4	SG on pile.	Ra ref.
6620	- LIGHT 72 200 feet outside channel limit.	30-36-21.370N 088-01-48.822W	Fl R 2.5s	17	4	TR on pile.	Ra ref.
6625	MOBILE AIRPORT APPROACH LIGHTS(4)	30-36-32.000N 088-03-20.000W	Q W	20		On platform on piles.	Private aid.
6630	- LIGHT 73 200 feet outside channel limit.	30-37-06.379N 088-02-03.074W	Q G	17	3	SG on pile.	Ra ref.
6635	- LIGHT 74 200 feet outside channel limit.	30-37-06.480N 088-01-52.659W	Q R	17	4	TR on pile.	Ra ref.
6640	- G RANGE FRONT LIGHT	30-36-27.376N 088-01-59.961W	Q G	25		KRW on skeleton tower on piles.	For downbound traffic. Visible 2° each side of range line.
6645	- G RANGE FRONT LIGHT PASSING LIGHT	30-36-27.368N 088-01-59.964W	Q W	11	5	On same structure as Mobile Channel G Range Front Light.	
6650	- G RANGE REAR LIGHT 1,669 yards, 181.7° from front light.	30-35-37.839N 088-02-01.663W	Iso G 6s	56		KRW on skeleton tower on piles.	Visible 2° each side of range line.
6655	- G RANGE REAR LIGHT PASSING LIGHT	30-35-37.854N 088-02-01.667W	Q W	14	4	On same structure as Mobile Channel G Range Rear Light.	
6660	- LIGHT 76	30-37-45.393N 088-01-52.475W	Fl R 2.5s	17	3	TR on pile.	Ra ref.
6665	- F RANGE FRONT LIGHT	30-37-48.653N 088-02-03.221W	Q G	25		KRW on skeleton tower on piles.	
6670	- F RANGE FRONT LIGHT PASSING LIGHT	30-37-48.659N 088-02-03.218W	Q W	12	5	On same structure as Mobile Channel F Range Front Light.	
6675	- F RANGE REAR LIGHT 1,714 yards, 354.4° from front light.	30-38-39.302N 088-02-08.918W	Iso G 6s	67		KRW on skeleton tower on piles.	
6680 7540	*Arlington Channel Lighted Buoy 1* 60 feet outside channel limit.	30-38-22.689N 088-01-59.991W	Fl G 2.5s		4	Green.	
6685	- LIGHT 78 200 feet outside channel limit.	30-38-28.668N 088-01-51.613W	Fl R 4s	17	5	TR on pile.	Ra ref.

Light List corrected through LNM week: 01/18

(1) No.	(2) Name and Location	(3) Position	(4) Characteristic	(5) Height	(6) Range	(7) Structure	(8) Remarks
	**ALABAMA - Eighth District**							

MOBILE BAY (Chart 11376)

Mobile Channel

(1) No.	(2) Name and Location	(3) Position	(4) Characteristic	(5) Height	(6) Range	(7) Structure	(8) Remarks
6690 7555	Arlington Channel Junction Buoy 60 feet outside channel limit.	30-38-40.688N 088-02-01.991W					Green can with red band.
6695	- LIGHT 82 200 feet outside channel limit.	30-38-58.824N 088-01-49.766W	Fl R 2.5s	17	3	TR on pile.	Ra ref.
6697	MOBILE TURNING BASIN LIGHT A	30-40-03.442N 088-01-42.621W	Fl W 4s	20	3		
6700	USS ALABAMA PARK FISHING PIER LIGHT	30-40-58.540N 088-00-46.760W	Fl G 2.5s			On east end fishing pier.	Private aid.

TENNESSEE - TOMBIGBEE WATERWAY (Alabama) - Eighth District

Mobile Bay (Chart 11376)

Mobile River

From mile 0.0 to mile 45.2, the river is marked with numerous unlisted daybeacons and unlighted buoys which are periodically relocated to meet minor changing conditions.

(1) No.	(2) Name and Location	(3) Position	(4) Characteristic	(5) Height	(6) Range	(7) Structure	(8) Remarks
6705	LL&E DOLPHIN LIGHTS (2)	30-42-53.000N 088-02-15.000W	Fl R 2.5s	17		On breasting dolphin.	Private aid.
6710	- TERMINAL LIGHT	30-43-39.000N 088-02-36.000W	F G	25		Pole.	Private aid.
6712	ARC TERMINAL MOORING DOLPHIN LIGHTS	30-43-17.808N 088-02-23.189W	Fl R 2.5s			Marks outermost upstream and downstream dolphins.	Private aid.
6715	Chickasaw Creek Junction Buoy C	30-44-16.619N 088-02-36.646W				Green can with red band.	
6720	SPANISH RIVER LIGHT	30-46-15.689N 088-01-22.812W	Fl R 2.5s	17	3	TR on pile.	Ra ref.
6722	MOBILE COUNTY SCIENTIFIC MONITORING PLATFORM LIGHT A	30-46-55.500N 088-04-25.400W	Fl Y 2.5s			On pile.	Private aid.
6723	*Genesis Pipeline Lighted Danger Buoy*	30-46-49.980N 088-00-54.470W	Fl W 2.5s			Marks submerged rock.	Private aid.
6725	TWELVE MILE ISLAND LIGHT	30-47-06.444N 088-00-40.396W	Fl R 2.5s	17	3	TR on pile.	Ra ref.
6750	Big Bayou Canot West Danger Daybeacon	30-48-40.250N 087-59-27.639W				NW on pile worded DANGER FIXED BRIDGE.	
6755	Big Bayou Canot East Danger Daybeacon	30-48-39.886N 087-59-24.057W				NW on pile worded DANGER FIXED BRIDGE.	
6765	SCOTT BRIDGE COMPANY BRIDGE ASSEMBLY STRUCTURE LIGHTS (2)	30-54-47.050N 087-57-41.530W	Fl R 2.5s			Marks structure outermost corners.	Private aid.

TOMBIGBEE RIVER

From mile 45.2 to mile 410 the river is marked with numerous unlisted daybeacons and unlighted buoys which are periodically relocated to meet minor changing conditions.

(1) No.	(2) Name and Location	(3) Position	(4) Characteristic	(5) Height	(6) Range	(7) Structure	(8) Remarks
6770	ALABAMA ELECTRIC SOUTH BARGE UNLOADING FACILITY LIGHTS (2) RDB Mile 89.0.	. .	Fl G 2.5s			On mooring cells.	Private aid.
6775	ALABAMA ELECTRIC COOP UNLOADING FACILITY LIGHTS (2) RDB mile 89.5	. .	Fl G 6s			On mooring dolphins.	Private aid.
6780	Boise Cascade Water Intake Buoy LDB mile 89.5	31-29-24.000N 087-54-19.000W				Red.	Private aid.

Weyerhaeuser Water Intake

(1) No.	(2) Name and Location	(3) Position	(4) Characteristic	(5) Height	(6) Range	(7) Structure	(8) Remarks
6785	- LIGHT A	33-26-09.000N 088-26-26.000W	Fl G 6s	36		NW on pile.	Private aid.
6790	- LIGHT B	33-26-07.000N 088-26-31.000W	Fl (2)R 6s	36		NW on pile.	Private aid.
6795	- LIGHT C	33-26-11.000N 088-26-27.000W	Fl G 6s	36		NW on pile.	Private aid.

Light List corrected through LNM week: 01/18

(1) No.	(2) Name and Location	(3) Position	(4) Characteristic	(5) Height	(6) Range	(7) Structure	(8) Remarks
		TENNESSEE - TOMBIGBEE WATERWAY (Alabama) - Eighth District					
	TOMBIGBEE RIVER						
	Weyerhaeuser Water Intake						
6800	- LIGHT D	33-26-10.000N 088-26-31.000W	Fl (2)R 6s	36		NW on pile.	Private aid.
	ALABAMA RIVER						
6800.05	- CELLULOSE PILING LIGHT LDB Mile 69.9	31-34-37.980N 087-31-09.620W	Fl R 2.5s			Marks outermost upstream piling.	Private aid.
6801	UNITED LAND COMPANY DOLPHIN LIGHTS (2) LDB Mile 353.3		Fl R 2.5s	15		On dolphins.	Private aid.

BLACK WARRIOR RIVER

From mile 217 to mile 385.5, the river is marked with numerous unlisted daybeacons and unlighted buoys which are periodically relocated to meet minor changing conditions.

Holt Lock and Bankhead Lake buoys and daybeacons have been discontinued and waterways marked with unlisted, unlighted buoys.

Mulberry Fork
From mile 385.6 to mile 399.7, the river is marked with unlisted daybeacons and unlighted buoys which are periodically relocated to meet minor changing condtions.

Locust Fork
From mile 387.0 to mile 390.8, the river is marked with unlisted daybeacons and unlighted buoys which are periodically relocated to meet minor changing conditions.

(1) No.	(2) Name and Location	(3) Position	(4) Characteristic	(5) Height	(6) Range	(7) Structure	(8) Remarks
6802	Lyon Park Range Front Day beacon					KWR on pile.	Private aid.
6803	Lyon Park Range Rear Day beacon					KWR on pile.	Private aid.
		ALABAMA - Eighth District					
	SANTA ROSA SOUND TO DAUPHIN ISLAND (Chart 11378)						
	Mobile Bay						
	Bon Secour River						
6805 33770	- LIGHT 2	30-17-02.338N 087-45-23.122W	Fl R 2.5s	17	3	TR on pile.	Ra ref.
6810	- Day beacon 3 20 feet outside channel limit.	30-17-07.798N 087-45-15.840W				SG on pile.	Ra ref.
6815	- Day beacon 4	30-17-05.725N 087-45-15.956W				TR on pile.	Ra ref.
6820	- Day beacon 5	30-17-12.898N 087-45-05.280W				SG on pile.	Ra ref.
6825	- Day beacon 6 20 feet outside channel limit.	30-17-12.425N 087-45-03.855W				TR on pile.	Ra ref.
6830	- Day beacon 7	30-17-28.125N 087-45-00.255W				SG on pile.	Ra ref.
6835	- Day beacon 8	30-17-27.743N 087-44-56.842W				TR on pile.	Ra ref.
6840	- Day beacon 9	30-17-43.324N 087-44-55.555W				SG on pile.	Ra ref.
6845	- Day beacon 10	30-17-42.505N 087-44-54.192W				TR on pile.	Ra ref.
6850	- Day beacon 11	30-17-49.281N 087-44-38.635W				SG on pile.	Ra ref.
	South Fork Channel						
6855	- Day beacon SF	30-17-47.118N 087-44-38.357W				JR on pile.	Ra ref.
6860	- Day beacon 2	30-17-45.383N 087-44-42.253W				TR on pile.	Ra ref.
6865	- Day beacon 3	30-17-44.724N 087-44-33.954W				SG on pile.	Ra ref.
6870	- Day beacon 5	30-17-40.724N 087-44-28.954W				SG on pile.	Ra ref.

(1) No.	(2) Name and Location	(3) Position	(4) Characteristic	(5) Height	(6) Range	(7) Structure	(8) Remarks
			ALABAMA - Eighth District				
	SANTA ROSA SOUND TO DAUPHIN ISLAND (Chart 11378)						
	Mobile Bay						
	Bon Secour River						
6875	- Day beacon 14	30-17-53.870N 087-44-21.244W				TR on pile.	Ra ref.
6880	- Day beacon 16 40 feet outside channel limit.	30-18-00.624N 087-44-13.954W				TR on pile.	Ra ref.
6885	- Day beacon 18 40 feet outside channel limit.	30-18-05.424N 087-44-07.254W				TR on pile.	Ra ref.
6890	- Day beacon 20 40 feet outside channel limit.	30-18-08.224N 087-44-01.254W				TR on pile.	Ra ref.
6895	- Day beacon 22 40 feet outside channel limit.	30-18-09.423N 087-43-51.553W				TR on pile.	Ra ref.
6900	- Day beacon 24 40 feet outside channel limit.	30-18-11.793N 087-43-37.715W				TR on pile.	Ra ref.
6905	- Day beacon 26 40 feet outside channel limit.	30-18-23.423N 087-43-36.453W				TR on pile.	Ra ref.
6910	- Day beacon 28 40 feet outside channel limit.	30-18-33.223N 087-43-35.453W				TR on pile.	Ra ref.
6915	- Day beacon 30 40 feet outside channel limit.	30-18-40.222N 087-43-25.853W				TR on pile.	Ra ref.
6920	- Day beacon 31 30 feet outside channel limit.	30-18-46.522N 087-43-19.853W				SG on pile.	Ra ref.
6925	- Day beacon 32 30 feet outside channel limit.	30-18-44.158N 087-43-08.100W				TR on pile.	Ra ref.
6930	- Day beacon 33 30 feet outside channel limit.	30-18-44.722N 087-43-07.952W				SG on pile.	Ra ref.
6935	- Day beacon 34 30 feet outside channel limit.	30-18-42.778N 087-42-55.560W				TR on pile.	Ra ref.
6940	- Day beacon 36 30 feet outside channel limit.	30-18-49.722N 087-42-47.952W				TR on pile.	Ra ref.
6945	- Day beacon 37 30 feet outside channel limit.	30-19-00.058N 087-42-49.140W				SG on pile.	Ra ref.
6950	- Day beacon 38 30 feet outside channel limit.	30-19-00.722N 087-42-45.952W				TR on pile.	Ra ref.
	MOBILE BAY (Chart 11376)						
	Mobile Bay						
	Mobile Channel						
6955	AUBURN UNIVERSITY RESEARCH LIGHT A	30-18-38.441N 087-47-10.670W	Fl Y 2.5s	12		On platform on piles.	Private aid.
	Mobile Bay						
6960	WEEKS BAY ENTRANCE LIGHT 1	30-22-12.838N 087-51-17.040W	Fl G 4s	30	5	SG on platform.	Ra ref.
6963	NOAA BON SECOUR BAY DANGER BREAKWATER LIGHT	30-19-15.162N 087-47-25.445W	Fl W 2.5s			Marks shoreline restoration breakwater structure.	Private aid.
6963.01	NOAA BON SECOUR BAY DANGER BREAKWATER LIGHT	30-19-17.260N 087-47-29.969W	Fl W 2.5s			Marks shoreline restoration breakwater structure.	Private aid.

Light List corrected through LNM week: 01/18

(1) No.	(2) Name and Location	(3) Position	(4) Characteristic	(5) Height	(6) Range	(7) Structure	(8) Remarks
			ALABAMA - Eighth District				
	MOBILE BAY (Chart 11376)						
	Mobile Bay						
6963.02	NOAA BON SECOUR BAY DANGER BREAKWATER LIGHT	30-19-30.741N 087-47-56.618W	Fl W 2.5s			Marks shoreline restoration breakwater structure.	Private aid.
6963.03	NOAA BON SECOUR BAY DANGER BREAKWATER LIGHT	30-19-21.655N 087-47-38.951W	Fl W 2.5s			Marks shoreline restoration breakwater structure.	Private aid.
6963.04	NOAA BON SECOUR BAY DANGER BREAKWATER LIGHT	30-19-23.822N 087-47-43.441W	Fl W 2.5s			Marks shoreline restoration breakwater structure.	Private aid.
6963.05	NOAA BON SECOUR BAY DANGER BREAKWATER LIGHT	30-19-26.069N 087-47-47.875W	Fl W 2.5s			Marks shoreline restoration breakwater structure.	Private aid.
6963.06	NOAA BON SECOUR BAY DANGER BREAKWATER LIGHT	30-19-28.405N 087-47-52.241W	Fl W 2.5s			Marks shoreline restoration breakwater structure.	Private aid.
6963.07	NOAA BON SECOUR BAY DANGER BREAKWATER LIGHT	30-19-30.741N 087-47-56.618W	Fl W 2.5s			Marks shoreline restoration breakwater structure.	Private aid.
6963.08	NOAA BON SECOUR BAY DANGER BREAKWATER LIGHT	30-19-47.831N 087-48-20.166W	Fl W 2.5s			Marks shoreline restoration breakwater structure.	Private aid.
6963.09	NOAA BON SECOUR BAY DANGER BREAKWATER LIGHT	30-19-36.167N 087-48-04.759W	Fl W 2.5s			Marks shoreline restoration breakwater structure.	Private aid.
6963.11	NOAA BON SECOUR BAY DANGER BREAKWATER LIGHT	30-19-39.217N 087-48-08.511W	Fl W 2.5s			Marks shoreline restoration breakwater structure.	Private aid.
6963.12	NOAA BON SECOUR BAY DANGER BREAKWATER LIGHT	30-19-42.019N 087-48-12.434W				Marks shoreline restoration breakwater structure.	Private aid.
6963.13	NOAA BON SECOUR BAY DANGER BREAKWATER LIGHT	30-19-44.742N 087-48-16.470W	Fl W 2.5s			Marks shoreline restoration breakwater structure.	Private aid.
6963.14	NOAA BON SECOUR BAY DANGER BREAKWATER LIGHT	30-19-47.831N 087-48-20.166W	Fl W 2.5s			Marks shoreline restoration breakwater structure.	Private aid.
6963.15	NOAA BON SECOUR BAY DANGER BREAKWATER LIGHT	30-19-50.981N 087-48-23.793W	Fl W 2.5s			Marks shoreline restoration breakwater structure.	Private aid.
6963.16	NOAA BON SECOUR BAY DANGER BREAKWATER LIGHT	30-19-53.535N 087-48-27.977W	Fl W 2.5s			Marks shoreline restoration breakwater structure.	Private aid.
6963.17	NOAA BON SECOUR BAY DANGER BREAKWATER LIGHT	30-19-56.396N 087-48-31.912W	Fl W 2.5s			Marks shoreline restoration breakwater structure.	Private aid.
6963.18	NOAA BON SECOUR BAY DANGER BREAKWATER LIGHT	30-19-59.605N 087-48-35.482W	Fl W 2.5s			Marks shoreline restoration breakwater structure.	Private aid.
6963.19	NOAA BON SECOUR BAY DANGER BREAKWATER LIGHT	30-20-03.022N 087-48-38.779W	Fl W 2.5s			Marks shoreline restoration breakwater structure.	Private aid.

(1) No.	(2) Name and Location	(3) Position	(4) Characteristic	(5) Height	(6) Range	(7) Structure	(8) Remarks
	ALABAMA - Eighth District						
	MOBILE BAY (Chart 11376)						
	Mobile Bay						
6963.21	NOAA BON SECOUR BAY DANGER BREAKWATER LIGHT	30-20-06.528N 087-48-41.951W	Fl W 2.5s			Marks shoreline restoration breakwater structure.	Private aid.
	SANTA ROSA SOUND TO DAUPHIN ISLAND (Chart 11378)						
	Mobile Bay						
	Bon Secour River						
6963.22	NOAA BON SECOUR BAY DANGER BREAKWATER LIGHT	30-20-10.284N 087-48-44.712W	Fl W 2.5s			Marks shoreline restoration breakwater structure.	Private aid.
6963.23	NOAA BON SECOUR BAY DANGER BREAKWATER LIGHT	30-20-13.650N 087-48-48.010W	Fl W 2.5s			Marks shoreline restoration breakwater structure.	Private aid.
6965	Alabama Marine Resources Division Danger Day beacons (4)	30-23-12.300N 087-53-08.820W				NW on pile. DANGER - SUBMERGED WRECK.	Marks submerged obstruction. Private aid.
	MOBILE BAY (Chart 11376)						
	Mobile Bay						
6968	- DANGER LIGHT A	30-19-00.998N 087-57-56.868W	Q W	17	3	NW on pile worded "DANGER PIPE"	Ra ref.
6970	MULLET POINT LIGHT 2	30-24-17.722N 087-55-14.688W	Fl R 4s	30	5	TR on platform.	Ra ref.
6972	ADCNR LEGACY REEF SPECIAL LIGHTS (10)	30-15-59.800N 087-58-26.570W	Fl Y 2.5s			Marks submerged obstructions.	Private aid.
6974	ADCNR POINT CLEAR REEF SPECIAL LIGHTS (6)	30-27-54.060N 087-57-43.920W	Fl Y 2.5s			Marks submerged obstructions.	Private aid.
6975	Klondike Fishing Reef Day beacons (8)	30-27-24.000N 087-56-06.000W				NW on piles worded DANGER SUBMERGED FISHING REEF.	Private aid.
6980	GREAT POINT CLEAR LIGHT 4	30-28-41.927N 087-57-18.352W	Fl R 4s	37	5	TR on platform	Ra ref.
	Grand Hotel Yacht Basin						
7015	- Day beacon 1	30-29-13.374N 087-56-17.115W				SG on pile.	Private aid.
7025	- LIGHT 3	30-29-14.307N 087-56-06.012W	Fl G 4s	15		SG on pile.	Private aid.
7030	- LIGHT 2	30-29-12.770N 087-56-05.924W	Fl R 4s	15		TR on pile.	Private aid.
	Mobile Bay						
7035	Battles Wharf Fishing Reef Day beacons (2)	30-29-42.000N 087-56-00.000W				NW on piles worded DANGER FISHING REEFS.	Marks perimeter 150 ft square fishing reef. Private aid.
7040	Upper Bay Barge Fishing Reef Day beacons (5)	30-34-42.000N 087-56-54.000W				NW on piles. worded DANGER SUBMERGED FISHING REEF.	Marks perimeter 150ft. square fishing reef. Private aid.
	Fly Creek						
7045	- ENTRANCE LIGHT 2	30-32-38.128N 087-54-32.441W	Fl R 4s	17	4	TR on pile.	Ra ref.
7050	- Day beacon 3	30-32-38.696N 087-54-29.282W				SG on pile.	Ra ref.
7055	- Day beacon 4	30-32-36.209N 087-54-26.417W				TR on pile.	Ra ref.
7060	- Buoy 5	30-32-37.270N 087-54-24.603W				Green can.	
7065	- Day beacon 6	30-32-34.268N 087-54-17.310W				TR on pile.	Ra ref.

(1) No.	(2) Name and Location	(3) Position	(4) Characteristic	(5) Height	(6) Range	(7) Structure	(8) Remarks
	ALABAMA - Eighth District						
	MOBILE BAY (Chart 11376)						
	Fly Creek						
7070	- Buoy 7	30-32-34.986N 087-54-16.723W				Green can.	
	Blakeley River						
7143	ALGAE SYSTEMS AQUACULTURE SPECIAL LIGHTS (13)	30-37-49.930N 087-55-23.100W	Fl Y 2.5s			Marks aquaculture dock.	Private aid.
	Tensaw River						
7145	Corps Of Engineers Survey Station Daybeacon					NR on pile.	Maintained by U.S. Army Corps of Engineers. Aid maintained by U.S. Army Corps of Engineers.
7150	LOWER HALL LANDING DOCK LIGHT	30-49-08.000N 087-54-57.000W	F R	15		On pole.	Maintained by U. S. Maritime Commission.
	Dauphin Island Channel						
7155	- LIGHT 1	30-15-13.302N 088-03-22.682W	Q G	17	3	SG on pile.	Ra ref.
7160	- Daybeacon 2	30-15-16.613N 088-03-25.953W				TR on pile.	Ra ref.
7165	- Daybeacon 3	30-15-10.054N 088-03-33.540W				SG on pile.	
7170	- Daybeacon 4	30-15-14.840N 088-03-35.049W				TR on pile.	Ra ref.
7175	- Daybeacon 5	30-15-09.496N 088-03-41.351W				SG on pile.	Ra ref.
7180	- Daybeacon 6	30-15-12.933N 088-03-42.847W				TR on pile.	Ra ref.
7185	- Daybeacon 7	30-15-09.239N 088-03-48.715W				SG on pile.	Ra ref.
7190	- Daybeacon 8	30-15-11.982N 088-03-49.642W				TR on pile.	Ra ref.
7195	- Daybeacon 9	30-15-07.860N 088-04-01.303W				SG on pile.	Ra ref.
7200	- Daybeacon 10	30-15-10.300N 088-04-01.429W				TR on pile.	Ra ref.
7205	- LIGHT 12 50 feet outside channel limit.	30-15-08.148N 088-04-19.468W	Q R	17	3	TR on pile.	Ra ref.
7210	- LIGHT 14	30-15-07.239N 088-04-32.787W	Fl R 4s	17	3	TR on pile.	Ra ref.
7215	- Daybeacon 16	30-15-07.198N 088-04-38.280W				TR on pile.	Ra ref.
7220	- LIGHT 17	30-15-05.398N 088-04-44.640W	Q G	11	3	SG on pile.	Ra ref.
7225	FORT GAINES POINT WRECK LIGHT WR1	30-14-59.732N 088-04-23.995W	Q G	17	3	On single pile.	Ra ref.
7230	DAUPHIN ISLAND SPIT LIGHT D	30-15-00.306N 088-04-05.796W	Q W	17	5	NR on dolphin.	Ra ref.
7235	Sand Reef Oyster Reef Daybeacons (5)	30-16-12.000N 088-05-40.000W				NW on piles worded DANGER SUBMERGED FISHING REEFS.	Private aid.
7240	Alabama Oyster Reef Daybeacons (38)	30-19-42.000N 088-05-06.000W				NW on pile worded DANGER SUBMERGED OYSTER REEF.	Private aid.
7245	Alabama Oyster Reef Buoys (6)	30-17-12.200N 088-06-54.600W				White with orange bands and diamond worded DANGER OYSTER REEF.	Private aid.

Light List corrected through LNM week: 01/18

(1) No.	(2) Name and Location	(3) Position	(4) Characteristic	(5) Height	(6) Range	(7) Structure	(8) Remarks
	ALABAMA - Eighth District						
	MOBILE BAY (Chart 11376)						
	Dauphin Island Channel						
7250	West-Side Fishing Reef Day beacons (5)	30-20-36.000N 088-03-54.000W				NW on piles worded DANGER SUBMERGED FISHING REEFS.	Private aid.
	Fowl River						
	Lights and daybeacons are 50 feet outside channel limit.						
7255	- Day beacon 1	30-26-53.683N 088-04-57.119W				SG on pile.	Ra ref.
7260	- LIGHT 2	30-26-57.718N 088-04-56.400W	Fl R 2.5s	17	4	TR on dolphin.	Ra ref.
7265	- Day beacon 3	30-26-58.741N 088-05-17.285W				SG on pile.	Ra ref.
7270	- Day beacon 4	30-27-01.723N 088-05-16.890W				TR on pile.	Ra ref.
7275	- Day beacon 5	30-27-04.708N 088-05-44.995W				SG on pile.	Ra ref.
7280	- LIGHT 6	30-27-07.138N 088-05-40.860W	Fl R 6s	17	4	TR on dolphin.	Ra ref.
7285	- Day beacon 7	30-27-08.459N 088-05-56.995W				SG on pile.	Ra ref.
7290	- Day beacon 8	30-27-10.467N 088-05-57.086W				TR on pile.	Ra ref.
7295	- Day beacon 9	30-27-12.071N 088-06-14.137W				SG on pile.	Ra ref.
7300	- LIGHT 10	30-27-14.158N 088-06-14.040W	Q R	17	3	TR on dolphin.	Ra ref.
7305	- Day beacon 12	30-27-04.838N 088-06-29.586W				TR on pile.	Ra ref.
7310	- OBSTRUCTION LIGHT 12A	30-27-02.289N 088-06-31.086W	Q R	17	3	TR on pile.	
7312	MOBILE BAY NATIONAL ESTUARY DANGER BREAKWATER LIGHT	30-27-00.630N 088-06-28.180W	Fl W 2.5s			Marks shoreline restoration breakwater structure.	Private aid.
7312.01	MOBILE BAY NATIONAL ESTUARY DANGER BREAKWATER LIGHT	30-26-59.160N 088-06-25.070W	Fl W 2.5s			Marks shoreline restoration breakwater structure.	Private aid.
7312.02	MOBILE BAY NATIONAL ESTUARY DANGER BREAKWATER LIGHT	30-26-55.680N 088-06-23.980W	Fl W 2.5s			Marks shoreline restoration breakwater structure.	Private aid.
7312.03	MOBILE BAY NATIONAL ESTUARY DANGER BREAKWATER LIGHT	30-26-51.320N 088-06-23.760W	Fl W 2.5s			Marks shoreline restoration breakwater structure.	Private aid.
7315	- Day beacon 13	30-26-50.873N 088-06-36.399W				SG on pile.	Ra ref.
7320	- Day beacon 14	30-26-51.651N 088-06-38.387W				TR on pile.	Ra ref.
7325	- Day beacon 15	30-26-38.338N 088-06-44.280W				SG on pile.	Ra ref.
7330	- Day beacon 16	30-26-39.709N 088-06-47.997W				TR on pile.	Ra ref.
7333	ANKERSEN AQUACULTURE SPECIAL LIGHTS (4)	30-29-00.965N 088-06-00.139W	Fl Y 2.5s			Marks outermost corners of aquaculture farm.	Private aid.
	Theodore Ship Channel						
7335	- OUTER RANGE FRONT LIGHT	30-28-36.002N 088-00-43.096W	Q W	25		KRW on skeleton tower on piles.	Visible all around; higher intensity 1.5° each side of range line.

ALABAMA - Eighth District

MOBILE BAY (Chart 11376)
Theodore Ship Channel

(1) No.	(2) Name and Location	(3) Position	(4) Characteristic	(5) Height	(6) Range	(7) Structure	(8) Remarks
7340	- OUTER RANGE REAR LIGHT 1,667 yards, 123.6° from front light.	30-28-08.618N 087-59-55.506W	Iso W 6s	67		KRW on skeleton tower on piles.	Visible 4° each side of rangeline.
7345	- OUTER RANGE REAR LIGHT PASSING LIGHT	30-28-08.618N 087-59-55.506W	Fl W 4s	15	3	On same structure as Theodore Ship Channel Outer Range Rear Light.	
7350 6535	- LIGHT 1 350 feet outside channel limit.	30-28-38.703N 088-01-08.485W	Q G	17	3	SG on pile.	Ra ref.
7355 6545	- JUNCTION LIGHT T	30-28-58.365N 088-01-11.700W	Fl (2+1)G 6s	17	4	JG on pile.	Ra ref.
7360	- LIGHT 3 290 feet outside channel limit.	30-28-54.205N 088-01-22.843W	Fl G 2.5s	17	4	SG on pile.	Ra ref.
7365	- LIGHT 5 190 feet outside channel limit.	30-29-14.169N 088-01-56.954W	Fl G 4s	17	4	SG on pile.	Ra ref.
7370	- LIGHT 6 280 feet outside channel limit.	30-29-19.423N 088-01-51.411W	Fl R 4s	17	3	TR on pile.	Ra ref.
7375	- LIGHT 7 225 feet outside channel limit.	30-29-41.515N 088-02-43.823W	Fl G 2.5s	17	3	SG on pile.	Ra ref.
7380	- LIGHT 8 300 feet outside channel limit.	30-29-47.461N 088-02-39.126W	Fl R 2.5s	17	3	TR on pile.	Ra ref.
7385	- Buoy 9 300 feet outside channel limit.	30-30-10.197N 088-03-35.372W				Green can.	
7390	- LIGHT 10 240 feet outside channel limit.	30-30-16.482N 088-03-30.879W	Fl R 4s	17	3	TR on dolphin.	Ra ref.
7395	- LIGHT 11 270 feet outside channel limit.	30-30-36.824N 088-04-21.083W	Fl G 2.5s	17	3	SG on pile.	Ra ref.
7400	- LIGHT 12 270 feet outside channel limit.	30-30-44.809N 088-04-20.933W	Fl R 2.5s	17	3	TR on pile.	Ra ref.
7405	- LIGHT 13 380 feet outside channel limit.	30-30-53.900N 088-04-52.900W	Fl G 4s	17	4	SG on pile.	Ra ref.
7410	- Anchorage Day beacon A	30-30-58.300N 088-05-04.800W				NY on pile.	Ra ref.
7415	- LIGHT 14 270 feet outside channel limit.	30-31-08.675N 088-05-00.965W	Q R	17	3	TR on pile.	Ra ref.
7420	- Day beacon 15 285 feet outside channel limit.	30-31-09.953N 088-05-18.897W				SG on pile.	Ra ref.
7425	- LIGHT 16 260 feet outside channel limit.	30-31-17.431N 088-05-16.715W	Fl R 2.5s	17	3	TR on pile.	Ra ref.
7430	- LIGHT 17 155 feet outside channel limit.	30-31-21.210N 088-05-36.048W	Fl G 2.5s	17	3	SG on pile.	Ra ref.
7435	- LIGHT 18 160 feet outside channel limit.	30-31-24.717N 088-05-31.498W	Fl R 2.5s	17	3	TR on pile.	Ra ref.
7440	- LIGHT 22 200 feet outside channel limit.	30-31-52.989N 088-06-22.994W	Q R	17	3	TR on pile.	Ra ref.

Light List corrected through LNM week: 01/18

(1) No.	(2) Name and Location	(3) Position	(4) Characteristic	(5) Height	(6) Range	(7) Structure	(8) Remarks
		ALABAMA - Eighth District					
	MOBILE BAY (Chart 11376)						
7445	Hollingers Island Fishing Reef Day beacons (5)	30-32-06.000N 088-03-12.000W				NW on piles worded DANGER SUBMERGED FISHING REEFS.	Private aid.
	Dog River Channel						
7450	- Day beacon 1	30-32-45.474N 088-01-36.614W				SG on pile.	Ra ref.
7455	- Day beacon 2	30-32-49.024N 088-01-39.444W				TR on pile.	Ra ref.
7460	- LIGHT 3	30-33-18.044N 088-02-28.239W	Fl G 4s	17	4	SG on pile.	Ra ref.
7465	- Day beacon 4	30-33-19.443N 088-02-27.216W				TR on pile.	Ra ref.
7470	- Day beacon 5	30-33-49.636N 088-03-19.972W				SG on pile.	Ra ref.
7475	- LIGHT 6	30-33-57.425N 088-03-26.429W	Fl R 2.5s	17	3	TR on pile.	Ra ref.
7480	- Day beacon 7	30-33-58.847N 088-04-12.831W				SG on pile.	Ra ref.
7485	- LIGHT 8	30-34-00.327N 088-04-12.694W	Fl R 4s	17	4	TR on pile.	Ra ref.
7490	- Day beacon 9	30-33-59.178N 088-04-24.532W				SG on pile.	Ra ref.
7495	- Day beacon 10	30-34-01.117N 088-04-24.097W				TR on pile.	Ra ref.
7500	- LIGHT 11	30-34-00.407N 088-04-35.371W	Fl G 2.5s	17	4	SG on pile.	Ra ref.
7505	- Day beacon 12	30-34-01.903N 088-04-35.445W				TR on pile.	Ra ref.
7510	- Day beacon 13	30-33-57.153N 088-04-53.693W				SG on pile.	Ra ref.
7515	- Day beacon 14	30-33-59.067N 088-04-53.856W				TR on pile.	Ra ref.
7520	- LIGHT 15	30-33-53.542N 088-05-04.253W	Fl G 4s	21	4	SG on pile.	Ra ref.
7525	- Day beacon 16	30-33-56.295N 088-05-04.895W				TR on pile.	Ra ref.
7530	Brookley Hole Site Fishing Reef Day beacons (2)	30-37-42.000N 088-03-24.000W				NW on piles worded DANGER SUBMERGED FISHING REEFS.	Private aid.
	Arlington Channel						
7535	Arlington Docks Site Fishing Reef Day beacons (4)	30-38-30.000N 088-02-30.000W				NW on pile worded DANGER SUBMERGED FISHING REEFS.	Private aid.
7540 6680	- *Lighted Buoy 1* 60 feet outside channel limit.	30-38-22.689N 088-01-59.991W	Fl G 2.5s		4	Green.	
7545	- OUTBOUND RANGE FRONT LIGHT	30-38-28.556N 088-01-47.021W	Q W	20		KRW on skeleton tower on piles.	Visible all around; higher intensity on rangeline.
7550	- OUTBOUND RANGE REAR LIGHT 209 yards, 109.1° from front light.	30-38-26.525N 088-01-40.232W	Iso W 6s	35		KRW on skeleton tower on piles.	Visible all around; higher intensity on rangeline.
7555 6690	- Junction Buoy 60 feet outside channel limit.	30-38-40.688N 088-02-01.991W				Green can with red band.	
7560	- LIGHT 3	30-38-34.055N 088-02-13.295W	Q G	17	3	SG on dolphin.	
7565	- LIGHT 4	30-38-37.397N 088-02-12.168W	Fl R 2.5s	17	3	TR on pile.	Ra ref.

(1) No.	(2) Name and Location	(3) Position	(4) Characteristic	(5) Height	(6) Range	(7) Structure	(8) Remarks
	ALABAMA - Eighth District						
	**MOBILE BAY (Chart 11376)**						
	**Arlington Channel**						
7570	- LIGHT 5	30-38-38.720N 088-02-28.209W	Fl G 6s	17	4	SG on pile.	Ra ref.
7575	- LIGHT 6	30-38-42.193N 088-02-27.667W	Fl R 6s	17	4	TR on pile.	Ra ref.
7580	- LIGHT 7	30-38-42.700N 088-02-40.246W	Fl G 2.5s	17	4	SG on pile.	Ra ref.
7585	- Day beacon 8	30-38-46.413N 088-02-40.704W				TR on pile.	Ra ref.
7590	- LIGHT 9	30-38-48.579N 088-03-00.515W	Fl G 6s	17	4	SG on pile.	Ra ref.
7595	- Day beacon 10	30-38-52.202N 088-02-59.662W				TR on pile.	Ra ref.
7600	- LIGHT 11	30-38-53.304N 088-03-16.433W	Fl G 2.5s	17	3	SG on pile.	Ra ref.
7605	- LIGHT 12	30-38-58.798N 088-03-17.933W	Fl R 4s	17	3	TR on pile.	Ra ref.
7610	- LIGHT 14	30-39-05.267N 088-03-20.954W	Fl R 2.5s	17	3	TR on pile.	Ra ref.
7615	- RANGE FRONT LIGHT	30-39-00.219N 088-03-33.016W	Q R	33		KRW on skeleton tower on piles.	Visible all around; higher intensity on rangeline.
7620	- RANGE REAR LIGHT 255 yards, 289.3° from front light.	30-39-03.080N 088-03-42.594W	Oc R 4s	55		KRW on skeleton tower.	Visible all around; higher intensity on rangeline.
7625	Choctaw Pass Fishing Reef Day beacons (4)	30-39-48.000N 088-01-12.000W				NW on piles worded DANGER SUBMERGED FISHING REEFS.	Private aid.
	**DAUPHIN ISLAND TO DOG KEYS PASS (Chart 11374)**						
	**Mississippi Sound**						
7632	ADCNR DANGER BREAKWATER LIGHTS (6)	30-19-14.160N 088-13-37.330W	Fl W 2.5s			Marks marsh restoration breakwater.	Private aid.
7632.01	ADCNR DANGER BREAKWATER LIGHTS (6)	30-19-11.240N 088-13-20.290W	Fl W 2.5s			Marks marsh restoration breakwater.	Private aid.
7635	Sunken Shrimpboat Fishing Reef Day beacons (5)	30-18-18.000N 088-16-24.000W				NW on piles worded DANGER SUBMERGED FISHING REEFS.	Private aid.
7640	ISLE AUX HERBES WRECK LIGHT	30-18-17.896N 088-16-26.571W	Fl W 2.5s	17	5	NW on pile worded DANGER WRECK.	Ra ref.
7645	BAYOU LA BATRE WRECK LIGHT WR 2	30-21-21.958N 088-16-30.900W	Q R	17	3	TR on pile.	Ra ref.
7650	- LIGHT WR 6	30-20-34.534N 088-20-55.945W	Fl W 4s	17	4	NW on pile.	
	**Bayou La Batre**						
7660 34320	- LIGHT 3	30-14-51.823N 088-25-32.550W	Fl G 4s	17	4	SG-TY on pile.	Ra ref.
7665 34315	- LIGHT 5	30-15-16.571N 088-20-45.385W	Q G	17	3	SG-TY on pile.	Ra ref.
7670	- Buoy 7	30-15-53.973N 088-19-53.602W				Green can.	
7675	- Buoy 8	30-16-10.747N 088-19-25.307W				Red nun.	
7680	- WRECK LIGHT WR	30-16-13.950N 088-19-16.564W	Q R	17	3	TR on pile.	Ra ref.
7685	- LIGHT 10	30-16-29.014N 088-18-58.237W	Fl R 2.5s	17	3	TR on pile.	Ra ref.
7690	- Buoy 11	30-16-56.507N 088-18-48.901W				Green can.	

(1) No.	(2) Name and Location	(3) Position	(4) Characteristic	(5) Height	(6) Range	(7) Structure	(8) Remarks
		ALABAMA - Eighth District					
	DAUPHIN ISLAND TO DOG KEYS PASS (Chart 11374)						
	Mississippi Sound						
	Bayou La Batre						
7695	- Buoy 12	30-17-23.854N 088-18-35.303W				Red nun.	
7700	- LIGHT 13	30-17-52.403N 088-18-25.615W	Fl G 2.5s	17	3	SG on pile.	Ra ref.
7705	- Buoy 14	30-18-19.824N 088-18-11.920W				Red nun.	
7710	- Buoy 15	30-18-46.251N 088-18-02.105W				Green can.	
7715	- LIGHT 16	30-19-15.533N 088-17-48.456W	Fl R 6s	17	4	TR on pile.	Ra ref.
7720	- Buoy 17	30-19-44.078N 088-17-38.648W				Green can.	
7725	- Buoy 18	30-20-11.269N 088-17-25.037W				Red nun.	
7730	- LIGHT 19	30-20-39.688N 088-17-15.255W	Fl G 4s	17	4	SG on pile.	Ra ref.
7735	- Day beacon 20	30-21-07.467N 088-17-01.340W				TR on pile.	Ra ref.
7740	- Day beacon 21	30-21-35.798N 088-16-51.983W				SG on pile.	Ra ref.
7745	- LIGHT 22	30-22-02.839N 088-16-38.152W	Fl R 4s	17	3	TR on pile.	Ra ref.
7748	CITY OF BAYOU LA BATRE DANGER LIGHT	30-22-04.862N 088-16-36.573W	Fl W 2.5s			Marks submerged outfall diffuser.	Private aid.
7750	- Day beacon 23	30-22-31.790N 088-16-28.926W				SG on pile.	Ra ref.
7755	- LIGHT 24	30-22-54.057N 088-16-16.605W	Q R	17	3	TR on pile.	Ra ref.
7760	- Day beacon 25	30-23-00.130N 088-16-17.687W				SG on pile.	Ra ref.
7762	MOBILE COUNTY SCIENTIFIC MONITORING PLATFORM LIGHT B	30-24-21.300N 088-14-53.100W	Fl Y 2.5s			On pile.	Private aid.
7763	*Point Aux Pins Special Lighted Buoys (5)*	30-22-57.120N 088-18-48.060W	Fl Y 2.5s			Marks perimeter of oyster farm.	Private aid.
	Bayou Coden						
7765	- JUNCTION LIGHT BC	30-22-19.842N 088-16-30.945W	Fl (2+1)R 6s	17	3	JR on pile.	Ra ref.
7770	- Day beacon 1	30-22-28.004N 088-16-08.480W				SG on pile.	Ra ref.
7775	- Day beacon 2	30-22-26.424N 088-16-07.842W				TR on pile.	Ra ref.
7780	- LIGHT 4 50 feet outside channel limit.	30-22-34.534N 088-15-45.538W	Fl R 2.5s	17	3	TR on pile.	Ra ref.
7785	- Day beacon 3	30-22-36.822N 088-15-44.282W				SG on pile.	Ra ref.
7790	- Day beacon 5	30-22-27.106N 088-15-10.113W				SG on pile.	Ra ref.
7795	- Day beacon 6	30-22-25.171N 088-15-10.748W				TR on pile.	Ra ref.
7800	- Day beacon 7	30-22-18.479N 088-14-39.717W				SG on pile.	Ra ref.
7805	- LIGHT 8 50 feet outside channel limit.	30-22-15.814N 088-14-37.618W	Q R	17	3	TR on pile.	Ra ref.
7810	- Day beacon 9	30-22-20.061N 088-14-37.447W				SG on pile.	Ra ref.
7815	- LIGHT 10 50 feet outside channel limit.	30-22-32.641N 088-14-27.939W	Fl R 4s	17	3	TR on pile.	Ra ref.

Light List corrected through LNM week: 01/18

(1) No.	(2) Name and Location	(3) Position	(4) Characteristic	(5) Height	(6) Range	(7) Structure	(8) Remarks
			ALABAMA - Eighth District				
	DAUPHIN ISLAND TO DOG KEYS PASS (Chart 11374)						
	Mississippi Sound						
	Bayou Coden						
7820	- Day beacon 11	30-22-33.874N 088-14-29.278W				SG on pile.	Ra ref.
	Mississippi Sound						
7822	PORTERSVILLE OYSTER COMPANY SPECIAL LIGHTS (4)	30-21-21.000N 088-11-35.010W	Fl W 2.5s			Marks aquaculture farm perimeter.	Private aid.
7823	AUBURN UNIVERSITY OYSTER FARM SPECIAL LIGHTS (4)	30-20-59.690N 088-11-36.340W	Fl Y 2.5s			Marks aquaculture farm perimeter.	Private aid.
7825	Portersville Bay Day beacon A Marks end of discharge line.	30-22-44.000N 088-15-58.000W				JR on pile.	Private aid.
7825.01	ALMA BRYANT AQUACULTURE SPECIAL LIGHTS A THRU R	30-22-25.800N 088-19-10.980W	Fl Y 2.5s			Marks the aquaculture farm perimeter.	Private aid.
7826	SANDY BAY OYSTER COMPANY SPECIAL LIGHTS (6)	30-22-48.260N 088-18-42.020W	Fl Y 2.5s			Marks perimeter of aquaculture farm.	Private aid.
7826.05	SANDY BAY OYSTER COMPANY SPECIAL LIGHTS (6)	30-22-46.350N 088-18-43.650W	Fl Y 2.5s			Marks perimeter of aquaculture farm.	Private aid.
7826.21	AUBURN UNIVERSITY PORTERSVILLE BAY OYSTER FARM SPECIAL LIGHT A	30-21-56.100N 088-12-58.140W	Fl Y 2.5s			Marks perimeter of aquaculture farm.	Private aid.
7826.22	AUBURN UNIVERSITY PORTERSVILLE BAY OYSTER FARM SPECIAL LIGHT B	30-21-51.450N 088-12-55.500W	Fl Y 2.5s			Marks perimeter of aquaculture farm.	Private aid.
7826.23	AUBURN UNIVERSITY PORTERSVILLE BAY OYSTER FARM SPECIAL LIGHT C	30-21-47.200N 088-12-56.360W	Fl Y 2.5s			Marks perimeter of aquaculture farm.	Private aid.
7826.24	AUBURN UNIVERSITY PORTERSVILLE BAY OYSTER FARM SPECIAL LIGHT D	30-21-42.440N 088-12-58.100W	Fl Y 2.5s			Marks perimeter of aquaculture farm.	Private aid.
7826.25	AUBURN UNIVERSITY PORTERSVILLE BAY OYSTER FARM SPECIAL LIGHT E	30-21-37.520N 088-12-59.490W	Fl Y 2.5s			Marks perimeter of aquaculture farm.	Private aid.
7826.26	AUBURN UNIVERSITY PORTERSVILLE BAY OYSTER FARM SPECIAL LIGHT F	30-21-41.330N 088-13-02.300W	Fl Y 2.5s			Marks perimeter of aquaculture farm.	Private aid.
7826.27	AUBURN UNIVERSITY PORTERSVILLE BAY OYSTER FARM SPECIAL LIGHT G	30-21-45.480N 088-13-04.190W	Fl Y 2.5s			Marks perimeter of aquaculture farm.	Private aid.
7826.28	AUBURN UNIVERSITY PORTERSVILLE BAY OYSTER FARM SPECIAL LIGHT H	30-21-51.700N 088-13-04.190W	Fl Y 2.5s			Marks perimeter of aquaculture farm.	Private aid.
7826.29	AUBURN UNIVERSITY PORTERSVILLE BAY OYSTER FARM SPECIAL LIGHT I	30-21-56.500N 088-13-03.500W	Fl Y 2.5s			Marks perimeter of aquaculture farm.	Private aid.
7826.31	AUBURN UNIVERSITY PORTERSVILLE BAY OYSTER FARM SPECIAL LIGHT J	30-21-58.280N 088-13-02.300W	Fl Y 2.5s			Marks perimeter of aquaculture farm.	Private aid.
7826.32	SHASHY AQUACULTURE FARM SPECIAL LIGHT A	30-22-10.960N 088-14-02.710W	Fl Y 2.5s			Marks southeastern corner of aquaculture farm.	Private aid.
7826.33	SHASHY AQUACULTURE FARM SPECIAL LIGHT B	30-22-10.990N 088-14-03.070W	Fl Y 2.5s			Marks northwestern corner of aquaculture farm.	Private aid.

Light List corrected through LNM week: 01/18

(1) No.	(2) Name and Location	(3) Position	(4) Characteristic	(5) Height	(6) Range	(7) Structure	(8) Remarks
			ALABAMA - Eighth District				
	DAUPHIN ISLAND TO DOG KEYS PASS (Chart 11374)						
	Mississippi Sound						
7827	ADCNR WEST DAUPHIN ISLAND EAST DANGER LIGHT	30-14-42.960N 088-14-25.200W	Fl W 2.5s			Marks southeast corner of submerged obstructions.	Private aid.
7827.01	ADCNR WEST DAUPHIN ISLAND EAST DANGER LIGHT	30-14-44.580N 088-14-25.200W	Fl W 2.5s			Marks northeast corner of submerged obstructions.	Private aid.
7827.02	ADCNR WEST DAUPHIN ISLAND EAST DANGER LIGHT	30-14-42.840N 088-14-35.460W	Fl W 2.5s			Marks northwest corner of submerged obstructions.	Private aid.
7827.03	ADCNR WEST DAUPHIN ISLAND EAST DANGER LIGHT	30-14-41.040N 088-14-34.500W	Fl W 2.5s			Marks southwest corner of submerged obstructions.	Private aid.
7827.04	ADCNR WEST DAUPHIN ISLAND MIDDLE DANGER LIGHT	30-14-24.600N 088-16-14.940W	Fl W 2.5s			Marks southeast corner of submerged obstructions.	Private aid.
7827.05	ADCNR WEST DAUPHIN ISLAND MIDDLE DANGER LIGHT	30-14-30.720N 088-16-18.300W	Fl W 2.5s			Marks northeast corner of submerged obstructions.	Private aid.
7827.06	ADCNR WEST DAUPHIN ISLAND MIDDLE DANGER LIGHT	30-14-26.100N 088-16-30.600W	Fl W 2.5s			Marks northwest corner of submerged obstructions.	Private aid.
7827.07	ADCNR WEST DAUPHIN ISLAND MIDDLE DANGER LIGHT	30-14-19.860N 088-16-27.060W	Fl W 2.5s			Marks southwest corner of submerged obstructions.	Private aid.
7827.08	ADCNR WEST DAUPHIN ISLAND WEST DANGER LIGHT	30-14-10.020N 088-17-31.200W	Fl W 2.5s			Marks southeast corner of submerged obstructions.	Private aid.
7827.09	ADCNR WEST DAUPHIN ISLAND WEST DANGER LIGHT	30-14-11.700N 088-17-31.620W	Fl W 2.5s			Marks northeast corner of submerged obstructions.	Private aid.
7827.11	ADCNR WEST DAUPHIN ISLAND WEST DANGER LIGHT	30-14-09.720N 088-17-41.460W	Fl W 2.5s			Marks northwest corner of submerged obstructions.	Private aid.
7827.12	ADCNR WEST DAUPHIN ISLAND WEST DANGER LIGHT	30-14-08.160N 088-17-41.100W	Fl W 2.5s			Marks southwest corner of submerged obstructions.	Private aid.
7840	PETIT BOIS PASS LIGHT P	30-13-52.857N 088-19-52.709W	Fl W 2.5s	20	5	NR on piles.	Ra ref.
			MISSISSIPPI - Eighth District				
	PASCAGOULA HARBOR (Chart 11375)						
	Horn Island Pass						
7850 310	- Lighted Buoy HI	30-08-30.049N 088-34-40.125W	Mo (A) W		5	Red and white stripes with red spherical topmark.	
7855	- Lighted Buoy 1	30-09-15.262N 088-34-00.576W	Q G		3	Green.	
7860	- Lighted Buoy 2	30-09-10.431N 088-33-54.011W	Q R		3	Red.	
7865	- Lighted Buoy 3	30-09-58.052N 088-33-17.700W	Fl G 2.5s		3	Green.	
7870	- Lighted Buoy 4	30-09-53.249N 088-33-11.244W	Fl R 2.5s		3	Red.	
7875	- Lighted Buoy 5	30-10-40.850N 088-32-34.846W	Fl G 4s		4	Green.	

Light List corrected through LNM week: 01/18

(1) No.	(2) Name and Location	(3) Position	(4) Characteristic	(5) Height	(6) Range	(7) Structure	(8) Remarks
			MISSISSIPPI - Eighth District				
	PASCAGOULA HARBOR (Chart 11375)						
	Horn Island Pass						
7880	- Lighted Buoy 6	30-10-35.971N 088-32-28.329W	Fl R 4s		3		Red.
7885	- Lighted Buoy 7	30-11-24.463N 088-31-52.469W	Fl G 2.5s		3		Green.
7890	- Lighted Buoy 8	30-11-19.367N 088-31-45.329W	Fl R 2.5s		3		Red.
7895	- ENTRANCE RANGE FRONT LIGHT	30-12-49.968N 088-30-19.663W	Fl W 2.5s (NIGHT) Fl W 2.5s (DAY)	26 29			Visible 2° each side of rangeline.
7900	- ENTRANCE RANGE REAR LIGHT 1666 yards, 041.1° from front light.	30-13-27.289N 088-29-42.235W	Iso W 6s (NIGHT) Iso W 6s (DAY)	94 91		KRW on skeleton tower on pile.	Visible 2° each side of range line.
7905	- ENTRANCE RANGE REAR LIGHT PASSING LIGHT	30-13-27.289N 088-29-42.235W	Fl W 4s	40	5		On same structure as Horn Island Pass Entrance Range Rear Light.
7910	- Lighted Buoy 9	30-11-48.654N 088-31-25.948W	Fl G 4s		4		Green.
7915	- Lighted Buoy 10	30-11-44.287N 088-31-20.063W	Fl R 4s		3		Red.
7920	- Lighted Buoy 11	30-12-12.022N 088-31-02.713W	Fl G 2.5s		4		Green.
7925	- Lighted Buoy 12	30-12-07.721N 088-30-56.662W	Fl R 2.5s		3		Red.
7930	- Lighted Buoy 13	30-12-25.232N 088-30-53.206W	Q G		4		Green.
7935	- Lighted Buoy 14	30-12-22.381N 088-30-43.614W	Q R		4		Red.
7940	- Lighted Buoy 16	30-12-45.153N 088-30-34.622W	Fl R 2.5s		3		Red.
7945	- Lighted Buoy 17	30-12-56.056N 088-30-39.519W	Fl G 2.5s		4		Green.
7950	- Lighted Buoy 18	30-12-57.734N 088-30-28.681W	Fl R 2.5s		3		Red.
	Pascagoula Channel						
7955	- Lighted Buoy 19	30-13-18.289N 088-30-27.782W	Q G		3		Green.
7960	- D RANGE FRONT LIGHT	30-12-57.520N 088-30-15.435W	Q W	27		KRW on skeleton tower on piles.	Visible 2° each side of range line.
7965	- D RANGE FRONT LIGHT PASSING LIGHT	30-12-57.520N 088-30-15.435W	Fl W 4s	29	3		On same structure as Pascagoula Channel Range D Front Light.
7970	- D RANGE REAR LIGHT 506 yards, 175° from front light.	30-12-42.563N 088-30-13.603W	Iso W 6s	60		KRW on skeleton tower.	Visible 2° each side of rangeline.
7975	- Lighted Buoy 20	30-13-23.815N 088-30-14.708W	Q R		3		Red.
7980	PETIT BOIS ISLAND OBSTRUCTION LIGHT 2 Marks rip rap.	30-13-22.943N 088-29-11.015W	Q R	17	4	TR on dolphin.	Ra ref.
7985	- Lighted Buoy 21	30-13-27.159N 088-30-24.793W	Fl G 2.5s		3		Green.
7990	- A RANGE FRONT LIGHT	30-17-57.603N 088-30-52.167W	Fl R 2.5s (NIGHT) Fl W 2.5s (DAY)	31 34			Lighted throughout 24 hours. Night range visible 1.5° each side of rangeline. Passing light visible all around.
7992	- A RANGE FRONT PASSING LIGHT	30-17-57.603N 088-30-52.167W	Fl R 2.5s	36			On same structure as Pascagoula Channel A Range Front Light.

(1) No.	(2) Name and Location	(3) Position	(4) Characteristic	(5) Height	(6) Range	(7) Structure	(8) Remarks
			MISSISSIPPI - Eighth District				
	PASCAGOULA HARBOR (Chart 11375)						
	Pascagoula Channel						
7995	- A RANGE REAR LIGHT 1,666 yards, 354.1° from front light.	30-18-46.318N 088-30-58.141W	Iso R 6s (NIGHT) Iso W 6s (DAY)	94 91			Day range visible 0.5° each side of rangeline. Night range visible 1.5° each side of rangeline. Passing light visible all around.
8000	- Lighted Buoy 23	30-13-55.438N 088-30-27.498W	Fl G 2.5s		3		Green.
8005	- Lighted Buoy 24	30-13-56.340N 088-30-19.361W	Fl R 2.5s		3		Red.
8010	- Lighted Buoy 25	30-14-28.067N 088-30-29.775W	Fl G 4s		3		Green.
8015	- Lighted Buoy 26	30-14-28.661N 088-30-23.313W	Fl R 4s		3		Red.
8020	- Lighted Buoy 27	30-14-43.814N 088-30-31.316W	Fl G 6s		3		Green.
8025	Bayou La Batre Junction Lighted Buoy BB	30-14-44.380N 088-30-25.246W	Fl (2+1)R 6s		3		Red with green band.
8030 34330	- Lighted Buoy 29	30-15-24.404N 088-30-36.284W	Q G		3		Green with yellow triangle.
8035 34325	- Lighted Buoy 30	30-15-24.956N 088-30-30.218W	Q R		3		Red with yellow triangle.
8040	- Lighted Buoy 31	30-16-04.994N 088-30-41.253W	Fl G 4s		3		Green.
8045	- Lighted Buoy 32	30-16-05.634N 088-30-35.109W	Fl R 4s		3		Red.
8050	- Lighted Buoy 33	30-16-39.167N 088-30-45.422W	Fl G 2.5s		3		Green.
8055	- Lighted Buoy 34	30-16-39.690N 088-30-39.752W	Fl R 2.5s		3		Red.
8060	PASCAGOULA PIPELINE CHANNEL LIGHT A	30-16-29.200N 088-30-50.500W	Fl Y 2.5s	15		On pile.	Private aid.
8065	PASCAGOULA PIPELINE CHANNEL LIGHT C	30-16-06.000N 088-30-08.000W	Fl Y 2.5s	15		On pile.	Private aid.
8070	- WRECK LIGHT	30-16-50.754N 088-31-08.118W	Fl W 2.5s	17	5	NW on pile worded DANGER WRECK.	Ra ref.
8075	- Lighted Buoy 35 50 feet outside channel limit.	30-17-05.255N 088-30-49.220W	Q G		3		Green.
8080	- Lighted Buoy 36	30-17-10.948N 088-30-42.310W	Q R		3		Red.
8085	- Lighted Buoy 37	30-17-13.480N 088-30-53.356W	Fl G 2.5s		3		Green.
8090	Bayou Casotte Channel Junction Lighted Buoy BC	30-17-21.642N 088-30-51.654W	Fl (2+1)R 6s		3		Red with green band.
8095	- B RANGE FRONT LIGHT	30-16-56.532N 088-30-32.978W	Q W	25		KRW on skeleton tower on piles.	Visible all around; higher intensity on range line.
8100	- B RANGE REAR LIGHT 1,800 yards, 139.8° from front light.	30-16-15.649N 088-29-53.292W	Oc W 4s	64		KRW on skeleton tower on piles.	Visible 2° each side of range line.
8105	- B RANGE REAR LIGHT PASSING LIGHT	30-16-15.674N 088-29-53.284W	Fl W 4s	12	3	On same structure as Pascagoula Channel Range B Rear Light.	
8110	- C RANGE FRONT LIGHT	30-20-44.928N 088-34-15.120W	Fl R 2.5s (NIGHT) Fl W 2.5s (DAY)	63 65		On skeleton tower on piles.	Lighted throughout 24 hours. Visible 2° each side of rangeline.
8115	- C RANGE REAR LIGHT 1,381 yards, 319.8° from front light.	30-21-16.278N 088-34-45.639W	F R (NIGHT) F W (DAY)	122 120		On pile.	Lighted throughout 24 hours. Visible 2° each side of rangeline.
8120	- LIGHT 39 150 feet outside channel limit.	30-17-42.062N 088-31-21.853W	Fl G 2.5s	17	3	SG on pile.	Ra ref.

Light List corrected through LNM week: 01/18

(1) No.	(2) Name and Location	(3) Position	(4) Characteristic	(5) Height	(6) Range	(7) Structure	(8) Remarks
	MISSISSIPPI - Eighth District							

PASCAGOULA HARBOR (Chart 11375)
Pascagoula Channel

(1) No.	(2) Name and Location	(3) Position	(4) Characteristic	(5) Height	(6) Range	(7) Structure	(8) Remarks
8125	- LIGHT 40 150 feet outside channel limit.	30-17-46.321N 088-31-16.448W	Fl R 2.5s	17	3	TR on pile.	Ra ref.
8130	- LIGHT 41 150 feet outside channel limit.	30-18-12.721N 088-31-52.050W	Fl G 4s	17	4	SG on pile.	Ra ref.
8135	- LIGHT 42 150 feet outside channel limit.	30-18-18.721N 088-31-48.050W	Fl R 4s	17	3	TR on pile.	Ra ref.
8140	PASCAGOULA PIPELINE CHANNEL LIGHT E	30-18-03.000N 088-32-00.000W	Fl Y 2.5s	15		On pile.	Private aid.
8145	PASCAGOULA PIPELINE CHANNEL LIGHT F	30-18-04.000N 088-31-08.000W	Fl Y 2.5s	15		On pile.	Private aid.
8150	Spoil Bank Daybeacon 4	30-18-27.500N 088-32-34.000W				TR on pile.	Private aid.
8155	SPOIL BANK LIGHT 3	30-18-35.000N 088-32-41.000W	Fl G 2.5s	17		SG on dolphin.	Private aid.
8160	Spoil Bank Daybeacon 2	30-18-15.000N 088-32-51.500W				TR on pile.	Private aid.
8165	- SPOIL BANK WRECK LIGHT WR	30-18-21.072N 088-33-17.674W	Q G	17	3	On pile.	Ra ref.
8170	SPOIL BANK LIGHT 1	30-18-22.500N 088-32-58.500W	Fl G 2.5s	17		SG on dolphin.	Private aid.
8175	- LIGHT 43 150 feet outside channel limit.	30-18-43.720N 088-32-22.052W	Fl G 6s	17	4	SG on pile.	Ra ref.
8180	- LIGHT 44 150 feet outside channel limit.	30-18-47.720N 088-32-16.052W	Fl R 6s	17	4	TR on pile.	Ra ref.
8185	- LIGHT 45 150 feet outside channel limit.	30-19-16.720N 088-32-54.054W	Fl G 4s	17	4	SG on pile.	Ra ref.
8190	- LIGHT 46 150 feet outside channel limit.	30-19-21.000N 088-32-48.486W	Fl R 4s	17	3	TR on pile.	Ra ref.
8195	- LIGHT 47 150 feet outside channel limit.	30-19-47.264N 088-33-24.760W	Fl G 2.5s	17	3	SG on pile.	Ra ref.
8200	- LIGHT 48 150 feet outside channel limit.	30-19-52.117N 088-33-18.952W	Fl R 2.5s	17	3	TR on pile.	Ra ref.
8205	- LIGHT 49	30-20-19.340N 088-33-55.672W	Fl G 4s	17	4	SG on pile.	Ra ref.
8210	- LIGHT 50 150 feet outside channel limit.	30-20-24.129N 088-33-49.797W	Fl R 4s	17	4	TR on pile.	Ra ref.
8215	- *Lighted Buoy 51*	30-20-31.684N 088-34-05.252W	Q G		3	Green.	
8220	Yazoo Lake Entrance Bouy 2	30-20-36.198N 088-33-55.120W				Red nun.	
8222	Yazoo Channel Daybeacon 1	30-20-50.810N 088-33-35.790W				SG on pile.	Private aid.
8222.01	Yazoo Channel Daybeacon 2	30-20-50.340N 088-33-35.370W				TR on pile.	Private aid.
8225	- LIGHT 52 150 feet outside channel limit.	30-20-37.454N 088-33-57.388W	Q R	17	3	TR on pile.	Ra ref.
8227	Jackson County Barge Fleet Mooring Buoy	30-20-39.090N 088-34-52.300W				Barge fleet mooring buoy.	Private aid.
8227.11	Jackson County Barge Fleet Mooring Buoy	30-20-38.870N 088-34-54.400W				Barge fleet mooring buoy.	Private aid.
8227.12	Jackson County Barge Fleet Mooring Buoy	30-20-38.620N 088-34-56.790W				Barge fleet mooring buoy.	Private aid.
8227.13	Jackson County Barge Fleet Mooring Buoy	30-20-37.480N 088-34-59.500W				Barge fleet mooring buoy.	Private aid.

(1) No.	(2) Name and Location	(3) Position	(4) Characteristic	(5) Height	(6) Range	(7) Structure	(8) Remarks
	MISSISSIPPI - Eighth District						
	PASCAGOULA HARBOR (Chart 11375)						
	Pascagoula Channel						
8227.14	Jackson County Barge Fleet Mooring Buoy	30-20-35.510N 000-34-59.280W				Barge fleet mooring buoy.	Private aid.
8227.15	Jackson County Barge Fleet Mooring Buoy	30-20-33.540N 088-34-59.050W				Barge fleet mooring buoy.	Private aid.
8227.16	Jackson County Barge Fleet Mooring Buoy	30-20-31.570N 088-34-58.830W				Barge fleet mooring buoy.	Private aid.
8227.17	Jackson County Barge Fleet Mooring Buoy	30-20-29.600N 088-34-58.600W				Barge fleet mooring buoy.	Private aid.
8230	Pascagoula Navy Channel Buoy 1	30-20-31.574N 088-34-25.546W				Green can.	
8240	MISSISSIPPI GULF FISH REEF LIGHT A	30-15-57.000N 088-38-55.000W	Fl Y 6s	17		NY on pile.	Ra ref. Private aid.
	DAUPHIN ISLAND TO DOG KEYS PASS (Chart 11374)						
8245	*Pascagoula River Obstruction Lighted Buoy 2*	30-21-06.000N 088-33-58.200W	Fl R 2.5s			Red.	Private aid.
8250	*Pascagoula River Obstruction Lighted Buoy 4* Marks outer end of submerged ways.	30-21-19.800N 088-33-51.600W	Fl R 2.5s			Red.	Private aid.
8255	MISSISSIPPI POWER EAST TOWER LIGHT	30-22-15.000N 088-33-43.000W	Fl Y 2.5s	10		On pile cluster.	Private aid.
8260	MISSISSIPPI POWER WEST TOWER LIGHT	30-22-18.000N 088-33-51.000W	Fl Y 2.5s	10		On pile cluster.	Private aid.
	Krebs Lake Channel						
8265	- Junction Day beacon K	30-22-40.432N 088-33-50.587W				JR on pile.	Ra ref.
8270	- Buoy 3	30-22-47.330N 088-33-46.477W				Green can.	
8275	- Buoy 5	30-22-50.993N 088-33-42.056W				Green can.	
8280	- Buoy 7	30-22-53.746N 088-33-30.384W				Green can.	
8285	- Buoy 9	30-22-54.102N 088-33-19.446W				Green can.	
8290	- Buoy 11	30-22-48.718N 088-33-00.057W				Green can.	
	Pascagoula River						
8295	- Day beacon 4	30-22-46.698N 088-34-00.290W				TR on pile.	Ra ref.
8300	- Day beacon 5	30-22-58.536N 088-34-07.806W				SG on pile.	Ra ref.
8305	- Day beacon 6	30-23-19.195N 088-33-50.952W				TR on pile.	Ra ref.
8310	- Day beacon 7	30-23-36.984N 088-34-32.808W				SG on pile.	Ra ref.
8315	- Day beacon 8	30-23-54.174N 088-34-40.062W				TR on pile.	Ra ref.
8320	- Day beacon 10	30-24-08.657N 088-34-57.047W				TR on pile.	Ra ref.
8325	- LIGHT 11	30-24-19.917N 088-35-04.364W	Fl G 4s	17	4	SG on pile.	Ra ref.
8330	- Day beacon 12	30-24-44.108N 088-34-59.624W				TR on pile.	Ra ref.
8335	- LIGHT 14	30-24-54.476N 088-34-53.864W	Fl R 4s	17	3	TR on pile.	Ra ref.
8340	- Day beacon 16	30-25-09.791N 088-34-21.912W				TR on pile.	Ra ref.
8345	- Day beacon 17	30-25-13.623N 088-34-00.514W				SG on pile.	Ra ref.

Light List corrected through LNM week: 01/18

(1) No.	(2) Name and Location	(3) Position	(4) Characteristic	(5) Height	(6) Range	(7) Structure	(8) Remarks
			MISSISSIPPI - Eighth District				
	DAUPHIN ISLAND TO DOG KEYS PASS (Chart 11374)						
	Escatawpa River						
8350	- Day beacon 1	30-25-22.206N 088-33-31.182W				SG on pile.	Ra ref.
8355	- Day beacon 2	30-25-22.848N 088-33-10.206W				TR on pile.	Ra ref.
8360	- CUTOFF LIGHT 3	30-25-33.386N 088-32-27.898W	Fl G 4s	17	4	SG on pile.	Ra ref.
8365	- Day beacon 4	30-25-23.770N 088-32-17.083W				TR on pile.	Ra ref.
8370	- Day beacon 5	30-25-23.443N 088-32-06.606W				SG on pile.	Ra ref.
8375	- CUTOFF LIGHT 6	30-25-16.369N 088-31-57.417W	Fl R 4s	17	3	TR on skeleton tower.	Ra ref.
8380	- Day beacon 8	30-25-08.949N 088-31-42.105W				TR on pile.	Ra ref.
8385	- CUTOFF LIGHT 9	30-25-06.916N 088-31-28.896W	Fl G 4s	17	4	SG on skeleton tower on piles.	Ra ref.
	PASCAGOULA HARBOR (Chart 11375)						
	Bayou Casotte Channel						
8390	- A RANGE FRONT LIGHT	30-20-08.497N 088-30-45.808W	Fl G 2.5s (NIGHT) Fl W 2.5s (DAY)	45 48		Skeleton tower on piles.	
8395	- A RANGE FRONT LIGHT PASSING LIGHT	30-20-08.520N 088-30-45.812W	Fl W 4s	15	6	On same structure as Bayou Casotte Channel Range A Front Light.	
8400	- A RANGE REAR LIGHT 935 yards, 000.2° from front light.	30-20-36.227N 088-30-45.723W	Iso G 6s (NIGHT) Iso W 6s (DAY)	83 80		Skeleton tower on piles.	
8405	- D RANGE FRONT LIGHT	30-16-25.501N 088-30-46.543W	Q W	25		KRW on skeleton tower on piles.	Visible all around; higher intensity on rangeline.
8410	- D RANGE REAR LIGHT 1,339 yards, 180.2° from front light.	30-15-47.120N 088-30-46.642W	Iso W 6s	55		KRW on skeleton tower on piles.	
8415	- D RANGE REAR LIGHT PASSING LIGHT	30-15-45.746N 088-30-46.654W	Fl W 4s	14	4	On same structure as Bayou Casotte Channel D Rear Light.	
8420	- LIGHT 1 170 feet outside channel limit.	30-17-44.034N 088-30-50.241W	Fl G 2.5s	17	3	SG on pile.	Ra ref.
8425	- LIGHT 2 160 feet outside channel limit.	30-17-43.958N 088-30-42.481W	Fl R 2.5s	17	3	TR on pile.	Ra ref.
8430	- LIGHT 3 150 feet outside channel limit.	30-18-13.316N 088-30-49.907W	Fl G 4s	17	4	SG on pile.	Ra ref.
8435	- LIGHT 4 160 feet outside channel limit	30-18-13.254N 088-30-42.413W	Fl R 4s	17	3	TR on pile.	Ra ref.
8440	- PIPELINE LIGHT A	30-18-38.400N 088-30-54.210W	Fl Y 2.5s	15		On pile.	Private aid.
8445	- PIPELINE LIGHT B	30-18-43.700N 088-30-37.500W	Fl Y 2.5s			On pile.	Private aid.
8450	- LIGHT 5 140 feet outside channel limit.	30-18-43.832N 088-30-49.667W	Fl G 4s	17	4	SG on pile.	Ra ref.
8455	- LIGHT 6 150 feet outside channel limit.	30-18-43.786N 088-30-42.312W	Fl R 4s	17	3	TR on pile.	Ra ref.
8460	GULF LNG LIGHT 2	30-19-08.012N 088-30-34.354W	Fl R 6s	10		TR on pile.	Private aid.

Light List corrected through LNM week: 01/18

(1) No.	(2) Name and Location	(3) Position	(4) Characteristic	(5) Height	(6) Range	(7) Structure	(8) Remarks
	**MISSISSIPPI - Eighth District**						

PASCAGOULA HARBOR (Chart 11375)
Bayou Casotte Channel

(1) No.	(2) Name and Location	(3) Position	(4) Characteristic	(5) Height	(6) Range	(7) Structure	(8) Remarks
8465	GULF LNG LIGHT 4	30-19-14.499N 088-30-25.095W	Fl R 6s	10		TR on pile.	Private aid.
8470	- LIGHT 7 140 feet outside channel limit.	30-19-11.858N 088-30-49.618W	Fl G 2.5s	17	3	SG on pile.	Ra ref.
8475	- LIGHT 8 150 feet outside channel limit.	30-18-57.285N 088-30-42.646W	Fl R 2.5s	17	3	TR on pile.	Ra ref.
8480	BAYOU CASOTTE LIGHT 9	30-19-21.067N 088-30-49.047W	Fl G 2.5s	17	4	SG on pile.	Ra ref.
8485	- LIGHT 10 130 feet outside channel limit.	30-19-22.009N 088-30-42.170W	Q R	17	3	TR on pile.	Ra ref.
8490.01	- Lighted Buoy 10A	30-19-40.913N 088-30-40.420W	Fl R 6s		3	Red.	
8495	- LIGHT 11 125 feet outside channel limit.	30-19-39.405N 088-30-49.147W	Q G	17	3	SG on pile.	Ra ref.
8500	- LIGHT 11A	30-19-58.218N 088-30-53.851W	Fl G 6s	17	4	SG on pile.	Ra ref.
8505	- LIGHT 11B	30-20-04.696N 088-30-52.426W	Fl G 6s	17	4	SG on pile.	Ra ref.
8510	- B RANGE FRONT LIGHT	30-21-08.140N 088-30-22.085W	Q W	25		KRW on skeleton tower on piles.	Visible 2° each side of rangeline.
8515	- B RANGE REAR LIGHT 892 yards, 013.3° from front light.	30-21-33.315N 088-30-15.235W	Iso W 6s	38		KRW on skeleton tower on piles.	Visible 2° each side of rangeline.
8520.01	Bayou Casotte Lighted Buoy 12	30-21-08.550N 088-30-26.699W	Fl R 2.5s		3		
8522	Mississippi Phosphates Lighted Danger Buoy	30-21-07.360N 088-30-20.330W	Fl W 2.5s			Marks submerged pipe.	Private aid.
8525	CHEVRON DOCK 4 LIGHTS (2) Marks end of dock.	30-19-51.000N 088-30-39.000W	Fl R 2.5s	22		On dolphins.	Private aid.
8530	STANDARD OIL DOCK LIGHTS (2)	30-20-07.200N 088-30-34.100W	Fl R 2.5s	19		On mooring dolphin.	Private aid.
8535	CHEVRON NO. 4 DOCK LIGHTS (2)	30-20-11.000N 088-30-33.000W	Fl R 2.5s	21		On dolphins at end of dock.	Private aid.
8540	- C RANGE FRONT LIGHT	30-19-19.713N 088-30-51.889W	Q W	25		KWR on tower.	Visible all around; higher intensity beam on rangeline.
8545	- C RANGE REAR LIGHT 833 yards, 193.3° from front light.	30-18-55.637N 088-30-58.440W	Iso W 6s	36		KWR on tower.	Visible all around; higher intensity on rangeline.
8550	BAYOU CHICO JETTY LIGHT	30-20-15.900N 088-31-33.000W	Fl R 2.5s	15		On pile.	Private aid.
8555	MISSISSIPPI GULF FISH REEF LIGHT E	30-20-07.080N 088-31-56.040W	Fl Y 4s	17		NY on pile.	Ra ref. Private aid.
8560	MISSISSIPPI GULF FISH REEF LIGHT B	30-17-53.040N 088-35-53.040W	Fl Y 4s	17		NY on pile.	Ra ref. Private aid.

Pascagoula Bay

(1) No.	(2) Name and Location	(3) Position	(4) Characteristic	(5) Height	(6) Range	(7) Structure	(8) Remarks
8565	U.S.G.S. ROUND ISLAND MONITORING PLATFORM LIGHT	30-18-49.000N 088-35-00.000W	Fl Y 2.5s	35		On pile.	Private aid.
8570	- Channel Daybeacon 2	30-20-02.000N 088-36-03.000W				TR on pile.	Private aid.
8575	- Channel Daybeacon 4	30-20-39.000N 088-36-03.000W				TR on pile.	Private aid.
8578	Graveline Bayou Channel Daybeacon 1	30-21-13.310N 088-39-44.230W				SG on pile.	Private aid.
8578.01	Graveline Bayou Channel Daybeacon 2	30-21-13.150N 088-39-45.000W				TR on pile.	Private aid.

Light List corrected through LNM week: 01/18

(1) No.	(2) Name and Location	(3) Position	(4) Characteristic	(5) Height	(6) Range	(7) Structure	(8) Remarks
		MISSISSIPPI - Eighth District					
	PASCAGOULA HARBOR (Chart 11375)						
	Pascagoula Bay						
8578.02	Graveline Bayou Channel Day beacon 3	30-21-22.790N 088-39-42.990W				SG on pile.	Private aid.
8578.03	Graveline Bayou Channel Day beacon 4	30-21-22.540N 088-39-41.650W				TR on pile.	Private aid.
8578.04	Graveline Bayou Channel Day beacon 5	30-21-33.450N 088-39-40.440W				SG on pile.	Private aid.
8578.05	Graveline Bayou Channel Day beacon 6	30-21-33.210N 088-39-39.100W				TR on pile.	Private aid.
8578.06	Graveline Bayou Channel Day beacon 7	30-21-35.340N 088-39-40.000W				SG on pile.	Private aid.
8578.07	Graveline Bayou Channel Day beacon 8	30-21-35.200N 088-39-38.640W				TR on pile.	Private aid.
8578.08	Graveline Bayou Channel Day beacon 9	30-21-37.610N 088-39-10.840W				SG on pile.	Private aid.
8578.09	Graveline Bayou Channel Day beacon 10	30-21-38.410N 088-39-39.830W				TR on pile.	Private aid.
8578.11	Graveline Bayou Channel Day beacon 11	30-21-39.490N 088-39-43.380W				SG on pile.	Private aid.
8578.12	Graveline Bayou Channel Day beacon 12	30-21-40.400N 088-39-12.500W				TR on pile.	Private aid.
8578.13	Graveline Bayou Channel Day beacon 13	30-21-42.910N 088-39-50.830W				SG on pile.	Private aid.
8578.14	Graveline Bayou Channel Day beacon 14	30-21-44.180N 088-39-50.680W				TR on pile.	Private aid.
	Round Island						
8580	- BREAKWATER OBSTRUCTION LIGHTS (6)	30-17-28.980N 088-35-18.780W	Fl W 2.5s			NW on pile worded DANGER BREAKWATER	Private aid.
8585	MISSISSIPPI SOUND PIPELINE LIGHT CP-7	30-17-09.600N 088-35-44.770W	Q W	13		On pile.	Private aid.
8590	- NORTH SPIT LIGHT 2	30-19-26.661N 088-36-30.517W	Fl R 4s	17	4	TR on skeleton tower on piles.	Ra ref.
	DOG KEYS PASS TO WAVELAND (Chart 11372)						
	Dog Keys Pass						
8595	- Lighted Buoy 2	30-14-42.723N 088-46-56.091W	Fl R 2.5s		3	Red.	
8600	- Buoy 3 Marks shoal.	30-15-18.723N 088-46-28.090W				Green can.	
	Biloxi East Channel						
8639	DEER ISLAND BREAKWATER SOUTHEAST DANGER LIGHT	30-21-14.820N 088-49-54.660W	Fl W 2.5s			Marks southeast end of breakwater.	Private aid.
8640	DEER ISLAND BREAKWATER DANGER LIGHT	30-21-14.440N 088-49-57.700W	Fl W 2.5s			NW on pile worded DANGER.	Private aid.
8645	DEER ISLAND BREAKWATER DANGER LIGHT	30-21-17.840N 088-50-08.170W	Fl W 2.5s			NW on pile worded DANGER.	Private aid.
8650	DEER ISLAND BREAKWATER DANGER LIGHT	30-21-18.120N 088-50-07.940W	Fl W 2.5s			NW on pile worded DANGER.	Private aid.
8655	DEER ISLAND BREAKWATER DANGER LIGHT	30-21-21.300N 088-50-16.700W	Fl W 2.5s			NW on pile worded DANGER.	Private aid.
8660	DEER ISLAND BREAKWATER DANGER LIGHT	30-21-21.580N 088-50-16.460W	Fl W 2.5s			NW on pile worded DANGER.	Private aid.
8665	DEER ISLAND BREAKWATER DANGER LIGHT	30-21-25.150N 088-50-25.060W	Fl W 2.5s			NW on pile worded DANGER.	Private aid.
8670	DEER ISLAND BREAKWATER DANGER LIGHT	30-21-25.460N 088-50-24.880W	Fl W 2.5s			NW on pile worded DANGER.	Private aid.

Light List corrected through LNM week: 01/18

(1) No.	(2) Name and Location	(3) Position	(4) Characteristic	(5) Height	(6) Range	(7) Structure	(8) Remarks
	MISSISSIPPI - Eighth District						
	DOG KEYS PASS TO WAVELAND (Chart 11372)						
	Biloxi East Channel						
8675	DEER ISLAND BREAKWATER DANGER LIGHT	30-21-28.610N 088-50-33.540W	Fl W 2.5s			NW on pile worded DANGER.	Private aid.
8677	DEER ISLAND BREAKWATER NORTHWEST DANGER LIGHT	30-21-32.460N 088-50-44.820W	Fl W 2.5s			Marks northwest end of breakwater.	Private aid.
	Dog Keys Pass						
8680	Deer Island Wreck Day beacon DI	30-21-46.224N 088-52-54.618W				NW on pile worded DANGER WRECK.	
8685	MISSISSIPPI GULF KEESLER FISH REEF LIGHT	30-21-54.000N 088-53-00.000W	Fl Y 6s			NY on pile.	Private aid.
8690	DEER ISLAND WRECK LIGHT WR2	30-21-43.700N 088-52-54.100W	Q R	17	4	TR on pile.	Ra ref.
	Biloxi East Channel						
8695	- Day beacon 1	30-18-00.468N 088-46-33.971W				SG on pile.	Ra ref.
8700	- LIGHT 2	30-18-00.144N 088-46-29.444W	Fl R 6s	17	4	TR on pile.	Ra ref.
8705	- Day beacon 3	30-18-32.651N 088-46-33.966W				SG on pile.	Ra ref.
8710	- LIGHT 4	30-18-34.184N 088-46-29.135W	Fl R 4s	17	3	TR on pile.	Ra ref.
8715	- Day beacon 5	30-19-09.165N 088-46-33.904W				SG on pile.	Ra ref.
8720	- Day beacon 6	30-19-09.274N 088-46-28.922W				TR on pile.	Ra ref.
8725	- Day beacon 7	30-19-42.407N 088-46-33.949W				SG on pile.	Ra ref.
8730	- WRECK LIGHT WR7A	30-19-53.409N 088-46-55.530W	Q G	17	3	SG on pile.	Ra ref.
8735	- LIGHT 8	30-19-42.605N 088-46-28.681W	Fl R 2.5s	17	3	TR on pile.	Ra ref.
8740	- Day beacon 9	30-20-21.475N 088-46-34.393W				SG on pile.	Ra ref.
8745	- LIGHT 10	30-20-20.958N 088-46-28.408W	Q R	17	3	TR on pile.	Ra ref.
8750	- Day beacon 11	30-20-50.794N 088-46-47.888W				SG on pile.	Ra ref.
8755	- Day beacon 12	30-20-52.234N 088-46-43.691W				TR on pile.	Ra ref.
8760	- Day beacon 13	30-21-23.266N 088-47-05.465W				SG on pile	Ra ref.
8765	- LIGHT 14	30-21-23.475N 088-47-00.112W	Q R	17	3	TR on pile.	Ra ref.
8770	- Day beacon 16	30-21-47.698N 088-47-29.892W				TR on pile.	Ra ref.
8775	- Day beacon 17	30-22-07.977N 088-48-04.168W				SG on pile.	Ra ref.
8780	- LIGHT 18	30-22-11.634N 088-47-59.655W	Fl R 2.5s	17	3	TR on pile.	Ra ref.
8785	- Day beacon 20	30-22-36.716N 088-48-30.097W				TR on pile.	Ra ref.
8790	- Day beacon 21	30-22-55.277N 088-49-00.232W				SG on pile.	Ra ref.
8795	- LIGHT 22	30-22-59.146N 088-48-58.538W	Fl R 2.5s	17	3	TR on pile.	Ra ref.
8800	- Day beacon 24	30-23-23.047N 088-49-28.822W				TR on pile.	Ra ref.
8805	- LIGHT 26	30-23-38.525N 088-49-47.760W	Q R	17	3	TR on pile.	Ra ref.

Light List corrected through LNM week: 01/18

(1) No.	(2) Name and Location	(3) Position	(4) Characteristic	(5) Height	(6) Range	(7) Structure	(8) Remarks
			MISSISSIPPI - Eighth District				
	DOG KEYS PASS TO WAVELAND (Chart 11372)						
	Biloxi East Channel						
8810	- Day beacon 27	30-23-43.037N 088-50-01.448W				SG on pile.	Ra ref.
8815	- LIGHT 29	30-23-48.664N 088-50-12.174W	Fl G 2.5s	17	4	SG on pile.	Ra ref.
8820	- Day beacon 30	30-23-54.906N 088-50-12.026W				TR on pile.	Ra ref.
8825	- Day beacon 31	30-23-59.057N 088-50-25.708W				SG on pile.	Ra ref.
	Davis Bayou Channel						
8830	- Day beacon 1	30-23-31.610N 088-48-52.760W				SG on pile.	Private aid.
8830.01	- LIGHT 2	30-23-30.040N 088-48-51.900W	Fl R 2.5s			TR on pile.	Private aid.
8830.02	- Day beacon 4	30-23-31.420N 088-48-45.620W				TR on pile.	Private aid.
8830.03	- Day beacon 6	30-23-32.340N 088-48-42.050W				TR on pile.	Private aid.
8830.04	- Day beacon 3	30-23-34.730N 088-48-39.710W				SG on pile.	Private aid.
8830.05	- Day beacon 8	30-23-32.010N 088-48-32.620W				TR on pile.	Private aid.
8830.06	- DANGER LIGHT	30-23-33.320N 088-48-29.230W	Fl W 2.5s			NW on pile worded DANGER SUBMERGED ROCKS.	Private aid.
8830.07	- Day beacon 10	30-23-29.200N 088-48-19.000W				TR on pile.	Private aid.
8830.08	- Day beacon 12	30-23-28.430N 088-48-11.000W				TR on pile.	Private aid.
8830.09	- Day beacon 14	30-23-28.440N 088-48-06.150W				TR on pile.	Private aid.
8830.11	- Day beacon 5	30-23-29.720N 088-48-05.880W				SG on pile.	Private aid.
8830.12	- Day beacon 16	30-23-28.190N 088-47-57.300W				TR on pile.	Private aid.
8830.13	- Day beacon 18	30-23-27.780N 088-47-51.740W				TR on pile.	Private aid.
8830.14	- Day beacon 7	30-23-28.800N 088-47-50.230W				SG on pile.	Private aid.
8830.15	- Day beacon 9	30-23-27.960N 088-47-46.660W				SG on pile.	Private aid.
8830.16	- Day beacon 20	30-23-26.530N 088-47-46.250W				TR on pile.	Private aid.
8830.17	- Day beacon 22	30-23-24.460N 088-47-40.120W				TR on pile.	Private aid.
8830.18	- Day beacon 11	30-23-25.590N 088-47-39.860W				SG on pile.	Private aid.
8830.19	- Day beacon 24	30-23-19.780N 088-47-34.880W				TR on pile.	Private aid.
8830.21	- Day beacon 13	30-23-20.780N 088-47-34.000W				SG on pile.	Private aid.
8830.22	- Day beacon 26	30-23-15.430N 088-47-29.040W				TR on pile.	Private aid.
8831	Univ of Southern Mississippi Research Vessel Preferred Channel Day beacon B	30-23-30.966N 088-47-46.248W				JR on pile.	Private aid.
8950	OCEAN SPRINGS CHANNEL LIGHT 2	30-23-53.475N 088-49-37.930W	Fl R 2.5s	17	3	TR on dolphin.	
	Biloxi Channel						
8955	BILOXI LIGHT	30-23-42.000N 088-54-06.000W	Oc W 4s	61		White conical tower, black balustrade.	Higher intensity beam to south. Private aid.
8960	- Day beacon 1	30-21-35.081N 088-54-13.377W				SG on pile.	Ra ref.

77

Light List corrected through LNM week: 01/18

(1) No.	(2) Name and Location	(3) Position	(4) Characteristic	(5) Height	(6) Range	(7) Structure	(8) Remarks
		MISSISSIPPI - Eighth District					
	DOG KEYS PASS TO WAVELAND (Chart 11372)						
	Biloxi Channel						
8965	- LIGHT 2 100 feet outside channel limit.	30-21-35.677N 088-54-07.512W	Fl R 6s	17	4	TR on pile.	Ra ref.
8970	- LIGHT 4	30-22-07.163N 088-54-06.631W	Fl R 6s	17	4	TR on pile.	Ra ref.
8975	- Day beacon 5	30-22-37.517N 088-54-10.243W				SG on pile.	Ra ref.
8980	- LIGHT 6	30-22-35.429N 088-54-05.950W	Fl R 4s	17	3	TR on pile.	Ra ref.
8985	- LIGHT 8	30-22-58.852N 088-54-05.696W	Fl R 2.5s	17	3	TR on pile.	Ra ref.
8990	- Day beacon 9	30-23-14.338N 088-54-07.001W				SG on pile.	Ra ref.
8995	- LIGHT 10	30-23-14.614N 088-54-03.009W	Q R	17	3	TR on pile.	Ra ref.
9000	- LIGHT 12	30-23-21.714N 088-53-56.909W	Fl R 2.5s	17	3	TR on pile.	Ra ref.
9005	- Day beacon 14	30-23-25.242N 088-53-47.517W				TR on pile.	Ra ref.
9010	- Day beacon 16	30-23-25.714N 088-53-30.108W				TR on pile.	Ra ref.
9015	BILOXI SMALL CRAFT HARBOR ENTRANCE WEST LIGHT	30-23-26.400N 088-53-02.400W	Fl G 4s	12		SG on bulkhead.	Private aid.
9020	BILOXI SMALL CRAFT HARBOR ENTRANCE EAST LIGHT	30-23-26.400N 088-53-01.200W	Fl R 4s	12		TR on bulkhead.	Private aid.
9025	BILOXI COMMERCIAL DOCKING EAST ENTRANCE LIGHT	30-23-27.000N 088-53-12.000W	Fl R 2.5s	13		TR on bulkhead.	Private aid.
9030	BILOXI COMMERCIAL DOCKING WEST ENTRANCE LIGHT	30-23-27.000N 088-53-13.000W	Fl G 2.5s			SG on bulkhead.	Private aid.
9035	- LIGHT 18	30-23-23.741N 088-53-01.037W	Fl R 2.5s	17	3	TR on pile.	Ra ref.
9040	- Day beacon 20	30-23-22.315N 088-52-36.606W				TR on pile.	Ra ref.
9045	- LIGHT 21	30-23-23.943N 088-52-14.495W	Q G	17	3	SG on pile.	Ra ref.
9050	- Day beacon 22	30-23-20.000N 088-52-13.800W				TR on pile.	Ra ref.
9055	GRAND CASINO LIGHT	30-23-24.890N 088-51-56.120W	Fl G 2.5s	7		On barge.	Private aid.
9060	- Day beacon 24	30-23-17.100N 088-51-50.700W				TR on pile.	Ra ref.
9065	POINT CADET MARINA BREAKWATER LIGHT 1	30-23-18.100N 088-51-40.970W	Q G	12		SG atop breakwater wall.	Private aid.
9070	Point Cadet Marina Breakwater Day beacon 2	30-23-19.610N 088-51-40.970W				TR atop breakwater wall.	Private aid.
9075	POINT CADET MARINA BREAKWATER LIGHT 3	30-23-18.120N 088-51-36.130W	Fl G 4s	12		SG atop breakwater wall.	Private aid.
9080	Point Cadet Marina Breakwater Day beacon 4	30-23-18.130N 088-51-31.820W				TR atop breakwater wall.	Private aid.
9085	POINT CADET MARINA BREAKWATER LIGHT 5	30-23-18.170N 088-51-26.960W	Fl G 4s	12		SG atop breakwater wall.	Private aid.
9090	Point Cadet Marina Breakwater Day beacon 6	30-23-18.250N 088-51-25.630W				TR atop breakwater wall.	Private aid.
9095	- Day beacon 26	30-23-15.180N 088-51-34.465W				TR on pile.	Ra ref.
9100	- LIGHT 27	30-23-16.835N 088-51-22.457W	Q G	17	3	SG on dolphin.	Ra ref.
9105	- Day beacon 28	30-23-12.348N 088-51-08.301W				TR on pile.	Ra ref.

(1) No.	(2) Name and Location	(3) Position	(4) Characteristic	(5) Height	(6) Range	(7) Structure	(8) Remarks
		MISSISSIPPI - Eighth District					
	DOG KEYS PASS TO WAVELAND (Chart 11372)						
	Biloxi Channel						
9110	- LIGHT 30	30-23-11.115N 088-50-54.498W	Q R	17	3	TR on pile.	Ra ref.
9115	- Day beacon 32	30-23-18.754N 088-50-35.280W				TR on pile.	Ra ref.
9120	- LIGHT 34	30-23-24.185N 088-50-21.271W	Fl R 2.5s	17	3	TR on pile.	Ra ref.
9125	- Day beacon 35	30-23-36.716N 088-49-54.099W				SG on pile.	Ra ref.
	Ott Bayou Channel						
9130	- Day beacon 1	30-24-24.176N 088-51-01.640W				SG on pile.	Ra ref.
9135	- Day beacon 3	30-24-14.602N 088-51-23.245W				SG on pile.	Ra ref.
9140	- Day beacon 5	30-24-11.560N 088-51-26.418W				SG on pile.	Ra ref.
9145	- Day beacon 7	30-23-54.120N 088-51-29.160W				SG on pile.	Ra ref.
9150	PALACE CASINO MARINA ENTRANCE LIGHT 1	30-23-52.200N 088-51-36.300W	Fl G 4s			SG on pile.	Private aid.
9155	PALACE CASINO MARINA ENTRANCE LIGHT 2	30-23-52.200N 088-51-34.200W	Fl R 2.5s			TR on pile.	Private aid.
	Old Fort Bayou Channel						
9160	- Day beacon 1	30-25-24.521N 088-51-18.553W				SG on pile.	Private aid.
9160.01	- LIGHT 2	30-25-24.572N 088-51-16.814W	Fl R 2.5s			TR on pile.	Private aid.
9160.02	- Day beacon 3	30-25-29.203N 088-51-15.952W				SG on pile.	Private aid.
9160.03	- Day beacon 4	30-25-29.814N 088-51-13.801W				TR on pile.	Private aid.
9160.04	- Day beacon 6	30-25-35.066N 088-51-09.290W				TR on pile.	Private aid.
9160.05	- Day beacon 5	30-25-38.647N 088-51-04.864W				SG on pile.	Private aid.
9160.06	- Day beacon 8	30-25-36.628N 088-51-03.180W				TR on pile.	Private aid.
9160.07	- Day beacon 10	30-25-35.410N 088-50-55.782W				TR on pile.	Private aid.
9160.08	- Day beacon 7	30-25-35.471N 088-50-53.006W				SG on pile.	Private aid.
9160.09	- Day beacon 12	30-25-27.612N 088-50-46.853W				TR on pile.	Private aid.
9160.11	- Day beacon 14	30-25-23.164N 088-50-42.571W				TR on pile.	Private aid.
9160.12	- Day beacon 9	30-25-21.885N 088-50-37.136W				SG on pile.	Private aid.
9160.13	- Day beacon 16	30-25-17.356N 088-50-35.213W				TR on pile.	Private aid.
9160.14	- Day beacon 18	30-25-17.160N 088-50-24.691W				TR on pile.	Private aid.
9160.15	- Day beacon 11	30-25-19.399N 088-50-21.250W				SG on pile.	Private aid.
9160.17	- Day beacon 20	30-25-17.360N 088-50-21.613W				TR on pile.	Private aid.
9160.18	- LIGHT 22	30-25-16.972N 088-50-18.671W	Fl R 2.5s			TR on pile.	Private aid.
9160.19	- Day beacon 24	30-25-16.134N 088-50-14.724W				TR on pile.	Private aid.
9160.21	- Day beacon 26	30-25-12.805N 088-50-09.512W				TR on pile.	Private aid.
9160.22	- Day beacon 13	30-25-10.507N 088-50-00.480W				SG on pile.	Private aid.

Light List corrected through LNM week: 01/18

(1) No.	(2) Name and Location	(3) Position	(4) Characteristic	(5) Height	(6) Range	(7) Structure	(8) Remarks
		MISSISSIPPI - Eighth District					
	DOG KEYS PASS TO WAVELAND (Chart 11372)						
	Old Fort Bayou Channel						
9160.23	- Day beacon 28	30-25-07.108N 088-49-54.782W				TR on pile.	Private aid.
	Back Bay of Biloxi						
9260	- Buoy 2	30-24-42.919N 088-51-08.099W				Red nun.	
9265	- Day beacon 3	30-24-40.357N 088-51-14.800W				SG on pile.	Ra ref.
9270	- WRECK LIGHT WR3A	30-24-39.723N 088-51-30.315W	Q G	17	3	SG on pile.	Ra ref.
9275	- Day beacon 4	30-24-44.653N 088-51-43.526W				TR on pile.	Ra ref.
9280	- Day beacon 5	30-24-40.816N 088-51-43.029W				SG on pile.	Ra ref.
9285	- WRECK LIGHT WR5A	30-24-39.108N 088-52-18.682W	Q G	17	3	SG on pile.	Ra ref.
9290	- Day beacon 6	30-24-47.736N 088-52-30.012W				TR on pile.	Ra ref.
9295	- LIGHT 7 75 feet outside channel limit.	30-24-42.609N 088-52-31.675W	Oc G 4s	17	3	SG on dolphin.	Ra ref.
9300	- Day beacon 8	30-24-50.896N 088-52-42.856W				TR on pile.	Ra ref.
9305	BILOXI PORT COMMISSION FISHING DOCK LIGHT	30-24-47.713N 088-52-46.832W	Fl G 2.5s	19		On dolphins.	Private aid.
9310	- Day beacon 10	30-25-04.209N 088-53-00.908W				TR on pile.	Ra ref.
9315	AMERICAN COMMERCIAL DOLPHIN LIGHTS (4)	30-25-04.000N 088-53-13.000W	Fl G 2.5s	22		On dolphins.	Private aid.
9320	MISSISSIPPI POWER ELECTRICAL TOWER CROSSING LIGHT	30-25-19.000N 088-53-28.000W	Fl G 2.5s			On dolphin.	Private aid.
9325	MISSISSIPPI POWER ELECTRICAL TOWER CROSSING LIGHT	30-25-15.000N 088-53-28.000W	Fl R 2.5s			On dolphin.	Private aid.
9330	- Day beacon 12	30-25-35.808N 088-54-06.936W				TR on pile.	Ra ref.
9335	- Day beacon 14	30-25-32.505N 088-54-47.335W				TR on pile.	Ra ref.
9340	- Day beacon 16	30-25-22.312N 088-55-21.213W				TR on pile.	Ra ref.
9345	- Day beacon 18	30-25-03.353N 088-55-54.868W				TR on pile.	Ra ref.
9350	- Day beacon 19	30-25-12.712N 088-56-48.117W				SG on pile.	Ra ref.
9355	- Day beacon 20	30-25-18.712N 088-56-54.117W				TR on pile.	Ra ref.
9360	- Day beacon 22	30-25-14.140N 088-57-34.187W				TR on pile.	Ra ref.
9365	- Day beacon 23	30-25-10.007N 088-57-56.523W				SG on pile.	Ra ref.
9370	- Day beacon 24	30-25-06.843N 088-58-13.942W				TR on pile.	Ra ref.
9375	Biloxi River Day beacon 1	30-25-23.199N 088-58-46.522W				SG on pile.	Ra ref.
	Big Lake						
9380	- Junction Day beacon	30-24-58.514N 088-58-50.143W				JR on pile.	Ra ref.
9385	- Day beacon 26	30-24-54.917N 088-59-11.561W				TR on pile.	Ra ref.
9390	- Day beacon 28	30-24-48.036N 088-59-26.093W				TR on pile.	Ra ref.

Light List corrected through LNM week: 01/18

(1) No.	(2) Name and Location	(3) Position	(4) Characteristic	(5) Height	(6) Range	(7) Structure	(8) Remarks
			MISSISSIPPI - Eighth District				
	DOG KEYS PASS TO WAVELAND (Chart 11372)						
	Big Lake						
9395	- Day beacon 29	30-24-43.708N 088-59-26.256W				SG on pile.	Ra ref.
9400	- Day beacon 30	30-24-49.221N 088-59-32.315W				TR on pile.	Ra ref.
9405	- Day beacon 32	30-24-54.234N 088-59-41.524W				TR on pile.	Ra ref.
9410	- Day beacon 33	30-24-51.015N 088-59-43.228W				SG on pile.	Ra ref.
9415	- Day beacon 34	30-24-55.710N 088-59-55.767W				TR on pile.	Ra ref.
9420	- Day beacon 36	30-24-56.753N 089-00-07.268W				TR on pile.	Ra ref.
9425	U.S.G.S. GULFPORT MONITORING PLATFORM LIGHT	30-19-12.000N 088-58-33.000W	Fl Y 2.5s	37			Maintained by U.S. Geological Survey. Private aid.
9430	MISSISSIPPI POWER NORTH LIGHT	30-25-15.200N 089-00-04.500W	Q W			On platform.	Private aid.
9435	MISSISSIPPI POWER SOUTH LIGHT	30-25-10.900N 089-00-09.100W	Q W			On platform.	Private aid.
9440	WARREN PAVING BARGE DOCK LIGHTS (2)	30-25-24.000N 089-01-30.000W	Fl R 2.5s	20		On dock.	Private aid.
	Bernard Bayou						
9445	- LIGHT 1	30-24-57.412N 089-00-15.346W	Fl G 6s	17	4	SG on pile.	Ra ref.
9450	- LIGHT 2	30-25-07.411N 089-00-24.925W	Q R	17	3	TR on pile.	Ra ref.
9455	- LIGHT 3	30-25-36.709N 089-02-36.130W	Fl G 2.5s	17	3	SG on pile.	Ra ref.
9460	- LIGHT 5	30-25-34.409N 089-03-09.232W	Fl G 4s	17	4	SG on dolphin.	Ra ref.
9465	- LIGHT 9	30-25-27.108N 089-03-58.434W	Q G	17	3	SG on dolphin.	Ra ref.
9467	*Gulf Ship Lighted Containment Buoys (2)*	30-25-37.440N 089-02-47.580W	Fl W 2.5s			Marks upstream/downstream temporary containment area at shipyard slip.	Buoys deployed during dry dock operations only. Private aid.
9470	- LIGHT 11	30-25-37.255N 089-04-12.877W	Fl G 4s	17	4	SG on dolphin.	Ra ref.
9475.01	- *Lighted Buoy 13*	30-25-43.528N 089-04-24.528W	Fl G 2.5s		3		Green.
9480	MISSISSIPPI GULF FISHING REEF LIGHT B	30-15-24.000N 088-54-00.000W	Fl Y 6s	17		NY on pile.	Ra ref. Private aid.
9485	MISSISSIPPI GULF FISHING REEF LIGHT C	30-16-00.000N 088-57-42.000W	Fl Y 6s	17		NY on pile.	Ra ref. Private aid.
	Treasure Bay Casino Channel						
9490	- Day beacon 1	30-22-50.000N 088-57-17.000W				SG on pile.	Private aid.
9495	- Day beacon 2	30-22-50.000N 088-57-15.000W				TR on pile.	Private aid.
9500	- Day beacon 3	30-22-57.000N 088-57-17.000W				SG on pile.	Private aid.
9505	- Day beacon 4	30-22-57.000N 088-57-15.000W				TR on pile.	Private aid.
9510	- Day beacon 5	30-23-04.000N 088-57-17.000W				SG on pile.	Private aid.
9515	- Day beacon 6	30-23-04.000N 088-57-15.000W				TR on pile.	Private aid.
9520	- Day beacon 7	30-23-11.000N 088-57-17.000W				SG on pile.	Private aid.

Light List corrected through LNM week: 01/18

(1) No.	(2) Name and Location	(3) Position	(4) Characteristic	(5) Height	(6) Range	(7) Structure	(8) Remarks
			MISSISSIPPI - Eighth District				
	DOG KEYS PASS TO WAVELAND (Chart 11372)						
	Treasure Bay Casino Channel						
9525	- Day beacon 8	30-23-11.000N 088-57-15.000W				TR on pile.	Private aid.
9530	- Day beacon 9	30-23-18.000N 088-57-17.000W				SG on pile.	Private aid.
9535	- Day beacon 10	30-23-18.000N 088-57-15.000W				TR on pile.	Private aid.
	Broadwater Beach Hotel Marina Channel						
9540	- Day beacon 2	30-22-42.000N 088-57-50.820W				TR on pile.	Private aid.
9545	- Day beacon 3	30-22-51.910N 088-57-50.060W				SG on pile.	Private aid.
9550	- Day beacon 4	30-23-01.800N 088-57-51.120W				TR on pile.	Private aid.
9555	- Day beacon 5	30-22-22.210N 088-57-50.520W				SG on pile.	Private aid.
9560	- Day beacon 6	30-23-11.710N 088-57-50.360W				TR on pile.	Private aid.
9565	- Day beacon 7	30-23-15.880N 088-57-51.330W				SG on pile.	Private aid.
9570	- LIGHT	30-23-24.000N 088-57-54.000W	Fl W 5s	67		White cylindrical structure.	Private aid.
	MISSISSIPPI SOUND AND APPROACHES (Chart 11373)						
	Gulfport Ship Channel						
9575 340	- Lighted Buoy GP	30-07-09.931N 088-52-39.881W	Mo (A) W		4	Red and white stripes with red spherical topmark.	
9580 335	SHIP ISLAND LIGHT	30-12-45.414N 088-57-58.736W	Fl W 6s	82	6	Skeleton tower on concrete block. On same structure as Ship Channel Upper Reach Outbound Range Rear Light.	
9585	- Lighted Buoy 2 100 feet outside channel limit.	30-07-10.272N 088-53-49.179W	Fl R 2.5s		3	Red.	
9590	- Lighted Buoy 3 250 feet outside channel limit.	30-07-00.973N 088-54-44.357W	Fl G 4s		4	Green.	
9595	- Lighted Buoy 4 100 feet outside channel limit.	30-07-08.408N 088-54-44.618W	Fl R 4s		3	Red.	
9600	- Lighted Buoy 6 90 feet outside channel limit.	30-07-06.522N 088-55-39.553W	Q R		3	Red.	
9605	- Lighted Buoy 7 50 feet outside channel limit.	30-07-00.463N 088-55-50.316W	Q G		3	Green.	
9610	- Lighted Buoy 8 130 feet outside channel limit.	30-07-14.163N 088-55-53.440W	Oc R 4s		4	Red.	
9615	- Lighted Buoy 9 70 feet outside channel limit.	30-07-49.555N 088-56-30.876W	Fl G 2.5s		4	Green.	
9620	- Lighted Buoy 10 130 feet outside channel limit.	30-07-53.006N 088-56-25.317W	Fl R 2.5s		3	Red.	
9625	- Lighted Buoy 11 80 feet outside channel limit.	30-08-28.614N 088-57-02.980W	Fl G 4s		4	Green.	
9630	- Lighted Buoy 12 120 feet outside channel limit.	30-08-32.066N 088-56-57.419W	Fl (2)R 5s		3	Red.	
9635	- Lighted Buoy 13 120 feet outside channel limit.	30-09-07.619N 088-57-35.577W	Fl G 2.5s		4	Green.	

Light List corrected through LNM week: 01/18

(1) No.	(2) Name and Location	(3) Position	(4) Characteristic	(5) Height	(6) Range	(7) Structure	(8) Remarks
	MISSISSIPPI - Eighth District						
	MISSISSIPPI SOUND AND APPROACHES (Chart 11373)						
	Gulfport Ship Channel						
9640	- Lighted Buoy 14 120 feet outside channel limit.	30-09-11.122N 088-57-29.529W	Fl R 2.5s		3		Red.
	DOG KEYS PASS TO WAVELAND (Chart 11372)						
	Gulfport Ship Channel						
9645	- Lighted Buoy 15 90 feet outside channel limit.	30-09-46.725N 088-58-07.207W	Fl G 4s		3		Green.
9650	- Lighted Buoy 16 110 feet outside channel limit.	30-09-50.177N 088-58-01.646W	Fl R 4s		3		Red.
9655	- Lighted Buoy 17 90 feet outside channel limit.	30-10-25.777N 088-58-39.332W	Fl G 6s		3		Green.
9660	- Lighted Buoy 18 110 feet outside channel limit.	30-10-29.229N 088-58-33.769W	Fl R 6s		3		Red.
9665	- Lighted Buoy 20 100 feet outside channel limit.	30-11-08.350N 088-59-05.970W	Q R		3		Red.
9670	- Lighted Buoy 21 100 feet outside channel limit.	30-11-19.696N 088-59-23.653W	Q G		3		Green.
9675	GULFPORT MIDDLE REACH INBOUND RANGE FRONT LIGHT	30-15-58.575N 089-00-25.889W	Q W	25		KRW on skeleton tower on piles.	Visible all around; higher intensity 1.5° each side rangeline.
9680	GULFPORT MIDDLE REACH INBOUND RANGE REAR LIGHT 4,400 yards, 348.4° from front light.	30-18-06.375N 089-00-56.038W	Iso W 6s	69		KRW on skeleton tower on piles.	Visible on rangeline only.
9685	GULFPORT MIDDLE REACH CHANNEL INBOUND RANGE REAR PASSING LIGHT	30-18-06.372N 089-00-56.035W	Fl W 4s	20	5	On same structure as Gulfport Ship Channel Middle Reach Inbound Range Rear Light.	
9690	- Lighted Buoy 22 100 feet outside channel limit.	30-11-38.708N 088-59-21.199W	Oc R 4s		3		Red.
9695	- Lighted Buoy 23 100 feet outside channel limit.	30-12-12.108N 088-59-36.035W	Fl G 4s		3		Green.
9700	- Lighted Buoy 24 100 feet outside channel limit.	30-12-13.299N 088-59-29.336W	Fl R 6s		3		Red.
9705	SHIP ISLAND PASS ENTRANCE RANGE FRONT LIGHT	30-12-09.243N 089-00-00.284W	Q W (NIGHT) Q W (DAY)	39 37		Skeleton tower on piles.	Day: Visible 4° each side of range line. Night: Visible all around, higher intensity on range line.
9710	SHIP ISLAND PASS ENTRANCE RANGE REAR LIGHT 6000 yards, 324.5° from front light.	30-14-34.298N 089-01-59.409W	Oc W 4s (NIGHT) Oc W 4s (DAY)	117 115		Skeleton tower on piles.	Visible 2° each side of range line.
9715	SHIP ISLAND PASS ENTRANCE RANGE REAR PASSING LIGHT	30-14-34.298N 089-01-59.409W	Fl W 4s	43	6	On same structure as Ship Island Pass Range Rear Light.	
9720	- Lighted Buoy 25 100 feet outside channel limit.	30-12-56.970N 088-59-46.604W	Fl G 2.5s		3		Green.
9725	- Lighted Buoy 26 100 feet outside channel limit.	30-12-58.161N 088-59-39.905W	Fl R 2.5s		3		Red.

Light List corrected through LNM week: 01/18

(1) No.	(2) Name and Location	(3) Position	(4) Characteristic	(5) Height	(6) Range	(7) Structure	(8) Remarks
			MISSISSIPPI - Eighth District				
	DOG KEYS PASS TO WAVELAND (Chart 11372)						
	Gulfport Ship Channel						
9730	- LIGHT 27	30-13-21.813N 088-59-52.075W	Fl G 6s	17	4	SG on pile.	Ra ref.
9735	- LIGHT 28	30-13-22.670N 088-59-45.895W	Fl R 4s	17	3	TR on pile.	Ra ref.
9740	- LIGHT 29	30-13-51.295N 088-59-59.023W	Fl G 4s	17	4	SG on pile.	Ra ref.
9745	- LIGHT 30	30-13-52.462N 088-59-52.672W	Fl R 6s	17	4	TR on pile.	Ra ref.
9750	CHEVRON PIPELINE LIGHT A	30-14-02.900N 089-00-08.000W	Fl Y 2.5s	15		On pile.	Private aid.
9755	CHEVRON PIPELINE LIGHT B	30-14-12.600N 088-59-53.500W	Fl Y 2.5s	15		On pile.	Private aid.
9760	- LIGHT 31	30-14-20.777N 089-00-05.971W	Fl G 6s	17	4	SG on pile.	Ra ref.
9765	- LIGHT 32	30-14-21.967N 088-59-59.268W	Fl R 4s	17	3	TR on pile.	Ra ref.
9770	- LIGHT 33	30-14-50.149N 089-00-13.175W	Fl G 4s	17	4	SG on pile.	Ra ref.
9775	- LIGHT 34	30-14-51.449N 089-00-06.217W	Fl R 2.5s	17	3	TR on pile.	Ra ref.
9780	- LIGHT 35	30-15-19.741N 089-00-19.869W	Q G	17	3	SG on pile.	Ra ref.
9785	GULFPORT OBSTRUCTION LIGHT	30-14-03.022N 088-58-59.997W	Q W	35	6	NB on concrete structure.	
9790	GULFPORT UPPER REACH OUTBOUND RANGE FRONT LIGHT	30-13-50.741N 088-58-53.883W	Q W	35		KRW on pile.	Visible all around; higher intensity on the range line.
9795	GULFPORT UPPER REACH OUTBOUND RANGE REAR LIGHT 2,728 yards, 143.8° from front light.	30-12-45.414N 088-57-58.736W	Iso W 6s	81		KRW on skeleton tower on concrete pile. On same structure as Ship Island Light.	Visible 2° each side of rangeline.
9800	- LIGHT 36	30-15-34.760N 089-00-16.252W	Q R	17	3	TR on pile.	Ra ref.
9805	- LIGHT 37	30-15-40.645N 089-00-30.306W	Oc G 4s	17	4	SG on pile.	Ra ref.
9810	- LIGHT 39	30-16-04.604N 089-00-50.579W	Fl G 4s	17	4	SG on pile.	Ra ref.
9815	- LIGHT 40	30-16-08.083N 089-00-45.067W	Fl R 4s	17	3	TR on pile.	Ra ref.
9820 34385	- LIGHT 41	30-16-31.500N 089-01-13.828W	Fl G 2.5s	17	3	SG-SY on pile.	Ra ref.
9825 34380	- LIGHT 42	30-16-31.829N 089-01-05.614W	Iso R 6s	17	4	TR-SY on dolphin.	Ra ref.
9830 34395	- LIGHT 43	30-17-03.596N 089-01-40.858W	Iso G 6s	17	4	SG-TY on dolphin.	Ra ref.
9835 34390	- LIGHT 44	30-17-03.627N 089-01-32.419W	Fl R 2.5s	17	4	TR-TY on pile.	Ra ref.
9840	- LIGHT 45	30-17-24.439N 089-01-58.709W	Fl G 4s	17	4	SG on pile.	Ra ref.
9845	- LIGHT 46	30-17-27.959N 089-01-53.197W	Fl R 4s	17	3	TR on pile.	Ra ref.
9850	- LIGHT 47	30-17-48.676N 089-02-19.259W	Fl G 4s	17	4	SG on pile.	Ra ref.
9855	- LIGHT 48	30-17-52.196N 089-02-13.747W	Fl R 4s	17	3	TR on pile.	Ra ref.
9860	- LIGHT 49	30-18-12.913N 089-02-39.810W	Fl G 4s	17	4	SG on pile.	Ra ref.
9865	- LIGHT 50	30-18-16.433N 089-02-34.298W	Fl R 4s	17	3	TR on pile.	Ra ref.

(1) No.	(2) Name and Location	(3) Position	(4) Characteristic	(5) Height	(6) Range	(7) Structure	(8) Remarks
			MISSISSIPPI - Eighth District				
	DOG KEYS PASS TO WAVELAND (Chart 11372)						
	Gulfport Ship Channel						
9870	GULFPORT UPPER REACH INBOUND RANGE FRONT LIGHT	30-21-12.217N 089-05-07.514W	Q R	35		KRW on skeleton tower on piles.	Visible all around; higher intensity on the range line.
9875	GULFPORT UPPER REACH INBOUND RANGE REAR LIGHT 1,672 yards, 323.7° from front light.	30-21-52.325N 089-05-41.541W	Oc R 4s	81		KRW on skeleton tower on block.	Visible 2° each side of rangeline. Ra ref.
9880	- LIGHT 51	30-18-37.151N 089-03-00.364W	Fl G 4s	17	4	SG on pile.	Ra ref.
9885	- LIGHT 52	30-18-39.567N 089-02-54.095W	Fl R 4s	17	3	TR on pile.	Ra ref.
9890	- LIGHT 53	30-19-00.834N 089-03-20.628W	Fl G 2.5s	17	3	SG on pile.	Ra ref.
9895	- LIGHT 54	30-19-04.852N 089-03-15.556W	Fl R 2.5s	17	3	TR on pile.	Ra ref.
9905	- LIGHT 55	30-19-25.215N 089-03-41.160W	Fl G 4s	17	4	SG on pile.	Ra ref.
9910	- LIGHT 56	30-19-29.146N 089-03-35.962W	Fl R 4s	17	3	TR on pile.	Ra ref.
9915	- LIGHT 57	30-19-49.638N 089-04-01.806W	Fl G 6s	17	4	SG on pile.	Ra ref.
9920	- LIGHT 58	30-19-53.383N 089-03-56.519W	Fl R 6s	17	4	TR on pile.	Ra ref.
9925	- LIGHT 59	30-20-14.013N 089-04-22.786W	Fl G 4s	17	4	SG on pile.	Ra ref.
9930	- LIGHT 60	30-20-18.713N 089-04-18.131W	Fl R 4s	17	3	TR on pile.	Ra ref.
9935	- LIGHT 61	30-20-38.338N 089-04-43.148W	Fl G 2.5s	17	4	SG on pile.	Ra ref.
9940	- LIGHT 62	30-20-41.858N 089-04-37.637W	Fl R 2.5s	17	3	TR on pile.	Ra ref.
9945	- LIGHT 63	30-20-54.269N 089-04-56.576W	Q G	17	3	SG on pile.	Ra ref.
9950	PORT AUTHORITY DOLPHIN LIGHT	30-20-51.120N 089-05-12.180W	Fl R 6s			On dolphin.	Private aid.
9952	PORT OF GULFPORT MOORING PILE LIGHTS (4)	30-21-31.300N 089-05-33.370W	Fl W 2.5s			Marks T-pier mooring piles.	Private aid.
			GULF COAST (Louisiana) - Eighth District				
	DOG KEYS PASS TO WAVELAND (Chart 11372)						
	Courthouse Road Boat Launch Channel						
9955	- LIGHT 2	30-22-18.000N 089-02-40.000W	Fl R 2.5s	14		TR on pile.	Private aid.
9960	- Day beacon 3	30-22-22.000N 089-02-41.000W				SG on pile.	Private aid.
9965	- Day beacon 4	30-22-25.000N 089-02-40.000W				TR on pile.	Private aid.
9970	- Day beacon 5	30-22-28.000N 089-02-41.000W				SG on pile.	Private aid.
			MISSISSIPPI - Eighth District				
	DOG KEYS PASS TO WAVELAND (Chart 11372)						
	Gulfport Small Boat Harbor						
9975	- Buoy 1	30-20-42.770N 089-04-52.681W				Green can.	
9980	- LIGHT 3 30 feet outside channel limits.	30-20-35.504N 089-05-16.900W	Fl G 2.5s	17	4	SG on pile.	Ra ref.
9985	- Day beacon 4 30 feet outside channel limit.	30-20-37.887N 089-05-16.951W				TR on pile.	Ra ref.

Light List corrected through LNM week: 01/18

(1) No.	(2) Name and Location	(3) Position	(4) Characteristic	(5) Height	(6) Range	(7) Structure	(8) Remarks
	MISSISSIPPI - Eighth District						
	DOG KEYS PASS TO WAVELAND (Chart 11372)						
	Gulfport Small Boat Harbor						
9990	- LIGHT 5 30 feet outside channel limits.	30-20-47.470N 089-05-40.188W	Q G	17	3	SG on pile.	Ra ref.
9995	- Day beacon 6 30 feet outside channel limit.	30-20-49.279N 089-05-38.771W				TR on pile.	Ra ref.
10000	- Day beacon 5A 30 feet outside channel limit.	30-21-02.896N 089-05-52.307W				SG on pile.	Ra ref.
10005	- Buoy 6A	30-21-18.107N 089-06-00.112W				Red nun.	
10010	- LIGHT 7 30 feet outside channel limits.	30-21-18.748N 089-06-03.664W	Fl G 4s	17	4	SG on pile.	Ra ref.
10015	- Buoy 8	30-21-21.648N 089-05-58.436W				Red nun.	
10020	GULFPORT HARBOR LIGHTHOUSE	30-21-22.000N 089-05-12.000W	Fl W 4s	46		On skeleton tower.	Private aid.
	Gulfport Yacht Basin Channel						
10025	- LIGHT 2	30-21-13.046N 089-04-56.040W	Q R	17	4	TR on dolphin.	Ra ref.
10030	- Day beacon 3	30-21-14.919N 089-04-59.251W				SG on pile.	Ra ref.
10035	- LIGHT 4	30-21-20.395N 089-05-01.844W	Fl R 2.5s	17	3	TR on pile.	Ra ref.
10040	- Day beacon 5 20 feet outside channel limit.	30-21-24.534N 089-05-07.362W				SG on pile.	Ra ref.
10045	- LIGHT 6	30-21-29.207N 089-05-08.699W	Fl R 6s	17	3	TR on pile.	Ra ref.
10050	- Day beacon 7	30-21-30.495N 089-05-12.540W				SG on pile.	Ra ref.
10055	- LIGHT 8	30-21-32.412N 089-05-12.234W	Fl R 4s	20	3	TR on dolphin.	Ra ref.
10060	- Day beacon 9	30-21-33.614N 089-05-15.396W				SG on pile.	Ra ref.
10065	- LIGHT 10	30-21-35.960N 089-05-15.360W	Fl (2)R 5s	17	3	TR on pile.	Ra ref.
	Mississippi Sound						
10070	- PIPELINE LIGHT CP-5	30-13-39.050N 089-00-45.930W	Q W	13		On pile.	Private aid.
	Long Beach Harbor						
10075	- ENTRANCE LIGHT 1	30-20-25.000N 089-08-22.000W	Fl G 4s	14		SG on pile.	Private aid.
10080	- ENTRANCE LIGHT 2	30-20-26.000N 089-08-21.000W	Fl R 4s	14		TR on pile.	Private aid.
10085	- Day beacon 3	30-20-27.000N 089-08-24.000W				SG on pile.	Private aid.
10090	- Day beacon 4	30-20-28.000N 089-08-23.000W				TR on pile.	Private aid.
10095	- Day beacon 5	30-20-29.000N 089-08-26.000W				SG on pile.	Private aid.
10100	- Day beacon 6	30-20-30.000N 089-08-24.000W				TR on pile.	Private aid.
10105	- Day beacon 7	30-20-30.000N 089-08-27.000W				SG on pile.	Private aid.
10110	- Day beacon 8	30-20-31.000N 089-08-28.000W				TR on pile.	Private aid.
10115	- Day beacon 9	30-20-32.000N 089-08-28.000W				SG on pile.	Private aid.
10120	- Day beacon 10	30-20-33.000N 089-08-27.000W				TR on pile.	Private aid.
10125	- Day beacon 11	30-20-32.000N 089-08-29.000W				SG on pile.	Private aid.

Light List corrected through LNM week: 01/18

(1) No.	(2) Name and Location	(3) Position	(4) Characteristic	(5) Height	(6) Range	(7) Structure	(8) Remarks
			MISSISSIPPI - Eighth District				
	DOG KEYS PASS TO WAVELAND (Chart 11372)						
	Long Beach Harbor						
10130	- Day beacon 12	30-20-33.000N 089-08-29.000W				TR on pile.	Private aid.
10135	- Day beacon 13	30-20-32.000N 089-08-30.000W				SG on pile.	Private aid.
10140	- Day beacon 14	30-20-33.000N 089-08-31.000W				TR on pile.	Private aid.
	Cat Island Channel						
10145	- Buoy A	30-10-46.719N 089-07-25.133W				Red and white stripes.	
10150	- Buoy B	30-11-24.919N 089-08-33.635W				Red and white stripes.	
10155	- Buoy C	30-12-02.717N 089-09-48.138W				Red and white stripes.	
10160	- Buoy D	30-12-32.717N 089-10-59.141W				Red and white stripes.	
10165	- Buoy E	30-12-16.467N 089-12-32.245W				Red and white stripes.	
10170	- Buoy F	30-11-46.816N 089-13-30.247W				Red and white stripes.	
10175	- West Buoy 2	30-10-55.864N 089-14-49.015W				Red nun.	
10180	- West Buoy 4	30-10-00.697N 089-16-11.836W				Red nun.	
	Mississippi Sound						
	Pass Christian						
10185	- ENTRANCE EAST LIGHT 2	30-18-33.490N 089-14-13.672W	Fl R 6s	17	4	TR on pile.	Ra ref.
10190	- BREAKWATER LIGHT 4	30-18-37.354N 089-14-49.860W	Q R	20	3	TR on skeleton tower.	
10195	- ENTRANCE WEST LIGHT 1	30-18-15.160N 089-15-13.214W	Fl G 6s	17	4	SG on pile.	Ra ref.
10200	- ENTRANCE WEST LIGHT 2A	30-18-27.400N 089-14-59.444W	Fl R 2.5s	17	3	TR on pile.	Ra ref.
10202	Mississippi DMR Oyster Reef Buoys (8)	30-17-08.220N 089-14-43.140W				Marks oyster reef perimeter.	Private aid.
	St. Louis Bay						
	Bayou Portage Channel						
10205	- LIGHT 1	30-19-54.072N 089-18-18.089W	Q G	17	3	SG on dolphin.	Ra ref.
10210	- Day beacon 2	30-20-24.244N 089-17-53.252W				TR on pile.	Ra ref.
10215	- LIGHT 3	30-20-33.053N 089-17-51.575W	Q G	17	3	SG on pile.	Ra ref.
10220	- Day beacon 4	30-20-31.471N 089-17-41.726W				TR on pile.	Ra ref.
10225	- Day beacon 5	30-20-33.291N 089-17-14.641W				SG on pile.	Ra ref.
10230	- LIGHT 7	30-20-34.158N 089-16-37.623W	Fl G 4s	17	4	SG on dolphin.	Ra ref.
10235	- Day beacon 9	30-20-33.479N 089-16-13.545W				SG on pile.	Ra ref.
10240	- Buoy 12	30-20-30.120N 089-15-27.870W				Red nun.	
10245	- LIGHT 13	30-20-33.558N 089-15-18.652W	Q G	17	3	SG on dolphin.	Ra ref.
10250	- Buoy 14	30-20-24.790N 089-15-17.620W				Red nun.	
	Wolf River						
10255	- Preferred Channel Day beacon A	30-20-18.715N 089-18-01.011W				JG on pile.	Ra ref.
10260	- LIGHT 3	30-20-51.735N 089-18-01.420W	Fl G 4s	17	4	SG on dolphin.	Ra ref.

MISSISSIPPI - Eighth District

(1) No.	(2) Name and Location	(3) Position	(4) Characteristic	(5) Height	(6) Range	(7) Structure	(8) Remarks
	DOG KEYS PASS TO WAVELAND (Chart 11372)						
	St. Louis Bay						
	Wolf River						
10265	- LIGHT 5	30-21-16.293N 089-17-46.402W	Q G	17	3	SG on pile.	Ra ref.
	St. Louis Bay						
10270	NOAA BAY WAVELAND TIDE MONITORING PLATFORM LIGHT	30-19-34.510N 089-19-33.390W	Fl Y 2.5s	30		On platform.	Private aid.
10275	DUPONT DIFFUSER PLATFORM LIGHT 1	30-22-16.100N 089-19-05.200W	Fl W 4s	18		NW on protective structure worded DANGER SUBMERGED PIPE.	Private aid.
	Jourdan River Channel						
10280	- Day beacon 3	30-20-40.291N 089-19-31.688W				SG on pile.	Ra ref.
10285	- LIGHT 5	30-20-55.784N 089-19-57.118W	Fl G 4s	17	4	SG on pile.	Ra ref.
10290	- Day beacon 7	30-20-44.704N 089-20-31.669W				SG on pile.	Ra ref.
10295	- Day beacon 9	30-20-31.803N 089-21-06.407W				SG on pile.	Ra ref.
	Bay Cove Marina to Casino Magic Marina						
10300	- Day beacon 1	30-20-21.500N 089-21-18.000W				SG on pile.	Private aid.
10305	- Day beacon 2	30-20-18.000N 089-21-17.500W				TR on pile.	Private aid.
10310	- Day beacon 3	30-20-14.500N 089-21-17.000W				SG on pile.	Private aid.
	Mississippi Sound						
10315	U.S.G.S. PASS MARIANNE MONITORING PLATFORM LIGHT	30-14-17.000N 089-14-34.000W	Fl Y 2.5s	37			Maintained by U.S. Geological Survey. Private aid.
10320	- WRECK LIGHT WR4	30-15-33.568N 089-14-23.893W	Q R	17	3	TR on pile.	Ra ref.
10325	U.S. GEOLOGICAL SURVEY SCIENTIFIC MONITORING PLATFORM LIGHT (SBP)	30-07-22.100N 089-15-01.000W	Fl Y 2.5s	37		On pipe.	Private aid.
10330	SQUARE HANDKERCHIEF SHOAL LIGHT SH	30-15-49.135N 089-19-37.237W	Fl (2+1)G 6s	17	3	JG on pile.	Ra ref.
10335	SQUARE HANDKERCHIEF SHOAL LIGHT 2	30-15-59.779N 089-18-57.174W	Fl R 2.5s	17	4	TR on pile.	Ra ref.
10340	MISSISSIPPI GULF FISHING BANKS BREAKWATER LIGHT A	30-16-14.500N 089-18-49.000W	Fl Y 2.5s			NY on pile.	Marks Breakwater. Private aid.
10345	SQUARE HANDKERCHIEF SHOAL LIGHT 4	30-16-23.365N 089-18-58.347W	Fl R 4s	17	4	TR on pile.	Ra ref.
10350	HANCOCK COUNTY BOAT RAMP LIGHT 1	30-18-04.000N 089-19-40.000W	Fl G 2.5s	7		Marks end of jetty.	Private aid.
10355	HANCOCK COUNTY BOAT RAMP LIGHT 2	30-18-05.000N 089-19-39.000W	Fl R 2.5s	7		Marks end of jetty.	Private aid.
10357	CITY OF BAY ST. LOUIS DANGER LIGHTS (6)	30-18-43.900N 089-19-11.200W	Fl W 2.5s			Marks submerged pier debris.	Private aid.
10357.01	CITY OF BAY ST. LOUIS MUNICIPAL PIER LIGHT 1	30-18-40.700N 089-19-12.200W	Fl G 2.5s			Marks entrance of port side pier structure.	Private aid.
10357.02	CITY OF BAY ST. LOUIS MUNICIPAL PIER LIGHT 2	30-18-41.700N 089-19-12.700W	Fl R 2.5s			Marks entrance of starboard side pier structure.	Private aid.
	Mississippi Fishing Reef FR-MS-04						
10360	- Day beacon A	30-17-30.400N 089-20-12.500W				NY on pile worded FISHING REEF FR-MS-04.	Private aid.

Light List corrected through LNM week: 01/18

(1) No.	(2) Name and Location	(3) Position	(4) Characteristic	(5) Height	(6) Range	(7) Structure	(8) Remarks
	MISSISSIPPI - Eighth District						

DOG KEYS PASS TO WAVELAND (Chart 11372)
Mississippi Sound
Mississippi Fishing Reef FR-MS-04

10365	- Day beacon B	30-17-16.600N 089-21-00.100W				NY on pile worded FISHING REEF FR-MS-04.	Private aid.
10370	MISSISSIPPI GULF FISH REEF LIGHT F	30-16-55.200N 089-21-50.400W	Fl Y 6s			NY on pile.	Private aid.
10375	- LIGHT C	30-17-12.600N 089-20-36.100W	Fl Y 6s	7		NY on pile worded FISHING REEF FR-MS-04.	Private aid.
10380	GARFIELD LADNER MEMORIAL PIER LIGHT	30-16-50.020N 089-21-53.560W	Fl R 2.5s	10		On pier.	Private aid.

Mississippi Sound

10385	MISSISSIPPI DMR BREAKWATER DANGER LIGHTS (7)	30-15-10.140N 089-23-02.220W	Fl W 2.5s	10		NW on pile worded DANGER BREAKWATER.	Private aid.

WAVELAND TO CATAHOULA BAY (Chart 11367)
Bayou Caddy

10390	- LIGHT 1	30-13-51.905N 089-24-07.210W	Fl G 6s	17	4	SG on dolphin.	Ra ref.
10395	- Day beacon 2	30-14-03.172N 089-24-22.440W				TR on pile.	Ra ref.
10400	- Day beacon 3	30-14-09.294N 089-24-41.486W				SG on pile.	Ra ref.
10405	- LIGHT 4	30-14-22.139N 089-25-01.144W	Q R	17	3	TR on dolphin.	Ra ref.
10410	- LIGHT 5	30-14-17.909N 089-25-28.316W	Fl G 2.5s	17	3	SG on pile.	Ra ref.
10415	HANCOCK COUNTY BREALWATER DANGER LIGHT NORTH	30-14-23.100N 089-25-20.210W	Fl W 2.5s			NW on pile.	Private aid.
10420	HANCOCK COUNTY BREALWATER DANGER LIGHT SOUTH (10)	30-14-08.480N 089-24-47.230W	Fl W 2.5s			NW on pile.	Private aid.

LAKE BORGNE AND APPROACHES (Chart 11371)
Mississippi Sound

10425	U.S.G.S. ST. JOE PASS MONIITORING PLATFORM LIGHT	30-11-04.000N 089-25-34.000W	Fl Y 2.5s	37			Maintained by U.S. Geological Survey. Private aid.
10427	ROBERT CAMPO AQUACULTURE SPECIAL LIGHT A	30-01-40.320N 089-25-40.190W	Fl Y 2.5s			Marks perimeter corner of aquaculture farm.	Private aid.
10427.01	ROBERT CAMPO AQUACULTURE SPECIAL LIGHT B	30-01-37.600N 089-25-41.650W	Fl Y 2.5s			Marks perimeter corner of aquaculture farm.	Private aid.
10427.02	ROBERT CAMPO AQUACULTURE SPECIAL LIGHT C	30-01-37.120N 089-25-32.820W	Fl Y 2.5s			Marks perimeter corner of aquaculture farm.	Private aid.
10427.03	ROBERT CAMPO AQUACULTURE SPECIAL LIGHT D	30-01-34.670N 089-25-34.330W	Fl Y 2.5s			Marks perimeter corner of aquaculture farm.	Private aid.
10429	MISSISSIPPI DEPARTMENT OF ENVIRONMENTAL QUALITY DANGER LIGHT	30-10-41.340N 089-27-29.910W	Fl W 2.5s			Marks submerged breakwater structure.	Private aid.

LOUISIANA - Eighth District

WAVELAND TO CATAHOULA BAY (Chart 11367)
Pearl River Entrance Channel

10430 34640	- LIGHT 1 30 feet outside channel limit.	30-09-20.881N 089-31-29.549W	Fl G 4s	17	4	SG-TY on pile.	Ra ref.
10435	- Day beacon 3	30-09-37.207N 089-31-28.963W				SG on pile.	Ra ref.
10440	- Day beacon 5	30-09-53.016N 089-31-28.291W				SG on pile.	Ra ref.

LOUISIANA - Eighth District

WAVELAND TO CATAHOULA BAY (Chart 11367)
Pearl River Entrance Channel

(1) No.	(2) Name and Location	(3) Position	(4) Characteristic	(5) Height	(6) Range	(7) Structure	(8) Remarks
10445	- Day beacon 7	30-10-20.482N 089-31-26.070W				SG on pile.	Ra ref.
10450	- LIGHT 7A	30-10-58.271N 089-31-38.960W	Fl G 6s	17	3	SG on platform on piles.	Ra ref.
10455	- LIGHT 8	30-11-00.336N 089-31-28.214W	Fl R 4s	17	3	TR on pile.	Ra ref.
10457	MISSISSIPPI DEQ DANGER BREAKWATER LIGHT	30-10-59.060N 089-31-22.020W	Fl W 2.5s			Marks shoreline protection breakwater.	Private aid.
10457.01	MISSISSIPPI DEQ DANGER BREAKWATER LIGHT	30-10-59.300N 089-31-16.720W	Fl W 2.5s			Marks shoreline protection breakwater.	Private aid.
10457.02	MISSISSIPPI DEQ DANGER BREAKWATER LIGHT	30-10-59.020N 089-31-14.350W	Fl W 2.5s			Marks shoreline protection breakwater.	Private aid.
10457.03	MISSISSIPPI DEQ DANGER BREAKWATER LIGHT	30-11-00.300N 089-31-07.520W	Fl W 2.5s			Marks shoreline protection breakwater.	Private aid.
10457.04	MISSISSIPPI DEQ DANGER BREAKWATER LIGHT	30-11-00.540N 089-31-05.130W	Fl W 2.5s			Marks shoreline protection breakwater.	Private aid.
10457.05	MISSISSIPPI DEQ DANGER BREAKWATER LIGHT	30-11-02.190N 089-30-56.570W	Fl W 2.5s			Marks shoreline protection breakwater.	Private aid.
10457.06	MISSISSIPPI DEQ DANGER BREAKWATER LIGHT	30-11-05.270N 089-30-51.800W	Fl W 2.5s			Marks shoreline protection breakwater.	Private aid.
10457.07	MISSISSIPPI DEQ DANGER BREAKWATER LIGHT	30-11-00.300N 089-31-07.520W	Fl W 2.5s			Marks shoreline protection breakwater.	Private aid.
10457.08	MISSISSIPPI DEQ DANGER BREAKWATER LIGHT	30-11-02.240N 089-30-38.110W	Fl W 2.5s			Marks shoreline protection breakwater.	Private aid.
10457.09	MISSISSIPPI DEQ DANGER BREAKWATER LIGHT	30-11-02.440N 089-30-30.930W	Fl W 2.5s			Marks shoreline protection breakwater.	Private aid.
10457.11	MISSISSIPPI DEQ DANGER BREAKWATER LIGHT	30-11-00.390N 089-30-19.220W	Fl W 2.5s			Marks shoreline protection breakwater.	Private aid.
10457.12	MISSISSIPPI DEQ DANGER BREAKWATER LIGHT	30-11-00.500N 089-30-09.650W	Fl W 2.5s			Marks shoreline protection breakwater.	Private aid.
10457.13	MISSISSIPPI DEQ DANGER BREAKWATER LIGHT	30-10-58.810N 089-30-04.150W	Fl W 2.5s			Marks shoreline protection breakwater.	Private aid.
10457.14	MISSISSIPPI DEQ DANGER BREAKWATER LIGHT	30-10-56.900N 089-29-59.910W	Fl W 2.5s			Marks shoreline protection breakwater.	Private aid.
10457.15	MISSISSIPPI DEQ DANGER BREAKWATER LIGHT	30-10-56.150N 089-29-50.380W	Fl W 2.5s			Marks shoreline protection breakwater.	Private aid.
10457.16	MISSISSIPPI DEQ DANGER BREAKWATER LIGHT	30-10-57.780N 089-29-43.110W	Fl W 2.5s			Marks shoreline protection breakwater.	Private aid.
10457.17	MISSISSIPPI DEQ DANGER BREAKWATER LIGHT	30-10-59.270N 089-29-36.480W	Fl W 2.5s			Marks shoreline protection breakwater.	Private aid.
10457.18	MISSISSIPPI DEQ DANGER BREAKWATER LIGHT	30-10-59.990N 089-29-32.200W	Fl W 2.5s			Marks shoreline protection breakwater.	Private aid.
10457.28	MISSISSIPPI DEQ DANGER BREAKWATER LIGHT	30-10-36.562N 089-27-59.130W	Fl W 2.5s			Marks breakwater.	Private aid.
10457.29	MISSISSIPPI DEQ DANGER BREAKWATER LIGHT	30-10-32.804N 089-27-56.840W	Fl W 2.5s			Marks breakwater.	Private aid.
10457.31	MISSISSIPPI DEQ DANGER BREAKWATER LIGHT	30-10-31.483N 089-27-51.970W	Fl W 2.5s			Marks breakwater.	Private aid.

Light List corrected through LNM week: 01/18

(1) No.	(2) Name and Location	(3) Position	(4) Characteristic	(5) Height	(6) Range	(7) Structure	(8) Remarks
		LOUISIANA - Eighth District					
	WAVELAND TO CATAHOULA BAY (Chart 11367)						
	Pearl River Entrance Channel						
10457.32	MISSISSIPPI DEQ DANGER BREAKWATER LIGHT	30-10-32.433N 089-27-44.910W	Fl W 2.5s			Marks breakwater.	Private aid.
10457.33	MISSISSIPPI DEQ DANGER BREAKWATER LIGHT	30-10-33.979N 089-27-40.470W	Fl W 2.5s			Marks breakwater.	Private aid.
10457.34	MISSISSIPPI DEQ DANGER BREAKWATER LIGHT	30-10-38.495N 089-27-32.450W	Fl W 2.5s			Marks breakwater.	Private aid.
10457.35	MISSISSIPPI DEQ DANGER BREAKWATER LIGHT	30-10-45.203N 089-27-26.920W	Fl W 2.5s			Marks breakwater.	Private aid.
10457.36	MISSISSIPPI DEQ DANGER BREAKWATER LIGHT	30-10-53.429N 089-27-20.820W	Fl W 2.5s			Marks breakwater.	Private aid.
10457.37	MISSISSIPPI DEQ DANGER BREAKWATER LIGHT	30-11-00.001N 089-27-11.130W	Fl W 2.5s			Marks breakwater.	Private aid.
10457.38	MISSISSIPPI DEQ DANGER BREAKWATER LIGHT	30-11-00.085N 089-27-09.430W	Fl W 2.5s			Marks breakwater.	Private aid.
10457.39	MISSISSIPPI DEQ DANGER BREAKWATER LIGHT	30-11-01.549N 089-27-05.210W	Fl W 2.5s			Marks breakwater.	Private aid.
10457.41	MISSISSIPPI DEQ DANGER BREAKWATER LIGHT	30-11-08.034N 089-26-59.620W	Fl W 2.5s			Marks breakwater.	Private aid.
10457.42	MISSISSIPPI DEQ DANGER BREAKWATER LIGHT	30-11-14.153N 089-26-52.350W	Fl W 2.5s			Marks breakwater.	Private aid.
10457.43	MISSISSIPPI DEQ DANGER BREAKWATER LIGHT	30-11-15.831N 089-26-50.930W	Fl W 2.5s			Marks breakwater.	Private aid.
10457.44	MISSISSIPPI DEQ DANGER BREAKWATER LIGHT	30-11-23.714N 089-26-48.020W	Fl W 2.5s			Marks breakwater.	Private aid.
10457.45	MISSISSIPPI DEQ DANGER BREAKWATER LIGHT	30-11-33.649N 089-26-50.980W	Fl W 2.5s			Marks breakwater.	Private aid.
10457.46	MISSISSIPPI DEQ DANGER BREAKWATER LIGHT	30-11-39.868N 089-26-50.460W	Fl W 2.5s			Marks breakwater.	Private aid.
10457.47	MISSISSIPPI DEQ DANGER BREAKWATER LIGHT	30-11-40.977N 089-26-51.770W	Fl W 2.5s			Marks breakwater.	Private aid.
10457.48	MISSISSIPPI DEQ DANGER BREAKWATER LIGHT	30-11-41.323N 089-26-52.170W	Fl W 2.5s			Marks breakwater.	Private aid.
10457.49	MISSISSIPPI DEQ DANGER BREAKWATER LIGHT	30-11-53.420N 089-26-54.800W	Fl W 2.5s			Marks breakwater.	Private aid.
10457.51	MISSISSIPPI DEQ DANGER BREAKWATER LIGHT	30-12-03.263N 089-26-56.090W	Fl W 2.5s			Marks breakwater.	Private aid.
10457.52	MISSISSIPPI DEQ DANGER BREAKWATER LIGHT	30-12-05.917N 089-26-55.250W	Fl W 2.5s			Marks breakwater.	Private aid.
10457.53	MISSISSIPPI DEQ DANGER BREAKWATER LIGHT	30-12-08.692N 089-26-48.560W	Fl W 2.5s			Marks breakwater.	Private aid.
10457.54	MISSISSIPPI DEQ DANGER BREAKWATER LIGHT	30-12-19.085N 089-26-48.590W	Fl W 2.5s			Marks breakwater.	Private aid.
10457.55	MISSISSIPPI DEQ DANGER BREAKWATER LIGHT	30-12-34.230N 089-26-36.110W	Fl W 2.5s			Marks breakwater.	Private aid.
10457.56	MISSISSIPPI DEQ DANGER BREAKWATER LIGHT	30-12-38.901N 089-26-31.450W	Fl W 2.5s			Marks breakwater.	Private aid.
10457.57	MISSISSIPPI DEQ DANGER BREAKWATER LIGHT	30-12-39.889N 089-26-29.340W	Fl W 2.5s			Marks breakwater.	Private aid.
10457.58	MISSISSIPPI DEQ DANGER BREAKWATER LIGHT	30-12-40.748N 089-26-27.420W	Fl W 2.5s			Marks breakwater.	Private aid.
10457.59	MISSISSIPPI DEQ DANGER BREAKWATER LIGHT	30-12-42.227N 089-26-25.430W	Fl W 2.5s			Marks breakwater.	Private aid.
10457.61	MISSISSIPPI DEQ DANGER BREAKWATER LIGHT	30-12-51.776N 089-26-12.790W	Fl W 2.5s			Marks breakwater.	Private aid.
10457.62	MISSISSIPPI DEQ DANGER BREAKWATER LIGHT	30-12-56.964N 089-26-08.810W	Fl W 2.5s			Marks breakwater.	Private aid.
10457.63	MISSISSIPPI DEQ DANGER BREAKWATER LIGHT	30-13-04.396N 089-26-04.780W	Fl W 2.5s			Marks breakwater.	Private aid.
	Little Lake						
10460	- LIGHT 1	30-09-35.806N 089-37-49.344W	Fl G 2.5s	17	4	SG on dolphin.	Ra ref.
10465	- Buoy 2	30-09-30.210N 089-37-40.501W				Red nun.	
10470	- Day beacon 3	30-09-38.927N 089-37-40.934W				SG on pile.	Ra ref.

(1) No.	(2) Name and Location	(3) Position	(4) Characteristic	(5) Height	(6) Range	(7) Structure	(8) Remarks
			LOUISIANA - Eighth District				
	WAVELAND TO CATAHOULA BAY (Chart 11367)						
	Little Lake						
10475	- Day beacon 4	30-09-42.898N 089-37-29.843W				TR on pile.	Ra ref.
10480	- Day beacon 5	30-09-45.810N 089-37-34.201W				SG on pile.	Ra ref.
10485	- LIGHT 7	30-10-05.810N 089-37-04.400W	Fl G 4s	17	4	SG on pile.	Ra ref.
10490	- Day beacon 9	30-10-17.748N 089-36-38.661W				SG on pile.	Ra ref.
10495	- LIGHT 10	30-10-14.460N 089-36-35.194W	Fl R 6s	17	4	TR on pile.	Ra ref.
10500	- LIGHT 11	30-10-36.330N 089-36-04.497W	Fl G 2.5s	17	3	SG on dolphin.	Ra ref.
	Little Lake North Pass						
10505	- Day beacon 2	30-10-41.375N 089-36-02.210W				TR on pile.	Ra ref.
10510	- Day beacon 3	30-10-39.928N 089-36-24.672W				SG on pile.	Ra ref.
10515	- Buoy 5	30-10-43.028N 089-36-39.024W				Green can.	
	Little Lake						
10520	- Day beacon 13	30-10-46.709N 089-35-44.198W				SG on pile.	Ra ref.
10525	- LIGHT 14	30-10-42.606N 089-35-42.481W	Fl R 4s	17	3	TR on pile.	Ra ref.
10530	- LIGHT 15	30-11-01.209N 089-35-08.896W	Fl G 2.5s	17	3	SG on pile.	Ra ref.
10535	- Day beacon 16	30-10-53.940N 089-35-08.564W				TR on pile.	Ra ref.
10540	- Buoy 18	30-10-56.612N 089-34-50.296W				Red nun.	
10545	- Day beacon 19	30-11-03.704N 089-34-50.743W				SG on pile.	Ra ref.
			MISSISSIPPI - LOUISIANA - Eighth District				
	WAVELAND TO CATAHOULA BAY (Chart 11367)						
	Pearl River						
10550	- LIGHT 21	30-11-05.189N 089-34-48.589W	Q G	17	3	SG on dolphin.	Ra ref.
10555	- Day beacon 23	30-11-18.077N 089-35-04.569W				SG on pile.	Ra ref.
10560	- LIGHT 23A	30-11-40.028N 089-35-18.500W	Fl G 6s	17	4	SG on pile.	Ra ref.
10565	- Day beacon 24	30-11-42.230N 089-35-09.295W				TR on pile.	Ra ref.
10570	- LIGHT 25	30-12-00.525N 089-35-23.254W	Fl G 4s	17	4	SG on pile.	Ra ref.
	Port Bienville						
10575	- JUNCTION LIGHT PB	30-12-25.816N 089-35-34.224W	Fl (2+1)R 6s	17	3	JR on pile.	Ra ref.
10580	- Day beacon 2	30-12-34.707N 089-35-22.198W				TR on pile.	Ra ref.
10585	- Day beacon 3	30-12-55.762N 089-35-12.661W				SG on pile.	Ra ref.
	Pearl River						
10590	- LIGHT 30	30-12-44.093N 089-35-44.736W	Fl R 2.5s	17	3	TR on pile.	Ra ref.
10595	- Day beacon 31	30-12-54.178N 089-36-05.196W				SG on pile.	Ra ref.
10600	- Day beacon 33	30-13-05.206N 089-36-37.701W				SG on pile.	Ra ref.

MISSISSIPPI - LOUISIANA - Eighth District

WAVELAND TO CATAHOULA BAY (Chart 11367)
Pearl River

(1) No.	(2) Name and Location	(3) Position	(4) Characteristic	(5) Height	(6) Range	(7) Structure	(8) Remarks
10605	- LIGHT 35	30-13-15.022N 089-36-54.228W	Fl G 4s	17	4	SG on pile.	Ra ref.
10610	- Day beacon 36	30-13-20.296N 089-36-55.260W				TR on pile.	Ra ref.
10615	- Day beacon 38	30-13-33.756N 089-36-59.139W				TR on pile.	Ra ref.
10620	- Day beacon 40	30-14-48.790N 089-36-53.514W				TR on pile.	Ra ref.
10625	- Day beacon 41	30-14-54.766N 089-37-21.372W				SG on pile.	Ra ref.
10630	- LIGHT 43	30-15-27.702N 089-37-59.205W	Fl G 2.5s	17	3	SG on pile.	Ra ref.
10635	- Day beacon 45	30-15-42.202N 089-37-55.212W				SG on pile.	Ra ref.
10640	- Day beacon 48	30-15-58.318N 089-37-33.480W				TR on pile.	Ra ref.
10645	- Day beacon 49	30-16-07.690N 089-37-59.268W				SG on pile.	Ra ref.
10650	- Day beacon 50	30-16-42.586N 089-37-48.126W				TR on pile.	Ra ref.
10655	- Day beacon 51	30-17-08.038N 089-38-18.294W				SG on pile.	Ra ref.
10660	- Day beacon 52	30-17-16.900N 089-38-14.908W				TR on pile.	Ra ref.
10665	- Day beacon 55	30-17-32.008N 089-38-50.220W				SG on pile.	Ra ref.
10670	- Day beacon 57	30-18-20.344N 089-38-33.004W				SG on pile.	Ra ref.
10675	- LIGHT 59	30-18-27.838N 089-38-22.337W	Fl G 2.5s	17	3	SG on pile.	Ra ref.
10680	- Day beacon 60	30-18-28.066N 089-38-11.094W				TR on pile.	Ra ref.
10685	- Day beacon 61	30-18-33.169N 089-37-57.699W				SG on pile.	Ra ref.
10690	- LIGHT 62	30-18-53.196N 089-37-33.054W	Fl R 2.5s	17	3	TR on dolphin.	Ra ref.
10695	- Day beacon 63	30-19-05.734N 089-37-51.144W				SG on pile.	Ra ref.
10700	- Day beacon 63A	30-19-11.000N 089-37-52.000W				SG on pile.	Ra ref.
10705	- Day beacon 64	30-19-18.574N 089-37-45.414W				TR on pile.	Ra ref.
10710	- Day beacon 66	30-19-31.159N 089-37-51.039W				TR on pile.	Ra ref.
10715	- Day beacon 67	30-19-42.244N 089-37-58.884W				SG on pile.	Ra ref.
10720	- Day beacon 68	30-20-04.479N 089-37-48.039W				TR on pile.	Ra ref.
10725	- Day beacon 70	30-20-16.018N 089-37-50.532W				TR on pile.	Ra ref.
10730	- Day beacon 72	30-20-26.528N 089-37-59.344W				TR on pile.	Ra ref.
10735	- Day beacon 73	30-20-37.998N 089-38-06.011W				SG on pile.	Ra ref.

Light List corrected through LNM week: 01/18

(1) No.	(2) Name and Location	(3) Position	(4) Characteristic	(5) Height	(6) Range	(7) Structure	(8) Remarks
			LOUISIANA - Eighth District				
	WAVELAND TO CATAHOULA BAY (Chart 11367)						
	West Pearl River						
	River is marked with numerous unlisted, unlighted buoys which are periodically relocated to meet changing conditions.						
10740	- Buoy 1	30-09-40.710N 089-38-58.204W				Green can.	Ra ref.
10745	- Buoy 2	30-09-42.803N 089-38-53.000W				Red nun.	Ra ref.
10750	LAKE BORGNE LIGHT WR2	30-06-37.127N 089-30-44.506W	Q R	17	3	TR on pile.	
	LAKE BORGNE AND APPROACHES (Chart 11371)						
	Lake Borgne						
10755	NOAA SHELL BEACH TIDE MONITORING PLATFORM LIGHT	29-52-05.240N 089-40-23.510W	Fl Y 2.5s	30		On platform.	Private aid.
10758	BILOXI MARSH WILDLIFE MANAGEMENT AREA DANGER BREAKWATER LIGHT	29-52-53.480N 089-35-49.860W	Fl W 2.5s			Marks shoreline restoration breakwater.	Private aid.
10758.01	BILOXI MARSH WILDLIFE MANAGEMENT AREA DANGER BREAKWATER LIGHT	29-52-57.730N 089-35-42.890W	Fl W 2.5s			Marks shoreline restoration breakwater.	Private aid.
10758.02	BILOXI MARSH WILDLIFE MANAGEMENT AREA DANGER BREAKWATER LIGHT	29-53-03.420N 089-35-34.040W	Fl W 2.5s			Marks shoreline restoration breakwater.	Private aid.
10758.03	BILOXI MARSH WILDLIFE MANAGEMENT AREA DANGER BREAKWATER LIGHT	29-53-06.950N 089-35-26.360W	Fl W 2.5s			Marks shoreline restoration breakwater.	Private aid.
10758.04	BILOXI MARSH WILDLIFE MANAGEMENT AREA DANGER BREAKWATER LIGHT	29-53-11.780N 089-35-28.150W	Fl W 2.5s			Marks shoreline restoration breakwater.	Private aid.
10758.05	BILOXI MARSH WILDLIFE MANAGEMENT AREA DANGER BREAKWATER LIGHT	29-53-18.780N 089-35-27.450W	Fl W 2.5s			Marks shoreline restoration breakwater.	Private aid.
10758.06	BILOXI MARSH WILDLIFE MANAGEMENT AREA DANGER BREAKWATER LIGHT	29-53-28.170N 089-35-23.630W	Fl W 2.5s			Marks shoreline restoration breakwater.	Private aid.
10758.07	BILOXI MARSH WILDLIFE MANAGEMENT AREA DANGER BREAKWATER LIGHT	29-53-37.590N 089-35-23.370W	Fl W 2.5s			Marks shoreline restoration breakwater.	Private aid.
10758.08	BILOXI MARSH WILDLIFE MANAGEMENT AREA DANGER BREAKWATER LIGHT	29-53-46.690N 089-35-26.570W	Fl W 2.5s			Marks shoreline restoration breakwater.	Private aid.
10758.09	BILOXI MARSH WILDLIFE MANAGEMENT AREA DANGER BREAKWATER LIGHT	29-53-52.140N 089-35-24.880W	Fl W 2.5s			Marks shoreline restoration breakwater.	Private aid.
10758.11	BILOXI MARSH WILDLIFE MANAGEMENT AREA DANGER BREAKWATER LIGHT	29-54-01.370N 089-35-27.530W	Fl W 2.5s			Marks shoreline restoration breakwater.	Private aid.
10758.12	BILOXI MARSH WILDLIFE MANAGEMENT AREA DANGER BREAKWATER LIGHT	29-54-09.270N 089-35-29.380W	Fl W 2.5s			Marks shoreline restoration breakwater.	Private aid.
10758.13	BILOXI MARSH WILDLIFE MANAGEMENT AREA DANGER BREAKWATER LIGHT	29-54-14.270N 089-35-29.560W	Fl W 2.5s			Marks shoreline restoration breakwater.	Private aid.
10758.14	BILOXI MARSH WILDLIFE MANAGEMENT AREA DANGER BREAKWATER LIGHT	29-54-17.540N 089-35-29.770W	Fl W 2.5s			Marks shoreline restoration breakwater.	Private aid.

Light List corrected through LNM week: 01/18

(1) No.	(2) Name and Location	(3) Position	(4) Characteristic	(5) Height	(6) Range	(7) Structure	(8) Remarks
	**LOUISIANA - Eighth District**						

LAKE BORGNE AND APPROACHES (Chart 11371)

Lake Borgne

(1) No.	(2) Name and Location	(3) Position	(4) Characteristic	(5) Height	(6) Range	(7) Structure	(8) Remarks
10758.15	BILOXI MARSH WILDLIFE MANAGEMENT AREA DANGER BREAKWATER LIGHT	29-54-26.320N 089-35-30.310W	Fl W 2.5s			Marks shoreline restoration breakwater.	Private aid.
10758.16	BILOXI MARSH WILDLIFE MANAGEMENT AREA DANGER BREAKWATER LIGHT	29-54-36.450N 089-35-30.020W	Fl W 2.5s			Marks shoreline restoration breakwater.	Private aid.
10758.17	BILOXI MARSH WILDLIFE MANAGEMENT AREA DANGER BREAKWATER LIGHT	29-54-46.210N 089-35-28.470W	Fl W 2.5s			Marks shoreline restoration breakwater.	Private aid.
10758.18	BILOXI MARSH WILDLIFE MANAGEMENT AREA DANGER BREAKWATER LIGHT	29-54-55.730N 089-35-31.300W	Fl W 2.5s			Marks shoreline restoration breakwater.	Private aid.
10758.19	BILOXI MARSH WILDLIFE MANAGEMENT AREA DANGER BREAKWATER LIGHT	29-55-02.680N 089-35-31.690W	Fl W 2.5s			Marks shoreline restoration breakwater.	Private aid.
10758.21	BILOXI MARSH WILDLIFE MANAGEMENT AREA DANGER BREAKWATER LIGHT	29-55-08.900N 089-35-28.290W	Fl W 2.5s			Marks shoreline restoration breakwater.	Private aid.
10758.22	BILOXI MARSH WILDLIFE MANAGEMENT AREA DANGER BREAKWATER LIGHT	29-55-15.830N 089-35-20.090W	Fl W 2.5s			Marks shoreline restoration breakwater.	Private aid.
10758.23	BILOXI MARSH WILDLIFE MANAGEMENT AREA DANGER BREAKWATER LIGHT	29-55-23.930N 089-35-13.380W	Fl W 2.5s			Marks shoreline restoration breakwater.	Private aid.
10758.24	BILOXI MARSH WILDLIFE MANAGEMENT AREA DANGER BREAKWATER LIGHT	29-55-31.540N 089-35-07.020W	Fl W 2.5s			Marks shoreline restoration breakwater.	Private aid.
10758.25	BILOXI MARSH WILDLIFE MANAGEMENT AREA DANGER BREAKWATER LIGHT	29-55-37.060N 089-35-01.800W	Fl W 2.5s			Marks shoreline restoration breakwater.	Private aid.
10758.26	BILOXI MARSH WILDLIFE MANAGEMENT AREA DANGER BREAKWATER LIGHT	29-55-45.020N 089-34-55.020W	Fl W 2.5s			Marks shoreline restoration breakwater.	Private aid.
10758.27	BILOXI MARSH WILDLIFE MANAGEMENT AREA DANGER BREAKWATER LIGHT	29-55-50.160N 089-34-52.210W	Fl W 2.5s			Marks shoreline restoration breakwater.	Private aid.
10758.28	BILOXI MARSH WILDLIFE MANAGEMENT AREA DANGER BREAKWATER LIGHT	29-56-00.670N 089-34-48.610W	Fl W 2.5s			Marks shoreline restoration breakwater.	Private aid.
10758.29	BILOXI MARSH WILDLIFE MANAGEMENT AREA DANGER BREAKWATER LIGHT	29-56-10.260N 089-34-45.440W	Fl W 2.5s			Marks shoreline restoration breakwater.	Private aid.

Bayou Yscloskey

(1) No.	(2) Name and Location	(3) Position	(4) Characteristic	(5) Height	(6) Range	(7) Structure	(8) Remarks
10760	- LIGHT 2	29-52-20.292N 089-40-26.439W	Fl R 6s	17	4	TR on pile.	Ra ref.
10765	- Day beacon 3	29-52-11.792N 089-40-26.880W				SG on pile.	
10770	- Day beacon 4	29-52-07.819N 089-40-29.503W				TR on pile.	Ra ref.

Lake Borgne

(1) No.	(2) Name and Location	(3) Position	(4) Characteristic	(5) Height	(6) Range	(7) Structure	(8) Remarks
10775	PROCTOR POINT LIGHT	29-56-46.805N 089-42-30.236W	Fl W 6s	17	5	NB on dolphin.	Ra ref.

(1) No.	(2) Name and Location	(3) Position	(4) Characteristic	(5) Height	(6) Range	(7) Structure	(8) Remarks
	\multicolumn{7}{c}{**LOUISIANA - Eighth District**}						
	LAKE BORGNE AND APPROACHES (Chart 11371)						
	Lake Borgne						
10780	ALLIGATOR POINT LIGHT	30-01-10.394N 089-43-11.730W	Fl W 2.5s	17	3	NB on dolphin.	Ra ref.
	Bayou Dupre						
10785	- LIGHT 1	29-57-15.974N 089-49-22.122W	Fl G 6s	17	5	SG on dolphin.	Ra Ref.
10790	- Day beacon 2	29-57-11.332N 089-49-33.277W				TR on pile.	
10795	- Day beacon 3	29-57-01.671N 089-49-42.459W				SG on pile.	
10800	- Day beacon 4	29-56-54.345N 089-49-56.357W				TR on pile.	
10805	- Day beacon 5	29-56-45.903N 089-50-04.295W				SG on piles.	Ra ref.
10807	- LIGHT 6	29-56-36.135N 089-50-21.734W	Fl R 2.5s	17	3	TR on pile.	Ra ref.
10810	Mortello Castle Oyster Reef Day beacons (6)	29-56-33.000N 089-50-05.000W				NW on pile worded DANGER SUBMERGED OYSTER REEF.	Private aid.
10812	ST. BERNARD PARISH DANGER BREAKWATER LIGHT	29-56-34.500N 089-50-14.800W	Fl W 2.5s			Marks shoreline protection breakwater structure.	Private aid.
	Chef Menteur Pass						
10815	- LIGHT 2	30-02-13.051N 089-45-49.166W	Fl R 4s	17	5	TR on pile.	Ra ref.
10820 34710	- LIGHT 4	30-03-54.220N 089-47-19.230W	Fl R 2.5s	17	4	TR-TY on pile.	Ra ref.
10825 34715	- LIGHT 5	30-03-34.330N 089-47-44.384W	Fl G 2.5s	25	5	SG-SY on pile.	Ra ref.
10827	- *Lighted Buoy 6*	30-06-02.714N 089-48-59.962W	Fl R 4s		4	Red nun.	
10830	RIGOLETS BRIDGE APPROACH RANGE FRONT LIGHT	30-09-40.890N 089-38-30.319W	Q W	25		KRW on skeleton tower on piles.	
10835	RIGOLETS BRIDGE APPROACH RANGE REAR LIGHT 1,076 yards, 301.5° from front light.	30-09-57.603N 089-39-01.654W	Iso W 6s	47		KRW on skeleton tower on piles.	Visible 2° each side of rangeline.
	The Rigolets						
10840	- LIGHT 2	30-09-39.710N 089-39-07.405W	Fl R 6s	17	4	TR on dolphin.	Ra ref.
10845	- LIGHT 3	30-10-23.845N 089-41-19.744W	Fl G 4s	17	4	SG on dolphin.	Ra ref.
10850	- LIGHT 4	30-10-00.707N 089-43-00.214W	Fl R 4s	17	3	TR on dolphin.	Ra ref.
10855	*Louisiana State University Oceanographic Lighted Buoy B*	30-10-19.200N 089-43-48.000W	Fl Y 4s			Yellow.	Private aid.
10860	FORT PIKE ENTRANCE LIGHT 1	30-09-52.388N 089-44-09.458W	Fl G 6s	17	4	SG on pile.	Ra ref.
10865	- LIGHT 5	30-10-29.476N 089-44-35.795W	Fl G 4s	17	4	SG on dolphin.	Ra ref.
10870	- LIGHT 6	30-10-40.680N 089-45-17.917W	Fl R 2.5s	17	3	TR on pile.	Ra ref.
	LAKES PONTCHARTRAIN AND MAUREPAS (Chart 11369)						
10875	Lake Pontchartrain Rockpile Inner Day beacon	30-09-55.033N 089-44-57.261W				NW on pile worded DANGER ROCKS.	
10880	Lake Pontchartrain Rockpile Outer Day beacon	30-09-52.334N 089-44-56.967W				NW on pile worded DANGER ROCKS.	
10885	Fritchie Marsh Weir Danger Day beacons (4)	30-13-45.000N 089-44-47.500W				NW on pile worded DANGER DO NOT PROCEED.	Marks weir. Private aid.

Light List corrected through LNM week: 01/18

(1) No.	(2) Name and Location	(3) Position	(4) Characteristic	(5) Height	(6) Range	(7) Structure	(8) Remarks
			LOUISIANA - Eighth District				
	LAKES PONTCHARTRAIN AND MAUREPAS (Chart 11369)						
	North Shore Channel						
10890	- Day beacon 3	30-10-51.266N 089-45-38.523W				SG on pile.	Ra ref.
10895	- Day beacon 5	30-11-06.602N 089-45-53.079W				SG on pile.	
10900	- Day beacon 7	30-11-24.056N 089-46-14.535W				SG on pile.	
	Lakeshore Estates Channel						
10905	Lakeshore Estates East Channel Day beacon 1	30-11-32.420N 089-46-01.440W				SG on pile.	Private aid.
10910	Lakeshore Estates East Channel Day beacon 3	30-11-39.040N 089-45-58.550W				SG on pile.	Private aid.
10915	Lakeshore Estates East Channel Day beacon 5	30-11-45.660N 089-45-55.660W				SG on pile.	Private aid.
10920	Lakeshore Estates East Channel Junction Day beacon B	30-11-33.310N 089-45-58.610W				JR on pile.	Private aid.
10925	Lakeshore Estates Southeast Channel Day beacon 1	30-11-34.970N 089-45-53.370W				SG on pile.	Private aid.
10930	Lakeshore Estates Southeast Channel Day beacon 3	30-11-36.630N 089-45-48.130W				SG on pile.	Private aid.
	North Shore Channel						
10935	- LIGHT 8	30-11-48.345N 089-46-28.262W	Q R	17	3	TR on pile.	Ra ref.
10940	- Day beacon 9	30-11-45.175N 089-46-37.646W				SG on pile.	Ra ref.
10945	- Day beacon 11	30-11-45.461N 089-47-07.056W				SG on pile.	Ra ref.
10950	- Day beacon 13	30-11-45.587N 089-47-37.598W				SG on pile.	Ra ref.
10955	- Day beacon 15	30-11-45.492N 089-48-02.424W				SG on pile.	Ra ref.
	Eden Isles Channel						
10960	- Day beacon 1	30-12-38.000N 089-48-35.000W				SG on dolphin.	Private aid.
10965	- Day beacon 2	30-12-35.000N 089-48-00.000W				SG on pile.	Private aid.
10970	- Day beacon 3	30-12-42.000N 089-47-57.000W				SG on pile.	Private aid.
10975	- Day beacon 4	30-12-40.000N 089-47-56.000W				TR on pile.	Private aid.
10977	*FR-LA-71-A*	30-11-39.134N 089-50-15.544W	Fl Y 2.5s			Marks northwest corner of reef site.	Private aid.
10977.01	*FR-LA-71-B*	30-11-39.134N 089-50-10.784W	Fl Y 2.5s			Marks northeast corner of reef site.	Private aid.
10977.02	*FR-LA-71-C*	30-11-35.020N 089-50-10.784W	Fl Y 2.5s			Marks southeast corner of reef site.	Private aid.
10977.03	*FR-LA-71-D*	30-11-35.020N 089-50-15.544W	Fl Y 2.5s			Marks southwest corner of reef site.	Private aid.
10980	*FR-LA-70-A*	30-10-12.234N 089-50-47.040W	Fl Y 2.5s			Marks northwest corner of reef site.	Private aid.
10985	*FR-LA-70-B*	30-10-12.234N 089-50-42.274W	Fl Y 2.5s			Marks northeast corner of reef site.	Private aid.
10990	*FR-LA-70-C*	30-10-08.112N 089-50-42.274W	Fl Y 2.5s			Marks southeast corner of reef site.	Private aid.
10995	*FR-LA-70-D*	30-10-08.112N 089-50-47.040W	Fl Y 2.5s			Marks southwest corner of reef site.	Private aid.
	LAKES PONTCHARTRAIN AND MAUREPAS (Chart 11369)						
11000	IRISH BAYOU LIGHT 1	30-08-29.676N 089-51-31.734W	Fl G 6s	17	4	SG on pile.	Ra ref.
	North Shore Beach						
11005	- Day beacon 1	30-13-06.000N 089-49-48.000W				SG on pile.	Private aid.

Light List corrected through LNM week: 01/18

(1) No.	(2) Name and Location	(3) Position	(4) Characteristic	(5) Height	(6) Range	(7) Structure	(8) Remarks
			LOUISIANA - Eighth District				
	LAKES PONTCHARTRAIN AND MAUREPAS (Chart 11369)						
	North Shore Beach						
11010	- Day beacon 2	30-13-06.000N 089-49-45.000W				TR on pile.	Private aid.
11015	- Day beacon 3	30-13-12.000N 089-49-48.000W				SG on pile.	Private aid.
11020	- Day beacon 4	30-13-12.000N 089-49-45.000W				TR on pile.	Private aid.
	Bayou Bonfouca Channel						
11025	- LEADING LIGHT	30-14-59.073N 089-51-57.694W	Iso W 6s	17	5	NB on dolphin.	Visible all around.
11030	- LIGHT 2	30-13-06.258N 089-51-57.956W	Fl R 4s	17	4	TR on dolphin.	
11035	- Day beacon 3	30-13-30.167N 089-52-04.100W				SG on pile.	
11040	- Day beacon 4	30-14-00.706N 089-51-56.239W				TR on pile.	
11045	- LIGHT 5	30-14-24.699N 089-52-04.782W	Fl G 2.5s	17	3	SG on pile.	
11050	- Day beacon 6	30-14-38.705N 089-51-56.239W				TR on pile.	
11055	- Day beacon 8	30-14-49.668N 089-51-56.122W				TR on pile.	
11060	- LIGHT 10	30-14-55.287N 089-51-55.764W	Q R	17	3	TR on pile.	
11065	Southern Railway East Lake Pontchartrain Mooring Buoy	30-12-00.000N 089-50-00.000W				White with blue band.	Private aid.
	LAKES PONTCHARTRAIN AND MAUREPAS (Chart 11369)						
11070	LAKE PONCHATRAIN TIE IN PLATFORM LIGHT	30-09-06.560N 089-53-47.050W	Q R	14		On concrete platform.	Private aid.
	Lincoln Beach						
11075	- Day beacon	30-04-26.521N 089-57-13.749W				NW on pile worded DANGER SPOIL AREA.	Private aid.
11080	- Danger Day beacon East Breakwater (2)	30-04-21.420N 089-57-03.240W				NW on pile worded DANGER ROCK JETTY.	Private aid.
11085	- Danger Day beacon West Breakwater (2)	30-04-12.200N 089-57-19.760W				NW on pile worded DANGER ROCK JETTY.	Private aid.
	Lacombe Bayou						
11090	- ENTRANCE LIGHT 2	30-15-04.477N 089-57-05.690W	Fl R 4s	17	4	TR on dolphin.	
11095	- Entrance Day beacon 4	30-15-18.976N 089-57-00.980W				TR on pile.	Ra ref.
11100	- LIGHT 5	30-15-35.699N 089-56-56.878W	Fl G 2.5s	17	4	SG on pile.	Ra ref.
	South Shore Harbor Marina						
11105	- Safe Water Mark	30-02-58.000N 090-01-10.000W				MR on pile.	Private aid.
11110	- LIGHT 1	30-02-47.000N 090-00-53.000W	Fl G 2.5s			SG on pile.	Private aid.
11115	- LIGHT 2	30-02-44.000N 090-00-56.000W	Fl R 2.5s			TR on pile.	Private aid.
11120	- LIGHT 3	30-02-43.000N 090-00-49.000W	Fl G 2.5s			SG on pile.	Private aid.
11125	- LIGHT 4	30-02-39.000N 090-00-50.000W	Fl R 2.5s			TR on pile.	Private aid.
11130	- LIGHT 5	30-02-39.000N 090-00-44.000W	Fl G 2.5s			SG on pile.	Private aid.
11135	- LIGHT 6	30-02-36.000N 090-00-47.000W	Fl R 2.5s			TR on pile.	Private aid.
11140	- LIGHT 7	30-02-35.000N 090-00-39.000W	Fl G 2.5s			SG on pile.	Private aid.
11145	- LIGHT 8	30-02-33.000N 090-00-43.000W	Fl R 2.5s			TR on pile.	Private aid.

Light List corrected through LNM week: 01/18

(1) No.	(2) Name and Location	(3) Position	(4) Characteristic	(5) Height	(6) Range	(7) Structure	(8) Remarks
			LOUISIANA - Eighth District				
	LAKES PONTCHARTRAIN AND MAUREPAS (Chart 11369)						
	South Shore Harbor Marina						
11150	- LIGHT 9	30-02-28.000N 090-00-35.000W	Fl G 2.5s			SG on pile.	Private aid.
11155	- LIGHT 10	30-02-32.000N 090-00-44.000W	Fl R 2.5s			TR on pile.	Private aid.
11160	- LIGHT 11	30-02-23.000N 090-00-43.000W	Fl G 2.5s			SG on pile.	Private aid.
11165	- LIGHT 13	30-02-30.000N 090-00-46.000W	Fl G 2.5s			SG on pile.	Private aid.
	LAKES PONTCHARTRAIN AND MAUREPAS (Chart 11369)						
11170	LAKEFRONT AIRPORT APPROACH LIGHTS (6)	30-03-36.000N 090-01-48.000W	F Y	15		Marks steel walkway supporting approach lights.	Private aid.
11175	UNO SURVEY LIGHT B	30-09-52.000N 090-04-55.000W	Fl Y 4s	10		On pile.	Private aid.
11180	NEW CANAL LIGHT	30-01-37.760N 090-06-47.550W	Fl (2)W 5s	15		On skeleton pole.	Private aid.
	New Canal						
11185	- WEST JETTY LIGHT 2	30-01-42.174N 090-06-45.630W	Fl R 4s	25	5	TR on pile.	
	Bayou Castine						
11190	- LIGHT 1	30-20-50.460N 090-03-47.508W	Fl G 4s	17	4	SG on pile.	
11195	- LIGHT 2	30-20-49.064N 090-03-45.729W	Fl R 4s	17	4	TR on pile.	
	Mariners Village Marina						
11200	- Day beacon 1	30-21-42.000N 090-05-26.000W				SG on pile.	Private aid.
11205	- LIGHT 2	30-21-43.000N 090-05-24.000W	Fl W 2.5s			TR on dolphin.	Private aid.
11210	- Day beacon 3	30-21-44.000N 090-05-26.000W				SG on pile.	Private aid.
11215	- Day beacon 4	30-25-45.000N 090-05-24.000W				TR on pile.	Private aid.
11220	- Day beacon 5	30-21-46.000N 090-05-26.000W				SG on pile.	Private aid.
11225	- Day beacon 6	30-21-48.000N 090-05-24.000W				TR on pile.	Private aid.
	Lake Pontchartrain						
11230	- SLAB STORAGE EAST LIGHTS (2)	30-21-39.365N 090-05-38.447W	Q W	20		On concrete slab.	Private aid.
11235	- SLAB STORAGE WEST LIGHTS (2)	30-21-32.870N 090-05-41.727W	Q W			On concrete slab.	Private aid.
	Lake Pontchartrain Causeway Cut No.1						
11239	CAUSEWAY BRIDGE ELECTRICAL DISTRIBUTION LIGHTS (19)	30-11-02.000N 090-07-32.000W	Q W	26		On west bridge span.	Marks power distribution vaults on west span of bridge. Private aid.
11240	- LIGHT 1	30-14-32.200N 090-05-53.300W	Fl G 4s	15		SG on pile.	Private aid.
11245	- LIGHT 2	30-15-11.600N 090-05-46.100W	Fl R 4s	15		TR on pile.	Private aid.
11250	- LIGHT 3	30-14-46.100N 090-06-20.700W	Fl G 4s	15		SG on pile.	Private aid.
11255	- LIGHT 4	30-15-05.900N 090-06-17.300W	Fl R 4s	15		TR on pile.	Private aid.
11260	- LIGHT 5	30-14-54.100N 090-07-21.600W	Fl G 4s	15		SG on pile.	Private aid.
11265	- LIGHT 6	30-15-13.900N 090-07-18.200W	Fl R 4s	15		TR on pile.	Private aid.
11270	- LIGHT 7	30-14-48.400N 090-07-52.800W	Fl G 4s	15		SG on pile.	Private aid.
11275	- LIGHT 8	30-15-28.100N 090-07-46.000W	Fl R 4s	15		TR on pile.	Private aid.

Light List corrected through LNM week: 01/18

(1) No.	(2) Name and Location	(3) Position	(4) Characteristic	(5) Height	(6) Range	(7) Structure	(8) Remarks
	LOUISIANA - Eighth District						

LAKES PONTCHARTRAIN AND MAUREPAS (Chart 11369)
Lake Pontchartrain Causeway Cut No. 2

(1) No.	(2) Name and Location	(3) Position	(4) Characteristic	(5) Height	(6) Range	(7) Structure	(8) Remarks
11280	- LIGHT 1	30-07-38.300N 090-07-05.600W	Fl G 4s	15		SG on pile.	Private aid.
11285	- LIGHT 2	30-08-17.600N 090-06-58.800W	Fl R 4s	15		TR on pile.	Private aid.
11290	- LIGHT 3	30-07-51.800N 090-07-33.800W	Fl G 4s	15		SG on pile.	Private aid.
11295	- LIGHT 4	30-08-11.300N 090-07-30.000W	Fl R 4s	15		TR on pile.	Private aid.
11300	- LIGHT 5	30-07-59.700N 090-08-34.300W	Fl G 4s	15		SG on pile.	Private aid.
11305	- LIGHT 6	30-08-19.600N 090-08-30.900W	Fl R 4s	15		TR on pile.	Private aid.
11310	- LIGHT 7	30-07-53.800N 090-09-05.600W	Fl G 4s	15		SG on pile.	Private aid.
11315	- LIGHT 8	30-08-33.100N 090-08-58.700W	Fl R 4s	15		TR on pile.	Private aid.

Tchefuncta River

(1) No.	(2) Name and Location	(3) Position	(4) Characteristic	(5) Height	(6) Range	(7) Structure	(8) Remarks
11320	- RANGE FRONT LIGHT	30-22-42.539N 090-10-10.172W	Q W	25		KRW on skeleton tower.	Visible all around; higher intensity on rangeline.
11322	TOWN OF MADISONVILLE TCHEFUNCTE RIVER LIGHTHOUSE BREAKWATER LIGHTS (3)	30-22-42.400N 090-10-08.500W	Fl W 2.5s			Marks breakwater structure.	Private aid.
11325	- RANGE REAR LIGHT 141 yards, 016° from front light.	30-22-46.622N 090-10-08.822W	Iso W 6s	49		White conical tower.	Visible all around; higher intensity on rangeline.
11330	- LIGHT 2	30-22-03.334N 090-10-21.792W	Fl R 4s	17	3	TR on pile.	
11335	- Day beacon 4	30-22-19.094N 090-10-16.467W				TR on pile.	
11340	- Day beacon 6	30-22-37.738N 090-10-10.032W				TR on pile.	
11345	- Day beacon 8	30-22-36.161N 090-09-50.892W				TR on pile.	
11350	- Day beacon 10	30-22-36.047N 090-09-39.664W				TR on pile.	

Port Louis Channel

(1) No.	(2) Name and Location	(3) Position	(4) Characteristic	(5) Height	(6) Range	(7) Structure	(8) Remarks
11355	PORT LOUIS ENTRANCE CHANNEL LIGHT 1	30-22-29.000N 090-12-20.000W	Fl G 2.5s			SG on pile.	Private aid.
11360	PORT LOUIS ENTRANCE CHANNEL LIGHT 2	30-22-29.480N 090-12-18.980W	Fl R 2.5s			TR on pile.	Private aid.
11365	PORT LOUIS ENTRANCE CHANNEL TOWER LIGHTS	30-22-33.860N 090-12-21.750W	Mo (A) W			MR on pile.	LIGHTS FLASH IN UNISON. Private aid.
11370	- Day beacon 3	30-22-38.240N 090-12-24.510W				SG on pile.	Private aid.
11375	- Day beacon 4	30-22-38.720N 090-12-23.070W				TR on pile.	Private aid.
11380	- Day beacon 5	30-22-47.480N 090-12-28.610W				SG on pile.	Private aid.
11385	- Day beacon 6	30-22-47.960N 090-12-27.160W				TR on pile.	Private aid.
11390	- Day beacon 7	30-22-56.720N 090-12-32.700W				SG on pile.	Private aid.
11395	- Day beacon 8	30-22-57.200N 090-12-31.260W				TR on pile.	Private aid.
11400	- LIGHT 9	30-23-05.170N 090-12-36.320W	Fl G 2.5s			SG on pile.	Private aid.
11405	- LIGHT 10	30-23-05.440N 090-12-34.810W	Fl R 2.5s			TR on pile.	Private aid.
11410	- Day beacon 11	30-23-13.570N 090-12-36.390W				SG on pile.	Private aid.
11415	- Day beacon 12	30-23-13.550N 090-12-34.850W				TR on pile.	Private aid.

Light List corrected through LNM week: 01/18

(1) No.	(2) Name and Location	(3) Position	(4) Characteristic	(5) Height	(6) Range	(7) Structure	(8) Remarks
	LOUISIANA - Eighth District						
	LAKES PONTCHARTRAIN AND MAUREPAS (Chart 11369)						
	Lake Pontchartrain						
11420	NEW ORLEANS VOR PLATFORM LIGHTS (9)	30-01-54.000N 090-10-30.000W	F R	17		On square platform.	Private aid.
	Koch Gateway Pipeline						
11425	- LIGHT A1	30-04-39.100N 090-17-34.200W	Fl Y 2.5s	15			Private aid.
11430	- LIGHT B1	30-05-57.000N 090-16-33.000W	Fl Y 2.5s	17			Private aid.
11435	- LIGHT C	30-06-39.000N 090-16-03.000W	Fl Y 2.5s	17			Private aid.
11440	- LIGHT C1	30-07-14.000N 090-15-23.000W	Fl Y 2.5s	15			Private aid.
11445	- LIGHT D	30-07-57.000N 090-14-56.000W	Fl Y 2.5s	17			Private aid.
11450	- LIGHT D1	30-08-36.000N 090-14-10.000W	Fl R 4s	17			Private aid.
11455	- LIGHT E	30-09-25.600N 090-13-38.000W	Fl Y 2.5s	17			Private aid.
	Lake Pontchartrain						
11460	UNO SURVEY LIGHT A	30-01-56.016N 090-11-43.941W	Fl Y 4s	10		On pile.	Maintained by U.N.O. Private aid.
	Koch Gateway Pipeline						
11465	- LIGHT E1	30-10-04.800N 090-12-53.700W	Fl Y 2.5s	17			Private aid.
11470	- LIGHT F	30-10-52.000N 090-12-23.000W	Fl Y 2.5s	18			Private aid.
11475	- LIGHT F1	30-11-30.000N 090-11-43.000W	Fl Y 2.5s	17			Private aid.
11480	- LIGHT G	30-12-17.500N 090-11-16.700W	Fl Y 2.5s	18			Private aid.
11485	- LIGHT H	30-13-41.000N 090-10-15.000W	Fl Y 2.5s	17			Private aid.
11490	- LIGHT I1	30-15-41.000N 090-08-28.000W	Fl Y 2.5s	17			Private aid.
11495	- LIGHT J	30-16-22.000N 090-08-02.000W	Fl Y 2.5s	17			Private aid.
11500	- LIGHT J1	30-16-56.500N 090-07-22.100W	Fl Y 2.5s	15			Private aid.
11505	- LIGHT K	30-17-37.000N 090-06-54.000W	Fl Y 2.5s	18			Private aid.
11510	- LIGHT K1	30-18-12.300N 090-06-12.900W	Fl Y 2.5s	15			Private aid.
11515	- LIGHT L	30-18-52.000N 090-05-41.000W	Fl Y 2.5s	17			Private aid.
11520	- LIGHT L1	30-19-14.000N 090-05-10.000W	Fl Y 2.5s	15			Private aid.
11525	- LIGHT M	30-19-39.000N 090-04-52.000W	Fl Y 2.5s	18			Private aid.
11530	- LIGHT M1	30-20-05.000N 090-04-00.000W	Fl Y 2.5s	15			Private aid.
	Lake Pontchartrain						
11535	- POWER LINE LIGHTS (45)	30-04-54.000N 090-24-06.000W	Q W	11		On power line structure.	Private aid.
11540	ENTERGY TOWER LIGHTS (2)	30-02-38.700N 090-14-12.700W	Fl R 2.5s			Steel dolphins.	MARKS ELEVATED CLEARANCE FOR FOR ELECTRICAL TRANSMISSION POWER LINES. Private aid.
11545	ENTERGY TOWER LIGHTS (2)	30-02-36.300N 090-14-09.500W	Fl G 2.5s			Steel dolphin.	MARKS ELEVATED CLEARANCE FOR ELECTRICAL TRANSMISSION POWER LINE. Private aid.
11550	- NORTHWEST POWER LINE LIGHTS (12)	30-22-59.000N 090-11-51.000W	Q W			On power line structures.	Private aid.

Light List corrected through LNM week: 01/18

(1) No.	(2) Name and Location	(3) Position	(4) Characteristic	(5) Height	(6) Range	(7) Structure	(8) Remarks
		LOUISIANA - Eighth District					
	LAKES PONTCHARTRAIN AND MAUREPAS (Chart 11369)						
	Lake Pontchartrain						
11555	LUMCON ENVIROMENTAL MONITORING STATION LIGHT	30-18-52.680N 090-16-49.860W	Fl Y 2.5s			On platform.	Private aid.
11557	TANGIPAHOA PARISH DANGER BREAKWATER LIGHTS (2)	30-18-51.191N 090-17-20.400W	Fl W 2.5s			Marks shoreline breakwater.	Private aid.
11557.01	TANGIPAHOA PARISH DANGER BREAKWATER LIGHTS (2)	30-19-06.671N 090-17-10.679W	Fl W 2.5s			Marks shoreline breakwater.	Private aid.
11557.02	TANGIPAHOA PARISH DANGER BREAKWATER LIGHTS (2)	30-19-32.087N 090-16-54.480W	Fl W 2.5s			Marks shoreline breakwater.	Private aid.
11557.03	TANGIPAHOA PARISH DANGER BREAKWATER LIGHTS (3)	30-19-54.552N 090-16-37.919W	Fl W 2.5s			Marks shoreline breakwater.	Private aid.
	Tangipahoa River						
11560	- LIGHT 2	30-19-41.684N 090-15-39.545W	Fl R 4s	17	3	TR on dolphin.	
11565	- Day beacon 4	30-19-58.056N 090-16-03.117W				TR on pile.	
11570	- LIGHT 8	30-20-12.511N 090-16-26.662W	Fl R 4s	17	4	TR on dolphin.	
	Pass Manchac South Channel						
11575	- LIGHT 1	30-16-29.318N 090-18-43.112W	Fl G 4s	17	4	SG on pile.	
11580	- Day beacon 3	30-16-50.921N 090-18-32.533W				SG on pile.	Ra ref.
11585	- Day beacon 5	30-17-12.176N 090-18-22.280W				SG on pile.	Ra ref.
11590	- LIGHT 7	30-17-32.968N 090-18-11.542W	Fl G 2.5s	17	4	SG on pile.	
11592	PASS MANCHAC LIGHTHOUSE WRECK LIGHT WR8	30-17-46.329N 090-17-53.090W	Q R	17	4	TR on pile.	Ra ref.
	LAKES PONTCHARTRAIN AND MAUREPAS (Chart 11369)						
11595	Williams Land Company Danger Daybeacon South	30-19-52.000N 090-24-42.000W				NW on pile.	Worded: DANGER BARRICADE AHEAD. Private aid.
11600	*Williams Land Company Danger Lightd Buoy*	30-19-53.000N 090-24-43.000W				White with Orange Bands and Open Face Diamond.	Marks Barricade on Private Canal. Private aid.
11605	Williams Land Company Danger Daybeacon North	30-20-07.000N 090-24-45.000W				NW on pile.	Worded: Danger barricade Ahead. Private aid.
	Lake Maurepas						
11610	- Day beacon 2	30-17-26.407N 090-25-04.118W				TR on pile.	
11615	- Day beacon 4	30-17-39.537N 090-25-21.826W				TR on pile.	
11620	- LIGHT 6	30-17-41.866N 090-26-01.204W	Fl R 4s	17	4	TR on dolphin.	
11625	TICKFAW RIVER LIGHT 1	30-20-29.736N 090-28-30.447W	Fl G 4s	17	4	SG on dolphin.	
11630	*Tickfaw River Lighted Buoy 3*	30-20-42.148N 090-28-24.591W	Q G		3	Green.	
11635	*Tickfaw River Buoy 5*	30-20-48.502N 090-28-26.585W				Green can.	
11640	*Blind River Lighted Buoy 2*	30-12-25.970N 090-34-48.480W	Fl R 4s		3	Red.	
11645	*Blind River Lighted Buoy 4*	30-12-30.165N 090-35-21.852W	Q R		3	Red.	
	Amite River						
11650	- ENTRANCE LIGHT	30-17-49.888N 090-33-28.614W	Fl W 4s	25	4	NW on skeleton tower.	

Light List corrected through LNM week: 01/18

(1) No.	(2) Name and Location	(3) Position	(4) Characteristic	(5) Height	(6) Range	(7) Structure	(8) Remarks
\multicolumn{8}{c}{**LOUISIANA - Eighth District**}							
	LAKES PONTCHARTRAIN AND MAUREPAS (Chart 11369)						
	Lake Maurepas						
	Amite River						
11652	- Buoy 3	30-17-58.024N 090-33-26.979W				Green can.	
11654	- Buoy 5	30-18-03.392N 090-33-33.086W				Green can.	
	LAKE BORGNE AND APPROACHES (Chart 11371)						
11665	CAL-KY PIPELINE LIGHT CP-4B	30-07-58.430N 089-05-02.000W	Fl Y 2.5s	13		Pile.	Private aid.
	CHANDELEUR AND BRETON SOUNDS (Chart 11363)						
	Chandeleur Sound						
11670	CAL-KY PIPELINE LIGHT CP55	30-02-55.000N 089-06-34.000W	Fl Y 2.5s	15		Pile.	Private aid.
11675	CAL-KY PIPELINE LIGHT CP4A	29-58-41.000N 089-07-51.000W	Fl Y 2.5s	13		Pile.	Private aid.
11680	CAL-KY PIPELINE LIGHT CP4	29-54-11.000N 089-09-16.000W	Fl Y 2.5s	10			Private aid.
11690	CAL-KY PIPELINE LIGHT CP3A	29-44-43.000N 089-13-02.680W	Fl Y 2.5s	13		Concrete pile.	Private aid.
	Mississippi River - Gulf Outlet						
11705	- PIPELINE LIGHT 27 (C-1)	29-31-27.356N 089-10-16.710W	Q G	20		Pile structure.	Private aid.
11710	- PIPELINE LIGHT 28 (C-2)	29-31-34.574N 089-10-10.263W	Q R	20		Pile structure.	Private aid.
	MISSISSIPPI RIVER - Venice to New Orleans (Chart 11364)						
	Mississippi River - Gulf Outlet						
11715	- Day beacon 62 150 feet outside channel limit.	29-40-40.343N 089-23-08.122W				TR on pile.	Ra ref.
11720	- Day beacon 68	29-42-25.506N 089-25-40.908W				TR on pile.	Ra ref.
11723	STATE OF LOUISIANA MISSISSIPPI RIVER GULF OUTLET DANGER LIGHT	29-49-19.190N 089-35-38.240W	Fl W 2.5s			Marks channel closure structure.	Private aid.
11723.01	STATE OF LOUISIANA MISSISSIPPI RIVER GULF OUTLET DANGER LIGHT	29-49-17.250N 089-35-39.970W	Fl W 2.5s			Marks channel closure structure.	Private aid.
11723.02	STATE OF LOUISIANA MISSISSIPPI RIVER GULF OUTLET DANGER LIGHT	29-49-15.320N 089-35-41.680W	Fl W 2.5s			Marks channel closure structure.	Private aid.
11723.03	STATE OF LOUISIANA MISSISSIPPI RIVER GULF OUTLET DANGER LIGHT	29-49-33.720N 089-35-53.890W	Fl W 2.5s			Marks channel closure.	Private aid.
11723.04	STATE OF LOUISIANA MISSISSIPPI RIVER GULF OUTLET DANGER LIGHT	29-49-29.200N 089-36-04.810W	Fl W 2.5s			Marks channel closure.	Private aid.
11723.05	STATE OF LOUISIANA MISSISSIPPI RIVER GULF OUTLET DANGER LIGHT	29-49-17.820N 089-35-31.770W	Fl W 2.5s			Marks channel closure.	Private aid.
11723.06	STATE OF LOUISIANA MISSISSIPPI RIVER GULF OUTLET DANGER LIGHT	29-49-09.120N 089-35-38.060W	Fl W 2.5s			Marks channel closure.	Private aid.
11730	- LIGHT 96	29-50-31.663N 089-37-22.681W	Q R	17	3	TR on pile.	Ra ref.
11735	- LIGHT 97	29-50-46.853N 089-38-45.054W	Fl G 2.5s	17	3	SG on pile.	Ra ref.
11740	- Day beacon 98	29-50-56.236N 089-38-43.094W				TR on dolphin.	Ra ref.
11745	- LIGHT 101	29-51-23.773N 089-40-49.564W	Fl G 2.5s	17	3	SG on pile.	
11750	- LIGHT 102	29-51-30.734N 089-40-47.636W	Fl R 2.5s	17	3	TR on skeleton tower on piles.	
11755	- LIGHT 103 150 feet outside channel limit.	29-51-53.129N 089-42-32.923W	Q G	17	4	SG on skeleton tower on piles.	

LOUISIANA - Eighth District

(1) No.	(2) Name and Location	(3) Position	(4) Characteristic	(5) Height	(6) Range	(7) Structure	(8) Remarks
MISSISSIPPI RIVER - Venice to New Orleans (Chart 11364)							
Mississippi River - Gulf Outlet							
11760	- LIGHT 104	29-52-00.273N 089-42-29.292W	Q R	17	3	TR on skeleton tower on piles.	
11765	- LIGHT 105	29-52-29.230N 089-43-45.561W	Fl G 2.5s	17	4	SG on pile.	
11770	- LIGHT 106	29-52-35.962N 089-43-41.991W	Fl R 2.5s	17	4	TR on dolphin.	
11775	- LIGHT 107 150 feet outside channel limit.	29-53-04.747N 089-44-56.293W	Fl G 4s	30	4	SG on skeleton tower on piles.	
11780	- LIGHT 108	29-53-11.157N 089-44-51.208W	Fl R 4s	17	4	TR on pile.	Ra ref.
11790	- LIGHT 112	29-54-17.806N 089-47-00.522W	Fl R 2.5s	30	4	TR on skeleton tower on piles.	
11795	- LIGHT 113	29-54-58.217N 089-48-36.675W	Q G	30	4	SG on skeleton tower on piles.	
11800	- LIGHT 114	29-55-04.240N 089-48-31.143W	Q R	30	4	TR on skeleton tower on piles.	
11840	- PIPELINE LIGHT 123A	29-59-20.000N 089-54-04.000W	Fl Y 2.5s	15		NW on pile.	Private aid.
11850	- PIPELINE LIGHT 124A	29-59-27.000N 089-53-57.000W	Fl Y 2.5s	15		NW on pile.	Private aid.
11853	ORLEANS LEVEE DISTRICT BAYOU BIENVENUE FLOODGATE LIGHT 2	30-00-09.180N 089-54-08.360W	Fl R 2.5s			Marks southeast gate wall.	Private aid.
11853.01	ORLEANS LEVEE DISTRICT BAYOU BIENVENUE FLOODGATE LIGHT 1	30-00-08.600N 089-54-08.540W	Fl G 2.5s			Marks southwest gate wall.	Private aid.
11853.02	ORLEANS LEVEE DISTRICT BAYOU BIENVENUE FLOODGATE LIGHT 3	30-00-08.930N 089-54-09.850W	Fl G 2.5s			Marks northwest gate wall.	Private aid.
11853.03	ORLEANS LEVEE DISTRICT BAYOU BIENVENUE FLOODGATE LIGHT 4	30-00-09.530N 089-54-09.640W	Fl R 2.5s			Marks northeast gate wall.	Private aid.
11855	- LIGHT 125	30-00-02.312N 089-54-53.514W	Fl G 4s	17	4	SG on dolphin.	
11860	- LIGHT 126 150 feet outside channel limit.	30-00-04.256N 089-54-42.754W	Fl R 4s	30	4	TR on skeleton tower on piles.	
11865	- LIGHT 127 105 feet outside channel limit.	30-00-19.272N 089-55-23.766W	Fl G 2.5s	17	4	SG on dolphin.	
11870	- LIGHT 128	30-00-18.317N 089-55-01.961W	Fl R 2.5s	17	4	TR on dolphin.	
WAVELAND TO CATAHOULA BAY (Chart 11367)							
Mississippi River - Gulf Outlet							
11875 34725	- JUNCTION LIGHT MRGO	30-00-27.566N 089-55-18.004W	Fl (2+1)R 6s	30	3	JR-SY on skeleton tower on piles.	
11880 34730	- LIGHT 129	30-00-19.410N 089-55-53.972W	Fl G 4s	17	4	SG-SY on pile.	
11885 34735	MICHOUD DOCK LIGHTS (2)	30-00-24.000N 089-56-03.000W	Fl R 2.5s	6			Private aid.
11890 34740	GRANT STREET DISCHARGE LIGHT	30-00-14.000N 089-56-59.000W	Fl R 2.5s	10		On dolphin.	Private aid.
11900 34750	AMID STATION DISCHARGE LIGHTS (2)	29-59-52.000N 090-00-35.000W	Fl R 2.5s			On dolphins.	Private aid.
CHANDELEUR AND BRETON SOUNDS (Chart 11363)							
Breton Sound							
11905	CALIFORNIA BAY PIPELINE LIGHT CP3	29-36-40.000N 089-19-08.000W	Q W	10			Private aid.
MISSISSIPPI RIVER - Venice to New Orleans (Chart 11364)							
Breton Sound							
11908	Nature Conservancy Danger Day beacon	29-44-34.480N 089-28-12.500W				Marks submerged shoreline protection.	Private aid.

(1) No.	(2) Name and Location	(3) Position	(4) Characteristic	(5) Height	(6) Range	(7) Structure	(8) Remarks
		LOUISIANA - Eighth District					

MISSISSIPPI RIVER - Venice to New Orleans (Chart 11364)

Breton Sound

(1) No.	(2) Name and Location	(3) Position	(4) Characteristic	(5) Height	(6) Range	(7) Structure	(8) Remarks
11908.01	Nature Conservancy Danger Day beacon	29-44-38.360N 089-28-10.420W				Marks submerged shoreline protection.	Private aid.
11908.02	Nature Conservancy Danger Day beacon	29-44-41.960N 089-28-08.220W				Marks submerged shoreline protection.	Private aid.
11908.03	Nature Conservancy Danger Day beacon	29-44-45.420N 089-28-05.560W				Marks submerged shoreline protection.	Private aid.
11908.04	Nature Conservancy Danger Day beacon	29-44-48.730N 089-28-02.320W				Marks submerged shoreline protection.	Private aid.
11908.05	Nature Conservancy Danger Day beacon	29-44-52.040N 089-27-58.900W				Marks submerged shoreline protection.	Private aid.
11910	CALIFORNIA BAY PIPELINE LIGHT CP2	29-29-31.000N 089-26-14.000W	Q W	10			Private aid.
11915	CALIFORNIA BAY PIPELINE LIGHT CP1	29-25-11.000N 089-29-48.000W	Q R	10			Private aid.

Quarantine Bay Channel

(1) No.	(2) Name and Location	(3) Position	(4) Characteristic	(5) Height	(6) Range	(7) Structure	(8) Remarks
11920	- LIGHT 2	29-25-02.000N 089-28-27.000W	Fl R 4s			TR on pile.	Private aid.
11925	- LIGHT 3	29-25-02.000N 089-28-27.000W	Fl G 4s			SG on pile.	Private aid.
11930	- LIGHT 4	29-25-03.000N 089-28-28.000W	Fl R 4s	17		TR on pile.	Private aid.
11935	- LIGHT 5	29-24-54.000N 089-28-30.000W	Fl G 4s			SG on pile.	Private aid.
11940	- LIGHT 6	29-25-03.000N 089-28-48.000W	Fl R 4s	17		TR on pile.	Private aid.
11945	- LIGHT 8	29-25-03.000N 089-28-52.000W	Fl R 4s			TR on pile.	Private aid.
11950	- LIGHT 9	29-24-57.000N 089-29-11.000W	Fl G 4s	17		SG on pile.	Private aid.
11955	- LIGHT 10	29-25-02.000N 089-29-12.000W	Fl R 4s	17		TR on pile.	Private aid.
11960	- LIGHT 12	29-25-02.000N 089-29-15.000W	Fl R 4s	17		TR on pile.	Private aid.
11965	- LIGHT 14	29-24-54.000N 089-29-18.000W	Fl R 4s			TR on pile.	Private aid.
11970	- LIGHT 16	29-24-38.000N 089-29-43.000W	Fl R 4s	7		TR on pile.	Private aid.
11975	- LIGHT 18	29-24-25.000N 089-30-09.000W	Fl R 4s	17		TR on pile.	Private aid.
11980	- LIGHT 20	29-24-19.000N 089-30-21.000W	Fl R 4s	17		TR on pile.	Private aid.
11985	- LIGHT 22	29-24-12.000N 089-30-30.000W	Fl R 4s	17		TR on pile.	Private aid.
11990	- LIGHT 24	29-24-11.000N 089-30-45.000W	Fl R 4s	17		TR on pile.	Private aid.
11995	- LIGHT 30	29-23-49.000N 089-31-07.000W	Fl R 4s	17		TR on pile.	Private aid.
12000	- LIGHT 34	29-23-35.000N 089-31-14.000W	Fl R 4s	17		TR on pile.	Private aid.
12005	- LIGHT 36	29-23-34.000N 089-31-14.000W	Fl R 4s	17		TR on pile.	Private aid.
12010	- LIGHT 38	29-23-32.000N 089-31-16.000W	Fl R 4s	17		TR on pile.	Private aid.
12015	- LIGHT 40	29-23-00.000N 089-31-24.000W	Fl R 4s			TR on pile.	Private aid.
12020	- LIGHT 42	29-23-16.000N 089-31-28.000W	Fl R 4s	17		TR on pile.	Private aid.
12022	MOEM BONNIES BAY PIPELINE LIGHT A	29-23-55.980N 089-34-19.960W	Fl Y 2.5s			Marks submerged pipeline.	Private aid.
12022.01	MOEM BONNIES BAY PIPELINE LIGHT B	29-23-57.090N 089-34-21.350W	Fl Y 2.5s			Marks submerged pipeline.	Private aid.

Light List corrected through LNM week: 01/18

(1) No.	(2) Name and Location	(3) Position	(4) Characteristic	(5) Height	(6) Range	(7) Structure	(8) Remarks
		LOUISIANA - Eighth District					
	MISSISSIPPI RIVER - Venice to New Orleans (Chart 11364)						
	Breton Sound						
	Quarantine Bay Channel						
12025	QUARANTINE BAY NORTH CHANNEL LIGHT 2	29-25-44.000N 089-30-58.000W	Fl R 4s	17		TR on pile.	Private aid.
	California Bay						
12030	UPSTREAM EXPLORATION PALMETTO PROSPECT DANGER OBSTRUCTION LIGHT	29-28-12.000N 089-31-53.000W	Fl W 2.5s			Marks piling obstruction.	Private aid.
12030.01	UPSTREAM EXPLORATION PALMETTO PROSPECT DANGER OBSTRUCTION LIGHT	29-28-15.000N 089-32-04.000W	Fl W 2.5s			Marks piling obstruction.	Private aid.
12030.02	UPSTREAM EXPLORATION PALMETTO PROSPECT DANGER OBSTRUCTION LIGHT	29-28-18.000N 089-32-15.000W	Fl W 2.5s			Marks piling obstruction.	Private aid.
12030.03	UPSTREAM EXPLORATION PALMETTO PROSPECT DANGER OBSTRUCTION LIGHT	29-28-20.000N 089-32-26.000W	Fl W 2.5s			Marks piling obstruction.	Private aid.
12030.04	UPSTREAM EXPLORATION PALMETTO PROSPECT DANGER OBSTRUCTION LIGHT	29-28-23.000N 089-32-37.000W	Fl W 2.5s			Marks piling obstruction.	Private aid.
12030.05	UPSTREAM EXPLORATION PALMETTO PROSPECT DANGER OBSTRUCTION LIGHT	29-28-26.000N 089-32-47.000W	Fl W 2.5s			Marks piling obstruction.	Private aid.
12030.06	UPSTREAM EXPLORATION PALMETTO PROSPECT DANGER OBSTRUCTION LIGHT	29-28-28.000N 089-32-58.000W	Fl W 2.5s			Marks piling obstruction.	Private aid.
12030.07	UPSTREAM EXPLORATION PALMETTO PROSPECT DANGER OBSTRUCTION LIGHT	29-28-26.000N 089-33-05.000W	Fl W 2.5s			Marks piling obstruction.	Private aid.
12030.08	UPSTREAM EXPLORATION PALMETTO PROSPECT DANGER OBSTRUCTION LIGHT	29-28-20.000N 089-33-12.000W	Fl W 2.5s			Marks piling obstruction.	Private aid.
12030.09	UPSTREAM EXPLORATION PALMETTO PROSPECT DANGER OBSTRUCTION LIGHT	29-28-12.000N 089-33-16.000W	Fl W 2.5s			Marks piling obstruction.	Private aid.
12030.11	UPSTREAM EXPLORATION PALMETTO PROSPECT DANGER OBSTRUCTION LIGHT	29-28-03.000N 089-33-21.000W	Fl W 2.5s			Marks piling obstruction.	Private aid.
12030.12	UPSTREAM EXPLORATION PALMETTO PROSPECT DANGER OBSTRUCTION LIGHT	29-27-54.000N 089-33-25.000W	Fl W 2.5s			Marks piling obstruction.	Private aid.
12030.13	UPSTREAM EXPLORATION PALMETTO PROSPECT SEDIMENT CURTAIN DANGER LIGHT	29-28-26.000N 089-33-11.000W	Fl W 2.5s			Marks sediment curtain piling obstruction.	Private aid.
12030.14	UPSTREAM EXPLORATION PALMETTO PROSPECT SEDIMENT CURTAIN DANGER LIGHT	29-28-23.000N 089-33-08.000W	Fl W 2.5s			Marks sediment curtain piling obstruction.	Private aid.
12030.15	UPSTREAM EXPLORATION PALMETTO PROSPECT SEDIMENT CURTAIN DANGER LIGHT	29-28-17.000N 089-33-18.000W	Fl W 2.5s			Marks sediment curtain piling obstruction.	Private aid.
12030.16	UPSTREAM EXPLORATION PALMETTO PROSPECT SEDIMENT CURTAIN DANGER LIGHT	29-28-25.000N 089-33-14.000W	Fl W 2.5s			Marks sediment curtain piling obstruction.	Private aid.

Light List corrected through LNM week: 01/18

(1) No.	(2) Name and Location	(3) Position	(4) Characteristic	(5) Height	(6) Range	(7) Structure	(8) Remarks
			LOUISIANA - Eighth District				
	MISSISSIPPI RIVER - Venice to New Orleans (Chart 11364)						
	Breton Sound						
	California Bay						
12030.17	UPSTREAM EXPLORATION PALMETTO PROSPECT SEDIMENT CURTAIN DANGER LIGHT	29-28-06.000N 089-33-23.000W	Fl W 2.5s			Marks sediment curtain piling obstruction.	Private aid.
12030.18	UPSTREAM EXPLORATION PALMETTO PROSPECT SEDIMENT CURTAIN DANGER LIGHT	29-28-06.000N 089-33-18.000W	Fl W 2.5s			Marks sediment curtain piling obstruction.	Private aid.
12030.19	UPSTREAM EXPLORATION PALMETTO PROSPECT SEDIMENT CURTAIN DANGER LIGHT	29-27-55.000N 089-33-28.000W	Fl W 2.5s			Marks sediment curtain piling obstruction.	Private aid.
12030.21	UPSTREAM EXPLORATION PALMETTO PROSPECT SEDIMENT CURTAIN DANGER LIGHT	29-27-52.000N 089-33-23.000W	Fl W 2.5s			Marks sediment curtain piling obstruction.	Private aid.
12030.22	UPSTREAM EXPLORATION PALMETTO PROSPECT SEDIMENT CURTAIN DANGER LIGHT	29-27-48.000N 089-33-28.000W	Fl W 2.5s			Marks sediment curtain piling obstruction.	Private aid.
12030.23	UPSTREAM EXPLORATION PALMETTO PROSPECT SEDIMENT CURTAIN DANGER LIGHT	29-28-26.000N 089-33-06.000W	Fl W 2.5s			Marks sediment curtain piling obstruction.	Private aid.
12030.24	UPSTREAM EXPLORATION PALMETTO PROSPECT SEDIMENT CURTAIN DANGER LIGHT	29-28-29.000N 089-33-08.000W	Fl W 2.5s			Marks sediment curtain piling obstruction.	Private aid.
12030.25	UPSTREAM EXPLORATION PALMETTO PROSPECT SEDIMENT CURTAIN DANGER LIGHT	29-28-20.000N 089-33-11.000W	Fl W 2.5s			Marks sediment curtain piling obstruction.	Private aid.
12030.26	UPSTREAM EXPLORATION PALMETTO PROSPECT SEDIMENT CURTAIN DANGER LIGHT	29-28-22.000N 089-33-15.000W	Fl W 2.5s			Marks sediment curtain piling obstruction.	Private aid.
12030.27	UPSTREAM EXPLORATION PALMETTO PROSPECT SEDIMENT CURTAIN DANGER LIGHT	29-28-10.000N 089-33-16.000W	Fl W 2.5s			Marks sediment curtain piling obstruction.	Private aid.
12030.28	UPSTREAM EXPLORATION PALMETTO PROSPECT SEDIMENT CURTAIN DANGER LIGHT	29-28-12.000N 089-33-21.000W	Fl W 2.5s			Marks sediment curtain piling obstruction.	Private aid.
12030.29	UPSTREAM EXPLORATION PALMETTO PROSPECT SEDIMENT CURTAIN DANGER LIGHT	29-28-02.000N 089-33-20.000W	Fl W 2.5s			Marks sediment curtain piling obstruction.	Private aid.
12030.31	UPSTREAM EXPLORATION PALMETTO PROSPECT SEDIMENT CURTAIN DANGER LIGHT	29-28-01.000N 089-33-26.000W	Fl W 2.5s			Marks sediment curtain piling obstruction.	Private aid.
12030.32	UPSTREAM EXPLORATION PALMETTO PROSPECT SEDIMENT CURTAIN DANGER LIGHT	29-27-57.000N 089-33-21.000W	Fl W 2.5s			Marks sediment curtain piling obstruction.	Private aid.
12030.33	UPSTREAM EXPLORATION PALMETTO PROSPECT SEDIMENT CURTAIN DANGER LIGHT	29-27-47.000N 089-33-26.000W	Fl W 2.5s			Marks sediment curtain piling obstruction.	Private aid.
12030.34	UPSTREAM EXPLORATION PALMETTO PROSPECT SEDIMENT CURTAIN DANGER LIGHT	29-27-49.000N 089-33-31.000W	Fl W 2.5s			Marks sediment curtain piling obstruction.	Private aid.
12032	MOEM GASPER BAY PIPELINE LIGHT A	29-27-46.530N 089-34-50.700W	Fl Y 2.5s			Marks submerged pipeline.	Private aid.

Light List corrected through LNM week: 01/18

(1) No.	(2) Name and Location	(3) Position	(4) Characteristic	(5) Height	(6) Range	(7) Structure	(8) Remarks
			LOUISIANA - Eighth District				
	MISSISSIPPI RIVER - Venice to New Orleans (Chart 11364)						
	Breton Sound						
12070	TELEGRAPH POINT LIGHT	29-29-42.000N 089-30-12.000W	Fl W 3s	20		On dolphin.	Private aid.
12072	MOEM LONG BAY PIPELINE LIGHT A	29-29-31.640N 089-34-39.860W	Fl Y 2.5s			Marks submerged pipeline.	Private aid.
	Black Bay Channel						
12075	- LIGHT 1	29-33-06.000N 089-30-18.000W	Fl W 4s	10		SG on piles.	Private aid.
12080	HELIS BLACK BAY CHANNEL LIGHT 2	29-33-37.500N 089-30-36.500W	Fl R 4s			TR on pile.	Private aid.
12085	HELIS BLACK BAY CHANNEL LIGHT 3	29-33-36.500N 089-30-42.100W	Fl G 4s			SG on pile.	Private aid.
12090	HELIS BLACK BAY CHANNEL LIGHT 4	29-33-51.800N 089-30-51.000W	Fl R 4s			TR on pile.	Private aid.
12095	HELIS BLACK BAY CHANNEL LIGHT 5	29-33-50.300N 089-30-53.900W	Fl G 4s			SG on pile.	Private aid.
12100	HELIS BLACK BAY CHANNEL LIGHT 6	29-34-03.700N 089-30-59.100W	Fl R 4s			TR on pile.	Private aid.
12105	HELIS BLACK BAY CHANNEL LIGHT 7	29-34-03.800N 089-34-02.700W	Fl G 4s			SG on pile.	Private aid.
12110	HELIS BLACK BAY CHANNEL LIGHT 9	29-34-31.000N 089-31-00.300W	Fl G 4s			SG on pile.	Private aid.
12115	HELIS BLACK BAY CHANNEL LIGHT 11	29-34-47.100N 089-31-03.500W	Fl G 4s			SG on pile.	Private aid.
12120	HELIS BLACK BAY CHANNEL LIGHT 13	29-34-56.900N 089-31-09.300W	Fl G 4s			SG on pile.	Private aid.
12125	HELIS BLACK BAY CHANNEL LIGHT 15	29-34-58.100N 089-31-23.400W	Fl G 4s			SG on pile.	Private aid.
12130	HELIS STONE ISLAND REMEDIATION PROJECT DANGER LIGHTS (3)	29-34-49.290N 089-31-56.640W	Fl W 2.5s	15		NW on pile.	Worded: DANGER ROCKS. Private aid.
12135	HELIS BLACK BAY CHANNEL LIGHT 17	29-35-00.600N 089-31-57.800W	Fl G 4s			SG on pile.	Private aid.
12140	HELIS BLACK BAY CHANNEL LIGHT 19	29-35-00.600N 089-31-57.800W	Fl G 4s			SG on pile.	Private aid.
12145	HELIS BLACK BAY CHANNEL LIGHT 21	29-35-01.800N 089-32-12.300W	Fl G 4s			SG on pile.	Private aid.
12150	HELIS BLACK BAY CHANNEL LIGHT 23	29-35-06.600N 089-32-29.300W	Fl G 4s			SG on pile.	Private aid.
	West Black Bay Channel						
12345	- LIGHT 78A	29-35-07.800N 089-33-02.100W	Fl W 4s			On dolphin.	Private aid.
12350	U.S. GEOLOGICAL SURVEY SCIENTIFIC MONITORING PLATFORM LIGHT (PP)	29-35-08.700N 089-36-21.500W	Fl Y 2.5s	37		On pipe.	Private aid.
	Bayou Terre Aux Boeufs						
12355	- Day beacon 2	29-37-13.261N 089-29-11.695W				TR on pile.	Ra ref.
12360	- Day beacon 3	29-37-07.446N 089-29-14.842W				SG on pile.	Ra ref.
12365	- Day beacon 5	29-37-25.866N 089-30-53.997W				SG on pile.	
12370	- Day beacon 6	29-38-03.372N 089-32-25.433W				TR on pile.	Ra ref.
12375	- Day beacon 7	29-39-31.058N 089-33-50.453W				SG on pile.	Ra ref.
12376	MOEM BLACK BAY PIPELINE LIGHT A	29-39-44.940N 089-36-40.850W	Fl Y 2.5s			Marks submerged pipeline.	Private aid.
12376.01	MOEM BAYOU TERRA AUX PIPELINE LIGHT A	29-40-33.270N 089-36-57.150W	Fl Y 2.5s			Marks submerged pipeline.	Private aid.
12376.02	MOEM LAKE JEAN LOUIS PIPELINE LIGHT A	29-42-58.880N 089-38-14.590W	Fl Y 2.5s			Marks submerged pipeline.	Private aid.
12376.03	MOEM LAKE JEAN LOUIS PIPELINE LIGHT B	29-44-43.460N 089-39-09.960W	Fl Y 2.5s			Marks submerged pipeline.	Private aid.

Light List corrected through LNM week: 01/18

(1) No.	(2) Name and Location	(3) Position	(4) Characteristic	(5) Height	(6) Range	(7) Structure	(8) Remarks
			LOUISIANA - Eighth District				
MISSISSIPPI RIVER - Venice to New Orleans (Chart 11364)							
Bayou Terre Aux Boeufs							
12376.04	MOEM MIDDLE BAYOU PIPELINE LIGHT A	29-46-36.280N 089-40-11.930W	Fl Y 2.5s			Marks submerged pipeline.	Private aid.
12376.05	MOEM CROOKED BAYOU PIPELINE LIGHT A	29-48-04.830N 089-41-01.580W	Fl Y 2.5s			Marks submerged pipeline.	Private aid.
12377	Nature Conservancy Bayou Palo Day beacon 2	29-40-03.981N 089-32-06.988W				TR on pile.	Private aid.
12377.01	Nature Conservancy Lake Fortuna Danger Day beacons (4)	29-40-09.411N 089-32-08.248W				NW on pile.	Private aid.
12377.02	Nature Conservancy Lake Fortuna Danger Day beacons (3)	29-40-21.615N 089-31-57.100W				NW on pile.	Private aid.
12377.03	Nature Conservancy Bayou Numa Day beacon 1	29-40-26.873N 089-31-51.120W				SG on pile.	Private aid.
12377.04	Nature Conservancy Bayou Numa Day beacon 2	29-40-25.844N 089-31-49.820W				TR on pile.	Private aid.
12377.05	Nature Conservancy Lake Fortuna Danger Day beacons (5)	29-40-26.587N 089-31-40.470W				NW on pile.	Private aid.
12377.06	Nature Conservancy Lake Fortuna Danger Day beacons (4)	29-40-39.033N 089-31-47.090W				NW on pile.	Private aid.
12377.07	Nature Conservancy Cat Pass Cut Day beacon 1	29-40-52.114N 089-31-47.370W				SG on pile.	Private aid.
12377.08	Nature Conservancy Lake Eloi Danger Day beacons (5)	29-45-03.461N 089-26-14.900W				NW on pile.	Private aid.
12377.09	Nature Conservancy Lake Eloi South Cut Day beacon 1	29-45-09.923N 089-26-22.470W				SG on pile.	Private aid.
12377.11	Nature Conservancy Lake Eloi South Cut Day beacon 2	29-45-15.005N 089-26-24.650W				TR on pile.	Private aid.
12377.12	Nature Conservancy Lake Eloi Danger Day beacons (3)	29-45-16.301N 089-26-23.850W				NW on pile.	Private aid.
12377.13	Nature Conservancy Lake Eloi Danger Day beacon (3)	29-45-25.598N 089-26-25.440W				NW on pile.	Private aid.
12377.14	Nature Conservancy Lake Eloi Center Cut Day beacon 1	29-45-28.089N 089-26-27.950W				SG on pile.	Private aid.
12377.15	Nature Conservancy Lake Eloi Center Cut Day beacon 2	29-45-29.633N 089-26-30.230W				TR on pile.	Private aid.
12377.16	Nature Conservancy Lake Eloi Danger Day beacons (5)	29-45-33.583N 089-26-32.940W				NW on pile.	Private aid.
12377.17	Nature Conservancy Lake Eloi North Cut Day beacon 1	29-45-46.440N 089-26-26.610W				SG on pile.	Private aid.
12378	CPRA ELOI POINT DANGER BREAKWATER LIGHTS 1-30	29-45-23.740N 089-25-00.714W	Fl W 2.5s			Marks shoreline restoration breakwater.	Private aid.
12378.01	CPRA ELOI POINT DANGER BREAKWATER LIGHTS 31-49	29-46-07.500N 089-24-31.320W	Fl W 2.5s			Marks shoreline restoration breakwater.	Private aid.
12378.02	CPRA ELOI POINT DANGER BREAKWATER LIGHTS 50-67	29-46-47.590N 089-21-58.250W	Fl W 2.5s			Marks shoreline restoration breakwater.	Private aid.
12378.03	CRCL Danger Day beacons (6)	29-45-18.560N 089-26-55.210W				Marks submerged oyster beds.	Private aid.
CHANDELEUR AND BRETON SOUNDS (Chart 11363)							
Baptiste Collette Bayou							
12380	- ENTRANCE LIGHT	29-24-43.445N 089-18-33.599W	Oc W 4s	17	4	NG on piles.	Ra ref.
12385	- LIGHT 1 50 feet outside channel limit.	29-24-16.678N 089-18-28.712W	Fl G 2.5s	17	4	SG on dolphin.	Ra ref.
12390	- LIGHT 2	29-24-16.396N 089-18-33.977W	Fl R 2.5s	17	4	TR on dolphin.	Ra ref.
12395	- LIGHT 3 50 feet outside channel limit.	29-23-57.926N 089-18-26.575W	Fl G 6s	17	4	SG on pile.	Ra ref.

Light List corrected through LNM week: 01/18

(1) No.	(2) Name and Location	(3) Position	(4) Characteristic	(5) Height	(6) Range	(7) Structure	(8) Remarks
	LOUISIANA - Eighth District						
	CHANDELEUR AND BRETON SOUNDS (Chart 11363)						
	Baptiste Collette Bayou						
12400	- Day beacon 4	29-23-45.291N 089-18-30.128W				TR on pile.	Ra ref.
12405	- LIGHT 5 50 feet outside channel limit.	29-23-35.551N 089-18-23.415W	Fl G 4s	17	4	SG on pile.	Ra ref.
12410	- LIGHT 6 50 feet outside channel limit.	29-23-21.693N 089-18-26.012W	Fl R 6s	17	4	TR on pile.	Ra ref.
12415	- LIGHT 7	29-23-03.054N 089-18-18.071W	Fl G 6s	17	4	SG on pile.	Ra ref.
12420	- Day beacon 8 50 feet outside channel limit.	29-23-03.551N 089-18-23.878W				TR on pile.	Ra ref.
12425	- LIGHT 9 50 feet outside channel limit.	29-22-42.382N 089-18-14.943W	Fl G 4s	17	4	SG on dolphin.	
12430	- LIGHT 10	29-22-41.990N 089-18-20.161W	Fl R 4s	17	3	TR on pile.	
12435	- Day beacon 11 45 feet outside channel limit.	29-22-29.423N 089-18-13.204W				SG on pile.	Ra ref.
12440	- Day beacon 12 45 feet outside channel limit.	29-22-22.728N 089-18-16.806W				TR on pile.	Ra ref.
12445	- LIGHT 13 45 feet outside channel limit.	29-22-04.324N 089-18-08.878W	Fl G 2.5s	17	3	SG on pile.	Ra ref.
12450	- LIGHT 14 45 feet outside channel limit.	29-22-03.413N 089-18-13.846W	Fl R 2.5s	17	3	TR on pile.	Ra ref.
12455	- Day beacon 15 50 feet outside channel limit.	29-21-45.091N 089-18-05.964W				SG on pile.	
12460	- Day beacon 16 50 feet outside channel limit.	29-21-45.702N 089-18-10.966W				TR on pile.	Ra ref.
12465	- LIGHT 17 50 feet outside channel limit.	29-21-34.978N 089-18-03.657W	Fl G 2.5s	17	3	SG on pile.	Ra ref.
12470	- LIGHT 18 50 feet outside channel limit.	29-21-35.141N 089-18-09.267W	Fl R 2.5s	17	3	TR on pile.	
12475	- Day beacon 19 50 feet outside channel limit.	29-19-14.529N 089-18-54.799W				SG on pile.	
12480	- Day beacon 20 50 feet outside channel limit.	29-18-52.152N 089-19-11.078W				TR on pile.	Ra ref.
12485	EMELINE PASS WRECK LIGHT WR2	29-18-13.702N 089-18-28.446W	Q R	17	3	TR on pile.	Ra ref.
	MISSISSIPPI RIVER DELTA (Chart 11361)						
	Baptiste Collette Bayou						
12490	- Day beacon 21	29-18-04.456N 089-19-34.272W				SG on pile.	Ra ref.
12495	- Day beacon 22 50 feet outside channel limit.	29-18-07.504N 089-19-41.785W				TR on pile.	Ra ref.
12500	- LIGHT 23	29-17-55.264N 089-19-47.203W	Q G	17	3	SG on pile.	Ra ref.
12505	- LIGHT 25	29-17-34.605N 089-20-49.355W	Fl G 2.5s	17	3	SG on pile.	
12510	MAIN PASS LOADING DOCK LIGHT	29-15-20.000N 089-14-06.000W	Fl W 2s	12			Private aid.

Light List corrected through LNM week: 01/18

(1) No.	(2) Name and Location	(3) Position	(4) Characteristic	(5) Height	(6) Range	(7) Structure	(8) Remarks
		LOUISIANA - Eighth District					
	MISSISSIPPI RIVER DELTA (Chart 11361)						
	Lonesome Bayou						
12515	- LIGHT 2	29-14-24.000N 089-03-43.000W	Q R	15		TR on dolphin.	Private aid.
12520	- Day beacon 4	29-13-17.000N 089-03-38.000W				TR on pile.	Private aid.
12525	- Day beacon 6	29-13-11.000N 089-03-33.000W				TR on pile.	Private aid.
12530	- Day beacon 8	29-13-04.000N 089-03-28.000W				TR on pile.	Private aid.
12535	- Day beacon 10	29-12-57.000N 089-03-23.000W				TR on pile.	Private aid.
	Pass A Loutre						
12540	SHELL PIPELINE CORPORATION DOCK LIGHT	29-09-06.000N 089-14-06.000W	F W	10		White rectangular day mark.	Private aid.
12545	GARDEN ISLAND BAY 214-160 CHANNEL LIGHT 1	29-06-21.000N 089-11-01.000W	Q G	14		SG on pile.	Private aid.
12550	JOHNSON PASS LIGHT 1	29-05-24.000N 089-09-42.000W	Fl W 2.5s	12		On dolphin.	Private aid.
12552	CRIMSON GULF PIPELINE MARKER LIGHT A	29-09-03.010N 089-13-10.830W	Fl Y 2.5s			Western mark.	Private aid.
12552.01	CRIMSON GULF PIPELINE MARKER LIGHT B	29-09-03.010N 089-13-10.600W	Fl Y 2.5s			Eastern mark,	Private aid.
	Redfish Bay						
	S.L. 11107 Pipeline						
12555	Redfish Bay Sl 11107 Pipeline Day beacon A	29-05-54.000N 089-05-24.000W				NW on pile.	Private aid.
12560	Redfish Bay Sl 11107 Pipeline Day beacon B	29-05-54.000N 089-05-30.000W				NW on pile.	Private aid.
12565	Redfish Bay Sl 11107 Pipeline Day beacon C	29-06-00.000N 089-05-36.000W				NW on pile.	Private aid.
12570	Redfish Bay Sl 11107 Pipeline Day beacon D	29-06-00.000N 089-05-42.000W				NW on pile.	Private aid.
	South Pass						
12575	- Lighted Buoy 2	28-58-49.331N 089-06-52.575W	Fl R 2.5s		4	Red.	
12580	- Lighted Buoy 3	28-58-53.282N 089-07-19.159W	Fl G 4s		4	Green.	
12585	- Buoy 3A	28-59-11.637N 089-08-03.569W				Green can.	
12590	- LIGHT 4	28-59-22.625N 089-08-11.241W	Q R	24	4	TR on pile.	Ra ref.
12591	- LIGHT 3B	28-59-28.198N 089-08-21.510W	Fl G 2.5s	17	4	SG on pile.	Ra ref.
12592	- DANGER LIGHT A	28-59-30.613N 089-08-16.355W	Fl W 2.5s	17	4	NW on pile.	Ra ref.
12593	- DANGER LIGHT B	28-59-36.929N 089-08-20.989W	Fl W 4s	17	4	NW on pile.	Ra ref.
12595	- Day beacon 5	28-59-40.453N 089-08-30.051W				SG on pile.	Ra ref.
12596	- LIGHT 6	28-59-42.931N 089-08-26.697W	Fl R 2.5s	17	4	TR on pile.	Ra ref.
12596.01	- LIGHT 5A	28-59-45.419N 089-08-34.320W	Q G	17	4	SG on pile.	Ra ref.
12596.02	- Danger Day beacon C	28-59-51.883N 089-08-35.161W				NW on pile.	Ra ref.
12596.03	- LIGHT 7	28-59-54.409N 089-08-48.308W	Fl G 4s	17	4	SG on pile.	Ra ref.
12596.04	- DANGER LIGHT D	29-00-00.007N 089-08-44.546W	Fl W 2.5s	17	4	NW on pile.	Ra ref.
12596.05	- Danger Day beacon E	29-00-07.526N 089-08-54.751W				NW on pile.	Ra ref.
12596.06	- LIGHT 8	29-00-14.264N 089-09-03.059W	Fl R 4s	17	4	TR on pile.	Ra ref.

Light List corrected through LNM week: 01/18

(1) No.	(2) Name and Location	(3) Position	(4) Characteristic	(5) Height	(6) Range	(7) Structure	(8) Remarks
			LOUISIANA - Eighth District				

MISSISSIPPI RIVER DELTA (Chart 11361)

South Pass

(1) No.	(2) Name and Location	(3) Position	(4) Characteristic	(5) Height	(6) Range	(7) Structure	(8) Remarks
12597	PORT EADS MARINA LOWER DOCK LIGHT	29-00-55.000N 089-09-59.000W	Fl G 2.5s			Marks lower end of dock.	Private aid.
12597.01	PORT EADS MARINA UPPER DOCK LIGHT	29-00-58.000N 089-10-03.000W	Fl G 2.5s			Marks upper end of dock.	Private aid.
12605	PICAYUNE BAYOU LIGHT 9	29-01-36.825N 089-10-54.173W	Iso G 6s	17	4	SG on pile.	Ra ref.
12610	OYSTERVILLE LIGHT 9A	29-03-12.345N 089-12-13.250W	Iso G 6s	17	4	SG on piles.	
12612	- Buoy 9B	29-03-36.700N 089-12-23.800W				Green can.	
12615	- Lighted Buoy 9C	29-04-30.021N 089-12-50.831W	Fl G 4s		4	Green can.	
12620	OLD GRAND BAYOU LIGHT 10	29-04-32.314N 089-12-44.845W	Iso R 6s	17	4	TR on pile.	Ra Ref.
12622	- Buoy 9D	29-04-46.108N 089-13-02.566W				Green can.	
12625	SOUTHERN NATURAL GAS SOUTH PASS DOCK A LIGHT	29-05-06.000N 089-13-12.000W	Fl R 4s	8		On boat dock.	Private aid.
12630	SOUTHERN NATURAL GAS SOUTH PASS DOCK B LIGHT	29-04-54.000N 089-13-24.000W	Fl G 4s	8		On boat dock.	Private aid.
12632	CLAYTON WILLIAMS ENERGY SOUTH PASS PIPELINE LIGHT	29-05-17.560N 089-13-37.640W	Fl Y 2.5s			NW on pile.	Private aid.
12632.01	CLAYTON WILLIAMS ENERGY SOUTH PASS PIPELINE LIGHT	29-05-09.710N 089-13-30.570W	Fl Y 2.5s			NW on pile.	Private aid.
12632.02	CLAYTON WILLIAMS ENERGY SOUTH PASS PIPELINE LIGHT	29-05-02.010N 089-13-23.290W	Fl Y 2.5s			NW on pile.	Private aid.
12635	UPPER CAVE LIGHT 11	29-06-02.272N 089-14-09.037W	Iso G 6s	17	4	SG on dolphin.	
12640	- LIGHT 11A	29-06-52.871N 089-14-32.579W	Fl G 2.5s	17	4	SG on pile.	Ra ref.
12642	- Lighted Buoy 11B	29-07-07.560N 089-14-29.100W	Fl G 2.5s		3	Green can.	
12645	- LIGHT 13	29-07-23.088N 089-14-34.516W	Iso G 6s	17	4	SG on pile.	Ra ref.
12650	DEPOT POINT LIGHT 14	29-07-59.512N 089-14-31.843W	Iso R 6s	17	4	TR on skeleton tower on piles.	
12655	- LIGHT 14 A	29-08-24.280N 089-14-47.123W	Iso R 6s	17	4	TR on pile.	
12660	CYPRESS LEADING LIGHT	29-08-01.574N 089-14-47.549W	Iso W 6s	42		NB on skeleton tower on piles.	Visible 6° either side of 166° to the light..
12665	- LIGHT 15	29-08-28.409N 089-15-00.454W	Iso G 6s	17	4	SG on pile.	Ra ref.
12670	- LIGHT 16	29-09-05.673N 089-14-58.798W	Fl R 2.5s	17	4	TR on pile.	Ra ref.

Southwest Pass

(1) No.	(2) Name and Location	(3) Position	(4) Characteristic	(5) Height	(6) Range	(7) Structure	(8) Remarks
12680 430	- Entrance Lighted Buoy SW	28-52-39.100N 089-25-55.000W	Mo (A) W		5	Red and white stripes with red spherical topmark.	
12685	- ENTRANCE RANGE FRONT LIGHT	28-54-34.456N 089-25-55.186W	F W	20		KRW on skeleton tower on piles.	Visible 1.5° each side of rangeline.
12690	- ENTRANCE RANGE REAR LIGHT 383 yards, 000.3° from front light.	28-54-45.822N 089-25-55.099W	F W	65		KRW on skeleton tower on piles.	Visible 1.5° each side of rangeline.
12695	- Lighted Buoy 1 150 feet outside channel limit.	28-53-41.261N 089-26-00.572W	Fl G 2.5s		4	Green.	

(1) No.	(2) Name and Location	(3) Position	(4) Characteristic	(5) Height	(6) Range	(7) Structure	(8) Remarks
		LOUISIANA - Eighth District					
	MISSISSIPPI RIVER DELTA (Chart 11361)						
	Southwest Pass						
12700	- ENTRANCE EAST RANGE FRONT LIGHT	28-54-33.742N 089-25-53.446W	Q R	21		NR on tower on piles.	Visible 1.5° each side of rangeline.
12705	- ENTRANCE EAST RANGE FRONT PASSING LIGHT	28-54-34.518N 089-25-53.454W	Q W	23	5	On same structure as Southwest Pass Entrance East Range Front Light.	
12710	- ENTRANCE EAST RANGE REAR LIGHT 544 yards, 000.1° from front light.	28-54-49.848N 089-25-53.414W	Iso R 6s	45		NR on tower on piles.	Visible only on the east quarter of SWP Entrance Channel.
12715	- ENTRANCE WEST RANGE FRONT LIGHT	28-54-34.667N 089-25-56.898W	Q G	21		NG on dolphin.	Visible 1.5° each side of rangeline.
12720	- ENTRANCE WEST RANGE REAR LIGHT 414 yards, 359.9° from front light.	28-54-46.747N 089-25-56.857W	Iso G 6s	45		NG on skeleton tower on piles.	Visible 1.5° each side of rangeline.
12725	- LEADING LIGHT	28-53-59.115N 089-26-15.579W	Q W (NIGHT) Q W (NIGHT)	30	5	NB on pile.	
12730	- EAST JETTY END LIGHT 4	28-54-19.891N 089-25-45.460W	Iso R 6s (NIGHT) Iso R 6s (NIGHT)	38	5	TR on red skeleton tower on piles.	Higher intensity beam up channel.
12735	- *East Jetty End Lighted Buoy 4A*	28-54-16.743N 089-25-48.869W	Fl R 4s		3	Red.	
12740 420	- **Entrance Light**	28-54-21.376N 089-25-43.025W	Fl W 10s	122 85	12	Tower on white dwelling on piles.	RACON: K (- . -) Emergency light of reduced intensity: Fl W 10s.
12745	- B RANGE FRONT LIGHT	28-55-01.185N 089-25-09.466W	Q W	25		KRW on skeleton tower on piles.	Visible 5.5° each side of rangeline.
12750	- B RANGE FRONT PASSING LIGHT	28-54-57.015N 089-25-13.835W	Fl W 2.5s	17	4	On same structure as Southwest Pass Range B Front Light.	
12755	- B RANGE REAR LIGHT 541 yards, 42.8° from front light.	28-55-12.966N 089-24-57.051W	Iso W 6s	41		KRW on skeleton tower on piles.	
12760	- B EAST RANGE FRONT LIGHT	28-55-04.345N 089-25-03.845W	Q R	20		KWR on skeleton tower on piles.	Visible 1.5° each side of rangeline.
12765	- B EAST RANGE REAR LIGHT 302 yards, 42.4° from front light.	28-55-10.959N 089-24-56.971W	Iso R 6s	35		KWR on skeleton tower on piles.	Visible 1.5° each side of rangeline.
12770	- B WEST RANGE FRONT LIGHT	28-55-06.197N 089-25-06.551W	Q G	20		KWG on skeleton tower on piles.	Visible 1.5° each side of rangeline.
12775	- B WEST RANGE REAR LIGHT 309 yards, 043.0° from front light.	28-55-12.891N 089-24-59.440W	Iso G 6s	35		KWG on skeleton tower on piles.	Visible 1.5° each side of rangeline.
12780	- LIGHT 5	28-56-11.153N 089-24-36.851W	Iso G 6s	41	5	SG on skeleton tower on piles.	
12785	- LIGHT 6	28-56-16.440N 089-24-12.480W	Iso R 6s	45	4	TR on skeleton tower on piles.	
12790	- LIGHT 7	28-56-50.914N 089-24-09.528W	Fl G 2.5s	45	5	SG on skeleton tower on piles.	
12795	- LIGHT 8	28-57-05.615N 089-23-38.008W	Fl R 2.5s	35	9	TR on skeleton tower on piles.	

(1) No.	(2) Name and Location	(3) Position	(4) Characteristic	(5) Height	(6) Range	(7) Structure	(8) Remarks
	LOUISIANA - Eighth District						
	MISSISSIPPI RIVER DELTA (Chart 11361)						
	Southwest Pass						
12800	- LIGHT 9	28-57-57.112N 089-23-17.552W	Iso G 6s	45	5	SG on skeleton tower on piles.	
12805	- LIGHT 10	28-58-35.495N 089-22-23.624W	Iso R 6s	45	5	TR on skeleton tower on piles.	
12810	- LIGHT 11	28-58-51.844N 089-22-30.890W	Iso G 6s	45	5	SG on skeleton tower on piles.	
12815	- LIGHT 12	28-59-28.023N 089-21-38.932W	Fl R 4s	45	4	TR on skeleton tower on piles.	
12820	- LIGHT 14	29-00-08.111N 089-21-05.026W	Iso R 6s	45	5	TR on skeleton tower on piles.	
12825	- LIGHT 16	29-00-46.114N 089-20-35.531W	Iso R 6s	40	5	TR on skeleton tower on piles.	
12830	- LIGHT 17	29-01-19.478N 089-20-29.602W	Fl G 2.5s	40	5	SG on skeleton tower on piles.	
12835	- LIGHT 18	29-01-23.765N 089-20-06.152W	Fl R 2.5s	45	9	TR on skeleton tower on piles.	
12845	CHEVRON PIER LIGHT	29-02-19.000N 089-19-33.200W	Q W	6		On dock.	Private aid.
12855	CHEVRON BOAT DOCK LIGHT	29-02-21.000N 089-19-13.000W	Fl R 4s	7		On dolphin.	Private aid.
12860	**Double Bayou Light 19**	29-02-49.035N 089-19-10.331W	Fl G 2.5s	45	10	SG on skeleton tower on piles. 45	
12865	ENERGY PARTNERS OUTFALL LIGHT	29-02-57.800N 089-18-43.200W	Fl R 4s			On pile.	Private aid.
12870	SHELL TERMINAL LOADING DOCK LIGHTS (2)	29-03-18.000N 089-18-32.000W	F R	25		On dock.	Private aid.
12875	- LIGHT 21	29-03-41.640N 089-18-39.360W	Iso G 6s	45	5	SG on skeleton tower on piles.	
12880	- LIGHT 22 200 feet outside channel limit.	29-03-58.740N 089-18-00.660W	Q R	40	5	TR on skeleton tower on piles.	
12885	**Scotts Canal Light 23**	29-05-08.825N 089-17-10.958W	Fl G 2.5s	45	10	SG on skeleton tower on mud sills. 15	
12890	- LIGHT 24	29-05-08.172N 089-16-50.205W	Fl R 2.5s	37	5	TR on skeleton tower on piles.	
12895	SCOTTS CANAL LANDING LIGHT	29-05-13.000N 089-17-03.000W	Fl W 3s	10			Private aid.
12900	- LIGHT 26	29-06-26.718N 089-16-06.816W	Iso R 6s	45	4	TR on skeleton tower.	
12905	- LIGHT 27	29-07-11.011N 089-16-01.016W	Fl G 2.5s	45	5	SG on skeleton tower on piles.	
12910	- HEAD RANGE FRONT LIGHT	29-07-56.340N 089-15-24.600W	F W	35		KRW on skeleton tower on piles.	Visible 2° each side of rangeline.
12915	- HEAD RANGE FRONT LIGHT PASSING LIGHT	29-07-54.812N 089-15-24.183W	Fl W 4s	17	5	On same structure as Southwest Pass Head Range Front Light.	
12920	- HEAD RANGE REAR LIGHT 315 yards, 183° from front light.	29-07-45.789N 089-15-25.207W	F W	48		KRW on skeleton tower on mud sills.	Visible 2° each side of rangeline.
12925	- HEAD EAST RANGE FRONT LIGHT	29-07-50.430N 089-15-21.509W	Q R	25		KWR on skeleton tower on piles.	Visible 4° each side of rangeline.
12930	- HEAD EAST RANGE REAR LIGHT 400 yards, 183° from front light.	29-07-38.551N 089-15-22.249W	Iso R 6s	40		KWR on skeleton tower on piles.	Visible 4° each side of rangeline.
12935	- HEAD WEST RANGE FRONT LIGHT	29-07-50.774N 089-15-27.149W	Q G	25		KWG on skeleton tower on piles.	Visible 4° each side of rangeline.
12940	- HEAD WEST RANGE REAR LIGHT 400 yards, 183° from front light.	29-07-38.848N 089-15-27.873W	Iso G 6s	40		KWG on skeleton tower on piles.	Visible 4° each side of rangeline.

Light List corrected through LNM week: 01/18

(1) No.	(2) Name and Location	(3) Position	(4) Characteristic	(5) Height	(6) Range	(7) Structure	(8) Remarks
	**MISSISSIPPI RIVER (Louisiana) - Eighth District**						

MISSISSIPPI RIVER DELTA (Chart 11361)

Head of Passes to New Orleans
Designations left descending bank (LDB) and right descending bank (RDB) are as seen from a vessel going downstream Mileage given indicates the number of miles above Head of Passes Junction Light.

(1) No.	(2) Name and Location	(3) Position	(4) Characteristic	(5) Height	(6) Range	(7) Structure	(8) Remarks
12945	HEAD OF PASSES JUNCTION LIGHT	29-08-52.769N 089-15-05.546W	Fl (2+1)R 6s		6	JR on skeleton tower on piles.	
12950	CUBITS GAP RANGE FRONT LIGHT	29-10-00.296N 089-15-13.002W	Q G			KRW on skeleton tower on piles.	Visible 2° each side of rangeline.
12955	CUBITS GAP RANGE REAR LIGHT 272 yards, 151.2° from front light.	29-09-53.144N 089-15-08.717W	F G			KRW on skeleton tower on piles.	Visible 2° each side of rangeline.
12960	PILOTTOWN A RANGE FRONT LIGHT	29-10-06.749N 089-15-16.574W	Q W			KRW on skeleton tower.	
12965	PILOTTOWN A RANGE REAR LIGHT 298 yards, 001.6° from front light.	29-10-15.591N 089-15-16.113W	Iso W 6s			KRW on skeleton tower.	
12970	PILOTTOWN A EAST RANGE FRONT LIGHT	29-10-11.168N 089-15-12.919W	Q R			KWR on skeleton tower on piles.	Visible 4° each side of rangeline.
12975	PILOTTOWN A EAST RANGE REAR LIGHT 400 yards, 003° from front light.	29-10-22.859N 089-15-12.321W	Iso R 6s			KWR on skeleton tower on piles.	Visible 4° each side of rangeline.
12980	PILOTTOWN A WEST RANGE FRONT LIGHT	29-10-11.441N 089-15-18.539W	Q G			KWG on skeleton tower on piles.	Visible 4° each side of rangeline.
12985	PILOTTOWN A WEST RANGE REAR LIGHT 415 yards, 001.8° from front light.	29-10-23.778N 089-15-17.845W	Iso G 6s			KWG on skeleton tower on piles.	Visible 4° each side of rangeline.
12990	Pilottown Anchorage Lower Day beacon 1.5	29-10-13.619N 089-16-06.123W				NY on pile.	Ra ref.
12995	*Pilottown Lighted Buoy 1* RDB mile 1.6.	29-10-22.469N 089-15-39.811W	Q G		4	Green.	
13000	PILOTTOWN WINGDAM LIGHT 2	29-10-27.086N 089-15-25.006W	Fl R 2.5s		5	TR on skeleton tower on piles.	
13005	RIVER PILOTS WINGDAM LIGHT	29-10-45.000N 089-15-34.000W	F R			On pile.	Private aid.
13010	RIVER PILOTS WHARF LIGHT	29-10-43.000N 089-15-32.000W	F R			Pile.	Private aid.
13015	PILOTTOWN TERMINAL WING DAM LIGHT	29-11-00.000N 089-15-39.000W	Q R				Private aid.
13020	*Cubits Gap Lighted Buoy 3* RDB mile 2.6.	29-11-11.790N 089-16-01.723W	Fl G 4s		4	Green.	
13025	CUBITS GAP LIGHT 4 LDB mile 2.8.	29-11-32.645N 089-15-51.579W	Iso R 6s		5	TR on skeleton tower on piles.	
13030	*Old Quarantine Station Lighted Buoy A* RDB mile 3.6.	29-12-00.626N 089-16-31.838W	Fl (2+1)G 6s		4	Green and red bands.	
13035	OLD QUARANTINE STATION LIGHT 6 LDB mile 3.5.	29-12-07.257N 089-16-17.248W	Fl R 4s		4	TR on skeleton tower on piles.	
13040	SPENCES LIGHT 6A LDB mile 3.5.	29-14-24.365N 089-17-54.300W	Fl R 6s		4	TR on skeleton tower on piles.	
13045	Pilottown Anchorage Upper Day beacon 6.7	29-14-04.401N 089-18-22.579W				NY on pile.	Ra ref.
13050	WEST POINT LIGHT 7 RDB mile 7.7.	29-14-48.143N 089-19-02.282W	Fl G 4s		4	SG on skeleton tower on piles.	
13055	WILDER FLATS LIGHT 8 LDB mile 7.7.	29-15-08.609N 089-18-42.866W	Fl R 2.5s		5	TR on skeleton tower on piles	
13060	Lower Venice Anchorage Lower Day beacon 8.0	29-15-15.079N 089-18-51.307W				NY on pile.	Ra ref.
13065	Lower Venice Anchorage Upper Day beacon 9.6	29-16-10.988N 089-20-00.055W				NY on pile.	Ra ref.
13070	JUMP LIGHT 9 RDB mile 9.8.	29-15-47.915N 089-20-22.137W	Fl G 6s		4	SG on skeleton tower on piles.	

Light List corrected through LNM week: 01/18

(1) No.	(2) Name and Location	(3) Position	(4) Characteristic	(5) Height	(6) Range	(7) Structure	(8) Remarks
		MISSISSIPPI RIVER (Louisiana) - Eighth District					
	MISSISSIPPI RIVER DELTA (Chart 11361)						
	Head of Passes to New Orleans						
	Designations left descending bank (LDB) and right descending bank (RDB) are as seen from a vessel going downstream. Mileage given indicates the number of miles above Head of Passes Junction Light.						
13075	*Jump Shoal Lighted Buoy 10* Mile 9.3, marks western edge of shoal.	29-15-50.231N 089-20-02.632W	Fl R 4s		4	Red.	
13080	Upper Venice Anchorage Lower Day beacon 10.0	29-16-24.652N 089-20-16.271W				NY on pile.	Ra ref.
13085	*Jump Shoal Lighted Buoy 10A* Mile 10.1.	29-16-20.838N 089-20-34.415W	Fl R 2.5s		5	Red.	
13090	THE JUMP WHARF LIGHTS (3) RDB mile 10.5.	29-16-32.000N 089-21-08.000W	F W				Aid maintained by U.S. Army Corps of Engineers.
13095	Upper Venice Anchorage Upper Day beacon 11.2	29-17-10.436N 089-20-59.882W				NY on pile.	Ra ref.
13100	GETTY DOCK LIGHTS (3) RDB mile 11.9.	29-17-28.000N 089-21-57.000W	F G				HORN: 1 BLAST EV 20S (2S BL). Private aid.
	MISSISSIPPI RIVER - Venice to New Orleans (Chart 11364)						
	Head of Passes to New Orleans						
	Designations left descending bank (LDB) and right descending bank (RDB) are as seen from a vessel going downstream. Mileage given indicates the number of miles above Head of Passes Junction Light.						
13105	MICHELLA LIGHT 14 LDB mile 13.5.	29-18-49.149N 089-22-18.757W	Iso R 6s		7	TR on skeleton tower on piles.	
13110	Boothville Anchorage Lower Day beacon 12.2	29-17-36.808N 089-22-00.126W				NY on pile.	Ra ref.
13115	OLGA LIGHT 16 LDB mile 16.3.	29-20-45.454N 089-24-09.934W	Iso R 6s		5	TR on skeleton tower on piles.	
13120	ST ANNE LIGHT 18 LDB mile 18.0.	29-21-44.187N 089-25-55.330W	Fl R 4s		5	TR on skeleton tower on piles.	
13125	*Fort Jackson Lighted Buoy A*	29-21-17.206N 089-25-31.256W	Fl (2+1)G 6s		4	Green with red bands.	
13130	Boothville Anchorage Upper Day beacon 18.5	29-21-18.093N 089-26-02.285W				NY on pile.	Ra ref.
13135	BOOTHVILLE WATER INTAKE LIGHT RDB mile 18.7.	29-21-31.000N 089-26-15.000W	Q G			On intake structure.	Private aid.
13140	FORT JACKSON LIGHT 19 RDB mile 19.2.	29-21-39.242N 089-26-50.859W	Iso G 6s		7	SG on skeleton tower on piles.	
13145	ST PHILIPS BEND LIGHT 20 LDB mile 19.6.	29-22-00.220N 089-27-04.098W	Iso R 6s		5	TR on skeleton tower on piles.	
13150	HARVEY LIGHT 20A LDB mile 20.5.	29-21-48.409N 089-27-40.498W	Fl R 4s		5	TR on skeleton tower on piles.	
13155	BAYOU PETIT LIARD LIGHT 21 RDB mile 21.1.	29-20-48.804N 089-28-00.744W	Iso G 6s		5	SG on skeleton tower on piles.	
13160	BAYOU GRAND LIARD LIGHT 21A RDB mile 21.9.	29-20-23.808N 089-28-56.520W	Fl G 2.5s		5	SG on skeleton tower on piles.	
13165	BOLIVAR POINT LIGHT 22 LDB mile 22.0.	29-20-47.045N 089-28-51.282W	Iso R 6s		4	TR on pile.	
13170	*Triumph Shoal Lighted Buoy 23* Mile 23.2, marks northern edge of shoal.	29-21-03.353N 089-30-12.966W	Fl G 4s		4	Green.	
13175	Ostrica Anchorage Lower Day beacon 23.0	29-20-41.326N 089-29-54.654W				NY on pile.	Ra ref.
13180	NEPTUNE LIGHT 24 LDB mile 23.9.	29-21-32.623N 089-30-35.881W	Iso R 6s		5	TR on skeleton tower on piles.	Ra ref.
13185	Ostrica Anchorage Upper Day beacon 24.4	29-21-19.987N 089-31-11.486W				NY on pile.	Ra ref.
13190	TANKER LOADING DOCK LIGHT LDB mile 25.7.	29-22-05.000N 089-32-04.000W	F R			On pile.	Private aid.

Light List corrected through LNM week: 01/18

(1) No.	(2) Name and Location	(3) Position	(4) Characteristic	(5) Height	(6) Range	(7) Structure	(8) Remarks
	MISSISSIPPI RIVER (Louisiana) - Eighth District

MISSISSIPPI RIVER - Venice to New Orleans (Chart 11364)

Head of Passes to New Orleans
Designations left descending bank (LDB) and right descending bank (RDB) are as seen from a vessel going downstream Mileage given indicates the number of miles above Head of Passes Junction Light.

(1) No.	(2) Name and Location	(3) Position	(4) Characteristic	(5) Height	(6) Range	(7) Structure	(8) Remarks
13195	CAL-KY OSTRICA BARGE DOCK LIGHTS (2) RDB mile 27.1.	29-22-18.300N 089-33-12.200W	Q R				Private aid.
13200	CAL-KY EMPIRE TANKER DOCK LIGHTS (4) LDB mile 27.5.	29-22-20.000N 089-33-23.000W	Fl R 2.5s			On dolphin.	HORN: 1 BLAST EV 20S (2S BL). Private aid.
13205	CAL-KY EMPIRE BOAT DOCK LIGHT RDB mile 27.5.	29-22-00.200N 089-34-00.030W	Q W				Private aid.
13210	ALBERTA LIGHT 27 LDB mile 27.8.	29-22-20.188N 089-34-17.837W	Iso G 6s		5	SG on skeleton tower on piles.	
13215	EMPIRE WATER INTAKE LIGHTS (2) RDB mile 30.0.	29-23-46.000N 089-36-00.000W	F G				HORN: 1 BLAST EV 20S (2S BL). OPERATED CONTINUOUSLY THROUGHOUT THE YEAR. Private aid.
13220	TROPICAL BEND LOWER LIGHT 29 rDB mile 30.4.	29-24-06.031N 089-36-20.398W	Iso G 6s		4	SG on skeleton tower on piles.	
13225	POINT PLEASANT LOWER LIGHT 30 LDB mile 30.4.	29-24-16.768N 089-35-56.726W	Iso R 6s		5	TR on skeleton tower on piles.	
13230	POINT PLEASANT UPPER LIGHT 30A LDB mile 31.8.	29-25-07.006N 089-36-08.616W	Fl R 6s		4	TR on skeleton tower on piles.	
13235	TROPICAL BEND UPPER LIGHT 31 RDB mile 32.1.	29-25-31.618N 089-36-28.841W	Iso G 6s		7	SG on skeleton tower on piles.	
13240	SIXTY MILE POINT LIGHT 33 Marks shoal off RDB mile 33.0.	29-26-17.904N 089-36-09.458W	Q G		4	SG on skeleton tower on piles.	
13245	BAYOU LAMOQUE LIGHT 32 LDB mile 33.2.	29-26-32.917N 089-35-43.762W	Iso R 6s		5	TR on skeleton tower on piles.	
13250	*Sixty Mile Point Lighted Buoy A*	29-26-44.637N 089-36-09.473W	Fl (2+1)G 6s		4	Green with red bands.	
13255	BAYOU LAMOQUE LIGHT 32A LDB mile 33.6.	29-26-52.809N 089-35-50.170W	Q R		5	TR on skeleton tower on piles.	
13260	HARRIS BAYOU LIGHT 34 LDB mile 34.3.	29-27-21.565N 089-36-32.330W	Iso R 6s		4	TR on skeleton tower on piles.	
13265	BASS LOADING DOCK LIGHTS (2) LDB mile 35.2.	29-27-38.000N 089-37-30.000W	F W			On dolphin.	Private aid.
13270	HOME PLACE LIGHT 37 RDB mile 37.0.	29-27-23.991N 089-39-13.507W	Iso G 6s		6	SG on skeleton tower on piles.	
13275	HOME PLACE EAST LIGHT 38 LDB mile 37.5.	29-27-59.188N 089-39-42.446W	Iso R 6s		4	TR on skeleton tower on piles. On same structure as Port Sulphur Anchorage Lower Day beacon 35.7.	
13280	Port Sulphur Anchorage Lower Day beacon 37.5	29-27-59.248N 089-39-42.386W				NY on pile. On same structure as Home Place East Light 38.	
13285	FREEPORT MCMORAN ENERGY DOCK LOWER LIGHT RDB mile 39.0	29-28-22.000N 089-41-02.000W	Fl G 2.5s	15		On dock.	Private aid.
13290	FREEPORT MCMORAN ENERGY DOCK UPPER LIGHT RDB mile 39.0	29-28-25.000N 089-41-06.000W	Fl G 2.5s	15		On dock.	Private aid.

Light List corrected through LNM week: 01/18

(1) No.	(2) Name and Location	(3) Position	(4) Characteristic	(5) Height	(6) Range	(7) Structure	(8) Remarks
	MISSISSIPPI RIVER (Louisiana) - Eighth District						
	MISSISSIPPI RIVER - Venice to New Orleans (Chart 11364)						
	Head of Passes to New Orleans *Designations left descending bank (LDB) and right descending bank (RDB) are as seen from a vessel going downstream Mileage given indicates the number of miles above Head of Passes Junction Light.*						
13295	NESTOR CNL LIGHT 40 LDB mile 39.7.	29-29-10.291N 089-41-18.464W	Iso R 6s		7	TR on skeleton tower on piles. On same structure as Port Sulphur Anchorage Upper Day beacon 39.7.	
13300	Port Sulphur Anchorage Upper Day beacon 39.7	29-29-10.528N 089-41-18.446W				NY on pile. On same structure as Nester Canal Light 40.	
13305	HULING LIGHT 42 LDB mile 42.8.	29-31-13.444N 089-43-02.598W	Iso R 6s		4	TR on skeleton tower on piles.	
13310	POINT MICHELE LIGHT 43 RDB mile 43.2.	29-31-16.140N 089-43-45.225W	Iso G 6s		7	SG on skeleton tower on piles.	
13312	SOCOLA LIGHT 45 RDB mile 44.8.	29-32-01.000N 089-45-22.780W	Fl G 4s		5	SG on tower.	
13315	BOHEMIA LIGHT 46 LDB mile 44.9.	29-32-11.227N 089-44-55.124W	Iso R 6s		7	TR on skeleton tower on piles.	
13320	Magnolia Anchorage Lower Day beacon 45.5	29-32-14.418N 089-45-42.964W				NY on pile.	Ra ref.
13325	Magnolia Anchorage Upper Day beacon 47.6	29-33-40.920N 089-47-09.013W				NY on pile.	Ra ref.
13330	SULPHUR LOADING DOCK LIGHTS (2) RDB mile 49.0.	29-34-21.000N 089-48-04.000W	Fl G 2.5s			On dolphins.	Private aid.
13335	ROCK ISLAND DOCK LIGHTS (2) RDB mile 49.3.	29-34-50.000N 089-48-16.000W	Fl G 4s			On dolphins.	Private aid.
13340	Celeste Anchorage Lower Day beacon 49.8	29-34-43.677N 089-48-47.787W				NY on pile.	Ra ref.
13345	Celeste Anchorage Upper Day beacon 52.0	29-35-51.876N 089-50-37.271W				NY on pile.	Ra ref.
13350	FAVRET LIGHT 52 LDB mile 52.5.	29-36-18.633N 089-50-50.698W	Iso R 6s		5	TR on skeleton tower on piles.	
13355	POINT CELESTE LIGHT 53 RDB mile 52.8.	29-36-03.670N 089-51-16.521W	Fl G 6s		4	SG on skeleton tower on piles.	
13360	Davant Anchorage Lower Day beacon 52.8	29-36-22.680N 089-51-05.640W				NY on pile.	Ra ref.
13365	Davant Anchorage Upper Day beacon 53.9	29-36-36.674N 089-52-09.287W				NY on pile.	Ra ref.
13370	DEER RANGE LIGHT 55 RDB mile 55.4.	29-36-42.969N 089-53-42.046W	Iso G 6s		5	SG on skeleton tower.	
13375	*Electro-Coal Mooring Buoy Light L* LDB mile 55.0.	29-36-32.000N 089-52-10.500W	Fl W 2.5s			White.	Private aid.
13380	Electro Coal Mooring Buoy B	29-37-21.500N 089-54-14.000W				White	Private aid.
13385	Electro Coal Mooring Buoy C	29-37-20.000N 089-54-11.500W				White	Private aid.
13390	Electro Coal Mooring Buoy D	29-37-18.500N 089-54-09.000W				White	Private aid.
13395	Electro Coal Mooring Buoy E	29-37-16.500N 089-54-06.000W				White.	Private aid.
13400	Electro Coal Mooring Buoy F	29-36-43.000N 089-52-48.000W				White	Private aid.
13405	Electro Coal Mooring Buoy G	29-36-45.000N 089-52-46.000W				White	Private aid.
13410	Electro Coal Mooring Buoy H	29-36-38.500N 089-52-34.500W				White	Private aid.
13415	Electro Coal Mooring Buoy I	29-36-41.000N 089-52-32.500W				White	Private aid.
13420	Electro Coal Mooring Buoy J	29-36-34.500N 089-52-20.000W				White	Private aid.

Light List corrected through LNM week: 01/18

(1) No.	(2) Name and Location	(3) Position	(4) Characteristic	(5) Height	(6) Range	(7) Structure	(8) Remarks
	MISSISSIPPI RIVER (Louisiana) - Eighth District

MISSISSIPPI RIVER - Venice to New Orleans (Chart 11364)

Head of Passes to New Orleans

Designations left descending bank (LDB) and right descending bank (RDB) are as seen from a vessel going downstream. Mileage given indicates the number of miles above Head of Passes Junction Light.

(1) No.	(2) Name and Location	(3) Position	(4) Characteristic	(5) Height	(6) Range	(7) Structure	(8) Remarks
13425	Electro Coal Mooring Buoy K	29-36-37.000N 089-52-18.000W				White.	Private aid.
13430	ELECTRO-COAL TRANSFER DOCK LIGHTS (3) LDB mile 55.4.	29-36-55.000N 089-53-14.000W	Fl R 2.5s	12		On piles.	Horn: 1 blast ev 20s in unison (2S BL). Operated during low visibility. Private aid.
13435	Electro-Coal Lighted Mooring Buoy A LDB mile 56.0.	29-37-22.000N 089-54-14.500W	Fl W 2.5s			White.	Private aid.
13440	Citrus Lands Coal Terminal Lighted Mooring Buoy A RDB mile 56.	29-37-12.000N 089-54-17.000W	Q W				Private aid.
13445	Citrus Lands Coal Terminal Lighted Mooring Buoy B RDB mile 56.	29-36-56.000N 089-54-04.000W	Q W				Private aid.
13450	INTERNATIONAL MARINE TERMINAL DOCK LIGHTS (5) RDB mile 57.0.	29-37-20.000N 089-54-55.000W	Fl G 2.5s			On dock and dolphins.	Private aid.
13455	INTERNATIONAL MARINE TERMINALS DOLPHIN LIGHT RDB mile 57.0.	29-37-55.000N 089-55-44.000W	Fl G 2.5s	11		On dolphin.	Private aid.
13460	MYRTLE GROVE LIGHT 59 RDB mile 59.0.	29-38-16.756N 089-56-40.891W	Iso G 6s		5	SG on skeleton tower on mud sills.	
13465	POVERTY POINT LIGHT 60 LDB mile 59.9.	29-39-07.072N 089-57-10.794W	Iso R 6s		5	TR on pile.	
13470	IRONTON LIGHT 61 RDB mile 60.0.	29-38-54.173N 089-57-30.871W	Iso G 6s		5	SG on skeleton tower on piles.	
13475	MISSISSIPPI RIVER GRAIN ELEVATOR DOCK LIGHTS (2) RDB mile 61.5.	29-40-25.000N 089-57-51.000W	Q W			On mooring dolphins.	Private aid.
13480	BEAU SEJOUR LIGHT 62 LDB mile 61.5.	29-40-54.128N 089-57-37.322W	Iso R 6s		5	TR on skeleton tower.	
13485	BP ALLIANCE REFINERY COKE BARGE DOCK LIGHTS (2) RDB mile 62.0.	29-40-52.000N 089-58-03.000W	Q G			On mooring dolphin.	Private aid.
13490	BP ALLIANCE REFINERY COKE BARGE DOCK LIGHTS (2) RDB mile 62.5.	29-41-00.000N 089-58-07.000W	F G			On mooring dolphin.	Private aid.
13495	BP ALLIANCE REFINERY TANKER DOCK LIGHTS (4) RDB mile 63.0.	29-41-20.000N 089-58-20.000W	Fl G 2.5s			On dock.	Private aid.
13500	ENTERGY LOUISIANA SUBMERGED CABLE LIGHT LDB mile 63.5.	29-41-44.450N 089-58-46.510W	Fl G 2.5s			On dolphins.	Private aid.
13505	ENTERGY LOUISIANA SUBMERGED CABLE LIGHTS (2) RDB mile 63.5.	29-41-52.890N 089-58-18.820W	Fl R 2.5s			On dolphin.	Private aid.
13510	BRITISH PETROLEUM REFINERY DOCK LIGHTS (3) RDB mile 63.6.	29-41-40.000N 089-58-38.000W	Fl G 2.5s			On dolphins.	Private aid.
13515	Alliance Anchorage Lower Day beacon 63.8	29-41-59.662N 089-58-59.455W				NY on pile.	Ra ref.
13520	BELAIR LIGHT 66 LDB mile 65.7.	29-43-35.576N 089-59-12.586W	Iso R 6s		7	TR on skeleton tower on piles.	
13525	Alliance Anchorage Upper Day beacon 65.8	29-43-34.883N 089-59-46.278W				NY on pile.	Ra ref.
13530	LA GRANGE LIGHT 67 RDB mile 65.8.	29-43-34.883N 089-59-46.278W	Iso G 6s		5	SG on skeleton tower on block.	
13535	Wills Point Anchorage Lower Day beacon 66.5	29-44-32.060N 090-00-06.720W				NY on pile.	Ra ref.

Light List corrected through LNM week: 01/18

(1) No.	(2) Name and Location	(3) Position	(4) Characteristic	(5) Height	(6) Range	(7) Structure	(8) Remarks

MISSISSIPPI RIVER (Louisiana) - Eighth District

MISSISSIPPI RIVER - Venice to New Orleans (Chart 11364)

Head of Passes to New Orleans

Designations left descending bank (LDB) and right descending bank (RDB) are as seen from a vessel going downstream. Mileage given indicates the number of miles above Head of Passes Junction Light.

No.	Name and Location	Position	Characteristic	Height	Range	Structure	Remarks
13540	Wills Point Anchorage Upper Day beacon 67.6	29-45-02.799N 090-00-57.059W				NY on pile.	Ra ref.
13550	LIVE OAK LIGHT 69 RDB Mile 68.6.	29-45-28.498N 090-01-37.641W	Iso G 6s		5	SG on skeleton tower on piles.	
13555	Cedar Grove Anchorage Lower Day beacon 69.9	29-46-41.503N 090-01-30.423W				NY on pile.	Ra ref.
13560	OAKVILLE LIGHT 71 On same structure as Cedar Grove Anchorage Lower Day beacon Mile 69.9.	29-46-41.503N 090-01-30.423W	Iso G 6s		5	SG on skeleton tower on piles.	
13565	BERTRANDVILLE LIGHT 70 LDB Mile 70.0	29-46-34.810N 090-01-03.429W	Fl R 4s		3	TR on skeleton tower on piles.	
13570	Cedar Grove Anchorage Upper Day beacon 71.1	29-47-35.304N 090-01-00.882W				NY on pile.	Ra ref.
13575	*Dockside Elevator Lighted Mooring Buoys (5)* RDB mile 71.5.	29-47-44.000N 090-00-40.000W	Q W			White with blue band.	Private aid.
13580	OAK POINT DOLPHIN LIGHTS (2) RDB mile 72.3.	29-48-27.700N 090-00-27.900W	Fl G 2.5s			On dolphins.	Private aid.
13585	Belle Chasse Anchorage Lower Day beacon 73.1	29-49-12.058N 090-00-19.509W				NY on pile.	Ra ref.
13590	SCARSDALE LIGHT 76 LDB Mile 75.2.	29-50-18.458N 089-59-02.847W	Iso R 6s		5	TR on skeleton tower on piles.	
13595	Belle Chasse Anchorage Upper Day beacon 75.2	29-50-44.264N 089-59-16.720W				NY on pile.	Ra ref.
13600	RED STAR YEAST WHARF LIGHTS (2) RDB mile 75.4.	29-51-05.000N 089-58-59.000W	Fl G 2.5s	25			Private aid.
13605	BELLE CHASSE FERRY LANDING EAST BANK LIGHTS LDB mile 75.6.	29-50-55.000N 089-58-41.000W	Fl R 2.5s				Horn: 1 blast ev 20S (2S BL). Operated during low visibility. Private aid.
13610	BELLE CHASSE FERRY LANDING WEST BANK LIGHTS (2) RDB mile 75.7.	29-51-18.000N 089-58-53.000W	Fl G 2.5s				Horn: 1 blast ev 20S (2S BL). Operated during low visibility. Private aid.
13613	PLAQUEMINES PARISH WEST BANK FERRY MAINTENANCE DOCK MOORING LIGHTS (2)	29-51-13.360N 089-58-55.230W	Fl G 2.5s			Marks the upper and lower mooring dolphins.	Private aid.
13615	CCI PORT NICKEL DOCK LIGHTS (2) LDB mile 76.4.	29-51-38.400N 089-58-21.800W	Fl R 2.5s	12		On dock.	Private aid.
13620	CCI PORT NICKEL DOCK LIGHT LDB mile 76.6.	29-51-46.200N 089-58-20.300W	Fl R 2.5s	12		On dolphin.	Private aid.
13625	SHINGLE POINT APPROACH LIGHT 78 LDB Mile 77.8.	29-52-24.412N 089-58-17.103W	Fl R 4s		5	TR on skeleton tower on mud sill.	
13630	SHINGLE POINT LIGHT 80 LDB mile 78.0.	29-52-41.737N 089-57-59.270W	Iso R 6s		3	TR on skeleton tower on piles.	
13635	ENGLISH TURN BEND LIGHT 79 RDB Mile 78.0.	29-53-02.874N 089-58-07.057W	Iso G 6s		5	SG on skeleton tower.	
13640	ENGLISH TURN LIGHT 80A LDB mile 78.3.	29-52-40.890N 089-57-36.947W	Fl R 2.5s		5	TR on skeleton tower.	
13645	Lower 12 Mile Point Anchorage Lower Day beacon 78.6	29-53-02.476N 089-57-22.865W				NY on pile.	Ra ref.
13650	STOLT-NIELSON DOCK LIGHT	29-52-17.000N 089-56-44.000W	Fl R 2.5s			On dock.	Private aid.
13655	Lower 12 Mile Point Anchorage Upper Day beacon 80.8	29-52-06.236N 089-55-23.789W				NY on pile.	Ra ref.

Light List corrected through LNM week: 01/18

(1) No.	(2) Name and Location	(3) Position	(4) Characteristic	(5) Height	(6) Range	(7) Structure	(8) Remarks

MISSISSIPPI RIVER (Louisiana) - Eighth District

MISSISSIPPI RIVER - Venice to New Orleans (Chart 11364)

Head of Passes to New Orleans

Designations left descending bank (LDB) and right descending bank (RDB) are as seen from a vessel going downstream Mileage given indicates the number of miles above Head of Passes Junction Light.

(1) No.	(2) Name and Location	(3) Position	(4) Characteristic	(5) Height	(6) Range	(7) Structure	(8) Remarks
13660	TWELVE MILE POINT LIGHT 81 RDB mile 81.5.	29-52-08.448N 089-54-50.010W	Fl G 2.5s		4	SG on skeleton tower on piles.	
13665	POYDRAS LIGHT 82 LDB Mile 81.6.	29-51-52.038N 089-54-35.484W	Iso R 6s		5	TR on skeleton tower on piles.	Higher intensity beam up and down river.
13670	RIVER BEND LIGHT 84 LDB Mile 82.6	29-52-31.253N 089-53-59.441W	Fl R 4s		4	TR on skeleton tower on piles.	
13675	Lower 9 Mile Point Anchorage Lower Day beacon 82.7	29-52-52.498N 089-54-27.299W				NY on pile.	Ra ref.
13680	SHELL INTAKE DOLPHIN LIGHTS (3) LDB mile 82.9.	29-53-00.000N 089-53-59.000W	Fl R 2.5s			On dolphins.	Private aid.
13685	Lower 9 Mile Point Anchorage Upper Day beacon 85.0	29-54-38.209N 089-55-03.422W				NY on pile.	Ra ref.
13690	SAXONHOLM LIGHT 86 LDB Mile 86.0.	29-55-26.232N 089-55-27.828W	Iso R 6s		5	TR on pile.	Higher intensity beam up and down river.
13695	MURPHY WHARF LIGHTS (2) LDB mile 87.0.	29-55-31.000N 089-56-45.000W	F R			On dolphins.	Horn: 1 blast ev 20S (2S BL). Private aid.
13700	NEW ORLEANS WATER DISCHARGE DOLPHIN LIGHTS (4) RDB mile 87.5	29-55-15.000N 089-57-30.000W	Fl G 2.5s			On dolphin.	Private aid.
13705	SEWEGE AND WATER BOARD PIPELINE LIGHT A	29-55-04.000N 089-58-03.000W	Fl Y 2.5s			NW on pile. Worded: DANGER PIPELINE	Private aid.
13710	SEWEGE AND WATER BOARD PIPELINE LIGHT B	29-55-09.000N 089-58-03.000W	Fl Y 2.5s			NW on pile Worded: DANGER PIPELINE.	Private aid.
13715 34935	ALGIERS ALTERNATE ROUTE JUNCTION LIGHT A RDB mile 88.2.	29-55-11.922N 089-58-03.168W	Fl (2+1)G 6s		4	JG-TY on skeleton tower on piles.	
13720 34930	TENNECO DOCK LIGHTS (2) LDB mile 88.2.	29-55-33.000N 089-57-51.000W	Fl R 2.5s			On dolphins.	Private aid.
13725 34925	*Mobil St. Bernard Intake Lighted Buoy*	29-55-32.400N 089-57-54.000W	Fl R 4s			Red.	Private aid.
13730 34920	MERAUX INTAKE LIGHTS (7) LDB mile 88.5.	29-55-31.000N 089-56-42.000W	Fl R 2.5s				Private aid.
13735 34915	HUMBLE DOCK LIGHTS (3) LDB mile 88.6.	29-55-31.000N 089-56-47.000W	Fl R 2.5s			On dolphins.	Private aid.
13740 34910	CHALMETTE-ALGIERS WEST BANK FERRY LANDING LIGHTS (2) RDB mile 88.6.	29-55-18.600N 089-58-24.300W	Fl G 2.5s			On barge.	Horn: 1 blast ev 20S (2S BL). Private aid.
13745 34905	CHALMETTE-ALGIERS EAST BANK FERRY LANDING LIGHTS (2) LDB mile 88.7.	29-55-41.700N 089-58-15.500W	Fl R 2.5s			On dolphin and barge.	Private aid.
13750 34900	CHALMETTE ALGIERS WEST BANK MAINTENANCE LANDING LIGHTS (2) RDB mile 88.7.	29-55-20.100N 089-55-28.100W	Fl G 2.5s			On barge.	Private aid.
13755 34895	TENNECO DOCK LIGHTS (2) LDB mile 89.1.	29-55-45.000N 089-58-37.000W	F R				Private aid.
13760 34890	MOBIL ST. BENARD MOORING DOLPHIN LIGHTS (4) LDB mile 89.1	29-55-42.000N 088-58-30.000W	Fl R 2.5s			On dolphins.	Private aid.
13765 34885	TENNECO COKE WHARF LIGHT LDB mile 89.1.	29-55-49.000N 089-58-44.000W	Fl R 2.5s			On dolphin.	Private aid.

(1) No.	(2) Name and Location	(3) Position	(4) Characteristic	(5) Height	(6) Range	(7) Structure	(8) Remarks
	**MISSISSIPPI RIVER (Louisiana) - Eighth District**

MISSISSIPPI RIVER - Venice to New Orleans (Chart 11364)

Head of Passes to New Orleans
Designations left descending bank (LDB) and right descending bank (RDB) are as seen from a vessel going downstream Mileage given indicates the number of miles above Head of Passes Junction Light.

(1) No.	(2) Name and Location	(3) Position	(4) Characteristic	(5) Height	(6) Range	(7) Structure	(8) Remarks
13770 / 34880	KAISER UPPER LIGHT LDB mile 89.3.	29-55-48.000N 089-58-48.000W	F R			On multi-pile structure.	Private aid.
13780 / 34870	NORFOLK SOUTHERN CORPORATION LIGHT LDB mile 89.8	29-56-23.000N 089-59-42.000W	Fl R 2.5s			On wall.	Private aid.
13785 / 34865	CHALMETTE OBSTRUCTION LIGHT LDB mile 89.9.	29-56-00.000N 089-59-12.000W	Q R			On multi-pile structure.	Private aid.

NEW ORLEANS HARBOR (Chart 11368)

Head of Passes to New Orleans
Designations left descending bank (LDB) and right descending bank (RDB) are as seen from a vessel going downstream Mileage given indicates the number of miles above Head of Passes Junction Light.

(1) No.	(2) Name and Location	(3) Position	(4) Characteristic	(5) Height	(6) Range	(7) Structure	(8) Remarks
13790 / 34860	New Orleans General Anchorage Lower Day beacon 90.1	29-55-52.050N 089-59-40.614W				NY on pile.	Ra ref.
13795	PORT SHIP SERVICE DOCK LIGHT	29-55-57.563N 089-59-48.400W	Fl G 2.5s			On dock.	Private aid.
13800 / 34855	CHALMETTE NATIONAL PARK TOUR BOAT DOCK LIGHTS (2) LDB mile 90.3.	29-56-20.000N 089-59-38.000W	Fl R 2.5s			On dock.	Lights flash in unison. Private aid.
13805	SOUTHERN RAILWAY LIGHT LDB mile 90.4.	29-56-24.000N 089-59-48.000W	Fl R 2.5s			On fender.	Private aid.
13807	HARBOR TOWING & FLEETING DOWNSTREAM MOORING LIGHT RDB mile 90.49	29-56-00.600N 089-59-52.600W	Fl G 2.5s			Marks downstream mooring pile.	Private aid.
13807.01	HARBOR TOWING & FLEETING UPSTREAM MOORING LIGHT RDB mile 90.495	29-56-22.000N 090-00-27.700W	Fl G 2.5s			Marks upstream mooring pile.	Private aid.
13810 / 34850	New Orleans General Anchorage Upper Day beacon 90.5	29-56-15.030N 090-00-19.020W				NY on pile.	Ra ref.
13815 / 34845	Quarantine Anchorage Lower Day beacon 90.9	29-56-15.168N 090-00-19.242W				NY on pile.	Ra ref.
13820 / 34840	Quarantine Anchorage Upper Day beacon 91.6	29-56-36.900N 090-00-54.996W				NY on pile.	Ra ref.
13825 / 34835	DELERY STREET DISCHARGE LIGHT LDB mile 91.6.	29-56-59.000N 090-00-43.000W	Q R			On pile cluster.	Private aid.
13830 / 34830	FORSTALL STREET DISCHARGE LIGHT LDB mile 92.2.	29-57-19.000N 090-01-25.000W	F R			On dolphins.	Private aid.

Inner Harbor Navigation Canal

(1) No.	(2) Name and Location	(3) Position	(4) Characteristic	(5) Height	(6) Range	(7) Structure	(8) Remarks
13835 / 34760	- LIGHT 1	29-57-30.732N 090-01-48.254W	Fl G 2.5s		4	SG-TY on skeleton tower.	
13840 / 34755	- LIGHT 2	29-57-26.118N 090-01-35.250W	Q R		4	TR-SY on skeleton tower.	
13842	PORT OF NEW ORLEANS DOLPHIN LIGHT	29-59-14.900N 090-01-17.500W	Fl W 2.5s			Marks dolphin.	Private aid.
13845	DWYER ROAD DISCHARGE STATION LIGHT	30-00-58.000N 090-01-45.000W	Fl W 2.5s			NW on dolphin worded DANGER WATER DISCHARGE.	Private aid.

New Orleans Harbor

(1) No.	(2) Name and Location	(3) Position	(4) Characteristic	(5) Height	(6) Range	(7) Structure	(8) Remarks
13850 / 34765	GOVERNOR NICHOLLS LIGHT 94 LDB mile 94.3.	29-57-37.914N 090-03-23.070W	Fl R 4s		6	On skeleton tower. On same structure as Governor Nicholls Harbor Traffic Control Light.	Not operated when traffic control lights are in operation.

(1) No.	(2) Name and Location	(3) Position	(4) Characteristic	(5) Height	(6) Range	(7) Structure	(8) Remarks
			MISSISSIPPI RIVER (Louisiana) - Eighth District				
	NEW ORLEANS HARBOR (Chart 11368)						
	New Orleans Harbor						
13855 34770	**Governor Nicholls Harbor Traffic Control Light 94** LDB mile 94.3.	29-57-37.902N 090-03-22.872W	Fl G 5s		16	On skeleton tower. 94	Operated by Vessel Traffic Safety Office New Orleans during periods of high water. Controls one way traffic around Algiers Point.
13860 34775	ALGIERS POINT LIGHT 95	29-57-18.883N 090-03-19.092W	Q G		5	SG-SY on skeleton tower on piles.	
13865 34780	NEW ORLEANS POLICE MOORING DOLPHIN LIGHT LDB mile 94.8.	29-56-58.600N 090-03-43.800W	Fl R 2.5s			On dolphin.	Private aid.
13870 34785	UPPER ALGIERS FERRY LANDING LIGHTS (2) RDB mile 94.8.	29-57-12.000N 090-03-21.000W	Fl G 2.5s			On dock.	HORN: 1 BLAST EV 20S (2S BL). OPERATED DURING LOW VISIBILITY. Private aid.
13875 34790	CANAL STREET FERRY LANDING LIGHTS (2) LDB mile 94.8.	29-56-58.000N 090-03-43.000W	Fl R 2.5s			On dock.	HORN: 1 BLAST EV 20S (2S BL). OPERATED DURING LOW VISIBILITY. Private aid.
13880 34795	**Gretna Harbor Traffic Control Light 97** RDB mile 96.6.	29-55-33.156N 090-03-29.982W	Fl R 5s (NIGHT) Fl G 5s (NIGHT)		16 16	On skeleton tower. 25	Operated by Vessel Traffic Safety Office New Orleans during periods of high water. Controls one way traffic around Algiers Point.
13885 34800	GRETNA LIGHT 97 RDB mile 96.6.	29-55-33.162N 090-03-30.078W	Fl G 4s		6	SG-SY on skeleton tower on same structure as Gretna Harbor Traffic Control Light.	Not operated when traffic control lights are in operation.
13890 34805	GRETNA WATER INTAKE LIGHT RDB mile 96.7.	29-55-27.000N 090-03-38.000W	Fl G 2.5s			On dolphin.	Private aid.
13892 34808	GRETNA FERRY BOAT RAMP LIGHT	29-55-07.871N 090-04-00.494W	Fl W 2.5s			Marks outermost upstream piling designating the riverward end of boat ramp.	Private aid.
13895 34810	GRETNA FERRY LANDING LIGHTS (2) RDB mile 97.2.	29-55-06.000N 090-04-02.000W	Fl G 2.5s			On dock.	HORN: 1 BLAST EV 20S (2S BL). OPERATED DURING LOW VISIBILITY. Private aid.
13900 34815	JACKSON AVENUE FERRY LANDING LIGHTS (2) LDB mile 97.2.	29-55-20.000N 090-04-15.000W	Fl R 2.5s			On dock.	HORN: 1 BLAST EV 20S (2S BL). OPERATED DURING LOW VISIBILITY. Private aid.
13905 34820	INTERNATIONAL MATEX DOCK LIGHTS (4) RDB mile 97.3.	29-55-00.000N 090-04-18.000W	Fl G 2.5s			(2) on floating dock; (2) on outermost upstream and downstream dolphins.	Private aid.
13907	Kinder Morgan Dock 1 Mooring Buoys (3)	29-54-34.990N 090-05-28.670W					Private aid.
13907.01	Kinder Morgan Dock 2 Mooring Buoys (4)	29-54-37.680N 090-05-22.540W					Private aid.
13907.02	Kinder Morgan Dock 3 Mooring Buoy	29-54-39.030N 090-05-16.430W					Private aid.
13907.03	Kinder Morgan Dock 4 Mooring Buoys (5)	29-54-32.700N 090-05-37.480W					Private aid.
13910	MILAN STREET WHARF MOORING DOLPHIN LIGHT LDB mile 99.0	29-54-45.000N 090-05-58.000W	Fl R 2.5s			On dolphin.	Private aid.

Light List corrected through LNM week: 01/18

(1) No.	(2) Name and Location	(3) Position	(4) Characteristic	(5) Height	(6) Range	(7) Structure	(8) Remarks
	MISSISSIPPI RIVER (Louisiana) - Eighth District

NEW ORLEANS HARBOR (Chart 11368)

New Orleans Harbor

No.	Name and Location	Position	Characteristic	Height	Range	Structure	Remarks
13940	ST SERVICES DOCK LIGHTS RDB mile 101.3	29-54-45.000N 090-08-17.000W	Fl G 2.5s			On Dock.	Private aid.
13945	SIX MILE POINT LIGHT 102 LDB mile 101.4.	29-55-01.345N 090-08-04.155W	Q R		4	TR on tower.	
13950	WESTWEGO TRAFFIC LIGHT RDB mile 101.4.	29-54-51.534N 090-08-23.016W	Q R (NIGHT) Q G (NIGHT)		5 5	On skeleton tower.	Operated by Coast Guard Marine Safety Office New Orleans. Indicates to down bound traffic whether Gretna Harbor Traffic Control Light is red or green.

New Orleans to Baton Rouge

Designations left descending bank (LDB) and right descending bank (RDB) are as seen from a vessel going downstream. Low water buoys are not listed and their positions may be frequently shifted with changing stages and condition of the river.

No.	Name and Location	Position	Characteristic	Height	Range	Structure	Remarks
13955	WESTWEGO WATER INTAKE LIGHT RDB mile 101.5.	29-54-55.308N 090-08-22.464W	Fl G 2.5s			On dolphin.	Private aid.
13960	INTERNATIONAL MATEX TANK TERMINAL WALKWAY LIGHT RDB mile 101.6.	29-55-03.800N 090-08-27.900W	Fl G 2.5s			On walkway.	Private aid.
13965	NEW ORLEANS STEAMBOAT CO. DOCK LIGHT LDB mile 101.7.	29-55-13.000N 090-08-07.500W	Fl R 2.5s			On dolphin.	Private aid.
13970	CONTINENTAL BARGE UNLOADING DOCK LIGHT RDB mile 103.0	29-56-01.000N 090-08-32.000W	Fl G 2.5s			On pile.	Private aid.
13975	CONTINENTAL GRAIN COMPANY DOCK LIGHTS (4) RDB mile 103.1.	29-56-17.000N 090-08-32.000W	Fl G 2.5s			On dock.	Private aid.
13980	NINE MILE POINT FUEL OIL UNLOADING FACILITY LIGHTS (3) RDB mile 104.5.	29-56-55.000N 090-08-35.000W	Fl G 2.5s	29		On dock extremities.	Private aid.
13985	OAK STREET INTAKE LIGHTS (4) LDB mile 103.8.	29-57-06.000N 090-08-15.000W	Q R			On dolphin.	Private aid.
13990	NINE MILE POINT OBSTRUCTION LIGHTS (2) RDB mile 103.9.	29-56-55.000N 090-08-42.000W	F G			On dolphins.	Private aid.
13995	NEW ORLEANS RAW WATER INTAKE LIGHTS (5) LDB mile 104.1.	29-57-18.000N 090-08-23.000W	F R			On dolphins.	Private aid.

MISSISSIPPI RIVER - New Orleans to Baton Rouge (Chart 11370)

New Orleans to Baton Rouge

Designations left descending bank (LDB) and right descending bank (RDB) are as seen from a vessel going downstream. Low water buoys are not listed and their positions may be frequently shifted with changing stages and conditions of the river.

No.	Name and Location	Position	Characteristic	Height	Range	Structure	Remarks
14000	SOUTHPORT LIGHT 104 LDB Mile 104.7.	29-57-33.420N 090-09-04.392W	Iso R 6s		5	TR on skeleton tower on piles.	
14005	JEFFERSON INTAKE DOLPHIN LIGHTS (10) LDB mile 105.1.	29-57-12.000N 090-09-45.500W	Fl R 2.5s			On concrete dolphin.	HORN: 1 BLAST EV 20S (2S BL). Private aid.
14010	*Zito Lighted Mooring Buoy I* LDB mile 105.2	29-57-05.000N 090-09-45.000W	Q W			White with blue band.	Private aid.
14015	*Zito Lighted Mooring Buoy F* LDB mile 105.6	29-56-56.000N 090-09-56.000W	Q W			White with blue band.	Private aid.
14020	*Zito Lighted Mooring Buoy E* LDB mile 105.6	29-56-58.000N 090-09-59.000W	Q W			White with blue band.	Private aid.
14025	*Zito Lighted Mooring Buoy A* LDB mile 105.7	29-56-46.000N 090-10-08.000W	Q W			White with blue band.	Private aid.

Huey P. Long Bridge

No.	Name and Location	Position	Characteristic	Height	Range	Structure	Remarks
14035	Huey P Long Bridge Approach Buoy A	29-56-46.075N 090-09-57.629W				Red nun with green bands.	AIS - 993682000
14040	Huey P Long Bridge Approach Buoy B	29-56-42.112N 090-10-02.151W				Red nun with green bands.	AIS - 993682001

MISSISSIPPI RIVER (Louisiana) - Eighth District

MISSISSIPPI RIVER - New Orleans to Baton Rouge (Chart 11370)

New Orleans to Baton Rouge

Huey P. Long Bridge

(1) No.	(2) Name and Location	(3) Position	(4) Characteristic	(5) Height	(6) Range	(7) Structure	(8) Remarks
14045	Huey P Long Bridge Approach Buoy C	29-56-33.658N 090-10-11.886W				Red nun with green bands.	AIS - 993682002
14050	Huey P Long Bridge Approach Buoy D	29-56-29.952N 090-10-16.419W				Red nun with green bands.	AIS - 993682003
14055	Huey P Long Bridge Approach Buoy 1 RDB mile 106.0.	29-56-35.969N 090-09-56.698W				Green can.	AIS - 993682004
14060	12 MILE POINT LIGHT 110 LDB mile 109.0.	29-55-31.572N 090-12-14.442W	Q R		5	TR on skeleton tower.	

New Orleans to Baton Rouge

Designations left descending bank (LDB) and right descending bank (RDB) are as seen from a vessel going downstream Low water buoys are not listed and their positions may be frequently shifted with changing stages and conditions of the river.

(1) No.	(2) Name and Location	(3) Position	(4) Characteristic	(5) Height	(6) Range	(7) Structure	(8) Remarks
14065	WAGGAMAN LIGHT 109 RDB Mile 109.1.	29-55-18.042N 090-12-47.472W	Iso G 6s		5	SG on skeleton tower.	

Huey P. Long Bridge

(1) No.	(2) Name and Location	(3) Position	(4) Characteristic	(5) Height	(6) Range	(7) Structure	(8) Remarks
14070	PROVIDENCE LIGHT 112 LDB mile 111.3.	29-57-22.716N 090-13-26.202W	Q R		5	TR on skeleton tower.	
14072	EAST JEFFERSON LEVEE DISTRICT DOLPHIN LIGHT	29-57-23.630N 090-13-28.280W	Fl R 6s			Marks storm drainage discharge.	Private aid.

New Orleans to Baton Rouge

Designations left descending bank (LDB) and right descending bank (RDB) are as seen from a vessel going downstream Low water buoys are not listed and their positions may be frequently shifted with changing stages and conditions of the river.

(1) No.	(2) Name and Location	(3) Position	(4) Characteristic	(5) Height	(6) Range	(7) Structure	(8) Remarks
14075	J.P.& Sons Lighted Mooring Buoy A RDB mile 111.5	29-57-24.419N 090-13-48.419W	Q W			White with blue band.	Ra ref. Private aid.
14080	J.P.& Sons Lighted Mooring Buoy RDB mile 111.7	29-57-32.939N 090-13-59.098W	Q W			White with blue band.	Ra ref. Private aid.
14085	J.P.And Sons Lighted Mooring Buoy C	29-57-43.220N 090-14-13.150W	Q W			White with blue band.	Ra ref. Private aid.
14090	J.P.And Sons Lighted Mooring Buoy D	29-57-33.970N 090-14-01.070W	Q W			White with blue band.	Private aid.
14095	EAST JEFFERSON REGIONAL SEWAGE TREATMENT PLANT ONSTRUCTION LIGHTS (3) LDB mile 112.2	29-57-48.000N 090-13-56.000W	Fl R 2.5s			On dolphins.	Private aid.
14100	GUY MALLORY LIGHT 114 LDB mile 112.9.	29-58-20.076N 090-14-43.986W	Iso R 6s		4	TR on skeleton tower on piles.	
14105	LASALLE LANDING BARGE DOCK LIGHTS (2) LDB mile 113.0.	29-58-16.100N 090-14-49.030W	Fl R 4s			On docking barge.	Private aid.
14110	Lower Kenner Bend Anchorage Lower Day beacon 113.5	29-57-56.725N 090-15-08.257W				NY on pile.	Ra ref.
14115	CITY OF KENNER OUTFALL LIGHT Marks sewerage discharge extremities.	29-58-23.000N 090-15-50.000W	Q R			On dolphins.	Private aid.
14120	OAKLAND LIGHT 114A LDB mile 114.1.	29-58-26.382N 090-15-57.126W	Q R		5	TR on skeleton tower.	
14125	Lower Kenner Bend Anchorage Upper Day beacon 114.3	29-57-55.018N 090-16-07.919W				NY on pile.	Ra ref.
14130	FORTIER OBSTRUCTIONS LIGHTS (2) RDB mile 114.4.	29-57-56.000N 090-16-19.000W				On dolphins.	HORN: 1 BLAST EV 20S (2S BL). Private aid.
14135	Kenner Bend Anchorage Lower Day beacon 114.7	29-57-51.598N 090-16-25.799W				NY on pile.	Ra ref.
14140	FAIRVIEW A RANGE FRONT LIGHT LDB mile 115.0.	29-58-20.717N 090-16-53.631W	Q R			KRW on skeleton tower on sills.	

Light List corrected through LNM week: 01/18

(1) No.	(2) Name and Location	(3) Position	(4) Characteristic	(5) Height	(6) Range	(7) Structure	(8) Remarks

MISSISSIPPI RIVER (Louisiana) - Eighth District

MISSISSIPPI RIVER - New Orleans to Baton Rouge (Chart 11370)
New Orleans to Baton Rouge

Designations left descending bank (LDB) and right descending bank (RDB) are as seen from a vessel going downstream Low water buoys are not listed and their positions may be frequently shifted with changing stages and conditions of the river.

(1) No.	(2) Name and Location	(3) Position	(4) Characteristic	(5) Height	(6) Range	(7) Structure	(8) Remarks
14145	FAIRVIEW A RANGE REAR LIGHT 218 yards, 041.0° from front light.	29-58-25.598N 090-16-48.724W	Oc R 4s			KRW on skeleton tower on block.	
14150	FAIRVIEW WHARF LIGHTS (2) LDB mile 115.0.	29-58-16.000N 090-16-57.000W	Fl W 2.5s			On dolphins.	Private aid.
14155	CRESCENT SHIP BARGE DOCK LIGHTS (2) LDB mile 115.1	28-58-15.000N 090-17-05.000W	Fl G 2.5s				On docking barge. Private aid.
14160	*Mississippi River Wreck Lighted Buoy WR4* LDB mile 115.4.	29-58-00.585N 090-17-18.691W	Q R		3	Red.	
14170	Kenner Bend Anchorage Upper Day beacon 115.6	29-57-25.116N 090-17-31.848W				NY on pile.	Ra ref.
14185	ADM GRAIN COMPANY LIGHTS (2) RDB mile 117.6.	29-56-27.380N 090-18-39.340W	Fl G 2.5s	40		On dolphins.	Private aid.
14190	DAVIS CREVASSE RANGE FRONT LIGHT RDB mile 118.1.	29-55-58.696N 090-19-16.435W	Q R			KRW on skeleton tower on piles.	Visible all around; higher intensity on rangeline.
14195	DAVIS CREVASSE RANGE REAR LIGHT 213 yards, 221° from front light.	29-55-53.765N 090-19-21.357W	Iso R 6s			KRW on skeleton tower on piles.	Visible all around; higher intensity on rangeline.
14197	INTERNATIONAL MATEX TANK TERMINAL SOUTH DOCK LIGHTS (4) LDB mile 118.3.	29-56-18.400N 090-19-19.230W	Fl R 2.5s			Marks outermost dock facility structures.	Private aid.
14200	INTERNATIONAL MATEX TANK DOCK LIGHTS (7) LDB mile 118.6.	29-56-13.000N 090-19-45.000W	Fl R 2.5s				HORN (2): 1 BLAST EV 20S (2S BL). ON EACH END OF WHARF. OPERATED ONLY DURING LOW VISIBILITY. Private aid.
14205	DAVIS CREVASSE LIGHT 121 RDB mile 118.7.	29-55-51.450N 090-19-46.308W	Iso G 6s		4	SG on skeleton tower on concrete block.	
14210	MONSANTO FUEL DOCK LIGHT RDB mile 119.8.	29-55-53.000N 090-20-43.000W	F G			On dolphin.	Private aid.
14215	MONSANTO DOCK LIGHTS (3) RDB mile 119.9.	29-55-55.000N 090-20-54.000W	F G				Private aid.
14220	BUNGE DOCK LIGHTS (2) LDB mile 119.9.	29-56-00.349N 090-21-00.042W	F R				Private aid.
14225	DESTREHAN GRAIN LOADING DOCK LIGHTS (2) LDB mile 120.6.	29-56-23.000N 090-21-23.000W	F R				Private aid.
14230	*Tulane Fleeting Lower Lighted Mooring Buoy* LDB mile 121.0.	29-56-26.000N 090-21-55.000W	Q W			White with blue band.	Private aid.
14235	*Tulane Fleeting Upper Lighted Mooring Buoy* LDB mile 121.0.	29-56-32.000N 090-22-11.000W	Q W			White with blue band.	Private aid.
14240	*Hale Boggs Luling Bridge Approach Buoy A*	29-56-31.012N 090-22-21.069W				Red nun with green bands.	

NEW ORLEANS HARBOR (Chart 11368)
New Orleans to Baton Rouge

Designations left descending bank (LDB) and right descending bank (RDB) are as seen from a vessel going downstream Low water buoys are not listed and their positions may be frequently shifted with changing stages and condition of the river.

(1) No.	(2) Name and Location	(3) Position	(4) Characteristic	(5) Height	(6) Range	(7) Structure	(8) Remarks
14242	Hale Boggs Luling Bridge East Pier V-AIS	29-56-32.330N 090-22-24.290W					AIS - 993682005
14243	Hale Boggs Luling Bridge West Pier V-AIS	29-56-33.920N 090-22-27.890W					AIS - 993682006

Light List corrected through LNM week: 01/18

(1) No.	(2) Name and Location	(3) Position	(4) Characteristic	(5) Height	(6) Range	(7) Structure	(8) Remarks
	MISSISSIPPI RIVER (Louisiana) - Eighth District						

MISSISSIPPI RIVER - New Orleans to Baton Rouge (Chart 11370)

New Orleans to Baton Rouge

Designations left descending bank (LDB) and right descending bank (RDB) are as seen from a vessel going downstream Low water buoys are not listed and their positions may be frequently shifted with changing stages and conditions of the river.

No.	Name and Location	Position	Characteristic	Height	Range	Structure	Remarks
14245	Hale Boggs Luling Bridge Approach Buoy B	29-56-36.784N 090-22-32.791W				Red nun with green bands.	
14250	Hale Boggs Luling Bridge Approach Buoy C	29-56-38.922N 090-22-39.000W				Red nun with green bands.	
14255	26 MILE POINT LIGHT 122 LDB Mile 122.7.	29-57-14.712N 090-23-19.242W	Q R		5	TR on skeleton tower.	
14260	FASHION LIGHT 123 RDB mile 123.0.	29-57-03.186N 090-23-48.156W	Iso G 6s		4	SG on skeleton tower on piles.	
14265	ORION REFINERY DOCK 1 LIGHTS (2) LDB mile 125.3.	29-59-24.500N 090-24-12.000W	Fl R 2.5s			On dolphins.	Private aid.
14270	26 MILE FALSE POINT LIGHT 124 LDB Mile 123.7.	29-57-52.662N 090-23-31.932W	Fl R 4s		3	TR on skeleton tower.	
14275	ORION REFINERY DOCK 2 LIGHTS (2) LDB mile 125.	29-59-19.000N 090-24-05.000W	Fl R 2.5s			On dolphins.	Private aid.
14280	ORION REFINERY DOCK 3 LIGHTS (2) LDB mile 125.	29-59-13.000N 090-23-57.000W	Fl R 2.5s			On dolphins.	Private aid.
14285	ORION REFINERY DOCK 4 LIGHTS (2) LDB mile 125.	29-58-58.380N 090-23-46.110W	Fl R 2.5s			On dolphins.	Private aid.
14290	ORION REFINERY DOCK 5 LIGHTS (2) LDB mile 125.	29-58-54.000N 090-23-42.000W	Fl R 2.5s			On dolphins.	Private aid.
14300	SHELL PUMPING STATION OBSTRUCTION LIGHTS (2) LDB mile 125.9.	29-59-36.000N 090-24-30.000W	Fl R 2.5s			On dolphin.	Private aid.
14305	NORCO OBSTRUCTION LIGHTS (2) LDB mile 126.9.	29-59-48.000N 090-25-30.000W	Fl R 2.5s			On dolphins.	Private aid.
14310	Bonnet Carre Anchorage Lower Day beacon 127.3	29-59-55.314N 090-25-49.956W				NY on pile.	Ra ref.
14315	UNION CARBIDE WATER INTAKE LIGHTS (2) RDB mile 128.3.	29-59-35.000N 090-27-04.000W	Q W			On dolphins.	Private aid.
14320	UNION CARBIDE DOCK LIGHTS (3)	29-59-30.000N 090-26-48.000W	Fl G 2.5s	16		On dolphins.	Private aid.
14325	Bonnet Carre Anchorage Upper Day beacon 128.8	29-59-58.355N 090-27-19.512W				NY on pile.	Ra ref.
14330	OCCIDENTAL CHEMICAL MOORING FACILITY LIGHTS (3) RDB mile 128.9.	29-59-45.500N 090-27-35.100W	Fl G 2.5s			On mooring facility.	Private aid.
14335	MONTZ OBSTRUCTION LIGHT LDB mile 129.4.	30-00-06.000N 090-27-54.000W	F R			On dolphin.	Private aid.
14340	LITTLE GYPSY OIL UNLOADING FACILITY LIGHT LDB mile 129.5.	30-00-06.000N 090-27-58.000W	Fl R 2.5s			Marks dock.	Private aid.
14345	ENTERGY DOCK LOWER LIGHT RDB Mile 128.6.	30-00-06.800N 090-28-27.900W	Fl G 2.5s			On dolphin.	Private aid.
14350	ENTERGY INTAKE UPPER LIGHT RDB Mile 129.4.	30-00-10.500N 090-28-30.000W	Fl G 2.5s			On dolphin.	Private aid.
14355	ENTERGY DISCHARGE LIGHT RDB Mile 129.8.	30-00-01.800N 090-28-25.600W	Fl G 2.5s			On dolphin.	Private aid.
14360	ENTERGY WATERFORD LIGHTS (3) RDB mile 129.8.	29-59-49.000N 090-28-03.227W	Fl G 2.5s			On dolphin.	MARKS INTAKE AND DISCHARGE STRUCTURE. Private aid.

Light List corrected through LNM week: 01/18

(1) No.	(2) Name and Location	(3) Position	(4) Characteristic	(5) Height	(6) Range	(7) Structure	(8) Remarks
	**MISSISSIPPI RIVER (Louisiana) - Eighth District**						

MISSISSIPPI RIVER - New Orleans to Baton Rouge (Chart 11370)

New Orleans to Baton Rouge

Designations left descending bank (LDB) and right descending bank (RDB) are as seen from a vessel going downstream Low water buoys are not listed and their positions may be frequently shifted with changing stages and conditions of the river.

No.	Name and Location	Position	Characteristic	Height	Range	Structure	Remarks
14365	THIRTY FIVE MILE POINT LIGHT 130 LDB mile 130.0.	30-00-22.748N 090-28-12.632W	Q R		4	TR on skeleton tower.	
14370	GYPSY LIGHT 132 LDB mile 132.0.	30-01-57.936N 090-28-09.144W	Iso R 6s		4	TR on skeleton tower on piles.	
14375	BAYOU STEEL DOCK LIGHTS (2) LDB mile 132.4.	30-02-22.050N 090-28-16.600W	Fl R 2.5s			On each end of dock.	Private aid.
14380	BONNET CARRE CREVASSE LIGHT 132A LDB Mile 132.9.	30-02-49.448N 090-28-27.473W	Iso R 6s		5	TR on skeleton tower on piles.	
14385	*CGB Marine Services Lighted Mooring Buoy A* LDB mile 134.1	30-03-15.000N 090-29-46.000W	Q W			White with blue band.	Ra ref. Private aid.
14390	*CGB Marine Services Lighted Mooring Buoy B* LDB mile 134.3	30-03-16.000N 090-29-28.000W	Q W			White with blue band.	Ra ref. Private aid.
14395	BONNET CARRE POINT LIGHT 133 RDB Mile 133.5.	30-02-53.964N 090-29-25.500W	Iso G 6s		5	SG on skeleton tower on piles.	
14400	WOODLAND LIGHT 134 LDB mile 133.6.	30-03-15.099N 090-29-10.684W	Iso R 6s		4	TR on skeleton tower on piles.	
14405	*Laplace Anchorage 134.7 Lower Day beacon*	30-03-16.236N 090-30-18.006W				NY on pile.	Ra ref.
14410	LUCY LIGHT 135 RDB mile 134.9.	30-02-55.425N 090-30-20.130W	Iso G 6s		4	SG on skeleton tower.	
14415	*Laplace Anchorage Upper Day beacon 135.4*	30-03-08.917N 090-30-55.465W				NY on pile.	Ra ref.
14420	DUPONT BARGE DOCK LIGHTS (3) LDB mile 135.6.	30-03-12.000N 090-31-40.000W	Fl R 2.5s				HORN: 1 BLAST EV 20S (2S BL). Private aid.
14425	DUPONT WATER INTAKE LIGHTS (5) LDB mile 135.8.	30-03-33.000N 090-44-21.000W	Q R			On dolphins.	SIREN: 1blast ev 30s (10s bl). Private aid.
14430	*Capital Marine Lighted Mooring Buoy A* RDB mile 136.3	30-02-43.000N 090-31-43.000W	Q W			White with blue band.	Private aid.
14435	*Capital Marine Lighted Mooring Buoy B* RDB mile 136.5	30-02-42.000N 090-32-00.000W	Q W			White with blue band.	Private aid.
14440	CALIFORNIA LIGHT 137 RDB mile 136.6.	30-02-34.644N 090-32-04.026W	Q G		5	SG on skeleton tower.	
14445	*Triangle Fleet Lighted Mooring Buoy A* RDB mile 136.8.	30-02-41.000N 090-32-17.000W	Q W			White with blue band.	Private aid.
14450	*Triangle Fleet Lighted Mooring Buoy B* RDB mile 137.0.	30-02-42.000N 090-32-34.000W	Q W			White with blue band.	Private aid.
14455	OLEANDER LIGHT 138 LDB mile 137.0.	30-03-03.059N 090-32-35.879W	Q R		3	TR on skeleton tower on piles.	

NEW ORLEANS HARBOR (Chart 11368)

New Orleans to Baton Rouge

Designations left descending bank (LDB) and right descending bank (RDB) are as seen from a vessel going downstream Low water buoys are not listed and their positions may be frequently shifted with changing stages and condition of the river.

No.	Name and Location	Position	Characteristic	Height	Range	Structure	Remarks
14467	PORT OF SOUTH LOUISIANA FINGER PIER LIGHTS (2)	30-03-14.030N 090-33-56.940W	Fl R 2.5s			On pier.	Marks outermost corners of finger pier. Private aid.

Light List corrected through LNM week: 01/18

MISSISSIPPI RIVER (Louisiana) - Eighth District

MISSISSIPPI RIVER - New Orleans to Baton Rouge (Chart 11370)

New Orleans to Baton Rouge

Designations left descending bank (LDB) and right descending bank (RDB) are as seen from a vessel going downstream. Low water buoys are not listed and their positions may be frequently shifted with changing stages and conditions of the river.

(1) No.	(2) Name and Location	(3) Position	(4) Characteristic	(5) Height	(6) Range	(7) Structure	(8) Remarks
14470	GLOBALPLEX GENERAL CARGO DOCK LIGHTS (2) LDB mile 138.6	30-03-14.000N 090-33-55.000W	Q R			On dock.	Private aid.
14475	HALL-BUCK MARINE MOORING DOLPHIN LIGHTS (2) LDB mile 138.8	30-03-12.000N 090-34-12.000W	Fl R 2.5s			On dolphins.	Private aid.
14480	CARGILL GRAIN DOCK LIGHTS (3) LDB mile 139.4.	30-03-14.000N 090-34-53.000W	Fl R 2.5s			On each end of dock.	Private aid.
14485	CARGILL MOLASSES DOCK LIGHTS (2) LDB mile 139.8.	30-03-08.000N 090-35-21.000W	Fl R 2.5s			On dolphins.	Private aid.
14490	MARATHON REFINERY MOORING DOCK 1 LIGHTS (3) LDB mile 140.0.	30-03-04.000N 090-35-31.000W	Fl R 2.5s			On dock loading platform.	HORN: 1 BLAST EV 15S (2S BL). CONTINUOUSLY FROM NOV. 1 TO APR. 30. Private aid.
14495	MARATHON REFINERY MOORING DOCK 2 LIGHTS (3) LDB mile 140.2.	30-03-01.000N 090-35-40.000W	Fl R 2.5s			On dock loading platform.	HORN: 1 BLAST EV 20S (2S BL). Private aid.
14500	MARATHON REFINERY MOORING LIGHTS LDB mile 140.4.	30-02-54.000N 090-35-53.000W	Fl R 2.5s			On dock loading platform.	HORN: 1 BLAST EV 20S (2S BL). Private aid.
14505	MARATHON REFINERY DOCK 5 LIGHTS (2) LDB mile 140.5.	30-02-52.000N 090-35-59.000W	Fl R 2.5s			On dock.	HORN: 1 BLAST EV 20S (2S BL). Private aid.
14510	WHITE ROSE LIGHT 141 RDB mile 141.2.	30-02-11.441N 090-36-17.113W	Q G		3	SG on skeleton tower on piles.	
14515	WEGO LIGHT 141A RDB mile 142.3.	30-01-44.946N 090-37-08.010W	Iso G 6s		5	SG on skeleton tower.	
14520	BELLE POINT LIGHT 142 LDB mile 142.4.	30-02-10.968N 090-37-19.644W	Iso R 6s		4	TR on skeleton tower on piles.	
14525	MARQUEZ LIGHT 144 LDB mile 143.4.	30-02-28.284N 090-37-47.952W	Q R		4	TR on skeleton tower on piles.	
14527	PIN OAK TERMINAL UPSTREAM MOORING LIGHT LDB mile 144.1	30-03-08.857N 090-38-41.680W	Fl R 2.5s			Marks outermost upstream mooring structure.	Private aid.
14532	PIN OAK TERMINAL DOWNSTREAM MOORING LIGHT LDB mile 144.2	30-03-04.275N 090-38-31.270W	Fl R 2.5s			Marks outermost downstream mooring structure.	Private aid.
14535	CLARK OIL DOCK HORN AND LIGHTS (2) LDB mile 144.6.	30-03-12.000N 090-39-03.000W	Fl R 2.5s			On dolphins.	HORN: 1 BLAST EV 20S (2S BL). LOCATED BETWEEN LIGHTS. Private aid.
14540	HALL-BUCK MARINE DOCK LIGHTS (3) LDB mile 144.9.	30-03-12.000N 090-39-31.000W	Fl R 2.5s	12		On dock.	Private aid.
14545	KAISER BARGE DOCK LIGHT LDB mile 145.1.	30-03-15.000N 090-39-30.000W	Fl R 2.5s				Private aid.
14547	NORANDA ALUMINA DOWNSTREAM DOLPHIN LIGHT	30-03-08.237N 090-39-49.951W	Fl R 2.5s			Marks downstream mooring dolphin.	Private aid.
14547.01	NORANDA ALUMINA UPSTREAM DOLPHIN LIGHT	30-03-07.121N 090-39-53.114W	Fl R 2.5s			Marks upstream mooring dolphin.	Private aid.
14547.02	*Noranda Alumina Lighted Downstream Mooring Buoy*	30-03-07.730N 090-39-57.169W	Q W			White with blue band.	Private aid.
14547.03	*Noranda Alumina Lighted Middle Mooring Buoy*	30-03-07.358N 090-39-58.223W	Q W			White with blue band.	Private aid.
14547.04	*Noranda Alumina Lighted Upstream Mooring Buoy*	30-03-06.986N 090-39-59.277W	Q W			White with blue band.	Private aid.

Light List corrected through LNM week: 01/18

(1) No.	(2) Name and Location	(3) Position	(4) Characteristic	(5) Height	(6) Range	(7) Structure	(8) Remarks
\multicolumn{8}{c}{MISSISSIPPI RIVER (Louisiana) - Eighth District}							

MISSISSIPPI RIVER - New Orleans to Baton Rouge (Chart 11370)

New Orleans to Baton Rouge

Designations left descending bank (LDB) and right descending bank (RDB) are as seen from a vessel going downstream Low water buoys are not listed and their positions may be frequently shifted with changing stages and conditions of the river.

No.	Name and Location	Position	Characteristic	Height	Range	Structure	Remarks
14550	KAISER COKE DOCK LIGHTS (3) LDB mile 145.6.	30-16-11.000N 091-07-11.000W	Fl R 2.5s			On ends and center of 1,200 foot dock.	Private aid.
14555	Gramercy Bridge Approach Buoy 1 Mile 145.7.	30-02-45.215N 090-40-11.131W				Green can.	

NEW ORLEANS HARBOR (Chart 11368)

New Orleans to Baton Rouge

Designations left descending bank (LDB) and right descending bank (RDB) are as seen from a vessel going downstream Low water buoys are not listed and their positions may be frequently shifted with changing stages and condition of the river.

No.	Name and Location	Position	Characteristic	Height	Range	Structure	Remarks
14557	Gramercy Bridge West Pier V-AIS	30-02-39.960N 090-40-21.510W					AIS - 993682007
14558	Gramercy Bridge East Pier V-AIS	30-02-42.340N 090-40-16.950W					AIS - 993682008

MISSISSIPPI RIVER - New Orleans to Baton Rouge (Chart 11370)

New Orleans to Baton Rouge

Designations left descending bank (LDB) and right descending bank (RDB) are as seen from a vessel going downstream Low water buoys are not listed and their positions may be frequently shifted with changing stages and conditions of the river.

No.	Name and Location	Position	Characteristic	Height	Range	Structure	Remarks
14560	Gramercy Bridge Approach Buoy 3 Mile 145.9.	30-02-38.507N 090-40-25.727W				Green can.	
14565	Gramercy Bridge Approach Buoy 5 Mile 146.0.	30-02-36.515N 090-40-29.939W				Green can.	
14570	Lower Grand View Reach Anchorage Lower Day beacon 146.4	30-02-44.700N 090-40-49.800W				NY on pile.	Ra ref.
14575	GRAMERCY WATER INTAKE LIGHT LDB mile 146.6.	30-02-33.600N 090-41-05.700W	Fl R 2.5s			On dolphins.	Private aid.
14580	Lower Grand View Reach Anchorage Upper Day beacon 146.7	30-02-38.220N 090-41-01.800W				NY on pile.	Ra ref.
14585	Middle Grand View Reach Anchorage Lower Day beacon 146.8	30-02-34.146N 090-41-08.979W				NY on pile.	Ra ref.
14590	Middle Grand View Reach Anchorage Upper Day beacon 147.2	30-02-18.876N 090-41-31.587W				NY on pile.	
14595	LUTCHER INTAKE LIGHTS (2) LDB mile 147.3.	30-02-15.000N 090-41-35.000W	Fl R 2.5s			Piles.	Private aid.
14600	Upper Grand View Reach Anchorage Lower Day beacon 147.5	30-02-10.380N 090-41-45.780W				NY on pile.	Ra ref.
14605	CRESCENT LIGHT 147 RDB mile 148.8.	30-01-06.906N 090-42-27.102W	Q G		5	SG on skeleton tower.	
14610	Upper Grand View Reach Anchorage Upper Day beacon 148.8	30-01-20.680N 090-42-44.060W				NY on pile.	Ra ref.
14615	LAURA LIGHT 149 RDB mile 149.7.	30-00-48.516N 090-43-04.950W	Q G		5	SG on skeleton tower on piles.	
14620	VACHERIE LIGHT 149A RDB mile 150.0.	30-00-37.046N 090-43-38.219W	Iso G 6s		3	SG on pile.	
14625	J. W. STONE OIL DOCK LIGHTS (2) LDB mile 150.1.	30-00-56.000N 090-43-58.000W	Fl R 2.5s	15		On dolphins.	Private aid.
14630	PEAVEY DOCK LIGHTS (3) LDB mile 150.4.	30-00-57.000N 090-44-02.000W	Fl R 2.5s			On dolphins.	Private aid.
14635	HESTER LIGHT 152 LDB mile 151.7.	30-01-05.520N 090-45-24.654W	Iso R 6s		4	TR on skeleton tower on piles.	

Light List corrected through LNM week: 01/18

(1) No.	(2) Name and Location	(3) Position	(4) Characteristic	(5) Height	(6) Range	(7) Structure	(8) Remarks
		MISSISSIPPI RIVER (Louisiana) - Eighth District					

MISSISSIPPI RIVER - New Orleans to Baton Rouge (Chart 11370)

New Orleans to Baton Rouge

Designations left descending bank (LDB) and right descending bank (RDB) are as seen from a vessel going downstream Low water buoys are not listed and their positions may be frequently shifted with changing stages and conditions of the river.

(1) No.	(2) Name and Location	(3) Position	(4) Characteristic	(5) Height	(6) Range	(7) Structure	(8) Remarks
14640	LOWER BELMONT CROSSING LOWER SIDE RANGE FRONT LIGHT LDB mile 152.2.	30-01-07.659N 090-45-57.285W	F G			KWG on skeleton tower.	Visible all around; higher intensity on range line.
14645	LOWER BELMONT CROSSING LOWER SIDE RANGE REAR LIGHT 108 yards, 049.2° from front light.	30-01-09.625N 090-45-54.666W	F G			KWG on skeleton tower.	Visible all around; higher intensity on range line.
14650	LOWER BELMONT CROSSING RANGE FRONT LIGHT LDB mile 152.2.	30-01-07.491N 090-46-01.903W	F W			KRW on skeleton tower.	Visible 2° each side of range line. Lighted throughout 24 hours.
14655	LOWER BELMONT CROSSING RANGE REAR LIGHT 102 yards, 049.0° from front light.	30-01-09.488N 090-45-59.267W	F W			KRW on skeleton tower on piles.	Visible 2° each side of range line. Lighted throughout 24 hours.
14660	LOWER BELMONT CROSSING UPPER SIDE RANGE FRONT LIGHT LDB mile 152.2.	30-01-06.599N 090-46-07.464W	F R			KWR on skeleton tower.	Visible all around; higher intensity on range line.
14665	LOWER BELMONT CROSSING UPPER SIDE RANGE REAR LIGHT 132 yards, 049.2° from front light.	30-01-09.172N 090-46-04.044W	F R			KWR on skeleton tower.	Visible all around; higher intensity on range line.
14670	BELMONT LIGHT 154 LDB mile 152.9.	30-00-57.708N 090-46-41.982W	Q R		4	TR on skeleton tower on piles.	
14675	COLLEGE POINT LIGHT 156	29-59-07.236N 090-49-13.483W	Q R		4	TR on skeleton tower.	
14680	CHOTIN LIGHT 155 RDB mile 155.6.	29-59-05.382N 090-48-25.824W	Q G		3	SG on skeleton tower.	
14685	LAGAN LEADING LIGHT RDB Mile 156.2.	29-58-40.057N 090-49-18.090W	Iso W 6s		5	NB on skeleton tower.	
14690	RICHANNEL BEND LIGHT 157 RDB mile 156.4.	29-58-42.408N 090-49-24.240W	Q G		4	SG on skeleton tower.	
14693	YUHUANG CHEMICAL DOCK LIGHTS (2) RDB mile 157.4.	29-59-36.040N 090-50-02.400W	Fl G 2.5s			Marks outermost upstream / downstream corners of dock.	Private aid.
14695	ST. JAMES SUGAR DOCK LIGHTS (2) RDB mile 157.7.	29-59-56.000N 090-50-05.000W	F G			On dock.	Private aid.
14698	PLAINS DOCK LIGHTS (2)	30-00-03.260N 090-50-05.700W	Fl G 2.5s			Marks outermost upstream and outermost downstream mooring dolphins.	Private aid.
14700	DEPT. OF ENERGY DOCK LIGHTS (4) RDB mile 158.4.	30-00-37.000N 090-50-13.000W	Fl G 2.5s			On dolphins.	Private aid.
14705	*Ryan Walsh Stevedoring Co. Lower Lighted Mooring Buoy* LDB mile 158.7.	30-00-51.500N 090-49-55.300W	Fl W 4s			White with blue band.	Private aid.
14710	*Ryan Walsh Stevedoring Co. Upper Lighted Mooring Buoy* LDB mile 158.7.	30-00-37.700N 090-49-53.700W	Fl W 4s			White with blue band.	Private aid.
14715	ST. JAMES TERMINAL TANKER DOCK 3 DOLPHIN LIGHTS (4) RDB mile 158.8.	30-00-44.000N 090-50-14.500W	Fl G 2.5s			On dolphins.	Private aid.
14720	ST. JAMES TERMINAL DOCK LIGHTS (4) RDB mile 159.0.	30-01-07.000N 090-50-18.000W	Fl G 2.5s				Private aid.

Light List corrected through LNM week: 01/18

(1) No.	(2) Name and Location	(3) Position	(4) Characteristic	(5) Height	(6) Range	(7) Structure	(8) Remarks
		MISSISSIPPI RIVER (Louisiana) - Eighth District					

MISSISSIPPI RIVER - New Orleans to Baton Rouge (Chart 11370)

New Orleans to Baton Rouge

Designations left descending bank (LDB) and right descending bank (RDB) are as seen from a vessel going downstream Low water buoys are not listed and their positions may be frequently shifted with changing stages and conditions of the river.

(1) No.	(2) Name and Location	(3) Position	(4) Characteristic	(5) Height	(6) Range	(7) Structure	(8) Remarks
14725	SHELL PIPELINE CORP. DOCK LIGHTS (6) RDB mile 159.5.	29-09-05.000N 089-14-07.000W	Fl G 4s				Private aid.
14730	NUSTAR BARGE DOCK LIGHTS (4) RDB mile 159.7.	30-01-35.558N 090-50-22.903W	Fl G 4s	18		On platform with dolphins.	Private aid.
14735	KOCH TANKER DOCK LIGHTS (4) RDB mile 159.8.	30-01-45.000N 090-50-23.000W	Fl G 4s			Marks dock.	Private aid.
14740	CAPLINE TANKER DOCK LIGHTS (4) RDB mile 160.0	30-01-53.000N 090-50-24.000W	Fl G 2.5s			On dock extremities.	Private aid.
14745	MATADOR BARGE DOCK LIGHTS (2) RDB mile 160.2	30-02-11.000N 090-50-48.000W	Fl R 2.5s	18		On dock.	Private aid.
14750	ERGON TANKER DOCK LIGHTS (3) RDB mile 160.7.	30-02-32.000N 090-50-29.000W	Fl G 2.5s			On dolphins.	Private aid.
14755	RAVEN ENERGY TERMINAL LIGHTS (3) LDB mile 161.	30-02-48.390N 090-50-16.830W	Fl R 2.5s			On mooring dolphin.	Private aid.
14760	OCCIDENTAL CHEMICAL DOCK LIGHTS (3) LDB mile 161.4.	30-03-08.000N 090-50-24.000W	Fl R 2.5s	40		On dolphins.	Private aid.
14765	T.T. BARGE DOCK LIGHTS (2) RDB Mile 162.3	30-03-15.040N 090-50-49.684W	Fl G 2.5s	10		On dock.	Private aid.
14770	NITA LIGHT 162 LDB mile 162.2.	30-03-47.130N 090-51-00.510W	Iso R 6s		5	TR on pile.	
14775	BRILLIANT POINT LIGHT 163 RDB mile 163.5.	30-03-37.218N 090-52-22.434W	Iso G 6s		4	SG on skeleton tower.	
14780	ZEN-NOH GRAIN DOCK LIGHTS (3) LDB mile 163.8.	30-03-52.430N 090-52-30.070W	Fl R 2.5s			On grain dock.	Private aid.
14785	ST ALICE LIGHT 165 RDB mile 164.8.	30-03-40.740N 090-53-46.110W	Q G		5	SG on skeleton tower on piles.	
14795	CHEVRON CHEMICAL DOCK LIGHTS (7) RDB mile 166.0	30-06-55.000N 090-54-40.000W	Fl G 2.5s	10		On dolphins.	Private aid.
14800	SHELL OIL LOADING PLATFORM LIGHT RDB mile 166.1.	30-04-39.000N 090-54-32.000W	Fl G 4s			On loading platform.	Private aid.
14805	CHEVRON DOCK LIGHTS (2) RDB mile 166.8.	30-05-10.000N 090-54-45.000W	Fl G 2s			Piles.	Private aid.
14815	YARA NORTH AMERICA MOORING DOLPHIN LIGHT LDB mile 167	30-05-26.280N 090-54-28.610W	Fl R 2.5s			On mooring dolphin.	Private aid.
14820	AGRICO CHEMICAL DOCK LIGHTS (3) RDB mile 167.0.	30-05-19.900N 090-54-46.000W	Fl G 2.5s			On dock extremities.	LIGHTS FLASH IN UNISON. Private aid.
14825	EAGLE ASPHALT PRODUCTS LIGHTS (2) RDB mile 167.5.	30-06-01.720N 090-54-58.180W	Fl R 2.5s			On mooring dolphins.	Private aid.
14830	LAFARGE CEMENT COMPANY DOLPHIN LIGHTS (2) LDB mile 167.9.	30-06-16.000N 090-54-36.000W	Fl R 2.5s	10		On dolphins.	Private aid.

Sunshine Bridge Approach

(1) No.	(2) Name and Location	(3) Position	(4) Characteristic	(5) Height	(6) Range	(7) Structure	(8) Remarks
14835	- Buoy 1	30-05-46.671N 090-54-53.317W				Green can.	AIS - 993682009
14840	- Buoy A	30-05-47.288N 090-54-43.939W				Green can with red bands.	AIS - 993682010
14845	- Buoy B	30-05-58.176N 090-54-46.531W				Green can with red bands.	AIS - 993682011

Light List corrected through LNM week: 01/18

(1) No.	(2) Name and Location	(3) Position	(4) Characteristic	(5) Height	(6) Range	(7) Structure	(8) Remarks
	MISSISSIPPI RIVER (Louisiana) - Eighth District						

MISSISSIPPI RIVER - New Orleans to Baton Rouge (Chart 11370)
New Orleans to Baton Rouge
Sunshine Bridge Approach

No.	Name and Location	Position	Characteristic	Height	Range	Structure	Remarks
14850	- Buoy C	30-06-04.967N 090-54-48.271W				Green can with red bands.	AIS - 993682012

New Orleans to Baton Rouge

Designations left descending bank (LDB) and right descending bank (RDB) are as seen from a vessel going downstream Low water buoys are not listed and their positions may be frequently shifted with changing stages and conditions of the river.

No.	Name and Location	Position	Characteristic	Height	Range	Structure	Remarks
14855	STAR ENTERPRISE DOCK LIGHTS (4) LDB mile 168.1.	30-06-34.000N 090-54-41.000W	Fl R 2.5s			On dock.	Private aid.
14860	STAR ENTERPRISE NORTH DOCK LIGHTS (3) LDB mile 168.5.	30-06-43.000N 090-54-40.000W	Fl R 2.5s			On dock.	HORN: 1 BLAST EV 20S (2S BL). Private aid.
14865	IMPALA WAREHOUSING DOCK LIGHTS (2) LDB mile 169.2.	30-07-26.000N 090-54-55.000W	Q R				Private aid.
14870	*Impala Warehousing Lighted Mooring Buoy A* LDB mile 169.3	30-07-40.000N 090-55-08.000W	Q W			White with blue band.	Private aid.
14875	*Impala Warehousing Lighted Mooring Buoy B* LDB mile 169.5	30-07-29.000N 090-55-01.000W	Q W			White with blue band.	Private aid.
14880	IMPALA WAREHOUSING TERMINAL DOCK LIGHT LDB mile 169.5.	30-07-46.000N 090-55-08.000W	Fl R 2.5s			On dolphin.	Private aid.
14885	IMPALA WAREHOUSING DOLPHIN LIGHTS (2) LDB mile 170.3.	30-07-39.000N 090-55-03.000W	Fl R 2.5s			On dolphin.	Private aid.
14890	IMPALA WAREHOUSING LIGHT 170 LDB mile 170.6.	30-08-22.500N 090-55-59.900W	Q R		4	TR on skeleton tower on piles.	
14895	RIVER CEMENT COMPANY DOCK LIGHTS LDB mile 170.9.	30-08-25.000N 090-56-22.000W	Fl R 2.5s	21		On mooring dolphin.	Private aid.
14900	RIVERTON LIGHT 172 LDB mile 171.2.	30-08-13.248N 090-56-44.478W	Iso R 6s		5	TR on skeleton tower on concrete pad.	
14905	WADE HAMPTON LIGHT 173 RDB mile 172.0.	30-07-43.679N 090-56-31.260W	Iso G 6s		5	SG on skeleton tower.	
14910	RATEAU LIGHT 173A RDB mile 173.0.	30-06-27.672N 090-56-47.430W	Q G		4	SG on skeleton tower on piles.	
14915	CF INDUSTRIES NITROGEN DOLPHIN LIGHTS (2) RDB mile 173.4.	30-06-12.250N 090-57-24.230W	Fl G 2.5s			On dolphins.	Private aid.
14917	CF INDUSTRIES MOORING DOLPHIN LIGHTS (2) RDB mile 173.5	30-06-17.150N 090-57-09.365W	Fl W 2.5s			Marks upstream and downstream mooring dolphins.	Private aid.
14920	CF INDUSTRIES NITROGEN BARGE DOCK LIGHTS (2) RDB mile 173.6.	30-06-10.820N 090-57-34.520W	Fl G 2.5s			On dock.	Private aid.
14925	BRINGIER POINT LIGHT 174 LDB mile 173.7.	30-06-46.980N 090-57-07.920W	Q R		5	TR on skeleton tower on piles.	
14930	C. F. INDUSTRIES NITROGEN MOORING FACILITIES LIGHTS (3) RDB mile 173.7.	30-06-10.620N 090-57-47.830W	Fl G 2.5s			On dock extremities.	Private aid.
14935	PUMPKIN BEZETTE J RANGE FRONT LIGHT LDB mile 174.6.	30-06-49.767N 090-58-09.244W	F W			KRW on skeleton tower on sills.	Lighted throughout 24 hours.
14940	PUMPKIN BEZETTE J RANGE REAR LIGHT 242 yards, 085° from front light.	30-06-50.445N 090-58-00.226W	F W			KRW on skeleton tower on platform.	Lighted throughout 24 hours.
14945	PUMPKIN BEZETTE LIGHT 176 LDB mile 174.6.	30-06-49.767N 090-58-09.244W	Fl R 2.5s		5	TR on same structure as Range J Front Light.	
14947	Le Pelican Wreck V-AIS MM 175.3 RDB	30-06-37.000N 090-59-14.000W					AIS(1): 993682028

Light List corrected through LNM week: 01/18

(1) No.	(2) Name and Location	(3) Position	(4) Characteristic	(5) Height	(6) Range	(7) Structure	(8) Remarks
		MISSISSIPPI RIVER (Louisiana) - Eighth District					

MISSISSIPPI RIVER - New Orleans to Baton Rouge (Chart 11370)

New Orleans to Baton Rouge
Designations left descending bank (LDB) and right descending bank (RDB) are as seen from a vessel going downstream. Low water buoys are not listed and their positions may be frequently shifted with changing stages and conditions of the river.

(1) No.	(2) Name and Location	(3) Position	(4) Characteristic	(5) Height	(6) Range	(7) Structure	(8) Remarks
14950	BAYOU LAFOURCHE INTAKE LIGHTS (3) RDB mile 175.4.	30-06-37.000N 090-59-24.000W	Q G			On dolphins.	Private aid.
14950.01	Bayou Lafourche Intake V-AIS MM 175.4 RDB	30-06-38.070N 090-59-25.440W					AIS(1): 993682027
14955	SMOKE BEND RANGE FRONT LIGHT RDB mile 177.1.	30-06-36.996N 091-00-49.172W	Iso W 2s			KRW on skeleton tower on piles.	Visible all around; higher intensity on rangeline.
14960	SMOKE BEND RANGE REAR LIGHT 281 yards, 265° from front light.	30-06-36.279N 091-00-58.707W	Iso W 6s			KRW on skeleton tower on piles.	Visible all around; higher intensity on rangeline.
14965	EVAN HALL LIGHT 177 RDB Mile 177.9.	30-06-52.350N 091-01-52.130W	Iso G 6s		5	SG on skeleton tower.	
14970	MCMANOR LIGHT 179 RDB mile 178.5.	30-07-31.932N 091-02-11.754W	Q G		5	SG on skeleton tower on concrete block.	
14975	EIGHTY ONE MILE POINT LIGHT 180 LDB mile 178.8.	30-07-22.338N 091-01-32.214W	Q R		4	TR on skeleton tower.	
14980	GEM LIGHT 180A LDB Mile 180.9.	30-08-37.794N 090-59-47.892W	Iso R 6s		5	TR on skeleton tower on piles.	
14982	MATADOR DOCK LIGHTS (3) LDB 181.5.	30-09-11.000N 090-59-48.000W	Fl R 2.5s			Marks dock.	Private aid.
14985	PHILADELPHIA POINT C RANGE FRONT LIGHT RDB mile 182.5.	30-09-38.993N 091-00-22.813W	Iso W 2s			KRW on skeleton tower on sills.	Visible all around, higher intensity on rangeline. Lighted throughout 24 hours.
14990	PHILADELPHIA POINT C RANGE REAR LIGHT 167 yards, 166° from front light.	30-09-34.191N 091-00-21.397W	Iso W 6s			KRW on mud sills.	Visible all around; higher intensity on rangeline. Lighted throughout 24 hours.
14993	BASF IMTT GEISMAR DOCK LIGHTS (2)	30-11-14.720N 091-00-52.010W	Fl R 2.5s			Marks outermost upstream and outermost downstream dock structures.	Private aid.
14995	OSCA BARGE DOCK LIGHTS (2) LDB mile 184.1	30-11-44.800N 091-01-12.000W	Fl R 6s			On dolphins.	Private aid.
15000	NEW RIVER LIGHT 184 LDB mile 184.8.	30-11-53.766N 091-01-17.166W	Iso R 6s		5	TR on skeleton tower on piles.	
15005	MONOCHEM DOCK LIGHTS (2) LDB mile 184.8.	30-11-52.110N 091-01-19.500W	F R			On dolphins.	Private aid.
15010	HONEYWELL CHEMICAL DOCK LIGHTS (2) LDB mile 186.8.	30-12-55.000N 090-03-16.000W	Fl R 4s			On pier.	Private aid.
15015	COS-MAR LIGHTS (2) LDB mile 187.9.	30-13-03.000N 091-04-06.500W	Fl R 4s			Dolphins.	Private aid.
15020	RESCUE LIGHT 190 LDB mile 188.6.	30-12-58.179N 091-04-57.918W	Iso R 6s		4	TR on pile.	
15022	*Bear Industries Dolphin Lights (2)* LDB mile 189.3	30-12-51.341N 091-05-14.520W	Fl R 2.5s			Marks upstream and downstream dolphins.	Private aid.
15025	ALHAMBRA RANGE FRONT D LIGHT LDB mile 189.4.	30-12-44.078N 091-05-49.124W	Iso R 2s			KRW on skeleton tower on piles.	Visible all around; higher intensity on rangeline.
15030	ALHAMBRA RANGE REAR D LIGHT 278 yards, 043.9° from front light.	30-12-50.026N 091-05-42.532W	Iso R 6s			KRW on skeleton tower on mud sills.	Visible all around; higher intensity on rangeline.
15035	White Castle Lower Anchorage Daybeacon 190.4 RDB mile 190.4	30-11-51.780N 091-06-19.260W				NY on pile.	Ra ref.

MISSISSIPPI RIVER (Louisiana) - Eighth District

MISSISSIPPI RIVER - New Orleans to Baton Rouge (Chart 11370)

New Orleans to Baton Rouge

Designations left descending bank (LDB) and right descending bank (RDB) are as seen from a vessel going downstream Low water buoys are not listed and their positions may be frequently shifted with changing stages and conditions of the river.

(1) No.	(2) Name and Location	(3) Position	(4) Characteristic	(5) Height	(6) Range	(7) Structure	(8) Remarks
15040	White Castle Anchorage Upper Day beacon 191.1 RDB mile 191.1	30-11-28.260N 091-06-55.680W				NY on pile.	Ra ref.
15045	WHITE CASTLE RANGE FRONT LIGHT RDB mile 192.7.	30-10-36.374N 091-08-10.723W	F G			KRW on skeleton tower on piles.	
15050	WHITE CASTLE RANGE REAR LIGHT 164 yards, 224.0° from front light.	30-10-32.872N 091-08-14.604W	F G			KRW on skeleton tower on piles.	
15055	WHITE CASTLE LIGHT 193 RDB mile 193.5.	30-10-36.169N 091-09-09.496W	Q G		5	SG on skeleton tower.	
15060	EUREKA LIGHT 195 RDB mile 194.8.	30-11-23.538N 091-09-58.537W	Iso G 6s		4	SG on pile.	
15065	WHITE ALDER MEMORIAL LIGHT 195A RDB mile 195.2.	30-11-56.247N 091-10-07.888W	Q G		5	SG on skeleton tower on concrete block.	
15070	BAYOU GOULA BEND LIGHT 197 RDB mile 196.2.	30-12-53.988N 091-09-43.968W	Iso G 6s		5	SG on skeleton tower on piles.	
15075	BAYOU GOULA E RANGE FRONT LIGHT RDB mile 197.1.	30-13-25.791N 091-09-07.061W	F W			KRW on skeleton tower.	Visible all around; higher intensity on rangeline.
15080	BAYOU GOULA E RANGE REAR LIGHT 238 yards, 249° from front light.	30-13-23.247N 091-09-14.647W	F W			KRW on skeleton tower.	Visible all around; higher intensity on rangeline.
15085	SUNOCO TERMINAL DOLPHIN LIGHTS (2) LDB mile 198.2.	30-13-42.000N 091-07-59.000W	Fl R 2.5s			On dolphins.	Private aid.
15090	VIRGINIA RANGE FRONT LIGHT LDB mile 198.7.	30-14-00.054N 091-07-24.815W	F R			KRW on skeleton tower.	Visible all around; higher intensity on rangeline.
15095	VIRGINIA RANGE REAR LIGHT 176 yards, 068° from front light.	30-14-01.938N 091-07-19.194W	F R			KRW on skeleton tower.	Visible all around; higher intensity on rangeline.
15100	OLIN DOCK LIGHTS (3)	30-14-44.050N 091-06-28.570W	Fl R 4s			On dolphins.	Private aid.
15105	ST. GABRIEL DOCK LIGHT LDB mile 200.6.	30-19-23.000N 091-09-25.000W	Fl R 2.5s			On end of dock.	Private aid.
15110	ST GABRIEL LIGHT 202 LDB mile 200.7.	30-15-25.248N 091-06-22.560W	Q R		4	TR on skeleton tower on piles.	
15115	WILLOW GLENN WHARF LIGHTS (5) LDB mile 201.6.	30-16-09.000N 091-07-06.000W	Fl R 2.5s			On mooring dolphins on 1,050 foot dock.	Private aid.
15120	BAYOU PAUL LIGHT 204 LDB mile 202.1.	30-16-29.288N 091-07-34.026W	Iso R 6s		4	TR on skeleton tower on piles.	
15125	GRANADA RANGE F LOWER FRONT LIGHT LDB mile 203.2	30-16-52.271N 091-08-29.576W	Q G			NG on pile.	Visible 144° - 269°
15130	GRANADA RANGE F LOWER REAR LIGHT LDB mile 203.2	30-16-52.752N 091-08-24.403W	Iso G 6s			NG on pile.	Visible 144° - 269°
15135	GRANADA RANGE F FRONT LIGHT LDB mile 203.2.	30-16-53.137N 091-08-33.448W	F W			KRW on skeleton tower.	
15140	GRANADA RANGE F REAR LIGHT 274 yards, 083.7° from front light.	30-16-54.010N 091-08-24.134W	F W			KRW on skeleton tower.	
15145	GRANADA RANGE F UPPER FRONT LIGHT LDB mile 203.2	30-16-54.103N 091-08-36.284W	Q R			NR on pile.	Visible 144° - 269°

Light List corrected through LNM week: 01/18

(1) No.	(2) Name and Location	(3) Position	(4) Characteristic	(5) Height	(6) Range	(7) Structure	(8) Remarks
		MISSISSIPPI RIVER (Louisiana) - Eighth District					

MISSISSIPPI RIVER - New Orleans to Baton Rouge (Chart 11370)

New Orleans to Baton Rouge

Designations left descending bank (LDB) and right descending bank (RDB) are as seen from a vessel going downstream. Low water buoys are not listed and their positions may be frequently shifted with changing stages and conditions of the river.

(1) No.	(2) Name and Location	(3) Position	(4) Characteristic	(5) Height	(6) Range	(7) Structure	(8) Remarks
15150	GRANADA RANGE F UPPER REAR LIGHT LDB mile 203.2	30-16-54.748N 091-08-29.654W	Iso R 6s			NR on pile.	Visible 144° - 269°
15155	PETROUNITED TANKER DOCK LIGHTS (3) LDB mile 203.8.	30-16-58.500N 091-09-18.700W	Fl R 2.5s			On wharf and mooring dolphins.	Private aid.
15160	ASHLAND DOCK LIGHTS(2) RDB mile 204.8.	30-16-33.000N 091-10-19.200W	Fl G 4s			On ends of dock.	Private aid.
15165	GEORGIA PACIFIC WHARF LIGHTS (5) RDB mile 205.4.	30-16-31.000N 091-11-02.000W	Fl G 2.5s			On ends of wharf and mooring dolphins.	HORN: 1 BLAST EV 15S (3S BL). Private aid.
15170	ST LOUIS PLANTATION RANGE FRONT LIGHT RDB mile 206.8.	30-16-31.494N 091-12-19.089W	F G			KRW on skeleton tower.	
15175	ST LOUIS PLANTATION RANGE REAR LIGHT 219 yards, 263.6° from front light.	30-16-30.777N 091-12-26.542W	F G			KRW on skeleton tower.	
15180	PLAQUEMINE LIGHT 209 RDB mile 209.0.	30-17-41.400N 091-14-01.590W	Iso G 6s		4	SG on skeleton tower on pile.	Higher intensity beam up and down river.
15185	RELIANCE LIGHT 211 RDB mile 209.4.	30-18-23.108N 091-14-00.948W	Q G		5	SG on skeleton tower on concrete block.	
15190	PLAQUEMINE WHARF LIGHTS (3) RDB mile 209.9.	30-18-44.000N 091-13-32.500W	Fl G 2.5s			on dolphins.	HORN: 1 BLAST EV 20S (2S BL). Private aid.
15195	PLAQUEMINE BEND LIGHT 213 RDB mile 210.4.	30-19-04.140N 091-13-06.300W	Iso G 6s		4	SG on pile.	
15200	MEDORA G RANGE FRONT LIGHT RDB mile 211.4.	30-19-20.581N 091-12-07.151W	Fl W 2.5s			KRW on skeleton tower on mud sills.	Visible all around.
15205	MEDORA G RANGE REAR LIGHT 290 yards, 290.4° from front light.	30-19-22.738N 091-12-13.872W	Iso W 6s			KRW on skeleton tower on mud sills.	Visible all around.
15210	OLD HERMITAGE RANGE FRONT LIGHT LDB mile 213.4.	30-18-38.804N 091-09-56.703W	Iso R 2s			KRW on skeleton tower.	Visible all around; higher intensity on rangeline. Lighted nighttime only.
15215	OLD HERMITAGE RANGE REAR LIGHT 218 yards, 110° from front light.	30-18-36.565N 091-09-49.705W	Iso R 6s			KRW on skeleton tower.	Visible all around; higher intensity on rangeline. Lighted nighttime only.
15220	WADLINGTON LIGHT 214 LDB mile 214.0.	30-18-37.650N 091-09-23.808W	Iso R 6s		4	TR on skeleton tower.	
15225	MANCHAC BEND LIGHT 216 LDB mile 214.9.	30-19-02.574N 091-08-22.128W	Q R		4	TR on skeleton tower.	
15230	BURTVILLE LIGHT 216A LDB mile 215.6.	30-19-53.583N 091-08-17.331W	Iso R 6s		4	TR on skeleton tower.	
15235	LONGWOOD PLANTATION LIGHT 216B LDB mile 216.2.	30-20-14.718N 091-08-31.062W	Q R		5	TR on skeleton tower on piles.	
15240	MULBERRY GROVE LIGHT 218 LDB Mile 217.3.	30-20-50.190N 091-09-46.764W	Iso R 6s		3	TR on skeleton tower on piles.	
15245	RICHARD POWELL RANGE FRONT LIGHT LDB mile 214.9.	30-21-07.200N 091-10-52.785W	Oc W 4s			KRW on skeleton tower on sill.	Visible all around.
15250	RICHARD POWELL RANGE REAR LIGHT 200 yards, 060.9° from front light.	30-21-10.082N 091-10-46.802W	F W			KRW on skeleton tower.	Visible all around.

Light List corrected through LNM week: 01/18

(1) No.	(2) Name and Location	(3) Position	(4) Characteristic	(5) Height	(6) Range	(7) Structure	(8) Remarks
			MISSISSIPPI RIVER (Louisiana) - Eighth District				

MISSISSIPPI RIVER - New Orleans to Baton Rouge (Chart 11370)
New Orleans to Baton Rouge
Designations left descending bank (LDB) and right descending bank (RDB) are as seen from a vessel going downstream Low water buoys are not listed and their positions may be frequently shifted with changing stages and conditions of the river.

(1) No.	(2) Name and Location	(3) Position	(4) Characteristic	(5) Height	(6) Range	(7) Structure	(8) Remarks
15255	SARDINE POINT LIGHT 221 RDB mile 220.0.	30-20-16.011N 091-12-25.053W	Q G		3	SG on skeleton tower on mud sills.	
15260	NEW HOPE LIGHT 221A RDB mile 221.3.	30-20-11.806N 091-13-45.428W	Q G		3	SG on skeleton tower.	
15265	DOW CHEMICAL WHARF LIGHTS (5) RDB mile 221.8.	30-20-29.000N 091-14-23.000W	Fl G 2.5s			On dock extremities.	Private aid.
15270	ST DELPHINE LIGHT 223 RDB mile 222.3.	30-20-53.565N 091-14-47.190W	Iso G 6s		4	SG on skeleton tower on concrete block.	
15275	MISSOURI LIGHT 223A RDB mile 222.6.	30-21-14.914N 091-14-52.440W	Q G		3	SG on skeleton tower on concrete block.	
15280	RED EYE H RANGE FRONT LIGHT RDB mile 223.2.	30-21-46.138N 091-14-49.945W	F G			KRW on skeleton tower on mud sills.	
15280.01	RED EYE H LIGHT	30-21-46.138N 091-14-49.945W	Fl G 2.5s			On same structure as Red Eye H Range Front Light.	
15285	RED EYE H RANGE REAR LIGHT 233 yards, 226.5° from front light.	30-21-41.389N 091-14-55.712W	F G			KRW on skeleton tower.	
15295	Baton Rouge General Anchorage Lower Day beacon 225.8	30-23-31.841N 091-13-28.510W				NY on pile.	Ra ref.
15300	ARLINGTON RANGE FRONT LIGHT LDB mile 226.3.	30-23-40.604N 091-12-30.836W	F R			KRW on skeleton tower.	Visible all around; higher intensity on rangeline.
15305	ARLINGTON RANGE REAR LIGHT 233 yards, 047° from front light.	30-23-45.376N 091-12-25.033W	F R			KRW on skeleton tower.	Visible all around; higher intensity on rangeline.
15310	COLLEGE TOWN LIGHT 226 LDB mile 226.6.	30-24-12.834N 091-12-08.352W	Q R		4	TR on skeleton tower.	
15315	Baton Rouge General Anchorage Upper Day beacon 227.3	30-24-40.996N 091-12-32.042W				NY on tree.	Ra ref.
15320	GARTNESS LIGHT 228 LDB mile 227.8.	30-25-01.218N 091-11-47.298W	Q R		4	TR on skeleton tower on piles.	
15325	Lower Baton Rouge Anchorage Lower Day beacon 228.5	30-25-34.319N 091-11-37.859W				NY on pile.	Ra ref.
15330	Lower Baton Rouge Anchorage Upper Day beacon 229.0	30-26-08.231N 091-11-34.383W				NY on tree.	Ra ref.
15335	*Greater Baton Rouge Port Commission Lighted Mooring Buoy D* LDB mile 229.0.	30-25-54.000N 091-11-47.000W	Q W			White with blue band.	Private aid.
15340	*Greater Baton Rouge Port Commission Lighted Mooring Buoy C* LDB mile 229.0.	30-26-09.000N 091-11-44.000W	Q W			White with blue band.	Private aid.
15345	*Greater Baton Rouge Port Commission Lighted Mooring Buoy B* LDB mile 229.0.	30-26-09.000N 091-11-46.000W	Q W			White with blue band.	Private aid.
15350	*Greater Baton Rouge Port Commission Lighted Mooring Buoy A* LDB mile 229.0.	30-26-09.000N 091-11-48.000W	Q W			White with blue band.	Private aid.
15355	I-10 Bridge Approach Buoy E	30-26-15.433N 091-11-47.770W				Red nun with green bands.	AIS - 993682013
15360	I-10 Bridge Approach F V-AIS	30-26-28.652N 091-11-47.223W					AIS MMSI: 993682123

Light List corrected through LNM week: 01/18

(1) No.	(2) Name and Location	(3) Position	(4) Characteristic	(5) Height	(6) Range	(7) Structure	(8) Remarks
	MISSISSIPPI RIVER (Louisiana) - Eighth District						

MISSISSIPPI RIVER - New Orleans to Baton Rouge (Chart 11370)
New Orleans to Baton Rouge
Designations left descending bank (LDB) and right descending bank (RDB) are as seen from a vessel going downstream Low water buoys are not listed and their positions may be frequently shifted with changing stages and conditions of the river.

(1) No.	(2) Name and Location	(3) Position	(4) Characteristic	(5) Height	(6) Range	(7) Structure	(8) Remarks
15365	I-10 Bridge Approach Buoy G	30-26-31.640N 091-11-47.187W				Red nun with green bands.	AIS - 993682015
15370	BELLE OF BATON ROUGE DOCK LIGHTS (2) LDB mile 229.4	30-26-30.000N 091-11-32.000W	Fl R 2.5s			On piles.	Private aid.
15375	Middle Baton Rouge Anchorage Lower Day beacon 229.6	30-26-49.206N 091-12-04.794W				NY on pile.	Ra ref.
15380	Middle Baton Rouge Anchorage Upper Day beacon 229.8	30-26-55.674N 091-12-07.799W				NY on pile.	Ra ref.
15385	CASINO ROUGE BARRIER BARGE LIGHTS (2) LDB mile 230.4	30-27-38.800N 091-11-33.000W	Fl R 2.5s			On barrier barge.	Private aid.
15390	Upper Baton Rouge Anchorage Lower Day beacon 230.6	30-27-42.922N 091-11-32.455W				NY on tree.	Ra ref.
15395	Upper Baton Rouge Anchorage Upper Day beacon 231.0	30-27-53.256N 091-11-31.254W				NY on pile.	Ra ref.
15400	PLACID MOORING FACILITY LIGHTS (5) RDB mile 231.8.	30-28-26.260N 091-11-59.930W	Fl G 2.5s			On dolphins.	Private aid.
15405	EXXON REFINERY DOLPHIN AND DOCK LIGHTS (10) LDB mile 232.2.	30-29-10.000N 091-11-37.000W	Fl R 2.5s	50		On dolphin.	Private aid.
15410	INTERCONTINENTAL TERMINAL COMPANY DOLPHIN LIGHTS (3) RDB mile 232.4.	30-29-01.190N 091-11-58.380W	Fl G 2.5s			On dolphins.	Private aid.
15415	HALL-BUCK COKE TERMINAL DOCK LIGHTS (2) LDB mile 233.0.	30-29-37.000N 090-11-00.000W	Fl R 2.5s			On piles.	Private aid.
15420	FORMOSA PLASTICS LOWER DOCK LIGHTS (2) LDB mile 233.5.	30-30-04.000N 091-11-39.000W	Fl R 2.5s			On dolphins.	Private aid.
15425	FORMOSA PLASTICS UPPER DOCK LIGHTS (3) LDB mile 233.7	30-30-18.000N 091-11-39.000W	Fl R 2.5s			On dock.	Private aid.

NEW ORLEANS HARBOR (Chart 11368)
New Orleans to Baton Rouge
Designations left descending bank (LDB) and right descending bank (RDB) are as seen from a vessel going downstream Low water buoys are not listed and their positions may be frequently shifted with changing stages and condition of the river.

(1) No.	(2) Name and Location	(3) Position	(4) Characteristic	(5) Height	(6) Range	(7) Structure	(8) Remarks
15426	Baton Rouge Bridge Port Allen Pier South V-AIS	30-30-21.580N 091-11-56.970W					AIS - 993682021
15427	Baton Rouge Bridge Baton Rouge Pier South V-AIS	30-30-22.290N 091-11-49.640W					AIS - 993682017
15428	Baton Rouge Bridge Port Allen Pier North V-AIS	30-30-26.470N 091-11-56.960W					AIS - 993682020
15429	Baton Rouge Bridge Baton Rouge Pier North V-AIS	30-30-27.020N 091-11-49.620W					AIS - 993682016
	LOUISIANA - Eighth District						

MISSISSIPPI RIVER DELTA (Chart 11361)
Tiger Pass

(1) No.	(2) Name and Location	(3) Position	(4) Characteristic	(5) Height	(6) Range	(7) Structure	(8) Remarks
15430	- LIGHT 1 75 feet outside channel limit.	29-08-18.916N 089-27-04.832W	Fl G 4s	17	4	SG on dolphin.	Ra ref.
15440	- LIGHT 3 75 feet outside channel limit.	29-08-17.084N 089-26-32.512W	Fl G 2.5s	17	3	SG on dolphin.	Ra ref.
15445	- LIGHT 4	29-08-09.717N 089-26-30.168W	Fl R 2.5s	17	3	TR on dolphin.	Ra ref.
15450	- LIGHT 5 75 feet outside channel limit.	29-08-17.430N 089-26-10.731W	Q G	17	3	SG on dolphin.	Ra ref.

(1) No.	(2) Name and Location	(3) Position	(4) Characteristic	(5) Height	(6) Range	(7) Structure	(8) Remarks
	**LOUISIANA - Eighth District**						

MISSISSIPPI RIVER DELTA (Chart 11361)

Tiger Pass

(1) No.	(2) Name and Location	(3) Position	(4) Characteristic	(5) Height	(6) Range	(7) Structure	(8) Remarks
15455	- LIGHT 6	29-08-12.566N 089-26-09.667W	Q R	17	3	TR on dolphin.	Ra ref.
15460	- DANGER LIGHT B 75 feet outside channel limit.	29-08-23.218N 089-25-49.170W	Fl W 2.5s	17	3	NW on dolphin worded DANGER JETTIES.	Ra ref.
15465	- Danger Day beacon C 75 feet outside channel limit.	29-08-19.821N 089-25-47.189W				NW on dolphin worded DANGER JETTIES.	Ra ref.
15470	- Danger Day beacon D 75 feet outside channel limit.	29-08-31.586N 089-25-29.666W				NW on pile worded DANGER CHANNEL SHOALED.	Ra ref.
15475	- Danger Day beacon E 75 feet outside channel limit.	29-08-27.951N 089-25-28.004W				NW on pile worded DANGER CHANNEL SHOALED.	
15480	- DANGER LIGHT F 75 feet outside channel limit.	29-08-36.215N 089-25-18.642W	Fl W 2.5s	17	3	NW on pile worded DANGER CHANNEL SHOALED.	Ra ref.
15485	- DANGER LIGHT G 75 feet outside channel limit.	29-08-32.112N 089-25-19.056W	Fl W 2.5s	17	3	NW on pile worded DANGER CHANNEL SHOALED.	Ra ref.
15495	- Danger Day beacon H	29-08-42.819N 089-24-55.189W				NW on pile worded DANGER CHANNEL SHOALED.	Ra ref.
15500	- Danger Day beacon I	29-08-53.040N 089-24-46.680W				NW on pile worded DANGER CHANNEL SHOALED.	Ra ref.
15525	- DANGER LIGHT J	29-09-09.940N 089-23-55.559W	Fl W 2.5s	17	3	NW on pile worded DANGER CHANNEL SHOALED.	Ra ref.
15530	- DANGER LIGHT K	29-09-08.122N 089-23-47.540W	Fl W 2.5s	17	3	NW on pile worded DANGER CHANNEL SHOALED.	Ra ref.
15535	- LIGHT 23	29-09-14.699N 089-23-43.287W	Fl G 4s	17	3	SG on pile.	Ra ref.
15540	- Buoy 24	29-09-18.474N 089-23-33.216W				Red nun.	
15545	- Day beacon 25	29-09-30.524N 089-23-20.519W				SG on pile.	
15550	- Day beacon 26	29-09-27.601N 089-23-19.889W				TR on pile.	Ra ref.
15555	- Day beacon 27	29-09-48.366N 089-22-47.099W				SG on pile.	
15560	- Day beacon 28	29-09-46.123N 089-22-44.594W				TR on pile.	
15565	- Day beacon 29	29-10-06.855N 089-22-26.510W				SG on pile.	Ra ref.
15570	- Day beacon 30	29-10-01.537N 089-22-27.920W				TR on pile.	Ra ref.
15575	- Day beacon 31	29-10-18.069N 089-22-09.133W				SG on pile.	Ra ref.
15580	- Day beacon 32	29-10-16.510N 089-22-05.799W				TR on pile.	Ra ref.
15585	- Day beacon 33	29-10-27.736N 089-22-01.499W				SG on pile.	
15590	- LIGHT 34	29-10-26.410N 089-21-57.921W	Fl R 6s	17	3	TR on pile.	Ra ref.
15595	- Day beacon 35	29-10-41.745N 089-21-55.173W				SG on pile.	

Light List corrected through LNM week: 01/18

(1) No.	(2) Name and Location	(3) Position	(4) Characteristic	(5) Height	(6) Range	(7) Structure	(8) Remarks
		LOUISIANA - Eighth District					
	MISSISSIPPI RIVER DELTA (Chart 11361)						
	Tiger Pass						
15600	- Day beacon 36	29-10-40.974N 089-21-52.035W				TR on pile.	Ra ref.
15605	- Day beacon 37	29-10-55.158N 089-21-53.235W				SG on pile.	Ra ref.
15610	- Day beacon 38	29-11-01.881N 089-21-47.719W				TR on pile.	Ra ref.
15612	- Buoy 38A	29-11-08.823N 089-21-47.159W				Red nun.	
15615	- Day beacon 39	29-11-16.998N 089-21-47.942W				SG on pile.	Ra ref.
15620	- Day beacon 40	29-11-15.620N 089-21-44.560W				TR on pile.	Ra ref.
15625	- LIGHT 41	29-11-28.163N 089-21-40.332W	Fl G 4s	17	3	SG on pile.	
15630	- Day beacon 42	29-11-24.443N 089-21-38.500W				TR on pile.	Ra ref.
15635	- Day beacon 43	29-11-42.965N 089-21-33.802W				SG on pile.	
15640	- LIGHT 44	29-11-41.621N 089-21-30.120W	Fl R 6s	17	3	TR on pile.	Ra ref.
15645	- Day beacon 45	29-11-55.185N 089-21-24.230W				SG on pile.	
15652	- Buoy 46	29-11-53.344N 089-21-22.059W				Red nun.	
15655	- Day beacon 47	29-12-20.545N 089-21-15.108W				SG on pile.	Ra ref.
15660	- Day beacon 48	29-12-19.980N 089-21-11.277W				TR on pile.	Ra ref.
15665	- Buoy 50	29-12-30.538N 089-21-08.050W				Red nun.	
15670	- Day beacon 51	29-12-46.621N 089-21-03.594W				SG on pile.	Ra ref.
15675	- LIGHT 52	29-12-55.271N 089-20-59.546W	Fl R 4s	17	3	TR on pile.	Ra ref.
15677	- Buoy 52A	29-13-05.455N 089-21-02.640W				Red nun.	
15680	- Buoy 53	29-12-54.665N 089-21-03.210W				Green can.	
15685	- Buoy 54	29-13-12.080N 089-21-02.650W				Red nun.	
15690	- Day beacon 55	29-13-26.810N 089-20-58.368W				SG on pile.	Ra ref.
15695	- LIGHT 56	29-13-42.841N 089-20-54.300W	Fl R 2.5s	17	3	TR on pile.	Ra ref.
15700	- Buoy 58	29-14-06.260N 089-21-28.037W				Red nun.	
15705	DYNEGY LPG DOCK NO. 1 LIGHT	29-13-26.000N 089-23-33.000W	Fl G 2.5s	40		On dock.	Private aid.
15710	DYNEGY LPG DOCK NO.2 LIGHT	29-13-30.000N 089-23-30.000W	Fl G 2.5s	40		On dock.	Private aid.
	BARATARIA BAY AND APPROACHES (Chart 11358)						
	Empire Waterway						
15725	- DANGER LIGHT A	29-14-56.717N 089-36-28.544W	Fl W 2.5s	17	4	NW on pile worded DANGER JETTIES.	Ra ref.
15727	CPRA BARATARIA BASIN SCIENTIFIC PLATFORM LIGHT	29-18-15.880N 089-35-49.230W	Q W			Marks scientific platform structure.	Private aid.
15728	*Great Lakes Dredge & Dock Lighted Danger Buoys (20)*	29-21-25.936N 089-35-47.851W	Fl W 2.5s			Marks submerged dredge pipeline.	Private aid.
15728.01	*Great Lakes Dredge & Dock Lighted Danger Buoys (20)*	29-15-25.104N 089-36-22.539W	Fl W 2.5s			Marks submerged dredge pipeline.	Private aid.

Light List corrected through LNM week: 01/18

(1) No.	(2) Name and Location	(3) Position	(4) Characteristic	(5) Height	(6) Range	(7) Structure	(8) Remarks
		LOUISIANA - Eighth District					
	BARATARIA BAY AND APPROACHES (Chart 11358)						
	Empire Waterway						
15728.02	GREAT LAKES DREDGE & DOCK LIGHTED DANGER MARKS (8)	29-21-49.116N 089-35-55.078W	Fl W 2.5s			Marks submerged spoil area.	Private aid.
15728.03	GREAT LAKES DREDGE & DOCK LIGHTED DANGER MARKS (8)	29-21-13.953N 089-35-41.864W	Fl W 2.5s			Marks submerged spoil area.	Private aid.
15728.04	GREAT LAKES DREDGE & DOCK LIGHTED DANGER MARKS (8)	29-20-17.486N 089-35-34.745W	Fl W 2.5s			Marks submerged spoil area.	Private aid.
15728.05	GREAT LAKES DREDGE & DOCK LIGHTED DANGER MARKS (8)	29-19-35.875N 089-36-06.105W	Fl W 2.5s			Marks submerged spoil area.	Private aid.
15728.06	GREAT LAKES DREDGE & DOCK LIGHTED DANGER MARKS (8)	29-18-02.445N 089-35-52.720W	Fl W 2.5s			Marks submerged spoil area.	Private aid.
15728.07	GREAT LAKES DREDGE & DOCK LIGHTED DANGER MARKS (8)	29-16-48.601N 089-36-02.706W	Fl W 2.5s			Marks submerged spoil area.	Private aid.
15728.08	Great Lakes Dredge & Dock Lighted Danger Buoy	29-21-56.147N 089-35-56.088W	Fl W 2.5s			Marks submerged dredge pipeline.	Private aid.
15728.09	Great Lakes Dredge & Dock Lighted Danger Buoy	29-20-43.172N 089-35-35.186W	Fl W 2.5s			Marks submerged dredge pipeline.	Private aid.
15728.11	Great Lakes Dredge & Dock Lighted Danger Buoys (4)	29-18-55.737N 089-36-12.210W	Fl W 2.5s			Marks submerged dredge pipeline.	Private aid.
15728.12	Great Lakes Dredge & Dock Lighted Danger Buoys (3)	29-17-41.945N 089-35-54.910W	Fl W 2.5s			Marks submerged dredge pipeline.	Private aid.
15728.13	Great Lakes Dredge & Dock Lighted Danger Buoys (2)	29-22-45.117N 089-35-37.543W	Fl W 2.5s			Marks submerged dredge pipeline.	Private aid.
15728.14	Great Lakes Dredge & Dock Lighted Danger Buoy	29-21-17.804N 089-35-43.442W	Fl W 2.5s			Marks submerged dredge pipeline.	Private aid.
15728.15	Great Lakes Dredge & Dock Lighted Danger Buoys (3)	29-19-29.501N 089-36-12.802W	Fl W 2.5s			Marks submerged dredge pipeline.	Private aid.
15728.16	Great Lakes Dredge & Dock Lighted Danger Buoy	29-14-52.582N 089-35-58.347W	Fl W 2.5s			Marks submerged dredge pipeline.	Private aid.
15728.17	Great Lakes Dredge & Dock Lighted Danger Buoy	29-14-43.486N 089-35-40.368W	Fl W 2.5s			Marks submerged dredge pipeline.	Private aid.
15728.18	Great Lakes Dredge & Dock Lighted Danger Buoy	29-14-37.949N 089-35-40.368W	Fl W 2.5s			Marks submerged dredge pipeline.	Private aid.
15728.19	Great Lakes Dredge & Dock Lighted Danger Buoy	29-14-32.410N 089-34-55.798W	Fl W 2.5s			Marks submerged dredge pipeline.	Private aid.
15728.21	Great Lakes Dredge & Dock Lighted Danger Buoy	29-14-26.863N 089-34-33.483W	Fl W 2.5s			Marks submerged dredge pipeline.	Private aid.
15728.22	Great Lakes Dredge & Dock Lighted Danger Buoy	29-14-34.574N 089-34-23.059W	Fl W 2.5s			Marks submerged dredge pipeline.	Private aid.
15728.23	Great Lakes Dredge & Dock Lighted Danger Buoy	29-14-48.263N 089-33-53.199W	Fl W 2.5s			Marks submerged dredge pipeline.	Private aid.
15728.24	Great Lakes Dredge & Dock Lighted Danger Buoy	29-14-50.105N 089-33-51.707W	Fl W 2.5s			Marks submerged dredge pipeline.	Private aid.
15728.25	Great Lakes Dredge & Dock Lighted Danger Buoy	29-16-17.866N 089-36-28.040W	Fl W 2.5s			Marks submerged spoil.	Private aid.
15728.26	Great Lakes Dredge & Dock Lighted Danger Buoy	29-16-17.670N 089-36-16.176W	Fl W 2.5s			Marks submerged spoil.	Private aid.
15728.27	Great Lakes Dredge & Dock Lighted Danger Buoy	29-16-15.231N 089-36-16.669W	Fl W 2.5s			Marks submerged spoil.	Private aid.
15728.28	Great Lakes Dredge & Dock Lighted Danger Buoy	29-16-13.414N 089-36-17.028W	Fl W 2.5s			Marks submerged spoil.	Private aid.
15728.29	Great Lakes Dredge & Dock Lighted Danger Buoy	29-16-10.965N 089-36-17.533W	Fl W 2.5s			Marks submerged spoil.	Private aid.
15728.31	Great Lakes Dredge & Dock Lighted Danger Buoy	29-16-11.054N 089-36-23.550W	Fl W 2.5s			Marks submerged spoil.	Private aid.
15728.32	Great Lakes Dredge & Dock Lighted Danger Buoy	29-18-22.248N 089-35-58.046W	Fl W 2.5s			Marks submerged spoil.	Private aid.
15728.33	Great Lakes Dredge & Dock Lighted Danger Buoy	29-18-22.640N 089-35-57.701W	Fl W 2.5s			Marks submerged spoil.	Private aid.
15728.34	Great Lakes Dredge & Dock Lighted Danger Buoy	29-18-20.520N 089-35-55.213W	Fl W 2.5s			Marks submerged spoil.	Private aid.

(1) No.	(2) Name and Location	(3) Position	(4) Characteristic	(5) Height	(6) Range	(7) Structure	(8) Remarks
			LOUISIANA - Eighth District				
	BARATARIA BAY AND APPROACHES (Chart 11358)						
	Empire Waterway						
15728.35	Great Lakes Dredge & Dock Lighted Danger Buoy	29-18-20.181N 089-35-55.625W	Fl W 2.5s			Marks submerged spoil.	Private aid.
15728.36	Great Lakes Dredge & Dock Lighted Danger Buoy	29-18-18.805N 089-35-53.840W	Fl W 2.5s			Marks submerged spoil.	Private aid.
15728.37	Great Lakes Dredge & Dock Lighted Danger Buoy	29-18-15.948N 089-35-52.607W	Fl W 2.5s			Marks submerged spoil.	Private aid.
15728.38	Great Lakes Dredge & Dock Lighted Danger Buoy	29-18-15.806N 089-35-53.148W	Fl W 2.5s			Marks submerged spoil.	Private aid.
15728.39	Great Lakes Dredge & Dock Lighted Danger Buoy	29-18-18.507N 089-35-54.314W	Fl W 2.5s			Marks submerged spoil.	Private aid.
15728.41	Great Lakes Dredge & Dock Lighted Danger Buoy	29-16-14.220N 089-36-15.875W	Fl W 2.5s			Marks submerged pipeline.	Private aid.
15728.42	Great Lakes Dredge & Dock Lighted Danger Buoy	29-16-13.942N 089-36-13.050W	Fl W 2.5s			Marks submerged pipeline.	Private aid.
15728.43	Great Lakes Dredge & Dock Lighted Danger Buoy	29-15-55.492N 089-36-20.177W	Fl W 2.5s			Marks submerged pipeline.	Private aid.
15728.44	Great Lakes Dredge & Dock Lighted Danger Buoy	29-15-54.931N 089-36-16.663W	Fl W 2.5s			Marks submerged pipeline.	Private aid.
15728.45	Great Lakes Dredge & Dock Lighted Danger Buoy	29-19-33.400N 089-36-09.380W	Fl W 2.5s			Marks submerged pipeline.	Private aid.
15728.46	Great Lakes Dredge & Dock Lighted Danger Buoy	29-19-33.980N 089-36-09.350W	Fl W 2.5s			Marks submerged pipeline.	Private aid.
	Adams Bay						
15730	MEYERS CANAL LIGHT 1	29-22-22.000N 089-39-57.000W	Fl G 2.5s	15		SG on dolphin.	Private aid.
15735	- LIGHT 3	29-22-46.159N 089-38-28.811W	Fl G 4s	17	4	SG on dolphin.	
15738	EXXON-MOBIL BASTIAN BAY PIPELINE LIGHT A	29-20-06.740N 089-38-26.410W	Fl Y 2.5s			Marks submerged pipeline.	Private aid.
15740	- Lighted Buoy 13	29-22-17.619N 089-36-05.985W	Fl G 4s		4	Green.	
15742	EXXON-MOBIL EAST PILING LIGHTS (20-25)	29-24-32.600N 089-49-07.320W	Fl W 2.5s			Marks pilings.	Private aid.
15742.01	EXXON-MOBIL EAST PILING LIGHTS (26-30)	29-22-34.720N 089-44-29.090W	Fl W 2.5s			Marks pilings.	Private aid.
15742.02	EXXON-MOBIL EAST PILING LIGHTS (31-35)	29-21-15.700N 089-41-48.680W	Fl W 2.5s			Marks pilings.	Private aid.
15742.03	EXXON-MOBIL EAST PILING LIGHTS (36-41)	29-21-44.450N 089-34-34.320W	Fl W 2.5s			Marks pilings.	Private aid.
15743	SHELLEY FARM SF1 SPECIAL LIGHTS (6)	29-18-56.343N 089-44-09.494W	Fl Y 2.5s			Marks perimeter of aquaculture farm.	Private aid.
15743.01	SHELLEY FARM SF2 SPECIAL LIGHTS (6)	29-18-53.460N 089-43-33.952W	Fl Y 2.5s			Marks perimeter of aquaculture farm.	Private aid.
15743.02	SHELLEY FARM SF3 SPECIAL LIGHTS (6)	29-19-06.416N 089-43-12.984W	Fl Y 2.5s			Marks perimeter of aquaculture farm.	Private aid.
15743.03	SHELLEY FARM SF4 SPECIAL LIGHTS (6)	29-19-20.406N 089-42-18.384W	Fl Y 2.5s			Marks perimeter of aquaculture farm.	Private aid.
	Bay Batiste						
	Pend Oreille-Bay Batiste						
15745	- South Channel Day beacon 4	29-26-25.657N 089-51-35.905W				TR on pile.	Private aid.
15750	- South Channel Day beacon 6	29-26-34.949N 089-51-49.138W				TR on pile.	Private aid.
15755	- South Channel Day beacon 8	29-26-44.241N 089-52-02.372W				TR on pile.	Private aid.
15757	- Main Channel Day beacon 4	29-24-44.982N 089-53-18.390W				TR on pile.	Private aid.
15760	- Main Channel Day beacon 6	29-25-09.375N 089-52-41.502W				TR on pile.	Private aid.
15765	- Main Channel Day beacon 8	29-25-38.921N 089-52-08.768W				TR on pile.	Private aid.
15770	- Main Channel Day beacon 10	29-26-06.582N 089-51-36.707W				TR on pile.	Private aid.
15775	- Main Channel Day beacon 12	29-26-25.765N 089-51-07.084W				TR on pile.	Private aid.

(1) No.	(2) Name and Location	(3) Position	(4) Characteristic	(5) Height	(6) Range	(7) Structure	(8) Remarks
		LOUISIANA - Eighth District					
	BARATARIA BAY AND APPROACHES (Chart 11358)						
	Bay Batiste						
	Pend Oreille-Bay Batiste						
15780	- North Channel Day beacon 2	29-26-51.900N 089-51-01.500W				TR on pile.	Private aid.
15785	- North Channel Day beacon 4	29-26-54.353N 089-51-16.282W				TR on pile.	Private aid.
	LL & E S.L. 12036-1 Channel						
15790	- Day beacon 2	29-26-44.397N 089-51-00.154W				TR on pile.	Private aid.
15795	- Day beacon 4	29-26-57.245N 089-59-51.645W				TR on pile.	Private aid.
15800	- Day beacon 6	29-27-10.092N 089-50-43.135W				TR on pile.	Private aid.
	BARATARIA AND BAYOU LAFOURCHE WATERWAY (Chart 11365)						
	Barataria Pass						
15802	EXXON MOBIL PIPELINE LIGHT B	29-59-25.000N 089-53-42.000W	Fl Y 2.5s	15		Marks pipeline.	Private aid.
15805	- Buoy 1	29-14-28.152N 089-54-46.518W				Green can.	
15810	- Buoy 2	29-14-34.817N 089-54-42.254W				Red nun.	
15815	- Buoy 3	29-14-49.818N 089-55-12.995W				Green can.	
15820	- Buoy 4	29-14-55.982N 089-55-05.851W				Red nun.	
15825	- *Lighted Buoy 5*	29-15-07.752N 089-55-35.598W	Fl G 2.5s		3	Green can.	
15830	- *Lighted Buoy 6*	29-15-16.938N 089-55-30.312W	Fl R 6s		4	Red.	
15835	- Buoy 7	29-15-22.561N 089-55-52.399W				Green can.	
15840	- Buoy 8	29-15-31.342N 089-55-47.439W				Red nun.	
15845	- Buoy 9	29-15-47.261N 089-56-20.683W				Green can.	
15850	- Buoy 10	29-15-53.383N 089-56-13.797W				Red nun.	
15855	- Buoy 11	29-16-06.815N 089-56-43.256W				Green can.	
15857	GRAND TERRE LAB CANAL ENTRANCE LIGHT 1	29-16-48.000N 089-56-42.000W	Q G	12		On pile cluster.	Private aid.
15857.01	GRAND TERRE LAB CANAL ENTRANCE LIGHT 2	29-16-46.000N 089-56-46.000W	Q R			On pile cluster.	Private aid.
15860	U.S. GEOLOGICAL SURVEY SCIENTIFIC MONITORING PLATFORM LIGHT (JP)	29-16-22.200N 089-56-48.500W	Fl Y 2.5s	37		On pipe.	Private aid.
15865	Fort Livingston Danger Day beacon A	29-16-20.280N 089-56-36.550W				NW on pile worded DANGER ROCKS.	Private aid.
15870	FORT LIVINGSTON DANGER LIGHT B	29-16-19.300N 089-56-38.100W	Fl W 2.5s			NW on pile worded DANGER ROCKS.	Private aid.
15875	FORT LIVINGSTON DANGER LIGHT C	29-16-18.680N 089-56-42.300W	Fl W 2.5s			NW on pile worded DANGER ROCKS.	Private aid.
15880	Fort Livingston Danger Day beacon D	29-16-21.550N 089-56-46.570W				NW on piles worded DANGER ROCKS.	Private aid.
15885	Fort Livingston Danger Day beacon E	29-16-22.660N 089-56-46.870W				NW on pile worded DANGER ROCKS.	Private aid.
15890	- SURVEY LIGHT A	29-16-16.270N 089-56-40.970W				On four pile cluster.	Private aid.
15895	GRAND ISLE STATE PARK FISH PIER LIGHTS (2)	29-15-40.000N 089-57-00.000W	Fl W 3s	25		End of fishing piers on pilings.	Private aid.
15900	GRAND ISLE FISHING JETTY LIGHT	29-15-44.700N 089-56-56.110W	Q R	17		On pile structure.	Private aid.

LOUISIANA - Eighth District

BARATARIA AND BAYOU LAFOURCHE WATERWAY (Chart 11365)

Barataria Pass

(1) No.	(2) Name and Location	(3) Position	(4) Characteristic	(5) Height	(6) Range	(7) Structure	(8) Remarks
15905	Grand Isle Breakwater East Danger Day beacon	29-15-28.700N 089-56-53.900W				NW on pile. WORDED: DANGER BREAKWATER.	Private aid.
15910	Grand Isle Breakwater West Danger Day beacon	29-15-22.300N 089-57-03.700W				NW on pile. WORDED: DANGER BREAKWATER.	Private aid.

Bayou Rigaud

(1) No.	(2) Name and Location	(3) Position	(4) Characteristic	(5) Height	(6) Range	(7) Structure	(8) Remarks
15915	- Lighted Buoy 1	29-16-24.689N 089-57-17.318W	Fl G 2.5s		4	Green.	
15920	- Buoy 2	29-16-30.178N 089-57-21.728W				Red nun.	Ra ref.
15925	- Buoy 3 60 feet outside channel limit.	29-16-14.181N 089-57-25.291W				Green can.	Ra ref.
15930	- Buoy 3A	29-16-06.899N 089-57-32.931W				Green can.	Ra ref.
15935	- Buoy 4	29-16-11.977N 089-57-37.238W				Red nun.	Ra ref.
15940	- ENTRANCE LEADING LIGHT	29-15-59.900N 089-57-48.434W	Q W	17	5	NB on dolphin.	Ra ref.

Grand Isle Turning Basin

(1) No.	(2) Name and Location	(3) Position	(4) Characteristic	(5) Height	(6) Range	(7) Structure	(8) Remarks
15945.01	- Day beacon 1	29-16-02.223N 089-57-33.782W					Ra ref.
15950.01	- Day beacon 2	29-16-01.831N 089-57-35.169W					Ra ref.
15955.01	- Day beacon 3	29-15-59.997N 089-57-33.458W					Ra ref.
15960	- Buoy 3A	29-15-54.240N 089-57-31.302W				Green can.	
15965.01	- Day beacon 4	29-15-57.843N 089-57-34.898W					Ra ref.

Bayou Rigaud

(1) No.	(2) Name and Location	(3) Position	(4) Characteristic	(5) Height	(6) Range	(7) Structure	(8) Remarks
15970	- Day beacon 5	29-15-57.652N 089-57-39.539W				SG on pile.	Ra ref.
15975	FIFI ISLAND DANGER BREAKWATER LIGHT	29-15-51.890N 089-57-49.452W	Fl W 2.5s			Marks breakwater structure.	Private aid.
15975.01	FIFI ISLAND DANGER BREAKWATER LIGHT	29-15-51.300N 089-57-47.840W	Fl W 2.5s			Marks breakwater structure.	Private aid.
15975.02	FIFI ISLAND DANGER BREAKWATER LIGHT	29-15-54.630N 089-57-48.210W	Fl W 2.5s			Marks breakwater structure.	Private aid.
15975.03	FIFI ISLAND DANGER BREAKWATER LIGHT	29-15-54.030N 089-57-46.540W	Fl W 2.5s			Marks breakwater structure.	Private aid.
15975.04	FIFI ISLAND DANGER BREAKWATER LIGHT	29-15-57.350N 089-57-46.820W	Fl W 2.5s			Marks breakwater structure.	Private aid.
15975.05	FIFI ISLAND DANGER BREAKWATER LIGHT	29-15-56.710N 089-57-45.180W	Fl W 2.5s			Marks breakwater structure.	Private aid.
15975.06	FIFI ISLAND DANGER BREAKWATER LIGHT	29-16-00.060N 089-57-45.390W	Fl W 2.5s			Marks breakwater structure.	Private aid.
15975.07	FIFI ISLAND DANGER BREAKWATER LIGHT	29-15-59.400N 089-57-43.740W	Fl W 2.5s			Marks breakwater structure.	Private aid.
15975.08	FIFI ISLAND DANGER BREAKWATER LIGHT	29-16-02.140N 089-57-44.670W	Fl W 2.5s			Marks breakwater structure.	Private aid.
15975.09	FIFI ISLAND DANGER BREAKWATER LIGHT	29-16-01.330N 089-57-42.570W	Fl W 2.5s			Marks breakwater structure.	Private aid.
15980	- LIGHT 6	29-15-52.100N 089-57-45.682W	Fl R 2.5s	17	3	TR on pile.	Ra ref.
15990	- LIGHT 7	29-15-54.132N 089-57-41.591W	Fl G 4s	17	4	SG on pile.	Ra ref.
15995	- Day beacon 8	29-15-25.597N 089-58-06.313W				TR on pile.	Ra ref.

Light List corrected through LNM week: 01/18

(1) No.	(2) Name and Location	(3) Position	(4) Characteristic	(5) Height	(6) Range	(7) Structure	(8) Remarks
			LOUISIANA - Eighth District				
	BARATARIA AND BAYOU LAFOURCHE WATERWAY (Chart 11365)						
	Bayou Rigaud						
16000	- Day beacon 10	29-15-17.158N 089-58-30.688W				TR on pile.	Ra ref.
16002	EXXON-MOBIL WEST PILING LIGHTS (1-6)	29-19-18.820N 089-58-36.510W	Fl W 2.5s			Marks pilings.	Private aid.
16005	- Day beacon 12	29-15-05.705N 089-58-51.130W				TR on pile.	Ra ref.
16010	- Day beacon 14	29-14-48.211N 089-59-17.094W				TR on pile.	Ra ref.
16015	- Day beacon 16	29-14-29.836N 089-59-54.670W				TR on pile.	Ra ref.
16020	- Day beacon 18	29-14-25.060N 090-00-13.489W				TR on pile.	Ra ref.
16022	Nature Conservancy Grand Isle Southwest Danger Day beacons (5)	29-13-44.571N 090-01-02.247W				NW on pile.	Private aid.
16022.01	Nature Conservancy Grand Isle Southwest Danger Day beacons (5)	29-13-54.716N 090-00-50.651W				NW on pile.	Private aid.
16022.02	Nature Conservancy Grand Isle Southwest Danger Day beacons (3)	29-13-59.844N 090-00-33.160W				NW on pile.	Private aid.
16022.03	Nature Conservancy Fifi Island Northeast Danger Day beacons (5)	29-15-38.431N 089-58-17.647W				NW on pile.	Private aid.
16022.04	Nature Conservancy Fifi Island Northeast Danger Day beacons (2)	29-15-46.512N 089-58-18.514W				NW on pile.	Private aid.
	Barataria Bay						
16025	- PIPELINE LIGHT H	29-15-55.219N 089-58-18.935W	Fl Y 2.5s	16		NW on pile worded DO NOT ANCHOR OR DREDGE.	Private aid.
	BARATARIA BAY AND APPROACHES (Chart 11358)						
	Barataria Bay						
	Lake Grand Ecaille						
16030	- LIGHT A	29-23-51.000N 089-47-45.000W	Fl Y 4s	12		NW on pile.	Private aid.
16035	- LIGHT B	29-23-53.000N 089-47-46.000W	Fl Y 4s	12		NW on pile.	Private aid.
16038	FREEPORT MCMORAN LAKE GRANDE ECAILLE DANGER LIGHTS (74)	29-22-39.900N 089-46-47.200W	Fl W 2.5s			Marks perimeter of navigation obstructions.	Private aid.
16040	- LIGHT 1 SG on dolphin.	29-23-33.000N 089-47-36.000W	Q W	12			Private aid.
16045	- PIPELINE LIGHT	29-23-31.000N 089-47-53.000W	Q R	10		On pile.	Private aid.
16048	GRAND ISLE PORT COMMISSION SPECIAL LIGHT A	29-13-10.530N 090-02-39.970W	Fl Y 2.5s			Marks perimeter of oyster farm.	Private aid.
16048.01	GRAND ISLE PORT COMMISSION SPECIAL LIGHT B	29-13-08.590N 090-02-36.090W	Fl Y 2.5s			Marks perimeter of oyster farm.	Private aid.
16048.02	GRAND ISLE PORT COMMISSION SPECIAL LIGHT C	29-13-14.690N 090-02-32.130W	Fl Y 2.5s			Marks perimeter of oyster farm.	Private aid.
16048.03	GRAND ISLE PORT COMMISSION SPECIAL LIGHT D	29-13-12.960N 090-02-32.130W	Fl Y 2.5s			Marks perimeter of oyster farm.	Private aid.
16048.04	GRAND ISLE PORT COMMISSION SPECIAL LIGHT E	29-13-22.450N 090-02-22.460W	Fl Y 2.5s			Marks perimeter of oyster farm.	Private aid.
16048.05	GRAND ISLE PORT COMMISSION SPECIAL LIGHT F	29-13-26.140N 090-02-29.820W	Fl Y 2.5s			Marks perimeter of oyster farm.	Private aid.

(1) No.	(2) Name and Location	(3) Position	(4) Characteristic	(5) Height	(6) Range	(7) Structure	(8) Remarks
		LOUISIANA - Eighth District					
	BARATARIA BAY AND APPROACHES (Chart 11358)						
	Barataria Bay						
16050	Shell Reef Day beacon	29-20-39.849N 089-56-26.901W				NW on piles worded DANGER.	Ra ref.
16051	*Jules Melancon Aquaculture Farm Special Lighted Buoy A*	29-18-07.896N 089-56-14.851W	Fl Y 2.5s			Marks perimeter of aquaculture farm.	Private aid.
16051.01	*Jules Melancon Aquaculture Farm Special Lighted Buoy B*	29-18-07.750N 089-56-06.599W	Fl Y 2.5s			Marks perimeter of aquaculture farm.	Private aid.
16051.02	*Jules Melancon Aquaculture Farm Special Lighted Buoy C*	29-18-00.240N 089-56-06.613W	Fl Y 2.5s			Marks perimeter of aquaculture farm.	Private aid.
16051.03	*Jules Melancon Aquaculture Farm Special Lighted Buoy D*	29-18-00.359N 089-56-17.782W	Fl Y 2.5s			Marks perimeter of aquaculture farm.	Private aid.
	NEW ORLEANS TO CALCASIEU RIVER (Chart 11352)						
	Lake Five						
16055	- Channel Day beacon 2	29-31-24.000N 089-57-01.000W				TR on pile.	Private aid.
16060	- Channel Day beacon 4	29-31-25.000N 089-57-18.000W				TR on pile.	Private aid.
16065	- Channel Day beacon 6	29-31-27.000N 089-57-36.000W				TR on pile.	Private aid.
16070	- Channel Day beacon 8	29-31-29.000N 089-57-53.000W				TR on pile.	Private aid.
16075	- Channel Day beacon 10	29-31-22.000N 089-58-09.000W				TR on pile.	Private aid.
16080	- Channel Day beacon 12	29-31-15.000N 089-58-24.000W				TR on pile.	Private aid.
16085	- Channel Day beacon 14	29-31-16.000N 089-58-36.000W				TR on pile.	Private aid.
16090	- Channel Day beacon 18	29-31-13.000N 089-58-51.000W				TR on pile.	Private aid.
	BARATARIA AND BAYOU LAFOURCHE WATERWAYS (Chart 11365)						
	Barataria Waterway						
	Lights and daybeacons located 50 feet outside channel limit.						
16095	CAL-KY PIPELINE LIGHT	29-16-36.000N 089-57-24.000W	Q W	24		NW on pile worded DO NOT ANCHOR OR DREDGE.	Private aid.
16100	- ENTRANCE LIGHT 1	29-16-41.931N 089-57-30.914W	Fl G 4s	17	4	SG on dolphin.	Ra ref.
16105	- ENTRANCE LIGHT 2	29-16-45.547N 089-57-27.106W	Q R	17	4	TR on pile.	Ra ref.
16110	BARATARIA BAY PIPELINE LIGHT E	29-16-48.203N 089-57-28.441W	Fl Y 2.5s	16		NW on pile worded DO NOT ANCHOR OR DREDGE.	Private aid.
16115	BARATARIA BAY PIPELINE LIGHT F	29-16-41.919N 089-57-32.705W	Fl Y 2.5s	16		NW on pile worded DO NOT ANCHOR OR DREDGE.	Private aid.
16120	- Buoy 2A	29-16-49.965N 089-57-36.222W				Red nun.	
16125	- Day beacon 3	29-16-59.411N 089-57-55.160W				SG on pile.	Ra ref.
16130	- Day beacon 4	29-17-02.987N 089-57-52.442W				TR on pile.	Ra ref.
16135	Entrance East Side Dredging Range Front Day beacon	29-17-06.000N 089-57-54.000W				Black diamond day mark on pile.	Fl W light will be displayed during dredging operations. Range marks edge of channel for dredging purposes. Maintained by U.S. Army Corps of Engineers. Aid maintained by U.S. Army Corps of Engineers.

LOUISIANA - Eighth District

BARATARIA AND BAYOU LAFOURCHE WATERWAYS (Chart 11365)

Barataria Waterway
Lights and daybeacons located 50 feet outside channel limit.

(1) No.	(2) Name and Location	(3) Position	(4) Characteristic	(5) Height	(6) Range	(7) Structure	(8) Remarks
16140	Entrance East Side Dredging Range Rear Day beacon	29-17-30.000N 089-58-18.000W				Black diamond day mark on pile.	Fl W light will be displayed during dredging operations. Range marks edge of channel for dredging purposes. Maintained by U.S. Army Corps of Engineers. Aid maintained by U.S. Army Corps of Engineers.
16145	Entrance Centerline Dredging Range Front Day beacon	29-17-06.000N 089-57-54.000W				Black diamond day mark on pile.	Fl W light will be displayed during dredging operations. Range marks edge of channel for dredging purposes. Maintained by U.S. Army Corps of Engineers. Aid maintained by U.S. Army Corps of Engineers.
16150	Entrance Centerline Dredging Range Rear Day beacon	29-17-30.000N 089-58-24.000W				Black diamond day mark on pile.	Fl W light will be displayed during dredging operations. Range marks edge of channel for dredging purposes. Maintained by U.S. Army Corps of Engineers. Aid maintained by U.S. Army Corps of Engineers.
16155	Entrance West Side Dredging Range Front Day beacon	29-17-06.000N 089-57-54.000W				Black diamond day mark on pile.	Fl W light will be displayed during dredging operations. Range marks edge of channel for dredging purposes. Maintained by U.S. Army Corps of Engineers. Aid maintained by U.S. Army Corps of Engineers.
16160	Entrance West Side Dredging Range Rear Day beacon	29-17-30.000N 089-58-24.000W				Black diamond day mark on pile.	Fl W light will be displayed during dredging operations. Range marks edge of channel for dredging purposes. Maintained by U.S. Army Corps of Engineers. Aid maintained by U.S. Army Corps of Engineers.
16165	- LIGHT 5	29-17-25.054N 089-58-26.589W	Fl G 2.5s	17	4	SG on pile.	Ra ref.
16170	- LIGHT 6	29-17-26.942N 089-58-21.928W	Fl R 2.5s	17	3	TR on pile.	Ra ref.
16175	- Day beacon 7	29-17-55.454N 089-58-42.916W				SG on pile.	Ra ref.
16180	- Day beacon 8	29-17-57.537N 089-58-38.640W				TR on pile.	Ra ref.
16182	EXXON-MOBIL BAY DES ILETTES PIPELINE LIGHT	29-17-58.800N 089-58-45.450W	Fl Y 2.5s			Marks submerged buried pipeline.	Private aid.
16185	- LIGHT 8A	29-18-22.537N 089-58-51.655W	Fl R 2.5s	17	3	TR on pile.	Ra ref.
16188	*Jules Melancon Aquaculture Special Lighted Buoy A*	29-18-21.616N 090-02-02.086W	Fl Y 2.5s			Marks perimeter of oyster farm.	Private aid.
16188.01	*Jules Melancon Aquaculture Special Lighted Buoy B*	29-18-31.627N 090-02-05.077W	Fl Y 2.5s			Marks perimeter of oyster farm.	Private aid.
16188.02	*Jules Melancon Aquaculture Special Lighted Buoy C*	29-18-26.624N 090-02-09.770W	Fl Y 2.5s			Marks perimeter of oyster farm.	Private aid.
16190	- Day beacon 9	29-18-21.716N 089-58-54.323W				SG on pile.	Ra ref.

Light List corrected through LNM week: 01/18

(1) No.	(2) Name and Location	(3) Position	(4) Characteristic	(5) Height	(6) Range	(7) Structure	(8) Remarks
		LOUISIANA - Eighth District					
	BARATARIA AND BAYOU LAFOURCHE WATERWAYS (Chart 11365)						
	Barataria Waterway						
	Lights and daybeacons located 50 feet outside channel limit.						
16195	- Day beacon 10	29-18-43.030N 089-59-00.431W				TR on pile.	Ra ref.
16200	- Day beacon 11	29-18-40.276N 089-59-02.949W				SG on pile.	Ra ref.
16205.01	- *Lighted Buoy 13*	29-19-07.560N 089-59-08.276W	Fl G 4s		4	Green.	
16210	- LIGHT 14	29-19-07.681N 089-59-05.689W	Fl R 4s	17	3	TR on pile.	Ra ref.
16215	- LIGHT 15	29-19-58.271N 089-59-08.127W	Fl G 6s	17	4	SG on pile.	Ra ref.
16220	- Day beacon 16	29-19-58.586N 089-59-04.583W				TR on pile.	Ra ref.
16222	CPRA BARATARIA BASIN SCIENTIFIC PLATFORM LIGHT	29-20-01.050N 089-59-18.600W	Q W			Marks scientific platform structure.	Private aid.
16225	- LIGHT 18	29-20-55.932N 089-59-03.085W	Fl R 6s	17	4	TR on pile.	Ra ref.
16230.01	- *Lighted Buoy 19*	29-21-50.045N 089-59-04.701W	Fl G 2.5s		4	Green.	
16235	- LIGHT 20	29-21-50.726N 089-59-00.149W	Fl R 2.5s	17	3	TR on pile.	Ra ref.
16240	- Day beacon 21	29-22-08.098N 089-59-06.432W				SG on pile.	Ra ref.
16245	- Day beacon 22	29-22-10.537N 089-59-01.750W				TR on pile.	Ra ref.
16250	- Day beacon 23	29-22-33.907N 089-59-10.133W				SG on pile.	Ra ref.
16255	- LIGHT 24	29-22-30.371N 089-59-03.915W	Fl R 4s	17	3	TR on pile.	Ra ref.
16260	- LIGHT 25	29-22-58.652N 089-59-12.878W	Fl G 4s	17	4	SG on pile.	Ra ref.
16265	- Day beacon 26	29-22-58.245N 089-59-07.925W				TR on pile.	Ra ref.
16270	- Day beacon 27	29-23-19.976N 089-59-15.454W				SG on pile.	Ra ref.
16275	- LIGHT 28	29-23-20.279N 089-59-11.357W	Fl R 2.5s	17	3	TR on pile.	Ra ref.
	Mobil State Lease 356-2 Channel						
16280	- Day beacon 1	29-23-43.625N 089-59-19.794W				SG on pile.	Private aid.
16285	- Day beacon 3	29-23-42.003N 089-59-33.012W				SG on pile.	Private aid.
16290	- Day beacon 5	29-23-43.856N 089-59-37.876W				SG on pile.	Private aid.
16295	- Day beacon 7	29-23-59.895N 089-59-42.818W				SG on pile.	Private aid.
16300	- Day beacon 9	29-24-10.974N 089-59-44.390W				SG on pile.	Private aid.
16305	- Day beacon 11	29-24-23.931N 089-59-46.209W				SG on pile.	Private aid.
16310	- Day beacon 13	29-24-28.886N 089-59-50.060W				SG on pile.	Private aid.
16315	- Day beacon 15	29-24-26.965N 090-00-02.755W				SG on pile.	Private aid.
	Barataria Waterway						
	Lights and daybeacons located 50 feet outside channel limit.						
16320	- Day beacon 29	29-23-43.748N 089-59-19.038W				SG on pile.	Ra ref.
16325	- Day beacon 30	29-23-44.568N 089-59-15.467W				TR on pile.	Ra ref.

LOUISIANA - Eighth District

BARATARIA AND BAYOU LAFOURCHE WATERWAYS (Chart 11365)

Barataria Waterway
Lights and daybeacons located 50 feet outside channel limit.

(1) No.	(2) Name and Location	(3) Position	(4) Characteristic	(5) Height	(6) Range	(7) Structure	(8) Remarks
16330	- LIGHT 31	29-24-21.072N 089-59-24.735W	Fl G 6s	17	4	SG on pile.	Ra ref.
16335	- LIGHT 32	29-24-21.262N 089-59-20.727W	Fl R 6s	17	4	TR on pile.	Ra ref.
16340	- Day beacon 33	29-24-58.795N 089-59-30.259W				SG on pile.	Ra ref.
16345	- Day beacon 34	29-25-15.239N 089-59-29.766W				TR on pile.	Ra ref.
16347	EXXON-MOBIL WEST PILING LIGHTS (7-12)	29-26-52.710N 090-01-01.390W	Fl W 2.5s			Marks pilings.	Private aid.
16350	- Day beacon 35	29-25-37.733N 089-59-36.860W				SG on pile.	Ra ref.
16355	- LIGHT 35A Marks submerged obstruction.	29-25-59.729N 089-59-40.512W	Q G	17	4	SG on pile.	Ra ref.
16360	- LIGHT 36	29-26-16.050N 089-59-39.134W	Fl R 4s	17	3	TR on pile.	Ra ref.
16365	- Day beacon 37	29-26-29.787N 089-59-45.506W				SG on pile.	Ra ref.
16370	- Day beacon 38	29-27-12.089N 089-59-49.060W				TR on pile.	Ra ref.
16375	- LIGHT 39	29-28-00.486N 090-00-01.591W	Q G	17	3	SG on pile.	Ra ref.
16380	- LIGHT 40	29-28-02.604N 089-59-59.128W	Q R	17	3	TR on pile.	Ra ref.
16385	- Buoy 41	29-28-17.880N 090-00-13.741W				Green can.	
16390	- Buoy 42	29-28-17.285N 090-00-09.739W				Red nun.	
16395	- LIGHT 43	29-28-31.194N 090-00-26.387W	Fl G 2.5s	17	3	SG on pile.	Ra ref.
16400	- LIGHT 44	29-28-33.816N 090-00-22.068W	Fl R 2.5s	17	3	TR on pile.	Ra ref.
16405	- Day beacon 46	29-28-59.921N 090-00-39.893W				TR on pile.	Ra ref.
16407	LLOX MANILLA VILLAGE PILING LIGHTS (2)	29-29-11.000N 089-59-39.000W	Fl W 2.5s			Marks barge mooring pilings.	Private aid.
16410	- Day beacon 47	29-29-17.461N 090-01-01.629W				SG on pile.	Ra ref.
16415	- Buoy 48	29-29-31.784N 090-01-01.261W				Red nun.	
16420	- LIGHT 50	29-29-41.615N 090-01-06.255W	Fl R 4s	17	3	TR on pile.	Ra ref.
16425	- LIGHT 51	29-29-56.088N 090-01-17.103W	Fl G 4s	17	4	SG on pile.	Ra ref.
16430	BAY DE CHENE PIPELINE LIGHT A	29-27-10.000N 090-01-57.000W	Fl Y 2.5s	10		NW on dolphin worded DANGER SUBMERGED PIPELINE.	Private aid.
16435	BAY DE CHENE PIPELINE LIGHT B	29-27-06.000N 090-02-24.000W	Fl Y 2.5s			NB on dolphin worded DANGER SUBMERGED PIPELINE.	Private aid.
16440	- PIPELINE LIGHT 1A	29-33-12.000N 090-02-36.000W				On dolphin.	Private aid.
16445	- PIPELINE LIGHT 2A	29-33-12.000N 090-02-42.000W				On dolphin.	Private aid.
16450	TEXACO PIPELINE MARKER LIGHT B	29-34-54.845N 090-03-42.655W	Fl Y 2.5s	10		NW on dolphin worded DANGER SUBMERGED PIPELINE.	Private aid.

(1) No.	(2) Name and Location	(3) Position	(4) Characteristic	(5) Height	(6) Range	(7) Structure	(8) Remarks
		LOUISIANA - Eighth District					
	BARATARIA AND BAYOU LAFOURCHE WATERWAYS (Chart 11365)						
	Barataria Waterway						
	Lights and daybeacons located 50 feet outside channel limit.						
16455	TEXACO PIPELINE MARKER LIGHT A	29-34-54.804N 090-03-38.630W	Fl Y 2.5s	10		NW on dolphin worded DANGER SUBMERGED PIPELINE.	Private aid.
16460	- PIPELINE LIGHT 1	29-34-59.000N 090-03-40.000W	Fl Y 2.5s	12		On dolphin.	Private aid.
16465	- PIPELINE LIGHT 2	29-35-00.000N 090-03-35.000W	Fl Y 2.5s	12		On dolphin.	Private aid.
	Dupre Cut						
16470	- LIGHT 1	29-34-40.357N 090-03-33.162W	Fl G 4s	17	4	SG on pile.	Ra ref.
16475	- LIGHT 2	29-35-15.684N 090-03-50.302W	Fl R 4s	17	3	TR on pile.	Ra ref.
16480	- LIGHT 3	29-36-03.283N 090-04-21.994W	Fl G 2.5s	17	3	SG on pile.	Ra ref.
16485	- LIGHT 4	29-36-04.476N 090-04-19.292W	Fl R 2.5s	17	3	TR on pile.	Ra ref.
16490	- Day beacon 5	29-36-40.471N 090-04-44.262W				SG on pile.	Ra ref.
16495	- Day beacon 6	29-36-41.474N 090-04-40.640W				TR on pile.	Ra ref.
16500	- LIGHT 7	29-37-23.491N 090-05-09.132W	Fl G 4s	17	4	SG on pile.	Ra ref.
16505	- LIGHT 8	29-37-25.406N 090-05-04.924W	Fl R 4s	17	3	TR on pile.	Ra ref.
	Bayou Dupont Canal Weir						
16510	- LIGHT 2	29-38-34.000N 090-05-44.700W	Q R			TR on pile clusters.	Private aid.
16515	- Day beacon 1	29-38-34.700N 090-05-44.900W				SG on pile clusters.	Private aid.
16520	- Danger Day beacons (2)	29-38-35.000N 090-05-43.450W				NW on pile worded DANGER OBSTRUCTION DO NOT PROCEED.	Private aid.
16525	- Danger Day beacon	29-38-34.500N 090-05-43.000W				NW on pile worded DANGER OBSTRUCTION DO NOT PROCEED.	Private aid.
16530	- Danger Buoys (2)	29-38-35.210N 090-05-43.580W				TR on pile cluster.	Private aid.
16535	- LIGHT 4	29-38-35.110N 090-05-42.610W	Q R			SG on pile cluster.	Private aid.
16540	- LIGHT 3	29-38-35.480N 090-05-42.780W	Q G			SG on pile.	Private aid.
16542	The Pen Southshore Danger Day beacons (8)	29-38-34.400N 090-05-41.800W				NW on pile. Marks shoreline restoration structure.	Private aid.
16542.01	The Pen Southshore Danger Day beacons (8)	29-38-34.200N 090-05-09.500W				NW on pile. Marks shoreline restoration structure.	Private aid.
16542.02	The Pen Southshore Danger Day beacons (6)	29-38-16.500N 090-04-33.800W				NW on pile. Marks shoreline restoration structure.	Private aid.
16542.03	The Pen Southshore Danger Day beacons (2)	29-38-02.000N 090-04-03.200W				NW on pile. Marks shoreline restoration structure.	Private aid.

Light List corrected through LNM week: 01/18

(1) No.	(2) Name and Location	(3) Position	(4) Characteristic	(5) Height	(6) Range	(7) Structure	(8) Remarks
		LOUISIANA - Eighth District					
	BARATARIA AND BAYOU LAFOURCHE WATERWAYS (Chart 11365)						
	Barataria Waterway						
	Dupre Cut						
16545	- LIGHT 10	29-38-44.676N 090-05-52.951W	Fl R 2.5s	17	4	TR on pile.	Ra ref.
16550	BAYOU RIGOLETTES LIGHT 1	29-39-58.138N 090-06-43.394W	Fl G 4s	17	4	SG on pile.	Ra ref.
16555	BAYOU RIGOLETTES LIGHT 2	29-40-01.221N 090-06-44.070W	Fl R 4s	17	3	TR on pile.	Ra ref.
	Goose Bayou Weir						
16560	- LIGHT 2	29-41-30.830N 090-05-31.600W	Q R			TR on pile cluster.	Private aid.
16565	- LIGHT 1	29-41-31.240N 090-05-31.640W	Q G			SG on pile cluster.	Private aid.
16570	- Danger Day beacon (2)	29-41-31.000N 090-05-30.800W				NW on piles worded DANGER OBSTRUCTION PROCEED WITH CAUTION.	Private aid.
16575	- Danger Day beacon (4)	29-41-30.000N 090-05-30.800W				NW on pile worded DANGER OBSTRUCTION DO NOT PROCEED.	Private aid.
16580	- LIGHT 4	29-41-30.770N 090-05-29.940W	Q R			TR on pile cluster.	Private aid.
16585	- LIGHT 3	29-41-31.190N 090-05-29.940W	Q G			SG on pile cluster.	Private aid.
	BARATARIA AND BAYOU LAFOURCHE WATERWAYS (Chart 11365)						
16590	Barataria Bay S.L. 10061 Pipeline Day beacon	29-24-38.000N 089-54-24.000W				NW on dolphin.	Private aid.
	Bayou St. Denis						
16595	- Day beacon 2	29-27-10.171N 089-58-29.171W				TR on pile.	Ra ref.
16600	- LIGHT 3	29-27-21.713N 089-59-13.184W	Fl G 6s	17	5	SG on pile.	Ra ref.
16605	- LIGHT 5	29-28-09.494N 089-59-45.000W	Fl G 4s	17	4	SG on pile.	Ra ref.
	Caminada Bay						
16610	CAMINADA PASS JETTY LIGHT	29-11-56.700N 090-02-27.960W	Q R	10		On dolphin.	Private aid.
16615	- PIPELINE MARKER LIGHT A	29-12-34.000N 090-02-36.000W	Fl Y 2.5s	15		NW on dolphin worded DO NOT ANCHOR OR DREDGE	Private aid.
16616	CPRA BAY ST. HONORE SOUTHWEST DANGER BREAKWATER LIGHT	29-12-30.770N 090-03-40.700W	Fl W 2.5s			Marks shoreline breakwater.	Private aid.
16616.01	CPRA BAY ST. HONORE SOUTHWEST DANGER BREAKWATER LIGHT	29-12-32.240N 090-03-34.710W	Fl W 2.5s			Marks shoreline breakwater.	Private aid.
16616.02	CPRA BAY ST. HONORE NORTHEAST DANGER BREAKWATER LIGHT	29-13-26.110N 090-02-42.910W	Fl W 2.5s			Marks shoreline breakwater.	Private aid.
16616.03	CPRA BAY ST. HONORE NORTHEAST DANGER BREAKWATER LIGHT	29-13-26.590N 090-02-32.040W	Fl W 2.5s			Marks shoreline breakwater.	Private aid.
16617	CPRA BARATARIA BASIN SCIENTIFIC PLATFORM LIGHT	29-13-52.880N 090-02-54.680W	Q W			Marks scientific platform structure.	Private aid.
	Bayou St. Denis						
	Caminada Bay Channel						
16619	CAMINADA PASS LIGHT 1	29-11-29.640N 090-02-44.170W	Fl G 2.5s			SG on pile.	Private aid.
16619.01	CAMINADA PASS LIGHT 2	29-11-36.000N 090-02-32.740W	Fl R 2.5s			TR on pile.	Private aid.

Light List corrected through LNM week: 01/18

(1) No.	(2) Name and Location	(3) Position	(4) Characteristic	(5) Height	(6) Range	(7) Structure	(8) Remarks
		LOUISIANA - Eighth District					
	BARATARIA AND BAYOU LAFOURCHE WATERWAYS (Chart 11365)						
	Bayou St. Denis						
	Caminada Bay Channel						
16619.02	CAMINADA PASS LIGHT 3	29-12-21.100N 090-02-58.860W	Fl G 2.5s			SG on pile.	Private aid.
16619.03	CAMINADA PASS LIGHT 4	29-11-45.770N 090-02-46.140W	Fl R 2.5s			TR on pile.	Private aid.
	Caminada Bay						
16660	Bay Rambo Demonstration Oyster Reef Daybeacons (2)	29-21-02.260N 090-07-54.430W				NW on pile worded DANGER SUBMERGED OYSTER REEF.	Private aid.
16665	Harrison Family Barricade Unl. Buoy	29-21-18.232N 090-05-21.495W				White with orange band worded DANGER BARRACADE AHEAD.	Private aid.
	Little Lake						
16670	- CHANNEL LIGHT 1	29-31-57.000N 090-09-51.000W	Q W	14		SG on pile.	Private aid.
16675	- CHANNEL LIGHT 3	29-31-57.000N 090-09-36.000W	Q W	14		SG on pile.	Private aid.
16680	- CHANNEL LIGHT 5	29-31-56.000N 090-09-18.000W	Q W	14		SG on pile.	Private aid.
16685	- WELL CHANNEL LIGHT 1	29-32-50.000N 090-09-59.000W	Q W	14		SG on pile.	Private aid.
16690	- WELL CHANNEL LIGHT 2	29-32-48.000N 090-09-39.000W	Q W	14		TR on pile.	Private aid.
16692	EXXON-MOBIL WEST PILING LIGHTS (13-19)	29-32-46.260N 090-09-31.540W	Fl W 2.5s			Marks pilings.	Private aid.
16695	BAY L'OURSE ENTRANCE LIGHT 2	29-31-02.000N 090-10-47.000W	Fl W 4s	10		TR on pile.	Private aid.
16832	LAFOURCHE PARISH LITTLE LAKE DANGER LIGHT	29-34-09.750N 090-11-53.930W	Fl W 2.5s			Marks rock shoreline.	Private aid.
16832.01	LAFOURCHE PARISH LITTLE LAKE DANGER LIGHT	29-34-05.980N 090-11-40.260W	Fl W 2.5s			Marks rock shoreline.	Private aid.
16832.02	LAFOURCHE PARISH LITTLE LAKE DANGER LIGHT	29-34-05.950N 090-11-36.740W	Fl W 2.5s			Marks rock shoreline.	Private aid.
16832.03	LAFOURCHE PARISH LITTLE LAKE DANGER LIGHT	29-34-17.260N 090-11-18.590W	Fl W 2.5s			Marks rock shoreline.	Private aid.
16832.04	LAFOURCHE PARISH LITTLE LAKE DANGER LIGHT	29-34-14.100N 090-11-25.720W	Fl W 2.5s			Marks rock shoreline.	Private aid.
16832.05	LAFOURCHE PARISH LITTLE LAKE DANGER LIGHT	29-34-20.340N 090-11-03.690W	Fl W 2.5s			Marks rock shoreline.	Private aid.
16832.06	LAFOURCHE PARISH LITTLE LAKE DANGER LIGHT	29-34-20.550N 090-10-46.280W	Fl W 2.5s			Marks rock shoreline.	Private aid.
16832.07	LAFOURCHE PARISH LITTLE LAKE DANGER LIGHT	29-34-19.720N 090-10-33.790W	Fl W 2.5s			Marks rock shoreline.	Private aid.
16832.08	LAFOURCHE PARISH LITTLE LAKE DANGER LIGHT	29-34-19.350N 090-10-27.540W	Fl W 2.5s			Marks rock shoreline.	Private aid.
16832.09	LAFOURCHE PARISH LITTLE LAKE DANGER LIGHT	29-34-20.470N 090-10-22.120W	Fl W 2.5s			Marks rock shoreline.	Private aid.
16832.11	LAFOURCHE PARISH LITTLE LAKE DANGER LIGHT	29-34-17.120N 090-10-21.800W	Fl W 2.5s			Marks rock shoreline.	Private aid.
16832.12	LAFOURCHE PARISH LITTLE LAKE DANGER LIGHT	29-34-13.750N 090-10-15.070W	Fl W 2.5s			Marks rock shoreline.	Private aid.
16832.13	LAFOURCHE PARISH LITTLE LAKE DANGER LIGHT	29-34-12.540N 090-09-58.770W	Fl W 2.5s			Marks rock shoreline.	Private aid.
16832.14	LAFOURCHE PARISH LITTLE LAKE DANGER LIGHT	29-34-17.470N 090-09-44.320W	Fl W 2.5s			Marks rock shoreline.	Private aid.
16832.15	LAFOURCHE PARISH LITTLE LAKE DANGER LIGHT	29-34-21.360N 090-09-45.110W	Fl W 2.5s			Marks rock shoreline.	Private aid.
16832.16	LAFOURCHE PARISH LITTLE LAKE DANGER LIGHT	29-34-31.070N 090-10-01.840W	Fl W 2.5s			Marks rock shoreline.	Private aid.
16832.17	LAFOURCHE PARISH LITTLE LAKE DANGER LIGHT	29-34-34.240N 090-10-03.060W	Fl W 2.5s			Marks rock shoreline.	Private aid.

Light List corrected through LNM week: 01/18

(1) No.	(2) Name and Location	(3) Position	(4) Characteristic	(5) Height	(6) Range	(7) Structure	(8) Remarks
		LOUISIANA - Eighth District					
	BARATARIA AND BAYOU LAFOURCHE WATERWAYS (Chart 11365)						
	Little Lake						
16832.18	LAFOURCHE PARISH LITTLE LAKE DANGER LIGHT	29-34-48.510N 090-10-10.040W	Fl W 2.5s			Marks rock shoreline.	Private aid.
16832.19	LAFOURCHE PARISH LITTLE LAKE DANGER LIGHT	29-34-54.940N 090-10-13.140W	Fl W 2.5s			Marks rock shoreline.	Private aid.
16832.21	LAFOURCHE PARISH LITTLE LAKE DANGER LIGHT	29-34-58.130N 090-10-16.940W	Fl W 2.5s			Marks rock shoreline.	Private aid.
16832.22	LAFOURCHE PARISH LITTLE LAKE DANGER LIGHT	29-35-09.160N 090-10-01.210W	Fl W 2.5s			Marks rock shoreline.	Private aid.
16835	SUPERIOR CANAL ENTRANCE LIGHT 2	29-30-21.000N 090-12-57.000W	Fl W 4s	10		TR on pile.	Private aid.
	NEW ORLEANS TO CALCASIEU RIVER (Chart 11352)						
	Lake Salvador						
16840	COUBA ISLAND CANAL ENTRANCE LIGHT 1	29-48-00.000N 090-12-14.000W	Q W	17		SG on dolphin.	Private aid.
16845	BAYOU COUBA LIGHT 1	29-47-08.122N 090-14-05.800W	Fl G 6s	17	4	SG on dolphin.	
16850	BRIDGELINE PIPELINE LIGHT A	29-41-00.000N 090-11-23.700W	Fl Y 2.5s	15		NW on pile worded DANGER DO NOT ANCHOR OR DREDGE.	Private aid.
16855	BRIDGELINE PIPELINE LIGHT B	29-41-09.870N 090-11-23.710W	Fl Y 2.5s	15		NW on pile worded DANGER DO NOT ANCHOR OR DREDGE.	Private aid.
16860	BAYOU PEROT ENTRANCE LIGHT 2	29-41-28.360N 090-12-37.398W	Fl R 4s	17	4	TR on pile.	
16865	- SOUTHEAST PIPELINE LIGHT A	29-40-27.000N 090-13-19.000W	Fl Y 2.5s	13		On dolphin.	Private aid.
16870	- SOUTHEAST PIPELINE LIGHT B	29-40-58.000N 090-13-52.000W	Fl Y 2.5s	13		On dolphin.	Private aid.
16875	- SOUTHEAST PIPELINE LIGHT C	29-41-29.000N 090-14-25.000W	Fl Y 2.5s	13		On dolphin.	Private aid.
16880	- NORTHWEST PIPELINE LIGHT B	29-42-52.000N 090-16-33.000W	Fl Y 2.5s	13		On dolphin.	Private aid.
16885	- NORTHWEST PIPELINE LIGHT C	29-43-10.000N 090-17-19.000W	Fl Y 2.5s	13		On dolphin.	Private aid.
16890	- NORTHWEST PIPELINE LIGHT D	29-43-28.000N 090-18-04.000W	Fl Y 2.5s	13		On dolphin.	Private aid.
16895	- NORTHWEST PIPELINE LIGHT E	29-43-47.000N 090-18-49.000W	Fl Y 2.5s	13		On dolphin.	Private aid.
16900	BAYOU DES ALLEMANDS LIGHT 1	29-41-52.340N 090-20-26.728W	Fl G 4s	17	4	SG on dolphin.	
16905	BRIDGELINE PIPELINE LIGHT C	29-41-01.770N 090-11-15.380W	Fl Y 2.5s	15		NW on pile worded: DANGER DO NOT ANCHOR OR DREDGE.	Private aid.
	Petit Lac des Allemands						
16910	- Channel Buoy 1	29-46-54.190N 090-26-15.130W				Green can.	Private aid.
16915	- Channel Buoy 2	29-47-06.700N 090-26-13.800W				Red nun.	Private aid.
16920	- Channel Buoy 3	29-47-05.030N 090-26-35.190W				Green can.	Private aid.
16925	- Channel Buoy 4	29-47-06.700N 090-26-33.970W				Red nun.	Private aid.
16930	- Channel Buoy 5	29-47-15.810N 090-26-53.040W				Green can.	Private aid.
16935	- Channel Buoy 6	29-47-17.560N 090-26-51.960W				Red nun.	Private aid.
16940	- Channel Buoy 7	29-47-26.560N 090-27-11.080W				Green can.	Private aid.
16945	- Channel Buoy 8	29-47-28.430N 090-27-10.330W				Red nun.	Private aid.
16950	- Channel Buoy 9	29-47-39.000N 090-27-29.210W				Green can.	Private aid.

(1) No.	(2) Name and Location	(3) Position	(4) Characteristic	(5) Height	(6) Range	(7) Structure	(8) Remarks
		LOUISIANA - Eighth District					
	NEW ORLEANS TO CALCASIEU RIVER (Chart 11352)						
	Petit Lac des Allemands						
16955	- Channel Buoy 10	29-27-41.240N 090-27-28.130W				Red nun.	Private aid.
16960	- Channel Buoy 11	29-47-53.160N 090-27-47.070W				Green can.	Private aid.
16965	- Channel Buoy 12	29-47-54.000N 090-27-45.990W				Red nun.	Private aid.
	BARATARIA AND BAYOU LAFOURCHE WATERWAYS (Chart 11365)						
	Belle Pass						
16970 615	- Entrance Lighted Buoy 2	29-04-15.965N 090-13-40.336W	Q R		4	Red.	
16975	- Entrance Lighted Buoy 1	29-04-18.052N 090-13-53.034W	Q G		4	Green.	
16980	- RANGE FRONT LIGHT	29-05-54.934N 090-13-23.367W	Q G	25		KRW on platform.	Visible all around; higher intensity 1.5° each side of rangeline.
16982	- RANGE FRONT PASSING LIGHT	29-05-54.934N 090-13-23.367W	Q G	27	4	On same structure as Belle Pass Range Front Light.	
16985	- RANGE REAR LIGHT 3,067 yards, 011.1° from front light.	29-07-24.356N 090-13-03.406W	Iso G 6s	67		KRW on platform.	Visible only on rangeline.
16990	- RANGE REAR LIGHT PASSING LIGHT	29-07-24.356N 090-13-03.406W	Fl G 4s	12	4	On same structure as Belle Pass Range Rear Light.	
16995	- WEST JETTY LIGHT 3	29-04-45.708N 090-13-45.960W	Fl G 2.5s	17	5	SG on pile.	Ra ref.
17000	- EAST JETTY LIGHT 4	29-04-43.893N 090-13-32.579W	Fl R 2.5s	17	5	TR on pile.	Ra ref.
17005	- ENTRANCE LIGHT 6	29-05-04.026N 090-13-31.214W	Fl R 4s	17	3	TR on pile.	Ra ref.
17010	- ENTRANCE LIGHT 8	29-05-27.501N 090-13-26.661W	Fl R 6s	17	4	TR on pile.	Ra ref.
	TIMBALIER AND TERREBONNE BAYS (Chart 11357)						
	Terrebonne Bay						
17015	- PIPELINE LIGHT A	29-05-10.700N 090-33-25.500W	Q W	11		On pile.	Private aid.
17020	- PIPELINE LIGHT B	29-05-36.700N 090-33-16.100W	Q W			On pile.	Private aid.
17025	- PIPELINE LIGHT C	29-06-00.500N 090-31-46.400W	Q W			On pile.	Private aid.
17030	- 1249-18 CHANNEL LIGHT 1	29-05-47.000N 090-31-42.000W	Q W	10		SG on pile.	Private aid.
17035	- 1249-18 Channel Day beacon 3	29-05-46.000N 090-31-42.000W				SG on pile.	Private aid.
17040	- 1249-18 Channel Day beacon 5	29-05-39.000N 090-31-41.000W				SG on pile.	Private aid.
17045	- 1249-18 Channel Day beacon 7	29-05-32.000N 090-31-40.000W				SG on pile.	Private aid.
17050	- 1249-18 Channel Day beacon 9	29-05-27.000N 090-31-38.000W				SG on pile.	Private aid.
17055	- 1249-18 Channel Day beacon 11	29-05-22.000N 090-31-36.000W				SG on pile.	Private aid.
17060	- 1249-18 Channel Day beacon 13	29-05-19.000N 090-31-36.000W				SG on pile.	Private aid.
17065	- 1249-18 Channel Day beacon 15	29-05-17.000N 090-31-35.000W				SG on pile.	Private aid.
17070	- PIPELINE LIGHT D	29-06-27.900N 090-30-19.800W	Q W			On pile.	Private aid.
17075	- PIPELINE LIGHT E	29-06-43.400N 090-29-49.300W	Q W			On pile.	Private aid.
17080	- PIPELINE LIGHT F	29-06-41.600N 090-29-07.300W	Q W			On pile.	Private aid.

(1) No.	(2) Name and Location	(3) Position	(4) Characteristic	(5) Height	(6) Range	(7) Structure	(8) Remarks
	LOUISIANA - Eighth District						
	TIMBALIER AND TERREBONNE BAYS (Chart 11357)						
	Terrebonne Bay						
17085	- PIPELINE LIGHT G	29-06-41.300N 090-29-04.500W	Q W			On pile.	Private aid.
	Caillou Island Channel						
17090	- Day beacon 2	29-05-32.000N 090-29-47.000W				TR on pile.	Private aid.
17095	- Day beacon 4	29-05-30.000N 090-29-42.000W				TR on pile.	Private aid.
17100	- Day beacon 6	29-05-28.000N 090-29-36.000W				TR on pile.	Private aid.
17105	- Day beacon 8	29-05-25.000N 090-29-30.000W				TR on pile.	Private aid.
	Timbalier Island 2703 Well 1						
17110	- CHANNEL LIGHT 2	29-04-29.000N 090-28-12.000W	Q R	15		TR on four pile platform.	Private aid.
17115	- Day beacon 4	29-04-24.000N 090-28-14.000W				TR on piles.	Private aid.
17120	- Day beacon 6	29-04-19.000N 090-28-15.000W				TR on pile.	Private aid.
17125	- Day beacon 8	29-04-14.000N 090-28-17.000W				TR on pile.	Private aid.
17130	- Day beacon 10	29-04-11.000N 090-28-20.000W				TR on pile.	Private aid.
	Timbalier Island 2703 Well 4						
17135	- CHANNEL LIGHT 2	29-04-44.000N 090-27-20.000W	Q W	15		TR on four pile platform.	Private aid.
17140	- Day beacon 4	29-04-14.000N 090-27-15.000W				TR on piles.	Private aid.
17145	- Day beacon 6	29-04-10.000N 090-27-14.500W				TR on pile.	Private aid.
17150	- Day beacon 8	29-04-05.000N 090-27-14.000W				TR on piles.	Private aid.
	Timbalier - Terrebonne Bay						
17155	- LIGHT 1	29-09-56.087N 090-34-54.321W	Fl G 2.5s	17	4	SG on pile.	Ra ref.
17160	- LIGHT 3	29-09-54.394N 090-33-49.356W	Fl G 4s	17	4	SG on pile.	Ra ref.
17165	- LIGHT 7	29-09-51.038N 090-31-39.118W	Fl G 6s	17	4	SG on pile.	Ra ref.
17170	- LIGHT 11	29-09-47.647N 090-29-28.881W	Fl G 4s	17	4	SG on pile.	Ra ref.
17175	- LIGHT 15	29-09-44.222N 090-27-18.647W	Fl G 6s	17	4	SG on pile.	Ra ref.
17180	- LIGHT 19	29-09-40.760N 090-25-08.410W	Fl G 4s	17	4	SG on pile.	Ra ref.
17185	- LIGHT 23	29-09-37.264N 090-22-58.187W	Fl G 6s	17	4	SG on pile.	Ra ref.
17190	- LIGHT 27	29-09-33.805N 090-20-48.260W	Q G	17	4	SG on pile.	Ra ref.
17195	- LIGHT 29	29-09-02.501N 090-19-55.774W	Fl G 6s	17	4	SG on pile.	Ra ref.
17200	- LIGHT 31	29-08-30.347N 090-19-04.067W	Fl G 4s	17	4	SG on pile.	Ra ref.
17205	- LIGHT 33	29-07-58.188N 090-18-12.367W	Fl G 6s	17	4	SG on pile.	Ra ref.
17210	- LIGHT 36	29-07-24.027N 090-17-21.089W	Q R	17	4	TR on pile.	Ra ref.
17215	- LIGHT 38	29-07-40.143N 090-16-33.757W	Fl R 4s	17	4	TR on pile.	Ra ref.
17217.01	- LIGHT 39	29-08-08.727N 090-15-15.871W	Fl G 4s	17	4	SG on dolphin.	Ra ref.

Light List corrected through LNM week: 01/18

LOUISIANA - Eighth District

TIMBALIER AND TERREBONNE BAYS (Chart 11357)

Timbalier - Terrebonne Bay

(1) No.	(2) Name and Location	(3) Position	(4) Characteristic	(5) Height	(6) Range	(7) Structure	(8) Remarks
17220	- LIGHT 40	29-07-56.547N 090-15-46.944W	Fl R 6s	17	4	TR on pile.	Ra ref.
17222	- LIGHT 40A	29-08-05.121N 090-15-19.551W	Fl R 2.5s	17	4	TR on pile.	Ra ref.
17224.01	- LIGHT 41	29-08-14.440N 090-15-00.676W	Fl G 2.5s	17	4	SG on dolphin.	Ra ref.
17225	- LIGHT 42	29-08-13.285N 090-14-57.983W	Q R	17	4	TR on pile.	Ra ref.
17227.01	- LIGHT 43	29-08-21.084N 090-14-54.678W	Fl G 4s	17	4	SG on dolphin.	Ra ref.
17230	- Junction Lighted Buoy TB	29-09-54.797N 090-36-00.136W	Fl (2+1)R 6s		4	Red with green band.	

Timbalier Bay

(1) No.	(2) Name and Location	(3) Position	(4) Characteristic	(5) Height	(6) Range	(7) Structure	(8) Remarks
17240	LAKE RACCOURCI FIELD ENTRANCE LIGHT 2	29-11-11.000N 090-25-07.000W	Fl R 4s	14		TR on dolphin.	Private aid.
17245	BAYOU BLUE ENTRANCE LIGHT	29-12-09.000N 090-16-08.000W	Fl W 4s	12		SG on dolphin.	Private aid.

Bayou Rosa

(1) No.	(2) Name and Location	(3) Position	(4) Characteristic	(5) Height	(6) Range	(7) Structure	(8) Remarks
17250	- ENTRANCE LIGHT 1	29-13-39.000N 090-18-00.000W	Fl W 4s	14		SG on pile.	Private aid.
17255	- Buoy 3	29-13-44.000N 090-17-56.000W				Green can.	Private aid.
17260	- Buoy 5	29-13-50.000N 090-17-52.000W				Green can.	Private aid.
17265	- Buoy 7	29-13-55.000N 090-17-47.000W				Green can.	Private aid.
17270	- Buoy 9	29-14-00.000N 090-17-43.000W				Green can.	Private aid.
17275	- Buoy 11	29-14-06.000N 090-17-39.000W				Green can.	Private aid.
17280	- Buoy 13	29-14-11.000N 090-17-35.000W				Green can.	Private aid.
17285	- Buoy 15	29-14-16.000N 090-17-31.000W				Green can.	Private aid.
17290	- Buoy 17	29-14-22.000N 090-17-27.000W				Green can.	Private aid.
17295	- Buoy 19	29-14-28.000N 090-17-25.000W				Green can.	Private aid.

Little Lake

(1) No.	(2) Name and Location	(3) Position	(4) Characteristic	(5) Height	(6) Range	(7) Structure	(8) Remarks
17300	- LIGHT 21	29-14-47.000N 090-16-57.000W	Fl W 4s	14		SG on piles.	Private aid.
17305	- Buoy 23	29-14-47.000N 090-16-50.000W				Green can.	Private aid.
17310	- Buoy 25	29-14-46.000N 090-16-43.000W				Green can.	Private aid.
17315	- Buoy 27	29-14-45.000N 090-16-36.000W				Green can.	Private aid.
17320	- Buoy 29	29-14-45.000N 090-16-28.000W				Green can.	Private aid.
17325	- Buoy 31	29-14-44.000N 090-16-21.000W				Green can.	Private aid.
17330	- Buoy 33	29-14-43.000N 090-16-14.000W				Green can.	Private aid.
17335	- Buoy 35	29-14-42.000N 090-16-06.000W				Green can.	Private aid.
17340	- Buoy 37	29-14-42.000N 090-15-59.000W				Green can.	Private aid.
17345	- Buoy 39	29-14-41.000N 090-15-52.000W				Green can.	Private aid.
17350	- Buoy 41	29-14-40.000N 090-15-44.000W				Green can.	Private aid.
17355	- Buoy 43	29-14-40.000N 090-15-37.000W				Green can.	Private aid.

(1) No.	(2) Name and Location	(3) Position	(4) Characteristic	(5) Height	(6) Range	(7) Structure	(8) Remarks
		LOUISIANA - Eighth District					
	TIMBALIER AND TERREBONNE BAYS (Chart 11357)						
	Little Lake						
17360	- Buoy 45	29-14-39.000N 090-15-30.000W				Green can.	Private aid.
17365	- Buoy 47	29-14-38.000N 090-15-23.000W				Green can.	Private aid.
17368	BAYOU ROSA OYSTER FARM SPECIAL LIGHTS (4)	29-14-32.570N 090-15-20.853W	Fl Y 2.5s			Marks perimeter of aquaculture farm.	Private aid.
17368.01	Bayou Rosa Oyster Farm Special Lighted Buoy E	29-14-27.295N 090-15-19.806W	Fl Y 2.5s			Marks perimeter of aquaculture farm.	Private aid.
	TIMBALIER AND TERREBONNE BAYS (Chart 11357)						
17370	LAKE RACCOURCI PIPELINE MARKER LIGHT	29-14-21.400N 090-20-23.400W	Q R	17		On pile.	Private aid.
	Chinaman Bayou						
17375	- Day beacon 1	29-17-27.685N 090-21-04.162W				SG on pile.	Private aid.
17380	- Day beacon 3	29-17-39.546N 090-20-50.896W				SG on pile.	Private aid.
17385	- Day beacon 5	29-17-41.771N 090-20-43.002W				SG on pile.	Private aid.
17390	- Day beacon 7	29-17-41.769N 090-20-26.357W				SG on pile.	Private aid.
17395	- Day beacon 9	29-17-44.792N 090-20-14.987W				SG on pile.	Private aid.
17400	- Day beacon 11	29-17-54.217N 090-20-05.165W				SG on pile.	Private aid.
17405	- Day beacon 13	29-18-02.975N 090-20-04.552W				SG on pile.	Private aid.
17410	- Day beacon 15	29-18-10.691N 090-20-06.587W				SG on pile.	Private aid.
17415	- Day beacon 17	29-18-19.835N 090-20-17.340W				SG on pile.	Private aid.
17420	- Day beacon 19	29-18-27.390N 090-20-25.487W				SG on pile.	Private aid.
17425	USACE BAYOU BLUE METERING STATION LIGHT	29-32-36.500N 090-24-00.700W	Fl Y 2.5s			On pile.	Private aid.
	Lake La Graisse						
17440	- ENTRANCE LIGHT 1	29-10-55.416N 090-35-00.552W	Fl G 4s	17	4	SG on pile.	Ra ref.
17445	- LIGHT 2	29-12-25.964N 090-34-50.006W	Fl R 2.5s	17	4	TR on dolphin.	Ra ref.
17450	- LIGHT 4	29-13-30.003N 090-35-45.825W	Fl R 4s	20	4	TR on dolphin.	Ra ref.
17455	- LIGHT 5	29-13-56.706N 090-36-11.470W	Fl G 6s	17	4	SG on dolphin.	Ra ref.
17460	- LIGHT 7	29-14-37.983N 090-35-29.025W	Fl G 4s	17	4	SG on dolphin.	Ra ref.
	Bayou Pointe au Chien						
17462.03	TLCD BARGE FLOODGATE DOLPHIN LIGHT 1	29-25-04.330N 090-26-53.120W	Fl G 2.5s			Marks starboard side entry dolphin.	Private aid.
17462.04	TLCD BARGE FLOODGATE DOLPHIN LIGHT 2	29-25-04.610N 090-26-52.440W	Fl R 2.5s			Marks port side entry dolphin.	Private aid.
17462.05	TLCD BARGE FLOODGATE DOLPHIN LIGHT 3	29-25-06.630N 090-26-54.370W	Fl G 2.5s			Marks starboard side exit dolphin.	Private aid.
17462.06	TLCD BARGE FLOODGATE DOLPHIN LIGHT 4	29-25-06.910N 090-26-53.690W	Fl R 2.5s			Marks port side exit dolphin.	Private aid.
	NEW ORLEANS TO CALCASIEU RIVER (Chart 11352)						
	Lake Boudreaux						
17475	- Buoy 1	29-22-07.207N 090-40-36.511W				Green can.	
17480	- Buoy 2	29-22-09.238N 090-40-28.733W				Red nun.	
17485	- Buoy 3	29-22-13.459N 090-40-27.798W				Green can.	

Light List corrected through LNM week: 01/18

(1) No.	(2) Name and Location	(3) Position	(4) Characteristic	(5) Height	(6) Range	(7) Structure	(8) Remarks
			LOUISIANA - Eighth District				
	NEW ORLEANS TO CALCASIEU RIVER (Chart 11352)						
	Lake Boudreaux						
17490	- Buoy 4	29-22-22.117N 090-40-12.847W				Red nun.	
17495	- Buoy 5	29-22-28.677N 090-40-09.647W				Green can.	
17500	- Lighted Buoy 7	29-22-50.598N 090-39-50.680W	Fl G 4s		4	Green can.	
17505	- Buoy 9	29-23-00.840N 090-39-43.680W				Green can.	
17510	- Buoy 11	29-23-11.487N 090-39-35.351W				Green can.	
17515	- Buoy 13	29-23-36.795N 090-39-18.318W				Green can.	
17520	- Lighted Buoy 15	29-23-50.049N 090-39-12.026W	Q G		3	Green can.	
17525	- Buoy 17	29-23-43.374N 090-38-50.448W				Green can.	
17530	- Lighted Buoy 19	29-23-38.047N 090-38-29.566W	Fl G 4s		4	Green can.	
			POINT AU FER TO MARSH ISLAND (Chart 11351)				
	ISLES DERNIERES TO POINT AU FER (Chart 11356)						
	Company Canal saltwater Control						
17535	- FLOODGATE LIGHT 1	29-37-38.180N 090-33-27.690W	Fl G 2.5s			SG on dolphin.	Private aid.
17540	- STRUCTURE LIGHT 2	29-37-38.180N 090-33-26.730W	Fl R 2.5s			TR on dolphin.	Private aid.
17545	- STRUCTURE WEST OBSTRUCTION LIGHT	29-37-39.300N 090-33-28.600W				On barge.	On west side of floodgate. (QG open) (QR closed).
							Private aid.
17550	- STRUCTURE EAST OBSTRUCTION LIGHT	29-37-39.000N 090-33-27.000W	Q R			On receiving structure cassion.	Private aid.
17555	- STRUCTURE LIGHT 3	29-37-39.970N 090-33-27.670W	Fl G 2.5s			SG dolphin.	Private aid.
17560	- STRUCTURE LIGHT 4	29-37-39.970N 090-33-26.720W	Fl R 2.5s			TR dolphin.	Private aid.
17565	- STRUCTURE MOVEABLE OBSTRUCTION LIGHT	29-37-38.500N 090-33-26.700W	Q R			On barge.	Shows only when floodgate closed.
							Private aid.
			LOUISIANA - Eighth District				
	CATAHOULA BAY TO WAX LAKE OUTLET (Chart 11355)						
	Bayou Petit Caillou Flood Canal						
17570	- EAST LIGHT Marks right side of floodgate for inbound traffic.	29-32-53.000N 090-37-58.000W	Fl R 2.5s			On gatewall.	Private aid.
17575	- WEST LIGHT Marks left side of floodgate for inbound traffic.	29-32-53.000N 090-37-58.000W				On gatewall.	(FL G 2.5s open) (FL R 2.5s closed). Private aid.
17578	BAYOU PETIT CAILLOU FLOODGATE DOLPHIN LIGHT 1	29-17-45.550N 090-38-55.320W	Fl G 2.5s			Marks dolphin cluster.	Private aid.
17578.01	BAYOU PETIT CAILLOU FLOODGATE DOLPHIN LIGHT 2	29-17-46.210N 090-38-53.810W	Fl R 2.5s			Marks dolphin cluster.	Private aid.
17578.02	BAYOU PETIT CAILLOU FLOODGATE DOLPHIN LIGHT 3	29-17-49.180N 090-38-55.160W	Fl G 2.5s			Marks dolphin cluster.	Private aid.
17578.03	BAYOU PETIT CAILLOU FLOODGATE DOLPHIN LIGHT 4	29-17-49.130N 090-38-53.830W	Fl R 2.5s			Marks dolphin cluster.	Private aid.
	Placid Canal						
17580	- FLOODGATE LIGHT 1	29-20-29.179N 090-37-54.712W	Fl G 2.5s			SG on pile cluster.	Private aid.

Light List corrected through LNM week: 01/18

(1) No.	(2) Name and Location	(3) Position	(4) Characteristic	(5) Height	(6) Range	(7) Structure	(8) Remarks
			LOUISIANA - Eighth District				
	CATAHOULA BAY TO WAX LAKE OUTLET (Chart 11355)						
	Placid Canal						
17585	- FLOODGATE LIGHT 2	29-20-29.530N 090-37-54.642W	Fl R 2.5s			TR on pile.	Private aid.
17590	- FLOODGATE LIGHT 3	29-20-29.436N 090-37-56.381W	Fl G 2.5s			SG on pile.	Private aid.
17595	- FLOODGATE LIGHT 4	29-20-29.787N 090-37-56.381W	Fl R 2.5s			TR on pile.	Private aid.
17600	- FLOODGATE SIDEWALL STRUCTURE LIGHTS(2)	29-20-29.671N 090-37-55.440W	Fl W 2.5s			On barge structure.	Marks each sidewall of floodgate. Private aid.
17605	- FLOODGATE CENTER GATE LIGHT	29-20-29.447N 090-37-55.272W	F R			On barge structure.	Shows only when center floodgate closed. Private aid.
17610	- FLOODGATE SIDEWALL CAISSON LIGHTS(2)	29-20-29.649N 090-37-55.479W	F R			On caisson structure.	Marks each sidewall caisson structure. Private aid.
17615	- FLOODGATE NORTHWEST PILING LIGHT	29-20-30.037N 090-37-56.503W	Fl W 2.5s			On pile cluster.	Private aid.
17620	- FLOODGATE SOUTHWEST PILING LIGHT	29-20-29.079N 090-37-56.935W	Fl W 2.5s			On pile cluster.	Private aid.
17625	- FLOODGATE NORTHEAST PILING LIGHT	29-20-29.785N 090-37-53.421W	Fl W 2.5s			On pile cluster.	Private aid.
17630	- FLOODGATE SOUTHEAST PILING LIGHT	29-20-28.325N 090-37-53.472W	Fl W 2.5s			On pile cluster.	Private aid.
	Bush Canal						
17635	- FLOODGATE LIGHT 1	29-22-06.079N 090-36-07.085W	Fl G 2.5s			SG on pile.	Private aid.
17640	- FLOODGATE LIGHT 2	29-22-06.448N 090-36-06.117W	Fl R 2.5s			TR on pile.	Private aid.
17645	- FLOODGATE LIGHT 3	29-22-07.809N 090-36-09.406W	Fl G 2.5s			SG on pile.	Private aid.
17650	- FLOODGATE LIGHT 4	29-22-08.688N 090-36-09.123W	Fl R 2.5s			TR on pile.	Private aid.
17655	- FLOODGATE SIDEWALL STRUCTURE LIGHTS (2)	29-22-07.031N 090-36-08.164W	Fl W 2.5s			On barge structure.	Marks each sidewall of floodgate. Private aid.
17660	- FLOODGATE CENTER GATE LIGHT	29-22-07.132N 090-36-07.767W	F R			On barge structure.	Shows only when center floodgate closed. Private aid.
17665	- FLOODGATE SIDEWALL CAISSON LIGHTS (2)	29-22-07.060N 090-36-08.202W	F R			On caisson structure.	Marks each sidewall caisson structure. Private aid.
17670	- FLOODGATE SOUTHEAST PILING LIGHT	29-22-05.012N 090-36-07.513W	Fl W 2.5s			On pile cluster.	Private aid.
17675	- FLOODGATE NORTHEAST PILING LIGHT	29-22-07.210N 090-36-05.691W	Fl W 2.5s			On pile cluster.	Private aid.
	TIMBALIER AND TERREBONNE BAYS (Chart 11357)						
	Cat Island Pass						
17680 680	- *Lighted Buoy CI*	29-00-12.927N 090-33-54.912W	Mo (A) W		5	Red and white stripes with red spherical topmark.	
17685	- *Lighted Buoy 1*	29-01-09.059N 090-34-05.325W	Fl G 6s		4	Green.	
17690	- *Lighted Buoy 3*	29-02-09.393N 090-34-13.517W	Fl G 2.5s		4	Green.	
17695	- *Buoy 4*	29-02-12.384N 090-34-02.843W				Red nun.	
17700	- *Buoy 5*	29-02-38.085N 090-34-24.291W				Green can.	
17705	- *Lighted Buoy 7*	29-03-08.419N 090-34-34.426W	Fl G 4s		4	Green.	
17710	- *Lighted Buoy 9*	29-03-34.530N 090-34-42.758W	Fl G 4s		4	Green.	
17715	- *Buoy 10*	29-03-36.177N 090-34-36.477W				Red nun.	

Light List corrected through LNM week: 01/18

(1) No.	(2) Name and Location	(3) Position	(4) Characteristic	(5) Height	(6) Range	(7) Structure	(8) Remarks
	LOUISIANA - Eighth District						
	TIMBALIER AND TERREBONNE BAYS (Chart 11357)						
	Cat Island Pass						
17720	- Lighted Buoy 11	29-04-01.681N 090-34-52.271W	Q G		3	Green.	
17725	- Lighted Buoy 12	29-04-03.794N 090-34-42.009W	Q R		3	Red.	
17730	- Buoy 13	29-04-32.364N 090-34-59.838W				Green can.	
17735	- Buoy 14	29-04-33.588N 090-34-51.024W				Red nun.	
17740	- Lighted Buoy 15	29-05-00.920N 090-34-55.561W	Fl G 4s		4	Green.	
17745	- Buoy 17	29-05-28.644N 090-34-47.172W				Green can.	
	CATAHOULA BAY TO WAX LAKE OUTLET (Chart 11355)						
	Houma Navigation Canal						
17750	- Lighted Buoy 1	29-05-56.868N 090-34-39.132W	Q G		3	Green.	
17755	- Lighted Buoy 2	29-05-58.630N 090-34-31.955W	Q R		3	Red.	
17760	- Buoy 3	29-06-23.015N 090-34-48.016W				Green can.	Ra ref.
17765	- Buoy 4	29-06-49.782N 090-34-43.518W				Red nun.	Ra ref.
17770	- A RANGE FRONT LIGHT	29-11-24.532N 090-36-42.134W	Q W	25		KRW on piles.	
17775	- A RANGE REAR LIGHT 2,336 yards, 340° from front light.	29-12-30.646N 090-37-09.330W	Iso W 6s	55		KRW on tower.	
17780	- Lighted Buoy 5	29-07-06.500N 090-34-58.500W	Fl G 4s		4	Green.	
17785	- Buoy 6	29-07-31.422N 090-35-04.364W				Red nun.	Ra ref.
17790	- Buoy 7	29-07-54.829N 090-35-18.319W				Green can.	Ra ref.
17795	- Buoy 8	29-08-22.828N 090-35-25.318W				Red nun.	Ra ref.
17800	- LIGHT 9	29-08-41.231N 090-35-38.154W	Fl G 2.5s	17	3	SG on pile.	Ra ref.
17805	- Buoy 10	29-09-07.827N 090-35-43.318W				Red nun.	Ra ref.
17810	- Buoy 11	29-09-27.758N 090-35-57.038W				Green can.	
17815	- LIGHT 13	29-10-14.697N 090-36-17.627W	Fl G 6s	17	4	SG on pile.	Ra ref.
17820	- Buoy 14	29-10-22.652N 090-36-11.260W				Red nun.	
17835	- Buoy 16	29-10-58.000N 090-36-29.000W				Red nun.	Ra ref.
17840	- LIGHT 17	29-11-11.537N 090-36-44.612W	Q G	17	4	SG on pile.	Ra ref.
17845	- Buoy 18	29-11-16.985N 090-36-41.182W				Red nun.	Ra ref.
17850	- Buoy 18A	29-11-28.723N 090-36-53.347W				Red nun.	
17855	- B RANGE FRONT LIGHT	29-11-13.199N 090-36-33.594W	Q W	25		KRW on tower.	
17860	- B RANGE REAR LIGHT 1330 yards, 129.8° from front light.	29-10-47.935N 090-35-58.997W	Iso W 6s	65		KRW on steel tower.	Ra ref.

(1) No.	(2) Name and Location	(3) Position	(4) Characteristic	(5) Height	(6) Range	(7) Structure	(8) Remarks
	LOUISIANA - Eighth District							

CATAHOULA BAY TO WAX LAKE OUTLET (Chart 11355)
Houma Navigation Canal

(1) No.	(2) Name and Location	(3) Position	(4) Characteristic	(5) Height	(6) Range	(7) Structure	(8) Remarks
17865	- B RANGE REAR LIGHT PASSING LIGHT	29-10-47.935N 090-35-58.997W	Fl W 4s	14	5	On same structure as Houma Navigation Canal Range B Rear Light.	
17870	- LIGHT 19	29-11-30.979N 090-37-00.135W	Fl G 2.5s	17	3	SG on piles.	Ra ref.
17875	- Buoy 20	29-12-00.821N 090-37-36.317W				Red nun.	
17880	- LIGHT 21	29-12-12.816N 090-38-00.127W	Fl G 4s	17	4	SG on pile.	Ra ref.
17885	- LIGHT 22	29-12-32.588N 090-38-17.736W	Fl R 6s	17	4	TR on pile.	Ra ref.
17890	- LIGHT 23	29-12-41.920N 090-38-41.481W	Fl G 6s	17	4	SG on pile.	Ra ref.
17895	- LIGHT 24	29-13-00.905N 090-38-56.641W	Fl R 4s	17	3	TR on pile.	Ra ref.
17900	- LIGHT 25	29-13-17.934N 090-39-29.345W	Fl G 4s	17	4	SG on pile.	Ra ref.
17905	- LIGHT 26	29-13-42.716N 090-39-54.676W	Fl R 2.5s	17	3	TR on pile.	Ra ref.
17910	- LIGHT WR28	29-18-05.367N 090-42-49.549W	Q R	17	3	TR on pile.	Ra ref.
17911	SHORT CUT CANAL LIGHT 1	29-33-18.920N 090-42-24.010W	Fl G 2.5s				Private aid.
17911.01	SHORT CUT CANAL LIGHT 2	29-33-20.110N 090-42-18.911W	Fl R 2.5s				Private aid.
17911.02	SHORT CUT CANAL LIGHT 3	29-33-28.060N 090-42-19.000W	Fl G 2.5s				Private aid.
17911.03	SHORT CUT CANAL LIGHT 4	29-33-28.707N 090-42-14.801W	Fl R 2.5s				Private aid.
17912	- FLOODGATE LIGHT	29-19-39.800N 090-43-47.200W	Fl W 2.5s			On dolphin.	Private aid.
17912.01	- FLOODGATE LIGHT	29-19-42.300N 090-43-41.200W	Fl W 2.5s			On dolphin.	Private aid.
17912.02	- FLOODGATE LIGHT 2	29-19-43.000N 090-43-43.500W	Fl R 2.5s			TR on dolphin.	Private aid.
17912.03	- FLOODGATE LIGHT 1	29-19-41.800N 090-43-46.400W	Fl G 2.5s			SG on dolphin.	Private aid.
17912.04	- FLOODGATE BARGE LIGHT	29-19-44.400N 090-43-44.400W	F R			On barge gate.	Marks barge gate when closed. Private aid.
17912.05	- FLOODGATE BARGE LIGHT	29-19-45.800N 090-43-44.600W	F R			On barge gate.	Marks center of barge gate when closed. Private aid.
17912.06	- FLOODGATE BARGE LIGHT	29-19-46.800N 090-43-45.700W	F R			On barge gate.	Marks barge gate when closed. Private aid.
17912.07	- FLOODGATE LIGHT 3	29-19-49.300N 090-43-50.500W	Fl G 2.5s			SG on dolphin.	Private aid.
17912.08	- FLOODGATE LIGHT 4	29-19-50.500N 090-43-47.600W	Fl R 2.5s			TR on dolphin.	Private aid.
17912.09	- FLOODGATE LIGHT	29-19-50.000N 090-43-52.800W	Fl W 2.5s			On dolphin.	Private aid.

TIMBALIER AND TERREBONNE BAYS (Chart 11357)
Lake Pelto

(1) No.	(2) Name and Location	(3) Position	(4) Characteristic	(5) Height	(6) Range	(7) Structure	(8) Remarks
17915	BLACK ELK ENERGY TANK BATTERY LIGHTS (3)	29-04-20.340N 090-38-29.310W	Q W	6		On pile.	Private aid.
17920	BLACK ELK ENERGY FLOW LINE LIGHT	29-04-20.200N 090-38-30.390W	Q W	6		On pile.	Private aid.
17930	- LIGHT LP	29-04-42.833N 090-42-20.045W	Fl W 6s	17	3	NB on dolphin.	Ra ref.
17935	BAYOU SALE CHANNEL LIGHT	29-06-39.000N 090-44-31.000W	Fl W 4s	10		On a dolphin.	Private aid.

Light List corrected through LNM week: 01/18

(1) No.	(2) Name and Location	(3) Position	(4) Characteristic	(5) Height	(6) Range	(7) Structure	(8) Remarks
	LOUISIANA - Eighth District						

TIMBALIER AND TERREBONNE BAYS (Chart 11357)
Caillou Boca

No.	Name and Location	Position	Characteristic	Height	Range	Structure	Remarks
17938	- DANGER LIGHT A	29-04-04.721N 090-47-56.120W	Q W	17	3	NW on pile worded DANGER CHANNEL SHOALED.	Ra ref.
17940	- Day beacon B	29-04-06.012N 090-48-09.588W				NR on pile.	Ra ref.
17943	- Shoal Day beacon	29-03-55.879N 090-48-09.160W				NG on pile.	Ra ref.
17955	- Day beacon C	29-03-11.927N 090-50-27.666W				NG on pile.	Ra ref.

ISLES DERNIERES TO POINT AU FER (Chart 11356)

No.	Name and Location	Position	Characteristic	Height	Range	Structure	Remarks
17970	CALLIOU BAY BARGE LOADING DOCK LIGHT	29-07-31.000N 090-53-27.000W	Q W	6		On dock.	Private aid.

Bayou Grand Caillou

No.	Name and Location	Position	Characteristic	Height	Range	Structure	Remarks
17975	USACE WEST GRAND CAILLOU METERING STATION LIGHT	29-20-30.100N 090-44-20.300W	Fl Y 2.5s			On pile.	Private aid.
17980	USACE EAST GRAND CAILLOU METERING STATION LIGHT	29-20-54.700N 090-43-52.200W	Fl Y 2.5s			On pile.	Private aid.
17982	- FLOODGATE LIGHT	29-20-35.700N 090-44-11.200W	Fl W 2.5s			On pile.	Private aid.
17982.01	- FLOODGATE LIGHT	29-20-32.200N 090-44-09.700W	Fl W 2.5s			On pile.	Private aid.
17982.02	- FLOODGATE LIGHT 2	29-20-35.000N 090-44-11.700W	Fl R 2.5s			TR on dolphin.	Private aid.
17982.03	- FLOODGATE LIGHT 1	29-20-32.800N 090-44-11.100W	Fl G 2.5s			SG on dolphin.	Private aid.
17982.04	- FLOODGATE BARGE LIGHT	29-20-33.800N 090-44-16.100W	F R			On barge gate.	Marks barge gate when closed. Private aid.
17082.05	- FLOODGATE BARGE LIGHT	29-20-33.900N 090-44-17.300W	F R			On barge gate.	Marks center of barge gate when closed. Private aid.
17982.06	- FLOODGATE BARGE LIGHT	29-20-33.300N 090-44-18.400W	F R			On barge gate.	Marks barge gate when closed. Private aid.
17982.07	- FLOODGATE LIGHT 4	29-20-33.100N 090-44-20.000W	Fl R 2.5s			TR on dolphin.	Private aid.
17982.08	- FLOODGATE LIGHT 3	29-20-30.900N 090-44-19.400W	Fl G 2.5s			SG on dolphin.	Private aid.
17982.09	- FLOODGATE LIGHT	29-20-33.500N 090-44-20.800W	Fl W 2.5s			On pile.	Private aid.
17982.11	- FLOODGATE LIGHT	29-20-30.500N 090-44-19.700W	Fl W 2.5s			On pile.	Private aid.
17984	*LDWF Special Lighted Buoy A*	29-06-14.800N 091-03-06.700W	Fl Y 2.5s			Marks submerged reef obstruction.	Private aid.
17984.01	*LDWF Special Lighted Buoy B*	29-06-26.700N 091-03-14.800W	Fl Y 2.5s			Marks submerged reef obstruction.	Private aid.
17984.02	*LDWF Special Lighted Buoy C*	29-06-32.600N 091-03-29.300W	Fl Y 2.5s			Marks submerged reef obstruction.	Private aid.
17985	- ENTRANCE LIGHT GC	29-09-05.115N 090-58-52.154W	Fl W 6s	17	3	NG on pile.	Ra ref.
17990	- *Entrance Lighted Buoy 1*	29-09-33.594N 090-57-46.661W	Fl G 4s		3	Green can.	
17995	- ENTRANCE LIGHT 5	29-10-24.455N 090-56-37.747W	Fl G 2.5s	17	4	SG on pile.	Ra ref.
18000	- Buoy 10	29-10-49.118N 090-56-07.278W				Red nun.	
18005	- Day beacon 11	29-11-14.586N 090-55-40.903W				SG on pile.	Ra ref.
18010	- Buoy 12	29-11-50.299N 090-55-12.250W				Red nun.	
18015	- Buoy 13	29-12-07.354N 090-54-49.327W				Green can.	

Light List corrected through LNM week: 01/18

(1) No.	(2) Name and Location	(3) Position	(4) Characteristic	(5) Height	(6) Range	(7) Structure	(8) Remarks
		LOUISIANA - Eighth District					
	ISLES DERNIERES TO POINT AU FER (Chart 11356)						
	Bayou Grand Caillou						
18020	- Buoy 15	29-12-25.027N 090-54-43.080W				Green can.	
18025	- Buoy 16	29-12-24.610N 090-54-30.910W				Red nun.	
18030	- Buoy 17	29-12-39.582N 090-54-28.962W				Green can.	
18035	- Buoy 18	29-12-36.420N 090-54-20.640W				Red nun.	
18040	- Buoy 18A	29-12-34.638N 090-53-55.826W				Red nun.	
18045	- Buoy 19	29-12-42.738N 090-54-08.881W				Green can.	
18050	- Buoy 20	29-12-28.917N 090-53-40.160W				Red nun.	
18055	- Buoy 22	29-12-19.740N 090-53-21.240W				Red nun.	
18060	- Buoy 22A	29-12-13.109N 090-53-00.337W				Red nun.	
18065	- Day beacon 23	29-12-22.212N 090-52-49.482W				SG on pile.	Ra ref.
18070	- Day beacon 24	29-12-50.285N 090-52-30.829W				TR on pile.	
18075	- Buoy 25	29-12-57.594N 090-51-55.836W				Green can.	
18080	- Day beacon 27	29-13-07.242N 090-51-32.208W				SG on pile.	Ra ref.
18085	- Buoy 28	29-13-03.362N 090-51-24.150W				Red nun.	
18090	- Buoy 29	29-13-04.365N 090-51-02.065W				Green can.	
18095	- Day beacon 31	29-13-07.809N 090-50-54.333W				SG on pile.	Ra ref.
	TIMBALIER AND TERREBONNE BAYS (Chart 11357)						
	Bayou Grand Caillou						
18100	- Buoy 32	29-13-14.492N 090-50-38.146W				Red nun.	
18105	- Buoy 33	29-13-21.900N 090-49-58.434W				Green can.	
18110	- Buoy 35	29-13-16.683N 090-49-44.396W				Green can.	
18115	- Buoy 36	29-13-13.470N 090-49-42.066W				Red nun.	
18120	- Day beacon 39	29-13-23.808N 090-49-08.923W				SG on pile.	Ra ref.
18125	- Day beacon 40	29-13-33.620N 090-48-51.374W				TR on pile.	Ra ref.
18130	- Buoy 41	29-13-32.079N 090-48-59.078W				Green can.	
18135	- Day beacon 43	29-15-19.284N 090-47-27.550W				SG on pile.	Ra ref.
18140	- Day beacon 44	29-15-16.177N 090-47-17.486W				TR on pile.	Ra ref.
18145	- Day beacon 46	29-15-08.549N 090-46-54.582W				TR on pile.	Ra ref.
18155	- Day beacon 48	29-15-19.916N 090-46-39.131W				TR on pile.	Ra ref.
18160	- Day beacon 50	29-15-38.316N 090-46-06.299W				TR on pile.	Ra ref.
18165	- Day beacon 52	29-16-28.670N 090-46-00.094W				TR on pile.	Ra ref.
18170	- Day beacon 54	29-17-00.341N 090-45-59.244W				TR on pile.	Ra ref.

(1) No.	(2) Name and Location	(3) Position	(4) Characteristic	(5) Height	(6) Range	(7) Structure	(8) Remarks
			LOUISIANA - Eighth District				
	ISLES DERNIERES TO POINT AU FER (Chart 11356)						
18172	TEXAS GAS TRANSMISSION PIPELINE LIGHTS (6)	29-10-32.290N 090-58-37.420W	Fl Y 2.5s			Marks pipeline crossing.	Private aid.
18175	CAILLOU BAY BOAT LANDING LIGHT	29-10-40.000N 090-58-59.000W	Fl W 2.5s	6		On wharf.	Private aid.
18180	GRAND BAYOU DULARGE OBSTRUCTION LIGHT WR2	29-11-38.772N 090-58-18.134W	Q R	17	3	TR on pile.	
18185	Grand Bayou Du Large Shoal Buoy 3	29-11-58.846N 090-57-27.994W				Green can.	
18190	GRAND BAYOU DULARGE OBSTRUCTION LIGHT WR4	29-12-55.113N 090-56-57.662W	Q R	17	3	TR on pile.	
18195	U.S. GEOLOGICAL SURVEY SCIENTIFIC MONITORING PLATFORM LIGHT (TP)	29-15-08.000N 090-55-18.000W	Fl Y 2.5s	37		On pipe.	Private aid.
18200	LAKE MECHANT PIPELINE LIGHT	29-16-24.000N 090-56-36.000W	Fl Y 2.5s	12		NW on pile cluster.	Private aid.
	Bayou Dularge						
18205	- FLOODGATE LIGHT A	29-20-09.211N 090-50-35.351W	Fl R 2.5s	12		On pile.	Private aid.
18210	- FLOODGATE LIGHT B	29-20-08.982N 090-50-36.669W	Fl G 2.5s	9		On pile.	Private aid.
18215	- FLOODGATE LIGHT C	29-20-08.319N 090-50-36.174W	Fl R 2.5s	9		On pile.	Private aid.
18220	- FLOODGATE TRAFFIC LIGHT	29-20-09.124N 090-50-34.976W		12		On pile.	Traffic light displays Fl R 2.5s when closed. Displays Fl G 2.5s when open. Private aid.
18225	- FLOODGATE LIGHT D	29-20-09.783N 090-50-35.067W	Fl G 2.5s	9		On pile.	Private aid.
18230	- FLOODGATE LIGHT E	29-20-09.287N 090-50-34.696W	Fl R 2.5s	9		On pile.	Private aid.
18232	FALGOUT CANAL FLOODGATE LIGHT 1	29-24-57.830N 090-47-23.510W	Fl G 2.5s			Marks port side of floodgate.	Private aid.
18232.03	FALGOUT CANAL FLOODGATE LIGHT 2	29-24-56.090N 090-47-23.840W	Fl R 2.5s			Marks starboard side of floodgate.	Private aid.
18232.06	FALGOUT CANAL FLOODGATE LIGHT 3	29-24-56.490N 090-47-18.110W	Fl G 2.5s			Marks port side of floodgate.	Private aid.
18232.09	FALGOUT CANAL FLOODGATE LIGHT 4	29-24-54.800N 090-47-18.660W	Fl R 2.5s			Marks port side of floodgate.	Private aid.
	ISLES DERNIERES TO POINT AU FER (Chart 11356)						
18235	FINA PIPELINE LIGHT A	29-25-03.130N 090-47-54.410W	Fl Y 2.5s	5		NW on platform. worded: DO NOT ANCHOR OR DREDGE.	Private aid.
	NEW ORLEANS TO CALCASIEU RIVER (Chart 11352)						
	Lake Decade						
18240	LAKE DE CADE LIGHT 2	29-24-54.000N 090-50-00.000W	Fl R 4s	15		TR on dolphin.	Private aid.
18245	LAKE DE CADE LIGHT 28	29-22-48.000N 090-54-12.000W	Fl R 4s	15		TR on dolphin.	Private aid.
	Jug Lake						
18250	- Danger Day beacons(4)	29-22-27.000N 090-56-07.000W				NW on pile worded DANGER DO NOT PROCEED.	Marks weir. Private aid.
18255	- Danger Day beacons (4)	29-22-47.000N 090-56-25.000W				NW on pile worded DANGER DO NOT PROCEED.	Marks weir. Private aid.
18260	- Danger Day beacons (4)	29-22-39.000N 090-57-25.000W				NW on pile worded DANGER DO NOT PROCEED.	Marks weir. Private aid.
18265	Bayou La Loutre Danger Day beacons (8)	29-22-28.000N 090-57-25.000W				NW on pile worded DANGER PROCEED WITH CAUTION.	Marks Riprap. Private aid.
	South Louisiana Electric Co Op						
18270	- LIGHT A	29-21-01.699N 090-57-26.960W	Q W	15		On power pole.	Private aid.

Light List corrected through LNM week: 01/18

(1) No.	(2) Name and Location	(3) Position	(4) Characteristic	(5) Height	(6) Range	(7) Structure	(8) Remarks
			LOUISIANA - Eighth District				
	NEW ORLEANS TO CALCASIEU RIVER (Chart 11352)						
	Jug Lake						
	South Louisiana Electric Co Op						
18275	- LIGHT B	29-20-31.614N 090-56-57.120W	Q W	15		On power pole.	Private aid.
18280	- LIGHT C	29-20-34.924N 090-56-58.066W	Q W	15		On power pole.	Private aid.
18285	- LIGHT D	29-20-48.088N 090-57-08.258W	Q W	15		On power pole.	Private aid.
18290	- LIGHT E	29-20-53.720N 090-57-19.433W	Q W	15		On power pole.	Private aid.
18295	- LIGHT F	29-20-55.873N 090-57-21.700W	Q W	15		On power pole.	Private aid.
18300	- LIGHT G	29-21-49.787N 090-57-47.403W	Q W	15		On power pole.	Private aid.
18305	- LIGHT H	29-22-07.077N 090-58-23.557W	Q W	15		On power pole.	Private aid.
18310	- LIGHT I	29-21-48.544N 090-59-15.922W	Q W	15		On power pole.	Private aid.
18315	- LIGHT J	29-21-50.729N 090-59-05.674W	Q W	15		On power pole.	Private aid.
	NEW ORLEANS TO CALCASIEU RIVER (Chart 11352)						
18320	UNOCAL PIPELINE OBSTRUCTION LIGHT	29-22-06.000N 090-58-25.000W	Fl G 2.5s				Private aid.
18323	Lafourche-Terrebonne Soil & Conservation District Information Marks (2)	29-24-09.484N 090-56-35.115W				Marks debris barrier on Superior Canal.	Private aid.
	Bayou Decade						
18325	- LIGHT 1	29-21-59.000N 090-57-44.000W	Fl G 2.5s	12		SG on pile.	Marks weir. Private aid.
18330	- Danger Day beacons 4	29-21-59.100N 090-57-44.100W				NW on pile worded DANGER OBSTRUCTION PROCEED WITH CAUTION.	Marks weir. Private aid.
18335	- LIGHT 2	29-21-59.000N 090-57-44.100W	Fl R 2.5s	12		TR on pile.	Marks weir. Private aid.
18340	- Danger Day beacons 6	29-22-07.000N 090-58-33.000W				NW on pile worded DANGER DO NOT PROCEED.	Marks weir. Private aid.
18345	Voss Canal Danger Day beacons(8)	29-21-58.000N 090-59-32.000W				NW on pile worded DANGER PROCEED WITH CAUTION.	Marks riprap. Private aid.
	ISLES DERNIERES TO POINT AU FER (Chart 11356)						
18355	USACE BAY WALLACE METERING STATION LIGHT	29-37-29.000N 091-01-25.900W	Fl Y 2.5s			On pile.	Private aid.
18360	LSU PLATFORM LIGHT OB1	29-14-14.400N 091-08-01.800W	Q W	12		On platform.	Private aid.
	POINT AU FER TO MARSH ISLAND (Chart 11351)						
	East Atchafalaya Bay						
18365	- Channel Day beacon 2	29-24-36.000N 091-13-00.000W				TR on pile.	Private aid.
18370	- Channel Day beacon 4	29-24-36.000N 091-13-00.000W				TR on pile.	Private aid.
18375	- Channel Day beacon 10	29-25-24.000N 091-12-48.000W				TR on pile.	Private aid.
18380	- Channel Day beacon 12	29-25-30.000N 091-12-48.000W				TR on pile.	Private aid.
18385	- Channel Day beacon 14	29-25-36.000N 091-12-54.000W				TR on pile.	Private aid.
18390	- Channel Day beacon 16	29-25-42.000N 091-13-00.000W				TR on pile.	Private aid.
18395	- Channel Day beacon 18	29-25-53.200N 091-13-02.800W				TR on pile.	Private aid.
18400	- Channel Day beacon 20	29-26-00.000N 091-13-12.000W				TR on pile.	Private aid.

Light List corrected through LNM week: 01/18

(1) No.	(2) Name and Location	(3) Position	(4) Characteristic	(5) Height	(6) Range	(7) Structure	(8) Remarks
			LOUISIANA - Eighth District				
	POINT AU FER TO MARSH ISLAND (Chart 11351)						
	East Atchafalaya Bay						
18405	- Channel Day beacon 22	29-26-06.000N 091-13-18.000W				TR on pile.	Private aid.
18410	- Channel Day beacon 24	29-26-06.000N 091-13-24.000W				TR on pile.	Private aid.
18415	- Channel Day beacon 26	29-26-06.000N 091-13-30.000W				TR on pile.	Private aid.
18420	- Channel Day beacon 28	29-26-06.000N 091-13-42.000W				TR on pile.	Private aid.
18425	- Channel Day beacon 30	29-26-06.000N 091-13-48.000W				TR on pile.	Private aid.
18430	- Channel Day beacon 32	29-26-06.000N 091-14-00.000W				TR on pile.	Private aid.
18435	- Channel Day beacon 34	29-26-06.000N 091-14-06.000W				TR on pile.	Private aid.
18440	- Channel Day beacon 38	29-26-20.200N 091-14-20.800W				TR on pile.	Private aid.
18445	- Channel Day beacon 40	29-26-24.000N 091-14-24.000W				TR on pile.	Private aid.
18450	- Channel Day beacon 42	29-26-24.000N 091-14-30.000W				TR on pile.	Private aid.
18455	- Channel Day beacon 44	29-26-30.000N 091-14-36.000W				TR on pile.	Private aid.
18460	- Channel Day beacon 46	29-26-30.000N 091-14-48.000W				TR on pile.	Private aid.
18465	- Channel Day beacon 48	29-26-36.000N 091-14-54.000W				TR on pile.	Private aid.
18470	- Channel Day beacon 50	29-26-36.000N 091-15-06.000W				TR on pile.	Private aid.
18475	- Channel Day beacon 52	29-26-36.000N 091-15-18.000W				TR on pile.	Private aid.
18480	- Channel Day beacon 54	29-26-36.000N 091-15-24.000W				TR on pile.	Private aid.
18485	- Channel Day beacon 58	29-26-46.000N 091-15-29.200W				TR on pile.	Private aid.
18490	- Channel Day beacon 59	29-26-48.000N 091-15-30.000W				SG on pile.	Private aid.
18495	- Channel Day beacon 60	29-26-54.000N 091-15-24.000W				TR on pile.	Private aid.
18500	- Channel Day beacon 64	29-27-12.000N 091-15-30.000W				TR on pile.	Private aid.
18505	- Channel Day beacon 66	29-27-24.000N 091-15-36.000W				TR on pile.	Private aid.
18510	- Channel Day beacon 74	29-27-56.800N 091-15-49.600W				TR on pile.	Private aid.
18515	- Channel Day beacon 76	29-28-06.400N 091-15-53.800W				TR on pile.	Private aid.
	Atchafalaya Channel						
18520	- *Lighted Buoy 1*	29-10-43.054N 091-33-21.796W	Fl G 2.5s		4	Green.	
18525	- *Lighted Buoy 2*	29-10-37.322N 091-33-14.219W	Fl R 2.5s		4	Red.	
18530	- *Lighted Buoy 3*	29-11-29.818N 091-32-39.585W	Fl G 4s		4	Green.	
18535	- Buoy 4	29-11-27.543N 091-32-32.971W				Red nun.	
18540	- Buoy 5	29-12-16.960N 091-31-57.559W				Green can.	
18545	- Buoy 6	29-12-13.311N 091-31-52.150W				Red nun.	
18550	- *Lighted Buoy 7*	29-13-04.361N 091-31-15.655W	Fl G 2.5s		4	Green.	
18555	- Buoy 8	29-13-00.631N 091-31-10.429W				Red nun.	
18560	- Buoy 9	29-13-53.629N 091-30-32.296W				Green can.	

Light List corrected through LNM week: 01/18

(1) No.	(2) Name and Location	(3) Position	(4) Characteristic	(5) Height	(6) Range	(7) Structure	(8) Remarks
		LOUISIANA - Eighth District					
	POINT AU FER TO MARSH ISLAND (Chart 11351)						
	Atchafalaya Channel						
18565	- Lighted Buoy 10	29-13-50.755N 091-30-27.198W	Fl R 4s		3	Red.	
18570	- Lighted Buoy 11	29-14-42.213N 091-29-49.334W	Fl G 4s		4	Green.	
18575	- Buoy 12	29-14-38.775N 091-29-44.927W				Red nun.	
18580	- Buoy 13	29-15-28.790N 091-29-08.097W				Green can.	
18585	- Lighted Buoy 15	29-16-17.399N 091-28-25.083W	Fl G 6s		4	Green.	
18590	- Lighted Buoy 14	29-15-26.065N 091-29-02.974W	Fl R 2.5s		3	Red.	
18595	- Buoy 16	29-16-13.059N 091-28-20.853W				Red nun.	
18600	- Day beacon 17	29-17-04.597N 091-27-43.230W				SG on pile.	Ra ref.
18605	USACE TEST PLATFORM A LIGHT	29-16-35.580N 091-27-56.100W	Fl Y 2.5s	12		NY on platform.	Private aid.
18610	- LIGHT 18	29-17-00.378N 091-27-37.754W	Fl R 4s	17	3	TR on pile.	Ra ref.
18615	- LIGHT 19	29-17-52.042N 091-27-00.621W	Fl G 2.5s	17	3	SG on dolphin.	Ra ref.
18620	- Day beacon 20	29-17-48.097N 091-26-55.120W				TR on dolphin.	Ra ref.
18625.01	- Day beacon 21	29-18-40.355N 091-26-18.323W				SG on dolphin.	Ra ref.
18630	- LIGHT 22	29-18-35.328N 091-26-13.476W	Fl R 2.5s	17	3	TR on pile.	Ra ref.
18632	PORT OF MORGAN CITY SPECIAL LIGHT A	29-19-05.090N 091-25-47.160W	Fl Y 2.5s			Marks scientific data monitoring platform.	Private aid.
18632.01	PORT OF MORGAN CITY SPECIAL LIGHT B	29-22-23.100N 091-23-02.040W	Fl Y 2.5s			Marks scientific data monitoring platform.	Private aid.
18635	USACE TEST PLATFORM B LIGHT	29-19-15.500N 091-25-25.500W	Fl Y 2.5s	12		NY on platform.	Private aid.
18640	- LIGHT 24	29-19-22.697N 091-25-31.187W	Fl R 4s	17	3	TR on pile.	Ra ref.
18645	- LIGHT 23	29-19-26.500N 091-25-38.576W	Fl G 4s	17	4	SG on pile.	Ra ref.
18650	USACE TEST PLATFORM C LIGHT	29-20-33.400N 091-25-56.900W	Fl Y 2.5s	12		NY on platform.	Private aid.
18655	- LIGHT 25 100 feet outside channel limit.	29-20-13.711N 091-24-56.934W	Fl G 6s	17	4	SG on pile.	Ra ref.
18660	- LIGHT 26	29-20-08.676N 091-24-50.160W	Fl R 6s	17	4	TR on pile.	Ra ref.
18665	- LIGHT 27 100 feet outside channel limit.	29-21-01.245N 091-24-14.546W	Fl G 4s	17	4	SG on pile.	Ra ref.
18670	USACE TEST PLATFORM D LIGHT	29-20-36.500N 091-23-46.700W	Fl Y 2.5s	12		NY on platform.	Private aid.
18675	USACE TEST PLATFORM E LIGHT	29-21-14.200N 091-24-40.700W	Fl Y 2.5s	12		NY on platform.	Private aid.
18680	- LIGHT 28	29-20-56.519N 091-24-07.746W	Fl R 4s	17	4	TR on pile.	Ra ref.
18685	- LIGHT 29 100 feet outside channel limit.	29-21-37.074N 091-23-42.456W	Fl G 2.5s	17	3	SG on pile.	Ra ref.
18690	- LIGHT 30	29-21-33.860N 091-23-34.523W	Fl R 2.5s	17	3	TR on pile.	Ra ref.
18700	- LIGHT 33	29-22-19.830N 091-23-03.710W	Fl G 4s	17	4	SG on pile.	

Light List corrected through LNM week: 01/18

(1) No.	(2) Name and Location	(3) Position	(4) Characteristic	(5) Height	(6) Range	(7) Structure	(8) Remarks
		LOUISIANA - Eighth District					
	POINT AU FER TO MARSH ISLAND (Chart 11351)						
	Atchafalaya Channel						
18705	- LIGHT 34	29-22-15.782N 091-22-57.799W	Fl R 4s	17	3	TR on pile.	Ra ref.
18710	- LIGHT 35 125 feet outside channel limit.	29-23-04.461N 091-22-27.125W	Fl G 2.5s	17	3	SG on pile.	Ra ref.
18715	- LIGHT 36 125 feet outside channel limit.	29-23-00.030N 091-22-20.545W	Fl R 2.5s	17	3	TR on pile.	Ra ref.
18720	- LIGHT 37 125 feet outside channel limit.	29-23-45.632N 091-21-48.356W	Fl G 4s	17	4	SG on pile.	Ra ref.
18725	- LIGHT 38 125 feet outside channel limit.	29-23-40.331N 091-21-42.023W	Fl R 4s	17	3	TR on pile.	Ra ref.
18730	- LIGHT 40 125 feet outside channel limit.	29-24-21.739N 091-21-06.821W	Fl R 6s	17	4	TR on pile.	Ra ref.
18735	- LIGHT 39 125 feet outside channel limit.	29-24-34.176N 091-21-05.841W	Fl G 6s	17	4	SG on pile.	Ra ref.
18740	- LIGHT 41 125 feet outside channel limit.	29-25-04.484N 091-20-40.840W	Fl G 4s	17	4	SG on pile.	Ra ref.
18745	- LIGHT 42 125 feet outside channel limit.	29-25-00.715N 091-20-34.424W	Fl R 4s	17	3	TR on pile.	Ra ref.
18750	- LIGHT 43 125 feet outside channel limit.	29-25-48.763N 091-20-02.014W	Fl G 2.5s	17	3	SG on pile.	Ra ref.
18755	- LIGHT 44 125 feet outside channel limit.	29-25-33.401N 091-20-05.615W	Fl R 2.5s	17	3	TR on pile.	Ra ref.
18760	- LIGHT 45	29-26-18.096N 091-19-37.732W	Fl G 4s	17	4	SG on pile.	Ra ref.
18765	- LIGHT 46	29-26-16.001N 091-19-26.764W	Fl R 4s	17	3	TR on pile.	Ra ref.
	Amerada Pass Channel						
18770	- Day beacon 2	29-26-25.800N 091-19-45.400W				TR on pile.	Private aid.
18775	- Day beacon 4	29-26-28.800N 091-19-50.400W				TR on pile.	Private aid.
18780	- Day beacon 6	29-26-28.800N 091-19-56.400W				TR on pile.	Private aid.
18785	- Day beacon 8	29-26-31.800N 091-19-57.400W				TR on pile.	Private aid.
18790	- Day beacon 10	29-26-34.800N 091-19-58.400W				TR on pile.	Private aid.
18795	- Day beacon 11	29-26-40.800N 091-19-59.400W				SG on pile.	Private aid.
18800	- Day beacon 12	29-26-58.800N 091-20-06.400W				TR on pile.	Private aid.
18805	- Day beacon 13	29-26-49.800N 091-20-03.400W				SG on pile.	Private aid.
18810	NOAA ATCHAFALAYA BAY TIDE MONITORING PLATFORM LIGHT	29-26-58.540N 091-20-17.150W	Fl Y 2.5s	25		On platform.	Private aid.
	Atchafalaya Channel						
18815	- LIGHT 47 125 feet outside channel limit.	29-26-38.651N 091-19-09.327W	Q G	17	3	SG on pile.	Ra ref.
18820	- LIGHT 48 125 feet outside channel limit.	29-26-31.400N 091-19-02.456W	Q R	17	3	TR on pile.	Ra ref.
18825	- LIGHT 51 125 feet outside channel limit.	29-26-51.484N 091-18-29.677W	Fl G 2.5s	17	3	SG on pile.	Ra ref.

Light List corrected through LNM week: 01/18

(1) No.	(2) Name and Location	(3) Position	(4) Characteristic	(5) Height	(6) Range	(7) Structure	(8) Remarks
	LOUISIANA - Eighth District						
	POINT AU FER TO MARSH ISLAND (Chart 11351)						
	Atchafalaya Channel						
18830	- LIGHT 52 200 yards, outside channel limit.	29-26-39.441N 091-18-36.373W	Fl R 2.5s	17	3	TR on pile.	Ra ref.
18835	- LIGHT 53	29-27-06.275N 091-17-55.623W	Fl G 4s	17	4	SG on pile.	Ra ref.
18840.01	- LIGHT 54	29-26-53.283N 091-17-48.459W	Fl R 4s	17	3	TR on pile.	Ra ref.
18846	- LIGHT 55	29-27-17.200N 091-17-31.203W	Fl G 6s	17	3	SG on pile.	Ra ref.
18850.01	- Day beacon 56	29-27-17.412N 091-17-02.323W				TR on pile.	Ra ref.
18856	- Day beacon 57	29-27-49.223N 091-17-03.556W				SG on pile.	Ra ref.
18861	- LIGHT 58	29-27-58.936N 091-16-32.698W	Fl R 6s	17	3	TR on pile.	Ra ref.
18865	- LIGHT 59	29-28-38.769N 091-16-39.428W	Fl G 2.5s	17	4	SG on pile.	Ra ref.
	Atchafalaya River						
18876	- LIGHT 2	29-28-46.811N 091-16-16.929W	Fl R 2.5s	17	3	TR on pile.	Ra ref.
18877	- LIGHT 3	29-29-12.053N 091-16-27.962W	Fl G 2.5s	17	3	SG on pile.	Ra ref.
18880	- LIGHT 4	29-29-37.033N 091-16-06.415W	Fl R 4s	17	3	TR on pile.	Ra ref.
18885	- LIGHT 5	29-29-59.980N 091-16-15.564W	Fl G 4s	17	3	SG on pile.	Ra ref.
18890	- LIGHT 6	29-30-12.636N 091-15-55.100W	Q R	17	3	TR on pile.	Ra ref.
18895	- LIGHT 7	29-30-36.977N 091-16-16.136W	Fl G 2.5s	17	4	SG on pile.	Ra ref.
18901	- LIGHT 9	29-32-04.973N 091-16-14.642W	Fl G 2.5s	17	3	SG on pile.	Ra ref.
18906	- LIGHT 10	29-32-05.788N 091-15-56.193W	Fl R 2.5s	17	3	TR on pile.	Ra ref.
18911	- LIGHT 8	29-31-25.038N 091-16-04.025W	Fl R 2.5s	17	3	TR on pile.	Ra ref.
18915	- LIGHT 11	29-32-20.703N 091-16-01.882W	Fl G 4s	17	3	SG on pile.	Ra ref.
18921	- LIGHT 12	29-32-21.840N 091-15-39.555W	Fl R 6s	17	3	TR on pile.	Ra ref.
18963	- JUNCTION LIGHT C	29-32-30.307N 091-14-53.843W	Fl (2+1)R 6s	17	3	JR on pile.	Ra ref.
	Avoca Island Cutoff Channel						
18970.01	- Day beacon 1	29-32-18.790N 091-14-44.891W				SG on pile.	Ra ref.
18973	- LIGHT 2	29-32-12.017N 091-14-47.013W	Fl R 2.5s	17	3	TR on pile.	Ra ref.
18975	- Day beacon 4	29-33-15.952N 091-12-30.856W				TR on pile.	Ra ref.
18980	- Day beacon 6	29-34-02.074N 091-12-11.154W				TR on pile.	Ra ref.
	NEW ORLEANS TO CALCASIEU RIVER (Chart 11352)						
	Atchafalaya River						
	Avoca Island Cutoff Channel						
18985	- LIGHT 7	29-35-39.038N 091-11-43.870W	Fl G 4s	17	4	SG on pile.	Ra ref.
18990	- Day beacon 8	29-35-44.908N 091-10-24.483W				TR on pile.	Ra ref.

Light List corrected through LNM week: 01/18

(1) No.	(2) Name and Location	(3) Position	(4) Characteristic	(5) Height	(6) Range	(7) Structure	(8) Remarks
	**LOUISIANA - Eighth District**						

NEW ORLEANS TO CALCASIEU RIVER (Chart 11352)
Atchafalaya River
Avoca Island Cutoff Channel

(1) No.	(2) Name and Location	(3) Position	(4) Characteristic	(5) Height	(6) Range	(7) Structure	(8) Remarks
18995	- Day beacon 9	29-35-40.226N 091-09-59.183W				SG on pile.	Ra ref.
19000	- Day beacon 10	29-35-33.234N 091-09-57.058W				TR on pile.	Ra ref.
19005	- LIGHT 11	29-35-42.408N 091-09-33.180W	Fl G 2.5s	17	3	SG on pile.	Ra ref.
19010	- Day beacon 12	29-35-39.602N 091-09-25.812W				TR on pile.	Ra ref.
19015	- LIGHT 13	29-36-15.466N 091-09-10.371W	Fl G 4s	17	4	SG on pile.	Ra ref.
19020	- Day beacon 14	29-36-23.226N 091-08-43.887W				TR on pile.	Ra ref.
19025	- LIGHT 15	29-36-37.670N 091-08-23.806W	Fl G 6s	17	4	SG on pile.	Ra. ref.
19027	BAYOU CHENE LIGHT 1	29-37-21.724N 091-05-23.941W	Fl G 2.5s			Marks the northwest fender dolphin.	Private aid.
19027.01	BAYOU CHENE LIGHT 2	29-37-17.413N 091-05-23.787W	Fl R 2.5s			Marks the southwest fender dolphin.	Private aid.
19027.02	BAYOU CHENE LIGHT 3	29-37-21.795N 091-05-21.952W	Fl G 2.5s			Marks the northeast fender dolphin.	Private aid.
19027.03	BAYOU CHENE LIGHT 4	29-37-17.472N 091-05-21.771W	Fl R 2.5s			Marks the southeast fender dolphin.	Private aid.
19027.04	BAYOU CHENE NORTH DANGER LIGHT	29-37-22.090N 091-05-22.770W	Fl W 2.5s			Marks the north rock wall.	Private aid.
19027.05	BAYOU CHENE SOUTH DANGER LIGHT	29-37-17.060N 091-05-22.770W	Fl W 2.5s			Marks the south rock wall.	Private aid.

POINT AU FER TO MARSH ISLAND (Chart 11351)
Atchafalaya River
Avoca Island Cutoff Channel

(1) No.	(2) Name and Location	(3) Position	(4) Characteristic	(5) Height	(6) Range	(7) Structure	(8) Remarks
19030	BURKE CANAL 7 BARRACADE LIGHT	29-36-06.000N 091-08-06.000W	Fl W 2.5s			On pontoon gate.	Private aid.

Atchafalaya River

(1) No.	(2) Name and Location	(3) Position	(4) Characteristic	(5) Height	(6) Range	(7) Structure	(8) Remarks
19035.01	- LIGHT 13	29-32-47.783N 091-14-56.665W	Fl G 6s	17	3	SG on pile.	Ra ref.
19040.01	- Day beacon 15	29-33-05.511N 091-14-23.608W				SG on pile.	Ra ref.
19045.01	- Day beacon 17	29-33-26.620N 091-14-08.037W				SG on pile.	Ra ref.
19050.01	- LIGHT 16	29-33-20.911N 091-13-54.202W	Fl R 2.5s	17	3	TR on pile.	Ra ref.
19055.01	- LIGHT 19	29-34-13.992N 091-13-51.459W	Fl G 4s	17	3	SG on pile.	Ra ref.
19060.01	- LIGHT 21	29-34-35.321N 091-13-53.534W	Fl G 2.5s	17	3	SG on pile.	Ra ref.
19065.01	- LIGHT 20	29-34-25.408N 091-13-38.916W	Fl R 4s	17	3	TR on pile.	Ra ref.

Bayou Shaffer

(1) No.	(2) Name and Location	(3) Position	(4) Characteristic	(5) Height	(6) Range	(7) Structure	(8) Remarks
19075	- ENTRANCE LIGHT 2	29-35-07.930N 091-13-06.654W	Fl R 2.5s	17	3	TR on pile.	Ra ref.
19080	VECTOR ENERGY CO. LOADING DOCK LIGHT	29-35-23.600N 091-12-55.300W	Fl G 2.5s	14		Dock.	Private aid.
19085	- *Lighted Wreck Buoy WR1*	29-40-30.689N 091-12-11.086W	Q G		3	Green.	

Atchafalaya River

(1) No.	(2) Name and Location	(3) Position	(4) Characteristic	(5) Height	(6) Range	(7) Structure	(8) Remarks
19090.01	- Day beacon 23	29-35-03.403N 091-13-57.934W				SG on pile.	Ra ref.

Light List corrected through LNM week: 01/18

(1) No.	(2) Name and Location	(3) Position	(4) Characteristic	(5) Height	(6) Range	(7) Structure	(8) Remarks
\multicolumn{8}{c}{LOUISIANA - Eighth District}

LOUISIANA - Eighth District

POINT AU FER TO MARSH ISLAND (Chart 11351)
Atchafalaya River

(1) No.	(2) Name and Location	(3) Position	(4) Characteristic	(5) Height	(6) Range	(7) Structure	(8) Remarks
19095.01	- LIGHT 24	29-35-30.640N 091-13-59.431W	Fl R 4s	17	3	TR on pile.	Ra ref.
19101	- LIGHT 25	29-35-34.029N 091-14-22.020W	Fl G 4s	17	3	SG on pile.	Ra ref.
19105.01	- LIGHT 26	29-36-30.450N 091-14-48.359W	Fl R 2.5s	17	3	TR-NW on pile.	VTS Berwick check point sign. Day beacon on same structure as light. Ra ref.
19108	- LIGHT 27	29-36-42.207N 091-15-14.599W	Fl G 6s	17	3	SG on pile.	Ra ref.
19111	- LIGHT 29	29-37-32.029N 091-15-31.776W	Fl G 4s	17	3	SG on pile.	Ra ref.
19115.01	- LIGHT 28	29-37-29.193N 091-15-21.967W	Q R	17	3	TR on pile.	Ra ref.
19125.01	- Day beacon 31	29-37-53.265N 091-14-49.807W				SG on pile.	Ra ref.
19131	- LIGHT 33	29-38-01.127N 091-14-38.330W	Fl G 2.5s	17	3	SG on pile.	Ra ref.
19136	- LIGHT 34	29-38-19.499N 091-14-17.933W	Fl R 4s	17	3	TR on pile.	Ra ref.
19140.01	- LIGHT 36	29-39-15.691N 091-14-26.161W	Fl R 2.5s	17	3	TR on pile.	Ra ref.

MORGAN CITY TO PORT ALLEN (Chart 11354)

(1) No.	(2) Name and Location	(3) Position	(4) Characteristic	(5) Height	(6) Range	(7) Structure	(8) Remarks
19145 35190	LITTLE WAX BAYOU JUNCTION LIGHT A	29-39-38.139N 091-14-32.559W	Fl (2+1)G 6s	30	5	JG-TY on dolphin.	
19150 35195	LITTLE WAX BAYOU LIGHT 1	29-39-24.390N 091-14-48.500W	Q G	17	4	SG-SY on pile.	Ra ref.
19155 35170	BERWICK BAY RANGE FRONT A LIGHT	29-41-10.099N 091-12-37.364W	Q R	19		KRW on skeleton tower on piles.	Visible from 054.6° to 215.6°.
19160 35175	BERWICK BAY RANGE REAR A LIGHT 139 yards, 160.6° from front light.	29-41-06.138N 091-12-35.823W	Iso R 6s	28		KRW on skeleton tower on piles.	Visible from 147.6° to 172.6°.
19165 35165	BERWICK LIGHT	29-41-39.000N 091-13-03.000W	Fl W 6s	45		Red tapered tower.	Private aid.
19170 35180	BERWICK BAY BRIDGE APPROACH DANGER RANGE FRONT LIGHT	29-41-46.704N 091-12-54.837W	Q Y	64		KGR-I on west side bridge abutment.	Visible downbound only. Range marks the western boundary of the suggested downbound course for approaching the bridges. NOTE: Range is not to be steered on.
19175 35185	BERWICK BAY BRIDGE APPROACH DANGER RANGE REAR LIGHT	29-41-43.612N 091-12-53.194W	Iso Y 6s	86		KGR-I on west side bridge abutment.	Visible downbound only. NOTE: Range is not to be steered on.
19180 35155	CONRAD DRYDOCK LIGHTS	29-42-00.000N 091-13-00.000W	Fl R 2.5s	25		On drydock and dolphin.	Private aid.
19185 35150	Berwick Locks Buoy 1	29-42-50.101N 091-13-21.841W				Green can with yellow triangle.	
19190	Berwick Lock Day beacon	29-43-00.636N 091-13-22.730W				NW on pile.	VTS Berwick check point sign.
19195	Drews Island Shoal Buoy 2	29-43-21.166N 091-12-54.160W				Red nun.	
19200	VALERO REFINING DOCK LIGHTS (2)	30-31-50.000N 091-44-35.000W	Fl G 2.5s	7		On dolphins.	Private aid.
19205	STOUTS POINT LIGHT 1	29-44-41.919N 091-13-50.256W	Fl G 4s	17	4	SG on pile. NW on pile.	VTS Berwick check point sign. Day beacon on same structure as light. Ra ref.
19210	P&P OIL LOADING DOCK LIGHT A	30-16-11.000N 091-35-11.000W	Fl R 2.5s	14		On square platform.	Private aid.

171

(1) No.	(2) Name and Location	(3) Position	(4) Characteristic	(5) Height	(6) Range	(7) Structure	(8) Remarks
		LOUISIANA - Eighth District					
	MORGAN CITY TO PORT ALLEN (Chart 11354)						
19215	VALERO DOLPHIN LIGHTS (2)	30-30-36.000N 091-45-00.000W	Fl G 2.5s	30		On dolphins.	Private aid.
19220	PORT KROTZ SPRINGS DOLPHIN LIGHTS	30-31-17.400N 091-44-13.800W	Fl G 2.5s	8		On dolphins.	Private aid.
19225	AVOYELLES PARISH PORT COMMISSION UNLOADING DOCK LIGHTS (2)	30-57-47.870N 091-48-24.200W	Fl G 2.5s			On barge dock.	Private aid.
	Lower Atchafalaya River						
19245	BERWICK-BAYOU VISTA INTAKE LIGHT	29-43-26.000N 091-14-20.000W	Q G	10		On pile.	Private aid.
	POINT AU FER TO MARSH ISLAND (Chart 11351)						
	Atchafalaya Bay						
19250	- LIGHT 1	29-27-24.000N 091-20-45.000W	Fl G 6s	9		SG on pile.	Private aid.
19255	- Day beacon 3	29-27-19.000N 091-20-40.000W				SG on pile.	Private aid.
19260	- Day beacon 5	29-27-17.000N 091-20-36.000W				SG on pile.	Private aid.
19265	- Day beacon 7	29-27-15.000N 091-20-34.000W				SG on pile.	Private aid.
19270	- Day beacon 9	29-27-15.000N 091-20-31.000W				SG on pile.	Private aid.
19275	- Day beacon 11	29-27-10.000N 091-20-27.000W				SG on pile.	Private aid.
19280	- Day beacon 13	29-27-08.000N 091-20-24.000W				SG on pile.	Private aid.
	Belle Isle 340-29 Channel						
19285	- Day beacon 1	29-29-55.000N 091-23-30.000W				SG on pile.	Private aid.
19290	- Day beacon 3	29-29-55.000N 091-23-31.000W				SG on pile.	Private aid.
19295	- Day beacon 5	29-29-57.000N 091-23-26.000W				SG on pile.	Private aid.
19300	- Day beacon 7	29-29-57.000N 091-23-37.000W				SG on pile.	Private aid.
19305	- Day beacon 9	29-29-59.000N 091-23-42.000W				SG on pile.	Private aid.
19310	- Day beacon 11	29-29-59.000N 091-23-43.000W				SG on pile.	Private aid.
19315	- Day beacon 13	29-30-01.000N 091-23-47.000W				SG on pile.	Private aid.
19320	- Day beacon 15	29-30-01.000N 091-23-48.000W				SG on pile.	Private aid.
	Atchafalaya Bay						
19325	- Well 36 Day beacon 1	29-30-07.000N 091-23-49.000W				SG on pile.	Private aid.
19330	- Well 36 Day beacon 3	29-30-11.000N 091-23-52.000W				SG on pile.	Private aid.
19335	- Well 36 Day beacon 5	29-30-16.000N 091-23-55.000W				SG on pile.	Private aid.
19340	- Well 36 Day beacon 7	29-30-20.000N 091-23-57.000W				SG on pile.	Private aid.
19345	- Well 36 Day beacon 9	29-30-22.000N 091-23-59.000W				SG on pile.	Private aid.
	Belle Isle 340-39 Channel						
19350	- Day beacon 1	29-30-10.000N 091-23-39.000W				SG on pile.	Private aid.
19355	- Day beacon 3	29-30-10.000N 091-23-40.000W				SG on pile.	Private aid.
19360	- Day beacon 5	29-30-11.000N 091-23-44.000W				SG on pile.	Private aid.
19365	- Day beacon 7	29-30-12.000N 091-23-46.000W				SG on pile.	Private aid.
19370	- Day beacon 9	29-30-13.000N 091-23-51.000W				SG on pile.	Private aid.

Light List corrected through LNM week: 01/18

(1) No.	(2) Name and Location	(3) Position	(4) Characteristic	(5) Height	(6) Range	(7) Structure	(8) Remarks
	\multicolumn{7}{c}{LOUISIANA - Eighth District}						

POINT AU FER TO MARSH ISLAND (Chart 11351)
Atchafalaya Bay
Belle Isle Well 38

(1) No.	(2) Name and Location	(3) Position	(4) Characteristic	(5) Height	(6) Range	(7) Structure	(8) Remarks
19375	- Day beacon 1	29-29-56.000N 091-24-43.000W				SG on pile.	Private aid.
19380	- Day beacon 3	29-29-56.000N 091-24-42.000W				SG on pile.	Private aid.
19385	- Day beacon 5	29-29-59.000N 091-24-38.000W				SG on pile.	Private aid.
19390	- Day beacon 7	29-29-59.000N 091-24-37.000W				SG on pile.	Private aid.
19395	- Day beacon 9	29-30-01.000N 091-24-34.000W				SG on pile.	Private aid.
19400	- Day beacon 11	29-30-02.000N 091-24-33.000W				SG on pile.	Private aid.
19405	- Day beacon 13	29-30-04.000N 091-24-29.000W				SG on pile.	Private aid.
19410	- Day beacon 15	29-30-05.000N 091-24-28.000W				SG on pile.	Private aid.
19415	- Day beacon 17	29-30-07.000N 091-24-24.000W				SG on pile.	Private aid.
19420	- Day beacon 19	29-30-07.000N 091-24-23.000W				SG on pile.	Private aid.
19425	- Day beacon 21	29-30-09.000N 091-24-19.000W				SG on pile.	Private aid.
19430	- Day beacon 23	29-30-10.000N 091-24-18.000W				SG on pile.	Private aid.
19435	- Day beacon 25	29-30-12.000N 091-24-15.000W				SG on pile.	Private aid.
19440	- Day beacon 27	29-30-13.000N 091-24-14.000W				SG on pile.	Private aid.
19445	- Day beacon 29	29-30-15.000N 091-24-10.000W				SG on pile.	Private aid.
19450	- Day beacon 31	29-30-15.000N 091-24-09.000W				SG on pile.	Private aid.
19455	- Day beacon 33	29-30-17.000N 091-24-05.000W				SG on pile.	Private aid.
19460	- Day beacon 35	29-30-18.000N 091-24-04.000W				SG on pile.	Private aid.
19465	- Day beacon 37	29-30-20.000N 091-24-00.000W				SG on pile.	Private aid.

Atchafalaya Bay

(1) No.	(2) Name and Location	(3) Position	(4) Characteristic	(5) Height	(6) Range	(7) Structure	(8) Remarks
19470	- Well 24 Day beacon 1	29-30-26.500N 090-22-51.000W				SG on pile.	Private aid.
19475	- Well 24 Day beacon 2	29-30-28.000N 090-22-56.000W				TR on pile.	Private aid.
19480	- Well 24 Day beacon 3	29-30-26.000N 090-22-54.000W				SG on pile.	Private aid.
19485	- Well 24 Day beacon 5	29-30-25.500N 091-23-57.000W				SG on pile.	Private aid.
19490	- Well 24 Day beacon 7	29-30-25.000N 091-23-00.000W				SG on pile.	Private aid.
19495	- Well 24 Day beacon 9	29-30-24.000N 091-23-07.000W				SG on pile.	Private aid.
19500	- Well 35 Day beacon 9	29-30-28.000N 091-23-14.000W				SG on pile.	Private aid.
19505	- LIGHT 1	29-25-18.000N 091-35-46.000W	Q G	9		Pile structure.	Private aid.
19510	- LIGHT 11	29-27-57.000N 091-34-24.000W	Q G	10		On pile.	Private aid.
19515	- LIGHT 12	29-30-59.000N 091-33-27.000W	Q R	10		On pile.	Private aid.

NEW ORLEANS TO CALCASIEU RIVER (Chart 11345)
Lake Fausse Pointe Channel

(1) No.	(2) Name and Location	(3) Position	(4) Characteristic	(5) Height	(6) Range	(7) Structure	(8) Remarks
19520	- LIGHT 1	30-04-54.000N 091-37-47.000W	Fl W 4s	8		SG on dolphin.	Private aid.

Light List corrected through LNM week: 01/18

(1) No.	(2) Name and Location	(3) Position	(4) Characteristic	(5) Height	(6) Range	(7) Structure	(8) Remarks
		LOUISIANA - Eighth District					
	NEW ORLEANS TO CALCASIEU RIVER (Chart 11345)						
	Lake Fausse Pointe Channel						
19525	- Day beacon 2	30-00-59.740N 091-39-26.510W				TR on pile.	Private aid.
19530	- Day beacon 4	30-00-59.820N 091-39-25.090W				TR on pile.	Private aid.
19535	- Day beacon 6	30-01-10.230N 091-39-12.850W				TR on pile.	Private aid.
19540	- Day beacon 8	30-01-19.670N 091-39-02.830W				TR on pile.	Private aid.
19545	- Day beacon 10	30-01-20.050N 091-39-02.310W				TR on pile.	Private aid.
19550	- Day beacon 12	30-01-25.260N 091-38-53.990W				TR on pile.	Private aid.
19555	- Day beacon 14	30-01-28.660N 091-38-45.810W				TR on pile.	Private aid.
19560	- Day beacon 16	30-01-28.840N 091-38-45.290W				TR on pile.	Private aid.
19565	- Day beacon 18	30-01-32.040N 091-38-38.510W				TR on pile.	Private aid.
19570	- Day beacon 20	30-01-35.090N 091-38-26.690W				TR on pile.	Private aid.
19575	- Day beacon 22	30-01-35.400N 091-38-25.390W				TR on pile.	Private aid.
19580	- Day beacon 24	30-01-38.330N 091-38-13.330W				TR on pile.	Private aid.
19585	- Day beacon 26	30-01-38.800N 091-38-02.630W				TR on pile.	Private aid.
19590	- Day beacon 28	30-01-38.720N 091-38-02.050W				TR on pile.	Private aid.
19595	- Day beacon 30	30-01-36.600N 091-37-54.710W				TR on pile.	Private aid.
19600	- Day beacon 32	30-01-31.350N 091-37-46.090W				TR on pile.	Private aid.
19605	- Day beacon 34	30-01-31.060N 091-37-47.630W				TR on pile.	Private aid.
19610	- Day beacon 36	30-01-24.870N 091-37-35.350W				TR on pile.	Private aid.
19615	- Day beacon 38	30-01-24.440N 091-37-30.690W				TR on pile.	Private aid.
19620	- Day beacon 40	30-01-26.930N 091-37-25.690W				TR on pile.	Private aid.
19625	- Day beacon 42	30-01-27.280N 091-37-25.290W				TR on pile.	Private aid.
19630	- Day beacon 44	30-01-25.690N 091-37-11.010W				TR on pile.	Private aid.
19635	- Day beacon 46	30-01-47.130N 091-37-27.450W				TR on pile.	Private aid.
19640	- Day beacon 48	30-01-47.580N 091-37-27.690W				TR on pile.	Private aid.
19645	- Day beacon 50	30-01-58.330N 091-37-32.970W				TR on pile.	Private aid.
19650	- Day beacon 52	30-02-09.500N 091-37-38.310W				TR on pile.	Private aid.
19655	- Day beacon 54	30-02-09.950N 091-37-38.490W				TR on pile.	Private aid.
19660	- Day beacon 56	30-02-21.780N 091-37-41.370W				TR on pile.	Private aid.
19665	- Day beacon 58	30-02-33.000N 091-37-42.630W				TR on pile.	Private aid.
19670	- Day beacon 60	30-02-34.800N 091-37-42.870W				TR on pile.	Private aid.
19675	- Day beacon 62	30-02-48.920N 091-37-44.330W				TR on pile.	Private aid.
19680	- Day beacon 64	30-02-53.630N 091-37-43.310W				TR on pile.	Private aid.

Light List corrected through LNM week: 01/18

(1) No.	(2) Name and Location	(3) Position	(4) Characteristic	(5) Height	(6) Range	(7) Structure	(8) Remarks
			LOUISIANA - Eighth District				
	NEW ORLEANS TO CALCASIEU RIVER (Chart 11345)						
	Lake Fausse Pointe Channel						
19685	- Day beacon 66	30-02-54.150N 091-37-43.650W				TR on pile.	Private aid.
19690	- Day beacon 68	30-03-00.150N 091-37-40.630W				TR on pile.	Private aid.
19695	- Day beacon 70	30-03-06.800N 091-37-36.250W				TR on pile.	Private aid.
19700	- Day beacon 72	30-03-07.170N 091-37-35.970W				TR on pile.	Private aid.
19705	- Day beacon 74	30-03-14.730N 091-37-28.570W				TR on pile.	Private aid.
19710	- Day beacon 76	30-03-21.190N 091-37-20.670W				TR on pile.	Private aid.
19715	- Day beacon 78	30-03-21.510N 091-37-20.270W				TR on pile.	Private aid.
19720	- Day beacon 80	30-03-26.670N 091-37-15.430W				TR on pile.	Private aid.
19725	- Day beacon 82	30-03-31.690N 091-37-12.530W				TR on pile.	Private aid.
19730	- Day beacon 84	30-03-37.050N 091-37-11.270W				TR on pile.	Private aid.
19735	- Day beacon 86	30-03-37.150N 091-37-10.990W				TR on pile.	Private aid.
19740	- Day beacon 88	30-03-44.270N 091-37-10.830W				TR on pile.	Private aid.
19745	- Day beacon 90	30-03-55.310N 091-37-11.550W				TR on pile.	Private aid.
	Loreauville Canal						
19748	- FLOOD CONTROL STRUCTURE LIGHT 1	30-01-08.900N 091-40-49.100W	Fl G 2.5s			Marks southeast entry dolphin.	Private aid.
19748.01	- FLOOD CONTROL STRUCTURE LIGHT 2	30-01-09.700N 091-40-49.400W	Fl R 2.5s			Marks northeast entry dolphin.	Private aid.
19748.02	- FLOOD CONTROL STRUCTURE LIGHT 3	30-01-09.400N 091-40-52.500W	Fl G 2.5s			Marks southwest entry dolphin.	Private aid.
19748.03	- FLOOD CONTROL STRUCTURE LIGHT 4	30-01-10.000N 091-40-51.500W	Fl R 2.5s			Marks northwest entry dolphin.	Private aid.
	POINT AU FER TO MARSH ISLAND (Chart 11351)						
	East Cote Blanche Bay						
	Bayou Sale Channel						
19750	BAYOU SALE ENTRANCE LIGHT 1	29-32-51.000N 091-32-09.000W	Fl G 3s	20		SG on dolphin.	HORN: 1 blast ev 20s (2s bl). Private aid.
19755	- Buoy 2	29-32-50.500N 091-32-01.800W				Red nun.	Private aid.
19760	- Buoy 3	29-32-51.900N 091-32-02.200W				Black can.	Private aid.
19765	- Buoy 4	29-32-52.100N 091-31-55.200W				Red nun.	Private aid.
19770	- Buoy 5	29-32-53.500N 091-31-55.700W				Black can.	Private aid.
19775	- Buoy 6	29-32-55.500N 091-31-47.500W				Red nun.	Private aid.
19780	- Buoy 7	29-32-55.100N 091-31-49.100W				Black can.	Private aid.
19785	- Buoy 8	29-32-55.300N 091-31-42.100W				Red nun.	Private aid.
19790	- Buoy 9	29-32-56.700N 091-31-42.600W				Black can.	Private aid.
19795	- Buoy 10	29-32-56.900N 091-31-35.600W				Red nun.	Private aid.
19800	- Buoy 11	29-32-58.300N 091-31-36.000W				Black can.	Private aid.
19805	- LIGHT 13	29-33-00.000N 091-31-00.500W	Q G	13		SG on dolphin.	Private aid.
19810	LUKES LANDING LIGHT 2	29-35-48.200N 091-32-56.900W	Fl R 4s	16		TR on dolphin.	Private aid.

Light List corrected through LNM week: 01/18

(1) No.	(2) Name and Location	(3) Position	(4) Characteristic	(5) Height	(6) Range	(7) Structure	(8) Remarks

LOUISIANA - Eighth District

POINT AU FER TO MARSH ISLAND (Chart 11351)
East Cote Blanche Bay
Bayou Sale Channel

No.	Name and Location	Position	Characteristic	Height	Range	Structure	Remarks
19815	LUKES LANDING LIGHT 1	29-35-51.200N 091-32-57.500W	Fl G 4s	16		SG on dolphin.	Private aid.
19817	Burns Point Channel Day beacon 1	29-34-34.320N 091-32-24.360W				SG on pile.	Private aid.
19817.01	Burns Point Channel Day beacon 2	29-34-33.240N 091-32-23.280W				TR on pile.	Private aid.
19817.02	Burns Point Channel Day beacon 3	29-34-33.600N 091-32-22.920W				SG on pile.	Private aid.
19817.03	Burns Point Channel Day beacon 4	29-34-32.520N 091-32-21.480W				TR on pile.	Private aid.
19817.04	Burns Point Channel Day beacon 5	29-34-32.880N 091-32-21.480W				SG on pile.	Private aid.
19817.05	Burns Point Channel Day beacon 6	29-34-31.800N 091-32-20.040W				TR on pile.	Private aid.
19817.06	Burns Point Channel Day beacon 7	29-34-32.160N 091-32-19.680W				SG on pile.	Private aid.
19817.07	Burns Point Channel Day beacon 8	29-34-31.080N 091-32-18.240W				TR on pile.	Private aid.
19817.08	Burns Point Channel Day beacon 9	29-34-31.440N 091-32-18.240W				SG on pile.	Private aid.
19817.09	Burns Point Channel Day beacon 10	29-34-31.080N 091-32-17.620W				TR on pile.	Private aid.
19817.11	Burns Point Channel Danger Day beacon	29-34-30.720N 091-32-17.160W				NW on bulkhead.	Private aid.
19817.12	Burns Point Channel Danger Day beacon	29-34-30.720N 091-32-16.800W				NW on bulkhead.	Private aid.
19817.13	Burns Point Channel Danger Day beacon	29-34-30.360N 091-32-16.440W				NW on bulkhead.	Private aid.
19817.14	Burns Point Channel Danger Day beacon	29-34-30.000N 091-32-16.080W				NW on bulkhead.	Private aid.
19817.15	Burns Point Channel Danger Day beacon	29-34-31.440N 091-32-17.880W				NW on bulkhead.	Private aid.

Louisiana Coastal Restoration Project

No.	Name and Location	Position	Characteristic	Height	Range	Structure	Remarks
19820	- East Danger Day beacon	29-38-17.000N 091-34-04.000W				NW on pile worded DANGER UNDERWATER OBSTRUCTION DO NOT PROCEED.	Marks east end of submerged dike., Private aid.
19825	- Middle Danger Day beacon	29-38-18.000N 091-34-06.000W				NW on pile worded DANGER UNDERWATER OBSTRUCTION DO NOT PROCEED.	Marks middle of submerged dike., Private aid.
19830	- West Danger Day beacon	29-38-18.000N 091-34-36.000W				NW on pile worded DANGER UNDERWATER OBSTRUCTION DO NOT PROCEED.	Marks west end of submerged dike., Private aid.

Atchafalaya River

No.	Name and Location	Position	Characteristic	Height	Range	Structure	Remarks
19835	E COTE BLAN BAY CANAL ENTRANCE LIGHT 1	29-38-08.000N 091-35-03.000W	Fl W 4s	14		SG on dolphin.	Private aid.

West Cote Blanche Bay
Charenton Canal Access

No.	Name and Location	Position	Characteristic	Height	Range	Structure	Remarks
19840.01	Charenton Canal Buoy 2	29-41-17.000N 091-38-36.000W				Red nun.	Private aid.
19845.01	Charenton Canal Buoy 4	29-41-32.000N 091-38-32.000W				Red nun.	Private aid.
19850.01	Charenton Canal Buoy 6	29-41-43.000N 091-38-28.000W				Red nun.	Private aid.
19855.01	Charenton Canal Buoy 8	29-41-58.000N 091-38-25.000W				Red nun.	Private aid.

Light List corrected through LNM week: 01/18

(1) No.	(2) Name and Location	(3) Position	(4) Characteristic	(5) Height	(6) Range	(7) Structure	(8) Remarks
			LOUISIANA - Eighth District				
	POINT AU FER TO MARSH ISLAND (Chart 11351)						
	West Cote Blanche Bay						
	Charenton Canal Access						
19860.01	Charenton Canal Buoy 10	29-42-12.000N 091-38-19.000W				Red nun.	Private aid.
19865.01	Charenton Canal Buoy 12	29-42-26.000N 091-38-13.000W				Red nun.	Private aid.
19870.01	Charenton Canal Buoy 14	29-42-39.000N 091-38-08.000W				Red nun.	Private aid.
19875.01	Charenton Canal Buoy 16	29-42-51.000N 091-38-03.000W				Red nun.	Private aid.
19880.01	Charenton Canal Buoy 18	29-43-05.000N 091-37-58.000W				Red nun.	Private aid.
19885.01	Charenton Canal Buoy 20	29-43-17.000N 091-37-53.000W				Red nun.	Private aid.
19890.01	Charenton Canal Buoy 22	29-43-29.000N 091-37-47.000W				Red nun.	Private aid.
19895.01	Charenton Canal Buoy 24	29-43-44.000N 091-37-40.000W				Red nun.	Private aid.
19900.01	Charenton Canal Buoy 26	29-43-58.000N 091-37-33.000W				Red nun.	Private aid.
19905.01	Charenton Canal Buoy 28	29-44-10.000N 091-37-27.000W				Red nun.	Private aid.
19910.01	Charenton Canal Buoy 30	29-44-22.000N 091-37-20.000W				Red nun.	Private aid.
19915.01	Charenton Canal Buoy 32	29-44-35.000N 091-37-13.000W				Red nun.	Private aid.
19920.01	Charenton Canal Buoy 34	29-44-47.000N 091-37-07.000W				Red nun.	Private aid.
19925.01	Charenton Canal Buoy 36	29-44-59.000N 091-37-00.000W				Red nun.	Private aid.
19930.01	Charenton Canal Buoy 38	29-45-04.000N 091-36-55.000W				Red nun.	Private aid.
19935.01	Charenton Canal Buoy 40	29-45-07.000N 091-36-48.000W				Red nun.	Private aid.
	WAX LAKE OUTLET TO FORKED ISLAND (Chart 11350)						
	West Cote Blanche Bay						
	Ivanhoe Canal						
19960	- LIGHT 2	29-44-09.200N 091-44-10.300W	Fl R 2.5s	20		TR on pile.	HORN: 1 blast ev 20s (2s bl). Private aid.
19990	- LIGHT 8	29-44-26.000N 091-44-16.000W	Fl R 2.5s	15		TR on pile.	Private aid.
20045	- LIGHT 19	29-44-56.200N 091-44-17.700W	Fl G 2.5s	13		SG on pile.	Private aid.
20050	- LIGHT 20	29-44-55.600N 091-44-16.000W	Fl R 2.5s	13		TR on pile.	Private aid.
20055	- LIGHT 21	29-45-01.000N 091-44-18.000W	Fl G 2.5s	13		SG on pile.	Private aid.
	VERMILION BAY AND APPROACHES (Chart 11349)						
	Mound Point						
20060	- WELL 340-2 LIGHT 2	29-27-35.000N 091-54-04.000W	Q R	17		TR on platform.	Private aid.
20065	- LIGHT 1	29-28-14.000N 091-54-36.000W	Fl G 3s	17		SG on dolphin.	Private aid.
20070	- Day beacon 3	29-28-16.000N 091-56-26.000W				SG on pile.	Private aid.
20075	- Day beacon 5	29-28-21.000N 091-54-21.000W				SG on pile.	Private aid.
20080	- Day beacon 7	29-28-25.000N 091-54-16.000W				SG on pile.	Private aid.
20085	- Day beacon 9	29-28-29.000N 091-54-12.000W				SG on pile.	Private aid.
20090	- Day beacon 12	29-28-32.000N 091-54-13.000W				TR on pile.	Private aid.

Light List corrected through LNM week: 01/18

(1) No.	(2) Name and Location	(3) Position	(4) Characteristic	(5) Height	(6) Range	(7) Structure	(8) Remarks
		LOUISIANA - Eighth District					
	VERMILION BAY AND APPROACHES (Chart 11349)						
	Mound Point						
20095	- Day beacon 14	29-28-34.000N 091-54-12.000W				TR on pile.	Private aid.
20100	- Day beacon 16	29-28-35.000N 091-54-10.000W				TR on pile.	Private aid.
20105	- Day beacon 18	29-28-35.000N 091-54-09.000W				TR on pile.	Private aid.
20110	- Day beacon 20	29-28-34.000N 091-54-08.000W				TR on pile.	Private aid.
	Southwest Pass - Vermilion Bay Channel						
20115	- LIGHT 3	29-32-18.888N 092-04-50.530W	Fl G 4s	17	4	SG on dolphin.	Ra ref.
20120	- LIGHT 4	29-32-15.105N 092-04-45.264W	Fl R 4s	17	3	TR on dolphin.	Ra ref.
20125	- LIGHT 5	29-33-41.336N 092-03-24.315W	Fl G 6s	17	4	SG on pile.	Ra ref.
20130	- LIGHT 7	29-34-36.661N 092-02-49.497W	Fl G 2.5s	17	3	SG on pile.	Ra ref.
20135	- LIGHT 10	29-34-55.780N 092-02-16.862W	Q R	17	3	TR on dolphin.	Ra ref.
20140	- LIGHT 11	29-35-15.101N 092-02-06.080W	Q G	17	3	SG on pile.	Ra ref.
20145	- LIGHT 13	29-35-13.207N 092-01-40.237W	Fl G 4s	17	4	SG on pile.	Ra ref.
20150	- LIGHT 14	29-35-06.002N 092-01-24.827W	Fl R 6s	17	3	TR on pile.	Ra ref.
20155	- LIGHT 15	29-35-34.812N 092-01-16.616W	Fl G 6s	17	4	SG on pile.	Ra ref.
20160	- LIGHT 16	29-35-26.038N 092-01-04.973W	Fl R 6s	17	4	TR on pile.	Ra ref.
20165	- LIGHT 17	29-35-58.077N 092-00-44.644W	Fl G 2.5s	17	4	SG on pile.	Ra ref.
20170	- LIGHT 18	29-35-50.975N 092-00-33.753W	Fl R 2.5s	17	3	TR on pile.	Ra ref.
20175	- LIGHT 19	29-36-24.590N 092-00-32.142W	Fl G 4s	17	4	SG on pile.	Ra ref.
20180	- LIGHT 20	29-36-12.552N 092-00-18.489W	Fl R 4s	17	3	TR on pile.	Ra ref.
20185	- LIGHT 21	29-36-44.543N 092-00-21.808W	Q G	17	3	SG on pile.	Ra ref.
	Vermilion Bay						
	Vermilion Bay Cutoff Channel						
	Lights and daybeacons 50 feet outside channel limits.						
20190	SOUTHWEST PASS - VERMILION BAY CHANNEL JUNCTION LIGHT A	29-37-11.505N 092-00-14.396W	Fl (2+1)R 6s	20	4	JR on pile.	Ra ref.
20195	SOUTHWEST PASS - VERMILION BAY CHANNEL LIGHT 22	29-38-09.554N 092-01-08.227W	Fl R 4s	17	3	TR on pile.	Ra ref.
20200	SOUTHWEST PASS - VERMILION BAY CHANNEL LIGHT 24	29-39-02.233N 092-01-55.603W	Fl R 6s	17	4	TR on pile.	Ra ref.
	Southwest Pass - Vermilion Bay Channel						
20205	- LIGHT 26	29-39-47.862N 092-02-37.796W	Fl R 2.5s	17	3	TR on pile.	Ra ref.
	Vermilion Bay						
	Vermilion Bay Cutoff Channel						
	Lights and daybeacons 50 feet outside channel limits.						
20210	SOUTHWEST PASS - VERMILION BAY CHANNEL LIGHT 28	29-40-36.199N 092-03-20.739W	Fl R 4s	17	3	TR on dolphin.	Ra ref.

Light List corrected through LNM week: 01/18

(1) No.	(2) Name and Location	(3) Position	(4) Characteristic	(5) Height	(6) Range	(7) Structure	(8) Remarks
		LOUISIANA - Eighth District					
	VERMILION BAY AND APPROACHES (Chart 11349)						
	Southwest Pass - Vermilion Bay Channel						
20215	- LIGHT 29	29-41-08.297N 092-04-00.700W	Fl G 2.5s	17	3	SG on pile.	Ra ref.
20220	- LIGHT 30	29-41-21.604N 092-03-58.673W	Fl R 2.5s	17	3	TR on pile.	Ra ref.
	Vermilion Bay						
	Vermilion Bay Cutoff Channel						
	Lights and daybeacons 50 feet outside channel limits.						
20225	SOUTHWEST PASS - VERMILION BAY CHANNEL LIGHT 32	29-42-14.370N 092-04-47.420W	Fl R 4s	17	3	TR on pile.	Ra ref.
	Southwest Pass - Vermilion Bay Channel						
20230	- LIGHT 34	29-42-57.582N 092-05-26.343W	Fl R 6s	17	4	TR on pile.	Ra ref.
20235	- LIGHT 35	29-43-39.953N 092-06-08.958W	Fl G 2.5s	17	3	SG on pile.	Ra ref.
	Vermilion Bay						
	Vermilion Bay Cutoff Channel						
	Lights and daybeacons 50 feet outside channel limits.						
20240	SOUTHWEST PASS - VERMILION BAY CHANNEL LIGHT 36	29-43-41.885N 092-06-06.071W	Fl R 2.5s	17	3	TR on pile.	Ra ref.
20245	SOUTHWEST PASS - VERMILION BAY CHANNEL LIGHT 37	29-44-27.484N 092-06-45.116W	Fl G 4s	17	4	SG on pile.	Ra ref.
20250	SOUTHWEST PASS - VERMILION BAY CHANNEL LIGHT 38	29-44-30.354N 092-06-41.381W	Fl R 4s	17	3	TR on pile.	Ra ref.
20255	Shell Day beacon 1	29-44-49.000N 092-11-56.800W				SG on pile.	Ra ref. Private aid.
20260	Shell Day beacon 2	29-44-48.560N 092-11-57.540W				TR on pile.	Private aid.
20265	Shell Day beacon 3	29-44-20.730N 092-11-20.740W				SG on pile.	Private aid.
20270	Shell Day beacon 4	29-44-19.870N 092-11-21.260W				TR on pile.	Private aid.
20275	Shell Day beacon 5	29-44-12.510N 092-10-30.140W				SG on pile.	Private aid.
20280	Shell Day beacon 6	29-44-11.570N 092-10-30.310W				TR on pile.	Private aid.
20285	Shell Day beacon 7	29-43-57.770N 092-09-42.960W				SG on pile.	Private aid.
20290	Shell Day beacon 8	29-43-57.360N 092-09-43.700W				TR on pile.	Private aid.
	Acadiana Navigation Channel						
20295	- LIGHT 1	29-38-01.565N 091-59-03.529W	Fl G 2.5s	17	4	SG on pile.	Ra ref.
20300	- LIGHT 4	29-38-23.368N 091-58-49.950W	Q R	17	4	TR on pile.	Ra ref.
20305	- LIGHT 6	29-40-02.834N 091-57-38.723W	Fl R 4s	17	3	TR on pile.	Ra ref.
20310	- LIGHT 8	29-41-44.290N 091-56-27.962W	Fl R 2.5s	17	4	TR on pile.	Ra ref.
20315	- LIGHT 9	29-42-36.302N 091-55-55.006W	Fl G 4s	17	4	SG on pile.	Ra ref.
20320	- LIGHT 12	29-43-25.746N 091-55-17.181W	Fl R 6s	17	4	TR on pile.	Ra ref.
20325	- LIGHT 14	29-45-07.202N 091-54-06.379W	Fl R 4s	17	4	TR on pile.	Ra ref.
20330	- LIGHT 16	29-46-48.657N 091-52-55.559W	Fl R 2.5s	17	4	TR on pile.	Ra ref.

Light List corrected through LNM week: 01/18

(1) No.	(2) Name and Location	(3) Position	(4) Characteristic	(5) Height	(6) Range	(7) Structure	(8) Remarks
			LOUISIANA - Eighth District				
	VERMILION BAY AND APPROACHES (Chart 11349)						
	Vermilion Bay						
	Acadiana Navigation Channel						
20332	LCPRA SHARK ISLAND DANGER LIGHT	29-46-59.642N 091-51-11.496W	Fl W 2.5s			Marks shoreline protection structure.	Private aid.
20332.01	LCPRA SHARK ISLAND DANGER LIGHT	29-46-51.563N 091-51-12.343W	Fl W 2.5s			Marks shoreline protection structure.	Private aid.
20332.02	LCPRA SHARK ISLAND DANGER LIGHT	29-46-44.853N 091-51-17.407W	Fl W 2.5s			Marks shoreline protection structure.	Private aid.
20332.03	LCPRA SHARK ISLAND DANGER LIGHT	29-46-36.000N 091-51-26.684W	Fl W 2.5s			Marks shoreline protection structure.	Private aid.
20335	- LIGHT 18	29-47-39.637N 091-52-20.583W	Fl R 4s	17	4	TR on pile.	Ra ref.
20340	- LIGHT 19	29-49-04.838N 091-51-26.799W	Fl G 4s	17	4	SG on pile.	Ra ref.
20345	- Day beacon 20	29-49-03.172N 091-51-21.107W				TR on pile.	Ra ref.
20350	- Day beacon 21	29-49-40.350N 091-51-04.845W				SG on pile.	Ra ref.
20355	- Day beacon 22	29-49-39.429N 091-51-02.757W				TR on pile.	Ra ref.
20357	BAYOU COMPANIES TEMPORARY MOORING LIGHTS (3)	29-56-13.830N 091-50-39.110W	Fl W 2.5s			Marks mooring piles.	Private aid.
20360	QUINTANA CANAL ENTRANCE LIGHT	29-44-02.000N 091-51-16.000W	Fl G 4s	13			Private aid.
20362	CYPREMORT POINT DANGER BREAKWATER LIGHT	29-43-31.200N 091-51-44.445W	Fl W 2.5s			Marks breakwater structure.	Private aid.
20362.01	CYPREMORT POINT DANGER BREAKWATER LIGHT	29-43-40.748N 091-51-32.109W	Fl W 2.5s			Marks breakwater structure.	Private aid.
20362.02	CYPREMORT POINT DANGER BREAKWATER LIGHT	29-43-50.201N 091-51-18.013W	Fl W 2.5s			Marks breakwater structure.	Private aid.
20362.03	CYPREMORT POINT DANGER BREAKWATER LIGHT	29-43-52.247N 091-51-18.696W	Fl W 2.5s			Marks breakwater structure.	Private aid.
20362.04	CYPREMORT POINT DANGER BREAKWATER LIGHT	29-43-59.634N 091-51-15.290W	Fl W 2.5s			Marks breakwater structure.	Private aid.
	Weeks Island Channel						
20365	- Day beacon 1	29-49-08.362N 091-50-04.702W				SG on pile.	Private aid.
20370	- Day beacon 3	29-49-05.346N 091-50-04.185W				SG on pile.	Private aid.
20375	- Day beacon 5	29-49-02.331N 091-50-03.668W				SG on pile.	Private aid.
20380	- Day beacon 7	29-48-59.315N 091-50-03.152W				SG on pile.	Private aid.
20385	- Day beacon 9	29-48-56.299N 091-50-02.635W				SG on pile.	Private aid.
20390	- Day beacon 11	29-48-53.284N 091-50-02.119W				SG on pile.	Private aid.
20395	- Day beacon 13	29-48-50.268N 091-50-01.603W				SG on pile.	Private aid.
20400	- Day beacon 15	29-48-47.251N 091-50-01.093W				SG on pile.	Private aid.
20405	- Day beacon 17	29-48-44.235N 091-50-00.582W				SG on pile.	Private aid.
20410	- Day beacon 19	29-48-39.659N 091-49-59.808W				SG on pile.	Private aid.

(1) No.	(2) Name and Location	(3) Position	(4) Characteristic	(5) Height	(6) Range	(7) Structure	(8) Remarks
	LOUISIANA - Eighth District						
	VERMILION BAY AND APPROACHES (Chart 11349)						
	Vermilion Bay						
	Weeks Island Channel						
20415	- Day beacon 21	29-48-33.708N 091-49-58.973W				SG on pile.	Private aid.
20420	- Day beacon 23	29-48-31.084N 091-49-57.491W				SG on pile	Private aid.
20425	- Day beacon 25	29-48-30.626N 091-49-50.356W				SG on pile	Private aid.
20430	- Day beacon 27	29-48-30.122N 091-49-37.675W				SG on pile	Private aid.
	Weeks Bay						
20435	- Spoil Banks Day beacon D	29-48-36.000N 091-49-59.000W				NW on pile.	Private aid.
20440	- Spoil Banks Day beacon H	29-48-32.000N 091-49-58.000W				NW on pile.	Private aid.
20445	- South Channel Day beacon 1	29-48-29.000N 091-49-38.000W				SG on pile.	Private aid.
20450	- South Channel Day beacon 3	29-48-26.000N 091-49-37.000W				SG on pile.	Private aid.
20455	- South Channel Day beacon 5	29-48-23.000N 091-49-36.000W				SG on pile.	Private aid.
20460	- South Channel Day beacon 7	29-48-20.000N 091-49-35.000W				SG on pile.	Private aid.
20465	U.S. GEOLOGICAL SURVEY SCIENTIFIC MONITORING PLATFORM LIGHT (SMP)	29-42-34.000N 091-52-57.000W	Fl Y 2.5s	37		On pipe.	Private aid.
	Avery Canal						
20470	- LIGHT 1	29-49-24.945N 091-54-05.739W	Fl G 2.5s	17	4	SG on dolphin.	Ra ref.
20475	- LIGHT 3	29-49-45.451N 091-54-18.650W	Fl G 4s	17	4	SG on dolphin.	Ra ref.
20480	- LIGHT 4	29-49-51.150N 091-54-24.767W	Fl R 4s	17	4	TR on pile.	
20485	- DANGER LIGHT NORTH	29-49-53.000N 091-54-30.000W	Fl W 2.5s			NW on pile worded DANGER ROCK SILL.	Private aid.
20490	- DANGER LIGHT SOUTH	29-49-52.000N 091-54-31.500W	Fl W 2.5s			NW on pile worded DANGER ROCK SILL.	Private aid.
20490.01	- SOUTHWEST DANGER LIGHT	29-49-54.010N 091-54-32.660W	Fl W 2.5s			Marks a rock weir.	Private aid.
20490.02	- NORTHWEST DANGER LIGHT	29-49-52.940N 091-54-33.230W	Fl W 2.5s			Marks a rock weir.	Private aid.
20495	CARGILL MOORING BARGE LIGHT	29-53-00.500N 091-55-52.500W	Fl R 2.5s			Marks mooring barge.	Private aid.
	Boston Bayou Channel						
20560	- ENTRANCE LIGHT 1	29-46-00.400N 092-01-00.900W	Fl G 4s	14		SG on dolphin.	Private aid.
20565	- LIGHT 7	29-46-54.000N 092-02-08.000W	Fl G 4s			SG on pile.	Private aid.
20570	- LIGHT 8	29-46-54.000N 092-02-05.000W	Fl R 4s			TR on pile.	Private aid.
	Freshwater Bayou						
20573	Vermilion Parish Danger Day beacons (6)	29-34-17.000N 092-11-16.000W				Marks submerged shoreline erosion protection structures.	Private aid.
20575	- LIGHT 3	29-29-24.697N 092-19-06.865W	Fl G 4s	17	4	SG on piles.	Ra ref.
20580	- LIGHT 4	29-29-22.446N 092-18-56.058W	Fl R 4s	17	4	TR on piles.	
20585	- Day beacon 5	29-30-05.394N 092-18-58.682W				SG on pile.	Ra ref.
20590	- LIGHT 6	29-30-03.972N 092-18-49.918W	Fl R 6s	17	4	TR on dolphin.	Ra ref.

Light List corrected through LNM week: 01/18

(1) No.	(2) Name and Location	(3) Position	(4) Characteristic	(5) Height	(6) Range	(7) Structure	(8) Remarks
			LOUISIANA - Eighth District				
	VERMILION BAY AND APPROACHES (Chart 11349)						
	Freshwater Bayou						
20595	- LIGHT 7	29-30-45.048N 092-18-49.015W	Fl G 4s	17	4	SG on dolphin.	Ra ref.
20600	- Day beacon 8	29-30-46.066N 092-18-42.691W				TR on pile.	Ra ref.
20605	- LIGHT 9	29-31-21.199N 092-18-41.279W	Fl G 6s	17	4	SG on dolphin.	Ra ref.
20610	- LIGHT 10	29-31-20.981N 092-18-36.203W	Fl R 4s	17	4	TR on dolphin.	Ra ref.
20615	- LIGHT 11 50 feet outside channel limit.	29-31-57.332N 092-18-33.420W	Fl G 2.5s	17	4	SG on dolphin.	Ra ref.
20620	- LIGHT 12 50 feet outside channel limit.	29-32-02.197N 092-18-27.922W	Fl R 2.5s	17	4	TR on dolphin.	Ra ref.
20625	- OBSTRUCTION LIGHT 13	29-32-23.940N 092-18-28.166W	Q G	17	3	SG on pile.	Ra ref.
20628	VERMILION PARISH TIGRE POINT DANGER BREAKWATER LIGHT	29-32-58.000N 092-14-11.000W	Fl W 2.5s			Marks oyster reef breakwaters.	Private aid.
20628.01	VERMILION PARISH TIGRE POINT DANGER BREAKWATER LIGHT	29-32-54.000N 092-14-20.000W	Fl W 2.5s			Marks oyster reef breakwaters.	Private aid.
20628.02	VERMILION PARISH TIGRE POINT DANGER BREAKWATER LIGHT	29-32-43.000N 092-14-40.000W	Fl W 2.5s			Marks oyster reef breakwaters.	Private aid.
20628.03	VERMILION PARISH TIGRE POINT DANGER BREAKWATER LIGHT	29-32-39.000N 092-14-49.000W	Fl W 2.5s			Marks oyster reef breakwaters.	Private aid.
20628.04	VERMILION PARISH TIGRE POINT DANGER BREAKWATER LIGHT	29-32-35.000N 092-14-57.000W	Fl W 2.5s			Marks oyster reef breakwaters.	Private aid.
20628.05	VERMILION PARISH TIGRE POINT DANGER BREAKWATER LIGHT	29-32-30.000N 092-15-06.000W	Fl W 2.5s			Marks oyster reef breakwaters.	Private aid.
20630	- LIGHT 14	29-35-29.939N 092-17-46.748W	Q R	17	3	TR on pile.	Ra ref.
20635	- LIGHT 16 60 feet outside channel limit.	29-37-36.795N 092-16-11.748W	Fl R 2.5s	17	3	TR on dolphin.	Ra ref.
20640	- LIGHT 18 60 feet outside channel limit.	29-39-50.086N 092-15-23.032W	Fl R 2.5s	17	3	TR on pile.	Ra ref.
20645	- LIGHT 20 60 feet outside channel limit.	29-43-37.788N 092-14-33.825W	Fl R 2.5s	17	3	TR on pile.	Ra ref.
20650	- LIGHT 22	29-44-37.387N 092-13-15.844W	Q R	17	3		
20657	- LIGHT 23	29-46-18.000N 092-10-42.000W	Fl G 2.5s	17	2	SG on pile.	
20658	- JUNCTION LIGHT FW	29-46-28.988N 092-10-13.742W	Fl (2+1)R 6s	17	2	JR-SY on pile.	
20659	INTRACOASTAL CITY LIGHT 1	29-46-33.222N 092-10-42.026W	Fl G 4s	17	2	SG on pile.	Ra ref.
20660	EXXON MOBIL FEE WELL NO.1 BREAKWATER LIGHTS (9)	29-33-50.000N 092-29-58.000W	Q W	10		On Dolphins.	Private aid.
	ROLLOVER BAYOU TO CALCASIEU PASS (Chart 11344)						
	Mermentau Channel						
20675	ROCKEFELLER REFUGE BREAKWATER DANGER LIGHT A	29-38-23.680N 092-47-09.020W	Fl W 2.5s			NW on pile.	Private aid.
20680	ROCKEFELLER REFUGE BREAKWATER DANGER LIGHT B	29-38-11.600N 092-46-41.720W	Fl W 2.5s			NW on pile.	Private aid.

Light List corrected through LNM week: 01/18

(1) No.	(2) Name and Location	(3) Position	(4) Characteristic	(5) Height	(6) Range	(7) Structure	(8) Remarks
	LOUISIANA - Eighth District						
	ROLLOVER BAYOU TO CALCASIEU PASS (Chart 11344)						
	Mermentau Channel						
20685	ROCKEFELLER REFUGE BREAKWATER DANGER LIGHT C	29-38-41.850N 092-47-43.490W	Fl W 2.5s			NW on pile.	Private aid.
20690	ROCKEFELLER REFUGE BREAKWATER DANGER LIGHT D	29-37-47.380N 092-47-05.670W	Fl W 2.5s			NW on pile.	Private aid.
	VERMILION BAY AND APPROACHES (Chart 11349)						
	Freshwater Bayou						
20695	ROCKEFELLER WILDLIFE REFUGE DANGER BREAKWATER LIGHTS (4)	29-38-56.730N 092-48-23.270W	Fl W 2.5s			NW on pile.	Marks oyster reef breakwaters. Private aid.
	ROLLOVER BAYOU TO CALCASIEU PASS (Chart 11344)						
	Mermentau Channel						
20700 1030	- Entrance Lighted Buoy 2	29-42-04.047N 093-00-34.389W	Fl (2)R 5s		4	Red.	
20715	- EAST JETTY LIGHT 6	29-43-18.636N 093-00-30.200W	Fl R 2.5s	21	3	TR on pile.	
20720	- WEST JETTY LIGHT 7	29-43-21.783N 093-00-41.480W	Fl G 2.5s	21	3	SG on pile.	
20725	- LIGHT 8	29-43-36.799N 093-00-36.630W	Fl R 6s	15	4	TR on dolphin.	
20727	FIELDWOOD PIPELINE DANGER LIGHTS (3)	29-44-46.380N 093-04-53.660W	Fl W 2.5s			NW on pile.	Private aid.
20730	ROUNDLAKE CANAL BARRACADE LIGHT 1	29-52-00.000N 092-39-01.000W	Fl G 4s	10		SG on pile.	Private aid.
20735	ROUNDLAKE CANAL BARRACADE LIGHT 2	29-52-00.000N 092-39-01.000W	Fl R 2.5s	10		TR on pile.	Private aid.
	FORKED ISLAND TO ELLENDER (Chart 11348)						
	Mermentau Channel						
20740	- Buoy 11	29-44-47.030N 093-00-39.939W				Green can.	
20745	- Buoy 12	29-44-46.305N 093-00-35.508W				Red nun.	
20750	- RANGE FRONT LIGHT	29-45-15.667N 093-00-36.401W	Q R (NIGHT) Q R (DAY)	17 17		On pile.	Visible 2° each side of rangeline.
20755	- RANGE REAR LIGHT 450 yards, 000.7° from front light.	29-45-29.037N 093-00-36.220W	Iso R 6s (NIGHT) Iso R 6s (DAY)	37 37		On skeleton tower.	Visible 2° each side of rangeline.
20760	- Buoy 15	29-45-03.153N 093-00-37.698W				Green can.	
20765	- Buoy 16	29-45-03.092N 093-00-34.577W				Red nun.	
20770	- Buoy 17	29-45-12.187N 093-00-40.975W				Green can.	
20775	- Buoy 18	29-45-14.762N 093-00-38.219W				Red nun.	
20780	- Buoy 21	29-45-20.451N 093-00-59.189W				Green can.	
20785	- Buoy 25	29-45-29.983N 093-01-14.701W				Green can.	
20790	- Buoy 26	29-45-38.241N 093-01-10.362W				Red nun.	
20795	- Buoy 27	29-45-56.373N 093-00-54.072W				Green can.	
	Upper Mud Lake						
20800	- Buoy 1	29-46-22.602N 092-55-13.728W				Green can.	
20805	- Buoy 2	29-46-20.322N 092-55-12.318W				Red nun.	
20810	- Buoy 3	29-46-30.321N 092-54-48.390W				Green can.	

Light List corrected through LNM week: 01/18

(1) No.	(2) Name and Location	(3) Position	(4) Characteristic	(5) Height	(6) Range	(7) Structure	(8) Remarks
		LOUISIANA - Eighth District					

FORKED ISLAND TO ELLENDER (Chart 11348)
Mermentau Channel
Upper Mud Lake

(1) No.	(2) Name and Location	(3) Position	(4) Characteristic	(5) Height	(6) Range	(7) Structure	(8) Remarks
20815	- Buoy 4	29-46-27.746N 092-54-47.863W				Red nun.	
20820	- Buoy 5	29-46-32.943N 092-54-30.810W				Green can.	
20825	- Buoy 6	29-46-30.602N 092-54-29.347W				Red nun.	
20830	- Buoy 7	29-46-28.838N 092-54-12.203W				Green can.	
20835	- Buoy 8	29-46-26.822N 092-54-12.217W				Red nun.	
20840	- Buoy 9	29-46-25.993N 092-53-58.849W				Green can.	
20845	- Buoy 10	29-46-23.954N 092-53-53.167W				Red nun.	
20850	- Buoy 11	29-46-27.381N 092-53-33.906W				Green can.	
20855	- Buoy 12	29-46-25.623N 092-53-33.972W				Red nun.	
20860	- Buoy 13	29-46-32.343N 092-53-18.018W				Green can.	
20865	- Buoy 14	29-46-30.903N 092-53-16.872W				Red nun.	
20870	- Buoy 15	29-46-40.310N 092-53-09.503W				Green can.	
20875	- Buoy 16	29-46-39.830N 092-53-07.651W				Red nun.	
20880	- Buoy 17	29-46-44.847N 092-53-08.934W				Green can.	
20885	- Buoy 18	29-47-08.550N 092-53-08.410W				Red nun.	
20890	- Buoy 19	29-47-07.525N 092-53-10.664W				Green can.	
20895	- Buoy 20	29-47-20.510N 092-53-03.889W				Red nun.	
20900	- Buoy 21	29-47-22.412N 092-53-05.813W				Green can.	

Mermentau Channel

(1) No.	(2) Name and Location	(3) Position	(4) Characteristic	(5) Height	(6) Range	(7) Structure	(8) Remarks
20905	CATFISH POINT LIGHT 1	29-52-00.313N 092-50-41.120W	Fl G 4s	17	4	SG on dolphin.	
20910	SOUTH GRAND LAKE LIGHT 2	29-50-00.000N 092-42-20.000W	Fl W 10s	21		TR on dolphin.	Private aid.

Grand Lake

(1) No.	(2) Name and Location	(3) Position	(4) Characteristic	(5) Height	(6) Range	(7) Structure	(8) Remarks
20919	TEBO POINT DANGER LIGHT	29-51-14.830N 092-48-38.090W	Fl W 2.5s			Marks rock dike.	Private aid.
20920	- LIGHT 3	29-52-58.570N 092-48-01.491W	Fl G 4s	17	5	SG on pile.	
20925	- LIGHT 4	29-53-29.066N 092-44-42.178W	Fl R 4s	17	4	TR on pile.	
20930	- LIGHT 5	29-56-07.102N 092-46-47.103W	Fl G 4s	17	4	SG on dolphin.	
20935	- LIGHT 6	29-57-06.897N 092-48-13.932W	Fl R 4s	17	5	TR on pile.	
20940	- LIGHT 8	29-57-40.723N 092-47-23.862W	Fl R 4s	17	4	TR on pile.	

Mermentau River Crossing

(1) No.	(2) Name and Location	(3) Position	(4) Characteristic	(5) Height	(6) Range	(7) Structure	(8) Remarks
20950 35295	- Buoy 1	29-58-17.998N 092-47-19.038W				Green can with yellow square.	
20954 35302	- LIGHT 2	29-58-23.457N 092-47-14.524W	Fl R 2.5s	17	3	TR-TY on pile.	
20955 35300	- Buoy 2A	29-58-24.653N 092-47-24.534W				Red nun with yellow triangle.	
20965 35310	- Buoy 4	29-58-23.751N 092-47-38.829W				Red nun with yellow triangle.	

(1) No.	(2) Name and Location	(3) Position	(4) Characteristic	(5) Height	(6) Range	(7) Structure	(8) Remarks
		LOUISIANA - Eighth District					
	FORKED ISLAND TO ELLENDER (Chart 11348)						
	Mermentau River Crossing						
20970 35315	- Buoy 5	29-58-16.440N 092-47-51.427W				Green can with yellow square.	
20975 35320	- Junction Buoy M	29-58-20.651N 092-48-04.118W				Red nun with green band and yellow triangle.	
20980 35325	- LIGHT 7	29-58-16.645N 092-48-10.590W	Fl G 2.5s	17	3	SG-SY on pile.	
20985	MERMENTAU RIVER WRECK LIGHT WR1	29-58-27.062N 092-48-05.828W	Q G	17	3	SG on pile.	
	Mermentau River						
20990	- Day beacon 1A	29-58-37.961N 092-48-10.710W				SG on pile.	
20995	- Day beacon 2	29-58-56.945N 092-48-08.528W				TR on pile.	
21000	- Day beacon 4	29-59-18.540N 092-47-36.036W				TR on pile.	Ra ref.
21005	- Day beacon 5	29-59-30.999N 092-47-20.774W				SG on pile.	
21010	- Day beacon 6	29-59-47.908N 092-47-17.843W				TR on pile.	
21015	WARREN PETROLEUM PILE LIGHT	30-00-11.000N 092-46-41.000W	Fl R 2.5s	6		On pile.	Private aid.
21020	- Day beacon 7	30-00-10.741N 092-46-34.450W				SG on pile.	
21025	- Day beacon 9	29-59-45.832N 092-46-18.835W				SG on pile.	
21030	- Day beacon 10	29-59-40.758N 092-46-28.527W				TR on pile.	
21035	- Day beacon 11	29-59-48.073N 092-45-47.385W				SG on pile.	
21040	- Day beacon 13	30-00-07.255N 092-45-25.495W				SG on pile.	
21045	- Day beacon 14	30-00-31.715N 092-45-13.276W				TR on pile.	
21050	- Day beacon 15	30-00-47.583N 092-45-18.172W				SG on pile.	
21055	- Day beacon 17	30-01-05.386N 092-45-29.586W				SG on pile.	
21060	- Day beacon 18	30-01-21.793N 092-46-00.479W				TR on pile.	
21065	- Day beacon 20	30-01-38.305N 092-46-00.431W				TR on pile.	
21070	- Day beacon 21	30-01-52.924N 092-45-28.320W				SG on pile.	
	Lake Arthur						
21075	- Day beacon 2	30-02-20.175N 092-44-52.805W				TR on pile.	
21080	- A RANGE FRONT LIGHT	30-02-17.003N 092-45-15.853W	Q W	25		KRW on skeleton tower on piles.	Visible all around; higher intensity on rangeline.
21085	- A RANGE REAR LIGHT 255 yards, 255.0° from front light.	30-02-15.062N 092-45-24.292W	Iso W 6s	35		KRW on skeleton tower on piles.	Visible all around; higher intensity on rangeline.
21090	- B RANGE FRONT LIGHT	30-03-00.737N 092-42-06.216W	Q W	17		KRW on dolphin.	Visible all around; higher intensity on rangeline.
21095	- B RANGE REAR LIGHT 399 yards, 074.8° from front light.	30-03-03.835N 092-41-53.085W	Iso W 6s	37		KRW on skeleton tower on piles.	Visible all around; higher intensity on rangeline.
21100	- Day beacon 4	30-02-25.640N 092-44-29.769W				TR on pile.	
21110	- LIGHT 8 50 feet outside channel limit.	30-02-35.081N 092-43-49.654W	Fl R 4s	17	4	TR on pile.	

Light List corrected through LNM week: 01/18

(1) No.	(2) Name and Location	(3) Position	(4) Characteristic	(5) Height	(6) Range	(7) Structure	(8) Remarks
		LOUISIANA - Eighth District					
	FORKED ISLAND TO ELLENDER (Chart 11348)						
	Lake Arthur						
21120	- Day beacon 12	30-02-44.048N 092-43-11.217W				TR on pile.	
21125	- Day beacon 14	30-02-48.289N 092-42-53.432W				TR on pile.	
21140	- LIGHT 20A	30-03-28.881N 092-41-43.566W	Fl R 4s	17	5	TR on pile.	
21145	- Day beacon 20	30-03-31.225N 092-41-42.288W				TR on pile.	
21150	- Day beacon 22	30-03-38.017N 092-41-22.954W				TR on pile.	
21155	- Day beacon 23	30-03-45.043N 092-41-18.024W				SG on pile.	
21160	- Day beacon 25	30-03-53.054N 092-41-08.234W				SG on pile.	
21165	- Day beacon 26	30-03-50.254N 092-41-01.806W				TR on pile.	
21170	- Day beacon 28	30-04-02.482N 092-40-46.536W				TR on pile.	
21175	- Day beacon 30	30-04-05.236N 092-40-23.184W				TR on pile.	
21180	- Day beacon 31	30-04-06.900N 092-40-04.169W				SG on pile.	
21185	- Day beacon 33	30-04-06.240N 092-39-51.896W				SG on pile.	
21190	PURE TRANSPORTATION CO. DOCK LIGHTS (3)	30-04-20.000N 092-38-05.000W	Q R		10	Black dolphin.	Private aid.
	ROLLOVER BAYOU TO CALCASIEU PASS (Chart 11344)						
	Calcasieu Channel						
21195 1010	- Lighted Buoy CC	29-20-00.870N 093-13-17.564W	Mo (A) W		4	Red and white stripes with red spherical topmark.	
21200	- Lighted Buoy 1 100 feet outside channel limit.	29-21-49.156N 093-13-24.664W	Fl G 2.5s		4	Green.	
21205	- Lighted Buoy 2 100 feet outside channel limit.	29-21-49.356N 093-13-14.134W	Fl R 2.5s		4	Red.	
21210	- Lighted Buoy 1A 100 feet outside channel limit.	29-22-49.155N 093-13-26.914W	Fl G 4s		4	Green.	
21215	- Lighted Buoy 2A	29-22-50.754N 093-13-15.003W	Fl R 4s		4	Red.	
	CALCASIEU RIVER AND LAKE (Chart 11347)						
	Calcasieu Channel						
21220	- Lighted Buoy 2B	29-27-20.544N 093-13-19.426W	Q R		3	Red.	
21225	- Lighted Buoy 3 100 feet outside channel limit.	29-28-58.834N 093-13-32.715W	Fl G 4s		4	Green.	
21230	- Lighted Buoy 4 100 feet outside channel limit.	29-28-59.037N 093-13-21.407W	Fl R 4s		4	Red.	
21235	- Lighted Buoy 5	29-30-00.857N 093-13-33.963W	Fl G 2.5s		4	Green.	
21240	- Lighted Buoy 6	29-30-01.113N 093-13-22.657W	Fl R 2.5s		3	Red.	
21245	- Lighted Buoy 7	29-30-52.503N 093-13-35.186W	Fl G 4s		4	Green.	
21250	- Lighted Buoy 8	29-31-07.921N 093-13-27.567W	Q R		3	Red.	
21255	- Lighted Buoy 9	29-31-14.763N 093-13-43.777W	Q G		3	Green.	
21260	- Lighted Buoy 11	29-31-52.276N 093-14-17.177W	Fl G 2.5s		4	Green.	

Light List corrected through LNM week: 01/18

(1) No.	(2) Name and Location	(3) Position	(4) Characteristic	(5) Height	(6) Range	(7) Structure	(8) Remarks
		LOUISIANA - Eighth District					
	CALCASIEU RIVER AND LAKE (Chart 11347)						
	Calcasieu Channel						
21265	- Lighted Buoy 12	29-31-58.369N 093-14-08.287W	Fl R 2.5s		3	Red.	
21270	- Lighted Buoy 14	29-32-47.352N 093-14-52.583W	Fl R 4s		3	Red.	
21275	- Lighted Buoy 15	29-33-28.310N 093-15-44.054W	Fl G 6s		4	Green.	
21280	- Lighted Buoy 16	29-33-34.900N 093-15-35.345W	Fl R 6s		4	Red.	
21285	- Lighted Buoy 18	29-34-22.654N 093-16-18.769W	Fl R 4s		3	Red.	
21290	- Lighted Buoy 19	29-35-04.911N 093-17-11.419W	Fl G 6s		4	Green.	
21295	- Lighted Buoy 20	29-35-11.106N 093-17-02.587W	Fl R 6s		4	Red.	
21300	- Lighted Buoy 22	29-35-58.705N 093-17-45.633W	Fl R 4s		4	Red.	
21305	- Lighted Buoy 23	29-36-39.254N 093-18-36.740W	Fl G 2.5s		4	Green.	
21310	- Lighted Buoy 24	29-36-46.207N 093-18-28.590W	Fl R 2.5s		3	Red.	
21315	- Lighted Buoy 27	29-37-27.330N 093-19-22.309W	Q G		3	Green.	
21320	- Lighted Buoy 28	29-37-34.615N 093-19-10.018W	Q R		3	Red.	
21325	- A RANGE FRONT LIGHT	29-47-07.531N 093-20-52.052W	Fl R 2.5s (NIGHT) Fl W 2.5s (DAY)	44 47		Skeleton tower on piles.	
21335	- A RANGE REAR LIGHT 1941 yards, 351.8° from front light.	29-48-04.593N 093-21-01.478W	F R (NIGHT) F W (DAY)	148 145		Skeleton tower on piles.	
21340	- Lighted Buoy 29	29-38-38.991N 093-19-34.160W	Fl G 2.5s		4	Green.	
21345	- Lighted Buoy 30	29-38-39.906N 093-19-22.878W	Fl (2)R 5s		3	Red.	
21350	- Lighted Buoy 31	29-39-35.630N 093-19-43.482W	Fl G 4s		4	Green.	
21355	- Lighted Buoy 32	29-39-37.348N 093-19-32.318W	Fl R 4s		3	Red.	
21360	- Lighted Buoy 33	29-40-35.503N 093-19-53.328W	Fl G 6s		4	Green.	
21365	- Lighted Buoy 34	29-40-37.363N 093-19-42.182W	Fl R 6s		4	Red.	
21370	- Lighted Buoy 35	29-41-34.659N 093-20-03.051W	Fl G 6s		4	Green.	
21375	- Lighted Buoy 36	29-41-37.438N 093-19-52.055W	Fl R 6s		4	Red.	
21380	- Lighted Buoy 37	29-42-35.180N 093-20-13.000W	Fl G 4s		4	Green.	Ra ref.
21385	- Lighted Buoy 38	29-42-35.406N 093-20-01.582W	Fl R 4s		3	Red.	
21390	- Lighted Buoy 39	29-43-32.862N 093-20-22.481W	Fl G 2.5s		4	Green.	
21395	- Lighted Buoy 40	29-43-32.444N 093-20-10.956W	Fl R 2.5s		3	Red.	
21400	- WEST JETTY LIGHT 41	29-44-39.428N 093-20-33.231W	Q G	30	4	SG on square tower, on piles.	
21405	- EAST JETTY LIGHT 42	29-44-41.369N 093-20-22.445W	Q R	30	4	TR on square tower on piles.	
21410	- LIGHT 47 100 feet outside channel limit.	29-45-58.262N 093-20-47.778W	Fl G 2.5s	17	4	SG on pile.	

187

Light List corrected through LNM week: 01/18

(1) No.	(2) Name and Location	(3) Position	(4) Characteristic	(5) Height	(6) Range	(7) Structure	(8) Remarks
			LOUISIANA - Eighth District				
	CALCASIEU RIVER AND LAKE (Chart 11347)						
	Calcasieu Channel						
21415	- LIGHT 48 100 feet outside channel limit.	29-46-02.180N 093-20-35.340W	Q R	17	3	TR on pile.	
21420	NOAA CALCASIEU PASS TIDE MONITORING PLATFORM LIGHT	29-46-05.400N 093-20-34.370W	Fl Y 2.5s	40		On platform.	Private aid.
21425	Monkey Island Daybeacon 2	29-46-38.311N 093-20-29.116W				TR on pile.	
21430	- LIGHT 50 130 feet outside channel limit.	29-46-40.678N 093-20-40.276W	Fl R 2.5s	17	3	TR on pile.	
21435	- LIGHT 52 50 feet outside channel limit.	29-47-55.033N 093-20-43.194W	Fl R 4s	17	4	TR on pile.	
21440	- LIGHT 53 130 feet outside channel limit.	29-48-09.441N 093-20-54.316W	Fl G 4s	17	4	SG on skeleton tower on piles.	
21445	St Johns Island Daybeacon 2	29-50-37.989N 093-19-39.954W				TR on pile.	
21447	*Calcasieu Lake Lighted Danger Buoy A*	29-50-45.770N 093-19-25.595W	Fl W 2.5s		3	White can.	Labeled "DANGER ROCKS".
21447.03	*Calcasieu Lake Lighted Danger Buoy B*	29-50-50.500N 093-18-57.500W	Fl W 4s		3	White can.	Labeled "DANGER ROCKS".
21447.06	*Calcasieu Lake Lighted Danger Buoy C*	29-50-56.117N 093-18-27.348W	Fl W 2.5s		3	White can.	Labeled "DANGER ROCKS".
21450	- LIGHT 56 130 feet outside channel limit.	29-49-17.506N 093-20-48.759W	Fl R 2.5s	17	4	TR on pile.	
21455	- LIGHT 57	29-49-50.503N 093-20-58.998W	Q G	30	3	SG on skeleton tower on piles.	
21460	OYSTER BAYOU WEIR LIGHT 1	29-48-41.470N 093-23-51.771W	Fl G 2.5s			SG on pile.	Private aid.
21465	OYSTER BAYOU WEIR LIGHT 2	29-48-41.088N 093-23-52.818W	Fl R 2.5s			TR on pile.	Private aid.
21470	OYSTER BAYOU WEIR LIGHT 3	29-48-39.461N 093-23-50.806W	Fl G 2.5s			SG on pile.	Private aid.
21475	OYSTER BAYOU WEIR LIGHT 4	29-48-39.079N 093-23-51.853W	Fl R 2.5s			TR on pile.	Private aid.
21480	OYSTER BAYOU WEIR DANGER LIGHT	29-48-42.520N 093-23-51.828W	Fl W 2.5s			NW on pile.	Private aid.
21485	OYSTER BAYOU WEIR DANGER LIGHT	29-48-42.627N 093-23-52.935W	Fl W 2.5s			NW on pile.	Private aid.
21490	OYSTER BAYOU WEIR DANGER LIGHT	29-48-38.172N 093-23-51.468W	Fl W 2.5s			NW on pile.	Private aid.
21495	OYSTER BAYOU WEIR DANGER LIGHT	29-48-38.596N 093-23-50.273W	Fl W 2.5s			NW on pile.	Private aid.
21500	OYSTER BAYOU EAST DANGER LIGHT	29-49-03.180N 093-22-24.231W	Fl W 2.5s			NW on pile.	Private aid.
21505	OYSTER BAYOU EAST DANGER LIGHT	29-49-02.181N 093-22-24.218W	Fl W 2.5s			NW on pile.	Private aid.
21510	OYSTER BAYOU EAST DANGER LIGHT	29-49-04.042N 093-22-23.376W	Fl W 2.5s			NW on pile.	Private aid.
21515	OYSTER BAYOU EAST DANGER LIGHT	29-49-04.017N 093-22-25.007W	Fl W 2.5s			NW on pile.	Private aid.
21520	OYSTER BAYOU EAST DANGER LIGHT	29-49-01.363N 093-22-23.715W	Fl W 2.5s			NW on pile.	Private aid.
21525	OYSTER BAYOU EAST DANGER LIGHT	29-49-01.347N 093-22-24.723W	Fl W 2.5s			NW on pile.	Private aid.
21530	- B RANGE FRONT LIGHT	29-50-14.771N 093-20-56.977W	Q W	33		KRW on skeleton tower on piles.	Visible 2° each side of rangeline.
21535	- B RANGE REAR LIGHT 689 Yards, 358.0 from front light.	29-50-35.204N 093-20-58.189W	Iso W 6s	60		KRW on skeleton tower on piles.	Visible 2° each side of rangeline.

LOUISIANA - Eighth District

CALCASIEU RIVER AND LAKE (Chart 11347)
Calcasieu Channel

(1) No.	(2) Name and Location	(3) Position	(4) Characteristic	(5) Height	(6) Range	(7) Structure	(8) Remarks
21540	- C RANGE FRONT LIGHT	29-48-54.767N 093-21-00.232W	Q W	30		KRW on skeleton tower.	Visible 2° each side of rangeline.
21545	- C RANGE FRONT LIGHT PASSING LIGHT	29-48-54.774N 093-21-00.221W	Fl G 2.5s	32	4	On same structure as Calcasieu Channel Range C Front Light.	
21550	- C RANGE REAR LIGHT 503 yards, 185.5° from front light.	29-48-39.859N 093-21-01.579W	Iso W 6s	55		KRW on skeleton tower.	Visible 2° each side of rangeline.
21555	- LIGHT 59	29-50-14.660N 093-20-56.922W	Fl G 2.5s	35	4	SG on skeleton tower on piles. Same structure as Calcasieu Channel Range B Front Light.	
21560	- LIGHT 60	29-50-19.478N 093-20-47.012W	Fl R 2.5s	17	4	TR on pile.	
21565	- LIGHT 61 130 feet outside channel limit.	29-51-09.587N 093-20-52.549W	Fl G 4s	17	4	SG on skeleton tower on piles.	
21570	- LIGHT 62 130 feet outside channel limit.	29-51-09.786N 093-20-43.010W	Fl R 4s	17	4	TR on pile.	
21575	- LIGHT 63 130 feet outside channel limit.	29-52-10.175N 093-20-46.128W	Fl G 6s	17	4	SG on pile.	
21577	NATURE CONSERVANCY CALCASIEU LAKE WEST COVE DANGER LIGHT	29-52-23.770N 093-25-57.380W	Fl W 2.5s			Marks shoreline reef.	Private aid.
21577.01	Nature Conservancy Calcasieu Lake West Cove Danger Day beacon	29-52-24.920N 093-25-54.580W	Fl W 2.5s			Marks shoreline reef.	Private aid.
21577.02	Nature Conservancy Calcasieu Lake West Cove Danger Day beacon	29-52-26.740N 093-25-50.480W	Fl W 2.5s			Marks shoreline reef.	Private aid.
21577.03	Nature Conservancy Calcasieu Lake West Cove Danger Day beacon	29-52-27.170N 093-25-49.140W	Fl W 2.5s			Marks shoreline reef.	Private aid.
21577.04	NATURE CONSERVANCY CALCASIEU LAKE WEST COVE DANGER LIGHT	29-52-28.410N 093-25-44.410W	Fl W 2.5s			Marks shoreline reef.	Private aid.
21577.05	Nature Conservancy Calcasieu Lake West Cove Danger Day beacon	29-52-28.780N 093-25-43.400W	Fl W 2.5s			Marks shoreline reef.	Private aid.
21577.06	Nature Conservancy Calcasieu Lake West Cove Danger Day beacon	29-52-30.810N 093-25-39.080W	Fl W 2.5s			Marks shoreline reef.	Private aid.
21577.07	Nature Conservancy Calcasieu Lake West Cove Danger Day beacon	29-52-31.540N 093-25-37.050W	Fl W 2.5s			Marks shoreline reef.	Private aid.
21577.08	Nature Conservancy Calcasieu Lake West Cove Danger Day beacon	29-52-32.720N 093-25-33.970W	Fl W 2.5s			Marks shoreline reef.	Private aid.
21577.09	NATURE CONSERVANCY CALCASIEU LAKE WEST COVE DANGER LIGHT	29-52-34.620N 093-25-29.670W	Fl W 2.5s			Marks shoreline reef.	Private aid.
21577.11	Nature Conservancy Calcasieu Lake West Cove Danger Day beacon	29-52-35.350N 093-25-28.200W	Fl W 2.5s			Marks shoreline reef.	Private aid.
21577.12	Nature Conservancy Calcasieu Lake West Cove Danger Day beacon	29-52-36.840N 093-25-24.050W	Fl W 2.5s			Marks shoreline reef.	Private aid.
21577.13	Nature Conservancy Calcasieu Lake West Cove Danger Day beacon	29-52-37.440N 093-25-22.560W	Fl W 2.5s			Marks shoreline reef.	Private aid.

Light List corrected through LNM week: 01/18

(1) No.	(2) Name and Location	(3) Position	(4) Characteristic	(5) Height	(6) Range	(7) Structure	(8) Remarks
			LOUISIANA - Eighth District				
	CALCASIEU RIVER AND LAKE (Chart 11347)						
	Calcasieu Channel						
21577.14	Nature Conservancy Calcasieu Lake West Cove Danger Day beacon	29-52-38.630N 093-25-10.550W	Fl W 2.5s			Marks shoreline reef.	Private aid.
21577.15	Nature Conservancy Calcasieu Lake West Cove Danger Day beacon	29-52-38.920N 093-25-17.080W	Fl W 2.5s			Marks shoreline reef.	Private aid.
21577.16	NATURE CONSERVANCY CALCASIEU LAKE WEST COVE DANGER LIGHT	29-52-39.800N 093-25-13.010W	Fl W 2.5s			Marks shoreline reef.	Private aid.
21577.17	Nature Conservancy Calcasieu Lake West Cove Danger Day beacon	29-52-40.370N 093-25-11.140W	Fl W 2.5s			Marks shoreline reef.	Private aid.
21577.18	Nature Conservancy Calcasieu Lake West Cove Danger Day beacon	29-52-41.720N 093-25-07.040W	Fl W 2.5s				Private aid.
21577.19	Nature Conservancy Calcasieu Lake West Cove Danger Day beacon	29-52-42.190N 093-25-05.780W	Fl R 2.5s			Marks shoreline reef.	Private aid.
21577.21	NATURE CONSERVANCY CALCASIEU LAKE WEST COVE DANGER LIGHT	29-52-43.580N 093-25-01.130W	Fl W 2.5s			Marks shoreline reef.	Private aid.
21580	- LIGHT 64 130 feet outside channel limit.	29-52-08.172N 093-20-37.317W	Fl R 6s	17	4	TR on pile.	
21585	- PIPELINE LIGHT A	29-52-18.000N 093-20-30.000W	Fl Y 2.5s	6		On piles worded DO NOT ANCHOR OR DREDGE.	Private aid.
21590	- PIPELINE LIGHT B	29-52-12.000N 093-20-47.000W	Fl Y 2.5s	17		On piles worded DO NOT ANCHOR OR DREDGE.	Private aid.
21595	- LIGHT 65 130 feet outside channel limit.	29-53-07.783N 093-20-41.556W	Fl G 4s	17	4	SG on skeleton tower on piles.	
21600	- LIGHT 66 130 feet outside channel limit.	29-53-08.971N 093-20-33.117W	Fl (2)R 5s	17	3	TR on pile.	
21605	- LIGHT 67 130 feet outside channel limit.	29-54-05.642N 093-20-35.770W	Fl G 4s	17	4	SG on pile.	
21610	- LIGHT 68 130 feet outside channel limit.	29-54-05.639N 093-20-27.708W	Fl R 4s	17	4	TR on pile.	
21615	- LIGHT 69 130 feet outside channel limit.	29-54-56.842N 093-20-30.939W	Fl G 2.5s	17	4	SG on pile.	
21620	- LIGHT 70	29-54-55.207N 093-20-23.380W	Fl R 2.5s	17	4	TR on pile.	
21625	- LIGHT 71 130 feet outside channel limit.	29-55-46.293N 093-20-26.175W	Fl G 4s	17	4	SG on pile.	
21630	- LIGHT 72	29-55-45.611N 093-20-18.785W	Fl R 4s	17	3	TR on skeleton tower on piles.	
21635	- LIGHT 73 130 feet outside channel limit.	29-56-43.274N 093-20-21.557W	Fl G 6s	17	4	SG on pile.	
21640	- LIGHT 74 130 feet outside channel limit.	29-56-42.656N 093-20-13.640W	Fl R 6s	17	4	TR on skeleton tower on piles.	
21645	- LIGHT 75	29-57-39.647N 093-20-16.580W	Fl G 4s	17	4	SG on pile.	
21650	- LIGHT 76	29-57-39.272N 093-20-08.557W	Fl R 2.5s	17	4	TR on pile.	
21655	- LIGHT 77 130 feet outside channel limit.	29-58-35.205N 093-20-11.420W	Fl G 4s	17	4	SG on skeleton tower on piles.	
21660	- LIGHT 78 130 feet outside channel limit.	29-58-34.911N 093-20-03.481W	Fl R 4s	17	4	TR on pile.	

(1) No.	(2) Name and Location	(3) Position	(4) Characteristic	(5) Height	(6) Range	(7) Structure	(8) Remarks
		LOUISIANA - Eighth District					
	CALCASIEU RIVER AND LAKE (Chart 11347)						
	Calcasieu Channel						
21665	- LIGHT 79	29-59-42.597N 093-20-05.095W	Fl G 6s	17	4	SG on skeleton tower on piles.	
21670	- LIGHT 80	29-59-32.769N 093-19-58.436W	Fl R 6s	17	4	TR on pile.	
21675	- LIGHT 81	30-00-27.082N 093-20-01.051W	Fl G 2.5s	17	4	SG on skeleton tower on piles.	
21680	- LIGHT 82	30-00-26.615N 093-19-54.042W	Fl R 2.5s	17	4	TR on skeleton tower on piles.	
21685	- LIGHT 83	30-01-19.532N 093-19-56.095W	Fl G 6s	17	4	SG on skeleton tower on piles.	
21690	- LIGHT 84	30-01-18.764N 093-19-48.558W	Fl R 6s	17	4	TR on pile.	
21695	CALCASIEU LAKE CHANNEL ENTRANCE LIGHT 2	30-01-25.500N 093-19-10.800W	Q R	10		TR on dolphin.	Private aid.
21700	- LIGHT 85 130 feet outside channel limit.	30-02-53.885N 093-19-47.314W	Fl G 4s	17	4	SG on pile.	Ra ref.
21705	Cameron LNG Day beacon A	30-02-04.257N 093-19-52.345W				On pile.	CONTROLLED AREA. Private aid.
21710	Cameron LNG Day beacon B	30-02-09.726N 093-19-44.037W				On pile.	CONTROLLED AREA. Private aid.
21715	Cameron LNG Day beacon C	30-02-19.995N 093-19-38.125W				On pile.	CONTROLLED AREA. Private aid.
21720	Cameron LNG Day beacon D	30-02-29.623N 093-19-42.256W				On pile.	CONTROLLED AREA. Private aid.
21725	CAMERON LNG FACILITY SOUTH JETTY LIGHT	30-02-05.844N 093-19-52.701W	Fl G 2.5s			On dolphin.	Private aid.
21730	- LIGHT 86 130 feet outside channel limit.	30-02-53.389N 093-19-40.121W	Fl R 4s	17	4	TR on pile.	
21735	CAMERON LNG FACILITY NORTH JETTY LIGHT	30-02-33.834N 093-19-50.147W	Fl G 2.5s			On dolphin.	Private aid.
21738	Cameron LNG Day beacon 1	30-02-42.000N 093-19-51.000W				Marks private channel.	Private aid.
21738.01	Cameron LNG Day beacon 2	30-02-44.000N 093-19-51.000W				Marks private channel.	Private aid.
21740	- D RANGE FRONT LIGHT	30-05-46.106N 093-19-28.142W	Iso R 2s (NIGHT) Iso W 2s (DAY)	27 30		Skeleton tower on piles.	Night: Visible 2° each side of rangeline. Day: Light visible only on rangeline. AIS - 993682018
21745	- D RANGE FRONT LIGHT PASSING LIGHT	30-05-46.016N 093-19-28.221W	Fl R 4s	32	4	On same structure as Calcasieu Channel Range D Front Light.	
21750	- D RANGE REAR LIGHT 790 yards, 004.5° from front light.	30-06-09.466N 093-19-26.010W	Iso R 6s (NIGHT) Iso W 6s (DAY)	63 60		Skeleton tower on piles.	Night: Visible only on the rangeline. Day: Light visible only on rangeline. AIS - 993682019
21755	- LIGHT 87 130 feet outside channel limit.	30-03-50.444N 093-19-42.924W	Fl G 6s	17	4	SG on skeleton tower on piles.	
21760	- LIGHT 88 130 feet outside channel limit.	30-03-51.343N 093-19-34.635W	Fl R 6s	17	4	TR on pile.	
21765	- LIGHT 89 130 feet outside channel limit.	30-04-40.448N 093-19-37.728W	Fl G 4s	17	4	SG on pile.	
21770	- LIGHT 90 130 feet outside channel limit.	30-04-38.357N 093-19-29.958W	Fl R 4s	17	4	TR on skeleton tower on piles.	
21775 35410	- LIGHT 91 50 feet outside channel limit.	30-05-18.123N 093-19-34.478W	Fl G 2.5s	17	4	SG-SY on skeleton tower on piles.	

(1) No.	(2) Name and Location	(3) Position	(4) Characteristic	(5) Height	(6) Range	(7) Structure	(8) Remarks

LOUISIANA - Eighth District

CALCASIEU RIVER AND LAKE (Chart 11347)
Calcasieu Channel

(1) No.	(2) Name and Location	(3) Position	(4) Characteristic	(5) Height	(6) Range	(7) Structure	(8) Remarks
21780 35405	- LIGHT 92	30-05-21.790N 093-19-24.920W	Fl R 2.5s	17	4	TR-SY on pile.	
21785 35390	DEVILS ELBOW LIGHT 1 90 yards outside channel limit.	30-05-48.804N 093-19-14.341W	Oc G 4s	17	3	SG-TY on pile.	Ra ref.
21790 35385	DEVILS ELBOW LIGHT 2 72 yards outside channel limit.	30-05-47.623N 093-19-01.149W	Oc R 4s	17	3	TR-SY on pile.	Ra ref.
21795 35380	DEVILS ELBOW LIGHT 3 88 yards outside channel limit.	30-06-16.399N 093-18-40.888W	Fl G 2.5s	17	3	SG-TY on pile.	Ra ref.
21800 35375	DEVILS ELBOW JUNCTION LIGHT	30-06-14.039N 093-18-27.324W	Fl (2+1)R 6s	20	3	JR-TY on skeleton tower.	
21805 35395	DEVILS ELBOW RANGE FRONT LIGHT	30-05-14.763N 093-19-47.153W	Q W	20		KRW-I on pile.	Visible all around; higher intensity on the rangeline.
21810 35400	DEVILS ELBOW RANGE REAR LIGHT 103 yards, 226.9° from front light.	30-05-12.642N 093-19-49.672W	Iso W 6s	40		KRW-1 on skeleton tower.	Visible all around; higher intensity on the rangeline.
21815	ALCOA METALS WEST DOLPHIN LIGHT	30-06-34.390N 093-17-56.620W	Fl G 2.5s			On dolphin.	Private aid.
21820	ALCOA METALS DOCK LIGHTS (2)	30-06-35.000N 093-17-46.000W	Fl G 2.5s			On pier.	Private aid.
21825	ALCOA METALS EAST DOLPHIN LIGHT	30-06-36.590N 093-17-38.860W	Fl G 2.5s			On mooring dolphin.	Private aid.
21830 35365	DEVILS ELBOW INDUSTRIAL CANAL RANGE FRONT LIGHT 5	30-06-27.801N 093-18-19.678W	Q G	20		KRW-I and SG on skeleton tower on piles.	Visible all around. Higher intensity on rangeline. KRW-I for inbound traffic. SG for outboard traffic.
21835 35370	DEVILS ELBOW INDUSTRIAL CANAL RANGE REAR LIGHT 192 yards, 046.4° from front light.	30-06-31.843N 093-18-14.816W	F G	37		KRW-I on skeleton tower on piles.	Visible all around. Higher intrnsity on rangeline. Ra ref.
21840	DEVILS ELBOW INDUSTRIAL CANAL LIGHT 7	30-06-31.788N 093-18-08.461W	Fl G 2.5s	17	3	SG on pile.	
21845	DEVILS ELBOW INDUSTRIAL CANAL LIGHT 8	30-06-27.305N 093-17-59.297W	Fl R 2.5s	17	3	TR on pile.	
21850	DEVILS ELBOW INDUSTRIAL CANAL LIGHT 10 30 yards outside the channel limit.	30-06-30.399N 093-17-39.700W	Oc R 4s	17	3	TR on pile.	Ra ref.
21855	TRUNKLINE LNG DOLPHIN LIGHTS (4)	30-06-35.940N 093-17-17.500W	Fl G 2.5s	19		On dolphin.	Private aid.

Calcasieu River

(1) No.	(2) Name and Location	(3) Position	(4) Characteristic	(5) Height	(6) Range	(7) Structure	(8) Remarks
21860	- LEADING LIGHT A	30-06-33.684N 093-20-05.010W	Iso W 6s	25	5	NB on skeleton tower on piles.	Visible all around; higher intensity on bearing 182°30`.
21865	- LIGHT 96	30-06-35.524N 093-19-55.451W	Fl R 2.5s	17	4	TR on skeleton tower on pile.	
21870	- LIGHT 97	30-06-44.157N 093-20-08.906W	Fl G 2.5s	17	4	SG on pile.	
21875	- LIGHT 98	30-06-46.160N 093-19-59.226W	Q R	17	4	TR on pile.	
21880	- LIGHT 99	30-06-58.337N 093-20-08.002W	Fl G 4s	17	4	SG on dolphin.	
21885	- LIGHT 100	30-06-57.779N 093-19-59.156W	Fl R 2.5s	17	4	TR on dolphin.	
21890	- LIGHT 101	30-07-27.974N 093-19-59.977W	Fl G 4s	17	4	SG on pile.	
21895	- LIGHT 102	30-07-26.180N 093-19-50.443W	Fl R 4s	17	4	TR on pile.	
21900	- LIGHT 103	30-07-51.301N 093-19-52.762W	Fl G 2.5s	17	4	SG on pile.	

Light List corrected through LNM week: 01/18

(1) No.	(2) Name and Location	(3) Position	(4) Characteristic	(5) Height	(6) Range	(7) Structure	(8) Remarks
			LOUISIANA - Eighth District				
	CALCASIEU RIVER AND LAKE (Chart 11347)						
	Calcasieu River						
21905	- E RANGE FRONT LIGHT	30-07-36.740N 093-19-44.491W	Q W	30		KRW on skeleton tower on piles.	Visible all around; higher intensity on rangeline.
21910	- E RANGE REAR LIGHT 713 yards, 173.6° from front light.	30-07-15.748N 093-19-41.338W	Iso W 6s	40		KRW on skeleton tower on piles.	Visible all around; higher intensity on rangeline.
21915	- LIGHT 104	30-08-05.370N 093-19-44.760W	Fl R 2.5s	17	4	TR on pile.	
21920	- REFINING DOCK LIGHTS (3)	30-08-08.000N 093-19-14.000W	Fl R 2.5s	13		On dolphins.	Private aid.
21925	- LIGHT 106	30-08-41.450N 093-19-50.034W	Fl R 4s	17	4	TR on skeleton tower on piles.	
21930	- LIGHT 108	30-09-10.793N 093-19-52.016W	Q R	17	4	TR on pile.	Ra ref.
21935	DAVISON CHEMICAL DOCK LIGHTS (2)	30-09-17.000N 093-19-55.000W	F G	13		On dolphin.	Private aid.
21940	CLIFTON RIDGE TANKER DOCK LIGHTS (2)	30-09-24.500N 093-19-48.600W	Fl G 2.5s	18		On each end of dock.	Private aid.
21945	CLIFTON RIDGE DOCK LIGHTS (3)	30-09-27.000N 093-14-46.000W	F W			On dock.	Private aid.
21950	- LIGHT 110	30-09-39.946N 093-19-08.613W	Fl R 2.5s	17	3	TR on pile.	
	Citgo Petroleum						
21955	- PIPELINE FACILITY DOLPHIN LIGHT	30-09-36.000N 093-19-25.000W	Fl G 2.5s	9		On dolphin.	Private aid.
21960	CALCASIEU RIVER LIGHT 109	30-09-43.055N 093-19-17.042W	Q G	17	4	SG on pile.	
21965	- MANUFACTURING COMPLEX BULKHEAD LIGHTS(2)	30-09-59.870N 093-19-13.920W	Fl G 2.5s	8		On bulkhead.	Private aid.
21970	- REFINING DOCK A LIGHTS (2)	30-10-24.000N 093-19-06.000W	Fl G 2.5s			On dock.	Private aid.
21975	- REFINING DOCK A TURNING LIGHT	30-10-18.900N 093-19-10.400W	Fl G 2.5s	14		On pile.	Private aid.
21980	- REFINING DOCK B LIGHTS (2)	30-10-24.000N 093-19-06.000W	Fl G 2.5s			On dock.	Private aid.
21985	CALCASIEU RIVER LIGHT 112	30-10-31.152N 093-19-00.673W	Q R	17	4	TR on pile.	
21990	- REFINING DOCK C LIGHTS (2)	30-10-42.000N 093-19-54.000W	Fl G 2.5s			On dock.	Private aid.
21995	- REFINING DOCK P LIGHTS (2)	30-10-54.000N 093-18-48.000W	Fl G 2.5s			On dock.	Private aid.
22000	- REFINING DOCK D LIGHTS (2)	30-11-54.000N 093-18-42.000W	Fl G 2.5s			On dock.	Private aid.
	Calcasieu River						
22005	- LIGHT 114	30-11-03.952N 093-18-19.395W	Fl R 2.5s	17	4	TR on pile.	
	Cline Canal						
22010	- Entrance Day beacon 1	30-11-52.400N 093-16-17.520W				SG on pile.	Private aid.
22015	- Entrance Day beacon 3	30-11-50.340N 093-16-13.220W				SG on pile.	Private aid.
22020	- Entrance Day beacon 5	30-11-49.100N 093-16-08.520W				SG on pile.	Private aid.
	Coon Island Channel						
22025	- LIGHT 1	30-12-19.211N 093-16-44.500W	Fl G 2.5s	17	4	SG on pile.	
22030	- LIGHT 2	30-12-21.825N 093-16-37.524W	Fl R 2.5s	17	4	TR on pile.	Ra ref.
22035	- A RANGE FRONT LIGHT	30-13-06.646N 093-16-53.636W	Q G	15		Skeleton tower.	Lighted throughout 24 hours.

Light List corrected through LNM week: 01/18

(1) No.	(2) Name and Location	(3) Position	(4) Characteristic	(5) Height	(6) Range	(7) Structure	(8) Remarks
		LOUISIANA - Eighth District					
	CALCASIEU RIVER AND LAKE (Chart 11347)						
	Calcasieu River						
	Coon Island Channel						
22040	- A RANGE REAR LIGHT 200 yards, 347° from front light.	30-13-13.784N 093-16-55.506W	Oc G 4s	34		Skeleton tower.	Higher intensity beam on rangeline.
22045	- Day beacon 1A	30-12-30.772N 093-16-46.499W				SG on pile.	
22050	- LIGHT 3	30-12-45.985N 093-16-51.023W	Fl G 4s	17	4	SG on pile.	
22055	- LIGHT 4	30-12-45.456N 093-16-45.448W	Fl R 4s	17	4	TR on pile.	
22060	- LIGHT 6	30-12-53.541N 093-16-47.181W	Fl R 6s	17	3	TR on pile.	
22065	PPG SOUTH LOADING TERMINAL DOCK LIGHTS (2)	30-12-52.300N 093-16-51.900W	F G	12		On sheerpipe caissons.	Private aid.
22070	- LIGHT 8	30-13-04.258N 093-16-47.702W	Fl R 2.5s	17	3	TR on pile.	
22075	PPG RIVERSIDE POWER HOUSE LIGHT	30-13-15.500N 093-16-47.700W	F G	10		On corner of structure.	Private aid.
22080	PPG CHLORINE LOADING DOCK LIGHT	30-13-22.200N 093-16-44.300W	F G	16		On corner of dock.	Private aid.
22085	PPG CAUSTIC LOADING DOCK LIGHTS (2)	30-13-26.000N 093-16-37.400W	F G	11		On sheerpipe caissons on ends of dock.	Private aid.
22090	- LIGHT 10 75 feet outside channel limit.	30-13-14.160N 093-16-44.358W	Fl R 4s	17	3	TR on pile.	
22095	- Day beacon 12	30-13-16.191N 093-16-41.302W				TR on pile.	
22100	- LIGHT 14	30-13-13.852N 093-16-33.428W	Fl R 6s	17	3	TR on pile.	
22105	- LIGHT 16	30-13-17.313N 093-16-28.450W	Fl R 2.5s	17	3	TR on pile.	
	Calcasieu River						
22110	- Buoy 115	30-11-52.381N 093-17-20.490W				Green can.	
22115	Bayou D'Inde Junction Buoy BD	30-11-53.686N 093-17-17.112W				Green can with red band.	
22120	- LIGHT 115A	30-12-23.401N 093-16-29.105W	Fl G 2.5s	17	4	SG on pile.	
22125	- LIGHT 116	30-12-17.917N 093-16-22.688W	Q R	17	4	TR on pile.	
22130	- LIGHT 117	30-12-26.424N 093-16-18.628W	Q G	17	4	SG on pile.	
22135	- LIGHT 118	30-12-20.780N 093-15-54.636W	Fl R 2.5s	17	4	TR on pile.	
22140	- LIGHT 119	30-12-43.009N 093-15-35.786W	Fl G 2.5s	17	4	SG on pile.	
22145	- LIGHT 120	30-12-35.743N 093-15-29.530W	Q R	17	4	TR on pile.	
22150	- PIER 7 LIGHT	30-12-40.000N 093-15-26.000W	Fl R 2.5s	15		On pier.	Private aid.
22155	LAKE CHARLES HARBOR DOCK LIGHT A	30-13-03.000N 093-15-33.000W	Fl R 2.5s	10		On dolphin.	Private aid.
22160	LAKE CHARLES HARBOR DOCK LIGHT B	30-13-08.000N 093-15-29.000W	Fl R 2.5s	10		On dolphin.	Private aid.
22165	- LIGHT 121	30-13-09.504N 093-15-40.560W	Q G	17	4	SG on pile.	
	Clooneys Loop						
22170	- LIGHT 2 130 feet outside channel limit.	30-13-03.856N 093-16-02.791W	Fl R 4s	17	4	TR on pile.	
22175	- LIGHT 3 130 feet outside channel limit.	30-13-06.484N 093-16-13.760W	Fl G 4s	17	4	SG on pile.	

(1) No.	(2) Name and Location	(3) Position	(4) Characteristic	(5) Height	(6) Range	(7) Structure	(8) Remarks
		LOUISIANA - Eighth District					
	CALCASIEU RIVER AND LAKE (Chart 11347)						
	Calcasieu River						
	Clooneys Loop						
22180	CONOCO DOCK 1 DOLPHIN LIGHT	30-13-54.000N 093-15-29.500W	Fl G 2.5s	12		On dolphin.	Private aid.
22185	CONOCO DOCK 1 LIGHTS (2)	30-13-53.800N 093-15-27.600W	Fl G 2.5s	16		On dock.	Private aid.
22190	CONOCO DOCK 2 LIGHTS (2)	30-13-53.500N 093-15-18.500W	Fl G 2.5s	16		On dock.	Private aid.
22195	CONOCO DOCK 2B LIGHTS(3)	30-13-48.780N 093-15-14.300W	Fl G 2.5s	10		On dolphin.	Private aid.
22200	CONOCO DOCK 3 LIGHTS (2)	30-13-48.100N 093-15-14.000W	Fl G 2.5s	16		On dock.	Private aid.
22205	CONOCO DOCK 3 DOLPHIN LIGHT	30-13-43.200N 093-15-10.000W	Fl G 2.5s	12		On dolphin.	Private aid.
	Calcasieu River						
22210	WESTLAKE DOCK LIGHT	30-13-11.000N 093-15-04.000W	F G	8		On concrete bridge pier.	Private aid.
22215	NORTH AMERICAN LAND COMPANY FUEL DOCK LIGHT A	30-13-10.000N 093-14-59.000W	Fl G 2.5s	9		On pier.	Private aid.
22220	NORTH AMERICAN LAND COMPANY FUEL DOCK LIGHT B	30-13-10.000N 093-15-00.000W	Fl G 2.5s	9		On pier.	Private aid.
22225	- LIGHT 122	30-13-08.479N 093-14-21.693W	Q R	17	4	TR on pile.	
22230	- Lighted Buoy 122A	30-13-17.225N 093-14-20.807W	Fl R 4s		3	Red.	
22235	- LIGHT 123	30-13-10.892N 093-14-33.222W	Q G	17	3	SG on skeleton tower.	
22240	- LIGHT 125	30-13-22.224N 093-14-30.590W	Fl G 2.5s	17	3	SG on pile.	
22245	- LIGHT 124	30-13-25.228N 093-14-23.981W	Fl R 2.5s	17	3	TR on pile.	
22250	- LIGHT 126	30-13-37.970N 093-14-36.714W	Fl R 4s	17	4	TR on pile.	
22255	- Day beacon 128	30-13-44.063N 093-14-40.664W				TR on pile.	
22260	- LIGHT 130	30-13-50.620N 093-14-42.399W	Fl R 4s	17	4	TR on pile.	
22265	WESTLAKE SHIP BERTH 13 DOCK LIGHTS (2)	30-13-53.000N 093-14-50.000W	Fl G 2.5s	11		On dock.	Private aid.
22270	- Day beacon 132	30-13-53.479N 093-14-38.878W				TR on pile.	
22275	- Day beacon 134	30-14-04.629N 093-14-39.784W				TR on pile.	
22280	- LIGHT 136	30-14-05.125N 093-14-44.278W	Fl R 6s	17	4	TR on pile.	
22285	- EROSION EAST LIGHTS (2)	30-14-33.000N 093-14-44.000W	Fl R 2.5s	10		On pile clusters.	Private aid.
22287	PORT OF LAKE CHARLES CONSTRUCTION DOCK LIGHTS (4)	30-14-41.630N 093-14-50.470W	Fl W 2.5s			Marks construction docks A and B.	Private aid.
22290	- EROSION WEST LIGHTS (2)	30-14-32.000N 093-14-51.000W	Fl G 2.5s	10		On pile clusters.	Private aid.
22295	LAKE CHARLES BULK TERMINAL NO.7 DOCK LIGHTS (2)	30-14-33.000N 093-13-03.000W	Fl R 2.5s	23			Private aid.
22298	MCMICHAEL DOCK LIGHT	30-18-42.000N 093-16-45.000W	Fl R 2.5s			Marks outermost upstream corner of dock.	Private aid.
		TEXAS - LOUISIANA - Eighth District					
	CALCASIEU PASS TO SABINE PASS (Chart 11341)						
	Sabine Bank Channel						
22300 1085	- Lighted Buoy SB	29-25-00.846N 093-40-00.586W	Mo (A) W		6	Red and white stripes with red spherical topmark.	

Light List corrected through LNM week: 01/18

(1) No.	(2) Name and Location	(3) Position	(4) Characteristic	(5) Height	(6) Range	(7) Structure	(8) Remarks
	TEXAS - LOUISIANA - Eighth District						
	CALCASIEU PASS TO SABINE PASS (Chart 11341)						
	Sabine Bank Channel						
22305	- Lighted Buoy 1 100 feet outside channel limit.	29-26-04.845N 093-40-06.240W	Fl G 4s		4		Green.
22310	- Lighted Buoy 2 100 feet outside channel limit.	29-26-05.844N 093-39-55.586W	Fl R 4s		4		Red.
22315	- Lighted Buoy 3 100 feet outside channel limit.	29-27-07.972N 093-40-06.543W	Fl G 6s		4		Green.
22320	- Lighted Buoy 4 100 feet outside channel limit.	29-27-07.842N 093-39-54.930W	Fl R 6s		4		Red.
22325	- Lighted Buoy 5 100 feet outside channel limit.	29-28-12.840N 093-40-05.585W	Fl G 2.5s		4		Green.
22330	- Lighted Buoy 6 100 feet outside channel limit.	29-28-12.840N 093-39-54.585W	Fl R 2.5s		3		Red.
22335	- Lighted Buoy 7	29-28-42.719N 093-40-06.087W	Q G		3		Green.
22340	- Lighted Buoy 8 50 feet outside channel limit.	29-28-55.839N 093-39-55.584W	Q R		3		Red.
22345	- Lighted Buoy 9	29-29-01.035N 093-40-15.293W	Q G		3		Green.
22350	- Lighted Buoy 11 100 feet outside channel limit.	29-29-20.377N 093-40-37.390W	Fl G 2.5s		4		Green.
22355	- Lighted Buoy 12 100 feet outside channel limit.	29-29-26.837N 093-40-27.585W	Fl R 2.5s		4		Red.
22360	- Lighted Buoy 13 100 feet outside channel limit.	29-30-15.455N 093-41-42.092W	Fl G 4s		4		Green.
22365	- Lighted Buoy 14 100 feet outside channel limit.	29-30-21.874N 093-41-33.473W	Fl R 4s		3		Red.
22370	- Lighted Buoy 17 100 feet outside channel limit.	29-31-38.031N 093-43-21.724W	Fl G 4s		4		Green.
22375	- Lighted Buoy 18 100 feet outside channel limit.	29-31-46.828N 093-43-10.585W	Fl R 2.5s		4		Red.
22380	- Lighted Buoy 21 100 feet outside channel limit.	29-33-03.194N 093-45-01.032W	Fl G 4s		4		Green.
22385	- Lighted Buoy 22 100 feet outside channel limit.	29-33-10.822N 093-44-51.085W	Fl R 4s		3		Red.
22390	- Lighted Buoy 25 100 feet outside channel limit.	29-34-27.600N 093-46-39.694W	Fl G 4s		4		Green.
22395	- Lighted Buoy 26 100 feet outside channel limit.	29-34-37.239N 093-46-31.347W	Fl R 4s		4		Red.
22400	- Lighted Buoy 29 100 feet outside channel limit.	29-35-53.812N 093-48-20.590W	Q G		3		Green.
22405	- Lighted Buoy 30 100 feet outside channel limit.	29-35-56.732N 093-48-06.663W	Q R		3		Red.
22410	SABINE PASS OUTER A RANGE FRONT LIGHT	29-39-18.922N 093-49-51.015W	Q G	39		KRW on skeleton tower on piles.	Visible 2° each side of rangeline.
22415	SABINE PASS OUTER A RANGE REAR LIGHT 1,003 yards 337.5° from front light.	29-39-46.432N 093-50-04.060W	Iso G 6s	70		KRW on skeleton tower on piles.	Visible 2° each side of rangeline.

Light List corrected through LNM week: 01/18

(1) No.	(2) Name and Location	(3) Position	(4) Characteristic	(5) Height	(6) Range	(7) Structure	(8) Remarks
	TEXAS - LOUISIANA - Eighth District						
	SABINE PASS AND LAKE (Chart 11342)						
	Sabine Bank Channel						
22420	- Lighted Buoy 31 200 feet outside channel limit.	29-36-43.075N 093-48-44.374W	Fl G 2.5s		4	Green.	
22425	- Lighted Buoy 32 200 feet outside channel limit.	29-36-47.510N 093-48-32.690W	Fl R 2.5s		3	Red.	
22430	- Lighted Buoy 33 200 feet outside channel limit.	29-37-39.807N 093-49-10.591W	Fl G 2.5s		4	Green.	
22435	- Lighted Buoy 34 200 feet outside channel limit.	29-37-43.807N 093-48-57.590W	Fl R 2.5s		3	Red.	
	Sabine Pass						
22440 1105	- **East Jetty Light**	29-38-40.574N 093-49-21.938W	Iso W 2s	42	8	Cylindrical tower on piles. 25	
22445	East Side Dredging Range Front Day beacon	29-40-00.000N 093-50-06.000W				Black square slatted day mark on skeleton tower.	Range marks edge of channel for dredging purposes. May show fixed amber light when dredging is in progress. Maintained by U.S. Army Corps of Engineers. Aid maintained by U.S. Army Corps of Engineers.
22450	East Side Dredging Range Rear Day beacon 1,350 yards, 338° from front day beacon					Orange square slatted day mark on skeleton tower.	Maintained by U.S. Army Corps of Engineers. May show fixed amber light when dredging is in progress. Aid maintained by U.S. Army Corps of Engineers.
22455	West Side Dredging Range Front Day beacon					Black square slatted day mark on skeleton tower.	Range marks edge of channel for dredging purposes. Maintained by U.S. Army Corps of Engineers. May show fixed amber light when dredging is in progress. Aid maintained by U.S. Army Corps of Engineers.
22460	West Side Dredging Range Rear Day beacon 1,740 yards, 338° from front day beacon.					Orange square slatted day mark on skeleton tower.	Maintained by U.S. Army Corps of Engineers. May show fixed amber light when dredging is in progress. Aid maintained by U.S. Army Corps of Engineers.
22465	- Lighted Buoy 18 50 feet outside channel limit.	29-38-36.814N 093-49-23.988W	Q R		3	Red.	
22470	- Lighted Buoy 17	29-38-37.861N 093-49-36.062W	Q G		3	Green.	
22475	- JETTY B RANGE FRONT LIGHT	29-41-37.207N 093-50-17.532W	Q R (NIGHT) Q W (DAY)	20 17			Visible 2° each side of rangeline.
22480	- JETTY B RANGE REAR LIGHT 600 yards, 347° from front light.	29-41-52.468N 093-50-21.484W	Oc R 4s (NIGHT) Oc W 4s (DAY)	50 47			Visible 2° each side of rangeline.

(1) No.	(2) Name and Location	(3) Position	(4) Characteristic	(5) Height	(6) Range	(7) Structure	(8) Remarks
			TEXAS - LOUISIANA - Eighth District				
	SABINE PASS AND LAKE (Chart 11342)						
	Sabine Pass						
22485	- *Lighted Buoy 19* 50 feet outside channel limit.	29-39-27.291N 093-49-48.391W	Fl G 2.5s		4		Green.
22490	- *Lighted Buoy 20* 50 feet outside channel limit.	29-39-28.802N 093-49-38.891W	Fl R 2.5s		3		Red.
22495	- *Lighted Buoy 21* 50 feet outside channel limit.	29-40-17.799N 093-50-01.591W	Fl G 2.5s		4		Green.
22500	- *Lighted Buoy 22* 50 feet outside channel limit.	29-40-19.921N 093-49-51.655W	Fl R 2.5s		3		Red.
22505	- *Lighted Buoy 26* 50 feet outside channel limit.	29-41-03.322N 093-50-00.498W	Q R		3		Red.
22510	Jetty Channel Dredging East Side Range Front Day beacon					Black triangular day mark on skeleton tower.	Range marks edge of channel for dredging purposes. Maintained by U.S. Army Corps of Engineers. Aid maintained by U.S. Army Corps of Engineers.
22515	Jetty Channel Dredging East Side Range Rear Day beacon					Orange square day mark on skeleton tower.	Range marks edge of channel for dredging purposes. Maintained by U.S. Army Corps of Engineers. Aid maintained by U.S. Army Corps of Engineers.
22520	Jetty Channel Dredging West Side Range Front Day beacon					Black triangular day mark on skeleton tower.	Range marks edge of channel for dredging purposes. Maintained by U.S. Army Corps of Engineers. Aid maintained by U.S. Army Corps of Engineers.
22525	Jetty Channel Dredging West Side Range Rear Day beacon					Orange square day mark on skeleton tower.	Range marks edge of channel for dredging purposes. Maintained by U.S. Army Corps of Engineers. Aid maintained by U.S. Army Corps of Engineers.
22530	- *Lighted Buoy 27*	29-41-21.511N 093-50-19.783W	Q G		3		Green.
22535	- C RANGE FRONT LIGHT	29-45-28.981N 093-53-24.448W	Iso R 2s (NIGHT) Iso W 2s (DAY)	27 25		Skeleton tower on piles.	Visible all around, higher intensity on rangeline.
22540	- C RANGE REAR LIGHT 1,123 yards, 323.0° from front light.	29-45-54.621N 093-53-44.193W	Iso R 6s (NIGHT) Iso W 6s (DAY)	70 67		Skeleton tower on piles.	Lighted throughout 24 hours. Visible 1° each side of rangeline.
22545	- C RANGE REAR LIGHT PASSING LIGHT	29-45-54.630N 093-53-44.202W	Fl R 4s	20	3	On same structure as Sabine Pass C Range Rear Light.	
22550	- *Lighted Buoy 29* 50 feet outside channel limit.	29-41-51.595N 093-50-42.891W	Fl G 2.5s		4		Green.
22555	- *Lighted Buoy 30*	29-41-53.649N 093-50-33.363W	Fl R 2.5s		3		Red.
22560	- *Lighted Buoy 32* 50 feet outside channel limit.	29-42-23.793N 093-50-57.192W	Fl R 4s		3		Red.

Light List corrected through LNM week: 01/18

(1) No.	(2) Name and Location	(3) Position	(4) Characteristic	(5) Height	(6) Range	(7) Structure	(8) Remarks
			TEXAS - LOUISIANA - Eighth District				
	SABINE PASS AND LAKE (Chart 11342)						
	Sabine Pass						
22565	- *Lighted Buoy 34* 50 feet outside channel limit.	29-42-54.816N 093-51-21.529W	Fl R 6s		3	Red nun.	
22570	- *Lighted Buoy 36*	29-43-27.790N 093-51-46.193W	Fl R 4s		3	Red.	
22575	- ANCHORAGE BASIN LIGHT A	29-44-05.068N 093-51-54.304W	Fl Y 4s	17	5	NY on dolphin.	
22580	- LNG WEST MOORING DOLPHIN LIGHT	29-44-32.800N 093-52-24.700W	Fl W 2.5s	19		Mooring dolphin.	Private aid.
22585	- LNG EAST MOORING DOLPHIN LIGHT	29-44-26.300N 093-52-13.500W	Fl W 2.5s	19		Mooring dolphin.	Private aid.
22590	- LNG WEST RANGE FRONT LIGHT	29-44-43.400N 093-52-07.700W	F G	35		KGW on tower.	Visible only from 175°T to 245°T. Private aid.
22595	- LNG WEST RANGE REAR LIGHT	29-44-48.300N 093-52-02.400W	F G	45		KGW on tower.	Visible only from 175°T to 245°T. Private aid.
22600	- LNG EAST RANGE FRONT LIGHT	29-44-42.000N 093-52-05.000W	F R	34		KRW on tower.	Visible only from 175°T to 245°T. Private aid.
22605	- LNG EAST RANGE REAR LIGHT	29-44-47.000N 093-52-01.400W	F R	45		KRW on tower.	Visible only from 175° to 245°. Private aid.
22610	- LIGHT 37	29-44-00.024N 093-52-22.408W	Q G	17	4	SG on pile.	
22615	- BATTLEGROUND STATE PARK ENTRANCE LIGHT 1	29-44-03.750N 093-52-28.450W	Fl G 6s			SG on pile.	Private aid.
22620	- Battleground State Park Day beacon 2	29-44-03.880N 093-52-28.770W				TR on pile.	Private aid.
22625	- *Anchorage Lighted Buoy B*	29-44-11.937N 093-52-13.977W	Fl Y 6s			Yellow.	Marks northern most point of anchorage.
22630	- LIGHT 38	29-44-34.146N 093-52-36.230W	Q R	17	3	TR on pile.	
22635	- LIGHT 39	29-45-04.456N 093-53-11.085W	Q G	17	4	SG on pile.	
	Chevron Sabine Facility Channel						
22640	Cox Sabine Facility Channel Channel Buoy 1	29-45-35.000N 093-53-19.000W				Green can.	Private aid.
22645	Cox Sabine Facility Channel Buoy 2	29-45-33.000N 093-53-13.000W				Red nun.	Private aid.
22650	Cox Sabine Facility Channel Buoy 3	29-45-39.000N 093-53-16.000W				Green can.	Private aid.
22655	Cox Sabine Facility Channel Buoy 4	29-45-38.000N 093-53-15.000W				Red nun.	Private aid.
22660	Cox Sabine Facility Channel Buoy 5	29-45-44.000N 093-53-13.000W				Green can.	Private aid.
22665	Cox Sabine Facility Channel Buoy 6	29-45-43.000N 093-53-12.000W				Red nun.	Private aid.
22670	Cox Sabine Facility Channel Buoy 7	29-45-47.000N 093-53-12.000W				Green can.	Private aid.
22675	Cox Sabine Facility Channel Buoy 8	29-45-46.000N 093-53-10.000W				Red nun.	Private aid.
22680	Cox Sabine Facility Channel Buoy 9	29-45-50.000N 093-53-10.000W				Green can.	Private aid.
22685	Cox Sabine Facility Channel Buoy 10	29-45-49.000N 093-53-08.000W				Red nun.	Private aid.
22690	Cox Sabine Facility Channel Buoy 11	29-45-53.000N 093-53-07.000W				Green can.	Private aid.
22695	Cox Sabine Facility Channel Buoy 12	29-45-52.000N 093-53-06.000W				Red nun.	Private aid.
22700	Cox Sabine Facility Channel Buoy 13	29-45-54.000N 093-53-06.000W				Green can.	Private aid.
22705	Cox Sabine Facility Channel Buoy 14	29-45-52.000N 093-53-05.000W				Red nun.	Private aid.

(1) No.	(2) Name and Location	(3) Position	(4) Characteristic	(5) Height	(6) Range	(7) Structure	(8) Remarks
		TEXAS - LOUISIANA - Eighth District					
	SABINE PASS AND LAKE (Chart 11342)						
	Sabine Pass						
	Chevron Sabine Facility Channel						
22710	Cox Sabine Facility Channel Buoy 15	29-45-56.000N 093-53-04.000W				Green can.	Private aid.
22715	Cox Sabine Facility Channel Buoy 16	29-45-52.000N 093-53-03.000W				Red nun.	Private aid.
22720	Cox Sabine Facility Channel Buoy 17	29-45-55.000N 093-53-01.000W				Green can.	Private aid.
22725	Cox Sabine Facility Channel Buoy 18	29-45-53.000N 093-53-02.000W				Red nun.	Private aid.
22730	Cox Sabine Facility Channel Danger Buoy A	29-45-31.000N 093-53-11.000W				White with orange diamond.	Private aid.
22735	Cox Sabine Facility Channel Danger Buoy B	29-45-32.000N 093-53-16.000W				White with orange diamond.	Private aid.
22740	Cox Sabine Facility Channel Danger Buoy C	29-45-37.000N 093-53-22.000W				White with orange diamond.	Private aid.
22745	Cox Sabine Facility Channel Danger Buoy D	29-45-47.000N 093-53-18.000W				White with orange diamond.	Private aid.
22750	Cox Sabine Facility Channel Danger Buoy E	29-45-52.000N 093-53-16.000W				White with orange diamond.	Private aid.
22755	Cox Sabine Facility Channel Danger Buoy F	29-45-57.000N 093-53-13.000W				White with orange diamond.	Private aid.
22760	Cox Sabine Facility Channel Rear Range Daymark	29-46-04.000N 093-53-00.000W				KRW on pile.	Private aid.
22765	Cox Sabine Facility Channel Front Range Daymark	29-46-01.000N 093-53-02.000W				KRW on pile.	Private aid.
	Sabine Lake						
	Scurlock Channel						
22770	TEXAS WATER BOARD RESEARCH LIGHT TOWER A	29-56-15.000N 093-48-30.000W	Fl Y 4s	6		NY on pile.	Ra ref. Private aid.
	Port Arthur Canal						
22780	- LIGHT 40	29-45-37.091N 093-53-51.180W	Q R	17	4	TR on pile.	
22785	- D RANGE FRONT LIGHT	29-45-16.162N 093-53-01.753W	Q W	37		Skeleton tower on piles.	Lighted throughout 24 hours.
22790	- D RANGE REAR LIGHT 727 yards, 108.1° from front light.	29-45-08.409N 093-52-38.658W	Iso W 6s	76		Skeleton tower on piles.	Lighted throughout 24 hours.
22795	Golden Pass LNG Berthing Lighted Entrance Buoy A	29-45-52.170N 093-55-00.310W	Fl Y 4s			Yellow.	Private aid.
22800	Golden Pass LNG Berthing Lighted Entrance Buoy B	29-46-03.750N 093-55-14.760W	Fl Y 4s			Yellow.	Private aid.
22805	Golden Pass LNG Berthing Lighted Entrance Buoy C	29-46-04.150N 093-55-36.120W	Fl Y 4s			Yellow.	Private aid.
22810	- E RANGE FRONT LIGHT	29-46-20.183N 093-56-12.962W	Q G	26		KRW on skeleton tower.	For upbound traffic. Visible for 2° each side of rangeline.
22815	- E RANGE FRONT LIGHT PASSING LIGHT	29-46-20.118N 093-56-12.973W	Q G	10	3	KRW on skeleton tower. On same structure as Port Arthur Canal Range E Front Light.	
22820	- E RANGE REAR LIGHT 550 yards, 291° from front light.	29-46-25.763N 093-56-29.683W	Iso G 6s	54		KRW on skeleton tower on piles.	Visible 2° each side of rangeline.
22825	- LIGHT 43	29-46-31.608N 093-56-28.060W	Fl G 2.5s	17	5	SG on pile.	
22830	- LIGHT 45	29-46-47.819N 093-56-42.446W	Q G	30	4	SG on skeleton tower on piles. Same structure as Port Arthur Canal Range F Front Light.	

Light List corrected through LNM week: 01/18

(1) No.	(2) Name and Location	(3) Position	(4) Characteristic	(5) Height	(6) Range	(7) Structure	(8) Remarks
			TEXAS - LOUISIANA - Eighth District				
	SABINE PASS AND LAKE (Chart 11342)						
	Port Arthur Canal						
22835	- F RANGE FRONT LIGHT	29-46-47.825N 093-56-42.450W	Q G	31		KRW on skeleton tower on piles. Same structure as Port Arthur Canal Light 45.	For downbound traffic. Visible 2° each side of rangeline.
22840	- F RANGE REAR LIGHT 635 yards, 162.3° from front light.	29-46-30.339N 093-56-36.043W	Iso G 6s	55		KRW on skeleton tower on piles.	Visible 2° each side of rangeline.
22845	- LIGHT 46	29-46-55.308N 093-56-37.869W	Q R	17	4	TR on pile.	
22850	- G RANGE FRONT LIGHT	29-49-34.309N 093-57-43.517W	Q G (NIGHT) Q W (DAY)	36 38			Ra ref. Lighted throughout 24 hours.
22855	- G RANGE REAR LIGHT 429 yards, 339.7° from front light.	29-49-46.431N 093-57-48.003W	Iso G 6s (NIGHT) Iso W 6s (DAY)	73 71			Ra ref. Lighted throughout 24 hours.
22860	- LIGHT 47	29-47-02.394N 093-56-52.924W	Fl G 4s	17	5	SG on pile.	
22865	- LIGHT 48	29-49-03.796N 093-57-26.798W	Fl R 4s	17	3	TR on pile.	
22867	TGS DEVELOPMENT PI DOCK MOORING PILE LIGHT	29-49-20.824N 093-57-24.441W	Fl R 6s			Marks outermost mooring pile.	Private aid.
22867.01	TGS DEVELOPMENT PI DOCK FRONT RANGE LIGHT	29-49-25.683N 093-57-11.435W	F G	69		KGW on tower.	Private aid.
22867.02	TGS DEVELOPMENT PI DOCK REAR RANGE LIGHT	29-49-27.990N 093-57-06.413W	F G	85		KGW on tower.	Private aid.
22870 35740	- LIGHT 49	29-49-23.493N 093-57-45.195W	Fl G 4s	17	4	SG-SY on pile.	
22875	TAYLOR BAYOU TURNING BASIN LIGHT 1	29-50-10.013N 093-58-05.857W	Fl G 4s	17	4	SG on pile.	
22876	OXBOW CALCINING DOCK LIGHT	29-50-08.800N 093-57-59.800W	Fl R 2.5s			Light marks outermost upstream dock structure.	Private aid.
22880	MOTIVA DOCK LIGHTS (2)	29-49-48.059N 093-57-33.505W	Fl R 2.5s			On dock.	Private aid.
	Sabine-Neches Canal						
22885 35735	- LIGHT 50	29-49-48.673N 093-57-12.315W	Fl R 2.5s	17	4	TR-SY on pile.	Ra ref.
22890 35730	- LIGHT 50A	29-50-20.211N 093-57-06.188W	Fl R 4s	17	3	TR-SY on pile.	Ra ref.
22895 35725	- LIGHT 51	29-50-48.687N 093-57-06.548W	Fl G 4s	17	4	SG-TY on pile.	
22900 35720	- LIGHT 52	29-50-45.168N 093-56-58.394W	Q R	17	4	TR-SY on pile.	
22905 35710	- H RANGE FRONT LIGHT	29-52-05.832N 093-55-49.118W	Q R	42		KRW-I on skeleton tower on block.	For upbound traffic Visible 2° each side of rangeline.
22910 35715	- H RANGE REAR LIGHT 326 yards, 040.0° from front light.	29-52-13.251N 093-55-41.974W	Iso R 6s	49		KRW on skeleton tower on concrete block.	
22915 35705	- LIGHT 52A	29-51-36.262N 093-56-12.650W	Fl R 2.5s	17	4	TR-SY on pile.	Ra ref.
22920 35700	- LIGHT 54	29-53-27.573N 093-54-37.275W	Fl R 4s	17	4	TR-SY on pile.	
22925 35695	- LIGHT 56	29-54-06.059N 093-53-55.405W	Fl R 4s	17	4	TR-SY on pile.	
22930 35690	- LIGHT 58	29-54-36.408N 093-53-29.077W	Fl R 4s	17	3	TR-SY on pile.	Ra ref.
22935 35685	- LIGHT 60	29-54-55.621N 093-53-10.641W	Fl R 2.5s	17	4	TR-SY on pile.	

Light List corrected through LNM week: 01/18

(1) No.	(2) Name and Location	(3) Position	(4) Characteristic	(5) Height	(6) Range	(7) Structure	(8) Remarks
		TEXAS - LOUISIANA - Eighth District					
	SABINE PASS AND LAKE (Chart 11342)						
	Sabine-Neches Canal						
22940 35680	- LIGHT 62	29-55-43.904N 093-52-26.839W	Fl R 4s	17	4	TR-SY on pile.	
22945 35670	- L RANGE FRONT LIGHT	29-56-35.682N 093-51-46.591W	Q W	32		KRW-I on skeleton tower on piles.	
22950 35675	- L RANGE REAR LIGHT 957 yards, 037.6° from front light.	29-56-58.197N 093-51-26.690W	Iso W 6s	56		KRW on skeleton tower on piles.	
22955 35655	- K RANGE FRONT LIGHT	29-56-04.480N 093-52-05.146W	Q W (NIGHT) Q W (DAY)	30 30			
22960 35660	- K RANGE FRONT PASSING LIGHT	29-56-04.480N 093-52-05.146W	Fl R 2.5s	15	3	On same structure as Neches Canal Range K Front Light.	
22965 35665	- K RANGE REAR LIGHT 1088 yards, 197.4° from front light.	29-55-34.101N 093-52-17.831W	Iso W 6s (NIGHT) Iso W 6s (DAY)	53 70			Visible only on rangeline. Lighted throughout 24 hours.
22970 35630	- M UPPER RANGE FRONT LIGHT	29-58-15.912N 093-51-10.204W	Q W	29		On skeleton tower.	For upbound traffic. Visible 2° each side of rangeline. Lighted throught 24 hours.
22975 35635	- M UPPER RANGE REAR LIGHT 745 yards, 020.1° from front light.	29-58-37.577N 093-51-01.130W	Iso W 6s	40		On skeleton tower on piles. On same structure as Neches River Outer Range R Rear Light.	
22980 35650	- LIGHT 64	29-56-56.521N 093-51-39.189W	Fl R 4s	17	4	TR-SY on pile.	Ra ref.
22985 35645	- Buoy 64A	29-57-33.927N 093-51-21.846W				Red nun with yellow square.	
22990	- LEADING LIGHT A	29-57-46.323N 093-51-09.403W	Fl W 4s	17	7	NR on dolphin.	
22995 35640	- LIGHT 65	29-57-57.250N 093-51-24.998W	Fl G 4s	17	4	SG-TY on pile.	
23000 35625	- LIGHT 66	29-58-04.708N 093-51-08.228W	Fl R 2.5s	17	4	TR-SY on pile.	
23005 35615	- N RANGE FRONT LIGHT	29-58-02.223N 093-51-44.648W	Q G (NIGHT) Q W (DAY)	35 38		On skeleton tower on piles.	For westbound traffic.
23010 35620	- N RANGE REAR LIGHT 984 yards, 250.1° from front light.	29-57-52.310N 093-52-16.094W	Iso G 6s (NIGHT) Iso W 6s (DAY)	91 89		On skeleton tower on piles.	Range is not effective inland of Sabine-Neches Canal Buoys 75 and 76.
	SABINE AND NECHES RIVER (Chart 11343)						
	Sabine-Neches Canal						
23015 35610	- Buoy 67	29-58-27.437N 093-50-36.611W				Green can with yellow triangle.	
23020 35605	- Buoy 68	29-58-22.031N 093-50-33.350W				Red nun with yellow square.	
23025 35600	- Buoy 69	29-58-32.871N 093-50-15.026W				Green can with yellow triangle.	
23030 35595	- Buoy 70	29-58-28.839N 093-50-12.653W				Red nun with yellow square.	
23035 35590	- Buoy 71	29-58-39.735N 093-49-53.000W				Green can with yellow triangle.	
23040 35585	- Buoy 72	29-58-35.623N 093-49-51.175W				Red nun with yellow square.	
23045 35580	- LIGHT 73	29-58-49.867N 093-49-23.096W	Fl G 4s	17	4	SG-TY on pile.	Ra ref.

(1) No.	(2) Name and Location	(3) Position	(4) Characteristic	(5) Height	(6) Range	(7) Structure	(8) Remarks
	TEXAS - LOUISIANA - Eighth District						
	SABINE AND NECHES RIVER (Chart 11343)						
	Sabine-Neches Canal						
23050 35575	- LIGHT 74	29-58-44.130N 093-49-21.324W	Fl R 4s	17	4	TR-SY on pile.	
23055 35570	- Buoy 75	29-58-57.979N 093-48-54.786W				Green can with yellow triangle.	
23060 35565	- Buoy 76	29-58-54.009N 093-48-51.394W				Red nun with yellow square.	
23065 35560	- Buoy 77	29-59-06.647N 093-48-27.556W				Green can with yellow triangle.	
23070 35555	- Buoy 78	29-59-02.422N 093-48-25.344W				Red nun with yellow square.	
23075 35550	- Buoy 79	29-59-12.709N 093-48-07.890W				Green can with yellow triangle.	
23080 35545	- Buoy 80	29-59-08.722N 093-48-05.484W				Red nun with yellow square.	
23085 35535	- O RANGE FRONT LIGHT	29-59-30.974N 093-47-02.276W	Q R	20		KRW on skeleton tower.	For eastbound traffic.
23090 35540	- O RANGE REAR LIGHT 954 yards, 070.3° from front light.	29-59-40.570N 093-46-31.661W	Fl R 4s	54		KRW on skeleton tower on mud sills.	
23095	- O RANGE REAR PASSING LIGHT	29-59-40.570N 093-46-31.661W	Fl R 4s	10	4	On same structure as Neches Canal Range O Rear Light.	
	Sabine River						
23100 35530	- LIGHT 1	29-59-51.077N 093-46-29.954W	Fl G 2.5s	17	4	SG-TY on pile.	Ra ref.
23105.01 35525.01	- *Lighted Buoy 2*	29-59-59.407N 093-46-14.851W	Fl R 4s		3	Red nun with yellow square.	
23110 35520	- Day beacon 4	30-00-50.085N 093-45-23.894W				TR-SY on pile.	
23115 35505	- LIGHT 5	30-00-51.162N 093-45-36.518W	Fl G 4s	17	4	SG-TY on skeleton tower on piles.	
23120 35510	- P RANGE FRONT LIGHT	30-01-06.720N 093-45-15.876W	Q W	24		KRW-I on skeleton tower on piles.	Visible 4° either side of rangeline.
23125 35515	- P RANGE REAR LIGHT 1,204 yards, 038.9° from front light.	30-01-34.543N 093-44-50.090W	Iso W 6s	47		KRW-I on skeleton tower on piles.	
23130 35500	- LIGHT 8	30-01-04.832N 093-44-51.420W	Fl R 2.5s	17	4	TR-SY on skeleton tower on piles.	
23135 35495	- Day beacon 10	30-01-13.405N 093-44-35.039W				TR-SY on pile.	
23140 35490	- LIGHT 11	30-01-21.578N 093-44-37.416W	Fl G 4s	17	4	SG-TY on pile.	
23145 35485	- LIGHT 13	30-01-38.960N 093-44-26.574W	Fl G 4s	17	4	SG-TY on pile.	
23150 35480	- Day beacon 13A	30-01-49.067N 093-44-24.648W				SG-TY on pile.	
23155 35475	- LIGHT 15	30-02-02.258N 093-44-24.174W	Fl G 4s	17	4	SG-TY on pile.	
23160 35470	DYNEGY MIDSTREAM DOCK LIGHTS(2)	30-02-09.000N 093-44-21.000W	Fl G 2.5s			On dolphins.	Private aid.
23165 35465	- LIGHT 16	30-02-16.838N 093-44-09.400W	Q R	17	4	TR-SY on pile.	
23170 35450	- OUTER Q RANGE FRONT LIGHT	30-02-22.394N 093-44-17.957W	Q W	25		KRW on skeleton tower on piles	Visible all around; higher intensity on rangeline.
23175 35455	- OUTER Q RANGE REAR LIGHT 464 yards, 231.6° from front light.	30-02-13.842N 093-44-30.362W	Iso W 6s	49		KRW on skeleton tower on mud sills.	Visible all around; higher intensity on rangeline.

Light List corrected through LNM week: 01/18

(1) No.	(2) Name and Location	(3) Position	(4) Characteristic	(5) Height	(6) Range	(7) Structure	(8) Remarks
			TEXAS - LOUISIANA - Eighth District				
	SABINE AND NECHES RIVER (Chart 11343)						
	Sabine River						
	Adams Bayou						
23180 35445	- LIGHT 2	30-02-55.205N 093-43-46.772W	Fl R 4s	17	3	TR-SY on pile.	
23185	DUPONT LIGHT 1	30-03-24.000N 093-44-30.000W	F G		22	On wharf.	Private aid.
23190	DUPONT LIGHT 3	30-03-24.000N 093-44-30.000W	F G		22	On wharf.	Private aid.
23195	DUPONT LIGHT 5	30-03-24.000N 093-44-30.000W	F G		22	On wharf.	Private aid.
	Sabine River						
23200 35440	- LIGHT 20	30-02-54.372N 093-43-27.260W	Fl R 2.5s	17	3	TR-SY on pile.	
23205 35435	- Day beacon 21	30-03-15.258N 093-43-17.086W				SG-TY on pile.	Ra ref.
23210 35430	- LIGHT 22	30-03-17.811N 093-43-07.540W	Fl R 4s	17	3	TR-TY on pile.	
23215	- Day beacon 23	30-03-33.330N 093-43-06.991W				SG on pile.	
23220	- LIGHT 24	30-03-39.864N 093-42-57.130W	Fl R 4s	17	4	TR on dolphin.	
23225	- Day beacon 25	30-03-43.570N 093-43-07.735W				SG on pile.	
23230	- Day beacon 26	30-04-10.026N 093-42-55.062W				TR on pile.	Ra ref.
23235	- LIGHT 27	30-03-56.626N 093-43-01.438W	Fl G 4s	17	4	SG on pile.	
23240	Conway Bayou Danger Day beacon A	30-04-05.228N 093-42-54.012W				NW on pile.	Ra ref.
23245	Conway Bayou Danger Day beacon B	30-03-33.449N 093-42-00.499W				NW on pile.	
23250	- Day beacon 29	30-04-12.995N 093-43-05.662W				SG on pile.	
23255	- LIGHT 31	30-04-43.808N 093-43-28.168W	Fl G 4s	17	4	SG on pile.	
23260	OLD RIVER OBSTRUCTION LIGHT 2	30-04-44.805N 093-43-31.819W	Q R	17	3	TR on pile.	Ra ref.
23265	OLD RIVER OBSTRUCTION LIGHT 2A	30-04-43.790N 093-43-33.390W	Q R	17	3	TR on pile.	Ra ref.
23270	- *Obstruction Lighted Buoy 53*	30-05-06.000N 093-43-24.000W	Q G			Green.	Private aid.
23275	NAVY PIER 10 LIGHTS (2)	30-05-50.400N 093-43-15.000W	Fl G 2.5s			On dolphin.	Maintained by U.S. Navy. Private aid.
	Orange County Pier						
23280	- LIGHT 6	30-06-01.000N 093-42-57.000W	Q G		10	On pile.	Private aid.
23285	- LIGHT 3	30-06-13.000N 093-42-51.000W	Q G			On pile.	Private aid.
23290	- LIGHT 2	30-06-18.000N 093-42-50.000W	Q G			On pile.	Private aid.
			TEXAS - Eighth District				
	SABINE AND NECHES RIVERS (Chart 11343)						
	Neches River						
23295	- *Lighted Buoy 2*	29-58-14.501N 093-51-18.114W	Q R		3	Red.	
23300	- LIGHT 6	29-58-33.456N 093-51-26.922W	Fl R 4s	17	3	TR on pile.	
23305	- LIGHT 7	29-58-30.932N 093-51-38.042W	Fl G 4s	17	4	SG on pile.	
23310	- Buoy 9	29-58-36.647N 093-51-47.041W				Green can.	
23315	- OUTER R RANGE FRONT LIGHT	29-58-41.404N 093-51-24.987W	Fl W 2.5s	23		On dolphin.	

Light List corrected through LNM week: 01/18

(1) No.	(2) Name and Location	(3) Position	(4) Characteristic	(5) Height	(6) Range	(7) Structure	(8) Remarks
			TEXAS - Eighth District				
	SABINE AND NECHES RIVERS (Chart 11343)						
	Neches River						
23320	- LIGHT 10	29-58-44.584N 093-51-44.740W	Fl R 2.5s	14	3	TR on pile.	Ra ref.
23325	- OUTER R RANGE REAR LIGHT 711 yards, 100.4° from front light.	29-58-37.577N 093-51-01.130W	Iso W 6s	49		On skeleton tower on piles. On same structure as Sabine-Neches Canal Upper Range M Rear Light.	
23330	FINA WHARF LIGHT 1	29-58-00.800N 093-52-00.800W	F G	22		On pile.	Private aid.
23335	FINA WHARF LIGHT 3	29-58-00.800N 093-52-00.800W	F G	22		On pile.	Private aid.
23340	FINA WHARF LIGHT 5	29-58-00.800N 093-52-00.800W	F G	22		On pile.	Private aid.
23345	- LIGHT 14	29-58-58.207N 093-52-47.029W	Fl R 4s	17	4	TR on skeleton tower on mud sills.	
23350	- LIGHT 19	29-59-05.018N 093-54-18.805W	Q G	17	4	SG on dolphin.	
23355	- LIGHT 20	29-59-14.613N 093-54-31.500W	Fl R 4s	17	3	TR on dolphin.	
23360	- LIGHT 22	29-59-25.886N 093-55-29.583W	Fl R 4s	17	3	TR on dolphin.	Ra ref.
23365	- S RANGE FRONT LIGHT	29-59-20.614N 093-55-38.020W	Q G	35		KRW on skeleton tower on mud sills.	For downbound traffic. Visible all around; higher intensity on rangeline.
23370	- S RANGE REAR LIGHT 131 yards, 113.2° from front light.	29-59-19.078N 093-55-33.910W	Iso G 6s	53		KRW on skeleton tower on mud sills.	
23375	TEXAS COMPANY WHARF LIGHTS (3)	29-59-36.000N 093-56-27.000W	Fl G 2.5s	10		On wharf.	Private aid.
23380	TEXAS PETROCHEMICAL NECHES RIVER WHARF LIGHTS (4)	29-59-37.000N 093-56-35.000W	Fl G 2.5s	10		On wharf.	Private aid.
23385	- LIGHT 26	29-59-56.691N 093-56-57.983W	Fl R 4s	17	4	TR on dolphin.	
23390	CITY OF PORT NECHES WHARF LIGHTS (2)	30-00-10.870N 093-57-19.580W	Fl G 2.5s	15			Private aid.
23395	- LIGHT 26A	30-00-18.716N 093-57-13.571W	Fl R 2.5s	17	4	TR on dolphin.	
23400	- LIGHT 28	30-00-44.504N 093-57-22.113W	Q R	17	4	TR on dolphin.	
23405	- LIGHT 29	30-00-40.882N 093-57-32.573W	Q G	17	3	SG on pile.	
23410	- LIGHT 30	30-00-54.350N 093-57-41.201W	Q R	17	4	TR on pile.	Ra ref.
23415	SMITH BLUFF LIGHT 1	30-00-39.000N 093-58-08.000W	Fl G 2.5s	20		Pile structure.	Private aid.
23420	SMITH BLUFF LIGHT 3	30-00-33.000N 093-58-26.000W	Fl G 2.5s	20		Pile structure.	Private aid.
23425	- LIGHT 34	30-00-35.420N 093-58-52.491W	Fl R 4s	17	3	TR on pile.	
23430	- T RANGE FRONT LIGHT	30-00-27.369N 093-58-41.632W	F G	37		On skeleton tower on block.	Lighted throughout 24 hours.
23435	- T RANGE REAR LIGHT 283 yards, 107.9° from front light.	30-00-24.787N 093-58-32.452W	F G	57		On skeleton tower on block.	Lighted throughout 24 hours.
23440	- U RANGE FRONT LIGHT	30-01-17.735N 094-01-41.161W	Fl G 2.5s	15		Skeleton tower on piles.	Lighted throughout 24 hours.
23445	- U RANGE REAR LIGHT 562 yards, 287.8° from front light.	30-01-22.840N 094-01-59.434W	Iso G 6s	41		Skeleton tower.	Lighted throughout 24 hours.
23450	- LIGHT 40	30-00-54.120N 094-00-06.700W	Fl R 4s	17	4	TR on pile.	

Light List corrected through LNM week: 01/18

(1) No.	(2) Name and Location	(3) Position	(4) Characteristic	(5) Height	(6) Range	(7) Structure	(8) Remarks
		TEXAS - Eighth District					
	SABINE AND NECHES RIVERS (Chart 11343)						
	Neches River						
23455	- LIGHT 40A	30-01-14.111N 094-01-18.658W	Fl R 2.5s	17	3	TR on pile.	
23460	- LIGHT 42	30-01-28.928N 094-01-41.548W	Q R	17	4	TR on pile.	
	Oiltanking Dock Channel						
23465	- Buoy 1	30-01-37.144N 094-01-58.620W				Green can.	Private aid.
23470	- Buoy 2	30-01-39.387N 094-01-59.292W				Red nun.	Private aid.
23475	- Buoy 3	30-01-36.255N 094-02-01.380W				Green can.	Private aid.
23480	- Buoy 4	30-01-37.874N 094-02-02.330W				Red nun.	Private aid.
23485	- Buoy 5	30-01-34.815N 094-02-04.623W				Green can.	Private aid.
23490	- Buoy 6	30-01-36.434N 094-02-05.573W				Red nun.	Private aid.
23495	- Buoy 7	30-01-33.374N 094-02-07.865W				Green can.	Private aid.
23500	- Buoy 8	30-01-34.993N 094-02-08.815W				Red nun.	Private aid.
	Neches River						
23506	ENTERPRISE PRODUCTS TERMINAL DOCK NORTH LIGHT	30-02-01.300N 094-02-01.400W	Fl G 2.5s			Marks upstream end of dock.	Private aid.
23506.01	ENTERPRISE PRODUCTS TERMINAL DOCK MIDDLE LIGHT	30-01-52.700N 094-02-01.300W	Fl G 2.5s			Marks outermost center of dock.	Private aid.
23506.02	ENTERPRISE PRODUCTS TERMINAL DOCK SOUTH LIGHT	30-01-43.100N 094-01-59.800W	Fl G 2.5s			Marks downstream end of dock.	Private aid.
23510	ENTERPRISE PRODUCTS MOORING DOLPHIN LIGHT	30-02-10.410N 094-02-03.758W	Fl G 2.5s			Marks mooring dolphin.	Private aid.
23515	- LIGHT 46	30-02-04.977N 094-01-52.508W	Fl R 4s	17	4	TR on pile.	
23520	- LIGHT 49	30-02-19.567N 094-01-55.991W	Fl G 4s	17	4	SG on dolphin.	
23525	STANDLOND CUT ENTRANCE LIGHT 2	30-02-25.800N 094-02-13.800W	Fl R 2.5s			TR on pile.	Private aid.
23530	- LIGHT 51	30-02-49.400N 094-01-45.277W	Q G	17	4	SG on pile.	
23535	- LIGHT 54	30-02-51.849N 094-01-37.754W	Fl R 4s	17	3	TR on pile.	
23540	- LIGHT 56	30-03-07.692N 094-01-38.426W	Q R	17	4	TR on skeleton tower on mud sills.	
23545	GULF STATES EROSION BARRIER LIGHTS (2)	30-03-22.000N 094-01-45.000W	Q R	13		On erosion barrier.	Private aid.
23550	- LIGHT 58	30-03-37.920N 094-01-58.650W	Q R	17	3	TR on dolphin.	
23555	- LIGHT 60	30-03-46.000N 094-02-12.497W	Q R	17	3	TR on dolphin.	
23560	NECHES INDUSTRIAL MORRING DOLPHIN LIGHTS (2)	30-34-02.000N 094-02-16.000W	Fl G 2.5s	43		On dolphins.	Private aid.
23565	- LIGHT 63	30-03-44.268N 094-02-29.772W	Fl G 4s	17	4	SG on pile.	
23570	POWER PLANT DIVERSION WALL LIGHTS (2)	30-03-56.000N 094-02-50.000W	Fl G 2.5s	4			Private aid.
23575	- LIGHT 66	30-04-08.718N 094-02-56.771W	Fl R 4s	17	4	TR on pile.	Ra ref.
23580	LOWER NECHES VALLEY DANGER LIGHT Marks submerged pipeline.	30-04-11.780N 094-03-11.590W	Fl W 2.5s			On steel pile.	Private aid.
23585	- LIGHT 68	30-04-26.612N 094-03-19.137W	Fl R 4s	17	4	TR on skeleton tower on piles.	

Light List corrected through LNM week: 01/18

(1) No.	(2) Name and Location	(3) Position	(4) Characteristic	(5) Height	(6) Range	(7) Structure	(8) Remarks
\multicolumn{8}{c}{**TEXAS - Eighth District**}							

SABINE AND NECHES RIVERS (Chart 11343)
Neches River

(1) No.	(2) Name and Location	(3) Position	(4) Characteristic	(5) Height	(6) Range	(7) Structure	(8) Remarks
23590	MOBIL CHEMICAL DOCK LIGHT 2	30-04-00.000N 094-03-33.000W	Fl G 2.5s	15		On wharf.	Private aid.
23595	MOBIL NO. 5 WHARF LIGHTS (2)	30-04-34.000N 094-04-52.000W	Fl G 2.5s	27		On dolphin.	Private aid.
23600	MOBIL NO. 4 WHARF LIGHTS (2)	30-04-36.000N 094-04-52.000W	Fl G 2.5s	30		On end of dock.	Private aid.
23605	MOBIL NO. 2 WHARF LIGHTS (2)	30-04-36.000N 094-04-16.000W	Fl G 2.5s	30		On end of dock.	Private aid.
23610	PORT OF BEAUMONT RO-RO DOCK LIGHTS (4)	30-04-32.000N 094-05-06.000W	F G	5		On dock ramp.	Private aid.
23615	PORT OF BEAUMONT GENERAL CARGO DOCK LIGHTS (2)	30-04-40.389N 094-04-46.667W	Fl R 2.5s	12		On dock.	Private aid.
23617	PORT OF BEAUMONT BULK TERMINAL DOWNSTREAM LIGHT	30-04-48.543N 094-05-01.701W	Fl R 2.5s			Marks the downstream corner of dock.	Private aid.
23617.01	PORT OF BEAUMONT BULK TERMINAL UPSTREAM LIGHT	30-04-51.298N 094-05-07.493W	Fl R 2.5s			Marks the upstream corner of dock.	Private aid.

GALVESTON BAY ENTRANCE (Chart 11324)
Galveston Bay Entrance Channel

(1) No.	(2) Name and Location	(3) Position	(4) Characteristic	(5) Height	(6) Range	(7) Structure	(8) Remarks
23620	- *Lighted Buoy 1* 150 feet outside channel limit.	29-15-59.533N 094-34-26.667W	Q G		4	Green.	
23625	- *Lighted Buoy 2* 150 feet outside channel limit.	29-16-07.281N 094-34-18.526W	Q R		4	Red.	
23630	- *Lighted Buoy 1A* 150 feet outside channel limit.	29-17-05.670N 094-35-51.216W	Fl G 4s		4	Green.	
23635	- *Lighted Buoy 2A* 150 feet outside channel limit.	29-17-12.207N 094-35-43.754W	Fl R 6s		4	Red.	
23650	- *Lighted Buoy 1B* 150 feet outside channel limit.	29-18-10.674N 094-37-17.138W	Q G		3	Green.	
23655	- *Lighted Buoy 2B* 150 feet outside channel limit.	29-18-21.030N 094-37-08.600W	Q R		3	Red.	
23660 1210	*Galveston Bay Entrance Lighted Buoy GA*	29-09-28.867N 094-25-53.670W	Mo (A) W		6	Red and white stripes with red spherical topmark.	
23665 1215	*Galveston Bay Entrance Traffic Lane Lighted Buoy A*	29-10-47.784N 094-27-35.533W	Fl Y 2.5s		5	Yellow.	
23670 1220	*Galveston Bay Entrance Traffic Lane Lighted Buoy C*	29-12-06.639N 094-29-17.469W	Fl Y 4s		6	Yellow.	
23675 1225	*Galveston Bay Entrance Traffic Lane Lighted Buoy E*	29-13-25.498N 094-30-59.436W	Fl Y 6s		5	Yellow.	
23680 1230	*Galveston Bay Entrance Lighted Buoy GB*	29-14-44.348N 094-32-41.467W	Mo (A) W		5	Red and white stripes with red shperical topmark.	AIS MMSI: 993682024
23686 1241	*Fieldwood-123-3 Lighted Buoy* Marks subsea installation.	29-13-31.445N 094-34-40.878W	Q R				Private aid.
23690	- A RANGE FRONT LIGHT	29-21-10.950N 094-42-44.305W	Fl W 2.5s (NIGHT) Fl W 2.5s (DAY)	37 40		On skeleton tower.	Lighted throughout 24 hours. Visible all around. Day light visible only on rangeline. Night light visible 1.5° each side of rangeline.
23695	- A RANGE REAR LIGHT 4,476 yards, 301.1° from front light	29-22-19.507N 094-44-54.325W	F W (NIGHT) F W (DAY)	125 122		Skeleton tower on block.	Lighted throughout 24 hours.
23700	- *Lighted Buoy 3* 100 feet outside channel limit.	29-19-11.852N 094-39-10.693W	Fl G 4s		4	Green.	

(1) No.	(2) Name and Location	(3) Position	(4) Characteristic	(5) Height	(6) Range	(7) Structure	(8) Remarks
		TEXAS - Eighth District					

GALVESTON BAY ENTRANCE (Chart 11324)
Galveston Bay Entrance Channel

(1) No.	(2) Name and Location	(3) Position	(4) Characteristic	(5) Height	(6) Range	(7) Structure	(8) Remarks
23705	- Lighted Buoy 4	29-19-20.662N 094-39-03.563W	Fl R 4s		3		Red.
23710	- Lighted Buoy 5	29-19-46.041N 094-40-15.530W	Fl G 2.5s		4		Green.
23715	- Lighted Buoy 6	29-19-55.341N 094-40-08.985W	Fl R 2.5s		3		Red.
23720	GALVESTON SOUTH JETTY LIGHT 5A	29-19-38.316N 094-41-16.514W	Iso G 6s	30	6	SG on pile.	Ra ref.
23725	GALVESTON NORTH JETTY LIGHT 6A	29-20-42.332N 094-40-34.075W	Iso R 6s	30	6	TR on pile.	Ra ref.
23730	- Lighted Buoy 7	29-20-20.025N 094-41-20.217W	Q G		3		Green.
23735	- Lighted Buoy 8	29-20-31.845N 094-41-15.409W	Q R		3		Red.
23740	- B RANGE FRONT LIGHT	29-21-18.422N 094-45-49.779W	Q G	25		KRW on skeleton tower on piles.	Visible all around; higher intensity 1.5° each side of rangeline.
23745	- B RANGE REAR LIGHT 1,296 yards, 282.2° from front light.	29-21-27.002N 094-46-33.997W	Iso G 6s	60		KRW on skeleton tower.	
23750	- B RANGE REAR LIGHT PASSING LIGHT	29-21-27.031N 094-46-33.986W	Fl W 4s	17	5	On same structure as Galveston Bay Entrance Channel Range B Rear Light.	
23755	- Lighted Buoy 7A	29-20-29.526N 094-42-06.114W	Fl G 2.5s		4		Green.

Galveston Bay

(1) No.	(2) Name and Location	(3) Position	(4) Characteristic	(5) Height	(6) Range	(7) Structure	(8) Remarks
23760	Galveston Entrance North Side Dredging Range Rear Day beacon					Black octagonal day mark on skeleton tower.	Range marks edge of channel for dredging purposes. Maintained by U.S. Army Corps of Engineers. May show fixed amber light when dredging is in progress. Aid maintained by U.S. Army Corps of Engineers.
23765	Galveston Entrance South Side Dredging Range Front Day beacon					Orange square day mark on skeleton tower.	Maintained by U.S. Army Corps of Engineers. May show fixed amber light when dredging is in progress. Aid maintained by U.S. Army Corps of Engineers.

Galveston Bay Entrance Channel

(1) No.	(2) Name and Location	(3) Position	(4) Characteristic	(5) Height	(6) Range	(7) Structure	(8) Remarks
23770	- Lighted Buoy 9	29-20-37.511N 094-42-54.991W	Q G		3		Green.
23775	- Lighted Buoy 10	29-20-50.696N 094-42-54.145W	Q R		3		Red.
23780	- C RANGE FRONT LIGHT	29-20-30.007N 094-46-57.941W	Q G	35		KRW on skeleton tower on piles.	Visible 2° each side of rangeline.
23785	- C RANGE REAR LIGHT 1,670 yards, 266° from front light.	29-20-26.716N 094-47-53.730W	Iso G 6s	72		KRW on skeleton tower on block.	Visible 2° each side of rangeline.
23790	- Lighted Buoy 11 100 feet outside channel limit.	29-20-32.349N 094-44-28.701W	Fl G 2.5s		4		Green.
23795	- Lighted Buoy 12 100 feet outside channel limit.	29-20-43.848N 094-44-47.201W	Fl R 2.5s		3		Red.

TEXAS - Eighth District

GALVESTON BAY ENTRANCE (Chart 11324)
Galveston Bay

(1) No.	(2) Name and Location	(3) Position	(4) Characteristic	(5) Height	(6) Range	(7) Structure	(8) Remarks
23800	Galveston Anchorage Lighted Buoy A Marks Northeast corner of anchorage area.	29-21-06.148N 094-42-52.099W	Fl Y 6s		4	Yellow.	
23805	Galveston Anchorage Lighted Buoy B Marks northwest corner of anchorage area.	29-21-15.848N 094-44-27.702W	Fl Y 6s		4	Yellow.	
23810	GALVESTON NORTH JETTY LIGHT WR2 Marks derelict wreck.	29-21-51.015N 094-44-38.933W	Q R	17	2	TR on pile.	
23815	Galveston Anchorage Lighted Buoy C	29-20-56.682N 094-46-06.797W	Fl Y 6s		4	Yellow.	

Galveston Bay Entrance Channel

(1) No.	(2) Name and Location	(3) Position	(4) Characteristic	(5) Height	(6) Range	(7) Structure	(8) Remarks
23820	- Lighted Buoy 16	29-20-39.798N 094-46-07.756W	Q R		3	Red.	

Galveston Bay

(1) No.	(2) Name and Location	(3) Position	(4) Characteristic	(5) Height	(6) Range	(7) Structure	(8) Remarks
23825 36060	Pelican Island Spit Shoal Lighted Buoy P	29-20-27.248N 094-46-20.704W	Fl (2+1)G 6s		4	Green with red bands.	

INTRACOASTAL WATERWAY (Texas) - Eighth District

GALVESTON BAY ENTRANCE (Chart 11324)
Galveston Outer Bar

(1) No.	(2) Name and Location	(3) Position	(4) Characteristic	(5) Height	(6) Range	(7) Structure	(8) Remarks
23830	North Side Dredging Range Rear Day beacon 1,335 yards, 282.5° from front day beacon.					Black square day mark on skeleton tower on piles.	F G light may be displayed during dredging operations. Maintained by U.S. Army Corps Engineers. Aid maintained by U.S. Army Corps of Engineers.
23835	South Side Dredging Range Front Day beacon	29-21-12.000N 094-45-48.000W				Black diamond day mark on pile structure.	Range marks edge of channel for dredging purposes. F G light may be displayed during dredging operations. Maintained by U.S. Army Corps of Engineers. Aid maintained by U.S. Army Corps of Engineers.
23840	South Side Dredging Range Rear Day beacon 1,335 yards, 282.5° from front day beacon.					Black square day mark on skeleton tower on piles.	F G light may be displayed during dredging operations. Maintained by U.S. Army Corps of Engineers. Aid maintained by U.S. Army Corps of Engineers.

Galveston Inner Bar

(1) No.	(2) Name and Location	(3) Position	(4) Characteristic	(5) Height	(6) Range	(7) Structure	(8) Remarks
23845	North Side Dredging Range Front Day beacon	29-20-30.000N 094-47-00.000W				Black diamond day mark on pile structure.	Range marks edge of channel for dredging purpose. F G light may be displayed during dredging operations. Maintained by U.S. Army Corps of Engineers. Aid maintained by U.S. Army Corps of Engineers.
23850	North Side Dredging Range Rear Day beacon 1,665 yards, 266°09` from front day beacon.					Black square day mark on skeleton tower.	F G light may be displayed during dredging operations. Maintained by U.S. Army Corps of Engineers. Aid maintained by U.S. Army Corps of Engineers.

Light List corrected through LNM week: 01/18

(1) No.	(2) Name and Location	(3) Position	(4) Characteristic	(5) Height	(6) Range	(7) Structure	(8) Remarks
			INTRACOASTAL WATERWAY (Texas) - Eighth District				
	GALVESTON BAY ENTRANCE (Chart 11324)						
	Galveston Inner Bar						
23855	South Side Dredging Range Front Day beacon	29-20-24.000N 094-46-42.000W				Black diamond day mark on pile structure.	Range marks edge of channel for dredging purposes. F G light may be displayed during dredging operations. Maintained by U.S. Army Corps of Engineers.
							Aid maintained by U.S. Army Corps of Engineers.
23860	South Side Dredging Range Rear Day beacon 1,665 yards, 266°09` from front day beacon.					Black square day mark on skeleton tower.	F G light may be displayed during dredging operations. Maintained by U.S. Army Corps of Engineers.
							Aid maintained by U.S. Army Corps of Engineers.
			TEXAS - Eighth District				
	GALVESTON BAY ENTRANCE (Chart 11324)						
	Galveston Channel						
23865 36065	- *Lighted Buoy 1* 50 feet outside channel limit.	29-20-16.349N 094-46-11.203W	Fl G 4s		4	Green with yellow square.	
23870 36070	- LIGHT 2	29-20-14.811N 094-46-35.752W	Q R	17	3	TR-TY on pile.	Ra ref.
23875	SEAWOLF FISHING PIER LIGHT	29-20-17.700N 094-46-41.330W	Fl Y 4s	16		On pier.	Private aid. Private aid.
23880 36075	- LIGHT 3	29-19-47.349N 094-46-28.703W	Fl G 2.5s	17	4	SG-SY on pile.	Ra ref.
23885 36080	GRASSO MARINE DOCK LIGHTS (2)	29-19-24.000N 094-46-52.000W	Fl R 2.5s	15		On end of dock.	Private aid.
23890 36085	GALVESTON ISLAND MARINA LIGHT	29-19-03.500N 094-46-40.000W	Q R	6			Private aid.
23895	GALVESTON TERMINAL DOCK LIGHT	29-18-42.600N 094-48-24.900W	Fl (2)R 6s			On dock.	Private aid.
	Houston Ship Channel						
23900 36055	- *Entrance Lighted Buoy 18*	29-21-05.030N 094-46-59.466W	Q R		3	Red with yellow square.	
23905	- ENTRANCE OUTER RANGE FRONT LIGHT	29-20-08.761N 094-46-10.178W	F G	30		KRW on skeleton tower.	For downbound traffic. Visible 2° each side of rangeline.
23910	- ENTRANCE OUTER RANGE REAR LIGHT 1,794 yards, 138.4° from front light.	29-19-30.473N 094-45-31.302W	F G	75		KRW on skeleton tower.	Visible 2° each side of rangeline.
23915	- ENTRANCE INNER RANGE FRONT LIGHT	29-22-39.548N 094-48-43.393W	Q G	28		KRW on skeleton tower on piles.	
23920	- ENTRANCE INNER RANGE REAR LIGHT 2,509 yards, 318.3° from front light.	29-23-35.190N 094-49-39.975W	Iso G 6s	60		KRW on skeleton tower on piles.	Visible 4° each side of rangeline.
23925	- ENTRANCE INNER RANGE REAR LIGHT PASSING LIGHT	29-23-35.190N 094-49-39.975W	Fl W 4s	12	5	On same structure as Galveston Channel Entrance Inner Range Rear Light.	
	Bolivar Roads Alternate Inbound Route						
23940	- RANGE FRONT LIGHT	29-22-53.291N 094-48-46.644W	Q G	27		KWR on skeleton tower on piles.	Visible all around; higher intensity 4° each side of centerline.
23945	- RANGE REAR LIGHT 1246 yards, 301.1° from front light.	29-23-12.421N 094-49-22.824W	Iso G 6s	56		KWR on skeleton tower on platform.	Visible 2° each side of rangeline.

Light List corrected through LNM week: 01/18

(1) No.	(2) Name and Location	(3) Position	(4) Characteristic	(5) Height	(6) Range	(7) Structure	(8) Remarks
	**TEXAS - Eighth District**						
	GALVESTON BAY ENTRANCE (Chart 11324)						
	Houston Ship Channel						
	Bolivar Roads Alternate Inbound Route						
23950	- RANGE REAR PASSING LIGHT	29-23-12.418N 094-49-22.830W	Fl W 4s	12	3	On same structure as Bolivar Roads Alternate Inbound Range Rear Light.	
	Houston Ship Channel						
23955	- Lighted Buoy 25	29-22-02.045N 094-48-11.508W	Fl G 4s		4	Green.	
23960	- Lighted Buoy 26	29-22-09.672N 094-48-02.712W	Q R		3	Red.	
23965	- Rock Pile Lighted Buoy 25A	29-22-11.249N 094-48-16.872W	Fl G 2.5s		4	Green.	
23970	LOWER GALVESTON BAY OUTER RANGE FRONT LIGHT	29-20-52.835N 094-47-31.413W	Fl G 2.5s (NIGHT) Fl G 2.5s (NIGHT) Fl W 2.5s (DAY)	39 45 42		On piles.	DAY: Visible 2° each side of range line. NIGHT: Visible all around, higher intensity on range line.
23975	LOWER GALVESTON BAY OUTER RANGE REAR LIGHT 3,632 yards, 156.2° from front light.	29-19-14.126N 094-46-41.808W	Oc G 4s (NIGHT) Oc W 4s (DAY)	135 132		On skeleton tower on piles.	Visible 2° each side of range line.
23980	LOWER GALVESTON BAY OUTER RANGE REAR LIGHT PASSING LIGHT	29-19-14.126N 094-46-41.808W	Fl W 4s	40	5	On same structure as Lower Galveston Bay Outer Range Rear Light.	
23985	- Lighted Buoy 27	29-22-41.778N 094-48-32.830W	Fl G 2.5s		4	Green.	Ra ref.
23990	- Lighted Buoy 28 265 feet outside channel limit.	29-22-45.951N 094-48-21.796W	Fl R 2.5s		3	Red.	
23995	- Lighted Buoy 29 235 feet outside channel limit.	29-23-12.789N 094-48-47.935W	Fl (2)G 6s		4	Green.	Ra ref.
24000	- Lighted Buoy 30	29-23-17.051N 094-48-37.352W	Fl (2)R 6s		3	Red.	Ra ref.
24005	- Lighted Buoy 31 235 feet outside channel limit.	29-23-44.072N 094-49-03.689W	Fl G 2.5s		4	Green.	
24010	- Lighted Buoy 32	29-23-47.970N 094-48-53.300W	Fl R 2.5s		3	Red.	Ra ref.
24015	- Lighted Buoy 33 235 feet outside channel limit.	29-24-25.251N 094-49-24.392W	Fl G 4s		4	Green.	
24020	- LIGHT 34	29-24-29.673N 094-49-11.736W	Fl R 4s	17	4	TR on pile.	
24025	- LIGHT 35 235 feet outside channel limit.	29-25-01.353N 094-49-43.641W	Fl G 6s	17	4	SG on pile.	Ra ref.
24030	- LIGHT 35A	29-25-23.935N 094-49-53.988W	Fl G 4s	17	4	SG on pile.	
24035	- WRECK LIGHT WR35B	29-25-22.341N 094-50-00.903W	Q G	17	3	SG on pile.	
	UPPER GALVESTON BAY (Chart 11327)						
	Houston Ship Channel						
24040	- LIGHT 36 235 feet outside channel limit.	29-25-05.490N 094-49-32.320W	Fl R 6s	17	4	TR on pile.	Ra ref.
24045	- LIGHT 37 235 feet outside channel limit.	29-25-37.749N 094-50-00.987W	Fl G 2.5s	17	4	SG on pile.	
24050	- LIGHT 38 235 feet outside channel limit.	29-25-41.738N 094-49-49.982W	Fl R 2.5s	17	3	TR on pile.	

Light List corrected through LNM week: 01/18

(1) No.	(2) Name and Location	(3) Position	(4) Characteristic	(5) Height	(6) Range	(7) Structure	(8) Remarks
		TEXAS - Eighth District					
	UPPER GALVESTON BAY (Chart 11327)						
	Houston Ship Channel						
24055	LOWER GALVESTON BAY INNER RANGE FRONT LIGHT	29-30-28.775N 094-52-21.864W	Fl G 2.5s (NIGHT) Fl W 2.5s (DAY)	40 43		On pile.	DAY: Visible 2° each side of range line. NIGHT: Visible all around, higher intensity on range line.
24060	LOWER GALVESTON BAY INNER RANGE REAR LIGHT 1999 yards, 336.2° from front light.	29-31-24.103N 094-52-49.263W	Iso G 6s (NIGHT) Iso W 6s (DAY)	118 115		On skeleton tower on piles.	Visible 2° each side of range line.
24065	LOWER GALVESTON BAY INNER RANGE REAR LIGHT PASSING LIGHT	29-31-24.116N 094-52-49.267W	Fl W 4s	40	6	On same structure as Lower Galveston Bay Inner Range Rear Light.	
24070	- LIGHT 39 235 feet outside channel limit.	29-26-13.968N 094-50-19.118W	Fl (2)G 6s	17	4	SG on pile.	Ra ref.
24075	- LIGHT 40 235 feet outside channel limit.	29-26-18.139N 094-50-08.371W	Fl (2)R 6s	17	3	TR on pile.	Ra ref.
24080	- LIGHT 41 235 feet outside channel limit.	29-26-50.196N 094-50-37.363W	Fl G 2.5s	17	4	SG on pile.	
24085	- LIGHT 42 235 feet outside channel limit.	29-26-54.240N 094-50-26.477W	Fl R 2.5s	17	3	TR on pile.	Ra ref.
24090	- LIGHT 43	29-27-26.423N 094-50-55.611W	Fl G 4s	17	4	SG on pile.	Ra ref.
24095	- LIGHT 44 235 feet outside channel limit.	29-27-30.403N 094-50-45.286W	Fl R 4s	17	3	TR on pile.	Ra ref.
24100	- LIGHT 45 235 feet outside channel limit.	29-28-02.595N 094-51-14.632W	Fl G 6s	17	4	SG on pile.	
24105	- LIGHT 46 235 feet outside channel limit.	29-28-06.629N 094-51-03.536W	Fl R 6s	17	4	TR on pile.	
24110	- LIGHT 47 235 feet outside channel limit.	29-28-38.480N 094-51-33.434W	Fl G 2.5s	17	4	SG on pile.	Ra ref.
24115	- LIGHT 48 235 feet outside channel limit.	29-28-42.854N 094-51-21.790W	Fl R 2.5s	17	4	TR on pile.	
24120	- LIGHT 49 235 feet outside channel limit.	29-29-15.170N 094-51-50.763W	Fl (2)G 6s	17	4	SG on pile.	
24125	- LIGHT 50 235 feet outside channel limit.	29-29-19.079N 094-51-40.051W	Fl (2)R 6s	17	4	TR on pile.	Ra ref.
	Trinity River Channel						
24130	- LIGHT 1	29-31-48.265N 094-48-56.932W	Fl G 2.5s	17	3	SG on pile.	Ra ref.
24135	- Day beacon 2	29-31-59.853N 094-48-35.704W				TR on pile.	Ra ref.
24140	- Day beacon 3	29-32-13.125N 094-48-21.273W				SG on pile.	Ra ref.
24155	- LIGHT 7	29-32-49.963N 094-47-26.053W	Fl G 4s	17	4	SG on pile.	Ra ref.
24160	- Day beacon 9	29-32-49.003N 094-46-46.431W				SG on pile.	Ra ref.
24165	- LIGHT 10	29-32-45.239N 094-46-20.476W	Fl R 2.5s	17	3	TR on pile.	Ra ref.

Light List corrected through LNM week: 01/18

(1) No.	(2) Name and Location	(3) Position	(4) Characteristic	(5) Height	(6) Range	(7) Structure	(8) Remarks
			TEXAS - Eighth District				
	UPPER GALVESTON BAY (Chart 11327)						
	Houston Ship Channel						
24170	- LIGHT 51	29-29-33.411N 094-51-59.586W	Q G	17	4	SG on pile.	Ra ref.
24175	- LIGHT 52	29-29-38.297N 094-51-49.771W	Q R	17	4	TR on pile.	Ra ref.
24180	- LIGHT 53	29-30-13.665N 094-52-30.536W	Fl G 2.5s	17	3	SG on pile.	
24185	- LIGHT 54	29-30-19.234N 094-52-21.177W	Fl R 2.5s	17	3	TR on pile.	Ra ref.
24190	Redfish Island Shoal South Day beacon	29-30-19.314N 094-53-08.999W				NR on pile.	Ra ref.
24195	REDFISH ISLAND SHOAL LIGHT	29-31-25.619N 094-53-38.860W	Fl W 6s	17	5	NG on pile.	
24200	Redfish Island Shoal North Day beacon	29-31-02.853N 094-53-55.918W				NG on pile.	
24205	UPPER GALVESTON BAY OUTER RANGE FRONT LIGHT	29-28-55.722N 094-51-23.968W	Q G	35		KRW on skeleton tower on piles.	Visible 2° each side of rangeline.
24210	UPPER GALVESTON BAY OUTER RANGE REAR LIGHT 1,492 yards, 146° from front light.	29-28-18.776N 094-50-55.604W	Iso G 6s	65		KRW on skeleton tower on piles.	Visible 2° each side of rangeline.
24215	UPPER GALVESTON BAY INNER RANGE FRONT LIGHT	29-37-08.370N 094-57-42.642W	Q W	25		KRW on piles.	Visible only on rangeline.
24220	UPPER GALVESTON BAY INNER RANGE REAR LIGHT 1,600 yards, 326° from front light.	29-37-47.439N 094-58-12.735W	Iso W 6s	65		KRW on skeleton tower on piles.	Visible only on rangeline.
24225	- LIGHT 55	29-30-46.615N 094-52-55.758W	Fl G 4s	17	4	SG on pile.	Ra ref.
24230	- LIGHT 56	29-30-52.058N 094-52-46.420W	Fl R 4s	17	4	TR on pile.	Ra ref.
24235	- LIGHT 57	29-31-19.438N 094-53-21.086W	Fl G 2.5s	17	4	SG on pile.	
24240	- LIGHT 58	29-31-24.864N 094-53-11.573W	Fl R 2.5s	17	4	TR on pile.	Ra ref.
24245	- LIGHT 59 500 feet from the channel centerline.	29-31-52.338N 094-53-46.310W	Fl (2)G 6s	17	4	SG on pile.	Ra ref.
24250	- LIGHT 60	29-31-57.730N 094-53-36.830W	Fl (2)R 6s	17	4	TR on pile.	Ra ref.
24255	- LIGHT 61	29-32-23.172N 094-54-10.122W	Fl G 2.5s	17	4	SG on pile.	
24260	- LIGHT 62	29-32-28.717N 094-54-00.588W	Fl R 2.5s	17	4	TR on pile.	Ra ref.
	South Boater Cut						
24265	- LIGHT 1 50 feet outside channel limit.	29-32-35.123N 094-53-12.168W	Fl G 4s	17	4	SG on pile.	Ra ref.
24270	- Day beacon 3 50 feet outside channel limit.	29-32-31.998N 094-53-37.014W				SG on pile.	
24275	- Day beacon 4 50 feet outside channel limit.	29-32-36.029N 094-53-37.621W				TR on pile.	
24280	- Day beacon 5 50 feet outside channel limit.	29-32-24.209N 094-54-39.338W				SG on pile.	
24285	- Day beacon 6 50 feet outside channel limit.	29-32-28.228N 094-54-39.947W				TR on pile.	
24290	- LIGHT 8	29-32-25.086N 094-55-04.797W	Fl R 4s	17	3	TR on pile.	

Light List corrected through LNM week: 01/18

(1) No.	(2) Name and Location	(3) Position	(4) Characteristic	(5) Height	(6) Range	(7) Structure	(8) Remarks
			TEXAS - Eighth District				
	UPPER GALVESTON BAY (Chart 11327)						
	Houston Ship Channel						
24295	- LIGHT 63	29-32-58.029N 094-54-36.846W	Fl G 4s	17	3	SG on pile.	
24300	- LIGHT 64	29-33-03.445N 094-54-27.361W	Fl R 4s	17	4	TR on pile.	Ra ref.
24305	- LIGHT 65	29-33-30.925N 094-55-02.101W	Fl G 6s	17	4	SG on pile.	
24310	- LIGHT 66	29-33-36.264N 094-54-52.553W	Fl R 6s	17	4	TR on pile.	Ra ref.
24315	- LIGHT 67	29-34-03.762N 094-55-27.378W	Fl G 2.5s	17	4	SG on pile.	
24320	- LIGHT 68 500 feet from the channel centerline.	29-34-09.129N 094-55-17.841W	Fl R 2.5s	17	3	TR on pile.	Ra ref.
24325	- LIGHT 69 500 feet from the channel centerline.	29-34-36.520N 094-55-52.572W	Fl (2)G 6s	17	4	SG on pile.	Ra ref.
24330	- LIGHT 70	29-34-41.837N 094-55-43.024W	Fl (2)R 6s	17	4	TR on pile.	Ra ref.
24335	- NORTH BOATER CUT LIGHT 1 50 feet outside channel limit.	29-35-30.765N 094-55-05.693W	Fl G 4s	17	3	SG on pile.	Ra ref.
24340	- North Boater Cut Day beacon 3 50 feet outside channel limit.	29-35-14.239N 094-55-33.851W				SG on pile.	Ra ref.
24345	- North Boater Cut Day beacon 4 50 feet outside channel limit.	29-35-15.850N 094-55-34.992W				TR on pile.	Ra ref.
24350	- North Boater Cut Day beacon 5 50 feet outside channel limit.	29-34-46.579N 094-56-20.521W				SG on pile.	Ra ref.
24355	- NORTH BOATER CUT LIGHT 6 50 feet outside channel limit.	29-34-48.100N 094-56-22.041W	Fl R 4s	17	3	TR on pile.	Ra ref.
24365	- LIGHT 71	29-35-09.351N 094-56-17.874W	Fl G 2.5s	17	4	SG on pile.	Ra ref.
24370	- LIGHT 72	29-35-14.708N 094-56-08.370W	Fl R 2.5s	17	4	TR on pile.	Ra ref.
24375	- LIGHT 73 500 feet from the channel centerline.	29-35-42.341N 094-56-43.260W	Fl G 4s	17	3	SG on pile.	Ra ref.
24380	- LIGHT 74 500 feet from the channel centerline.	29-35-47.708N 094-56-33.750W	Fl R 4s	17	3	TR on pile.	Ra ref.
24385	- LIGHT 75	29-36-26.600N 094-57-17.200W	Q G	17	4	SG on pile.	Ra ref.
24390	- LIGHT 76	29-36-30.696N 094-57-06.907W	Q R	17	4	TR on pile.	Ra ref.
24395	MORGANS POINT APPROACH OUTER RANGE FRONT LIGHT 2,361 yards, 161.7° from front light.	29-35-46.909N 094-56-56.298W	Fl G 2.5s (NIGHT) Fl W 2.5s (DAY)	40 38		Skeleton tower on piles.	Visible 2° each side of rangeline.
24400	MORGANS POINT APPROACH OUTER RANGE REAR LIGHT	29-34-40.313N 094-56-31.160W	Iso G 6s (NIGHT) Iso W 6s (DAY)	111 109			Visible 2° each side of rangeline.
24405	MORGANS POINT APPROACH CHANNEL OUTER RANGE REAR PASSING LIGHT	29-34-40.331N 094-56-31.144W	Fl W 4s	38	6	On same structure as Morgans Point Approach Outer Range Rear Light.	

Light List corrected through LNM week: 01/18

(1) No.	(2) Name and Location	(3) Position	(4) Characteristic	(5) Height	(6) Range	(7) Structure	(8) Remarks
TEXAS - Eighth District							

UPPER GALVESTON BAY (Chart 11327)

Houston Ship Channel

Five Mile Cut

(1) No.	(2) Name and Location	(3) Position	(4) Characteristic	(5) Height	(6) Range	(7) Structure	(8) Remarks
24410	- Buoy 2	29-36-33.018N 094-57-05.549W				Red nun.	
24415	- Buoy 4	29-36-35.501N 094-56-32.595W				Red nun.	
24420	- Buoy 6	29-36-36.689N 094-56-04.412W				Red nun.	
24425	- Day beacon 7	29-36-42.047N 094-55-18.043W				SG on pile.	

Bayport Ship Channel

(1) No.	(2) Name and Location	(3) Position	(4) Characteristic	(5) Height	(6) Range	(7) Structure	(8) Remarks
24430	- OUTER RANGE FRONT LIGHT	29-36-52.262N 094-57-07.388W	Q G (NIGHT) Q W (DAY)	28 28			
24435	- RANGE FRONT PASSING LIGHT	29-36-52.262N 094-57-07.388W	Fl W 4s	14	3		On same structure as Bayport Ship Channel Outer Range Front Light.
24440	- OUTER RANGE REAR LIGHT 3,500 yards, 88.9° from front light.	29-36-54.243N 094-55-08.460W	Iso G 6s (NIGHT) Iso W 6s (DAY)	96 96			
24445	- OUTER RANGE REAR LIGHT PASSING LIGHT	29-36-54.243N 094-55-08.460W	Fl W 4s	14	5		On same structure as Bayport Ship Channel Outer Range Rear Light.
24455	- JUNCTION LIGHT B 500 feet from the channel centerline.	29-37-09.589N 094-57-33.428W	Fl (2+1)G 6s	17	4	JG on pile.	Ra ref.
24460	- LIGHT 2	29-36-59.227N 094-57-38.517W	Fl R 2.5s	17	4	TR on pile.	
24465	- INNER RANGE FRONT LIGHT	29-36-47.054N 095-01-41.940W	Iso G 2s	30		KRW on pile.	
24467	LBC HOUSTON DIRECTIONAL SECTOR LIGHT	29-36-47.327N 095-01-40.496W	F R W G	160		On tower.	Long Range Light: FLG 269.4° to 269.2°. FG from 269.2° to 269.05°. GW from 269.05° to 268.85°. FW (on channel line) from 268.85° to 268.75°. RW from 268.75° to 268.55°. FR from 268.55° to 268.4°. FLR from 268.4° to 268.2°. Short Range Light: FG from 269.4° to 268.95°. FW (on channel line) from 268.95° to 268.65°. FR from 268.65° to 268.2°. Private aid.
24470	- INNER RANGE REAR LIGHT	29-36-46.544N 095-02-11.216W	Oc G 4s	71		KRW on skeleton tower.	Visible only on the channel line.
24475	- LIGHT 3	29-36-45.938N 094-57-32.762W	Fl G 2.5s	17	4	SG on pile.	Ra ref.
24480	- LIGHT 4	29-36-55.187N 094-57-50.113W	Fl R 2.5s	17	4	TR on pile.	Ra ref.
24485	- LIGHT 5	29-36-48.347N 094-57-49.888W	Fl G 4s	17	4	SG on pile.	
24490	- LIGHT 6	29-36-54.034N 094-58-41.069W	Fl R 4s	17	4	TR on pile.	
24495	- LIGHT 7	29-36-47.491N 094-58-40.800W	Fl G 6s	17	4	SG on pile.	Ra ref.
24500	- LIGHT 8	29-36-52.591N 094-59-32.030W	Fl R 2.5s	17	4	TR on pile	
24505	- LIGHT 9	29-36-46.394N 094-59-18.876W	Fl G 2.5s	17	4	SG on pile.	

TEXAS - Eighth District

(1) No.	(2) Name and Location	(3) Position	(4) Characteristic	(5) Height	(6) Range	(7) Structure	(8) Remarks
	UPPER GALVESTON BAY (Chart 11327)						
	Houston Ship Channel						
	Bayport Ship Channel						
24510	- LIGHT 11	29-36-44.636N 095-00-59.319W	Fl G 4s	17	4	SG on pile.	Ra ref.
	Houston Ship Channel						
24520	- LIGHT 78 500 feet from channel centerline.	29-37-12.523N 094-57-22.688W	Fl R 4s	17	3	TR on pile.	Ra ref.
24525	- LIGHT 81 500 feet from the channel centerline.	29-37-54.400N 094-57-50.400W	Fl G 2.5s	17	4	SG on pile.	
24530	- LIGHT 82	29-37-57.300N 094-57-39.600W	Fl R 2.5s	17	4	TR on pile.	Ra ref.
24535	- LIGHT 83	29-38-29.968N 094-58-03.880W	Fl G 4s	17	4	SG on pile.	
24540	- LIGHT 84	29-38-33.000N 094-57-53.100W	Fl R 4s	17	4	TR on pile.	
24545	- LIGHT 85	29-39-10.499N 094-58-19.199W	Fl G 6s	17	4	SG on pile.	Ra ref.
24550	- LIGHT 86	29-39-13.407N 094-58-08.439W	Fl R 6s	17	4	TR on dolphin.	Ra ref.
	HOUSTON SHIP CHANNEL (Chart 11328)						
	Houston Ship Channel						
24555	- LIGHT 87 500 feet from the channel centerline.	29-39-45.200N 094-58-32.300W	Fl G 2.5s	17	3	SG on pile.	Ra ref.
24560	- LIGHT 88	29-39-48.309N 094-58-21.507W	Fl R 2.5s	17	4	TR on pile.	Ra ref.
24565	- LIGHT 89	29-40-21.200N 094-58-44.600W	Fl (2)G 6s	17	5	SG on pile.	Ra ref.
24570	- LIGHT 89A 125 feet outside channel limit.	29-40-37.230N 094-58-50.689W	Fl G 4s	17	4	SG on pile.	Ra ref.
24575	- LIGHT 90	29-40-23.916N 094-58-35.015W	Fl (2)R 6s	17	4	TR on pile.	Ra ref.
24580	- LIGHT 90A	29-40-39.695N 094-58-41.011W	Fl R 4s	17	3	TR on pile.	Ra ref.
24585	MORGANS POINT APPROACH INNER RANGE FRONT LIGHT	29-41-22.490N 094-59-03.152W	Fl G 2.5s (NIGHT) Fl W 2.5s (DAY)	22 25		KRW on skeleton tower on piles.	Visible all around; higher intensity on the rangeline.
24590	MORGANS POINT APPROACH INNER RANGE REAR LIGHT 3,106 yards, 341.7° from front light.	29-42-50.096N 094-59-36.310W	Iso G 6s (NIGHT) Iso W 6s (DAY)	99 96		KRW on skeleton tower.	Visible only on the rangeline.
24595	- LIGHT 91	29-40-58.379N 094-58-59.529W	Fl G 2.5s	17	3	SG on dolphin.	Ra ref.
24600	- LIGHT 92	29-41-01.303N 094-58-49.226W	Fl R 2.5s	17	4	TR on pile.	Ra ref.
24605	BARBOURS CUT CROSSING RANGE FRONT LIGHT	29-40-42.360N 094-58-40.456W	Q R	25		KRW on skeleton tower on concrete block.	For downbound traffic. Visible 2° each side of rangeline.
24610	BARBOURS CUT CROSSING RANGE REAR LIGHT 223 yards, 146.8° from front light.	29-40-36.838N 094-58-39.298W	Iso R 6s	50		KRW on skeleton tower.	Visible 2° each side of rangeline.
	Cedar Bayou Channel						
24615	- Buoy 2	29-41-02.707N 094-58-47.453W				Red nun.	Ra ref.
24620.01	- Day beacon 3	29-41-11.158N 094-58-38.195W				SG on pile.	
24625	- Day beacon 6	29-41-13.216N 094-58-26.481W				TR on pile.	Ra ref.

Light List corrected through LNM week: 01/18

(1) No.	(2) Name and Location	(3) Position	(4) Characteristic	(5) Height	(6) Range	(7) Structure	(8) Remarks
			TEXAS - Eighth District				
	HOUSTON SHIP CHANNEL (Chart 11328)						
	Houston Ship Channel						
	Cedar Bayou Channel						
24630	- Buoy 8	29-41-16.632N 094-58-18.587W				Red nun.	
24635	- Day beacon 10	29-41-18.582N 094-58-07.116W				TR on pile.	Ra ref.
24645	- LIGHT 14 50 feet outside channel limit.	29-41-18.954N 094-57-55.182W	Fl R 4s	17	4	TR on pile.	Ra ref.
24650	- Day beacon 16	29-41-12.353N 094-57-41.141W				TR on pile.	Ra ref.
24655	- Day beacon 18	29-41-05.187N 094-57-24.988W				TR on pile.	Ra ref.
24660	- Day beacon 20	29-40-53.898N 094-57-00.770W				TR on pile.	Ra ref.
24665	- Day beacon 22	29-40-45.253N 094-56-41.860W				TR on pile.	Ra ref.
24670	- LIGHT 23	29-40-41.165N 094-56-27.119W	Fl G 4s	17	4	SG on pile.	
24675	- Day beacon 24	29-40-37.507N 094-56-27.727W				TR on pile.	Ra ref.
24680	- Day beacon 25	29-40-31.648N 094-56-16.631W				SG on pile.	
24685	- Day beacon 26	29-40-29.719N 094-56-18.550W				TR on pile.	Ra ref.
24690	- Day beacon 27	29-40-23.711N 094-56-08.127W				SG on pile.	Ra ref.
24695	- Day beacon 28	29-40-22.436N 094-56-10.081W				TR on pile.	Ra ref.
24700	- Day beacon 29	29-40-21.045N 094-56-02.164W				SG on pile.	Ra ref.
24705	- LIGHT 30	29-40-18.987N 094-55-54.580W	Fl R 4s	17	3	TR on pile.	Ra ref.
24710	- LIGHT 31	29-40-21.579N 094-55-54.248W	Fl G 4s	17	4	SG on pile.	Ra ref.
24715	- Day beacon 33	29-40-27.445N 094-55-48.154W				SG on pile.	Ra ref.
24720	- Day beacon 35	29-40-39.062N 094-55-45.335W				SG on pile.	Ra ref.
24725	- LIGHT 37	29-40-53.386N 094-55-37.140W	Fl G 6s	17	4	SG on pile.	
24730	- Day beacon 38	29-40-59.889N 094-55-20.325W				TR on pile.	Ra ref.
24735	- Day beacon 39	29-41-01.483N 094-55-22.250W				SG on pile.	
24740	- Day beacon 40	29-41-08.416N 094-55-11.631W				TR on pile.	Ra ref.
24745	- Day beacon 42	29-41-21.286N 094-55-11.112W				TR on pile.	Ra ref.
	Houston Ship Channel						
24750	BARBOURS CUT JUNCTION LIGHT BC	29-41-12.297N 094-59-10.000W	Fl (2+1)G 6s	17	4	JG pn pile.	Ra ref.
24752	ENTERPRISE PRODUCTS SPECIAL LIGHT A	29-41-09.110N 095-00-26.650W	Fl Y 2.5s			Marks turning point for mooring.	Private aid.
24755	- LIGHT 93 125 feet outside channel limit.	29-41-17.601N 094-59-12.513W	Fl G 4s	17	3	SG on pile.	Ra ref.
24760	UPPER MORGANS POINT INBOUND RANGE FRONT LIGHT	29-42-04.783N 095-00-02.395W	Q G	20		KRW on skeleton tower on piles.	Visible only on the rangeline.

TEXAS - Eighth District

HOUSTON SHIP CHANNEL (Chart 11328)

Houston Ship Channel

(1) No.	(2) Name and Location	(3) Position	(4) Characteristic	(5) Height	(6) Range	(7) Structure	(8) Remarks
24765	UPPER MORGANS POINT INBOUND RANGE FRONT PASSING LIGHT	29-42-04.800N 095-00-02.400W	Fl W 4s	15	3	On same structure as Upper Morgans Point Inbound Range Front Light.	
24770	UPPER MORGANS POINT INBOUND RANGE REAR LIGHT	29-42-09.496N 095-00-08.260W	Iso G 6s	35		KRW on skeleton tower on piles.	Visible on rangeline only.
24775	UPPER MORGANS POINT OUTBOUND RANGE FRONT LIGHT	29-41-00.209N 094-58-45.088W	Q R	20		KRW on skeleton tower on piles.	Visible all around, higher intensity on rangeline. Ra ref.
24780	UPPER MORGANS POINT OUTBOUND RANGE REAR LIGHT	29-40-57.130N 094-58-41.249W	Iso R 6s	37		KRW on skeleton tower on pile platform.	Visbile on rangeline only.
24785	- LIGHT 94 150 feet outside the channel limit.	29-41-22.971N 094-59-05.317W	Fl R 4s	17	4	TR on pile.	Ra ref.
24790.1	- *Lighted Buoy 95*	29-41-33.801N 094-59-32.672W	Fl G 6s		4	Green.	
24795	- LIGHT 96 120 feet outside the channel	29-41-39.482N 094-59-25.466W	Fl R 6s	17	4	TR on pile.	Ra ref.
24800	- LIGHT 97 120 feet outside the channel	29-41-48.382N 094-59-51.958W	Fl G 2.5s	17	4	SG on pile.	Ra ref.
24805	- LIGHT 98 150 feet outside the channel	29-41-55.083N 094-59-45.561W	Fl R 2.5s	17	4	TR on pile.	Ra ref.
24810	- LIGHT 99 100 feet outside the channel	29-41-53.432N 095-00-02.074W	Fl G 4s	17	4	SG on pile.	Ra ref.
24815	- LIGHT 100 150 feet outside the channel	29-42-01.321N 094-59-58.360W	Fl R 4s	17	4	TR on pile.	Ra ref.

Baytown Marina Channel

(1) No.	(2) Name and Location	(3) Position	(4) Characteristic	(5) Height	(6) Range	(7) Structure	(8) Remarks
24820	- Day beacon 1	29-42-08.930N 095-00-04.880W				SG on pile.	Private aid.
24825	- Day beacon 2	29-42-08.890N 095-00-03.400W				TR on pile.	Private aid.
24830	- Day beacon 3	29-42-24.000N 094-59-53.207W				SG on pile.	Private aid.
24835	- Day beacon 4	29-42-12.060N 095-00-03.070W				TR on pile.	Private aid.
24840	- Day beacon 5	29-42-13.770N 095-00-04.120W				SG on pile.	Private aid.
24845	- Day beacon 6	29-42-15.200N 095-00-02.460W				TR on pile.	Private aid.
24850	- Day beacon 7	29-42-17.850N 095-00-03.370W				SG on pile.	Private aid.
24855	- Day beacon 8	29-42-18.360N 095-00-01.850W				TR on pile.	Private aid.
24860	- Day beacon 9	29-42-22.440N 095-00-02.320W				SG on pile.	Private aid.
24865	- Day beacon 10	29-42-24.380N 095-00-00.790W				TR on pile.	Private aid.
24865.01	- Day beacon 11	29-42-24.990N 095-00-01.850W				SG on pile.	Private aid.
24870	- Day beacon 12	29-42-26.310N 095-00-00.530W				TR on pile.	Private aid.
24875	- LIGHT 13	29-42-27.130N 095-00-01.520W	Fl G 2.5s			SG on pile.	Private aid.

Baytown Goose Creek Channel

(1) No.	(2) Name and Location	(3) Position	(4) Characteristic	(5) Height	(6) Range	(7) Structure	(8) Remarks
24880	- Day beacon 1	29-42-26.410N 094-59-58.570W				SG on pile.	Private aid.
24885	- Day beacon 2	29-42-25.740N 094-59-58.100W				TR on pile.	Private aid.
24890	- Day beacon 3	29-42-25.480N 094-59-55.150W				SG on pile.	Private aid.

Light List corrected through LNM week: 01/18

(1) No.	(2) Name and Location	(3) Position	(4) Characteristic	(5) Height	(6) Range	(7) Structure	(8) Remarks
		TEXAS - Eighth District					
	HOUSTON SHIP CHANNEL (Chart 11328)						
	Houston Ship Channel						
	Baytown Goose Creek Channel						
24895	- Day beacon 4	29-42-23.910N 094-59-51.960W				TR on pile.	Private aid.
24900	- Day beacon 5	29-42-23.860N 094-59-49.390W				SG on pile.	Private aid.
24905	- Day beacon 6	29-42-22.790N 094-59-47.420W				TR on pile.	Private aid.
24910	- Day beacon 7	29-42-22.430N 094-59-44.360W				SG on pile.	Private aid.
24915	- Day beacon 8	29-42-21.910N 094-59-44.290W				TR on pile.	Private aid.
24920	- Day beacon 9	29-42-22.480N 094-59-42.660W				SG on pile.	Private aid.
24925	- Day beacon 10	29-42-21.950N 094-59-42.520W				TR on pile.	Private aid.
24930	- Day beacon 11	29-42-22.770N 094-59-40.590W				SG on pile.	Private aid.
24935	- Day beacon 12	29-42-22.240N 094-59-40.450W				TR on pile.	Private aid.
24940	- Day beacon 13	29-42-23.460N 094-59-38.940W				SG on pile.	Private aid.
24945	- Day beacon 14	29-42-23.060N 094-59-38.390W				TR on pile.	Private aid.
24950	- Day beacon 15	29-42-25.250N 094-59-35.680W				SG on pile.	Private aid.
24955	- Day beacon 16	29-42-24.830N 094-59-35.160W				TR on pile.	Private aid.
24960	- Day beacon 17	29-42-27.040N 094-59-34.120W				SG on pile.	Private aid.
24965	- Day beacon 18	29-42-26.810N 094-59-33.370W				TR on pile.	Private aid.
24970	- Day beacon 19	29-42-28.840N 094-59-33.330W				SG on pile.	Private aid.
24975	- Day beacon 20	29-42-30.510N 094-59-31.990W				TR on pile.	Private aid.
24980	- Day beacon 21	29-42-32.620N 094-59-31.750W				SG on pile.	Private aid.
24985	- Day beacon 22	29-42-34.090N 094-59-30.650W				TR on pile.	Private aid.
24990	- Day beacon 23	29-42-34.240N 094-59-31.190W				SG on pile.	Private aid.
24995	- Day beacon 24	29-42-36.080N 094-59-30.360W				TR on pile.	Private aid.
25000	- Day beacon 25	29-42-37.190N 094-59-30.970W				SG on pile.	Private aid.
25005	- Day beacon 26	29-42-38.170N 094-59-30.200W				TR on pile.	Private aid.
25010	- Day beacon 27	29-42-41.100N 094-59-30.860W				SG on pile.	Private aid.
25015	- Day beacon 28	29-42-41.070N 094-59-30.260W				TR on pile.	Private aid.
25020	- Day beacon 29	29-42-43.020N 094-59-30.820W				SG on pile.	Private aid.
25025	- Day beacon 30	29-42-45.910N 094-59-30.030W				TR on pile.	Private aid.
25027	- Day beacon 31	29-42-46.370N 094-59-30.580W				SG on pile.	Private aid.
	Baytown Marina Channel						
25030	- Day beacon 14	29-42-29.900N 094-59-59.610W				TR on pile.	Private aid.
25035	- Day beacon 15	29-42-30.010N 095-00-00.990W				SG on pile.	Private aid.
25040	- Day beacon 16	29-42-33.100N 094-59-58.860W				TR on pile.	Private aid.

(1) No.	(2) Name and Location	(3) Position	(4) Characteristic	(5) Height	(6) Range	(7) Structure	(8) Remarks
			TEXAS - Eighth District				
	HOUSTON SHIP CHANNEL (Chart 11328)						
	Houston Ship Channel						
	Baytown Marina Channel						
25045	- LIGHT 17	29-42-33.400N 095-00-00.340W	Fl G 2.5s			SG on pile.	Private aid.
25050	- Day beacon 18	29-42-33.400N 094-59-55.300W				TR on pile.	Private aid.
25055	- Day beacon 19	29-42-35.290N 095-00-00.450W				SG on pile.	Private aid.
	Houston Ship Channel						
25060	LOWER RED LIGHT BEND INBOUND RANGE FRONT LIGHT	29-42-07.589N 095-01-01.105W	Q G	19		KRW on skeleton tower on piles.	Visible all around, higher intensity on rangeline.
25065	LOWER RED LIGHT BEND INBOUND RANGE REAR LIGHT 71 yards, 277.1° from front light.	29-42-07.849N 095-01-03.494W	Iso G 6s	26		KRW on skeleton tower on piles.	
25070	LOWER RED LIGHT BEND OUTBOUND RANGE FRONT LIGHT	29-41-58.469N 094-59-50.514W	Q R	20		KRW on skeleton tower on piles.	Visible all around, higher intensity on rangeline.
25075	LOWER RED LIGHT BEND OUTBOUND RANGE REAR LIGHT 172 yards, 094.6° from front light.	29-41-57.877N 094-59-44.692W	Iso R 6s	32		KRW on skeleton tower on piles.	Visible all around, higher intensity on rangeline.
25080	- LIGHT 101 120 feet outside channel limit.	29-41-58.589N 095-00-23.948W	Fl G 6s	17	4	SG on pile.	Ra ref.
25085	- LIGHT 102 200 feet outside the channel limit.	29-42-07.604N 095-00-21.258W	Fl R 6s	17	4	TR on pile.	Ra ref.
25090	- LIGHT 101A 120 feet outside the channel limit.	29-42-01.451N 095-00-45.833W	Fl G 4s	17	4	SG on pile.	Ra ref.
25095	- LIGHT 102A 120 feet outside channel limit.	29-42-11.960N 095-00-46.440W	Fl R 4s	17	3	TR on pile.	Ra ref.
	HOUSTON SHIP CHANNEL (Chart 11329)						
	Houston Ship Channel						
25100	- LIGHT 103	29-42-15.069N 095-01-09.702W	Fl G 2.5s	17	4	SG on pile.	Ra ref.
	San Jacinto Bay Barge Channel						
25105	- Day beacon 1	29-42-14.040N 095-01-12.980W				SG on pile.	Private aid.
25107	- Day beacon 2	29-42-13.587N 095-01-22.334W				TR on pile.	Private aid.
25110	- Day beacon 3	29-42-11.083N 095-01-21.019W				SG on pile.	Private aid.
25115	- Day beacon 4	29-42-13.589N 095-01-31.851W				TR on pile.	Private aid.
25120	- Day beacon 5	29-42-10.240N 095-01-33.939W				SG on pile.	Private aid.
25123	- Day beacon 7	29-42-12.582N 095-01-40.471W				SG on pile.	Private aid.
25125	- Day beacon 6	29-42-15.713N 095-01-39.466W				TR on pile.	Private aid.
25130	- Day beacon 8	29-42-17.766N 095-01-47.398W				TR on pile.	Private aid.
25132	- Day beacon 9	29-42-15.344N 095-01-48.175W				SG on pile.	Private aid.
25135	- Day beacon 10	29-42-20.191N 095-01-56.404W				TR on pile.	Private aid.
25138	- Day beacon 11	29-42-17.798N 095-01-57.636W				SG on pile.	Private aid.
25140	- Day beacon 12	29-42-22.863N 095-02-06.194W				TR on pile.	Private aid.

Light List corrected through LNM week: 01/18

(1) No.	(2) Name and Location	(3) Position	(4) Characteristic	(5) Height	(6) Range	(7) Structure	(8) Remarks
		TEXAS - Eighth District					
	HOUSTON SHIP CHANNEL (Chart 11329)						
	Houston Ship Channel						
	San Jacinto Bay Barge Channel						
25142	- Day beacon 13	29-42-20.206N 095-02-06.667W				SG on pile.	Private aid.
25145	- Day beacon 14	29-42-25.171N 095-02-14.479W				TR on pile.	Private aid.
25150	- Day beacon 15	29-42-22.364N 095-02-14.979W				SG on pile.	Private aid.
25155	- Day beacon 16	29-42-28.047N 095-02-24.799W				TR on pile.	Private aid.
25158	- Day beacon 17	29-42-24.930N 095-02-24.300W				SG on pile.	Private aid.
25160	- Day beacon 18	29-42-30.747N 095-02-35.673W				TR on pile.	Private aid.
25162	- Day beacon 19	29-42-27.805N 095-02-35.763W				SG on pile.	Private aid.
25165	- Day beacon 20	29-42-33.215N 095-02-44.865W				TR on pile.	Private aid.
25168	- Day beacon 21	29-42-31.293N 095-02-48.670W				SG on pile.	Private aid.
25170	- Day beacon 22	29-42-36.917N 095-02-55.383W				TR on pile.	Private aid.
25175	- Day beacon 23	29-42-35.369N 095-03-03.752W				SG on pile.	Private aid.
25180	- Day beacon 24	29-42-39.344N 095-03-02.279W				TR on pile.	Private aid.
25185	- Day beacon 25	29-42-36.530N 095-03-07.471W				SG on pile.	Private aid.
25190	- Day beacon 26	29-42-42.490N 095-03-08.272W				TR on pile.	Private aid.
25195	- Day beacon 27	29-42-39.690N 095-03-13.057W				SG on pile.	Private aid.
25200	- Day beacon 28	29-42-46.335N 095-03-14.911W				TR on pile.	Private aid.
	Houston Ship Channel						
25205	- LIGHT 104	29-42-22.245N 095-01-02.429W	Fl R 2.5s	17	4	TR on pile.	Ra ref.
25210	- LIGHT 105	29-42-29.528N 095-01-17.861W	Fl G 4s	17	4	SG on pile.	Ra ref.
25215	- LIGHT 106	29-42-31.233N 095-01-07.518W	Fl R 4s	17	3	TR on pile.	Ra ref.
25220	- LIGHT 107	29-42-52.407N 095-01-19.351W	Fl G 6s	17	5	SG on pile.	Ra ref.
25230	UPPER RED LIGHT BEND INBOUND RANGE FRONT LIGHT	29-43-35.531N 095-01-13.709W	Q R	76		KRW on skeleton tower on piles.	For upbound traffic. Visible 2° each side of rangeline.
25235	UPPER RED LIGHT BEND INBOUND RANGE REAR LIGHT 910 yards, 358.25 from front light.	29-44-02.565N 095-01-13.595W	Oc R 4s	151		KRW on skeleton tower on concrete block.	Visible 4° each side of rangeline.
25240	UPPER RED LIGHT BEND OUTBOUND RANGE FRONT LIGHT	29-42-18.853N 095-01-15.963W	Q R	18		KRW on skeleton tower on piles.	Visible all around; higher intensity on rangeline.
25245	UPPER RED LIGHT BEND OUTBOUND RANGE REAR LIGHT 219 yards, 180.2° from front light.	29-42-12.360N 095-01-16.005W	Iso R 6s	26		KRW on skeleton tower on piles.	Visible 14° each side of rangeline.
25250	- LIGHT 109	29-43-15.232N 095-01-19.978W	Fl G 4s	17	5	SG on pile.	Ra ref.
25260	Exxon Black Duck Bay Obstruction Buoy	29-43-16.122N 095-00-50.856W				NW with orange band, orange diamond, worded DANGER.	Private aid.

Light List corrected through LNM week: 01/18

(1) No.	(2) Name and Location	(3) Position	(4) Characteristic	(5) Height	(6) Range	(7) Structure	(8) Remarks
			TEXAS - Eighth District				
	HOUSTON SHIP CHANNEL (Chart 11329)						
	Houston Ship Channel						
25265	- LIGHT 109A	29-43-25.302N 095-01-23.905W	Fl G 6s	17	4	SG on pile.	Ra ref.
25275	- LIGHT 111	29-43-39.378N 095-01-37.966W	Fl G 2.5s	17	4	SG on pile.	Ra ref.
25280	EXXON DOCK 2 LIGHT	29-43-37.000N 095-01-17.500W	Fl R 2.5s	20		On pilings.	Private aid.
25285	EXXON DOCK 5 LIGHT	29-43-39.400N 095-01-23.000W	Fl R 2.5s	22		On pilings.	Private aid.
	Baytown Bend Tower Obstruction						
25300	- LIGHT A	29-43-39.700N 095-01-41.400W	Q W			On base of lattice tower.	Private aid.
25305	- LIGHT B	29-43-41.200N 095-01-43.700W	Q W	12		On base of tower.	Private aid.
25310	- LIGHT C	29-43-52.200N 095-01-34.800W	Q W			On base of lattice tower.	Private aid.
25315	- LIGHT D	29-43-51.000N 095-01-29.300W	Q W			On base of lattice tower.	Private aid.
25317	CENTERPOINT ENERGY TOWER FOUNDATION PROTECTION CELL LIGHTS (6)	29-43-42.320N 095-01-47.572W	Fl W 2.5s			Marks highline tower foundation concrete protection cells.	Private aid.
	Houston Ship Channel						
25320	LOWER PEGGY'S LAKE INBOUND RANGE FRONT LIGHT	29-43-57.001N 095-03-08.953W	Q R (NIGHT) Q R (DAY)	70 73		KRW on skeleton tower on piles.	Visible 2° each side of rangeline.
25325	LOWER PEGGY'S LAKE INBOUND RANGE REAR LIGHT 533 yards, 274.9° from front light.	29-43-58.892N 095-03-26.973W	Iso R 6s (NIGHT) Iso R 6s (DAY)	132 138		KRW on skeleton tower on block. On same structure as Lower Crossover Outbound Range Rear Light.	Visible 2° each side of rangeline.
25330	LOWER PEGGY'S LAKE OUTBOUND RANGE FRONT LIGHT	29-43-43.789N 095-01-20.205W	Q R	97		KRW on skeleton tower on piles.	Visible 4° each side of rangeline. Lighted throughout 24 hours.
25335	LOWER PEGGY'S LAKE OUTBOUND RANGE REAR LIGHT 265 yards, 095.5 from front light.	29-43-42.828N 095-01-11.249W	Oc R 4s	137		Skeleton Tower on piles	Visible 4° each side of rangeline. Lighted throughout 24 hours.
25340	- Lighted Buoy 112	29-43-49.174N 095-01-36.234W	Fl R 4s		3	Red.	Ra ref.
25345	- LIGHT 111A	29-43-43.852N 095-01-53.164W	Fl G 2.5s	17	4	SG on pile.	Ra ref.
25349	- LIGHT 112A	29-43-52.703N 095-01-44.447W	Q R	17	3	TR on pile.	Ra ref.
25350	- LIGHT 112B	29-43-53.806N 095-01-54.394W	Fl R 2.5s	17	3	TR on pile.	Ra ref.
25355	- LIGHT 113	29-43-46.010N 095-02-16.134W	Fl G 4s	17	4	SG on pile.	
25360	- LIGHT 114	29-43-55.888N 095-02-15.616W	Fl R 4s	17	4	TR on pile.	
25365	- LIGHT 114A	29-43-55.600N 095-02-27.406W	Fl R 6s	17	4	TR on pile.	
25370	- LIGHT 113B	29-43-48.859N 095-02-38.022W	Fl G 4s	17	4	SG on pile.	Ra ref.
25380	- LIGHT 114B	29-43-57.007N 095-02-37.673W	Fl R 4s	17	4	TR on pile.	
25385	- LIGHT 115 118 feet outside channel limit.	29-43-51.000N 095-02-49.600W	Fl G 2.5s	17	4	SG on pile.	Ra ref.
25390	- LIGHT 116	29-44-02.568N 095-02-55.358W	Fl R 2.5s	17	4	TR on pile.	Ra ref.

Light List corrected through LNM week: 01/18

(1) No.	(2) Name and Location	(3) Position	(4) Characteristic	(5) Height	(6) Range	(7) Structure	(8) Remarks
		TEXAS - Eighth District					
	HOUSTON SHIP CHANNEL (Chart 11329)						
	Houston Ship Channel						
25392	BATTLEGROUND OIL BOSTCO TERMINAL DOWNSTREAM PILE LIGHT	29-43-52.860N 095-02-58.300W	Fl W 2.5s			Marks downstream pile.	Private aid.
25392.01	BATTLEGROUND OIL BOSTCO TERMINAL UPSTREAM PILE LIGHT	29-44-05.270N 095-03-19.400W	Fl W 2.5s			Marks upstream pile.	Private aid.
25392.02	BATTLEGROUND OIL BOSTCO TERMINAL UPSTREAM TURNING BASIN PILE LIGHT	29-44-11.050N 095-03-05.380W	Fl W 2.5s			Marks upstream turning basin piling.	Private aid.
25392.03	BATTLEGROUND OIL BOSTCO TERMINAL DOWNSTREAM TURNING BASIN PILE LIGHT	29-44-08.970N 095-03-01.710W	Fl W 2.5s			Marks downstream turning basin piling.	Private aid.
25394	BOSTCO PILING LIGHTS (2)	29-43-58.446N 095-03-07.642W	Fl W 2.5s				Private aid.
25395	UPPER PEGGY'S LAKE INBOUND RANGE FRONT LIGHT	29-44-24.840N 095-03-41.273W	Q R	25		KRW on skeleton tower on pile.	Visible all around; higher intensity on rangeline.
25400	UPPER PEGGY'S LAKE INBOUND RANGE REAR LIGHT 201 yards, 303.0° from front light.	29-44-28.089N 095-03-47.013W	Iso R 6s	35		KRW on skeleton tower on piles.	Visible 4° each side of rangeline.
25405	UPPER PEGGY'S LAKE OUTBOUND RANGE FRONT LIGHT	29-43-47.405N 095-02-38.809W	Q R	26		KRW on skeleton tower on piles.	Visible all around; higher intensity on rangeline.
25410	EXXON GOAT ISLAND DOCK LIGHT	29-44-02.300N 095-02-42.100W	Fl R 2.5s			On pile.	Private aid.
25415	UPPER PEGGY'S LAKE OUTBOUND RANGE REAR LIGHT 223 yards, 122.9° from front light.	29-43-43.801N 095-02-32.439W	Iso R 6s	35		KRW on skeleton tower on pile.	Visible 1.5° each side of rangeline.
25420	- LIGHT 117 125 feet outside channel limit.	29-44-09.200N 095-03-24.192W	Q G	17	3	SG on pile.	Ra ref.
25425	- LIGHT 118	29-44-16.468N 095-03-19.310W	Q R	17	4	TR on pile.	Ra ref.
25430	- LIGHT 117A	29-44-15.800N 095-03-32.400W	Fl G 4s	17	4	SG on pile.	Ra ref.
25435	- LIGHT 119 131 feet outside channel limit.	29-44-24.045N 095-03-38.822W	Fl G 2.5s	17	4	SG on pile.	Ra ref.
25440	- LIGHT 120	29-44-28.380N 095-03-30.449W	Fl R 2.5s	17	3	TR on pile.	Ra ref.
25445	- LIGHT 121 198 feet outside channel limit.	29-44-41.400N 095-03-48.900W	Fl G 4s	17	4	SG on pile.	
25450	- LIGHT 121A 135 feet outside channel limit.	29-45-08.200N 095-04-02.200W	Fl G 2.5s	17	4	SG on pile.	Ra ref.
25455	- LIGHT 122	29-44-45.300N 095-03-39.300W	Fl R 4s	17	4	TR on pile.	Ra ref.
25460	- LIGHT 122A	29-45-11.429N 095-03-51.921W	Fl R 2.5s	17	4	TR on pile.	Ra ref.
25465	CROSSOVER INBOUND RANGE FRONT LIGHT	29-45-35.950N 095-04-10.231W	Q G	32		KRW on skeleton tower on piles.	Visible only on the rangeline.
25470	CROSSOVER INBOUND RANGE FRONT PASSING LIGHT	29-45-35.950N 095-04-10.231W	Q R	10	3	KRW on skeleton tower on piles. On same structure as Crossover Inbound Range Front Light.	

Light List corrected through LNM week: 01/18

(1) No.	(2) Name and Location	(3) Position	(4) Characteristic	(5) Height	(6) Range	(7) Structure	(8) Remarks
	TEXAS - Eighth District						

HOUSTON SHIP CHANNEL (Chart 11329)
Houston Ship Channel

(1) No.	(2) Name and Location	(3) Position	(4) Characteristic	(5) Height	(6) Range	(7) Structure	(8) Remarks
25475	CROSSOVER INBOUND RANGE REAR LIGHT 552 yards, 333.5° from front light.	29-45-50.868N 095-04-18.040W	Iso G 6s	50		KRW on skeleton tower on piles.	Visible only on the rangeline.
25480	CROSSOVER OUTBOUND RANGE FRONT LIGHT	29-44-07.316N 095-03-25.909W	Q R (NIGHT) Q R (DAY)	33 30		KRW on skeleton tower on piles.	Visible 1.5° each side of rangeline (Day), Visible 14° each side of rangeline (Night).
25485	CROSSOVER OUTBOUND RANGE REAR LIGHT	29-44-01.476N 095-03-22.843W	Iso R 6s (NIGHT) Iso R 6s (DAY)	60 63		KRW on skeleton tower on piles. On same structure as Peggy`s Lake Inbound Range Rear Light.	Visible 2° each side of rangeline.
25490	- LIGHT 123 108 feet outside channel limit.	29-45-17.100N 095-04-06.700W	Fl G 6s	17	4	SG on pile.	Ra ref.
25495	- LIGHT 124 122 feet outside channel limit.	29-45-21.080N 095-03-58.122W	Fl R 6s	17	4	TR on pile.	Ra ref.
25500	- LIGHT 124A	29-45-28.904N 095-04-03.977W	Fl R 2.5s	17	4	TR on pile.	
25505	- LIGHT 125	29-45-28.057N 095-04-17.602W	Fl G 4s	17	4	SG on pile.	Ra ref.
25510	- LIGHT 125A	29-45-33.732N 095-04-27.190W	Fl G 2.5s	17	3	SG on pile.	Ra ref.
25515	- LIGHT 126 167 feet outside channel limit.	29-45-34.605N 095-04-10.671W	Q R	17	4	TR on pile.	Ra ref.
25520	- LIGHT 126A	29-45-41.299N 095-04-22.293W	Fl R 2.5s	17	3	TR on pile.	
25525	LYNCHBURG INBOUND RANGE FRONT LIGHT	29-45-57.213N 095-04-56.565W	Q R	17		KRW on dolphin.	Visible all around; higher intensity on rangeline.
25530	LYNCHBURG INBOUND RANGE REAR LIGHT	29-46-01.266N 095-05-03.599W	Iso R 6s	37		KRW on skeleton tower on piles.	Visible 4° each side of rangeline.
25535	LYNCHBURG OUTBOUND RANGE FRONT LIGHT	29-45-19.620N 095-03-55.410W	Q G	25		KRW on skeleton tower on piles.	Visible 4° each side of rangeline.
25540	LYNCHBURG OUTBOUND RANGE REAR LIGHT	29-45-16.667N 095-03-50.317W	Iso G 6s	35		KRW on skeleton tower on piles.	Visible 4° each side of rangeline.
25545	CIWA PIPELINE LIGHT A	29-45-38.000N 095-04-37.000W	Fl G 2.5s	6		On dolphin.	Private aid.
25550	CIWA PIPELINE LIGHT B	29-45-39.000N 095-04-38.000W	Fl G 2.5s	11		On 40 foot diameter steel dolphin.	Private aid.
25555	SAN JACINTO JUNCTION LIGHT SJ	29-45-57.440N 095-04-53.616W	Fl (2+1)R 6s	17	4	JR on pile.	Ra ref.

San Jacinto River
Positions of buoys frequently shifted with changing conditions.

(1) No.	(2) Name and Location	(3) Position	(4) Characteristic	(5) Height	(6) Range	(7) Structure	(8) Remarks
25560	- Buoy 2	29-46-21.090N 095-04-36.606W				Red nun.	
25565	- Buoy 4	29-46-30.369N 095-04-34.374W				Red nun.	
25570	- Buoy 6	29-46-43.619N 095-04-30.423W				Red nun.	
25575	- Buoy 8	29-46-58.520N 095-04-18.788W				Red nun.	
25580	- Buoy 10	29-47-05.072N 095-04-10.202W				Red nun.	
25585	- Buoy 11	29-47-40.103N 095-03-31.577W				Green can.	
25590	- Buoy 13	29-47-56.992N 095-03-33.155W				Green can.	

(1) No.	(2) Name and Location	(3) Position	(4) Characteristic	(5) Height	(6) Range	(7) Structure	(8) Remarks
		TEXAS - Eighth District					

HOUSTON SHIP CHANNEL (Chart 11329)
Houston Ship Channel
San Jacinto River
Positions of buoys frequently shifted with changing conditions.

(1) No.	(2) Name and Location	(3) Position	(4) Characteristic	(5) Height	(6) Range	(7) Structure	(8) Remarks
25595	- Buoy 14	29-48-02.136N 095-03-31.998W				Red nun.	
25600	- Lighted Buoy 15	29-48-06.886N 095-03-58.960W	Fl G 2.5s		4	Green.	
25605	- Buoy 16	29-48-14.356N 095-04-04.319W				Red nun.	
25610	- Lighted Buoy 17	29-48-10.200N 095-04-19.800W	Fl G 4s		4	Green.	
25615	- Buoy 18	29-48-12.740N 095-04-20.564W				Red nun.	
25620	- Buoy 19	29-48-03.692N 095-04-33.997W				Green can.	
25625	- Buoy 20	29-48-03.253N 095-04-42.028W				Red nun.	
25635	- Buoy 21	29-47-59.440N 095-04-41.727W				Green can.	
25640	- Buoy 22	29-47-55.200N 095-05-09.000W				Red nun.	
25660	- Buoy 26	29-48-30.600N 095-05-23.400W				Red nun.	
25665	- Buoy 27	29-48-10.800N 095-05-27.000W				Green can.	
25670	- Buoy 29	29-48-38.813N 095-05-28.205W				Green can.	
25680	- Buoy 32	29-48-46.419N 095-05-28.231W				Red nun.	

Houston Ship Channel

(1) No.	(2) Name and Location	(3) Position	(4) Characteristic	(5) Height	(6) Range	(7) Structure	(8) Remarks
25695	- LIGHT 127	29-45-42.947N 095-05-08.187W	Fl G 4s	17	4	SG on pile.	
25700	- LIGHT 128 170 feet outside channel limit.	29-45-53.752N 095-05-05.678W	Fl R 2.5s	17	3	TR on pile.	Ra ref.
25705	OLD RIVER TRANSMISSION TOWER LIGHT A	29-45-56.400N 095-05-15.500W	Fl R 2.5s			On transmission tower.	Private aid.
25710	OLD RIVER TRANSMISSION TOWER LIGHT B	29-45-50.500N 095-05-24.900W	Fl G 2.5s			On transmission tower.	Private aid.
25715	- LIGHT 129 50 feet outside 12 foot curve.	29-45-39.268N 095-05-14.168W	Q G	17	4	SG on pile.	Ra ref.
25720	- LIGHT 130	29-45-37.730N 095-05-30.964W	Fl R 2.5s	17	4	TR on pile.	Ra ref.
25725	- LIGHT 131	29-45-33.737N 095-05-20.914W	Fl G 2.5s	17	4	SG on pile.	Ra ref.
25730	- LIGHT 131A 115 feet outside channel limit.	29-45-17.018N 095-05-27.757W	Fl G 2.5s	17	4	SG on pile.	
25740	- LIGHT 133 260 feet outside channel limit.	29-45-09.010N 095-05-32.948W	Fl G 2.5s	17	3	SG on pile.	Ra ref.
25745	HOUSTON FUEL OIL TERMINAL EAST DOCK LIGHTS (2)	29-45-13.500N 095-05-47.200W	Fl R 2.5s			Marks east dock #4 location.	Private aid.
25750	HOUSTON FUEL OIL TERMINAL UPPER DOLPHIN LIGHT	29-45-02.000N 095-05-54.000W	Fl R 2.5s	21		On dolphin.	Private aid.
25755	HOUSTON FUEL OIL TERMINAL DOCK LIGHT	29-44-58.000N 095-05-59.000W	Fl R 2.5s	21		On dock.	Private aid.
25760	HOUSTON FUEL OIL TERMINAL LOWER DOLPHIN LIGHT	29-44-57.000N 095-06-03.000W	Fl R 2.5s	21		On dolphin.	Private aid.
25770	R & H Inc. Outfall Lighted Buoy	29-44-27.781N 095-06-24.720W	Fl W 4s			White with orange bands.	Private aid.

Light List corrected through LNM week: 01/18

(1) No.	(2) Name and Location	(3) Position	(4) Characteristic	(5) Height	(6) Range	(7) Structure	(8) Remarks
		TEXAS - Eighth District					
	HOUSTON SHIP CHANNEL (Chart 11329)						
	Houston Ship Channel						
25772	Clean Harbors Outfall Lighted Buoy	29-44-32.633N 095-06-17.389W	Fl W 4s			White with orange bands.	Private aid.
25773	Lubrizol Lighted Danger Buoy	29-44-23.840N 095-06-34.410W	Fl W 2.5s			White with orange bands.	Private aid.
25775	- LIGHT 139 150 feet outside channel limit.	29-44-16.819N 095-06-54.752W	Fl G 4s	17	4	SG on pile.	
25780	- LIGHT 144	29-44-12.430N 095-08-29.993W	Fl R 2.5s	17	4	TR on pile.	
25785.01	- Lighted Buoy 145	29-44-04.852N 095-08-28.884W	Fl G 4s		4		Green.
25787	KINDER MORGAN LIGHTED PIPELINE MARK	29-44-03.973N 095-08-48.637W	Fl W 2.5s			Marks pipeline south crossing point.	Private aid.
25787.01	KINDER MORGAN LIGHTED PIPELINE MARK	29-44-16.374N 095-08-47.475W	Fl W 2.5s			Marks pipeline north crossing point.	Private aid.
25790	- LIGHT 146 150 feet outside channel limit.	29-44-18.956N 095-09-15.502W	Fl R 4s	17	4	TR on pile.	
25795	- LIGHT 149 175 feet outside channel limit.	29-44-25.059N 095-09-34.301W	Fl G 2.5s	17	3	SG on pile.	
25800	- LIGHT 150 125 feet outside channel limit.	29-44-34.128N 095-09-33.932W	Fl R 2.5s	17	4	TR on pile.	
25810	- LIGHT 152 150 feet outside channel limit.	29-44-49.868N 095-10-02.803W	Fl R 2.5s	17	4	TR on pile.	
25815	- LIGHT 160	29-44-09.864N 095-12-21.778W	Fl R 2.5s	17	3	TR on pile.	
25820	- LIGHT 162 150 feet outside channel limit.	29-43-43.832N 095-12-36.961W	Fl R 4s	17	4	TR on pile.	
25823	KINDER MORGAN MOORING DOLPHIN LIGHT	29-43-36.633N 095-13-27.940W	Fl W 2.5s			Marks outermost upstream dock mooring dolphin.	Private aid.
25825	SIMS BAYOU DOCK LIGHTS (2)	29-43-02.100N 095-14-36.800W	Fl G 2.5s	13		On steel pile dolphin.	Private aid.
25830	VALERO REFINING FIRE PUMP DOCK LIGHTS (2)	29-43-32.800N 095-15-24.400W	Fl G 2.5s	17		On dock.	Private aid.
25835	VALERO REFINING CO. DOCK LIGHTS (2).	29-43-15.120N 095-14-59.020W	Fl G 2.5s	15		On dolphins.	Private aid.
25840	Fidelity Island Daybeacon 2	29-43-39.836N 095-15-27.310W				TR on pile.	
	GALVESTON BAY (Chart 11326)						
	Trinity Bay						
	Double Bayou Channel						
25845	- LIGHT 2 25 feet outside channel limit.	29-37-41.153N 094-45-56.343W	Fl R 4s	17	4	TR on pile.	Ra ref.
25855	- LIGHT 4	29-38-03.377N 094-44-48.361W	Fl R 4s	17	3	TR on pile.	Ra ref.
25865	- LIGHT 6	29-38-29.678N 094-43-25.034W	Fl R 2.5s	17	3	TR on pile.	Ra ref.
25875	- Daybeacon 8	29-38-36.814N 094-43-02.806W				TR on pile.	Ra ref.
25890	- Daybeacon 10	29-38-41.463N 094-42-48.790W				TR on pile.	Ra ref.
25900	- Daybeacon 11	29-38-53.454N 094-42-14.860W				SG on pile.	
25905	- LIGHT 12 20 feet outside channel limit.	29-38-52.293N 094-42-14.478W	Q R	17	3	TR on pile.	Ra ref.

Light List corrected through LNM week: 01/18

(1) No.	(2) Name and Location	(3) Position	(4) Characteristic	(5) Height	(6) Range	(7) Structure	(8) Remarks
	TEXAS - Eighth District						
	GALVESTON BAY (Chart 11326)						
	Trinity Bay						
	Anahuac Channel						
25910	- LIGHT 1	29-41-58.301N 094-44-09.132W	Fl G 6s	17	4	SG on pile.	
25915	- Day beacon 2 50 feet outside channel limit.	29-42-21.680N 094-43-49.745W				TR on pile.	
25925	- Day beacon 4 50 feet outside channel limit.	29-43-10.806N 094-43-12.709W				TR on pile.	
25940	- Day beacon 5	29-44-21.420N 094-42-25.620W				SG on pile.	Ra ref.
25945	- Day beacon 7	29-44-51.203N 094-42-04.907W				SG on pile.	Ra ref.
25950	- Day beacon 9	29-45-11.902N 094-41-49.307W				SG on pile.	Ra ref.
25955	- Day beacon 11	29-45-18.802N 094-41-42.706W				SG on pile.	Ra ref.
25960	- Day beacon 16	29-45-54.801N 094-41-11.206W				TR on pile.	
	Trinity River						
25970	City Of Liberty Weir Lighted Buoy 2	30-02-21.900N 094-49-27.000W	Q R			Red.	Marks rock weir. Private aid.
25975	City Of Liberty Weir Lighted Buoy 4	30-02-27.000N 094-49-27.800W	Q R			Red.	Marks rock weir. Private aid.
25980	City Of Liberty Weir Lighted Buoy 6	30-02-31.000N 094-49-28.900W	Q R			Red.	Marks rock weir. Private aid.
25985	City Of Liberty Weir Lighted Buoy 8	30-02-32.600N 094-49-31.400W	Q R			Red.	Marks rock weir. Private aid.
	Trinity Bay						
25990	- STATE TRACT 18-19A LIGHT 2	29-44-06.000N 094-45-34.000W	Q W	12		TR on dolphin.	Private aid.
25995	- STATE TRACT 22-23A LIGHT 2	29-44-13.000N 094-44-45.000W	Q W	12		TR on dolphin.	Private aid.
26000	Fisher Shoal Day beacon 1	29-39-30.815N 094-50-06.720W				SG on pile.	
	GALVESTON AND TEXAS CITY HARBORS (Chart 11324)						
	Texas City Channel *Buoys are located 60 to 150 feet outside channel limit.*						
26030	TEXAS CITY CUT A OUTER RANGE FRONT LIGHT	29-20-11.052N 094-45-19.145W	Q G	25		KRW on skeleton tower on piles.	For downbound traffic. Visible 2° each side of rangeline.
26035	TEXAS CITY CUT A OUTER RANGE REAR LIGHT 1,085 yards, 116.6° from front light.	29-19-56.530N 094-44-45.717W	Iso G 6s	65		KRW on skeleton tower on piles.	
26040	- Lighted Buoy 1	29-20-53.904N 094-47-13.069W	Fl G 4s		4	Green.	
26045	TEXAS CITY CUT A INNER RANGE FRONT LIGHT	29-22-24.657N 094-50-27.193W	Q G	25		KRW on skeleton tower on piles.	Visible all around; higher intensity on rangeline.
26050	TEXAS CITY CUT A INNER RANGE FRONT LIGHT PASSING LIGHT	29-22-24.657N 094-50-27.193W	Fl R 4s	17	4	On same structure as Texas City Channel Cut A Inner Range Front Light.	
26055	TEXAS CITY CUT A INNER RANGE REAR LIGHT 1,165 yards, 296.6° from front light.	29-22-34.877N 094-50-50.196W	Iso G 6s	60		KRW on skeleton tower on piles.	Visible 2° each side of rangeline.

Light List corrected through LNM week: 01/18

(1) No.	(2) Name and Location	(3) Position	(4) Characteristic	(5) Height	(6) Range	(7) Structure	(8) Remarks
		TEXAS - Eighth District					
	GALVESTON AND TEXAS CITY HARBORS (Chart 11324)						
	Texas City Channel						
	Buoys are located 60 to 150 feet outside channel limit.						
26060	- *Lighted Buoy 2*	29-21-18.484N 094-47-44.366W	Fl R 6s		4	Red.	
26065	- *Lighted Buoy 3*	29-21-11.966N 094-47-49.261W	Fl G 6s		4	Green.	
26070	- LIGHT 5	29-21-21.069N 094-48-17.879W	Fl G 2.5s	17	4	SG on pile.	
26075	- LIGHT 7	29-21-42.880N 094-49-00.655W	Fl G 4s	17	4	SG on pile.	
26080	TEXAS CITY DIKE BOAT RAMP LIGHT	29-22-02.000N 094-48-54.000W	Fl R 2.5s	8		On breakwater.	Private aid.
26085	- LIGHT 9	29-22-04.028N 094-49-50.938W	Q G	17	4	SG on pile.	
26090	- LIGHT 10	29-22-10.693N 094-49-47.354W	Fl R 2.5s	17	3	TR on pile.	Ra ref.
26095	TEXAS CITY CUT B OUTER RANGE FRONT LIGHT	29-22-00.027N 094-49-15.703W	Q R	30		KRW on piles.	Visible 2° each side of rangeline.
26100	TEXAS CITY CUT B OUTER RANGE FRONT PASSING LIGHT	29-22-00.027N 094-49-15.703W	Fl R 4s	17	3		On same structure as Texas City Channel Cut B Outer Range Front Light.
26105	TEXAS CITY CUT B OUTER RANGE REAR LIGHT 679 yards, 105.1° from front light.	29-21-54.776N 094-48-53.488W	Oc R 4s	67		KRW on skeleton tower on piles.	Visible 2° each side of rangeline.
26110	TEXAS CITY CUT B INNER RANGE FRONT LIGHT	29-22-54.607N 094-53-04.322W	Fl R 2.5s	26		KRW on skeleton tower on piles.	Visible all around; higher intensity 1.5° each side of rangeline.
26115	TEXAS CITY CUT B INNER REAR LIGHT 429 yards, 285.2° from front light.	29-22-57.947N 094-53-18.374W	Iso R 6s	56		KRW on skeleton tower on piles.	Visible 2° each side of rangeline.
26120	- LIGHT 12	29-22-28.221N 094-50-55.097W	Fl R 6s	17	4	TR on pile.	
26125	- LIGHT 11	29-22-21.187N 094-50-59.394W	Fl G 2.5s	17	4	SG on pile.	
26130	- LIGHT 14	29-22-40.902N 094-51-51.473W	Fl R 4s	17	3	TR on pile.	
26135	- LIGHT 15	29-22-34.659N 094-51-54.695W	Fl G 4s	17	4	SG on pile.	
26140	TEXAS CITY CUT C RANGE FRONT LIGHT	29-23-02.590N 094-52-42.055W	Iso G 2s	17		KRW on piles.	Visible all around; higher intensity on rangeline.
26145	TEXAS CITY CUT C RANGE REAR LIGHT 335 yards, 049.8° from front light.	29-23-09.163N 094-52-33.183W	Iso G 6s	35		KRW on piles.	Visible all around; higher intensity on rangeline.
26150	- LIGHT 17	29-22-45.616N 094-52-41.541W	Q G	17	4	SG on pile.	
26155	- LIGHT 18	29-22-54.126N 094-52-47.805W	Fl R 2.5s	17	3	TR on pile.	
26160	- LIGHT 19	29-22-45.073N 094-52-55.592W	Fl G 2.5s	17	4	SG on pile.	
26165	- LIGHT 21	29-22-38.479N 094-53-06.209W	Q G	17	4	SG on pile.	
26170	TEXAS CITY CANAL TURNING CELL LIGHT	29-21-51.000N 094-53-24.000W	Fl R 2.5s	13		On dolphin.	Private aid.
26175	- RANGE FRONT LIGHT	29-21-46.100N 094-53-21.373W	Q G	20		KRW on skeleton tower on piles.	Visible all around; higher intensity on rangeline.
26180	- RANGE REAR LIGHT 300 yards, 090° from front light.	29-21-46.104N 094-53-15.987W	Iso G 6s	30		KRW on skeleton tower on piles.	Visible all around; higher intensity on rangeline.

Light List corrected through LNM week: 01/18

(1) No.	(2) Name and Location	(3) Position	(4) Characteristic	(5) Height	(6) Range	(7) Structure	(8) Remarks
		TEXAS - Eighth District					
	GALVESTON AND TEXAS CITY HARBORS (Chart 11324)						
	Texas City Connection Channel						
26185	- Buoy 1	29-21-12.001N 094-48-51.428W				Green can.	
26190	- Buoy 2	29-21-17.356N 094-48-46.688W				Red nun.	
26195	- Buoy 3	29-21-21.022N 094-48-50.525W				Green can.	
26200	- Buoy 4	29-21-25.962N 094-48-46.297W				Red nun.	
26205	- Buoy 5	29-21-24.168N 094-48-49.321W				Green can.	
26210	- Buoy 6	29-21-35.848N 094-48-47.680W				Red nun.	
26215	- Buoy 7	29-21-30.996N 094-48-50.984W				Green can.	
	UPPER GALVESTON BAY (Chart 11327)						
	Dickinson Bayou Channel						
26220	- Day beacon 1	29-28-03.907N 094-51-32.065W				SG on pile.	Ra ref.
26225	- Day beacon 2	29-28-00.833N 094-52-45.721W				TR on pile.	Ra ref.
26230	- Buoy 3	29-27-40.516N 094-53-51.112W				Green can.	
26235	- LIGHT 4	29-27-44.907N 094-53-59.293W	Fl R 4s	17	4	TR on pile.	Ra ref.
26240	- Day beacon 5	29-27-37.239N 094-54-08.087W				SG on pile.	
26245	- Buoy 7	29-27-34.124N 094-54-20.098W				Green can.	
26250	- Day beacon 8	29-27-35.529N 094-54-32.683W				TR on pile.	
26255	- Buoy 9	29-27-28.770N 094-54-44.080W				Green can.	
26260	- Buoy 11	29-27-25.754N 094-54-57.403W				Green can.	
26265	- Buoy 13	29-27-24.161N 094-55-04.363W				Green can.	
26270	- LIGHT 14 60 feet outside channel limit.	29-27-25.222N 094-55-16.232W	Fl R 4s	17	4	TR on pile.	Ra ref.
26275	- Buoy 15	29-27-22.096N 094-55-17.010W				Green can.	
26280.01	- Buoy 17	29-27-29.638N 094-55-38.805W				Green can.	
26285	- Day beacon 19	29-27-37.732N 094-55-55.627W				SG on pile.	Ra ref.
26290	- Day beacon 21	29-27-45.881N 094-56-15.671W				SG on pile.	Ra ref.
26295	- Day beacon 22	29-27-49.522N 094-56-17.283W				TR on pile.	Ra ref.
26300	- Buoy 23	29-27-54.468N 094-56-35.117W				Green can.	
26305	- Buoy 25	29-27-59.733N 094-56-47.395W				Green can.	
26310	- LIGHT 27	29-28-05.888N 094-57-03.462W	Fl G 4s	17	4	SG on pile.	
26315	- Day beacon 29	29-27-57.968N 094-57-13.546W				SG on pile.	
	Galveston Bay						
26325	- Oyster Lease 404A Day beacons (4)	29-28-55.000N 094-53-31.000W				NW on pile, worded DANGER SUBMERGED OYSTER REEF.	Private aid.

Light List corrected through LNM week: 01/18

(1) No.	(2) Name and Location	(3) Position	(4) Characteristic	(5) Height	(6) Range	(7) Structure	(8) Remarks
			TEXAS - Eighth District				
	UPPER GALVESTON BAY (Chart 11327)						
	Galveston Bay						
26330	- Oyster Lease 405A Day beacons (4)	29-28-37.000N 094-52-54.000W				NW on pile, worded DANGER SUBMERGED OYSTER REEF.	Private aid.
26335	- Oyster Lease 406A Day beacons (4)	29-28-34.000N 094-53-30.000W				NW on pile, worded DANGER SUBMERGED OYSTER REEF.	Private aid.
26340	- Oyster Lease 407A Day beacons (4)	29-29-01.000N 094-53-47.000W				NW on pile, worded DANGER SUBMERGED OYSTER REEF.	Private aid.
26345	- Oyster Lease 411A Day beacons (4)	29-28-05.000N 094-52-31.000W				NW on pile, worded DANGER SUBMERGED OYSTER REEF.	Private aid.
26350	EAGLE POINT WRECK LIGHT WR1	29-29-15.430N 094-53-34.224W	Q G	17	3	SG on pile.	
26355	TEXAS CORINTHIAN YACHT CLUB PIER LIGHTS (2)	29-31-53.000N 095-00-05.000W	Fl R 2.5s			On pier.	Private aid.
	Clear Creek Channel						
26360	- Day beacon 1	29-33-06.848N 094-59-32.320W				SG on pile.	Ra ref.
26365	- LIGHT 2 60 feet from the channel limit.	29-33-09.805N 094-59-32.978W	Fl R 6s	17	4	TR on skeleton tower on piles.	Ra ref.
26370	- Day beacon 3	29-33-02.492N 095-00-00.429W				SG on pile.	Ra ref.
26375	- LIGHT 4 60 feet outside channel limit.	29-33-05.929N 095-00-01.023W	Fl R 4s	17	3	TR on pile.	
26380	- Day beacon 5	29-32-58.210N 095-00-27.991W				SG on pile.	Ra ref.
26385	- LIGHT 6	29-33-01.490N 095-00-26.962W	Fl R 2.5s	17	3	TR on pile.	Ra ref.
26390	- Day beacon 7	29-32-53.826N 095-00-57.741W				SG on pile.	Ra ref.
26395	- LIGHT 8	29-32-56.549N 095-00-57.256W	Q R	17	3	TR on pile.	Ra ref.
26400	- LIGHT 10	29-32-52.453N 095-01-41.617W	Q R	17	3	TR on pile.	
	GALVESTON BAY (Chart 11326)						
	Clear Creek Channel						
26410	- Buoy 11	29-33-05.668N 095-01-45.258W				Green can.	
26415	- LIGHT 13 50 feet outside channel limit.	29-33-07.360N 095-01-56.680W	Fl G 4s	17	4	SG on pile.	
26420	- Buoy 14	29-33-09.691N 095-01-56.858W				Red nun.	
26425	- Buoy 15	29-33-16.221N 095-02-33.056W				Green can.	
26430	- LIGHT 16	29-33-18.115N 095-02-33.096W	Fl R 4s	17	3	TR on pile.	
26435	- LIGHT 17 50 feet outside channel limit.	29-33-23.923N 095-03-07.579W	Q G	17	4	SG on pile.	
26440	- Buoy 18	29-33-25.582N 095-03-07.502W				Red nun.	
26445	- Buoy 19	29-33-16.599N 095-03-40.146W				Green can.	
26450	- LIGHT 20	29-33-17.744N 095-03-39.937W	Fl R 4s	17	4	TR on pile.	
26455	- Buoy 22	29-33-09.931N 095-04-11.996W				Red nun.	

Light List corrected through LNM week: 01/18

(1) No.	(2) Name and Location	(3) Position	(4) Characteristic	(5) Height	(6) Range	(7) Structure	(8) Remarks
	TEXAS - Eighth District						
	GALVESTON BAY (Chart 11326)						
	Clear Creek Channel						
26460	- LIGHT 23 50 feet outside channel limit.	29-33-08.286N 095-04-11.482W	Q G	17	4	SG on pile.	
26465	- Buoy 24	29-33-00.830N 095-04-23.247W				Red nun.	
	Lakewood Yacht Club Channel						
26475	- Day beacon 1	29-33-10.000N 095-01-55.000W				SG on pile.	Private aid.
26480	- Day beacon 3	29-33-13.000N 095-01-55.000W				SG on pile.	Private aid.
26485	- Day beacon 5	29-33-16.000N 095-01-55.000W				SG on pile.	Private aid.
26490	- Day beacon 7	29-33-19.000N 095-01-55.000W				SG on pile.	Private aid.
26495	- Day beacon 9	29-33-23.000N 095-01-56.000W				SG on pile.	Private aid.
26500	- Day beacon 11	29-33-25.000N 095-01-58.000W				SG on pile.	Private aid.
26510	- Day beacon 13	29-33-36.000N 095-02-00.000W				SG on pile.	Private aid.
26515	- Day beacon 14	29-33-27.000N 095-01-59.000W				TR on pile.	Private aid.
26520	- Day beacon 16	29-33-28.000N 095-01-59.000W				TR on pile.	Private aid.
	Watergate Marina Channel						
26525	- Day beacon 1	29-33-05.000N 095-02-02.000W				SG on pile.	Private aid.
26530	- LIGHT 2	29-33-07.000N 095-02-02.000W	Fl R 2.5s	10		TR on pile.	Private aid.
26535	- Day beacon 3	29-33-02.000N 095-02-06.000W				SG on pile.	Private aid.
26540	- Day beacon 4	29-33-03.000N 095-02-06.000W				TR on pile.	Private aid.
26545	- Junction Day beacon A	29-32-59.000N 095-02-10.000W				JG on pile.	Private aid.
26550	- Day beacon 6	29-33-01.000N 095-02-11.000W				TR on pile.	Private aid.
26555	- Day beacon 7	29-32-56.000N 095-02-13.000W				SG on pile.	Private aid.
26560	- Day beacon 8	29-32-57.000N 095-02-14.000W				TR on pile.	Private aid.
26565	- Day beacon 10	29-33-06.000N 095-02-06.000W				TR on pile.	Private aid.
26570	- BREAKWATER LIGHT 2	29-32-53.000N 095-02-16.000W	Q W	10		TR on end of breakwater.	Private aid.
26575	- LIGHT 9	29-32-52.000N 095-02-18.000W	Q G	10		SG on pile.	Private aid.
26580	- LIGHT 11	29-32-48.000N 095-02-24.000W	Q W			SG on breakwater bulkhead.	Private aid.
26585	- LIGHT 13	29-32-54.000N 095-02-24.000W	Q G			SG on breakwater bulkhead.	Private aid.
26590	- RANGE FRONT LIGHT	29-32-36.000N 095-02-36.000W	F G			KRW on post.	Private aid.
26595	- RANGE REAR LIGHT	29-32-42.000N 095-02-30.000W	F G			KRW on top of boat shed roof.	Private aid.
	Jarboe Bayou Channel						
26600	- Day beacon 2	29-32-53.000N 095-02-11.570W				TR on pile.	Private aid.
26605	- Day beacon 4	29-32-48.000N 095-02-08.000W				TR on pile.	Private aid.
26610	- Day beacon 6	29-32-44.000N 095-02-08.100W				TR on pile.	Private aid.
26615	- Day beacon 8	29-32-39.000N 095-02-09.060W				TR on pile.	Private aid.

Light List corrected through LNM week: 01/18

(1) No.	(2) Name and Location	(3) Position	(4) Characteristic	(5) Height	(6) Range	(7) Structure	(8) Remarks
			TEXAS - Eighth District				
	GALVESTON BAY (Chart 11326)						
	Waterford Harbor Channel						
26620	- JUNCTION LIGHT B	29-32-58.100N 095-02-13.500W	Fl (2+1)R 6s	15		JR on pile.	Private aid.
26625	- Day beacon 1	29-32-57.800N 095-02-17.200W				SG on pile.	Private aid.
26630	- Day beacon 2	29-32-58.300N 095-02-17.300W				TR on pile.	Private aid.
26635	- Day beacon 3	29-32-57.500N 095-02-21.000W				SG on pile.	Private aid.
26640	- Day beacon 4	29-32-58.000N 095-02-21.200W				TR on pile.	Private aid.
26645	- Day beacon 5	29-32-57.200N 095-02-24.700W				SG on pile.	Private aid.
26650	- Day beacon 6	29-32-51.700N 095-02-24.900W				TR on pile.	Private aid.
26655	- Day beacon 7	29-32-56.900N 095-02-29.000W				SG on pile.	Private aid.
26660	- Day beacon 8	29-37-57.400N 095-02-29.200W				TR on pile.	Private aid.
	Marina Del Sol Channel						
26665	- LIGHTED BUOY 1	29-33-24.000N 095-02-57.000W	Fl G 4s	16		Green.	Private aid.
26670	- Buoy 2	29-33-20.250N 095-02-55.250W				Red nun.	Private aid.
26675	- Day beacon 3	29-33-17.950N 095-02-55.000W				SG on pile.	Private aid.
26680	- Day beacon 4	29-33-17.950N 095-02-56.000W				TR on pile.	Private aid.
26685	- Day beacon 5	29-33-15.650N 095-02-55.750W				SG on pile.	Private aid.
26690	- Day beacon 6	29-33-15.650N 095-02-56.750W				TR on pile.	Private aid.
26695	- Day beacon 7	29-33-13.350N 095-02-56.500W				SG on pile.	Private aid.
26700	- Day beacon 8	29-33-13.350N 095-02-57.500W				TR on pile.	Private aid.
26705	- Day beacon 9	29-33-11.050N 095-02-57.250W				SG on pile.	Private aid.
26710	- Day beacon 10	29-33-11.050N 095-02-58.250W				TR on pile.	Private aid.
26715	- LIGHT 11	29-33-08.750N 095-02-58.000W	Fl G 2s			SG on pile.	Private aid.
26720	- LIGHT 12	29-33-08.750N 095-02-59.000W	Fl R 2s			TR on pile.	Private aid.
	Hilton Hotel Marina Channel						
26760	- Entrance Day beacon 1	29-33-20.750N 095-04-19.500W				SG on pile.	Private aid.
26765	- Entrance Day beacon 2	29-33-22.000N 095-04-22.000W				TR on pile.	Private aid.
26770	- RANGE FRONT	29-33-21.000N 095-04-27.700W	F G	12		On pile.	Private aid.
26775	- RANGE REAR 40 yards, 272.3° from front light.	29-33-21.100N 095-04-29.000W	F G	20		On building.	Private aid.
26780	- BREAKWATER LIGHT 3	29-33-20.500N 095-04-25.000W	F G	12		SG on pile.	Private aid.
26785	- BREAKWATER LIGHT 4	29-33-21.200N 095-04-25.000W	F R	12		TR on pile.	Private aid.
	Ideal Channel						
26790	- Day beacon 1	29-32-58.000N 095-04-21.000W				SG on pile.	Private aid.
26795	- LIGHT 2	29-32-56.000N 095-04-24.000W	Fl R 4s			TR on dolphin.	Private aid.
26800	- Day beacon 3	29-32-53.000N 095-04-15.000W				SG on pile.	Private aid.

Light List corrected through LNM week: 01/18

(1) No.	(2) Name and Location	(3) Position	(4) Characteristic	(5) Height	(6) Range	(7) Structure	(8) Remarks
			TEXAS - Eighth District				
	GALVESTON BAY (Chart 11326)						
	Ideal Channel						
26805	- Day beacon 4	29-32-51.000N 095-04-18.000W				TR on pile.	Private aid.
26810	- LIGHT 5	29-32-49.000N 095-04-16.000W	Q G			SG on dolphin.	Private aid.
26815	- Day beacon 6	29-32-47.000N 095-04-21.000W				TR on pile.	Private aid.
26820	- Day beacon 7	29-32-43.000N 095-04-23.000W				SG on pile.	Private aid.
26825	- Day beacon 8	29-32-44.000N 095-04-24.000W				TR on pile.	Private aid.
26830	- Day beacon 10	29-32-43.000N 095-04-27.000W				SG on pile.	Private aid.
	Plantation Channel						
26835	- LIGHT 1	29-32-45.000N 095-04-36.000W	Fl G 4s	11		SG on dolphin.	Private aid.
26840	- Day beacon 2	29-32-44.000N 095-04-37.000W				TR on pile.	Private aid.
26845	- Day beacon 3	29-32-42.000N 095-04-34.000W				SG on pile.	Private aid.
26850	CLEAR LAKE WHARF LIGHT #1	29-32-08.700N 095-04-41.800W	Fl G 4s	17		On dolphins.	Private aid.
26855	CLEAR LAKE WHARF LIGHT #2	29-31-09.000N 095-04-41.500W	Fl R 4s	17		On dolphins.	Private aid.
	Houston Yacht Club						
26900	SYLVAN BEACH BREAKWATER LIGHT 1	29-39-00.000N 095-00-36.000W	Fl G 2.5s	10		SG on pile.	Private aid.
	SAN LUIS BAY TO MATAGORDA BAY (Chart 11321)						
	Freeport Entrance						
26905 1315	- Lighted Buoy FP	28-52-36.699N 095-14-08.815W	Mo (A) W		5	Red and white stripes with red spherical topmark.	AIS MMSI: 993682025
26910	- Lighted Buoy 1	28-53-03.930N 095-14-42.886W	Fl G 4s		4	Green.	Ra ref.
26915	- Lighted Buoy 2	28-53-39.983N 095-15-03.961W	Fl R 4s		4	Red.	Ra ref.
	GALVESTON BAY TO CEDAR LAKES (Chart 11322)						
	Freeport Entrance						
26920	- Lighted Buoy 3	28-54-04.590N 095-15-47.757W	Fl G 4s		4	Green.	Ra ref.
26925	- Lighted Buoy 4	28-54-44.983N 095-16-11.641W	Fl R 4s		3	Red.	Ra ref.
26930	- Lighted Buoy 5	28-55-05.554N 095-16-50.235W	Fl G 2.5s		3	Green.	Ra ref.
26935	- Lighted Buoy 6	28-55-26.049N 095-16-55.851W	Fl R 2.5s		3	Red.	Ra ref.
26940	- LIGHT 7	28-55-42.393N 095-17-28.653W	Q G	17	5	SG on skeleton tower on block.	
26945	- LIGHT 8	28-55-50.759N 095-17-17.358W	Q R	22	5	TR on skeleton tower on block.	
26950	- LIGHT 10	28-56-25.116N 095-17-58.217W	Oc R 4s	17	4	TR on pile.	
26955	- LIGHT 11	28-56-24.007N 095-18-10.637W	Fl G 2.5s	17	3	SG on pile.	
26957	FREEPORT LNG DANGER LIGHT	28-56-27.300N 095-18-32.500W	Q W			Marks the end of breakwater structure.	Private aid.
26960 37380	- LIGHT 12	28-56-39.607N 095-18-21.359W	Q R	17	4	TR-SY on pile.	Ra ref.
26965	FREEPORT JETTY INBOUND RANGE FRONT LIGHT	28-56-37.415N 095-18-16.544W	Iso G 2s (NIGHT) Iso W 2s (DAY)	42 45		KRW on skeleton tower on piles.	Visible only on range line. Lighted throughout 24 hours.

(1) No.	(2) Name and Location	(3) Position	(4) Characteristic	(5) Height	(6) Range	(7) Structure	(8) Remarks
	TEXAS - Eighth District							

GALVESTON BAY TO CEDAR LAKES (Chart 11322)

Freeport Entrance

(1) No.	(2) Name and Location	(3) Position	(4) Characteristic	(5) Height	(6) Range	(7) Structure	(8) Remarks
26970	FREEPORT JETTY INBOUND RANGE FRONT LIGHT PASSING LIGHT	28-56-37.415N 095-18-16.544W	Q W	17	5	On same structure as Freeport Jetty Inbound Range Front Light.	
26975	FREEPORT JETTY INBOUND RANGE REAR LIGHT 2,470 yards, 315.7° from front light.	28-57-31.525N 095-19-12.869W	Oc G 4s (NIGHT) Oc W 4s (DAY)	146 143		KRW on skeleton tower on block.	Visible only on rangeline. Lighted throughout 24 hours.
26980	DOW CHEMICAL A-14 DOCK LIGHT	28-56-43.000N 095-18-25.000W	Fl R 2.5s	19		On dolphin.	Private aid.
26985	DOW CHEMICAL A-13 DOCK LIGHT	28-56-49.700N 095-18-27.700W	Fl R 2.5s	19		On dolphin.	Private aid.
26990	Freeport Jetty Channel North Edge Dredging Range Front Day beacon.					Red square day mark on skeleton tower.	Range marks edge of channel for dredging purposes. Maintained by U.S. Army Corps of Engineers. May show fixed amber light when dredging is in progress. Aid maintained by U.S. Army Corps of Engineers.
26995	Freeport Jetty Channel South Edge Dredging Range Front Day beacon					Red square day mark on skeleton tower.	Range marks edge of channel for dredging purposes. Maintained by U.S. Army Corps of Engineers. May show fixed amber light when dredging is in progress Aid maintained by U.S. Army Corps of Engineers.
27000	Freeport Jetty Channel South Edge Dredging Range Rear Day beacon 380 yards, 317.5° from front day beacon.					Red square day mark on skeleton tower.	Maintained by U.S. Army Corps of Engineers. May show fixed amber light when dredging is in progress. Aid maintained by U.S. Army Corps of Engineers.
27005	FREEPORT HARBOR OUTBOUND RANGE FRONT LIGHT	28-56-35.855N 095-18-09.908W	Q R	25		KRW on skeleton tower.	Visible 2° each side of rangeline.
27010	FREEPORT HARBOR OUTBOUND RANGE REAR LIGHT 367 yards, 81.4° from front light.	28-56-37.138N 095-17-57.589W	F R	50		KRW on skeleton tower.	Visible 2° each side of rangeline.
27015	DOW CHEMICAL A-3A DOCK LIGHT	28-56-37.000N 095-19-09.000W	Fl R 2.5s	15		On dolphin.	Private aid.
27020	FREEPORT HARBOR LIGHT 20	28-56-06.893N 095-19-30.778W	Q R	30	5	TR on skeleton tower.	Visible 209° to 085°.
27025	FREEPORT HARBOR LIGHT 21	28-55-55.397N 095-19-39.242W	Fl G 2.5s	17	3	SG on pile.	
27030	FREEPORT HARBOR LIGHT 22	28-56-06.893N 095-19-42.778W	Q R	30	5	TR on skeleton tower.	Visible 271° to 161°.
27035	PHILLIPS PETROLEUM DOCK LIGHTS (2)	28-56-04.000N 095-19-51.000W	F G	14		On Dock.	Private aid.

San Bernard River

(1) No.	(2) Name and Location	(3) Position	(4) Characteristic	(5) Height	(6) Range	(7) Structure	(8) Remarks
27040	PHILLIPS PETROLEUM DOLPHIN LIGHTS (2)	28-54-00.000N 095-30-29.000W	Fl G 2.5s			On dolphins.	Private aid.

CEDAR LAKES TO ESPIRITU SANTO BAY (Chart 11319)

(1) No.	(2) Name and Location	(3) Position	(4) Characteristic	(5) Height	(6) Range	(7) Structure	(8) Remarks
27045 1375	COLORADO RIVER WEST JETTY ENTRANCE LIGHT 1	28-35-27.975N 095-59-03.871W	Fl G 2.5s	17	4	SG on pile with platform.	
27047 1377	COLORADO RIVER EAST JETTY ENTRANCE OBSTRUCTION LIGHT	28-35-25.974N 095-58-48.871W	Q W	20	4	NB on platform.	

Light List corrected through LNM week: 01/18

(1) No.	(2) Name and Location	(3) Position	(4) Characteristic	(5) Height	(6) Range	(7) Structure	(8) Remarks
			TEXAS - Eighth District				
	CEDAR LAKES TO ESPIRITU SANTO BAY (Chart 11319)						
27050 1380	COLORADO RIVER EAST JETTY ENTRANCE LIGHT 2	28-35-27.720N 095-58-57.498W	Fl R 2.5s	17	4	TR on skeleton tower.	
	MATAGORDA BAY (Chart 11317)						
	Matagorda Bay						
	Matagorda Ship Channel						
	Lights and daybeacons located 150 feet outside channel limits.						
27100 1365	- Approach Lighted Buoy MSC	28-12-01.026N 096-05-12.882W	Mo (A) W		5	Red and white stripes with red spherical topmark.	
27105 1360	*Enron-106-17 Lighted Buoy* Marks subsea installation.	28-11-10.000N 096-23-07.000W	Q R			Red.	SIGN: ENRON MI BLK 586 RA REF. Private aid.
27110 1385	- **Entrance Light**	28-25-18.466N 096-19-05.915W	Fl W 10s	64	5	On same structure as Matagorda Ship Channel Range B Rear Light.	Obscured from 257° to 040°.
27117 1392	- Entrance Lighted Buoy MB	28-23-01.012N 096-17-00.897W	Mo (A) W		6	Red and white stripes with red spherical topmark.	
27120	- A RANGE FRONT LIGHT	28-26-34.408N 096-20-42.437W	Iso W 2s (NIGHT) Iso W 2s (DAY)	22 24		On pile with platform.	Visible all around; higher intensity 1.5° each side of rangeline.
27125	- A RANGE REAR LIGHT 1,239 yards, 316.7° from front light.	28-27-34.016N 096-21-46.138W	Iso W 6s (NIGHT) Iso W 6s (DAY)	78 76		On skeleton tower on piles.	Lighted throughout 24 hours.
27130	- A RANGE REAR PASSING LIGHT	28-27-34.016N 096-21-46.138W	Fl W 4s	21	4	On same structure as Matagorda Ship Channel Range A Rear Light.	
27135	- Lighted Buoy 1	28-23-38.111N 096-17-38.750W	Fl G 4s		4	Green.	
27140	- Lighted Buoy 2	28-23-41.842N 096-17-31.962W	Fl (2)R 5s		4	Red.	
27145	- Lighted Buoy 3	28-24-14.977N 096-18-18.120W	Fl G 2.5s		4	Green.	
27150	- Lighted Buoy 4	28-24-19.086N 096-18-11.824W	Fl R 2.5s		3	Red.	
27155	- Lighted Buoy 7	28-24-48.507N 096-18-54.448W	Q G		3	Green.	
27160	- Lighted Buoy 8 250 feet outside channel limit.	28-24-54.092N 096-18-48.716W	Q R		3	Red.	
27165	- LIGHT 11	28-25-34.457N 096-19-46.130W	Fl G 2.5s	25	8	SG on skeleton tower on concrete block.	Higher intensity beam up and down channel.
27170	- B RANGE FRONT LIGHT	28-25-40.582N 096-19-37.172W	Q W	20		KRW on skeleton tower on block.	Visible 2° each side of rangeline.
27175	- B RANGE FRONT LIGHT PASSING LIGHT	28-25-40.621N 096-19-37.261W	Fl R 4s	23	3	On same structure as Matagorda Ship Channel Range B Front Light.	
27180	- B RANGE REAR LIGHT 1,192 yards, 128.7° from front light.	28-25-18.466N 096-19-05.915W	Oc W 4s	62		KRW on skeleton tower block. On same structure as Matagorda Bay Entrance Light.	
27185	- Lighted Buoy 13	28-26-02.944N 096-20-14.360W	Q G		3	Green.	
27190	- Lighted Buoy 14	28-26-12.606N 096-20-16.809W	Q R		3	Red.	
27195	- LIGHT 17	28-26-28.798N 096-20-49.898W	Fl G 2.5s	17	4	SG on pile.	Ra ref.
27200	- Lighted Buoy 18	28-26-32.677N 096-20-46.417W	Fl R 2.5s		3	Red.	

(1) No.	(2) Name and Location	(3) Position	(4) Characteristic	(5) Height	(6) Range	(7) Structure	(8) Remarks
		TEXAS - Eighth District					
	MATAGORDA BAY (Chart 11317)						
	Matagorda Bay						
	Matagorda Ship Channel						
	Lights and daybeacons located 150 feet outside channel limits.						
27205	- LIGHT 19	28-26-51.726N 096-21-22.210W	Oc G 4s	17	3	SG on pile.	Ra ref.
27210	- LIGHT 20	28-26-55.590N 096-21-18.725W	Oc R 4s	20	4	TR on skeleton tower on piles.	
27212	- LIGHT 21	28-27-12.540N 096-21-51.789W	Fl G 4s	17	3	SG on pile.	Ra ref.
27213	- LIGHT 22	28-27-16.287N 096-21-48.345W	Fl R 4s	17	3	TR on pile.	Ra ref.
27215	- LIGHT 23	28-27-38.861N 096-22-28.839W	Q G	17	3	SG on pile.	Ra ref.
27220	- LIGHT 24	28-27-42.548N 096-22-25.342W	Q R	17	3	TR on pile.	Ra ref.
27225	- LIGHT 25	28-28-02.188N 096-23-02.128W	Fl G 4s	17	4	SG on pile.	Ra ref.
27230	- LIGHT 26	28-28-06.055N 096-22-58.631W	Fl R 4s	17	3	TR on pile.	Ra ref.
27235	- LIGHT 27	28-28-25.693N 096-23-35.421W	Fl G 2.5s	17	3	SG on pile.	Ra ref.
27240	- LIGHT 28	28-28-29.560N 096-23-31.924W	Fl R 2.5s	17	3	TR on dolphin.	Ra ref.
27245	- LIGHT 29	28-28-49.196N 096-24-08.719W	Oc G 4s	17	3	SG on pile.	Ra ref.
27250	- LIGHT 30	28-28-53.063N 096-24-05.221W	Oc R 4s	17	4	TR on pile.	Ra ref.
27255	- LIGHT 31	28-29-12.697N 096-24-42.020W	Q G	17	3	SG on pile.	Ra ref.
27260	- LIGHT 32	28-29-16.564N 096-24-38.521W	Q R	17	3	TR on pile.	Ra ref.
27265	- LIGHT 33	28-29-35.991N 096-25-15.342W	Fl G 2.5s	17	3	SG on pile.	Ra ref.
27270	- LIGHT 34	28-29-40.062N 096-25-11.827W	Fl R 2.5s	17	3	TR on pile.	Ra ref.
27275	- LIGHT 35	28-29-59.691N 096-25-48.636W	Fl G 4s	17	4	SG on pile.	Ra ref.
27280	- LIGHT 36	28-30-03.558N 096-25-45.137W	Fl R 4s	17	3	TR on pile.	Ra ref.
27285	- LIGHT 37	28-30-23.139N 096-26-22.001W	Q G	17	3	SG on pile.	Ra ref.
27290	- LIGHT 38	28-30-27.052N 096-26-18.450W	Q R	17	3	TR on pile.	Ra ref.
27295	- LIGHT 39	28-30-46.676N 096-26-55.267W	Oc G 4s	17	4	SG on pile.	Ra ref.
27300	- LIGHT 40	28-30-50.543N 096-26-51.768W	Oc R 4s	17	4	TR on pile.	Ra ref.
27305	- LIGHT 41	28-31-10.165N 096-27-28.589W	Fl G 2.5s	17	3	SG on pile.	Ra ref.
27310	- LIGHT 42	28-31-14.032N 096-27-25.090W	Fl R 2.5s	17	3	TR on pile.	Ra ref.
27315	- LIGHT 43	28-31-33.613N 096-28-01.916W	Fl G 4s	17	4	SG on pile.	Ra ref.
27320	- LIGHT 44	28-31-37.519N 096-27-58.416W	Fl R 4s	17	3	TR on pile.	Ra ref.
27325	- LIGHT 45	28-31-57.136N 096-28-35.245W	Q G	17	3	SG on pile.	Ra ref.
27330	- LIGHT 46	28-32-01.003N 096-28-31.746W	Q R	17	3	TR on pile.	Ra ref.

Light List corrected through LNM week: 01/18

(1) No.	(2) Name and Location	(3) Position	(4) Characteristic	(5) Height	(6) Range	(7) Structure	(8) Remarks
			TEXAS - Eighth District				
	MATAGORDA BAY (Chart 11317)						
	Matagorda Bay						
	Matagorda Ship Channel						
	Lights and daybeacons located 150 feet outside channel limits.						
27335	- C RANGE FRONT LIGHT	28-35-58.887N 096-34-14.604W	Q W	25		KRW on skeleton tower on piles.	Visible 2° each side of rangeline.
27340	- C RANGE FRONT LIGHT PASSING LIGHT	28-35-58.887N 096-34-14.604W	Q W	27	5	KRW on skeleton tower on piles.	On same structure as Matagorda Ship Channel Range C Front Light.
27345	- C RANGE REAR LIGHT 2,000 yards, 308.5° from front light.	28-36-35.723N 096-35-07.043W	Oc W 4s	60		KRW on skeleton tower on piles.	Visible 2° each side of rangeline.
27350	- C RANGE REAR LIGHT PASSING LIGHT	28-36-35.723N 096-35-07.043W	Fl W 4s	15	5	On same structure as Matagorda Ship Channel Range C Rear Light.	
27355	- LIGHT 47	28-32-20.618N 096-29-08.578W	Fl G 2.5s	17	3	SG on dolphin.	Ra ref.
27360	- LIGHT 48	28-32-24.485N 096-29-05.080W	Fl R 2.5s	17	3	TR on pile.	Ra ref.
27365	- LIGHT 49	28-32-44.098N 096-29-41.919W	Oc G 4s	17	4	SG on pile.	Ra ref.
27370	- LIGHT 50	28-32-47.965N 096-29-38.418W	Oc R 4s	17	4	TR on pile.	Ra ref.
27375	- LIGHT 51	28-33-07.576N 096-30-15.261W	Q G	17	3	SG on pile.	Ra ref.
27380	- LIGHT 52	28-33-11.443N 096-30-11.760W	Q R	17	3	TR on pile.	Ra ref.
27385	LAVACA PIPELINE LIGHT A	28-33-08.750N 096-30-19.510W	Fl Y 4s	15		On dolphin.	Private aid.
27390	LAVACA PIPELINE LIGHT B	28-33-14.720N 096-30-14.940W	Fl Y 4s			On dolphin.	Private aid.
27395	- LIGHT 53	28-33-34.291N 096-30-53.211W	Fl G 2.5s	17	3	SG on pile.	Ra ref.
27400	- LIGHT 54	28-33-38.158N 096-30-49.710W	Fl R 2.5s	17	3	TR on pile.	Ra ref.
27405	- LIGHT 55	28-33-54.458N 096-31-22.017W	Fl G 4s	17	4	SG on pile.	Ra ref.
27410	- LIGHT 56	28-33-58.391N 096-31-18.458W	Fl R 4s	17	3	TR on pile.	Ra ref.
27415	ONYX PIPELINE LIGHT B	28-34-17.000N 096-31-42.000W	Q R	8		NW on pile worded DANGER PIPELINE CROSSING.	Private aid.
27420	ONYX PIPELINE LIGHT A	28-34-09.000N 096-31-48.000W	Q G	8		NW on pile worded DANGER PIPELINE CROSSING.	Private aid.
27425	ONYX PIPELINE EAST LIGHT	28-34-20.000N 096-31-38.000W	Q R	8		NR on pile worded DANGER PIPELINE CROSSING.	Private aid.
27430	ONYX PIPELINE WEST LIGHT	28-34-05.000N 096-31-52.000W	Q G	8		NR on pile worded DANGER PIPELINE CROSSING.	Private aid.
27435	- LIGHT 57	28-34-17.994N 096-31-55.313W	Fl G 2.5s	17	3	SG on pile.	Ra ref.
27440	- LIGHT 58	28-34-21.861N 096-31-51.812W	Fl R 2.5s	17	3	TR on pile.	Ra ref.
27445	- LIGHT 59	28-34-41.436N 096-32-28.672W	Oc G 4s	17	4	SG on pile.	Ra ref.
27450	- LIGHT 60	28-34-45.330N 096-32-25.171W	Oc R 4s	17	4	TR on pile.	Ra ref.

Light List corrected through LNM week: 01/18

(1) No.	(2) Name and Location	(3) Position	(4) Characteristic	(5) Height	(6) Range	(7) Structure	(8) Remarks
		TEXAS - Eighth District					

MATAGORDA BAY (Chart 11317)
Matagorda Bay
Matagorda Ship Channel
Lights and daybeacons located 150 feet outside channel limits.

(1) No.	(2) Name and Location	(3) Position	(4) Characteristic	(5) Height	(6) Range	(7) Structure	(8) Remarks
27455	- LIGHT 61	28-35-04.929N 096-33-02.035W	Fl G 4s	17	4	SG on pile.	Ra ref.
27460	- LIGHT 62	28-35-08.795N 096-32-58.534W	Fl R 4s	17	3	TR on pile.	Ra ref.
27465	- LIGHT 63	28-35-28.392N 096-33-35.402W	Fl G 2.5s	17	3	SG on pile.	Ra ref.
27470	- LIGHT 64	28-35-32.259N 096-33-31.901W	Fl R 2.5s	17	3	TR on pile.	Ra ref.
27475	- LIGHT 65	28-35-39.872N 096-33-51.730W	Q G	17	3	SG on pile.	Ra ref.
27480	- LIGHT 66	28-35-46.144N 096-33-48.048W	Q R	17	3	TR on pile.	Ra ref.
27485	PORT LAVACA CHANNEL JUNCTION LIGHT PL	28-35-50.039N 096-34-00.254W	Fl (2+1)G 6s	17	3	JG on pile.	Ra ref.
27490	- E RANGE FRONT LIGHT	28-38-57.333N 096-33-56.867W	Q R	28		KRW on skeleton tower on mud sills.	Visible 2° each side of rangeline.
27492	- E RANGE FRONT LIGHT PASSING LIGHT	28-38-57.333N 096-33-56.867W	Fl W 4s	17	4	On same structure as Matagorda Ship Channel E Range Front Light.	
27495	- E RANGE REAR LIGHT 1,494 yards, 001.4° from front light.	28-39-41.700N 096-33-55.632W	Oc R 4s	66		KRW on skeleton tower on mud sills.	Visible 2° each side of rangeline.
27500	- LIGHT 67	28-36-03.722N 096-34-04.672W	Q G	17	3	SG on pile.	Ra ref.
27505	- LIGHT 68	28-36-02.263N 096-33-56.858W	Q R	17	3	TR on pile.	Ra ref.
27510	- D RANGE FRONT LIGHT	28-35-46.227N 096-34-02.456W	Q G	25		KRW on skeleton tower on piles.	Visible 2° each side of rangeline.
27515	- D RANGE FRONT LIGHT PASSING LIGHT	28-35-46.227N 096-34-02.456W	Fl W 4s	27	5	On same structure as Matagorda Ship Channel Range D Front Light.	
27520	- D RANGE REAR LIGHT 658.167 yards, 181.3° from front light.	28-35-26.682N 096-34-02.962W	Oc G 4s	47		KRW on skeleton tower on piles.	
27525	- D RANGE REAR LIGHT PASSING LIGHT	28-35-26.682N 096-34-02.962W	Fl W 4s	18	5	On same structure as Matagorda Ship Channel Range D Rear Light.	
27530	- LIGHT 69	28-36-29.520N 096-34-03.941W	Fl G 2.5s	17	3	SG on pile.	Ra ref.
27535	- LIGHT 70	28-36-29.397N 096-33-58.334W	Fl R 2.5s	17	3	TR on pile.	Ra ref.
27540	- LIGHT 71	28-36-55.319N 096-34-03.210W	Fl G 4s	17	4	SG on pile.	Ra ref.
27545	- LIGHT 72	28-36-55.196N 096-33-57.602W	Fl R 4s	17	3	TR on pile.	Ra ref.
27550	- LIGHT 73	28-37-21.118N 096-34-02.478W	Fl G 4s	17	4	SG on pile.	Ra ref.
27555	- LIGHT 74	28-37-20.995N 096-33-56.869W	Fl R 4s	17	3	TR on pile.	Ra ref.
27560	- LIGHT 75	28-37-46.917N 096-34-01.747W	Fl G 2.5s	17	3	SG on pile.	Ra ref.
27565	- LIGHT 76	28-37-46.793N 096-33-56.138W	Fl R 2.5s	17	3	TR on pile.	Ra ref.
27570	- G RANGE FRONT LIGHT	28-38-07.503N 096-34-05.513W	Q W	17		KRW on tower.	Visible all around; higher intensity on rangeline.

Light List corrected through LNM week: 01/18

(1) No.	(2) Name and Location	(3) Position	(4) Characteristic	(5) Height	(6) Range	(7) Structure	(8) Remarks
	**TEXAS - Eighth District**						
	MATAGORDA BAY (Chart 11317)						
	Matagorda Bay						
	Matagorda Ship Channel						
	Lights and daybeacons located 150 feet outside channel limits.						
27575	- G RANGE REAR LIGHT 115 yards, 231.7° from front light.	28-38-05.399N 096-34-08.594W	Iso W 6s	25		KRW on tower.	Visible all around; higher intensity on rangeline.
27580	- LIGHT 77	28-38-00.863N 096-34-01.351W	Q G	17	3	SG on pile.	Ra ref.
27585	- LIGHT 78	28-38-03.110N 096-33-53.110W	Q R	17	3	TR on pile.	Ra ref.
27590 27655	MATAGORDA SHIP JUNCTION LIGHT A	28-38-10.288N 096-33-55.798W	Fl (2+1)G 6s	17	4	JG on pile.	Ra ref.
27595	- LIGHT 79	28-38-24.344N 096-33-47.230W	Fl G 2.5s	17	3	SG on pile.	Ra ref.
27600	- LIGHT 80	28-38-18.075N 096-33-43.567W	Fl R 2.5s	17	3	TR on pile.	Ra ref.
27605	- F RANGE FRONT LIGHT	28-38-29.610N 096-33-40.074W	Q W	17		KRW on tower.	Visible all around; higher intensity on rangeline.
27610	- F RANGE REAR LIGHT 140 yards, 027.4° from front light.	28-38-33.241N 096-33-37.846W	Iso W 6s	25		KRW on tower.	
27615	- LIGHT 81	28-38-34.406N 096-33-30.216W	Q G	17	3	SG on Pile.	Ra ref.
27620	- LIGHT 82	28-38-31.087N 096-33-27.448W	Q R	17	4	TR on pile.	Ra ref.
	Point Comfort Turning Basin						
27625	- DOCK LIGHTS (6)	28-38-32.900N 096-32-58.400W	Fl R 2.5s	12		On dolphins.	Private aid.
27630	- NORTH SHOAL RANGE FRONT LIGHT	28-38-39.900N 096-32-56.800W	Q W	30		KGW on tower.	Marks shoal water. Private aid.
27635	- NORTH SHOAL RANGE REAR LIGHT	28-38-39.900N 096-32-55.600W	Fl W 2.5s	50		KGW on tower.	Marks shoal water. Private aid.
27640	- SOUTH SHOAL RANGE FRONT LIGHT	28-38-33.100N 096-32-56.700W	Q W	30		KGW on tower.	Marks shoal water. Private aid.
27645	- SOUTH SHOAL RANGE REAR LIGHT	28-38-33.200N 096-32-55.400W	Fl W 2.5s	50		KGW on tower.	Marks shoal water. Private aid.
27650	- PIER OBSTRUCTION LIGHT	28-38-36.900N 096-33-09.900W	Fl R 2.5s			On end of pier.	Private aid.
	Point Comfort Inner Channel						
27655 27590	MATAGORDA SHIP JUNCTION LIGHT A	28-38-10.288N 096-33-55.798W	Fl (2+1)G 6s	17	4	JG on pile.	Ra ref.
27660	- LIGHT 3	28-38-28.000N 096-34-00.000W	Fl G 4s	8		SG on pile.	Private aid.
27665	- LIGHT 4	28-38-29.000N 096-33-54.000W	Fl R 4s	10		TR on pile.	Private aid.
27670	- LIGHT 5	28-38-36.000N 096-34-02.000W	Fl W 4s	10		SG on pile.	Private aid.
27675	- LIGHT 6	28-38-52.000N 096-33-52.000W	Fl R 4s	10		TR on pile.	Private aid.
27680	- LIGHT 7	28-39-04.000N 096-33-53.000W	Fl G 4s	10		SG on pile.	Private aid.
27685	- LIGHT 8	28-39-30.000N 096-34-04.000W	Fl R 3s	10		TR on pile.	Private aid.
27690	POINT COMFORT RANGE A FRONT LIGHT	28-39-35.000N 096-34-11.000W	Fl W 4s	14		KRW on pile.	Private aid.
27695	POINT COMFORT RANGE A REAR LIGHT	28-39-41.000N 096-34-15.000W	Q W	19		KRW on piles.	Private aid.
	Lavaca Bay						
	Port Lavaca Channel						
27700	- LIGHT 1	28-36-01.204N 096-34-33.786W	Fl G 2.5s	17	4	SG on pile.	Ra ref.

Light List corrected through LNM week: 01/18

(1) No.	(2) Name and Location	(3) Position	(4) Characteristic	(5) Height	(6) Range	(7) Structure	(8) Remarks
	TEXAS - Eighth District						
	MATAGORDA BAY (Chart 11317)						
	Lavaca Bay						
	Port Lavaca Channel						
27705	- Day beacon 3	28-36-12.081N 096-34-57.496W				SG on pile.	Ra ref.
27710	- Buoy 6	28-36-24.511N 096-35-15.389W				Red nun.	
27715	- LIGHT 5 60 feet outside channel limit.	28-36-21.190N 096-35-17.362W	Fl G 6s	17	4	SG on pile.	Ra ref.
27720	- Day beacon 7	28-36-36.625N 096-35-50.393W				SG on pile.	Ra ref.
27725	- Day beacon 8	28-36-49.488N 096-36-09.819W				TR on pile.	Ra ref.
27730	- *Lighted Buoy 9*	28-36-48.278N 096-36-15.570W	Fl G 4s		4	Green can.	
27735	- Day beacon 10	28-36-58.327N 096-36-29.864W				TR on pile.	Ra ref.
27740	- Day beacon 11	28-36-55.988N 096-36-31.419W				SG on pile.	Ra ref.
27745	- Day beacon 12	28-37-04.250N 096-36-43.284W				TR on dolphin.	Ra ref.
27750	- LIGHT 13	28-37-01.879N 096-36-45.275W	Fl G 2.5s	17	4	SG on pile.	Ra ref.
27755	- Day beacon 14	28-37-11.801N 096-37-00.910W				TR on pile.	Ra ref.
27760	- Day beacon 15	28-37-09.656N 096-37-01.965W				SG on pile.	Ra ref.
27765	- LIGHT 16	28-37-20.066N 096-37-17.825W	Q R	17	4	TR on pile.	Ra ref.
	Nautical Landing Channel						
27770	- Day beacon 2	28-37-09.400N 096-37-02.300W				TR on pile.	Private aid.
27775	- Day beacon 4	28-37-07.300N 096-37-06.200W				TR on pile.	Private aid.
27780	- Day beacon 6	28-37-05.200N 096-37-09.900W				TR on pile.	Private aid.
27785	- Day beacon 8	28-37-03.600N 096-37-12.900W				TR on pile.	Private aid.
27790	- Day beacon 10	28-37-02.700N 096-37-12.400W				TR on pile.	Private aid.
	Port Lavaca Harbor of Refuge						
27795	- Day beacon 2 90 feet outside channel limit.	28-36-14.584N 096-35-13.935W				TR on pile.	Ra ref.
27800	- Day beacon 4 90 feet outside channel limit.	28-36-04.440N 096-35-37.036W				TR on pile.	Ra ref.
27805	- LIGHT WR 6 90 feet outside channel limit.	28-35-54.295N 096-36-00.136W	Q R	17	3	TR on pile.	Ra ref.
27810	- Day beacon 8 90 feet outside channel limit.	28-35-44.149N 096-36-23.235W				TR on pile.	Ra ref.
27815	- Day beacon 10 90 feet outside channel limit.	28-35-33.923N 096-36-46.506W				TR on pile.	Ra ref.
	Chocolate Bay Channel						
27820	- Buoy 1	28-36-01.000N 096-35-33.000W				Green can.	Private aid.
27825	- Buoy 3	28-35-45.000N 096-35-48.000W				Green can.	Private aid.
27830	- Buoy 5	28-35-32.000N 096-36-00.000W				Green can.	Private aid.

Light List corrected through LNM week: 01/18

(1) No.	(2) Name and Location	(3) Position	(4) Characteristic	(5) Height	(6) Range	(7) Structure	(8) Remarks
	TEXAS - Eighth District						
	MATAGORDA BAY (Chart 11317)						
	Lavaca Bay						
	Chocolate Bay Channel						
27835	- Buoy 7	28-35-20.000N 096-36-12.000W				Green can.	Private aid.
	Lavaca Bay Channel						
27840	- Day beacon 2	28-36-55.152N 096-36-09.600W				TR on pile.	Ra ref.
27845	- Day beacon 4	28-37-16.097N 096-35-56.995W				TR on pile.	Ra ref.
27850	- Day beacon 6	28-37-42.287N 096-35-41.117W				TR on pile.	Ra ref.
27855	- Day beacon 8	28-38-08.136N 096-35-26.502W				TR on dolphin.	Ra ref.
27860	- Day beacon 9	28-38-27.234N 096-35-19.252W				SG on pile.	Ra ref.
27865	- Day beacon 11	28-38-32.885N 096-35-18.917W				SG on pile.	Ra ref.
27870	- Day beacon 12 100 feet outside channel limit.	28-38-40.902N 096-35-18.936W				TR on pile.	Ra ref.
27880	- Day beacon 16	28-39-33.684N 096-36-02.184W				TR on pile.	Ra ref.
27885	- Day beacon 18	28-39-45.312N 096-35-57.828W				TR on pile.	Ra ref.
27895	- Day beacon 17	28-39-34.183N 096-36-08.917W				SG on pile.	Ra ref.
27900	- Day beacon 22	28-40-56.418N 096-34-54.258W				TR on pile.	Ra ref.
	Lavaca River						
27905	- Day beacon 2	28-41-20.922N 096-34-33.900W				TR on pile.	Ra ref.
27910	- Day beacon 3 150 feet outside channel limit.	28-41-51.792N 096-34-34.746W				SG on pile.	Ra ref.
	Lavaca Bay						
27915	- PIPELINE LIGHT A-8	28-33-08.570N 096-29-19.510W	Q Y	10		On pile.	Private aid.
27920	- PIPELINE LIGHT A-10	28-35-46.210N 096-31-27.210W	Q R			On pile.	Private aid.
27925	- PIPELINE LIGHT D-8	28-37-53.000N 096-32-27.910W	Q R			On pile.	Private aid.
	Matagorda Bay						
27928	SCHICKE POINT DANGER BREAKWATER LIGHT	28-37-43.150N 096-21-52.650W	Fl W 2.5s			Marks breakwater.	Private aid.
27928.01	SCHICKE POINT DANGER BREAKWATER LIGHT	28-37-40.680N 096-21-51.800W	Fl W 2.5s			Marks breakwater.	Private aid.
27928.02	SCHICKE POINT DANGER BREAKWATER LIGHT	28-37-37.970N 096-21-49.800W	Fl W 2.5s			Marks breakwater.	Private aid.
27928.03	Schicke Point Danger Breakwater Day beacon	28-37-36.330N 096-21-45.780W				Marks breakwater.	Private aid.
27928.04	SCHICKE POINT DANGER BREAKWATER LIGHT	28-37-34.820N 096-21-41.730W	Fl W 2.5s			Marks breakwater.	Private aid.
27928.05	Schicke Point Danger Breakwater Day beacon	28-37-35.390N 096-21-37.800W				Marks breakwater.	Private aid.
27928.06	SCHICKE POINT DANGER BREAKWATER LIGHT	28-37-35.960N 096-21-33.880W	Fl W 2.5s			Marks breakwater.	Private aid.
27928.07	SCHICKE POINT DANGER BREAKWATER LIGHT	28-37-36.350N 096-21-32.860W	Fl W 2.5s			Marks breakwater.	Private aid.
27928.08	Schicke Point Danger Breakwater Day beacon	28-37-37.880N 096-21-28.930W				Marks breakwater.	Private aid.
27928.09	SCHICKE POINT DANGER BREAKWATER LIGHT	28-37-39.390N 096-21-25.040W	Fl W 2.5s			Marks breakwater.	Private aid.

(1) No.	(2) Name and Location	(3) Position	(4) Characteristic	(5) Height	(6) Range	(7) Structure	(8) Remarks
		TEXAS - Eighth District					
	MATAGORDA BAY (Chart 11317)						
	Matagorda Bay						
27928.11	Schicke Point Danger Breakwater Day beacon	28-37-40.920N 096-21-21.130W				Marks breakwater.	Private aid.
27928.12	SCHICKE POINT DANGER BREAKWATER LIGHT	28-37-42.450N 096-21-17.240W	Fl W 2.5s			Marks breakwater.	Private aid.
27930	Well Point Day beacon 1	28-38-24.408N 096-17-10.929W				SG on pile.	Ra ref.
27935	TEXAS PARKS & WILDLIFE JETTY LIGHT	28-38-20.440N 096-19-24.000W	Q R		10	On jetty.	Private aid.
27937	JACKSON COUNTY CARANCAHUA BAY DANGER BREAKWATER LIGHTS (2)	28-44-09.450N 096-24-06.760W				Marks east and west ends of jetty.	Private aid.
	Matagorda Marine Education Channel						
27940	- Day beacon 1	28-41-11.000N 096-14-24.000W				SG on pile.	Private aid.
27945	- Day beacon 2	28-41-11.000N 096-14-23.000W				TR on pile.	Private aid.
27950	- Day beacon 3	28-41-18.000N 096-14-24.000W				SG on pile.	Private aid.
27955	- Day beacon 4	28-41-18.000N 096-14-23.000W				TR on pile.	Private aid.
27960	- Day beacon 5	28-41-25.000N 096-14-24.000W				SG on pile.	Private aid.
27965	- Day beacon 6	28-41-25.000N 096-14-23.000W				TR on pile.	Private aid.
	Matagorda Bay						
27970	Geological Survey Tide Gage Day beacon	28-44-20.000N 096-10-53.000W				NW on pile worded DANGER TIDE GAGE.	Private aid.
27975	Geological Survey Tide Gage Day beacon	28-37-52.000N 096-21-45.000W				NW on pile worded DANGER TIDE GAGE.	Private aid.
	Espiritu Santo Bay - Barroom Bay Navigation						
27980	- Day beacon 2	28-24-39.000N 096-25-14.000W				TR on pile.	Private aid.
27985	- Day beacon 4	28-24-00.700N 096-25-00.200W				TR on pile.	Private aid.
27990	- Day beacon 6	28-24-00.700N 096-25-00.200W				TR on pile.	Private aid.
27995	- Day beacon 8	28-24-00.700N 096-25-00.200W				TR on pile.	Private aid.
28000	- Day beacon 10	28-24-19.000N 096-25-36.000W				TR on pile.	Private aid.
28005	- Day beacon 12	28-24-00.700N 096-25-00.200W				TR on pile.	Private aid.
28010	- Day beacon 14	28-24-00.700N 096-25-00.200W				TR on pile.	Private aid.
28015	- Day beacon 16	28-24-00.700N 096-25-00.200W				TR on pile.	Private aid.
28020	- Day beacon 18	28-24-00.700N 096-25-00.200W				TR on pile.	Private aid.
28025	- Day beacon 22	28-24-00.700N 096-25-00.200W				TR on pile.	Private aid.
28030	- Day beacon 21	28-24-00.700N 096-25-00.200W				SG on pile.	Private aid.
28035	- Day beacon 22	28-24-00.700N 096-25-00.200W				TR on pile.	Private aid.
28040	- Day beacon 23	28-24-00.700N 096-25-00.200W				SG on pile.	Private aid.
28045	- Day beacon 25	28-24-00.700N 096-25-00.200W				SG on pile.	Private aid.
28050	- Day beacon 27	28-24-00.700N 096-25-00.200W				SG on pile.	Private aid.
28055	- Day beacon 29	28-24-00.700N 096-25-00.200W				SG on pile.	Private aid.

Light List corrected through LNM week: 01/18

(1) No.	(2) Name and Location	(3) Position	(4) Characteristic	(5) Height	(6) Range	(7) Structure	(8) Remarks
		TEXAS - Eighth District					
	MATAGORDA BAY (Chart 11317)						
	Espiritu Santo Bay - Barroom Bay Navigation						
28060	- Day beacon 31	28-24-00.700N 096-25-00.200W				SG on pile.	Private aid.
28065	- Day beacon 33	28-24-00.700N 096-25-00.200W				SG on pile.	Private aid.
28070	- Day beacon 35	28-28-00.700N 096-25-00.200W				SG on pile.	Private aid.
28075	- Day beacon 36	28-28-00.700N 096-25-00.200W				TR on pile.	Private aid.
28080	- Day beacon 38	28-24-00.700N 096-25-00.200W				TR on pile.	Private aid.
28085	- Day beacon 39	28-24-00.700N 096-25-00.200W				SG on pile.	Private aid.
28090	- Day beacon 40	28-24-00.700N 096-25-00.200W				TR on pile.	Private aid.
28095	- Day beacon 41	28-25-31.000N 096-24-33.000W				SG on pile.	Private aid.
28100	- Day beacon 42	28-24-00.700N 096-25-00.200W				TR on pile.	Private aid.
28105	- Day beacon 43	28-24-00.700N 096-25-00.200W				SG on pile.	Private aid.
28110	- Day beacon 44	28-24-00.700N 096-25-00.200W				TR on pile.	Private aid.
28115	- Day beacon 45	28-24-00.700N 096-25-00.200W				SG on pile.	Private aid.
28120	- Day beacon 46	28-24-00.700N 096-25-00.200W				TR on pile.	Private aid.
28125	- Day beacon 47	28-24-00.700N 096-25-00.200W				SG on pile.	Private aid.
28130	- Day beacon 48	28-24-00.700N 096-25-00.200W				TR on pile.	Private aid.
	ARANSAS PASS TO BAFFIN BAY (Chart 11307)						
28135 1430	*Aransas Pass Entrance Lighted Buoy AP*	27-47-34.122N 096-57-22.143W	Mo (A) W		6	Red and white stripes with red spherical topmark.	AIS MMSI: 993682026
28140	*Aransas Pass Lighted Buoy 3*	27-48-57.245N 097-00-29.513W	Fl G 4s		4	Green.	
28145	HARBOR ISLAND RANGE FRONT LIGHT	27-50-45.333N 097-03-41.196W	Iso G 2s (NIGHT) Iso W 2s (DAY)	67 65		Skeleton tower.	Visible 2° each side of rangeline. Lighted throughout 24 hours.
28150	HARBOR ISLAND RANGE REAR LIGHT 1,500 yards, 301.2° from front light.	27-51-08.414N 097-04-24.070W	F G (NIGHT) F W (DAY)	123 125		Skeleton tower.	Visible 2° each side of rangeline. Lighted throughout 24 hours.
	CORPUS CHRISTI BAY (Chart 11309)						
	Aransas Pass						
28155	- *Lighted Buoy 6* 90 feet outside channel limit.	27-49-31.128N 097-01-13.567W	Fl R 4s		4	Red.	
28160	- *Lighted Buoy 7*	27-49-41.984N 097-01-52.658W	Fl G 2.5s		4	Green.	
28165	- *Lighted Buoy 8*	27-49-52.161N 097-01-52.665W	Fl R 2.5s		3	Red.	
28170	- *Lighted Buoy 9*	27-50-01.815N 097-02-28.437W	Fl G 4s		4	Green.	
28175	- *Lighted Buoy 10*	27-50-09.412N 097-02-25.803W	Fl R 4s		3	Red.	
28180	DREDGING NORTH SIDE RANGE FRONT LIGHT	27-50-48.000N 097-03-36.000W	F Y	50		On white skeleton tower.	Range marks edge of channel for dredging purposes. Maintained by U.S. Army Corps of Engineers. Aid maintained by U.S. Army Corps of Engineers.

Light List corrected through LNM week: 01/18

(1) No.	(2) Name and Location	(3) Position	(4) Characteristic	(5) Height	(6) Range	(7) Structure	(8) Remarks
			TEXAS - Eighth District				
	CORPUS CHRISTI BAY (Chart 11309)						
	Aransas Pass						
28185	DREDGING NORTH SIDE RANGE REAR LIGHT 351 yards, 301° from front light.		F Y	70		On white skeleton tower.	Range marks edge of channel for dredging purposes. Maintained by U.S. Army Corps of Engineers.
							Aid maintained by U.S. Army Corps of Engineers.
28190	DREDGING SOUTH SIDE RANGE FRONT LIGHT	27-50-42.000N 097-03-42.000W	F Y	50		On white skeleton tower.	Range marks edge of channel for dredging purposes. Maintaind by U.S. Army Corps of Engineers.
							Aid maintained by U.S. Army Corps of Engineers.
28195	DREDGING SOUTH SIDE RANGE REAR LIGHT 306 yards, 301° from front light.		F Y	70		On white skeleton tower.	Range marks edge of channel for dredging purposes. Maintained by U.S. Army Corps of Engineers.
							Aid maintained by U.S. Army Corps of Engineers.
28200	UNIVERSITY OF TEXAS RESEARCH PIER LIGHTS (7)	27-50-16.200N 097-03-01.050W	Fl G 2.5s	19		On concrete pier.	Private aid.
28205	- LIGHT 11	27-50-30.864N 097-03-23.365W	Fl G 4s	22	4	SG on skeleton tower on piles.	
	Aransas Channel						
28210	- LIGHT 2	27-51-04.737N 097-03-50.416W	Fl R 2.5s	17	3	TR on pile.	Ra ref.
28215	- LIGHT 3 90 feet outside channel limit.	27-51-41.680N 097-04-39.781W	Fl G 2.5s	17	3	SG on pile.	
28220	- Day beacon 4	27-51-43.829N 097-04-35.811W				TR on pile.	Ra ref.
28225	- Day beacon 5 60 feet outside channel limit.	27-52-06.108N 097-05-05.548W				SG on pile.	
28230	- Day beacon 6 90 feet outside channel limit.	27-52-08.023N 097-05-03.406W				TR on pile.	
28235	- Day beacon 8	27-52-32.316N 097-05-30.243W				TR on pile.	Ra ref.
28240	- Day beacon 9	27-52-55.489N 097-05-59.641W				SG on pile.	
28245	- LIGHT 10 90 feet outside channel limit.	27-52-56.609N 097-05-57.083W	Fl R 4s	17	3	TR on pile.	
28250	- Day beacon 11	27-53-08.522N 097-06-14.015W				SG on pile.	
28255	- Day beacon 13 60 feet outside channel limit.	27-53-24.179N 097-06-31.694W				SG on pile.	
28260	- LIGHT 14 75 feet outside channel limit.	27-53-32.080N 097-06-36.346W	Q R	17	4	TR on dolphin.	
28265	- Day beacon 15	27-53-31.567N 097-06-45.683W				SG on pile.	
28270	- Day beacon 17	27-53-34.815N 097-06-57.300W				SG on pile.	
28275	- Day beacon 18 75 feet outside channel limit.	27-53-38.779N 097-07-03.297W				TR on pile.	
28280	- LIGHT 20 60 feet outside channel limit.	27-53-44.971N 097-07-29.852W	Fl R 2.5s	17	4	TR on dolphin.	
28285	- Day beacon 22	27-53-51.527N 097-07-57.077W				TR on pile.	

Light List corrected through LNM week: 01/18

(1) No.	(2) Name and Location	(3) Position	(4) Characteristic	(5) Height	(6) Range	(7) Structure	(8) Remarks
	TEXAS - Eighth District

CORPUS CHRISTI BAY (Chart 11309)

Aransas Channel

28290 39225	- LIGHT 23 50 feet outside channel limit.	27-53-51.523N 097-08-06.438W	Fl G 4s	17	4	SG-TY on pile.	
28295	- Day beacon 24	27-53-55.316N 097-08-07.742W				TR on pile.	

Corpus Christi Channel

28305	CORPUS CHRISTI CUT A EAST RANGE FRONT LIGHT	27-50-41.815N 097-03-13.687W	Q W	38		KRW on skeleton tower on piles.	
28310	CORPUS CHRISTI CUT A EAST RANGE REAR LIGHT 989 yards, 078.3° from front light.	27-50-47.194N 097-02-44.645W	Iso W 6s	93		KRW on skeleton tower on concrete block.	
28315	Port Aransas Harbor Day beacon 2	27-50-29.773N 097-03-45.220W				TR on pile.	
28320	PORT ARANSAS HARBOR LIGHT 3	27-50-30.093N 097-03-42.605W	Q G	17	3	SG on dolphin.	
28325	Port Aransas Harbor Day beacon 4	27-50-27.514N 097-03-39.257W				TR on pile.	
28330	Port Aransas Rock Groin Danger Day beacon	27-50-33.050N 097-05-00.220W				NW on pile worded: DANGER ROCK GROIN.	Private aid.
28335	PORT ARANSAS ROCK GROIN DANGER LIGHT	27-50-32.290N 097-05-00.640W	Fl W 2.5s			On pile.	Private aid.
28340	Port Aransas Rock Groin Danger Day beacon	27-50-33.060N 097-05-00.990W				NW on pile worded: DANGER ROCK GROIN.	Private aid.
28345	- LIGHT 1	27-50-18.504N 097-04-55.557W	Fl G 2.5s	17	3	SG on pile.	Ra ref.
28350	- LIGHT 7 150 feet outside channel limit.	27-50-04.012N 097-06-13.069W	Fl G 4s	17	4	SG on pile.	Ra ref.
28355	- LIGHT 8 150 feet outside channel limit.	27-50-12.662N 097-06-16.351W	Fl R 4s	17	3	TR on pile.	Ra ref.

Mustang Beach Channel

28360	- Entrance Day beacon 1	27-50-03.000N 097-06-24.000W				SG on piles.	Private aid.
28365	- EAST JETTY DANGER LIGHT	27-50-00.488N 097-06-21.587W	Fl W 2.5s	10		On pile.	Private aid.
28370	- East Jetty Danger Day beacon	27-49-57.555N 097-06-19.650W				NW on pile worded: DANGER JETTY.	Private aid.
28375	- East Jetty Danger Day beacon	27-49-59.201N 097-06-20.874W				NW on pile worded: DANGER JETTY.	Private aid.
28380	- Day beacon 1A	27-50-01.000N 097-06-23.000W				SG on piles.	Private aid.
28385	- Entrance Day beacon 2	27-50-02.000N 097-06-28.000W				TR on piles.	Private aid.
28390	- WEST JETTY DANGER LIGHT	27-50-00.120N 097-06-23.555W	Fl W 2.5s	10		On pile.	Private aid.
28395	- West Jetty Danger Day beacon	27-49-56.346N 097-06-24.123W				NW on pile worded: DANGER JETTY.	Private aid.
28400	- West Jetty Danger Day beacon	27-49-58.519N 097-06-23.704W				NW on pile worded: DANGER JETTY.	Private aid.
28405	- Day beacon 2A	27-50-00.000N 097-06-27.000W				TR on pile.	Private aid.
28410	- LIGHT 3	27-49-57.000N 097-06-22.000W	Fl G 4s	8		SG on pile.	Private aid.
28415	- Day beacon 3A	27-49-54.000N 097-06-22.000W				SG on pile.	Private aid.
28420	- LIGHT 4	27-49-57.000N 097-06-25.000W	Fl R 4s	8		TR on pile.	Private aid.
28425	- Day beacon 4A	27-49-54.000N 097-06-24.000W				TR on pile.	Private aid.
28430	- Day beacon 5	27-49-50.000N 097-06-22.000W				SG on pile.	Private aid.

Light List corrected through LNM week: 01/18

(1) No.	(2) Name and Location	(3) Position	(4) Characteristic	(5) Height	(6) Range	(7) Structure	(8) Remarks
	TEXAS - Eighth District						
	CORPUS CHRISTI BAY (Chart 11309) **Corpus Christi Channel** **Mustang Beach Channel**						
28435	- Day beacon 6	27-49-46.000N 097-06-22.000W				TR on pile.	Private aid.
28440	- Day beacon 7	27-49-45.000N 097-06-20.000W				SG on pile.	Private aid.
28445	- Day beacon 8	27-49-42.000N 097-06-21.000W				TR on pile.	Private aid.
28450	- Day beacon 9	27-49-38.000N 097-06-19.000W				SG on pile.	Private aid.
28455	- Day beacon 10	27-49-36.000N 097-06-19.000W				TR on pile.	Private aid.
28460	- Day beacon 11	27-49-33.000N 097-06-17.000W				TR on pile.	Private aid.
28465	- Day beacon 12	27-49-30.000N 097-06-18.000W				TR on pile.	Private aid.
28470	- Day beacon 13	27-49-28.000N 097-06-15.000W				SG on pile.	Private aid.
28475	- Day beacon 14	27-49-25.000N 097-06-16.000W				TR on pile.	Private aid.
28480	- Day beacon 16	27-49-19.000N 097-06-15.000W				TR on pile.	Private aid.
28485	- Day beacon 17	27-49-17.000N 097-06-13.000W				SG on pile.	Private aid.
28490	- Day beacon 18	27-49-15.000N 097-06-14.000W				TR on pile.	Private aid.
28495	- Day beacon 19	27-49-09.000N 097-06-11.000W				SG on pile.	Private aid.
28500	- Day beacon 20	27-49-03.000N 097-06-11.000W				TR on pile.	Private aid.
28505	- Day beacon 21	27-49-02.000N 097-06-10.000W				SG on pile.	Private aid.
28510	- LIGHT 22	27-49-01.000N 097-06-11.000W	Fl R 4s	8		TR on pile.	Private aid.
28515	- Day beacon 23	27-49-03.000N 097-06-10.000W				SG on pile.	Private aid.
28520	- Day beacon 23A	27-48-01.000N 097-06-08.000W				SG on pile.	Private aid.
28525	- Day beacon 24	27-48-58.000N 097-06-07.000W				TR on pile.	Private aid.
28530	- Day beacon 25	27-49-00.000N 097-06-07.000W				SG on pile.	Private aid.
28535	- Day beacon 26	27-48-56.000N 097-06-05.000W				TR on pile.	Private aid.
28540	- Day beacon 27	27-48-58.000N 097-06-02.000W				SG on pile.	Private aid.
28545	- Day beacon 28	27-48-52.000N 097-05-57.000W				TR on pile.	Private aid.
28550	- Day beacon 29	27-48-52.000N 097-05-55.000W				SG on pile.	Private aid.
28555	- Day beacon 30	27-48-49.000N 097-05-52.000W				TR on pile.	Private aid.
28560	- Day beacon 31	27-48-48.000N 097-05-49.000W				SG on pile.	Private aid.
28565	- Day beacon 32	27-48-45.000N 097-05-45.000W				TR on pile.	Private aid.
28570	- Day beacon 33	27-48-45.000N 097-05-43.000W				SG on pile.	Private aid.
28575	- Day beacon 34	27-48-04.000N 097-05-41.500W				TR on pile.	Private aid.
28580	- Day beacon 35	27-48-41.000N 097-05-37.000W				SG on pile.	Private aid.
28585	- Day beacon 36	27-48-40.000N 097-05-37.500W				TR on pile.	Private aid.
28590	- Day beacon 37	27-48-36.000N 097-05-34.000W				SG on pile.	Private aid.

Light List corrected through LNM week: 01/18

(1) No.	(2) Name and Location	(3) Position	(4) Characteristic	(5) Height	(6) Range	(7) Structure	(8) Remarks
	TEXAS - Eighth District						
	CORPUS CHRISTI BAY (Chart 11309)						
	Corpus Christi Channel						
	Mustang Beach Channel						
28595	- Day beacon 38	27-48-37.000N 097-05-32.000W				TR on pile.	Private aid.
	Corpus Christi Channel						
28600	- LIGHT 13 150 feet outside channel limit.	27-49-48.152N 097-07-35.807W	Fl G 6s	17	4	SG on pile.	Ra ref.
28605	- LIGHT 14 150 feet outside channel limit.	27-49-57.499N 097-07-38.078W	Fl R 6s	17	4	TR on dolphin.	Ra ref.
28607	RANSOM POINT DANGER BREAKWATER LIGHTS (5)	27-50-47.236N 097-08-20.843W	Fl W 2.5s			Marks breakwater structure.	Private aid.
28610	- LIGHT 19 150 feet outside channel limit.	27-49-35.183N 097-08-49.451W	Fl G 6s	17	4	SG on pile.	Ra ref.
28615	- LIGHT 20 150 feet outside channel limit.	27-49-43.325N 097-08-52.538W	Fl (2)R 5s	17	3	TR on pile.	Ra ref.
28620	CORPUS CHRISTI CUT A WEST RANGE FRONT LIGHT	27-48-30.183N 097-15-00.750W	Q G	24		KRW on skeleton tower on piles.	
28625	CORPUS CHRISTI CUT A WEST RANGE REAR LIGHT 1,984 yards, 258.2° from front light.	27-48-18.080N 097-16-05.610W	Iso G 6s	65		KRW on skeleton tower on piles.	Visible 1.5° each side of rangeline. Range is not effective seaward or Corpus Christi Channel Lights 19 and 20.
28630	- LIGHT 25 150 feet outside channel limit.	27-49-19.982N 097-10-11.426W	Fl G 4s	17	4	SG on pile.	Ra ref.
28635	- LIGHT 26 150 feet outside channel limit.	27-49-29.119N 097-10-15.256W	Fl R 4s	17	3	TR on pile.	Ra ref.
28640	- PIPELINE LIGHT A	27-49-19.000N 097-10-13.000W	Fl G 4s	20		Pile structure.	Private aid.
28645	- PIPELINE LIGHT B	27-49-28.000N 097-10-14.000W	Q R	20		Pile structure.	Private aid.
28650	- LIGHT 31 150 feet outside channel limit.	27-49-08.092N 097-11-16.541W	Fl G 2.5s	17	3	SG on pile.	Ra ref.
28655	- LIGHT 32	27-49-17.498N 097-11-15.658W	Fl R 2.5s	17	3	TR on pile.	Ra ref.
28660	- LIGHT 33 240 feet outside channel limit.	27-48-56.600N 097-12-13.500W	Fl G 2.5s	17	3		Ra ref.
28665	SUNOCO TERMINALS DOCK LIGHTS (2)	27-49-09.000N 097-11-57.000W	Fl R 2.5s	18		On dolphins.	Private aid.
28667	OXY INGLESIDE DOLPHIN LIGHTS (2)	27-49-03.530N 097-12-33.400W	Fl W 2.5s			Marks turning dolphin structure.	Private aid.
28668	Oxy Ingleside Facility Channel Front Range Day board	27-49-18.680N 097-12-29.400W				KRW marks private channel range.	Private aid.
28668.01	Oxy Ingleside Facility Channel Rear Range Day board	27-49-19.530N 097-12-29.350W				KRW marks private channel range.	Private aid.
28675	- LIGHT 36	27-49-00.751N 097-12-46.680W	Fl R 4s	17	3	TR on pile.	Ra ref.
28680	- LIGHT 37 150 feet outside channel limit.	27-48-46.691N 097-13-11.180W	Fl G 2.5s	17	3	SG on pile.	Ra ref.
28685	- LIGHT 38 100 feet outside channel limit.	27-48-54.491N 097-13-15.862W	Fl R 4s	17	3	TR on pile.	Ra ref.
28690	- LIGHT 43 200 feet outside channel limit.	27-48-35.032N 097-14-14.315W	Q G	17	3	SG on dolphin.	Ra ref.
28695	- LIGHT 44 200 feet outside channel.	27-48-43.106N 097-14-15.531W	Q R	17	3	TR on dolphin.	Ra ref.

Light List corrected through LNM week: 01/18

(1) No.	(2) Name and Location	(3) Position	(4) Characteristic	(5) Height	(6) Range	(7) Structure	(8) Remarks
			TEXAS - Eighth District				
	CORPUS CHRISTI BAY (Chart 11309)						
	Corpus Christi Channel						
28700	CORPUS CHRISTI CUT B EAST RANGE FRONT LIGHT	27-48-38.785N 097-13-41.116W	Fl W 2.5s (NIGHT) Fl W 2.5s (DAY)	37 40		Platform on pile.	Visible all around; higher intensity 4° each side of rangeline.
28705	CORPUS CHRISTI CUT B EAST RANGE FRONT LIGHT PASSING LIGHT	27-48-38.785N 097-13-41.116W	Q W	43	3	On same structure as Corpus Christi Channel Cut B East Range Front Light.	
28710	CORPUS CHRISTI CUT B EAST RANGE REAR LIGHT 5,049 yards, 089.8° from front light.	27-48-39.375N 097-10-52.319W	Iso W 6s (NIGHT) Iso W 6s (DAY)	128 125		Skeleton tower on piles.	Visible 2° each side of rangeline.
28715	CORPUS CHRISTI CUT B EAST RANGE REAR LIGHT PASSING LIGHT	27-48-39.375N 097-10-53.319W	Q Y	36	3	On same structure as Corpus Christi Channel Cut B East Range Rear Light.	
28720	- LIGHT 49 200 feet outside channel limit.	27-48-34.362N 097-15-31.081W	Fl G 2.5s	17	3	SG on dolphin.	Ra ref.
28725	- LIGHT 50 200 feet outside channel limit.	27-48-42.636N 097-15-31.130W	Fl R 2.5s	17	3	TR on dolphin.	Ra ref.
28730	- LIGHT 55 150 feet outside channel limit.	27-48-34.078N 097-16-47.102W	Fl G 4s	17	4	SG on dolphin.	Ra ref.
28735	- LIGHT 56	27-48-42.048N 097-16-47.209W	Fl R 4s	17	3	TR on dolphin.	Ra ref.
28740	Corpus Christi P/L Cross Buoy B	27-48-31.000N 097-16-54.000W				Yellow.	Private aid.
28745	Corpus Christi Pipeline Crossing Buoy A	27-48-42.000N 097-16-54.000W				Yellow.	Private aid.
28747	CORPUS CHRISTI BAY ALTERNATE ROUTE LEADING LIGHT	27-48-46.320N 097-17-26.710W	Fl W 2.5s	17	4		
28747.1	Corpus Christi Bay Alternate Route Daybeacon 7	27-47-09.822N 097-16-28.067W				SG on pile.	Ra ref.
28747.2	CORPUS CHRISTI BAY ALTERNATE ROUTE LIGHT 6	27-46-32.420N 097-15-25.857W	Fl R 4s	17	3	TR on pile.	Ra ref.
28747.3	Corpus Christi Bay Alternate Route Daybeacon 5	27-44-51.801N 097-14-44.077W				SG on pile.	Ra ref.
28747.4	CORPUS CHRISTI BAY ALTERNATE ROUTE LIGHT 4	27-44-37.003N 097-14-04.402W	Fl R 2.5s	17	3	TR on pile.	Ra ref.
28747.5	Corpus Christi Bay Alternate Route Daybeacon 3	27-43-48.284N 097-13-59.341W				SG on pile.	Ra ref.
28750	- LIGHT 61 150 feet outside channel limit.	27-48-33.795N 097-18-04.337W	Fl G 6s	17	4	SG on dolphin.	Ra ref.
28755	- LIGHT 62 200 feet outside channel limit.	27-48-41.701N 097-18-04.406W	Fl R 6s	17	4	TR on dolphin.	Ra ref.
28760	- LIGHT 67 200 feet outside channel limit.	27-48-33.432N 097-19-18.893W	Fl G 6s	17	4	SG on dolphin.	Ra ref.
28765	- LIGHT 68 200 feet outside channel limit.	27-48-41.394N 097-19-18.923W	Fl (2)R 5s	17	3	TR on dolphin.	Ra ref.
	CORPUS CHRISTI HARBOR (Chart 11311)						
	Corpus Christi Channel						
28770	CORPUS CHRISTI CUT B WEST RANGE FRONT LIGHT	27-48-37.009N 097-23-33.887W	Oc G 4s	55		KRW on building located south side of harbor entrance.	Visible 5° each side of rangeline.

Light List corrected through LNM week: 01/18

(1) No.	(2) Name and Location	(3) Position	(4) Characteristic	(5) Height	(6) Range	(7) Structure	(8) Remarks
	TEXAS - Eighth District						
	CORPUS CHRISTI HARBOR (Chart 11311)						
	Corpus Christi Channel						
28775	CORPUS CHRISTI CUT B WEST RANGE REAR LIGHT 2,600 yards, 269.7° from front light.	27-48-36.580N 097-25-00.684W	F G	101		KRW on skeleton tower, located south side of harbor entrance.	Visible 5° each side of rangeline.
28780	- LIGHT 73 200 feet outside channel limit.	27-48-33.099N 097-20-39.760W	Fl G 4s	17	4	SG on dolphin.	Ra ref.
28785	- LIGHT 74 150 feet outside channel limit.	27-48-41.060N 097-20-39.911W	Fl R 4s	17	3	TR on dolphin.	Ra ref.
28790	- LIGHT 79	27-48-32.778N 097-21-56.761W	Fl G 2.5s	17	3	SG on dolphin.	Ra ref.
28795	- LIGHT 80 150 feet outside channel limit.	27-48-40.672N 097-21-56.833W	Fl R 2.5s	17	3	TR on dolphin.	Ra ref.
28800	- LIGHT 82 200 feet outside channel limit.	27-48-40.438N 097-22-51.663W	Q R	17	3	TR on dolphin.	Ra ref.
28805	- LIGHT 85	27-48-35.140N 097-23-17.431W	Fl G 2.5s	17	3	SG on dolphin.	Ra ref.
28810	- LIGHT 86	27-48-45.420N 097-23-18.140W	Fl R 4s	30	3	TR on dolphin.	
28815	CORPUS CHRISTI HARBOR OUTER RANGE FRONT LIGHT	27-48-27.992N 097-22-03.261W	Q G	25		KRW on skeleton tower on piles.	Visible 2° each side of rangeline.
28820	CORPUS CHRISTI HARBOR OUTER RANGE REAR LIGHT 330 yards, 101.2° from front light.	27-48-26.098N 097-21-52.455W	Iso G 6s	42		KRW on skeleton tower on piles.	Visible 2° each side of rangeline.
	CORPUS CHRISTI BAY (Chart 11309)						
	Corpus Christi Channel						
28822	FLINT HILLS RESOURCES DANGER LIGHT	27-48-52.140N 097-25-09.180W	Fl W 2.5s			Marks outfall pipe.	Private aid.
	CORPUS CHRISTI HARBOR (Chart 11311)						
	Corpus Christi Channel						
28825	INDUSTRIAL CANAL RANGE FRONT LIGHT	27-49-14.418N 097-25-58.124W	Q G	47		KRW on skeleton tower on piles.	Visible 2° each side of rangeline.
28830	INDUSTRIAL CANAL RANGE REAR LIGHT 248 yards, 293.5° from front light.	27-49-17.444N 097-26-05.842W	F G	65		KRW on skeleton tower on mud sills.	Visible 2° each side of rangeline.
	Tule Lake Channel						
28835	- A RANGE FRONT LIGHT	27-49-29.729N 097-26-15.164W	Oc G 4s	45		On skeleton tower on piles.	Lighted throughout 24 hours.
28840	- A RANGE REAR LIGHT 616 yards, 066.8° from front light.	27-49-37.007N 097-25-56.274W	F G	63		KRW on skeleton tower on mud sills.	Lighted throughout 24 hours.
28850	- B RANGE FRONT LIGHT	27-49-13.316N 097-28-56.796W	Q G	55		KRW on skeleton tower on piles.	Visible all around; higher intensity on rangeline.
28855	- B RANGE REAR LIGHT 651 yards, 282.8° from front light.	27-49-17.605N 097-29-17.993W	Iso G 6s	75		KRW on skeleton tower on mud sills.	Visible all around; higher intensity on rangeline.
28860	- C RANGE FRONT LIGHT	27-48-52.553N 097-27-14.383W	Q G	35		KRW on skeleton tower.	Lighted throughout 24 hours.
28865	- C RANGE REAR LIGHT 175 yards, 102.2° from front light.	27-48-51.411N 097-27-08.678W	Iso G 6s	45		KRW on skeleton tower on mud sills.	Lighted throughout 24 hours.

Light List corrected through LNM week: 01/18

(1) No.	(2) Name and Location	(3) Position	(4) Characteristic	(5) Height	(6) Range	(7) Structure	(8) Remarks
	TEXAS - Eighth District						
	CORPUS CHRISTI HARBOR (Chart 11311)						
	Corpus Christi Channel						
	Tule Lake Channel						
28870	- DIRECTIONAL LIGHT D	27-49-42.982N 097-29-50.738W	F W	40	G W R	On skeleton tower.	Shows Fl G from 298.6° to 298.0°; F G from 298.0° to 297.5°; Alternating GW from 297.5° to 296.9°; F W (on channel line) from 296.9° to 296.5°; Alternating RW from 296.5° to 295.9°; F R from 295.9° to 295.5°; Fl R from 295.5° to 294.9°.
28875	- E RANGE FRONT LIGHT	27-49-01.908N 097-28-18.885W	Q G	26		KRW on skeleton tower.	Lighted throughuot 24 hours.
28880	- E RANGE REAR LIGHT 206 yards, 116.7° from front light.	27-48-59.162N 097-28-12.739W	Iso G 6s	37		KRW on skeleton tower on mud sills.	Lighted throughout 24 hours.
28885	- F RANGE FRONT LIGHT	27-49-05.737N 097-28-41.824W	Q G	55		KRW on skeleton tower on piles.	Visible all around; higher intensity on rangeline.
28890	- F RANGE REAR LIGHT 646 yards, 127.3° from front light.	27-48-54.090N 097-28-24.658W	Iso G 6s	80		KRW on skeleton tower on mud sills.	Visible all around; higher intensity on rangeline.
	Viola Channel						
28895	- G RANGE FRONT LIGHT	27-50-35.821N 097-30-54.534W	Iso G 2s	20		KRW on skeleton tower on sills.	Visible all around; higher intensity on rangeline.
28900	- G RANGE REAR LIGHT	27-50-43.972N 097-31-06.533W	Iso G 6s	41		KRW on skeleton tower.	Visible all around; higher intensity on rangeline.
28910	- H RANGE FRONT LIGHT	27-50-39.331N 097-31-31.380W	Q G	30		KRW on skeleton tower.	Lighted throughout 24 hours.
28915	- H RANGE REAR LIGHT 525 yards, 283.1° from front light.	27-50-42.992N 097-31-48.443W	Iso G 6s	41		KRW on skeleton tower on mud sills.	Lighted throughout 24 hours.
	CORPUS CHRISTI BAY (Chart 11309)						
	La Quinta Channel						
28920	- LIGHT 1	27-48-59.298N 097-13-13.438W	Fl G 4s	17	4	SG on pile.	
28925	- LIGHT 2	27-49-06.660N 097-13-06.928W	Fl R 4s	17	3	TR on pile.	Ra ref.
28930	- LIGHT 3	27-49-09.419N 097-13-27.170W	Fl G 2.5s	17	3	SG on pile.	
28935	- ENTRANCE RANGE FRONT LIGHT	27-49-14.915N 097-13-41.075W	Q W	17		KRW on piles.	Ra ref.
28940	- ENTRANCE RANGE REAR LIGHT 492 yards, 295.0° from front light.	27-49-21.062N 097-13-55.956W	Iso W 6s	24		KRW on piles.	Ra ref.
28945	- LIGHT 4	27-49-12.649N 097-13-19.200W	Fl R 2.5s	17	3	TR on pile.	
28950	- LIGHT 6	27-49-29.806N 097-13-29.744W	Fl R 4s	17	3	TR on pile.	
28955	- LIGHT 5	27-49-27.838N 097-13-35.807W	Fl G 4s	17	4	SG on pile.	Ra ref.
28960	- OUTER RANGE FRONT LIGHT	27-48-44.510N 097-13-11.467W	Q W	20		KRW on skeleton tower on piles.	Visible 2° each side of rangeline.
28965	- OUTER RANGE REAR LIGHT 888 yards, 156.2° from front light.	27-48-20.270N 097-12-59.816W	Iso W 6s	55		KRW on skeleton tower on pile.	Visible 2° each side of rangeline.
28970	- INNER RANGE FRONT LIGHT	27-52-31.866N 097-15-00.983W	Q G	26		KRW on skeleton tower on piles.	

Light List corrected through LNM week: 01/18

(1) No.	(2) Name and Location	(3) Position	(4) Characteristic	(5) Height	(6) Range	(7) Structure	(8) Remarks
\multicolumn{8}{c}{**TEXAS - Eighth District**}							
	CORPUS CHRISTI BAY (Chart 11309)						
	La Quinta Channel						
28975	- INNER RANGE REAR LIGHT 2,136 yards, 336.8° from front light.	27-53-30.190N 097-15-29.107W	Iso G 6s	64		KRW on skeleton tower on piles.	
28980	- LIGHT 7	27-49-58.336N 097-13-50.207W	Fl G 2.5s	17	3	SG on pile.	Ra ref.
28985	- LIGHT 8	27-50-02.657N 097-13-45.747W	Fl R 2.5s	17	3	TR on pile.	
29000	- LIGHT 10	27-50-24.688N 097-13-55.935W	Fl R 4s	17	3	TR on pile.	
29005	Jewel Fulton Channel Day beacon 1	27-50-34.494N 097-13-53.559W				SG on pile.	Ra ref.
29010	Jewel Fulton Channel Day beacon 3 50 feet outside channel limit.	27-50-40.860N 097-13-43.970W				SG on pile.	Ra ref.
29015	Jewel Fulton Channel Day beacon 4 60 feet outside channel limit.	27-50-38.627N 097-13-42.126W				TR on pile.	
	Peterson Builders Turning Basin Channel						
29020	- Day beacon 1	27-50-56.000N 097-13-18.000W				SG on pile.	Private aid.
29025	- Day beacon 2	27-50-56.000N 097-13-18.000W				TR on pile.	Private aid.
29030	- Day beacon 3	27-51-01.000N 097-13-16.000W				SG on pile.	Private aid.
29035	- Day beacon 4	27-50-57.000N 097-13-18.000W				TR on pile.	Private aid.
29040	- Front Range	27-50-56.000N 097-13-17.000W				KRW on pile.	Private aid.
29045	- Rear Range 160 yards, 054° from front light.	27-50-59.000N 097-13-13.000W				KRW on pile.	Private aid.
	La Quinta Channel						
29050	- LIGHT 11 100 feet outside the channel limit.	27-50-54.533N 097-14-17.893W	Fl G 6s	17	4	SG on dolphin.	
29055	- LIGHT 12 100 feet outside the channel limit.	27-50-57.210N 097-14-11.493W	Fl R 4s	17	3	TR on pile.	
29060	- Day beacon 13	27-51-32.727N 097-14-35.889W				SG on pile.	
29065	- LIGHT 14 170 feet outside the channel limit.	27-51-35.228N 097-14-30.145W	Fl R 4s	17	3	TR on pile.	
29070	DUPONT MOORING FACILITY LIGHTS (6)	27-52-11.000N 097-14-44.000W	Fl R 2.5s	19		On mooring facilities.	Private aid.
29075	- LIGHT 15 100 feet outside the channel limit.	27-52-07.403N 097-14-53.464W	Fl G 2.5s	17	3	SG on pile.	Ra ref.
29080	- LIGHT 17	27-52-24.338N 097-15-08.005W	Fl G 2.5s	17	3	SG on pile.	Ra ref.
29085	- LIGHT 18	27-52-33.064N 097-15-12.234W	Fl R 4s	17	3	TR on dolphin.	
29090	- LIGHT 19	27-52-29.155N 097-15-29.001W	Fl G 4s	17	4	SG on pile.	Ra ref.
29095	- LIGHT 20	27-52-36.615N 097-15-27.944W	Fl R 2.5s	17	3	TR on pile.	
29100	- LIGHT A	27-52-26.241N 097-15-51.822W	Fl W 4s	17	4	NG on pile.	
29101	- LIGHT 21	27-52-38.406N 097-16-08.401W	Fl G 2.5s	17	3	SG on pile.	Ra ref.
29101.03	- LIGHT 23	27-52-41.834N 097-16-26.252W	Q G	17	3	SG on pile.	Ra ref.

Light List corrected through LNM week: 01/18

(1) No.	(2) Name and Location	(3) Position	(4) Characteristic	(5) Height	(6) Range	(7) Structure	(8) Remarks
			TEXAS - Eighth District				
	CORPUS CHRISTI BAY (Chart 11309)						
	La Quinta Channel						
29101.06	- LIGHT 24	27-52-45.570N 097-16-50.106W	Fl R 4s	17	5	TR on pile.	Ra ref.
29101.09	- LIGHT 25	27-52-39.343N 097-16-48.502W	Fl G 6s	17	3	SG on pile.	Ra ref.
29101.12	- LIGHT 26	27-52-43.028N 097-17-05.339W	Fl R 4s	17	5	TR on pile.	Ra ref.
29101.15	- LIGHT 27	27-52-29.193N 097-16-54.970W	Fl G 4s	17	3	SG on pile.	Ra ref.
29101.18	- LIGHT 28	27-52-39.443N 097-17-13.264W	Fl R 2.5s	17	3	TR on pile.	Ra ref.
29101.21	- LIGHT 29	27-52-26.636N 097-17-10.935W	Fl G 2.5s	17	3	SG on pile.	Ra ref.
29101.24	PORT OF CORPUS CHRISTI LA QUINTA CHANNEL EXTENSION RANGE FRONT LIGHT	27-52-53.100N 097-17-05.430W	Q G			Marks front range.	Private aid.
29101.27	PORT OF CORPUS CHRISTI LA QUINTA CHANNEL EXTENSION RANGE REAR LIGHT	27-52-56.740N 097-17-23.120W	Fl G 6s			Marks rear range.	Private aid.
29102	- EXTENSION B RANGE FRONT LIGHT	27-52-35.237N 097-17-33.462W	Q W Q W	25 28		Skeleton tower on piles.	Visible 4° each side of rangeline. Lighted throughout 24 hours. Additional light visible all around.
29103	- EXTENSION B RANGE REAR LIGHT 233.393 yards, 258.3° from front light.	27-52-33.894N 097-17-41.116W	Iso W 6s (NIGHT) Iso W 6s (DAY)	50		Skeleton tower on piles.	Visible 4° each side of rangeline. Lighted throughout 24 hours.
29104	- EXTENSION B RANGE REAR LIGHT PASSING LIGHT	27-52-33.894N 097-17-41.116W	Fl W 4s	16	3	On same structure as La Quinta Channel Extension B Range Rear Light.	
	Rincon Industrial Park Channel						
	Rincon Canal						
29105	- Range Front Day beacon	27-50-34.751N 097-22-47.653W				KWR on dolphin.	Private aid.
29110	- Range Rear Day beacon 600 yards, 320° from front day beacon.	27-50-48.075N 097-22-59.080W				KWR on dolphin.	Private aid.
29115	- Day beacon 2 75 feet outside channel limit.	27-48-57.200N 097-21-16.400W				TR on pile.	Ra ref.
29120	- Day beacon 4	27-49-20.300N 097-21-37.500W				TR on pile.	Ra ref.
29125	- LIGHT 6	27-49-43.200N 097-21-58.500W	Fl R 4s	17	3	TR on pile.	Ra ref.
29130	- Day beacon 8 75 feet outside channel limits.	27-50-06.100N 097-22-19.600W				TR on pile.	Ra ref.
29135	- Day beacon 9	27-50-17.147N 097-22-32.545W				SG on pile.	Ra ref.
29140	- Day beacon 10	27-50-18.071N 097-22-31.253W				TR on pile.	Ra ref.
29142	COASTAL BENDS BAYS & ESTUARIES DANGER BREAKWATER LIGHT	27-51-04.065N 097-21-12.605W	Fl W 2.5s			Marks breakwater structure.	Private aid.
29145	- Buoy 11	27-50-27.636N 097-22-42.042W				Green can.	
29150	- Buoy 12	27-50-31.170N 097-22-46.338W				Red nun.	
29155	- Buoy 13	27-50-29.148N 097-22-51.114W				Green can.	

Light List corrected through LNM week: 01/18

TEXAS - Eighth District

(1) No.	(2) Name and Location	(3) Position	(4) Characteristic	(5) Height	(6) Range	(7) Structure	(8) Remarks
	CORPUS CHRISTI BAY (Chart 11309)						
	Rincon Industrial Park Channel						
	Rincon Canal						
29160	- Buoy 14	27-50-30.594N 097-22-54.144W				Red nun.	
	Corpus Christi Bay						
29165	- PIPELINE LIGHT A	27-49-56.000N 097-09-55.000W	Q R	9		On dolphin.	Private aid.
29170	- PIPELINE LIGHT B	27-48-37.000N 097-10-34.000W	Q R	9		On dolphin.	Private aid.
29175	- SPOIL BANK LIGHT	27-44-01.512N 097-16-32.842W	Fl W 4s	17	5	NW on pile worded DANGER SPOIL AREA.	Ra ref.
	University Beach						
29180	- Danger Day beacon A	27-42-51.660N 097-19-10.680W				NW on pile.	Private aid.
29185	- Danger Day beacon B	27-42-53.965N 097-19-09.947W				NW on pile worded DANGER ROCK GROIN.	Private aid.
29190	- Danger Day beacon C	27-42-55.409N 097-19-10.170W				NW on pile.	Private aid.
29195	- Danger Day beacon E	27-42-56.430N 097-19-12.077W				NW on pile.	Private aid.
29200	- Danger Day beacon D	27-42-54.980N 097-19-12.070W				NW on pile.	Private aid.
29205	- LIGHT	27-42-57.710N 097-19-14.635W	Fl G 2.5s			SG on plle.	Private aid.
29210	- Danger Day beacon G	27-42-58.843N 097-19-18.203W				NW on pile worded DANGER BREAKWATER.	Private aid.
29215	- Danger Day beacon F	27-42-56.620N 097-19-20.160W				NW on pile.	Private aid.
29220	- Danger Day beacon I	27-42-59.213N 097-19-19.819W				NW on pile worded DANGER ROCK GROIN.	Private aid.
29225	- Danger Day beacon H	27-42-57.660N 097-19-20.150W				NW on pile.	Private aid.
29230	- Danger Day beacon J	27-42-58.588N 097-19-21.666W				NW on pile worded DANGER ROCK GROIN.	Private aid.
29235	- Danger Day beacon K	27-42-56.110N 097-19-23.800W				NW on pile.	Private aid.
	Corpus Christi Bay						
29240	ALTA VISTA REEF LIGHT	27-45-56.128N 097-21-10.790W	Fl W 2.5s	17	5	NR on pile.	Ra ref.
29245	CORPUS CHRISTI LIGHT	27-47-24.700N 097-22-41.600W	Fl W 4s	17	6	NR on pile.	
29250	CORPUS CHRISTI BREAKWATER LIGHT 1	27-47-59.273N 097-23-09.523W	Fl G 2.5s	17	3	SG on pile.	
29255	Corpus Christi Breakwater Buoy WR1A	27-47-59.286N 097-23-10.563W				Green can.	
29260	CORPUS CHRISTI BREAKWATER LIGHT 2	27-48-01.015N 097-23-11.268W	Fl R 2.5s	17	3	TR on pile.	
29265	Corpus Christi Breakwater Buoy 3	27-47-58.884N 097-23-11.115W				Green can.	
	LAGUNA MADRE (Chart 11306)						
	Port Mansfield Channel						
29270	PORT MANSFIELD ENTRANCE LIGHT 2	26-33-54.540N 097-16-13.260W	Fl R 2.5s	25	5	TR on pile.	
29275	PORT MANSFIELD ENTRANCE LIGHT 3	26-33-44.880N 097-16-07.140W	Fl G 2.5s	25	5	SG on pile.	

(1) No.	(2) Name and Location	(3) Position	(4) Characteristic	(5) Height	(6) Range	(7) Structure	(8) Remarks

TEXAS - Eighth District

LAGUNA MADRE (Chart 11306)
Port Mansfield Channel

(1) No.	(2) Name and Location	(3) Position	(4) Characteristic	(5) Height	(6) Range	(7) Structure	(8) Remarks
29280	Port Mansfield Entrance North Side Dredging Range Front Day beacon	26-33-48.000N 097-17-06.000W				Black square day mark with orange stripe on pile.	Range marks edge of channel for dredging purposes. F G light will be exhibited during dredgng operations. Maintained by U.S. Army Corps of Engineers. Aid maintained by U.S. Army Corps of Engineers.
29285	Port Mansfield Entrance North Side Dredging Range Rear Day beacon 665 yards, 267° from front day beacon.					Black square day mark with orange stripe on pile.	F G light will be exhibited during dredging operations. Maintained by U.S. Army Corps of Engineers. Aid maintained by U.S. Army Corps of Engineers.
29290	Port Mansfield Entrance South Side Dredging Range Front Day beacon	26-33-48.000N 097-17-06.000W				Black square day mark with orange stripe on pile.	Range marks edge of channel for dredging purposes. F G light will be exhibited during dredging operations. Maintained by U.S. Army Corps of Engineers. Aid maintained by U.S. Army Corps of Engineers.
29295	Port Mansfield Entrance South Side Dredging Range Rear Day beacon 665 yards, 267° from front day beacon.					Black square day mark with vertical stripe on concrete pile.	F G light will be exhibited during dredging operations. Maintained by U.S. Army Corps of Engineers. Aid maintained by U.S. Army Corps of Engineers.
29300	- LIGHT 5 30 feet outside channel limit.	26-33-47.877N 097-16-37.205W	Fl G 4s	17	4	SG on pile.	
29305	- LIGHT 4 30 feet outside channel limit.	26-33-51.235N 097-16-35.343W	Fl R 4s	17	3	TR on pile.	
29310	- LIGHT 7 30 feet outside channel limit.	26-33-46.219N 097-17-28.370W	Fl G 6s	17	4	SG on pile.	
29315	- LIGHT 8 30 feet outside channel limit.	26-33-49.374N 097-17-28.280W	Fl R 6s	17	4	TR on pile.	
29320	- Day beacon 10	26-33-48.055N 097-18-00.789W				TR on pile.	
29325	- Day beacon 11	26-33-43.999N 097-18-30.600W				SG on pile.	Ra ref.
29330	- Day beacon 12	26-33-46.077N 097-18-53.938W				TR on pile.	
29335	- Day beacon 13	26-33-42.276N 097-19-12.528W				SG on pile.	Ra ref.
29340	- LIGHT 14 50 feet outside channel limit.	26-33-44.220N 097-19-34.900W	Fl R 4s	17	4	TR on dolphin.	
29345	- Day beacon 15	26-33-39.794N 097-19-58.830W				SG on pile.	Ra ref.
29350	- Day beacon 16	26-33-42.756N 097-20-19.094W				TR on pile.	Ra ref.
29355	- Day beacon 17	26-33-38.303N 097-20-42.944W				SG on pile.	Ra ref.
29360	- Day beacon 18	26-33-40.837N 097-21-03.522W				TR on pile.	Ra ref.
29365	- Day beacon 19	26-33-37.237N 097-21-24.923W				SG on pile.	Ra ref.

Light List corrected through LNM week: 01/18

(1) No.	(2) Name and Location	(3) Position	(4) Characteristic	(5) Height	(6) Range	(7) Structure	(8) Remarks
	TEXAS - Eighth District						
	LAGUNA MADRE (Chart 11306)						
	Port Mansfield Channel						
29370	- LIGHT 20 70 feet outside channel limit.	26-33-39.482N 097-21-47.949W	Fl R 4s	17	4	TR on pile.	Ra ref.
29375	- Day beacon 21	26-33-35.963N 097-22-10.086W				SG on pile.	Ra ref.
29380	- Day beacon 22	26-33-37.692N 097-22-31.233W				TR on pile.	Ra ref.
29385	- Day beacon 23	26-33-34.199N 097-22-50.641W				SG on pile.	
29390	- Day beacon 24	26-33-35.805N 097-23-14.178W				TR on pile.	
29395	- Day beacon 25	26-33-32.541N 097-23-39.528W				SG on pile.	Ra ref.
29400	- Day beacon 26	26-33-33.823N 097-24-01.326W				TR on pile.	Ra ref.
29405 41880	- Day beacon 27	26-33-31.533N 097-24-21.154W				SG-SY on pile.	Ra ref.
29410 41875	- JUNCTION LIGHT PM	26-33-33.128N 097-24-26.319W	Fl (2+1)R 6s	17	4	JR-TY on pile.	Ra ref.
29415	- RANGE FRONT LIGHT	26-33-29.496N 097-25-30.540W	Q R	20		KRW on tower on piles.	Visible 2° each side of rangeline, passing light visible all around.
29416	- RANGE FRONT PASSING LIGHT	26-33-29.496N 097-25-30.540W	Q R	22	3	On same structure as Port Mansfield Channel Range Front Light.	
29420	- RANGE REAR LIGHT 800 yards, 267.6° from front light.	26-33-28.418N 097-25-58.456W	Oc R 4s	77		KRW on skeleton tower on block.	Visible 2° each side of rangeline. F R aircraft warning light on tower.
29425	- Day beacon 29	26-33-29.655N 097-24-54.990W				SG on pile.	
29430	- Day beacon 30	26-33-31.551N 097-25-02.556W				TR on pile.	Ra ref.
29435	- Day beacon 31	26-33-28.137N 097-25-21.180W				SG on pile.	Ra ref.
29440	- Day beacon 32	26-33-30.498N 097-25-21.585W				TR on pile.	
29445	- Day beacon 33	26-33-27.795N 097-25-26.975W				SG on pile.	
29450	- Day beacon 34 50 feet outside channel limit.	26-33-29.661N 097-25-28.118W				TR on pile.	
	STOVER POINT TO BROWNSVILLE (Chart 11302)						
	Brazos Santiago Pass						
29455 1450	- Entrance Lighted Buoy BS	26-03-55.982N 097-06-34.990W	Mo (A) W		5	Red and white stripes with red spherical topmark.	
29460	Brazos Santiago Entrance Channel Lighted Buoy 2	26-04-03.445N 097-08-29.196W	Q R		4	Red.	
29465	BRAZOS SANTIAGO ENTRANCE RANGE FRONT LIGHT	26-03-56.938N 097-10-16.003W	Q G	37		KRW on skeleton tower on piles.	Visible all around; Higher intensity 1.5° each side of rangeline.
29470	BRAZOS SANTIAGO ENTRANCE RANGE REAR LIGHT 1,099 yards, 269.4° from front light.	26-03-56.679N 097-10-52.162W	Iso G 6s	72		KRW on skeleton tower on piles.	Visible 2° each side of rangeline.
29475	Brazos Santiago Entrance Channel Lighted Buoy 3	26-03-52.550N 097-08-29.112W	Q G		4	Green.	

Light List corrected through LNM week: 01/18

(1) No.	(2) Name and Location	(3) Position	(4) Characteristic	(5) Height	(6) Range	(7) Structure	(8) Remarks
	TEXAS - Eighth District						
	STOVER POINT TO BROWNSVILLE (Chart 11302)						
	Sea Ranch Marina Channel						
29480	- Day beacon 1	26-04-34.000N 097-10-02.000W				SG on pile.	Private aid.
29485	- Day beacon 2	26-04-05.000N 097-10-00.000W				TR on pile.	Private aid.
29490	- Day beacon 3	26-04-06.000N 097-10-00.000W				SG on pile.	Private aid.
29495	- Day beacon 4	26-04-06.000N 097-10-00.000W				TR on pile.	Private aid.
29500	- Day beacon 5	26-04-06.000N 097-10-00.000W				SG on pile.	Private aid.
29505	- Day beacon 6	26-04-06.000N 097-09-09.000W				TR on pile.	Private aid.
	South Padre Island						
29510	- Day beacon 1	26-04-09.568N 097-10-03.147W				SG on pile.	Ra ref.
29515	- Day beacon 2	26-04-18.944N 097-10-00.715W				TR on pile.	
29520	- Day beacon 3	26-04-23.684N 097-10-15.990W				SG on pile.	
29525	CAMERON COUNTY PARKS & RECREATION BOAT RAMP LIGHTS (3)	26-04-06.830N 097-09-48.830W	Fl R 2.5s	7		TR on pile.	Private aid.
29530	CAMERON COUNTY PARKS & RECREATION BOAT RAMP LIGHTS (3)	26-04-07.270N 097-09-48.970W	Fl G 2.5s	7		SG on pile.	Private aid.
29535	Cameron County Parks & Recreation Danger Day beacons (3)	26-04-07.020N 097-09-47.160W				NW on pile worded: DANGER ROCKS.	Private aid.
	Laguna Madre Channel						
29540	- Lighted Buoy 4	26-03-59.269N 097-10-02.756W	Q R		3	Red.	
29545	- Lighted Buoy 5	26-03-53.934N 097-10-00.653W	Q G		3	Green.	
29550	- RANGE FRONT LIGHT	26-04-04.849N 097-09-49.021W	Q G	36		KRW on skeleton tower on piles.	Visible 2° each side of rangeline.
29555	- RANGE FRONT LIGHT PASSING LIGHT	26-04-05.055N 097-09-49.178W	Q R	38	3	On same structure as Laguna Madre Channel Range Front Light.	
29560	- RANGE REAR LIGHT 823 yards, 055.7° from front light.	26-04-18.419N 097-09-26.500W	Iso G 6s	67		KRW on skeleton tower.	Visible 2° each side of rangeline.
29565	- LIGHT 9	26-03-42.786N 097-10-20.800W	Fl G 2.5s	17	3	SG on dolphin.	
29570	- LIGHT 10	26-03-47.882N 097-10-24.248W	Fl R 2.5s	17	3	TR on pile.	
29575	- LIGHT 15	26-03-27.961N 097-10-45.236W	Fl G 2.5s	17	3	SG on pile.	
29580	- LIGHT 16	26-03-32.563N 097-10-49.363W	Fl R 2.5s	17	3	TR on dolphin.	Ra ref.
29585	- LIGHT 21	26-03-09.903N 097-11-15.081W	Fl G 4s	17	3	SG on pile.	
29590	- LIGHT 22	26-03-14.275N 097-11-18.928W	Fl R 4s	17	3	TR on pile.	Ra ref.
29595	- LIGHT 26	26-03-00.429N 097-11-40.798W	Fl R 2.5s	17	3	TR on pile.	
29600	- LIGHT 27	26-02-54.993N 097-11-39.073W	Fl G 2.5s	17	4	SG on pile.	Ra ref.
29605	- LIGHT 28	26-02-52.134N 097-11-55.254W	Fl R 2.5s	17	4	TR on dolphin.	
29606	- LIGHT 29	26-02-47.547N 097-11-52.799W	Fl G 4s	17	3	SG on pile.	

(1) No.	(2) Name and Location	(3) Position	(4) Characteristic	(5) Height	(6) Range	(7) Structure	(8) Remarks
			TEXAS - Eighth District				
	STOVER POINT TO BROWNSVILLE (Chart 11302)						
	South Padre Island Channel						
29610	- Day beacon 1	26-05-07.800N 097-11-32.300W				SG on pile.	Private aid.
29615	- Day beacon 2	26-05-07.100N 097-11-31.900W				TR on pile.	Private aid.
29620	- Day beacon 3	26-05-11.400N 097-11-22.000W				SG on pile.	Private aid.
29625	- Day beacon 5	26-05-13.300N 097-11-11.200W				SG on pile.	Private aid.
29630	- Day beacon 7	26-05-13.600N 097-11-00.200W				SG on pile.	Private aid.
29635	- Day beacon 9	26-05-12.700N 097-10-49.500W				SG on pile.	Private aid.
29640	- Day beacon 11	26-05-10.800N 097-10-29.500W				SG on pile.	Private aid.
29645	- Day beacon 13	26-05-10.660N 097-10-28.390W				SG on pile.	Private aid.
29650	- Day beacon 14	26-05-15.000N 097-10-24.000W				TR on pile.	Private aid.
29655	- Day beacon 15	26-05-17.500N 097-10-24.000W				SG on pile.	Private aid.
29660	- Day beacon 16	26-05-23.250N 097-10-18.500W				TR on pile.	Private aid.
29665	- Day beacon 17	26-05-28.000N 097-10-16.450W				SG on pile.	Private aid.
29670	- Day beacon 18	26-05-33.500N 097-10-11.750W				TR on pile.	Private aid.
29675	- Day beacon 19	26-05-39.010N 097-10-09.540W				SG on pile.	Private aid.
29680	- Day beacon 20	26-05-38.600N 097-10-08.100W				TR on pile.	Private aid.
29685	- Day beacon 21	26-05-47.200N 097-10-09.700W				SG on pile.	Private aid.
29690	- Day beacon 22	26-05-47.200N 097-10-08.200W				TR on pile.	Private aid.
29695	- Day beacon 23	26-05-51.570N 097-10-09.820W				SG on pile.	Private aid.
29700	- Day beacon 25	26-06-07.320N 097-10-09.400W				SG on pile.	Private aid.
29705	- Day beacon 27	26-06-16.400N 097-10-15.220W				SG on pile.	Private aid.
29710	- Day beacon 29	26-06-25.570N 097-10-18.960W				SG on pile.	Private aid.
29715	- Day beacon 31	26-06-38.740N 097-10-21.590W				SG on pile.	Private aid.
29720	- Day beacon 33	26-06-47.500N 097-10-25.700W				SG on pile.	Private aid.
29725	- Day beacon 35	26-06-53.740N 097-10-28.460W				SG on pile.	Private aid.
29730	- Day beacon 36	26-06-53.750N 097-10-26.500W				TR on pile.	Private aid.
29735	- Day beacon 37	26-06-58.700N 097-10-24.200W				SG on pile.	Private aid.
29740	- Day beacon 38	26-06-58.700N 097-10-22.200W				TR on pile.	Private aid.
29745	- Day beacon 39	26-07-03.090N 097-10-20.340W				SG on pile.	Private aid.
29750	- Day beacon 41	26-07-14.530N 097-10-21.210W				SG on pile.	Private aid.
29755	- Day beacon 43	26-07-25.000N 097-10-26.400W				SG on pile.	Private aid.
29760	- Day beacon 44	26-07-25.000N 097-10-24.700W				TR on pile.	Private aid.
29765	- Day beacon 45	26-07-33.510N 097-10-30.430W				SG on pile.	Private aid.

Light List corrected through LNM week: 01/18

(1) No.	(2) Name and Location	(3) Position	(4) Characteristic	(5) Height	(6) Range	(7) Structure	(8) Remarks
			TEXAS - Eighth District				
	STOVER POINT TO BROWNSVILLE (Chart 11302)						
	South Padre Island Channel						
29770	- Day beacon 46	26-07-33.510N 097-10-28.700W				TR on pile.	Private aid.
29775	- Day beacon 47	26-07-40.380N 097-10-29.430W				SG on pile.	Private aid.
29780	- Day beacon 49	26-07-51.450N 097-10-34.870W				SG on pile.	Private aid.
29785	- Day beacon 51	26-07-57.060N 097-10-37.320W				SG on pile.	Private aid.
29787	GUILLOT PARASAIL PLATFORM LIGHTS (2)	26-07-47.990N 097-11-09.240W	Q W			Marks parasail barge platform.	Private aid.
29790	- South Danger Day beacon	26-05-42.000N 097-10-06.500W				NW on pile worded DANGER.	Private aid.
29795	- North Danger Day beacon	26-05-52.000N 097-10-06.500W				NW on pile worded DANGER.	Private aid.
	Port Isabel Channel						
29800	- JUNCTION LIGHT PI	26-02-45.608N 097-12-12.076W	Fl (2+1)R 6s	17	4	JR on pile.	
29805	- LIGHT 1	26-02-48.811N 097-12-19.109W	Fl G 4s	17	3	SG on pile.	
29810	- LIGHT 2	26-02-50.895N 097-12-09.471W	Fl R 4s	17	4	TR on pile.	
29815	- LIGHT 4	26-02-53.474N 097-12-19.260W	Fl R 2.5s	17	3	TR on pile.	Ra ref.
29820 42965	- LEADING LIGHT	26-02-50.856N 097-12-25.636W	Iso W 6s	17	5	NB on pile.	
29825 42955	- LIGHT 6	26-03-03.647N 097-12-29.536W	Q R	17	3	TR on dolphin.	
	Port Isabel Cutoff Channel						
29830 42940	HARLINGEN-PORT ISABEL LIGHT 90	26-03-39.189N 097-12-40.083W	Q R	17	3	TR-TY on dolphin.	Ra ref.
29835 42970	- LIGHT 1	26-02-41.939N 097-12-30.695W	Fl G 4s	17	4	SG-TY on dolphin.	Ra ref.
29840 42960	- LIGHT 3	26-03-01.758N 097-12-33.941W	Q G	17	3	SG-TY on pile.	
	Port Isabel Channel						
29845	LAGUNA MADRE WATER DISTRICT OUTFALL DANGER LIGHT	26-03-12.270N 097-12-40.440W	Fl W 2.5s			Marks diffuser outfall.	Private aid.
29850 42945	- LIGHT 8	26-03-15.080N 097-12-36.340W	Fl R 2.5s	17	3	TR-SY on dolphin.	
	Brownsville Channel						
29855 42975	- LIGHT 30	26-02-25.148N 097-12-39.788W	Fl R 4s	17	3	TR-TY on pile.	Ra ref.
29860 42980	- C RANGE FRONT LIGHT	26-02-16.482N 097-12-43.282W	Q G	25		KRW-I on skeleton tower on piles.	Visible all around; higher intensity on range line.
29865 42985	- C RANGE REAR LIGHT	26-02-37.482N 097-11-57.635W	Iso G 6s	65		KRW on skeleton tower on piles.	Visible 2° each side of rangeline.
29870 42990	- A RANGE FRONT LIGHT	26-01-50.708N 097-13-32.067W	Q W (NIGHT) Q W (NIGHT)	33 35		KRW-I on skeleton tower.	Visible all around; higher intensity 14° each side of rangeline.
29875 42995	- A RANGE REAR LIGHT 1,601 yards, 235.7° from front light.	26-01-24.321N 097-14-15.894W	Iso W 6s	60		KRW on skeleton tower.	Visible 2° each side of rangeline.
29880 43000	- LIGHT 31	26-02-01.835N 097-13-09.264W	Q G	17	3	SG-SY on pile.	Ra ref.
29885 43005	- LIGHT 32	26-02-06.093N 097-13-11.633W	Q R	17	3	TR-TY on pile.	Ra ref.
29890 43010	- LIGHT 34	26-01-53.815N 097-13-38.485W	Fl R 2.5s	17	3	TR-TY on pile.	Ra ref.

Light List corrected through LNM week: 01/18

(1) No.	(2) Name and Location	(3) Position	(4) Characteristic	(5) Height	(6) Range	(7) Structure	(8) Remarks
	TEXAS - Eighth District							

STOVER POINT TO BROWNSVILLE (Chart 11302)
Brownsville Channel

(1) No.	(2) Name and Location	(3) Position	(4) Characteristic	(5) Height	(6) Range	(7) Structure	(8) Remarks
29895 43015	- LIGHT 35	26-01-22.470N 097-14-34.736W	Fl G 4s	17	4	SG-SY on pile.	Ra ref.
29900 43020	- E RANGE FRONT LIGHT	26-01-22.652N 097-14-45.601W	Q W	33		KRW-I on skeleton tower on piles.	For downbound traffic. Visible all around; higher intensity 1.5° each side of rangeline.
29905 43025	- E RANGE REAR LIGHT 1,368 yards, 057.0° from front light.	26-01-44.065N 097-14-07.353W	Iso W 6s	63		KRW on skeleton tower on piles.	Visible 2° each side of rangeline.
29910 43030	- LIGHT 36	26-01-10.015N 097-15-13.456W	Q R	17	3	TR-TY on pile.	Ra ref.
29915 43035	- LIGHT 37	26-01-05.313N 097-15-11.452W	Q G	17	3	SG-SY on pile.	Ra ref.
29920 43040	- LIGHT 39	26-00-55.408N 097-15-28.497W	Fl G 4s	17	4	SG-SY on pile.	Ra ref.
29925 43045	- B RANGE FRONT LIGHT	26-00-52.470N 097-15-45.759W	Q R	35		KRW-I on skeleton tower on piles.	Visible all around; higher intensity 5.5° each side of rangeline.
29930 43050	- B RANGE REAR LIGHT	26-00-27.963N 097-16-39.127W	Iso R 6s	75		KRW on skeleton tower on piles.	Visible 2° each side of rangeline.
29935 43055	- LIGHT 40	25-59-55.487N 097-17-26.731W	Fl R 4s	17	3	TR-TY on pile.	
29940 43060	- LIGHT 41	25-59-50.651N 097-17-23.806W	Fl G 4s	17	4	SG-SY on pile.	
29945 43065	- LIGHT 42	25-59-24.254N 097-18-24.281W	Fl R 2.5s	17	3	TR-TY on pile.	
29950 43095	- D RANGE FRONT LIGHT	25-58-28.313N 097-19-56.658W	Q W	35		KRW-I on skeleton tower.	Visible all around; higher intensity 1.5° each side of rangeline.
29955 43100	- D RANGE REAR LIGHT	25-58-03.763N 097-20-40.411W	Iso W 6s	67		KRW on skeleton tower.	
29960 43070	- LIGHT 44	25-58-49.345N 097-19-26.229W	Fl R 4s	17	3	TR-TY on skeleton tower on piles.	
29965 43075	- G RANGE FRONT LIGHT	25-58-43.925N 097-19-22.137W	Q G	25		KRW-I on skeleton tower on piles.	Visible all around; higher intensity on rangeline.
29967 43072	- G RANGE FRONT LIGHT PASSING LIGHT	25-58-43.925N 097-19-22.137W	Q G	27	3	On same structure as Brownsville Channel G Range Front Light.	Visible all around.
29970 43080	- G RANGE REAR LIGHT 1,617 yards, 068.7 from front light.	25-59-00.459N 097-18-35.022W	Iso G 6s	58		KRW on skeleton tower.	Visible 2° each side of rangeline.
29975 43085	- LIGHT 45	25-58-33.011N 097-19-44.843W	Q G	17	3	SG-SY on pile.	Ra ref.
29980 43090	- LIGHT 46	25-58-38.077N 097-19-46.521W	Q R	17	3	TR-TY on pile.	Ra ref.
29985 43105	- LIGHT 48	25-58-25.077N 097-20-21.696W	Fl R 2.5s	17	3	TR-TY on dolphin.	
29990 43110	- F RANGE FRONT LIGHT	25-57-02.311N 097-24-11.346W	Fl G 2.5s (NIGHT) Fl W 2.5s (DAY)	45 47		KRW-I on skeleton tower.	Visible 2° each side of rangeline.
29995 43115	- F RANGE REAR LIGHT 3,870 yards, 249° from front light.	25-56-20.523N 097-26-10.086W	Oc G 4s (NIGHT) Oc W 4s (DAY)	98 95		KRW on skeleton tower.	Visible 2° each side of rangeline. Lighted throughout 24 hours.
30000	BROWNSVILLE LIQUID CARGO DOCK LIGHTS (4)	25-57-37.000N 097-22-22.000W	F G	11		On dock.	Private aid.
30005	BROWNSVILLE OIL DOCK NO. 3 LIGHTS (2)	25-57-34.000N 097-22-43.000W	F R	10		On dock.	Private aid.

Light List corrected through LNM week: 01/18

(1) No.	(2) Name and Location	(3) Position	(4) Characteristic	(5) Height	(6) Range	(7) Structure	(8) Remarks
	TEXAS - Eighth District						
	STOVER POINT TO BROWNSVILLE (Chart 11302)						
	Brownsville Channel						
30010	BROWNSVILLE CARGO DOCK NO.15 LIGHT	25-57-26.000N 097-22-47.000W	Fl G 2.5s	10		On dock.	Private aid.
30015	BROWNSVILLE BULK CARGO DOCK LIGHTS (2)	25-57-00.300N 097-23-00.100W	F G	11		On dock.	Private aid.
30020	BROWNSVILLE OIL DOCK NO. 2 LIGHTS (6)	25-57-21.000N 097-23-23.000W	F R	12		On dock.	Private aid.
30025	BROWNSVILLE OIL DOCK NO. 1 LIGHTS (2)	25-57-18.000N 097-23-30.000W	F R	10		On dock.	Private aid.
	INTRACOASTAL WATERWAY (Florida) - Eighth District						
	CARRABELLE TO APALACHICOLA BAY (Chart 11404)						
	St. George Sound						
30030	- LIGHT 2	29-46-29.937N 084-42-27.905W	Fl R 4s	17	4	TR-TY on pile.	Ra ref.
30035	- LIGHT 6	29-45-16.271N 084-44-33.771W	Fl R 6s	17	4	TR-TY on pile.	Ra ref.
30040	- LIGHT 8	29-44-33.989N 084-45-45.882W	Fl R 4s	17	3	TR-TY on dolphin.	Ra ref.
30045	- Day beacon 10	29-44-14.011N 084-46-35.312W				TR-TY on pile.	Ra ref.
30050	- Day beacon 12	29-44-07.765N 084-46-50.657W				TR-TY on pile.	Ra ref.
30055	- Day beacon 13	29-44-05.565N 084-46-47.813W				SG-SY on pile.	Ra ref.
30060	- LIGHT 14	29-43-56.733N 084-47-18.084W	Fl R 2.5s	17	3	TR-TY on piles.	Ra ref.
30065	- Day beacon 15	29-43-54.469N 084-47-15.396W				SG-SY on pile.	
30070	- Day beacon 16	29-43-49.358N 084-47-36.227W				TR-TY on pile.	Ra ref.
30075	- Day beacon 17	29-43-45.930N 084-47-36.498W				SG-SY on pile.	Ra ref.
30080	- Day beacon 18	29-43-37.480N 084-48-05.241W				TR-TY on pile.	Ra ref.
30085	- Day beacon 19	29-43-31.838N 084-48-11.226W				SG-SY on pile.	
30090	- LIGHT 20	29-43-27.511N 084-48-29.649W	Q R	17	3	TR-TY on pile.	
30095	- Buoy 21	29-43-21.714N 084-48-28.689W				Green can with yellow square.	
30100	- Buoy 22	29-43-18.944N 084-48-37.620W				Red nun with yellow triangle.	
30105	- LIGHT 24	29-42-56.163N 084-48-50.447W	Fl R 2.5s	17	3	TR-TY on dolphin.	
30110	- Day beacon 25	29-42-47.646N 084-48-46.570W				SG-SY on pile.	Ra ref.
	East Point Channel						
30115	- LIGHT 2	29-44-06.763N 084-52-17.666W	Fl R 2.5s	17	3	TR on dolphin.	
30120	- Day beacon 3	29-44-07.563N 084-52-18.366W				SG on pile.	
30125	- Day beacon 4	29-44-18.063N 084-52-24.166W				TR on pile.	Ra ref.
30130	- Buoy 5	29-44-17.163N 084-52-26.666W				Green can.	
	St. George Sound						
30135	- Day beacon 26	29-42-19.409N 084-49-02.550W				TR-TY on pile.	Ra ref.
30140	- Buoy 27	29-41-55.374N 084-49-06.457W				Green can with yellow square.	
30145	- LIGHT 28	29-41-56.656N 084-49-11.460W	Q R	17	3	TR-TY on pile.	

Light List corrected through LNM week: 01/18

INTRACOASTAL WATERWAY (Florida) - Eighth District

CARRABELLE TO APALACHICOLA BAY (Chart 11404)

St. George Sound

(1) No.	(2) Name and Location	(3) Position	(4) Characteristic	(5) Height	(6) Range	(7) Structure	(8) Remarks
30150	- LIGHT 30	29-41-45.828N 084-49-24.858W	Q R	17	3	TR-TY on pile.	
30155	- Buoy 31	29-41-40.585N 084-49-28.189W				Green can with yellow square.	
30160	- Day beacon 32	29-41-41.329N 084-49-45.555W				TR-TY on pile.	Ra ref.
30165	- LIGHT 34	29-41-36.807N 084-50-11.395W	Fl R 2.5s	17	3	TR-TY on pile.	
30170	- Day beacon 35	29-41-32.167N 084-50-14.597W				SG-SY on pile.	Ra ref.
30175	- Day beacon 36	29-41-29.985N 084-50-42.710W				TR-TY on pile.	Ra ref.
30180	- LIGHT 40	29-41-21.276N 084-51-21.688W	Fl R 4s	17	3	TR-TY on pile.	Ra ref.
30185	- Day beacon 41	29-41-18.312N 084-51-21.100W				SG-SY on pile.	
30190	- Buoy 44	29-41-14.122N 084-51-58.096W				Red nun with yellow triangle.	
30195	- Buoy 45	29-41-10.608N 084-51-58.712W				Green can with yellow square.	
30200	- Buoy 46	29-41-09.287N 084-52-17.398W				Red nun with yellow triangle.	
30205	- Buoy 47	29-41-07.231N 084-52-16.889W				Green can with yellow square.	

Apalachicola Bay

(1) No.	(2) Name and Location	(3) Position	(4) Characteristic	(5) Height	(6) Range	(7) Structure	(8) Remarks
30210	- Buoy 48	29-41-02.711N 084-52-44.627W				Red nun with yellow triangle.	
30215	- LIGHT 52	29-40-53.825N 084-53-35.939W	Fl R 4s	17	3	TR-TY on pile.	Ra ref.
30220	- Day beacon 53	29-40-50.756N 084-53-34.122W				SG-SY on pile.	Ra ref.
30225	- Day beacon 54	29-40-48.117N 084-54-02.766W				TR-TY on pile.	Ra ref.
30230	- LIGHT 58	29-40-39.790N 084-54-40.800W	Fl R 6s	17	4	TR-TY on pile.	Ra ref.
30235	- Day beacon 59	29-40-36.251N 084-54-40.595W				SG-SY on pile.	Ra ref.
30240	- Day beacon 60	29-40-32.751N 084-55-14.098W				TR-TY on pile.	Ra ref.
30245	- LIGHT 64	29-40-25.432N 084-55-49.098W	Fl R 4s	17	3	TR-TY on pile.	Ra ref.
30250	- Day beacon 65	29-40-22.691N 084-55-47.699W				SG-SY on pile.	Ra ref.
30255	- Day beacon 66	29-40-19.025N 084-56-19.861W				TR-TY on pile.	Ra ref.
30260	- LIGHT 70	29-40-11.761N 084-56-53.083W	Fl R 2.5s	16	3	TR-TY on pile.	Ra ref.
30265	- Day beacon 71	29-40-09.021N 084-56-51.947W				SG-SY on pile.	
30270	- Day beacon 74	29-40-01.043N 084-57-42.491W				TR-TY on pile.	Ra ref.
30275	- LIGHT 76	29-39-58.274N 084-57-57.283W	Q R	17	3	TR-TY on pile.	Ra ref.
30280	- Buoy 77	29-39-53.796N 084-57-58.137W				Green can with yellow square.	

Apalachicola River Entrance

(1) No.	(2) Name and Location	(3) Position	(4) Characteristic	(5) Height	(6) Range	(7) Structure	(8) Remarks
30285	- Buoy 1	29-40-12.731N 084-58-12.430W				Green can with yellow square.	
30290	- LIGHT 2	29-40-10.049N 084-58-07.595W	Fl R 2.5s	17	3	TR-TY on pile.	
30295	- Buoy 3	29-40-43.836N 084-58-18.471W				Green can with yellow square.	

Light List corrected through LNM week: 01/18

(1) No.	(2) Name and Location	(3) Position	(4) Characteristic	(5) Height	(6) Range	(7) Structure	(8) Remarks
	INTRACOASTAL WATERWAY (Florida) - Eighth District						
	CARRABELLE TO APALACHICOLA BAY (Chart 11404)						
	Apalachicola River Entrance						
30300	- LIGHT 4	29-40-38.769N 084-58-14.674W	Fl R 4s	17	3	TR-TY on pile.	Ra ref.
30305	- Buoy 4A	29-40-59.799N 084-58-19.495W					Red nun with yellow triangle.
30310	- Buoy 5	29-41-11.280N 084-58-23.894W					Green can with yellow square.
30315	- Buoy 6	29-41-11.499N 084-58-21.655W					Red nun with yellow triangle.
30320	- Buoy 7	29-41-28.813N 084-58-27.235W					Green can with yellow square.
30325	- Buoy 9	29-41-42.477N 084-58-29.934W					Green can with yellow square.
30330	- Buoy 10	29-41-42.830N 084-58-27.799W					Red nun with yellow triangle.
30335	- Buoy 11	29-41-55.920N 084-58-32.659W					Green can with yellow square.
30340	- Buoy 13	29-42-09.778N 084-58-35.244W					Green can with yellow square.
30345	- Buoy 14	29-42-09.889N 084-58-32.844W					Red nun with yellow triangle.
30350	- Buoy 15	29-42-22.473N 084-58-37.768W					Green can with yellow square.
30355	- Buoy 16	29-42-22.929N 084-58-35.718W					Red nun with yellow triangle.
30360	- Buoy 17	29-42-38.318N 084-58-40.838W					Green can with yellow square.
30365	- Buoy 18	29-42-38.299N 084-58-38.675W					Red nun with yellow triangle.
30370	- Buoy 19	29-42-49.599N 084-58-43.135W					Green can with yellow square.
30375	- Buoy 20	29-42-50.073N 084-58-41.008W					Red nun with yellow triangle.
30380	- Buoy 21	29-43-01.198N 084-58-45.297W					Green can with yellow square.
30385	- Buoy 22	29-43-01.578N 084-58-43.342W					Red nun with yellow triangle.
30390	- Buoy 24	29-43-08.819N 084-58-43.266W					Red nun with yellow triangle.
30395 2945	TWO MILE CHANNEL JUNCTION LIGHT TM	29-43-12.327N 084-58-49.464W	Fl (2+1)G 6s	17	3	JG-SY on pile.	Ra ref.
30400	- RANGE FRONT LIGHT	29-43-22.787N 084-58-48.427W	Q G	15		KRW-I on dolphin.	Visible all around; higher each side of rangeline.
30405	- RANGE REAR LIGHT 1,377 yards, 350.3° from front light.	29-44-03.105N 084-58-56.329W	F G	45		KRW-I on skeleton tower on piles.	
	APALACHICOLA BAY TO LAKE WIMICO (Chart 11402)						
	Apalachicola River						
30410	- LIGHT 2	29-43-40.932N 084-58-46.857W	Q R	17	3	TR-TY on pile.	Ra ref.
30415	- Day beacon 4	29-43-48.440N 084-58-49.861W				TR-TY on pile.	Ra ref.
30420	Scipio Creek Junction Buoy A	29-43-41.909N 084-58-53.010W					Green can with green band.
30425	- Buoy 5	29-43-53.994N 084-58-58.196W					Green can with yellow square.
30430	- Day beacon 6	29-43-54.789N 084-58-53.169W				TR-TY on pile.	Ra ref.
30435	- LIGHT 8	29-44-08.483N 084-59-03.039W	Fl R 2.5s	17	3	TR-TY on dolphin.	
30440	- LIGHT 10	29-44-28.103N 084-59-32.838W	Fl R 4s	17	3	TR-TY on dolphin.	
30445	- Buoy 13	29-45-32.411N 085-01-08.064W					Green can with yellow square.

Light List corrected through LNM week: 01/18

INTRACOASTAL WATERWAY (Florida) - Eighth District

APALACHICOLA BAY TO LAKE WIMICO (Chart 11402)

Apalachicola River

(1) No.	(2) Name and Location	(3) Position	(4) Characteristic	(5) Height	(6) Range	(7) Structure	(8) Remarks
30450	- Buoy 15	29-45-38.478N 085-01-16.114W				Green can with yellow square.	
30455	- Buoy 17	29-45-43.643N 085-01-23.840W				Green can with yellow square.	
30460	- Shoal Buoy 18	29-45-47.122N 085-01-22.329W				Red nun with yellow triangle.	
30465	- Buoy 19	29-45-46.041N 085-01-30.162W				Green can with yellow square.	
30470	- Day beacon 20	29-45-49.118N 085-01-33.101W				TR-TY on pile.	Ra ref.
30475	- Buoy 21	29-45-48.852N 085-01-41.632W				Green can with yellow square.	
30480	- Buoy 22	29-45-51.053N 085-01-39.140W				Red nun with yellow triangle.	
30485	- Buoy 24	29-45-59.222N 085-02-09.978W				Red nun with yellow triangle.	
30490	- Buoy 25	29-46-07.223N 085-02-30.005W				Green can with yellow square.	
30495	- Day beacon 26	29-46-22.738N 085-02-38.373W				TR-TY on pile.	Ra ref.
30500	- Day beacon 28	29-46-29.399N 085-02-45.983W				TR-TY on pile.	Ra ref.
30505	- Day beacon 30	29-46-34.219N 085-02-52.053W				TR-TY on pile.	Ra ref.

Jackson River

(1) No.	(2) Name and Location	(3) Position	(4) Characteristic	(5) Height	(6) Range	(7) Structure	(8) Remarks
30510	- LIGHT 2	29-46-46.136N 085-03-04.587W	Fl R 2.5s	17	3	TR-TY on dolphin.	
30515	- Buoy 3	29-46-53.293N 085-03-18.372W				Green can with yellow square.	
30520	- Day beacon 4	29-46-55.906N 085-03-16.281W				TR-TY on pile.	
30525	- Day beacon 6	29-47-03.466N 085-03-22.341W				TR-TY on pile.	Ra ref.
30530	- Buoy 7	29-47-01.551N 085-03-28.753W				Green can with yellow square.	
30535	- LIGHT 9	29-47-10.345N 085-03-38.795W	Fl G 2.5s	17	3	SG-SY on dolphin.	
30540	- Day beacon 10	29-47-13.495N 085-03-36.584W				TR-TY on pile.	Ra ref.

Lake Wimico

(1) No.	(2) Name and Location	(3) Position	(4) Characteristic	(5) Height	(6) Range	(7) Structure	(8) Remarks
30545	- LIGHT 1	29-46-38.755N 085-06-39.689W	Fl G 2.5s	17	3	SG-SY on pile.	Ra ref.
30550	- Day beacon 3	29-47-01.762N 085-07-11.960W				SG-SY on pile.	Ra ref.
30555	- Day beacon 4	29-47-03.971N 085-07-11.666W				TR-TY on pile.	Ra ref.
30560	- LIGHT 5 50 feet outside channel limit.	29-47-24.165N 085-07-44.982W	Fl G 4s	17	4	SG-SY on pile.	Ra ref.
30565	- Day beacon 6	29-47-26.801N 085-07-45.068W				TR-TY on pile.	Ra ref.
30570	- Day beacon 7	29-47-46.863N 085-08-18.746W				SG-SY on pile.	Ra ref.
30575	- Day beacon 8	29-47-48.378N 085-08-16.989W				TR-TY on pile.	Ra ref.
30580	- LIGHT 9	29-48-10.504N 085-08-53.561W	Fl G 2.5s	17	3	SG-SY on pile.	Ra ref.
30585	- Day beacon 10	29-48-12.688N 085-08-52.953W				TR-TY on pile.	Ra ref.
30590	- Day beacon 11	29-48-28.083N 085-09-19.813W				SG-SY on pile.	Ra ref.

Light List corrected through LNM week: 01/18

(1) No.	(2) Name and Location	(3) Position	(4) Characteristic	(5) Height	(6) Range	(7) Structure	(8) Remarks
\multicolumn{8}{c}{**INTRACOASTAL WATERWAY (Florida) - Eighth District**}							
\multicolumn{8}{l}{**APALACHICOLA BAY TO LAKE WIMICO (Chart 11402)**}							
\multicolumn{8}{l}{**Lake Wimico**}							
30595	- Day beacon 12	29-48-31.329N 085-09-19.833W				TR-TY on pile.	Ra ref.
30600	- LIGHT 13	29-49-01.918N 085-10-09.692W	Q G	17	3	SG-SY on pile.	Ra ref.
30605	- Day beacon 14	29-49-02.513N 085-10-05.661W				TR-TY on pile.	Ra ref.
30610	- LIGHT 15	29-49-11.849N 085-10-38.517W	Fl G 2.5s	17	3	SG-SY on pile.	Ra ref.
30612	FLORIDA DEPARTMENT OF AGRICULTURE INDIAN LAGOON SPECIAL LIGHT A	29-41-16.650N 085-14-03.830W	Fl Y 2.5s			Marks southwest corner of aquaculture farm perimeter,	Private aid.
30612.01	FLORIDA DEPARTMENT OF AGRICULTURE INDIAN LAGOON SPECIAL LIGHT B	29-41-16.900N 085-13-53.260W	Fl Y 2.5s			Marks southeast corner of aquaculture farm perimeter,	Private aid.
30612.02	FLORIDA DEPARTMENT OF AGRICULTURE INDIAN LAGOON SPECIAL LIGHT C	29-41-21.630N 085-13-53.260W	Fl Y 2.5s			Marks northeast corner of aquaculture farm perimeter,	Private aid.
30612.03	FLORIDA DEPARTMENT OF AGRICULTURE INDIAN LAGOON SPECIAL LIGHT D	29-41-21.380N 085-14-03.380W	Fl Y 2.5s			Marks northwest corner of aquaculture farm perimeter,	Private aid.
\multicolumn{8}{l}{**LAKE WIMICO TO EAST BAY (Chart 11393)**}							
\multicolumn{8}{l}{**Wetappo Creek**}							
30615	- Day beacon 1	30-01-37.000N 085-23-29.100W				SG-SY on pile.	Ra ref.
30620	- Buoy 1A	30-01-50.224N 085-23-39.022W				Green can with yellow square.	
30625	- Buoy 3	30-01-58.772N 085-23-40.868W				Green can with yellow square.	
30630	- Buoy 5	30-02-07.194N 085-23-42.078W				Green can with yellow square.	
30635	- Buoy 7	30-02-15.642N 085-23-44.540W				Green can with yellow square.	
30640	- Buoy 9	30-02-22.890N 085-23-46.638W				Green can with yellow square.	
30645	- LIGHT 10 25 feet outside channel limit.	30-02-25.300N 085-23-44.749W	Q R	17	3	TR-TY on pile.	Ra ref.
30650	- Buoy 11	30-02-26.826N 085-23-53.880W				Green can with yellow square.	
30655	- Buoy 13	30-02-29.007N 085-24-03.552W				Green can with yellow square.	
30660	- Buoy 14	30-02-35.958N 085-24-20.498W				Red nun with yellow triangle.	
30665	- Buoy 15	30-02-34.381N 085-24-21.892W				Green can with yellow square.	
30670	- Buoy 17	30-02-37.722N 085-24-32.369W				Green can with yellow square.	
30675	- Buoy 18	30-02-43.578N 085-24-48.684W				Red nun with yellow triangle.	
30680	- LIGHT 19 50 feet outside channel limit.	30-02-41.799N 085-24-48.254W	Fl G 2.5s	17	3	SG-SY on pile.	Ra ref.
30685	- Buoy 21	30-02-46.011N 085-25-01.896W				Green can with yellow square.	
30690	- Buoy 22	30-02-52.662N 085-25-16.908W				Red nun with yellow triangle.	
30695	- Buoy 23	30-02-51.156N 085-25-15.690W				Green can with yellow square.	
30700	- Buoy 25	30-02-54.054N 085-25-25.956W				Green can with yellow square.	

Light List corrected through LNM week: 01/18

(1) No.	(2) Name and Location	(3) Position	(4) Characteristic	(5) Height	(6) Range	(7) Structure	(8) Remarks
		INTRACOASTAL WATERWAY (Florida) - Eighth District					
	LAKE WIMICO TO EAST BAY (Chart 11393)						
	Wetappo Creek						
30705	- Buoy 27	30-02-58.424N 085-25-40.430W				Green can with yellow square.	
30710	- LIGHT 28	30-03-01.627N 085-25-47.313W	Q R	17	3	TR-TY on pile.	Ra ref.
30715	- Buoy 29	30-02-57.320N 085-25-47.476W				Green can with yellow square.	
30720	- Buoy 31	30-02-55.899N 085-25-51.342W				Green can with yellow square.	
30725	- Buoy 32	30-02-39.359N 085-26-12.722W				Red nun with yellow triangle.	
30730	- Buoy 33	30-02-38.460N 085-26-10.920W				Green can with yellow square.	
30735	- Buoy 35	30-02-28.026N 085-26-21.684W				Green can with yellow square.	
30740	- LIGHT 36	30-02-16.650N 085-26-37.376W	Fl R 2.5s	17	3	TR-TY pile.	Ra ref.
30745	- Buoy 37	30-02-15.204N 085-26-35.124W				Green can with yellow square.	
30750	- Day beacon 39	30-02-00.840N 085-26-42.715W				SG-SY on pile.	Ra ref.
30755	- Day beacon 41	30-01-52.246N 085-26-47.399W				SG-SY on pile.	Ra ref.
30760	- LIGHT 42	30-01-48.995N 085-26-53.437W	Fl R 2.5s	17	3	TR-TY on pile.	Ra ref.
30765	- Day beacon 43	30-01-33.211N 085-27-02.052W				SG-SY on pile.	Ra ref.
30770	- Day beacon 44	30-01-35.904N 085-27-03.749W				TR-TY on pile.	Ra ref.
30775	- Day beacon 46	30-01-29.142N 085-27-13.832W				TR-TY on pile.	Ra ref.
	East Bay						
30780	- LIGHT 1 190 feet outside channel limit.	30-01-26.022N 085-27-13.627W	Q G	17	3	SG-SY on pile.	
30785	- LIGHT 2	30-01-26.589N 085-27-28.660W	Q R	17	3	TR-TY on pile.	Ra ref.
30790	- Day beacon 3	30-01-23.201N 085-27-27.199W				SG-SY on pile.	Ra ref.
30795	- Day beacon 4	30-01-27.498N 085-27-42.132W				TR-TY on pile.	Ra ref.
30800	- Day beacon 6	30-01-30.271N 085-27-58.299W				TR-TY on pile.	Ra ref.
30805	- Day beacon 7	30-01-29.165N 085-28-04.511W				SG-SY on pile.	Ra ref.
30810	- LIGHT 8	30-01-33.582N 085-28-07.840W	Fl R 2.5s	17	3	TR-TY on pile.	Ra ref.
30815	- Day beacon 9	30-01-31.971N 085-28-22.946W				SG-SY on pile.	Ra ref.
30820	- Day beacon 10	30-01-37.590N 085-28-40.265W				TR-TY on pile.	Ra ref.
30825	- LIGHT 11	30-01-36.424N 085-28-58.433W	Q G	17	3	SG-SY on pile.	Ra ref.
30830	- Day beacon 12	30-01-43.845N 085-28-59.430W				TR-TY on pile.	Ra ref.
30835	- Day beacon 13	30-01-51.833N 085-29-10.610W				SG-SY on pile.	Ra ref.
30840	- Day beacon 13A	30-01-57.212N 085-29-15.359W				SG-SY on pile.	Ra ref.
30845	- LIGHT 14	30-02-04.304N 085-29-16.304W	Q R	17	3	TR-TY on pile.	Ra ref.

Light List corrected through LNM week: 01/18

(1) No.	(2) Name and Location	(3) Position	(4) Characteristic	(5) Height	(6) Range	(7) Structure	(8) Remarks

INTRACOASTAL WATERWAY (Florida) - Eighth District

LAKE WIMICO TO EAST BAY (Chart 11393)
East Bay

No.	Name and Location	Position	Characteristic	Height	Range	Structure	Remarks
30850	- LIGHT 15	30-02-15.398N 085-29-45.434W	Q G	17	4	SG-SY on pile.	Ra ref.
30855	- Buoy 16	30-02-17.166N 085-29-39.037W					Red nun with yellow triangle.
30860	- Day beacon 17	30-02-29.594N 085-29-49.901W				SG-SY on pile.	Ra ref.
30865	- Day beacon 18	30-02-40.636N 085-29-46.890W				TR-TY on pile.	Ra ref.
30870	- Day beacon 20	30-02-56.133N 085-29-49.599W				TR-TY on pile.	Ra ref.
30875	- Day beacon 22	30-03-08.126N 085-29-49.220W				TR-TY on pile.	Ra ref.
30880	- LIGHT 23	30-03-06.469N 085-29-55.158W	Fl G 2.5s	17	3	SG-SY on pile.	Ra ref.
30885	- LIGHT 25	30-03-21.646N 085-30-00.231W	Fl G 4s	17	4	SG-SY on pile.	Ra ref.
30890	- Day beacon 26	30-03-34.563N 085-30-04.751W				TR-TY on pile.	Ra ref.
30892	Richard Bayou Channel Day beacon 1	30-03-38.411N 085-29-35.473W				SG on pile.	Private aid.
30892.01	Richard Bayou Channel Day beacon 2	30-03-38.147N 085-29-35.318W				TR on pile.	Private aid.
30892.02	Richard Bayou Channel Day beacon 3	30-03-40.029N 085-29-31.846W				SG on pile.	Private aid.
30892.03	Richard Bayou Channel Day beacon 4	30-03-39.748N 085-29-31.730W				TR on pile.	Private aid.
30892.04	Richard Bayou Channel Day beacon 5	30-03-40.318N 085-29-28.876W				SG on pile.	Private aid.
30892.05	Richard Bayou Channel Day beacon 6	30-03-40.086N 085-29-29.969W				TR on pile.	Private aid.
30895	- LIGHT 28	30-03-52.784N 085-30-15.092W	Fl R 4s	17	3	TR-TY on pile.	Ra ref.
30900	- Day beacon 29	30-03-54.126N 085-30-22.759W				SG-SY on pile.	Ra ref.
30905	- LIGHT 35	30-04-19.050N 085-30-38.000W	Fl G 2.5s	17	3	SG-SY on pile.	Ra ref.
30910	- LIGHT 37	30-04-48.864N 085-31-07.970W	Q G	17	3	SG-SY on pile.	Ra ref.
30915	- Day beacon 38	30-05-10.014N 085-31-36.415W				TR-TY on pile.	Ra ref.
30920	- LIGHT 40	30-05-20.421N 085-31-58.449W	Fl R 2.5s	17	3	TR-TY on pile.	Ra ref.

EAST BAY TO WEST BAY (Chart 11390)

No.	Name and Location	Position	Characteristic	Height	Range	Structure	Remarks
30925	East Bay Day beacon 41	30-05-34.717N 085-32-28.354W				SG-SY on pile.	Ra ref.

East Bay
Cooks Bayou

No.	Name and Location	Position	Characteristic	Height	Range	Structure	Remarks
30930	- Day beacon 2	30-07-59.960N 085-30-39.240W				TR on pile.	Private aid.
30935	- Day beacon 3	30-08-01.660N 085-30-33.660W				SG on pile.	Private aid.
30940	- Day beacon 4	30-08-01.460N 085-30-29.140W				TR on pile.	Private aid.
30945	- Day beacon 5	30-08-00.630N 085-30-25.000W				SG on pile.	Private aid.

EAST BAY TO WEST BAY (Chart 11390)

No.	Name and Location	Position	Characteristic	Height	Range	Structure	Remarks
30950	EAST BAY LIGHT 43	30-06-12.728N 085-33-23.729W	Fl G 4s	17	4	SG-SY on pile.	
30955	Callaway Bayou Day beacon 2	30-06-50.888N 085-33-45.770W				TR on pile.	
30960	Callaway Bayou Day beacon 4	30-07-27.036N 085-33-48.099W				TR on pile.	

Light List corrected through LNM week: 01/18

(1) No.	(2) Name and Location	(3) Position	(4) Characteristic	(5) Height	(6) Range	(7) Structure	(8) Remarks
	INTRACOASTAL WATERWAY (Florida) - Eighth District							
	**EAST BAY TO WEST BAY (Chart 11390)**							
30963	Callaway Bayou Day beacon 1	30-08-28.200N 085-34-08.260W				SG on pile.	Private aid.
30963.01	Callaway Bayou Day beacon 3	30-08-32.630N 085-34-01.910W				SG on pile.	Private aid.
30963.02	Callaway Bayou Day beacon 5	30-08-35.570N 085-34-00.590W				SG on pile.	Private aid.
30963.03	Callaway Bayou Day beacon 2A	30-08-27.760N 085-34-08.000W				TR on pile.	Private aid.
30963.04	Callaway Bayou Day beacon 4A	30-08-29.820N 085-34-03.390W				TR on pile.	Private aid.
30963.05	Callaway Bayou Day beacon 6	30-08-34.880N 085-34-00.150W				TR on pile.	Private aid.
30963.06	Callaway Bayou Day beacon 8	30-08-34.650N 085-33-57.980W				TR on pile.	Private aid.
30963.07	Callaway Bayou Day beacon 10	30-08-33.080N 085-33-55.710W				TR on pile.	Private aid.
30965	EAST BAY LIGHT 45	30-06-10.729N 085-35-10.732W	Q G	17	3	SG-SY on pile.	Ra ref.
	**Shoal Point Bayou Channel**							
30970	- LIGHT 1	30-05-57.629N 085-35-20.882W	Fl G 2.5s	17	3	SG on dolphin.	
30975	- Buoy 2	30-05-53.354N 085-35-20.546W				Red nun.	Ra ref.
30980	- Buoy 3	30-05-47.200N 085-35-16.038W				Green can.	Ra ref.
30990	- Day beacon 7	30-05-25.390N 085-35-14.400W				SG on pile.	Ra ref.
30995	- Day beacon 9	30-05-15.950N 085-35-14.942W				SG on pile.	Ra ref.
	**St Andrew Bay**							
	**Long Point**							
31000	- Buoy 1	30-05-59.729N 085-36-16.734W				Green can with yellow square.	
31005	- LIGHT 2	30-06-08.367N 085-36-10.226W	Q R	17	3	TR-TY on pile.	
31010	- Buoy 3	30-06-08.636N 085-36-21.665W				Green can with yellow square.	
31015	- Buoy 4	30-06-11.635N 085-36-18.530W				Red nun with yellow triangle.	
31020	- Buoy 5	30-06-18.116N 085-36-36.355W				Green can with yellow square.	
31025	- Buoy 6	30-06-20.307N 085-36-33.329W				Red nun with yellow triangle.	
31030	- Buoy 7	30-06-24.242N 085-36-48.622W				Green can with yellow square.	
31035	- Buoy 8	30-06-29.729N 085-36-36.735W				Red nun with yellow triangle.	
	**St Andrew Bay**							
31040	PEARL BAYOU LIGHT 2	30-06-16.441N 085-36-46.724W	Fl R 4s	17	3	TR on dolphin.	
31045	PEARL BAYOU LIGHT 3	30-06-03.335N 085-36-54.746W	Fl G 4s	17	4	SG on pile.	
31050 3550	- LIGHT 29	30-07-22.535N 085-36-41.759W	Fl G 2.5s	17	3	SG-TY on pile.	Ra ref.
	**Gulf Power Electrical Tower**							
31055 3490	- DANGER LIGHT	30-07-49.570N 085-36-56.350W	Fl W 2.5s			NW on power line structure worded: DANGER OVERHEAD POWER LINE.	Private aid.
31060 3495	- DANGER LIGHTS(2)	30-07-44.890N 085-36-59.460W	Fl W 2.5s			NW on power line structure worded: DANGER OVERHEAD POWER LINE.	Private aid.

(1) No.	(2) Name and Location	(3) Position	(4) Characteristic	(5) Height	(6) Range	(7) Structure	(8) Remarks
\multicolumn{8}{c}{INTRACOASTAL WATERWAY (Florida) - Eighth District}							

EAST BAY TO WEST BAY (Chart 11390)

St Andrew Bay

Gulf Power Electrical Tower

(1) No.	(2) Name and Location	(3) Position	(4) Characteristic	(5) Height	(6) Range	(7) Structure	(8) Remarks
31065 3500	- DANGER LIGHTS (2)	30-07-38.920N 085-37-07.290W	Fl W 2.5s			NW on power line structure worded: DANGER OVERHEAD POWER LINE.	Private aid.
31070 3505	- DANGER LIGHT	30-07-33.790N 085-37-14.010W	Fl W 2.5s			NW on power line structure worded: DANGER OVERHEAD POWER LINE.	Private aid.

St Andrew Bay

(1) No.	(2) Name and Location	(3) Position	(4) Characteristic	(5) Height	(6) Range	(7) Structure	(8) Remarks
31075 3485	- LIGHT 28	30-07-39.529N 085-37-16.435W	Q R	17	3	TR-SY on pile.	Ra ref.
31080 3480	- Lighted Buoy 25	30-07-53.179N 085-37-53.445W	Fl G 2.5s		3	Green with yellow triangle.	
31085 3475	- Coast Guard Mooring Buoy	30-07-27.548N 085-38-12.044W					For use by USCG only.
31090 3470	- LIGHT 24	30-07-34.818N 085-38-32.747W	Fl R 4s	17	3	TR-SY on pile.	Ra ref.
31095 3465	- Lighted Buoy 21	30-08-01.827N 085-39-04.210W	Q G		4	Green with yellow triangle.	
31100 3460	- Lighted Buoy 20	30-08-19.803N 085-39-28.989W	Fl R 2.5s		3	Red with yellow square.	
31105 3455	- Lighted Buoy 19	30-08-33.926N 085-39-32.985W	Fl G 2.5s		3	Green can with yellow triangle.	
31110 3450	- LIGHT 18	30-08-34.642N 085-40-03.209W	Q R	17	3	TR-SY on pile.	
31115 3445	- Lighted Buoy 17	30-08-39.784N 085-39-57.886W	Q G		3	Green with yellow triangle.	
31120 3435	- Junction Lighted Buoy	30-08-59.377N 085-40-47.122W	Fl (2+1)G 6s		4	Green can with red band and yellow triangle.	
31125 3555	- West Lighted Buoy 3	30-09-03.503N 085-41-16.512W	Q G		3	Green with yellow square.	
31130 3560	- West Lighted Buoy 5	30-09-16.301N 085-41-52.343W	Fl G 4s		4	Green with yellow square.	
31135 3570	- West Lighted Buoy 6	30-09-29.544N 085-42-20.582W	Fl R 2.5s		3	Red with yellow triangle.	
31140 3575	- West Lighted Buoy 8	30-09-40.432N 085-42-36.298W	Fl R 4s		3	Red with yellow triangle.	
31145 3580	- West Lighted Buoy 9	30-09-50.184N 085-42-49.581W	Fl G 2.5s		4	Green with yellow square.	
31150 3585	- West Lighted Buoy 10	30-10-09.875N 085-43-00.709W	Fl R 4s		3	Red with yellow triangle.	
31155 3590	- West Lighted Buoy 11	30-09-57.727N 085-43-14.747W	Fl G 4s		4	Green with yellow square.	
31160 3595	- West Lighted Buoy 13	30-10-19.783N 085-43-29.111W	Fl G 2.5s		4	Green with yellow triangle.	
31165 3600	- WEST LIGHT 14	30-10-34.903N 085-44-10.493W	Fl R 4s	17	3	TR-TY on pile.	Ra ref.
31170 3680	Sulphur Point Buoy 1	30-10-55.897N 085-44-35.144W				Green can with yellow square.	
31175 3685	Sulphur Point Buoy 2	30-10-56.024N 085-44-27.033W				Red nun with yellow triangle.	
31180 3690	Sulphur Point Buoy 3	30-11-05.534N 085-44-34.567W				Green can with yellow square.	
31185 3695	Sulphur Point Buoy 4	30-11-03.488N 085-44-27.084W				Red nun with yellow triangle.	
31190 3710	Sulphur Point Buoy 5	30-11-27.511N 085-44-32.740W				Green can with yellow square.	

Light List corrected through LNM week: 01/18

(1) No.	(2) Name and Location	(3) Position	(4) Characteristic	(5) Height	(6) Range	(7) Structure	(8) Remarks
	INTRACOASTAL WATERWAY (Florida) - Eighth District						
	EAST BAY TO WEST BAY (Chart 11390)						
	St Andrew Bay						
31195 3715	Sulphur Point Buoy 6	30-11-26.748N 085-44-26.234W				Red nun with yellow triangle.	
31200 3720	Sulphur Point Buoy 7	30-11-36.130N 085-44-33.364W				Green can with yellow square.	
31205 3725	Sulphur Point Buoy 8	30-11-35.615N 085-44-23.871W				Red nun with yellow triangle.	
	EAST BAY TO WEST BAY (Chart 11390)						
31210	SHELL POINT LIGHT 5	30-12-42.996N 085-44-00.453W	Fl G 2.5s	17	3	SG-SY on pile.	Ra ref.
31215	SHELL POINT LIGHT 7	30-13-37.323N 085-44-10.599W	Fl G 4s	17	4	SG-SY on pile.	Ra ref.
31220	LONG POINT LIGHT 9	30-14-20.652N 085-44-59.701W	Fl G 6s	17	4	SG-SY on pile.	
31225	WEST BAY LIGHT 1	30-15-32.569N 085-46-28.953W	Fl G 4s	17	4	SG-SY on pile.	Ra ref.
31230	West Bay Daybeacon 3	30-15-36.821N 085-47-00.055W				SG-SY on pile.	Ra ref.
31235	West Bay Daybeacon 5	30-15-43.539N 085-47-40.123W				SG-SY on pile.	Ra ref.
31240	WEST BAY LIGHT 7	30-15-47.435N 085-47-59.764W	Fl G 2.5s	17	3	SG-SY on dolphin.	
31245	West Bay Buoy 8	30-15-50.529N 085-47-59.331W				Red nun with yellow triangle.	
31250	West Bay Buoy 9	30-15-50.495N 085-48-19.007W				Green can with yellow square.	
31255	West Bay Buoy 10	30-15-54.443N 085-48-20.866W				Red nun with yellow triangle.	
31260	West Bay Buoy 11	30-15-53.132N 085-48-32.446W				Green can with yellow square.	
31265	West Bay Buoy 12	30-15-56.709N 085-48-33.220W				Red nun with yellow triangle.	
31270	West Bay Buoy 13	30-15-57.112N 085-48-51.331W				Green can with yellow square.	
31275	West Bay Buoy 14	30-15-59.755N 085-48-49.626W				Red nun with yellow triangle.	
31280	WEST BAY LIGHT 15	30-15-59.690N 085-49-05.787W	Q G	17	3	SG-SY on dolphin.	
31285	West Bay Buoy 16	30-16-03.403N 085-49-04.170W				Red nun with yellow triangle.	
31290	West Bay Buoy 17	30-16-07.828N 085-49-23.842W				Green can with yellow square.	
31295	West Bay Buoy 18	30-16-10.313N 085-49-20.421W				Red nun with yellow triangle.	
31300	West Bay Buoy 19	30-16-13.855N 085-49-36.421W				Green can with yellow square.	
31305	West Bay Buoy 20	30-16-16.963N 085-49-35.453W				Red nun with yellow triangle.	
31310	West Bay Buoy 21	30-16-20.480N 085-49-49.896W				Green can with yellow square.	
31315	West Bay Buoy 22	30-16-22.107N 085-49-48.909W				Red nun with yellow triangle.	
31320	West Bay Buoy 23	30-16-26.833N 085-50-04.091W				Green can with yellow square.	
31325	West Bay Buoy 24	30-16-28.507N 085-50-03.109W				Red nun with yellow triangle.	
31327	WEST BAY OYSTER COMPANY SPECIAL LIGHTS (4)	30-15-31.254N 085-50-30.470W	Fl Y 2.5s			Marks the perimeter corners of aquaculture farm.	Private aid.
31330	West Bay Buoy 25	30-16-33.774N 085-50-18.409W				Green can with yellow square.	
31335	WEST BAY LIGHT 26	30-16-35.415N 085-50-16.737W	Q R	17	3	TR-TY on pile.	Ra ref.

Light List corrected through LNM week: 01/18

(1) No.	(2) Name and Location	(3) Position	(4) Characteristic	(5) Height	(6) Range	(7) Structure	(8) Remarks
	**INTRACOASTAL WATERWAY (Florida) - Eighth District**						
	**EAST BAY TO WEST BAY (Chart 11390)**						
31340	West Bay Buoy 27	30-16-44.175N 085-50-28.908W				Green can with yellow square.	
31345	West Bay Buoy 28	30-16-45.370N 085-50-27.385W				Red nun with yellow triangle.	
31350	West Bay Buoy 29	30-16-54.485N 085-50-39.428W				Green can with yellow square.	
31355	West Bay Buoy 30	30-16-56.055N 085-50-38.805W				Red nun with yellow triangle.	
31360	West Bay Buoy 31	30-17-04.901N 085-50-50.164W				Green can with yellow square.	
31365	West Bay Buoy 32	30-17-06.717N 085-50-49.675W				Red nun with yellow triangle.	
31370	West Bay Buoy 33	30-17-15.311N 085-51-00.713W				Green can with yellow square.	
31375	West Bay Buoy 34	30-17-16.530N 085-50-59.152W				Red nun with yellow triangle.	
31380	West Bay Buoy 35	30-17-25.770N 085-51-11.372W				Green can with yellow square.	
31385	West Bay Buoy 36	30-17-26.925N 085-51-09.768W				Red nun with yellow triangle.	
31390	West Bay Buoy 37	30-17-32.293N 085-51-17.903W				Green can with yellow square.	
31395	West Bay Buoy 38	30-17-33.408N 085-51-16.574W				Red nun with yellow triangle.	
31400	West Bay Daybeacon 39	30-17-49.674N 085-51-36.590W				SG-SY on pile.	
31402	West Bay Creek Wreck Buoy 1	30-18-40.638N 085-59-22.662W				Green can.	
	**WEST BAY TO SANTA ROSA SOUND (Chart 11385)**						
	**Choctawhatchee Bay**						
31405	- LIGHT 1	30-22-48.619N 086-07-02.955W	Fl G 2.5s	17	3	SG-SY on pile.	Ra ref.
31410	- Buoy 2	30-22-53.962N 086-07-11.373W				Red nun with yellow triangle.	
31415	- Buoy 3	30-22-56.171N 086-07-22.341W				Green can with yellow square.	
31420	- Buoy 4	30-23-03.560N 086-07-36.907W				Red nun with yellow triangle.	
31425	- Buoy 5	30-23-01.358N 086-07-37.588W				Green can with yellow square.	
31430	- Buoy 7	30-23-05.473N 086-07-49.384W				Green can with yellow square.	
31435	- Buoy 8	30-23-11.679N 086-07-59.681W				Red nun with yellow triangle.	
31440	- LIGHT 9	30-23-09.573N 086-08-01.142W	Fl G 4s	17	4	SG-SY on pile.	Ra ref.
31445	- Buoy 11	30-23-14.305N 086-08-13.208W				Green can with yellow square.	
31450	- Buoy 12	30-23-21.981N 086-08-26.338W				Red nun with yellow triangle.	
31455	- Buoy 13	30-23-19.595N 086-08-27.780W				Green can with yellow square.	
31460	- Buoy 15	30-23-23.901N 086-08-40.625W				Green can with yellow square.	
31465	- Buoy 16	30-23-32.132N 086-08-51.529W				Red nun with yellow triangle.	
31470	- LIGHT 17 45 feet outside channel limit.	30-23-29.421N 086-08-54.846W	Fl G 4s	17	4	SG-SY on pile.	
31475	- Buoy 18	30-23-39.492N 086-09-09.515W				Red nun with yellow triangle.	
31480	- Buoy 19	30-23-36.451N 086-09-12.038W				Green can with yellow square.	
31485	- Buoy 20	30-23-44.906N 086-09-22.580W				Red nun with yellow triangle.	

Light List corrected through LNM week: 01/18

(1) No.	(2) Name and Location	(3) Position	(4) Characteristic	(5) Height	(6) Range	(7) Structure	(8) Remarks
		INTRACOASTAL WATERWAY (Florida) - Eighth District					
	WEST BAY TO SANTA ROSA SOUND (Chart 11385)						
	Choctawhatchee Bay						
31490	- Buoy 21	30-23-42.135N 086-09-26.566W				Green can with yellow square.	
31495	- Buoy 22	30-23-51.969N 086-09-40.100W				Red nun with yellow triangle.	
31500	- LIGHT 23	30-23-49.341N 086-09-43.386W	Fl G 2.5s	17	3	SG-SY on pile.	
31505	- Buoy 25	30-23-53.515N 086-09-52.990W				Green can with yellow square.	
31507	FDOT CHOCTAWHATCHEE BAY TEMPORARY PIER OBSTRUCTION LIGHT	30-23-59.750N 086-10-07.160W	Q W			Marks west pier structure.	Private aid.
31507.01	FDOT CHOCTAWHATCHEE BAY TEMPORARY PIER OBSTRUCTION LIGHT	30-24-01.590N 086-10-06.310W	Q W			Marks east pier structure.	Private aid.
31510	- Buoy 26	30-24-07.968N 086-10-21.256W				Red nun with yellow triangle.	
31515	- Day beacon 27	30-24-09.049N 086-10-36.292W				SG-SY on pile.	
31520	- LIGHT 28	30-24-13.585N 086-10-33.652W	Q R	17	3	TR-TY on pile.	Ra ref.
31525	- Day beacon 29	30-24-21.838N 086-10-58.313W				SG-SY on pile.	Ra ref.
31530	- Day beacon 30	30-24-24.565N 086-10-54.966W				TR-TY on pile.	
31535	- Day beacon 33	30-24-33.407N 086-11-18.057W				SG-SY on pile.	
31540	- LIGHT 34	30-24-34.794N 086-11-12.631W	Fl R 2.5s	17	3	TR-TY on pile.	
31545	- Day beacon 35	30-24-43.738N 086-11-35.121W				SG-SY on pile.	Ra ref.
31550	- Day beacon 36	30-24-46.249N 086-11-32.092W				TR-TY on pile.	Ra ref.
31555	- Day beacon 39	30-24-53.511N 086-11-51.781W				SG-SY on pile.	
31560	- LIGHT 40	30-24-57.097N 086-11-49.504W	Fl R 4s	17	3	TR-TY on pile.	
31565	- Day beacon 45	30-25-16.192N 086-12-30.270W				SG-SY on pile.	
31570	- LIGHT 46	30-25-20.494N 086-12-27.983W	Fl R 6s	17	4	TR-TY on dolphin.	
	La Grange Bayou						
31575	- LIGHT 1	30-25-53.605N 086-12-32.153W	Q G	17	3	SG on pile.	Ra ref.
31580	- Day beacon 3	30-26-17.542N 086-11-47.114W				SG on pile.	
31585	- LIGHT 5	30-26-41.111N 086-11-02.012W	Fl G 4s	17	4	SG on pile.	Ra ref.
31590	- Day beacon 7	30-26-51.366N 086-10-42.259W				SG on pile.	
31595	- Day beacon 9	30-27-01.246N 086-10-23.558W				SG on pile.	Ra ref.
31600	- LIGHT 11	30-27-16.456N 086-09-55.782W	Fl G 4s	17	4	SG on pile.	
31605	- Day beacon 11A	30-27-19.276N 086-09-42.266W				SG on pile.	
31610	- Day beacon 13	30-27-21.220N 086-09-28.436W				SG on pile.	
31615	- LIGHT 14	30-27-18.710N 086-09-29.789W	Fl R 4s	17	3	TR on pile.	
31620	- Day beacon 15	30-27-22.930N 086-09-25.580W				SG on pile.	Ra ref.
31625	- Day beacon 16	30-27-32.352N 086-09-17.369W				TR on pile.	Ra ref.

Light List corrected through LNM week: 01/18

(1) No.	(2) Name and Location	(3) Position	(4) Characteristic	(5) Height	(6) Range	(7) Structure	(8) Remarks
	INTRACOASTAL WATERWAY (Florida) - Eighth District						
	**WEST BAY TO SANTA ROSA SOUND (Chart 11385)**						
	La Grange Bayou						
31630	- Day beacon 18	30-27-45.978N 086-09-09.377W				TR on pile.	Ra ref.
31635	- LIGHT 19	30-27-49.080N 086-09-09.928W	Fl G 4s	17	4	SG on dolphin.	
31640	- Day beacon 20	30-27-59.574N 086-08-46.337W				TR on pile.	
31645	- LIGHT 22	30-28-11.668N 086-08-26.373W	Fl R 4s	17	3	TR on dolphin.	
31650	- Day beacon 23	30-28-16.680N 086-08-24.720W				SG on pile.	
31655	- LIGHT 24	30-28-23.572N 086-08-15.626W	Fl R 4s	17	3	TR on pile.	Ra ref.
31660	- Day beacon 25	30-28-25.765N 086-08-18.366W				SG on pile.	
31665	- Day beacon 27	30-28-32.542N 086-08-19.657W				SG on pile.	Ra ref.
31670	American Commercial Lines Mooring Buoys (2)	30-26-40.000N 086-12-40.000W				White with blue band.	Private aid.
	Choctawhatchee Bay						
31675	- LIGHT 47	30-26-13.200N 086-14-31.516W	Fl G 4s	17	4	SG-SY on dolphin.	Ra ref.
31680	HAMMOCK POINT WRECK LIGHT	30-27-39.088N 086-18-13.839W	Fl W 2.5s	17	5	NW on pile.	
	Hogtown Bayou						
31685	- Day beacon 1	30-23-58.970N 086-14-11.730W				SG on pile.	Private aid.
31690	- Day beacon 2	30-23-56.870N 086-14-09.750W				TR on pile.	Private aid.
31695	- Day beacon 3	30-23-59.190N 086-13-59.610W				SG on pile.	Private aid.
31700	- Day beacon 4	30-23-57.790N 086-13-59.560W				TR on pile.	Private aid.
31705	- Day beacon 5	30-23-58.020N 086-13-50.630W				SG on pile.	Private aid.
31710	- Day beacon 6	30-23-56.600N 086-13-50.120W				TR on pile.	Private aid.
	Choctawhatchee Bay						
31715	- LIGHT 49	30-25-46.546N 086-18-46.627W	Fl G 4s	17	5	SG-SY on pile.	
	Sandestin Beach Channel						
31720	- LIGHT 1	30-23-45.000N 086-20-09.000W	Fl G 4s	12		SG on pile.	Private aid.
31725	- LIGHT 2	30-23-43.000N 086-20-11.000W	Fl R 4s	12		TR on pile.	Private aid.
31730	- LIGHT 3	30-23-45.500N 086-20-09.700W	Fl G 4s	12		SG on pile.	Private aid.
31735	- LIGHT 4	30-23-41.000N 086-20-07.000W	Fl R 4s	12		TR on pile.	Private aid.
31740	- Day beacon 5	30-23-43.600N 086-20-07.400W				SG on pile.	Private aid.
31745	- Day beacon 6	30-23-42.800N 086-20-07.900W				TR on pile.	Private aid.
31750	- Day beacon 7	30-23-41.700N 086-20-03.000W				SG on pile.	Private aid.
31755	- Day beacon 8	30-23-40.900N 086-20-05.400W				TR on pile.	Private aid.
31760	- Day beacon 9	30-23-39.200N 086-20-02.100W				SG on pile.	Private aid.
31765	- Day beacon 10	30-23-38.600N 086-20-02.500W				TR on pile.	Private aid.
31770	- LIGHT 11	30-23-37.300N 086-19-59.700W	Fl G 4s	12		SG on pile.	Private aid.
31775	- LIGHT 12	30-23-36.700N 086-20-00.100W	Fl R 4s	12		TR on pile.	Private aid.

Light List corrected through LNM week: 01/18

(1) No.	(2) Name and Location	(3) Position	(4) Characteristic	(5) Height	(6) Range	(7) Structure	(8) Remarks

INTRACOASTAL WATERWAY (Florida) - Eighth District

WEST BAY TO SANTA ROSA SOUND (Chart 11385)

Sandestin Beach Channel

(1) No.	(2) Name and Location	(3) Position	(4) Characteristic	(5) Height	(6) Range	(7) Structure	(8) Remarks
31780	- Day beacon 13	30-23-35.200N 086-19-57.000W				SG on pile.	Private aid.
31785	- Day beacon 14	30-23-35.000N 086-19-58.000W				TR on pile.	Private aid.
31790	- DAYBEACON 15	30-23-33.200N 086-19-54.500W				SG on pile.	Private aid.
31795	- Day beacon 16	30-23-32.500N 086-19-54.900W				TR on pile.	Private aid.
31800	- Day beacon 17	30-23-31.200N 086-19-52.100W				SG on pile.	Private aid.
31805	- Day beacon 18	30-23-30.600N 089-19-52.500W				TR on pile.	Private aid.
31810	- Day beacon 19	30-23-29.100N 086-19-49.400W				SG on pile.	Private aid.
31815	- Day beacon 20	30-23-28.500N 086-19-49.900W				TR on pile.	Private aid.
31820	- *Light 21*	30-23-27.200N 086-19-46.900W	Fl G 4s			SG on pile.	Private aid.
31825	- LIGHT 22	30-23-26.500N 086-19-47.300W	Fl R 4s	12		TR on pile.	Private aid.
31830	- Day beacon 23	30-23-11.000N 086-19-42.700W				SG on pile.	Private aid.
31835	- LIGHT 24	30-23-18.600N 086-19-46.700W	Fl R 4s			TR on pile.	Private aid.
31840	- Day beacon 25	30-23-07.800N 086-19-41.600W				SG on pile.	Private aid.
31845	- Day beacon 26	30-23-13.500N 086-19-46.100W				TR on pile.	Private aid.
31850	- Day beacon 28	30-23-10.500N 086-19-47.800W				TR on pile.	Private aid.
31855	- Day beacon 30	30-23-14.400N 086-19-38.700W				TR on pile.	Private aid.

Choctawhatchee Bay

(1) No.	(2) Name and Location	(3) Position	(4) Characteristic	(5) Height	(6) Range	(7) Structure	(8) Remarks
31860	- *Lighted Buoy 51*	30-25-46.807N 086-24-32.080W	Fl G 2.5s		3	Green with yellow square.	
31865	- Buoy 52	30-25-59.965N 086-24-31.270W				Red nun with yellow triangle.	
31870	- Buoy 53	30-25-53.402N 086-24-50.080W				Green can with yellow square.	
31875	- Buoy 54	30-26-00.358N 086-24-49.822W				Red nun with yellow triangle.	
31880	- Buoy 55	30-25-58.273N 086-25-17.733W				Green can with yellow square.	
31885	- Buoy 56	30-26-07.013N 086-25-15.178W				Red nun with yellow triangle.	
31890	- Buoy 57	30-25-59.969N 086-25-29.078W				Green can with yellow square.	
31895	- *Lighted Buoy 58*	30-26-08.888N 086-25-29.752W	Fl R 2.5s		3	Red with yellow triangle.	

Mid-Bay Marina Channel

(1) No.	(2) Name and Location	(3) Position	(4) Characteristic	(5) Height	(6) Range	(7) Structure	(8) Remarks
31900	- Day beacon 1	30-24-27.370N 086-25-25.450W				SG on pile.	Private aid.
31905	- Day beacon 3	30-24-26.410N 086-25-25.720W				SG on pile.	Private aid.
31910	- Day beacon 5	30-24-24.480N 086-25-26.300W				SG on pile.	Private aid.
31915	- Day beacon 7	30-24-22.560N 086-25-26.890W				SG on pile.	Private aid.
31920	- Day beacon 9	30-24-20.640N 086-25-27.520W				SG on pile.	Private aid.
31925	- Day beacon 11	30-24-18.740N 086-25-28.170W				SG on pile.	Private aid.
31930	- Day beacon 13	30-24-16.840N 086-25-28.860W				SG on pile.	Private aid.

INTRACOASTAL WATERWAY (Florida) - Eighth District

(1) No.	(2) Name and Location	(3) Position	(4) Characteristic	(5) Height	(6) Range	(7) Structure	(8) Remarks
WEST BAY TO SANTA ROSA SOUND (Chart 11385)							
Choctawhatchee Bay							
Mid-Bay Marina Channel							
31935	- Day beacon 15	30-24-14.940N 086-25-29.560W				SG on pile.	Private aid.
31940	- Day beacon 17	30-24-13.060N 086-25-30.290W				SG on pile.	Private aid.
Indian Bayou							
31945	- Day beacon 1	30-24-46.260N 086-26-55.280W				SG on pile.	Private aid.
31950	- Day beacon 2	30-24-46.320N 086-26-56.820W				TR on pile.	Private aid.
31955	- Day beacon 3	30-24-43.500N 086-26-55.200W				SG on pile.	Private aid.
31960	- Day beacon 4	30-24-43.380N 086-26-56.160W				TR on pile.	Private aid.
31965	- Day beacon 5	30-24-41.820N 086-26-54.960W				SG on pile.	Private aid.
31970	- Day beacon 6	30-24-41.700N 086-26-55.740W				TR on pile.	Private aid.
31975	- Day beacon 7	30-24-39.540N 086-26-54.540W				SG on pile.	Private aid.
31980	- Day beacon 8	30-24-39.360N 086-26-55.200W				TR on pile.	Private aid.
31985	- Day beacon 9	30-24-35.640N 086-26-53.820W				SG on pile.	Private aid.
31990	- Day beacon 10	30-24-35.520N 086-26-54.540W				TR on pile.	Private aid.
31995	- Day beacon 11	30-24-30.900N 086-26-52.680W				TR on pile.	Private aid.
32000	- Day beacon 12	30-24-30.660N 086-26-53.460W				SG on pile.	Private aid.
32005	- Day beacon 13	30-24-24.180N 086-26-55.080W				TR on pile.	Private aid.
32010	- Day beacon 14	30-24-24.840N 086-26-55.680W				SG on pile.	Private aid.
32015	- Day beacon 15	30-24-18.480N 086-27-01.620W				TR on pile.	Private aid.
32020	- Day beacon 16	30-24-18.720N 086-27-03.360W				TR on pile.	Private aid.
Choctawhatchee Bay							
32025	ROCKY BAYOU ENTRANCE LIGHT 1	30-29-02.098N 086-27-10.952W	Fl G 4s	17	4	SG on pile.	
Ward Cove							
32030	- Channel Day beacon 1	30-29-56.000N 086-26-52.000W				SG on pile.	Private aid.
32035	- LIGHT 2	30-29-54.000N 086-26-54.000W	Fl R 4s		4	TR on pile.	Private aid.
32040	- LIGHT 3	30-29-53.000N 086-26-49.000W	Fl G 4s		4	SG on pile.	Private aid.
32045	- Channel Day beacon 4	30-29-52.000N 086-26-46.000W				TR on pile.	Private aid.
Boggy Bayou							
32050	- LIGHT 1	30-27-36.234N 086-28-24.045W	Fl G 6s	17	4	SG on dolphin.	
32055	- LIGHT 3	30-28-45.024N 086-28-28.697W	Fl G 2.5s	17	3	SG on dolphin.	Ra ref.
32060	- Day beacon 4	30-28-49.832N 086-28-23.084W				TR on pile.	Ra ref.
32065	- Day beacon 5	30-28-52.036N 086-28-31.436W				SG on pile.	Ra ref.
32070	- Day beacon 6	30-29-32.458N 086-28-43.263W				TR on pile.	Ra ref.
32075	- Day beacon 7	30-29-32.626N 086-28-53.648W				SG on pile.	Ra ref.

Light List corrected through LNM week: 01/18

(1) No.	(2) Name and Location	(3) Position	(4) Characteristic	(5) Height	(6) Range	(7) Structure	(8) Remarks
		INTRACOASTAL WATERWAY (Florida) - Eighth District					
	WEST BAY TO SANTA ROSA SOUND (Chart 11385)						
	Choctawhatchee Bay						
	Boggy Bayou						
32080	- Day beacon 8	30-30-04.177N 086-28-57.652W				TR on pile.	
32085	- LIGHT 9	30-30-16.870N 086-29-03.506W	Fl G 4s	17	4	SG on pile.	
	Choctawhatchee Bay						
32090	Weekley Bayou Day beacon 1	30-29-03.308N 086-28-55.287W				SG on pile.	Ra ref.
32095	Weekley Bayou Day beacon 2	30-29-01.805N 086-28-59.550W				TR on pile.	
	WEST BAY TO SANTA ROSA SOUND (Chart 11385)						
32100	CHOCTAWHATCHEE BAY LIGHT 59	30-25-35.792N 086-29-21.042W	Q G	17	3	SG-SY on pile.	Ra ref.
32105	JOES BAYOU ENTRANCE CHANNEL LIGHT 2	30-25-06.394N 086-29-34.952W	Q R	17	3	TR on pile.	Ra ref.
32110	Joes Bayou Entrance Channel Day beacon 4	30-24-58.962N 086-29-31.964W				TR on pile.	
32115	CHOCTAWHATCHEE BAY LIGHT 61	30-24-29.700N 086-32-14.329W	Fl G 6s	17	4	SG-SY on pile.	Ra ref.
32120	BLACK POINT LIGHT 2	30-25-32.307N 086-33-19.979W	Fl R 2.5s	17	3	TR on pile.	
32125	Garnier Bayou Entrance Day beacon 4	30-25-51.971N 086-34-33.921W				TR on pile.	
32130	SMACK SHOAL LIGHT 3	30-25-33.679N 086-34-38.337W	Fl G 2.5s	17	3	SG on pile.	Ra ref.
32135	SMACK SHOAL LIGHT 5	30-25-40.143N 086-35-12.085W	Fl G 4s	17	4	SG on pile.	
	Santa Rosa Sound Entrance						
32140	- LIGHT 1	30-24-01.562N 086-33-37.788W	Fl G 2.5s	17	4	SG-SY on dolphin.	Visible all around, higher intensity on bearing 245°. Ra ref.
32145	- Buoy 2	30-24-08.690N 086-33-40.936W				Red nun with yellow triangle.	
32150	- Buoy 3	30-24-04.006N 086-33-51.680W				Green can with yellow square.	
32155	- Buoy 4	30-24-07.525N 086-33-51.974W				Red nun with yellow triangle.	
32160	- Buoy 5	30-24-04.609N 086-34-04.028W				Green can with yellow square.	
32165	- Buoy 6	30-24-07.210N 086-34-05.025W				Red nun with yellow triangle.	
32170	- Buoy 7	30-24-04.535N 086-34-16.479W				Green can with yellow square.	
32175	- Buoy 8	30-24-06.925N 086-34-18.135W				Red nun with yellow triangle.	
32180	- Buoy 9	30-24-04.916N 086-34-30.983W				Green can with yellow square.	
32185	- Buoy 10	30-24-06.840N 086-34-31.113W				Red nun with yellow triangle.	
32190	- Buoy 11	30-24-04.274N 086-34-41.205W				Green can with yellow square.	
32195	- Buoy 12	30-24-06.148N 086-34-41.296W				Red nun with yellow triangle.	
32200	- Buoy 13	30-24-03.206N 086-34-52.598W				Green can with yellow square.	
32205	- Buoy 14	30-24-06.107N 086-34-52.285W				Red nun with yellow triangle.	
32210	- Buoy 15	30-24-02.920N 086-35-05.028W				Green can with yellow square.	
32215	- Buoy 16	30-24-06.175N 086-35-06.080W				Red nun with yellow triangle.	

Light List corrected through LNM week: 01/18

(1) No.	(2) Name and Location	(3) Position	(4) Characteristic	(5) Height	(6) Range	(7) Structure	(8) Remarks
	INTRACOASTAL WATERWAY (Florida) - Eighth District						
	WEST BAY TO SANTA ROSA SOUND (Chart 11385)						
	Santa Rosa Sound						
32220	- Day beacon 4	30-24-07.659N 086-35-39.553W				TR-TY on pile.	Ra ref.
32225	- Day beacon 4A	30-24-06.427N 086-35-52.344W				TR-TY on pile.	Ra ref.
32230	- Day beacon 6	30-24-03.219N 086-36-21.830W				TR-TY on pile.	Ra ref.
32235	- Buoy 7	30-24-00.396N 086-36-20.558W				Green can with yellow square.	
32240	- Day beacon 8	30-24-02.592N 086-36-26.299W				TR-TY on pile.	Ra ref.
32245	- LIGHT 10 50 feet outside channel limit.	30-24-01.360N 086-36-42.231W	Q R	17	3	TR-TY on pile.	
32250	- Day beacon 14	30-24-01.818N 086-36-54.564W				TR-TY on pile.	
32255	- Day beacon 16	30-24-01.888N 086-37-03.560W				TR-TY on pile.	Ra ref.
32260	Fort Walton Lodge & Yacht Basin Day beacon 1	30-24-03.750N 086-37-15.000W				SG on pile.	Private aid.
32265	Fort Walton Lodge & Yacht Basin Day beacon 2	30-24-03.750N 086-37-13.120W				TR on pile.	Private aid.
32270	- Day beacon 20	30-24-04.077N 086-37-23.356W				TR-TY on pile.	Ra ref.
32275	- LIGHT 21	30-24-04.518N 086-37-42.722W	Fl G 2.5s	17	3	SG-SY on pile.	Ra ref.
32280	- Buoy 22	30-24-07.219N 086-37-48.532W				Red nun with yellow triangle.	
32285	- Buoy 23	30-24-05.739N 086-38-11.475W				Green can with yellow square.	
32290	- Day beacon 24	30-24-08.119N 086-38-19.433W				TR-TY on pile.	Ra ref.
32295	- Day beacon 26	30-24-07.219N 086-38-33.533W				TR-TY on pile.	Ra ref.
32300	- Day beacon 28	30-24-05.919N 086-38-47.434W				TR-TY on pile.	Ra ref.
32305	- Buoy 29	30-24-02.065N 086-38-55.975W				Green can with yellow square.	
32310	- LIGHT 30	30-24-04.864N 086-38-55.694W	Q R	17	3	TR-TY on pile.	
32315	- Buoy 31	30-24-06.292N 086-39-13.606W				Green can with yellow square.	
32320	- LIGHT 32	30-24-09.274N 086-39-11.382W	Q R	17	3	TR-TY on pile.	
32325	- Buoy 32A	30-24-10.082N 086-39-12.788W				Red nun with yellow triangle.	
32330	- Buoy 34	30-24-14.444N 086-39-16.528W				Red nun with yellow triangle.	
32335	- Buoy 35	30-24-18.218N 086-39-26.035W				Green can with yellow square.	
32340	- LIGHT 37 45 feet outside channel limit.	30-24-22.553N 086-39-33.346W	Q G	17	3	SG-SY on pile.	Ra ref.
32345	- Day beacon 39	30-24-23.203N 086-39-45.773W				SG-SY on pile.	Ra ref.
32350	- Day beacon 40	30-24-27.391N 086-40-02.584W				TR-TY on pile.	Ra ref.
32355	- Day beacon 41	30-24-24.018N 086-40-02.435W				SG-SY on pile.	Ra ref.
32360	- Day beacon 42	30-24-27.734N 086-40-12.657W				TR-TY on pile.	Ra ref.
32365	- LIGHT 43	30-24-25.882N 086-40-32.201W	Q G	17	3	SG-SY on pile.	Ra ref.

INTRACOASTAL WATERWAY (Florida) - Eighth District

WEST BAY TO SANTA ROSA SOUND (Chart 11385)
Santa Rosa Sound

(1) No.	(2) Name and Location	(3) Position	(4) Characteristic	(5) Height	(6) Range	(7) Structure	(8) Remarks
32370	- Day beacon 45	30-24-25.478N 086-40-38.559W				SG-SY on pile.	Ra ref.
32375	- Day beacon 47	30-24-22.218N 086-40-55.737W				SG-SY on pile.	Ra ref.
32380	- Day beacon 48	30-24-26.017N 086-40-57.137W				TR-TY on pile.	Ra ref.
32385	- Buoy 49	30-24-20.117N 086-41-09.737W				Green can with yellow square.	
32390	- Shoal Buoy 48A	30-24-20.088N 086-41-24.501W				Red nun with yellow triangle.	
32395	- LIGHT 50	30-24-20.032N 086-41-30.128W	Q R	17	3	TR-TY on pile.	
32400	- Buoy 51	30-24-16.918N 086-41-28.338W				Green can with yellow square.	
32405	- Buoy 52	30-24-20.817N 086-41-39.538W				Red nun with yellow triangle.	
32410	- Buoy 53	30-24-18.618N 086-41-44.431W				Green can with yellow square.	
32415	- Buoy 54	30-24-21.585N 086-41-50.389W				Red nun with yellow triangle.	
32420	- Buoy 55	30-24-18.974N 086-42-00.692W				Green can with yellow square.	
32425	- *Lighted Buoy 56*	30-24-22.200N 086-42-01.160W	Fl R 2.5s		3	Red with yellow triangle.	Ra ref.
32430	- Buoy 57	30-24-21.102N 086-42-09.351W				Green can with yellow square.	
32435	- Buoy 58	30-24-26.617N 086-42-22.838W				Red nun with yellow triangle.	
32440	- LIGHT 59	30-24-22.147N 086-42-17.563W	Fl G 2.5s	17	3	SG-SY on pile.	
32445	Hurlburt Field Marina Buoy 1	30-24-28.800N 086-42-34.800W				Green can.	Private aid.
32450	Hurlburt Field Marina Buoy 2	30-24-28.900N 086-42-33.900W				Red nun.	Private aid.
32455	- LIGHT 60 60 feet outside channel limit.	30-24-26.409N 086-42-38.901W	Fl R 2.5s	17	3	TR-TY on pile.	Ra ref.
32460	- Buoy 60A	30-24-26.758N 086-42-45.089W				Red nun with yellow triangle.	
32465	- Buoy 61	30-24-23.052N 086-42-39.400W				Green can with yellow square.	
32470	- Buoy 62	30-24-27.775N 086-42-53.347W				Red nun with yellow triangle.	
32475	- Buoy 63	30-24-25.717N 086-42-53.844W				Green can with yellow square.	
32480	- Buoy 64	30-24-29.160N 086-43-03.569W				Red nun with yellow triangle.	
32485	- Buoy 65	30-24-28.030N 086-43-13.065W				Green can with yellow square.	
32490	- LIGHT 66	30-24-31.565N 086-43-13.742W	Q R	17	3	TR-TY on pile.	Ra ref.
32495	- LIGHT 67	30-24-26.564N 086-43-39.146W	Q G	17	3	SG-SY on pile.	
32500	- Buoy 68	30-24-31.004N 086-43-39.081W				Red nun with yellow triangle.	
32505	- Buoy 69	30-24-19.917N 086-43-50.341W				Green can with yellow square.	
32510	- Buoy 69A	30-24-17.616N 086-43-55.041W				Green can with yellow square.	
32515	- Buoy 70	30-24-23.003N 086-43-52.254W				Red nun with yellow triangle.	
32520	- Buoy 70A	30-24-20.054N 086-43-56.914W				Red nun with yellow triangle.	

Light List corrected through LNM week: 01/18

INTRACOASTAL WATERWAY (Florida) - Eighth District

WEST BAY TO SANTA ROSA SOUND (Chart 11385)
Santa Rosa Sound

(1) No.	(2) Name and Location	(3) Position	(4) Characteristic	(5) Height	(6) Range	(7) Structure	(8) Remarks
32525	- LIGHT 71 60 feet outside channel limit.	30-24-12.329N 086-44-03.099W	Q G	17	3	SG-SY on pile.	
32530	- Buoy 72	30-24-16.371N 086-44-05.260W				Red nun with yellow triangle.	
32535	- Day beacon 73	30-24-08.671N 086-44-13.326W				SG-SY on pile.	Ra ref.
32540	- LIGHT 74	30-24-06.761N 086-44-34.771W	Q R	17	3	TR-TY on pile.	Ra ref.
32545	- Buoy 74A	30-24-04.944N 086-44-51.150W				Red nun with yellow triangle.	
32550	- LIGHT 75	30-24-03.195N 086-45-23.844W	Q G	17	3	SG-SY on pile.	Ra ref.
32555	- Buoy 75A	30-23-59.117N 086-45-32.544W				Green can with yellow square.	
32560	- Buoy 76	30-24-03.417N 086-45-33.744W				Red nun with yellow triangle.	
32565	- Buoy 77	30-23-52.617N 086-45-43.644W				Green can with yellow square.	
32570	- LIGHT 78	30-23-57.895N 086-45-46.286W	Fl R 2.5s	17	3	TR-TY on pile.	
32575	- Day beacon 79	30-23-47.065N 086-47-07.822W				SG-SY on pile.	Ra ref.
32580	- LIGHT 80	30-23-49.078N 086-47-39.602W	Fl R 4s	17	3	TR-TY on pile.	Ra ref.
32585	- LIGHT 81	30-23-54.076N 086-48-48.794W	Fl G 4s	17	4	SG-SY on pile.	
32590	- Day beacon 81A	30-23-47.917N 086-49-31.651W				SG-SY on pile.	Ra ref.
32595	- LIGHT 82	30-23-49.641N 086-49-54.501W	Fl R 2.5s	17	3	TR-TY on pile.	Ra ref.
32600	- Buoy 83	30-23-46.217N 086-49-55.452W				Green can with yellow square.	
32605	- Day beacon 84	30-23-52.017N 086-50-03.652W				TR-TY on pile.	Ra ref.
32610	- Day beacon 85	30-23-49.417N 086-50-13.452W				SG-SY on pile.	Ra ref.
32615	- LIGHT 87	30-23-51.916N 086-50-30.953W	Fl G 2.5s	17	3	SG-SY on pile.	
32620	- LIGHT 88	30-23-58.317N 086-51-01.554W	Q R	17	3	TR-TY on pile.	
32625	- Buoy 88A	30-23-54.817N 086-51-14.154W				Red nun with yellow triangle.	
32630	- Buoy 89	30-23-51.717N 086-51-12.854W				Green can with yellow square.	
32635	- Day beacon 89A	30-23-48.716N 086-51-23.854W				SG-SY on pile.	Ra ref.
32640	- LIGHT 90	30-23-53.982N 086-51-23.267W	Fl R 2.5s	17	3	TR-TY on pile.	
32645	- Day beacon 91	30-23-48.466N 086-51-40.069W				SG-SY on pile.	Ra ref.
32650	NAVARRE BEACH PIPELINE LIGHT	30-22-58.000N 086-51-53.000W	Fl Y 2.5s	13		NW on pile.	Private aid.
32655	NAVARRE PIPELINE LIGHT	30-24-02.000N 086-51-59.000W	Fl Y 2.5s	13		NW on pile.	Private aid.
32660	- Day beacon 92	30-23-50.516N 086-52-00.855W				TR-TY on pile.	Ra ref.
32665	- Day beacon 93	30-23-46.817N 086-51-59.756W				SG-SY on pile.	
32670	- Buoy 95	30-23-44.570N 086-52-16.094W				Green can with yellow square.	
32675	- Day beacon 96	30-23-44.828N 086-52-34.010W				TR-TY on pile.	Ra ref.

Light List corrected through LNM week: 01/18

(1) No.	(2) Name and Location	(3) Position	(4) Characteristic	(5) Height	(6) Range	(7) Structure	(8) Remarks
		INTRACOASTAL WATERWAY (Florida) - Eighth District					
	WEST BAY TO SANTA ROSA SOUND (Chart 11385)						
	Santa Rosa Sound						
32680	- Buoy 97	30-23-42.250N 086-52-35.596W				Green can with yellow square.	
32685	- Buoy 99	30-23-40.715N 086-52-48.379W				Green can with yellow square.	
32690	- Buoy 101	30-23-39.711N 086-52-58.160W				Green can with yellow square.	
32695	- LIGHT 102	30-23-39.536N 086-53-20.655W	Fl R 4s	17	3	TR-TY on pile.	Ra ref.
32700	- Buoy 103	30-23-37.055N 086-53-19.077W				Green can with yellow square.	
32705	- Day beacon 104	30-23-37.105N 086-53-35.809W				TR-TY on pile.	Ra ref.
32710	- Buoy 105	30-23-34.791N 086-53-35.852W				Green can with yellow square.	
32715	- Day beacon 106	30-23-35.816N 086-53-47.454W				TR-TY on pile.	Ra ref.
32720	- Buoy 107	30-23-31.897N 086-54-00.455W				Green can with yellow square.	
32725	- LIGHT 108	30-23-34.586N 086-53-59.904W	Fl R 6s	17	4	TR-TY on pile.	Ra ref.
32730	- Day beacon 110	30-23-33.257N 086-54-20.663W				TR-TY on pile.	Ra ref.
32735	- Buoy 111	30-23-28.419N 086-54-28.465W				Green can with yellow square.	
32740	- Buoy 113	30-23-27.037N 086-54-41.448W				Green can with yellow square.	
32745	- LIGHT 114	30-23-30.033N 086-54-42.347W	Fl R 4s	17	3	TR-TY on pile.	
32750	- Buoy 115	30-23-25.209N 086-54-56.631W				Green can with yellow square.	
32755	- Buoy 117	30-23-23.568N 086-55-10.265W				Green can with yellow square.	
32760	- Buoy 119	30-23-21.960N 086-55-24.824W				Green can with yellow square.	
32765	- LIGHT 121	30-23-19.110N 086-55-40.440W	Fl G 2.5s	17	3	SG-SY on pile.	
32770	- Day beacon 122	30-23-24.716N 086-55-41.562W				TR-TY on pile.	Ra ref.
32775	- LIGHT 123	30-23-06.717N 086-57-23.865W	Fl G 4s	17	4	SG-SY on pile.	Ra ref.
32780	- Shoal Day beacon 124	30-23-08.136N 086-58-35.564W				TR-TY on pile.	Ra ref.
32785	- LIGHT 125	30-22-56.417N 086-59-12.669W	Fl G 6s	17	4	SG-SY on pile.	Ra ref.
32790	- Day beacon 127	30-22-39.229N 087-00-18.279W				SG-SY on pile.	Ra ref.
32795	- LIGHT 129	30-22-24.330N 087-01-30.030W	Fl G 4s	17	4	SG-SY on pile.	
32800	- LIGHT 130	30-22-24.218N 087-02-05.274W	Fl R 4s	17	4	TR-TY on pile.	Ra ref.
	SANTA ROSA SOUND TO DAUPHIN ISLAND (Chart 11378)						
	Santa Rosa Sound						
32805	- LIGHT 131	30-21-34.856N 087-04-51.232W	Fl G 6s	17	4	SG-SY on pile.	Ra ref.
32810	East Santa Rosa Shores Channel Day beacon 2	30-22-04.000N 087-04-06.000W				TR on pile.	Ra ref. Private aid.
32815	East Santa Rosa Shores Channel Day beacon 4	30-22-05.000N 087-04-06.000W				TR on pile.	Ra ref. Private aid.

Light List corrected through LNM week: 01/18

(1) No.	(2) Name and Location	(3) Position	(4) Characteristic	(5) Height	(6) Range	(7) Structure	(8) Remarks
	INTRACOASTAL WATERWAY (Florida) - Eighth District							

SANTA ROSA SOUND TO DAUPHIN ISLAND (Chart 11378)
Santa Rosa Sound

(1) No.	(2) Name and Location	(3) Position	(4) Characteristic	(5) Height	(6) Range	(7) Structure	(8) Remarks
32820	East Santa Rosa Shores Channel Day beacon 5	30-22-30.000N 087-04-36.000W				SG on pile.	Ra ref. Private aid.
32825	East Santa Rosa Shore Channel Day beacon 6	30-22-31.000N 087-04-34.000W				TR on pile.	Private aid.
32830	East Santa Rosa Shores Day beacon 7	30-22-34.000N 087-04-36.600W				SG on pile.	Ra ref. Private aid.
32835	East Santa Rosa Shores Day beacon 8	30-22-34.000N 087-04-36.000W				TR on pile.	Ra ref. Private aid.
32840	Central Santa Rosa Shores Channel Day beacon 2	30-22-03.000N 087-04-08.000W				TR on pile.	Ra ref. Private aid.
32845	Central Santa Rosa Shores Channel Day beacon 4	30-22-04.000N 087-04-08.000W				TR on pile.	Ra ref. Private aid.
32850	Central Santa Rosa Shores Channel Day beacon 6	30-22-05.000N 087-04-08.000W				TR on pile.	Ra ref. Private aid.
32855	Central Santa Rosa Shores Channel Day beacon 8	30-22-34.000N 087-04-45.000W				TR on pile.	Ra ref. Private aid.
32860	Central Santa Rosa Shores Channel Day beacon 9	30-22-31.800N 087-04-45.600W				SG on pile.	Ra ref. Private aid.
32865	Center-West Crossing Santa Rosa 1	30-22-28.500N 087-04-49.000W				SG on pile.	Ra ref. Private aid.
32870	Center-West Crossing Santa Rosa 2	30-22-29.000N 087-04-51.000W				TR on pile.	Ra ref. Private aid.
32875	West Santa Rosa Shores Channel Day beacon 2	30-22-02.000N 087-04-09.000W				TR on pile.	Ra ref. Private aid.
32880	West Santa Rosa Shores Channel Day beacon 4	30-22-03.000N 087-04-09.000W				TR on pile.	Ra ref. Private aid.
32885	West Santa Rosa Shores Channel Day beacon 6	30-22-04.000N 087-04-09.000W				TR on pile.	Ra ref. Private aid.
32890	West Santa Rosa Shores Channel Day beacon 8	30-22-26.000N 087-04-51.400W				TR on pile.	Ra ref. Private aid.
32895	West Santa Rosa Shores Day beacon 9	30-22-28.400N 087-04-51.900W				SG on pile.	Ra ref. Private aid.
32900	West Santa Rosa Shores Channel Day beacon 10	30-22-28.400N 087-04-51.500W				TR on pile.	Ra ref. Private aid.
32905	West Santa Rosa Shores Day beacon 11	30-22-29.300N 087-04-52.000W				SG on pile.	Ra ref. Private aid.
32910	West Santa Rosa Shores Channel Day beacon 12	30-22-29.300N 087-04-51.600W				TR on pile.	Ra ref. Private aid.

Grand Canal Channel

(1) No.	(2) Name and Location	(3) Position	(4) Characteristic	(5) Height	(6) Range	(7) Structure	(8) Remarks
32915	- Day beacon 1	30-21-56.160N 087-06-53.520W				SG on pile.	Private aid.
32920	- LIGHT 2	30-21-56.100N 087-06-52.620W	Fl R 4s			TR on pile.	Ra ref. Private aid.

Light List corrected through LNM week: 01/18

(1) No.	(2) Name and Location	(3) Position	(4) Characteristic	(5) Height	(6) Range	(7) Structure	(8) Remarks
	INTRACOASTAL WATERWAY (Florida) - Eighth District						
	SANTA ROSA SOUND TO DAUPHIN ISLAND (Chart 11378)						
	Santa Rosa Sound						
	Grand Canal Channel						
32925	- Day beacon 3	30-21-58.200N 087-06-54.060W				SG on pile.	Private aid.
32930	- Day beacon 4	30-21-58.200N 087-06-53.280W				TR on pile.	Private aid.
32935	- Day beacon 5	30-22-00.120N 087-06-54.780W				SG on pile.	Private aid.
32940	- Day beacon 6	30-22-00.200N 087-06-53.750W				TR on pile.	Private aid.
32945	- Day beacon 7	30-22-01.920N 087-06-55.200W				SG on pile.	Private aid.
32950	- Day beacon 8	30-22-02.070N 087-06-54.330W				TR on pile.	Private aid.
32955	- Day beacon 9	30-22-03.780N 087-06-55.680W				SG on pile.	Private aid.
32960	- Day beacon 10	30-22-03.960N 087-06-54.840W				TR on pile.	Private aid.
	SANTA ROSA SOUND TO DAUPHIN ISLAND (Chart 11378)						
32965	*Santa Rosa Sound Lighted Buoy 133*	30-21-15.403N 087-08-31.647W	Fl G 2.5s		4	Green with yellow triangle.	
	Fish Bend South Channel						
32966	ESCAMBIA COUNTY FISH BEND SOUTH CHANNEL LIGHT 1	30-20-58.020N 087-07-52.780W	Fl G 6s				Private aid.
32966.01	ESCAMBIA COUNTY FISH BEND SOUTH CHANNEL LIGHT 2	30-22-57.970N 087-07-55.060W	Fl R 6s				Private aid.
32966.02	ESCAMBIA COUNTY FISH BEND SOUTH CHANNEL LIGHT 3	30-20-48.550N 087-07-52.530W	Fl G 6s				Private aid.
32966.03	ESCAMBIA COUNTY FISH BEND SOUTH CHANNEL LIGHT 4	30-20-48.510N 087-07-54.810W	Fl R 6s				Private aid.
32966.04	ESCAMBIA COUNTY FISH BEND SOUTH CHANNEL LIGHT 5	30-20-36.830N 087-07-52.220W	Fl G 6s				Private aid.
32966.05	ESCAMBIA COUNTY FISH BEND SOUTH CHANNEL LIGHT 6	30-20-37.530N 087-07-54.520W	Fl R 6s				Private aid.
32966.06	ESCAMBIA COUNTY FISH BEND SOUTH CHANNEL LIGHT 7	30-20-28.250N 087-08-00.570W	Fl G 6s				Private aid.
32966.07	ESCAMBIA COUNTY FISH BEND SOUTH CHANNEL LIGHT 8	30-20-29.530N 087-08-02.310W	Fl R 6s				Private aid.
32966.08	ESCAMBIA COUNTY FISH BEND SOUTH CHANNEL LIGHT 9	30-20-19.970N 087-08-08.640W	Fl G 6s				Private aid.
32966.09	ESCAMBIA COUNTY FISH BEND SOUTH CHANNEL LIGHT 10	30-20-21.240N 087-08-10.380W	Fl R 6s				Private aid.
32966.11	ESCAMBIA COUNTY FISH BEND SOUTH CHANNEL LIGHT 11	30-20-15.660N 087-08-12.830W	Fl G 6s				Private aid.
32966.12	ESCAMBIA COUNTY FISH BEND SOUTH CHANNEL LIGHT 12	30-20-16.930N 087-08-14.580W	Fl R 6s				Private aid.
32966.13	ESCAMBIA COUNTY FISH BEND SOUTH CHANNEL LIGHT 13	30-20-11.340N 087-08-17.030W	Fl G 6s				Private aid.
32966.14	ESCAMBIA COUNTY FISH BEND SOUTH CHANNEL LIGHT 14	30-20-12.700N 087-08-18.700W	Fl G 6s				Private aid.
32966.15	ESCAMBIA COUNTY FISH BEND SOUTH CHANNEL LIGHT 15	30-20-10.640N 087-08-25.190W	Fl G 6s				Private aid.

(1) No.	(2) Name and Location	(3) Position	(4) Characteristic	(5) Height	(6) Range	(7) Structure	(8) Remarks
	INTRACOASTAL WATERWAY (Florida) - Eighth District						
	SANTA ROSA SOUND TO DAUPHIN ISLAND (Chart 11378)						
	Fish Bend South Channel						
32966.16	ESCAMBIA COUNTY FISH BEND SOUTH CHANNEL LIGHT 16	30-20-11.810N 087-08-24.690W	Fl R 6s				Private aid.
	SANTA ROSA SOUND TO DAUPHIN ISLAND (Chart 11378)						
32970	Fishing Bend Obstruction Danger Buoy	30-20-25.200N 087-08-21.000W				White with orange WORDED: DANGER.	
32975	GRAND MARLIN MARINA ENTRANCE LIGHT 2	30-20-40.031N 087-08-56.445W	Fl R 2.5s			Marks marina entrance.	Private aid.
32980	Grand Marlin Marina Entrance Day beacon 1	30-20-38.507N 087-08-55.764W				Marks marina entrance.	Private aid.
	Little Sabine Bay						
32985	- Day beacon 2	30-20-33.000N 087-09-03.000W				TR on pile.	Private aid.
32990	- Day beacon 4	30-20-29.000N 087-09-00.000W				TR on pile.	Private aid.
32995	- Day beacon 5	30-20-24.000N 087-08-55.000W				SG on pile.	Private aid.
33000	- Day beacon 6	30-20-25.000N 087-08-58.000W				TR on pile.	Private aid.
33005	- Day beacon 7	30-20-24.000N 087-08-54.000W				SG on pile.	Private aid.
33010	- Day beacon 8	30-20-24.000N 087-08-56.000W				TR on pile.	Private aid.
33015	- Day beacon 9	30-20-20.000N 087-08-51.000W				SG on pile.	Private aid.
33020	- Day beacon 10	30-20-17.000N 087-08-51.000W				TR on pile.	Private aid.
33025	- Day beacon 12	30-20-12.000N 087-08-47.000W				TR on pile.	Private aid.
	Santa Rosa Sound						
33030	- LIGHT 140 75 feet outside channel limit.	30-20-49.483N 087-09-26.708W	Fl R 4s	17	3	TR-TY on pile.	Ra ref.
33035	- LIGHT 141 75 feet outside channel limit.	30-20-38.869N 087-09-34.008W	Fl (2)G 5s	17	4	SG-SY on pile.	Ra ref.
33040	- LIGHT 142	30-20-32.997N 087-10-00.661W	Fl R 2.5s	17	3	TR-TY on pile.	Ra ref.
33045	- LIGHT 144 100 feet outside channel limit.	30-20-23.842N 087-10-56.792W	Fl R 4s	17	3	TR-TY on pile.	
33047	ESCAMBIA COUNTY ARTIFICIAL REEF LIGHT A	30-19-39.900N 087-10-51.600W	Fl Y 2.5s			Marks southeast corner of reef.	Private aid.
33047.01	ESCAMBIA COUNTY ARTIFICIAL REEF LIGHT B	30-19-39.840N 087-10-52.740W	Fl Y 2.5s			Marks southwest corner of reef.	Private aid.
33047.02	ESCAMBIA COUNTY ARTIFICIAL REEF LIGHT C	30-19-40.860N 087-10-52.800W	Fl Y 2.5s			Marks northwest corner of reef.	Private aid.
33047.03	ESCAMBIA COUNTY ARTIFICIAL REEF LIGHT D	30-19-40.860N 087-10-51.660W	Fl Y 2.5s			Marks northeast corner of reef.	Private aid.
33050	- LIGHT 145	30-19-53.610N 087-13-53.348W	Fl G 2.5s	17	4	SG-SY on dolphin.	Ra ref.
	Pensacola Bay						
33055 4915	- Lighted Buoy 20	30-19-48.719N 087-15-17.895W	Q R		3	Red with yellow square.	
33060 4850	- NAVY RANGE FRONT LIGHT	30-20-04.514N 087-18-58.739W	Fl G 2.5s	34		KRW on skeleton tower on piles.	Visible all around; higher intensity 1.5° each side of range line.
33065 4855	- NAVY RANGE REAR LIGHT 300 feet, 273.5° from front light.	30-20-05.059N 087-19-09.065W	Iso G 6s	58		On skeleton tower on piles.	Visible 2° each side of rangeline.
33070 4905	- Lighted Buoy 18	30-19-53.498N 087-16-41.945W	Fl R 4s		3	Red with yellow square.	

(1) No.	(2) Name and Location	(3) Position	(4) Characteristic	(5) Height	(6) Range	(7) Structure	(8) Remarks
	INTRACOASTAL WATERWAY (Florida) - Eighth District						
	SANTA ROSA SOUND TO DAUPHIN ISLAND (Chart 11378)						
	Pensacola Bay						
33075 4870	- Lighted Buoy 17	30-20-01.719N 087-16-55.899W	Fl G 4s		4	Green with yellow triangle.	
33080 4845	- Lighted Buoy 16	30-19-55.719N 087-17-39.900W	Q R		3	Red with yellow square.	
33085 4840	- Lighted Buoy 15	30-20-15.224N 087-18-07.464W	Fl G 2.5s		4	Green with yellow triangle.	
	Pensacola-Mobile						
33090	- Buoy 1	30-20-03.919N 087-18-37.102W				Green can with yellow square.	
33095	- Lighted Buoy 2	30-20-09.946N 087-18-41.903W	Q R		3	Red with yellow triangle.	
33100	- Buoy 3	30-20-04.101N 087-18-47.590W				Green can with yellow square.	
33105	- Buoy 4	30-20-06.819N 087-18-50.303W				Red nun with yellow triangle.	
33110	- Buoy 5	30-19-57.355N 087-19-04.014W				Green can with yellow square.	
33115	- Shoal Buoy 5A	30-19-54.746N 087-19-18.343W				Green can with yellow square.	
33120	- Buoy 6	30-20-00.789N 087-19-02.863W				Red nun with yellow triangle.	
33125	- Buoy 6A	30-19-57.942N 087-19-13.125W				Red nun with yellow triangle.	
33130	- Buoy 6B	30-19-54.536N 087-19-26.463W				Red nun with yellow triangle.	
	INTRACOASTAL WATERWAY (Alabama) - Eighth District						
	SANTA ROSA SOUND TO DAUPHIN ISLAND (Chart 11378)						
	Pensacola-Mobile						
33132	- Buoy 8	30-19-51.647N 087-19-37.637W				Red nun with yellow triangle.	
	INTRACOASTAL WATERWAY (Florida) - Eighth District						
	SANTA ROSA SOUND TO DAUPHIN ISLAND (Chart 11378)						
	Pensacola-Mobile						
	Sherman Cove Marina						
33135	- Day beacon 1	30-19-52.000N 087-19-38.000W				SG on pile.	Private aid.
33140	- Day beacon 2	30-19-52.000N 087-19-38.000W				TR on pile.	Private aid.
33145	- Day beacon 3	30-19-55.000N 087-19-37.000W				SG on pile.	Private aid.
33150	- Day beacon 4	30-19-55.000N 087-19-36.000W				TR on pile.	Private aid.
33155	- Day beacon 5	30-19-57.000N 087-19-36.000W				SG on pile.	Private aid.
33160	- Day beacon 6	30-19-59.000N 087-19-35.000W				TR on pile.	Private aid.
33165	- Day beacon 7	30-19-59.000N 087-19-35.000W				SG on pile.	Private aid.
33170	- Day beacon 8	30-19-59.000N 087-19-32.000W				TR on pile.	Private aid.
33175	- Day beacon 9	30-20-00.000N 087-19-34.000W				SG on pile.	Private aid.
33180	- Day beacon 10	30-20-00.000N 087-19-32.000W				TR on pile.	Private aid.
	Pensacola-Mobile						
33185	- LIGHT 7	30-19-48.215N 087-19-34.815W	Fl G 2.5s	17	3	SG-SY on pile.	Ra ref.
33190	- LIGHT 10 Marks shoal off Trout Point.	30-19-26.046N 087-21-05.703W	Fl R 6s	17	4	TR-TY on pile.	
33195	- Buoy 11	30-19-01.274N 087-23-21.147W				Green can with yellow square.	

Light List corrected through LNM week: 01/18

(1) No.	(2) Name and Location	(3) Position	(4) Characteristic	(5) Height	(6) Range	(7) Structure	(8) Remarks
	**INTRACOASTAL WATERWAY (Florida) - Eighth District**						
	SANTA ROSA SOUND TO DAUPHIN ISLAND (Chart 11378)						
	Pensacola-Mobile						
	Grand Lagoon Boat Basin Channel						
33200	- Day beacon 1	30-19-10.400N 087-23-28.300W				SG on pile.	Private aid.
33205	- Day beacon 2	30-19-10.020N 087-23-27.000W				TR on pile.	Private aid.
33210	- Day beacon 3	30-19-11.100N 087-23-29.000W				SG on pile.	Private aid.
33215	- Day beacon 4	30-19-10.090N 087-23-27.700W				TR on pile.	Private aid.
33220	- Day beacon 5	30-19-11.800N 087-23-29.600W				SG on pile.	Private aid.
33225	- Day beacon 6	30-19-11.600N 087-23-28.300W				TR on pile.	Private aid.
33230	- Day beacon 8	30-19-12.200N 087-23-28.900W				TR on pile.	Private aid.
	Pensacola-Mobile						
33235	- LIGHT 12	30-19-03.306N 087-23-33.304W	Fl R 4s	17	3	TR-TY on pile.	
33240	- LIGHT 13	30-18-50.037N 087-23-25.853W	Fl G 2.5s	17	3	SG-SY on pile.	Ra ref.
33245	- Day beacon 15	30-18-29.010N 087-23-32.241W				SG-SY on pile.	Ra ref.
33250	- LIGHT 16	30-18-33.136N 087-23-42.396W	Fl R 2.5s	17	3	TR-TY on pile.	
33255	- Day beacon 17	30-18-20.363N 087-23-49.230W				SG-SY on pile.	Ra ref.
33260	- Shoal Buoy 17A	30-18-20.063N 087-23-58.698W				Green can.	
33265	- LIGHT 18	30-18-25.410N 087-23-51.062W	Q R	17	3	TR-TY on pile.	Ra ref.
33270	- Buoy 19	30-18-20.063N 087-24-10.488W				Green can with yellow square.	
33275	- Day beacon 20	30-18-23.742N 087-24-06.908W				TR-TY on pile.	Ra ref.
33280	- Buoy 21	30-18-21.373N 087-24-21.466W				Green can with yellow square.	
33285	- Buoy 21A	30-18-21.499N 087-24-27.424W				Green can with yellow square.	
33290	- Day beacon 22	30-18-24.112N 087-24-21.157W				TR-TY on pile.	Ra ref.
33295	- Day beacon 23	30-18-21.524N 087-24-34.465W				SG-SY on pile.	Ra ref.
33300	- Buoy 24	30-18-24.723N 087-24-36.916W				Red nun with yellow triangle.	
33305	- LIGHT 25	30-18-21.339N 087-24-49.876W	Q G	17	3	SG-SY on pile.	Ra ref.
33310	- Day beacon 26	30-18-25.465N 087-24-48.599W				TR-TY on pile.	Ra ref.
33315	- Buoy 28	30-18-30.846N 087-25-01.603W				Red nun with yellow triangle.	
33320	- Day beacon 29	30-18-32.706N 087-25-10.319W				SG-SY on pile.	Ra ref.
33325	- Day beacon 30	30-18-37.509N 087-25-12.165W				TR-TY on pile.	Ra ref.
33330	- LIGHT 31	30-18-38.746N 087-25-22.260W	Fl G 2.5s	17	3	SG-SY on pile.	Ra ref.
33335	- Shoal Buoy 31A	30-18-47.706N 087-25-43.873W				Green can with yellow square.	
33340	- Buoy 33	30-18-48.331N 087-25-49.426W				Green can with yellow square.	
33345	- LIGHT 35	30-18-45.654N 087-26-20.430W	Fl G 4s	17	4	SG-SY on pile.	Ra ref.

Light List corrected through LNM week: 01/18

(1) No.	(2) Name and Location	(3) Position	(4) Characteristic	(5) Height	(6) Range	(7) Structure	(8) Remarks
	INTRACOASTAL WATERWAY (Florida) - Eighth District						
	SANTA ROSA SOUND TO DAUPHIN ISLAND (Chart 11378)						
	Pensacola-Mobile						
33350	- Day beacon 36	30-18-47.947N 087-26-20.962W				TR-TY on pile.	Ra ref.
	Holiday Harbor Marina Channel						
33355	- Buoy 1	30-18-43.000N 087-26-24.000W				Green can.	Private aid.
33360	- Buoy 2	30-18-43.000N 087-26-24.000W				Red nun.	Private aid.
33365	- Day beacon 3	30-18-41.000N 087-26-25.000W				SG on pile.	Private aid.
33370	- Buoy 4	30-18-40.000N 087-26-26.000W				Red nun.	Private aid.
33375	- Day beacon 5	30-18-39.000N 087-26-24.000W				SG on pile.	Private aid.
33380	- Buoy 6	30-18-38.000N 087-26-25.000W				Red nun.	Private aid.
33385	- Day beacon 7	30-18-37.000N 087-26-24.000W				SG on pile.	Private aid.
33390	- Buoy 8	30-18-36.000N 087-26-24.000W				Red nun.	Private aid.
33395	- Day beacon 9	30-18-36.000N 087-26-24.000W				SG on pile.	Private aid.
33400	- Buoy 10	30-18-35.000N 087-26-23.000W				Red nun.	Private aid.
33405	- Day beacon 11	30-18-35.000N 087-26-21.000W				SG on pile.	Private aid.
	Pensacola-Mobile						
33410	- Day beacon 37	30-18-44.827N 087-26-34.445W				SG-SY on pile.	
33415	- LIGHT 39	30-18-44.517N 087-26-47.175W	Fl G 4s	17	4	SG-SY on pile.	Ra ref.
33420	- Buoy 39A	30-18-40.491N 087-26-59.961W				Green can.	
33425	- Day beacon 40	30-18-45.966N 087-26-53.094W				TR-I on pile.	
33430	- Buoy 41	30-18-37.723N 087-27-05.921W				Green can with yellow square.	
33435	- Buoy 42	30-18-39.309N 087-27-08.040W				Red nun with yellow triangle.	
33440	- Day beacon 43	30-18-30.978N 087-27-19.921W				SG-SY on pile.	Ra ref.
33445	- LIGHT 44 60 feet outside channel limit.	30-18-33.872N 087-27-22.419W	Q R	17	3	TR-TY on pile.	Ra ref.
33450	- Day beacon 46	30-18-31.398N 087-27-39.444W				TR-TY on pile.	Ra ref.
33455	- Day beacon 47	30-18-24.977N 087-28-02.507W				SG-SY on pile.	Ra ref.
33460	- Day beacon 48	30-18-28.112N 087-28-02.359W				TR-TY on pile.	Ra ref.
33465	- Day beacon 49	30-18-21.427N 087-28-26.545W				SG-SY on pile.	
33470	- Day beacon 50	30-18-24.962N 087-28-27.486W				TR-TY on pile.	
33475	- Day beacon 51	30-18-19.723N 087-28-48.925W				SG-SY on pile.	
33480	- Day beacon 52	30-18-22.500N 087-28-49.272W				TR-TY on pile.	Ra ref.
33485	- Day beacon 52A	30-18-19.478N 087-29-26.482W				TR-TY on pile.	Ra ref.
33490	- Day beacon 53	30-18-14.684N 087-29-27.612W				SG-SY on pile.	
33493	ALABAMA DCNR ONO ISLAND DANGER LIGHTS (6)	30-18-07.120N 087-29-31.260W	Fl W 2.5s			Marks submerged fishing reef.	Private aid.

(1) No.	(2) Name and Location	(3) Position	(4) Characteristic	(5) Height	(6) Range	(7) Structure	(8) Remarks
		INTRACOASTAL WATERWAY (Florida) - Eighth District					
	SANTA ROSA SOUND TO DAUPHIN ISLAND (Chart 11378)						
	Pensacola-Mobile						
33495	- LIGHT 55	30-18-13.861N 087-29-43.591W	Fl G 4s	17	4	SG-SY on pile.	
33500	- Day beacon 56	30-18-21.887N 087-30-01.268W				TR-TY on pile.	Ra ref.
33505	- LIGHT 57	30-18-17.724N 087-30-15.929W	Fl G 4s	17	4	SG-SY on pile.	
33510	- LIGHT 58	30-18-35.123N 087-30-24.529W	Fl R 2.5s	17	3	TR-TY on pile.	Ra ref.
		INTRACOASTAL WATERWAY (Alabama) - Eighth District					
	SANTA ROSA SOUND TO DAUPHIN ISLAND (Chart 11378)						
	Pensacola-Mobile						
33515	- LIGHT 59	30-18-49.273N 087-30-48.174W	Fl G 2.5s	17	4	SG-SY on pile.	Ra ref.
33520	- LIGHT 60	30-19-05.333N 087-30-58.336W	Fl R 4s	17	3	TR-TY on pile.	Ra ref.
33525	- LIGHT 61	30-19-00.295N 087-31-11.401W	Q G	17	3	SG-SY on pile.	Ra ref.
33530	- Day beacon 65	30-18-38.072N 087-31-44.080W				SG-I on pile.	
	Stone Quarry Channel						
33535	- Day beacon 2	30-18-42.900N 087-32-13.260W				TR on pile.	Private aid.
33540	- Day beacon 4	30-18-45.300N 087-32-13.260W				TR on pile.	Private aid.
33545	- Day beacon 6	30-18-46.800N 087-32-13.500W				TR on pile.	Private aid.
33550	- Day beacon 8	30-18-48.300N 087-32-13.500W				TR on pile.	Private aid.
	Pensacola-Mobile						
33555	- Day beacon 67 50 feet outside channel limit.	30-18-19.635N 087-32-08.805W				SG-SY on pile.	Ra ref.
33560	- LIGHT 68	30-18-21.620N 087-32-15.637W	Fl R 4s	17	3	TR-TY on pile.	Ra ref.
33565	- Day beacon 69	30-18-13.732N 087-32-30.158W				SG-SY on pile.	Ra ref.
33570	- LIGHT 70	30-18-18.114N 087-32-31.042W	Fl R 4s	17	3	TR-TY on pile.	
33575	- Day beacon 71	30-18-16.451N 087-33-16.927W				SG-SY on pile.	
33580	- Day beacon 72	30-18-21.348N 087-33-16.306W				TR-TY on pile.	Ra ref.
33585	- Day beacon 73	30-18-19.269N 087-33-50.279W				SG-SY on pile.	Ra ref.
		LOUISIANA - Eighth District					
	POINT AU FER TO MARSH ISLAND (Chart 11351)						
	Pensacola-Mobile						
	Bay La Launch Channel						
33590	- Day beacon 1	30-18-42.600N 087-34-08.640W				SG on pile.	Private aid.
33595	- Day beacon 2	30-18-43.980N 087-34-11.280W				TR on pile.	Private aid.
33600	- Day beacon 3	30-18-40.920N 087-34-07.320W				SG on pile.	Private aid.
33605	- Day beacon 4	30-18-42.120N 087-34-05.400W				TR on pile.	Private aid.
33610	- Day beacon 5	30-18-39.540N 087-34-06.240W				SG on pile.	Private aid.
33615	- Day beacon 6	30-18-40.920N 087-34-04.380W				TR on pile.	Private aid.

INTRACOASTAL WATERWAY (Alabama) - Eighth District

SANTA ROSA SOUND TO DAUPHIN ISLAND (Chart 11378)
Pensacola-Mobile

(1) No.	(2) Name and Location	(3) Position	(4) Characteristic	(5) Height	(6) Range	(7) Structure	(8) Remarks
33620	- LIGHT 74 50 feet outside channel limit.	30-18-26.093N 087-33-53.218W	Fl R 4s	17	3	TR-TY on pile.	
33625	- Day beacon 75	30-18-11.653N 087-34-08.266W				SG-SY on pile.	Ra ref.
33630	- Day beacon 76	30-18-15.642N 087-34-12.318W				TR-TY on pile.	Ra ref.
33635	- Day beacon 77	30-18-00.178N 087-34-29.479W				SG-SY on pile.	Ra ref.
33640	- LIGHT 78	30-18-04.694N 087-34-29.957W	Fl R 4s	17	3	TR-TY on pile.	
33645	- Day beacon 80	30-18-04.506N 087-34-34.090W				TR-TY on pile.	
33650	- Day beacon 81	30-18-02.044N 087-35-03.769W				SG-SY on pile.	
33655	- Day beacon 82	30-18-05.657N 087-35-04.383W				TR-TY on pile.	Ra ref.
33660	- Day beacon 84	30-18-06.322N 087-35-25.882W				TR-TY on pile.	Ra ref.
33665	- Day beacon 85	30-18-02.960N 087-35-33.348W				SG-SY on pile.	Ra ref.
33670	- LIGHT 86	30-18-06.829N 087-35-42.279W	Fl R 2.5s	17	3	TR-TY on pile.	Ra ref.
33675	- LIGHT 87	30-18-03.789N 087-36-10.063W	Fl G 4s	17	4	SG-SY on pile.	Ra ref.
33680	- Day beacon 88	30-18-06.712N 087-36-09.765W				TR-TY on pile.	Ra ref.
33685	- Day beacon 89	30-18-03.724N 087-36-30.940W				SG-SY on pile.	Ra ref.
33690	- Day beacon 90	30-18-06.193N 087-36-31.858W				TR-TY on pile.	Ra ref.
33695	- Day beacon 91 50 feet outside channel limit.	30-18-03.425N 087-36-45.054W				SG-SY on pile.	Ra ref.
33700	- Day beacon 92 50 feet outside channel limit.	30-18-06.038N 087-36-45.375W				TR-TY on pile.	Ra ref.
33705	- Day beacon 93	30-18-03.482N 087-37-08.143W				SG-SY on pile.	Ra ref.
33710	- Shoal Buoy 93A	30-18-02.996N 087-37-22.708W				Green can with yellow square.	
33715	- LIGHT 94	30-18-05.928N 087-37-20.476W	Fl R 4s	17	3	TR-TY on pile.	Ra ref.
33720	- Buoy 95	30-18-01.430N 087-37-27.546W				Green can with yellow square.	
33725	- Buoy 95A	30-17-59.993N 087-37-30.236W				Green can with yellow square.	
33728	SAUNDERS YACHTWORKS BASIN LIGHT 2	30-16-49.000N 087-40-32.500W	Fl R 2.5s			Marks dolphin.	Private aid.
33728.01	Saunders Yachtworks Basin Day beacon 1	30-16-49.000N 087-40-33.200W				Marks dolphin.	Private aid.
33730	- LIGHT 97	30-16-41.601N 087-43-23.903W	Fl G 2.5s	17	3	SG-SY on pile.	Ra ref.
33735	- Day beacon 99 50 feet outside channel limit.	30-16-41.992N 087-43-46.068W				SG-SY on pile.	Ra ref.
33740	- LIGHT 100 50 feet outside channel limit.	30-16-44.518N 087-43-45.691W	Fl R 4s	17	3	TR-TY on pile.	Ra ref.
33745	- LIGHT 101	30-16-42.790N 087-44-07.230W	Q G	17	3	SG-SY on pile.	Ra ref.

INTRACOASTAL WATERWAY (Alabama) - Eighth District

SANTA ROSA SOUND TO DAUPHIN ISLAND (Chart 11378)
Pensacola-Mobile

(1) No.	(2) Name and Location	(3) Position	(4) Characteristic	(5) Height	(6) Range	(7) Structure	(8) Remarks
33750	- Day beacon 102	30-16-45.895N 087-44-08.488W				TR-TY on pile.	Ra ref.
33755	- LIGHT 103	30-16-54.634N 087-45-08.646W	Fl G 4s	17	4	SG-SY on pile.	Ra ref.
33760	- Buoy 104	30-16-57.412N 087-45-07.497W				Red nun with yellow triangle.	
33765	- Day beacon 105 50 feet outside channel limit.	30-16-58.851N 087-45-22.527W				SG-SY on pile.	Ra ref.
33770 6805	BON SECOUR RIVER LIGHT 2	30-17-02.338N 087-45-23.122W	Fl R 2.5s	17	3	TR on pile.	Ra ref.
33775	- Buoy 106	30-17-03.105N 087-45-29.951W				Red nun with yellow triangle.	
33780	- Buoy 107	30-17-02.726N 087-45-41.957W				Green can with yellow square.	
33785	- LIGHT 108	30-17-06.429N 087-45-42.928W	Q R	17	3	TR-TY on pile.	Ra ref.
33790	- Buoy 109	30-17-03.010N 087-46-11.682W				Green can with yellow square.	
33795	- Buoy 110	30-17-05.660N 087-46-12.219W				Red nun with yellow triangle.	
33800	- LIGHT 111	30-17-02.642N 087-46-44.817W	Fl G 4s	17	4	SG-SY on pile.	Ra ref.
33805	- Day beacon 112 50 feet outside channel limit.	30-17-05.400N 087-46-45.381W				TR-TY on pile.	Ra ref.
33810	- Buoy 113	30-17-02.264N 087-47-14.367W				Green can with yellow square.	
33815	- Buoy 114	30-17-04.887N 087-47-15.892W				Red nun with yellow triangle.	
33820	- LIGHT 115	30-17-01.557N 087-47-47.075W	Fl G 4s	17	4	SG-SY on pile.	Ra ref.
33823	TERRYS LANDING OYSTER FARM SPECIAL LIGHTS (2)	30-15-18.880N 087-48-00.370W	Fl Y 2.5s			Marks the corner perimeters of aquaculture farm.	Private aid.
33825	- Day beacon 116 50 feet outside channel limit.	30-17-04.726N 087-47-46.962W				TR-TY on pile.	Ra ref.
33830	- Day beacon 117	30-17-01.121N 087-48-25.227W				SG-SY on pile.	Ra ref.
33835	- Day beacon 118	30-17-04.162N 087-48-24.802W				TR-TY on pile.	Ra ref.
33837	ALABAMA DCNR BON SECOUR BAY DANGER LIGHTS (6)	30-18-03.030N 087-48-26.310W	Fl W 2.5s			Marks submerged fishing reef.	Private aid.
33840	- LIGHT 119	30-17-01.589N 087-49-02.688W	Fl G 4s	17	4	SG-SY on pile.	Ra ref.
33845	- Day beacon 120 50 feet outside channel limit.	30-17-04.472N 087-49-02.929W				TR-TY on pile.	Ra ref.
33850	- Day beacon 121	30-17-01.335N 087-49-36.238W				SG-SY on pile.	Ra ref.
33855	- Day beacon 122	30-17-04.572N 087-49-36.675W				TR-TY on pile.	Ra ref.
33860	- LIGHT 123	30-17-00.939N 087-50-10.600W	Fl G 4s	17	4	SG-SY on pile.	Ra ref.
33865	- Day beacon 124	30-17-04.846N 087-50-12.066W				TR-TY on pile.	Ra ref.
33870	- Day beacon 125	30-17-01.381N 087-50-36.838W				SG-SY on pile.	Ra ref.

Light List corrected through LNM week: 01/18

(1) No.	(2) Name and Location	(3) Position	(4) Characteristic	(5) Height	(6) Range	(7) Structure	(8) Remarks
	INTRACOASTAL WATERWAY (Alabama) - Eighth District						
	SANTA ROSA SOUND TO DAUPHIN ISLAND (Chart 11378)						
	Pensacola-Mobile						
33875	- Day beacon 127 50 feet outside channel limit.	30-17-01.333N 087-51-00.705W				SG-SY on pile.	Ra ref.
33880	- Day beacon 129	30-17-01.306N 087-51-20.159W				SG-SY on pile.	Ra ref.
33885	- Day beacon 131 50 feet outside channel limit.	30-17-01.426N 087-51-47.035W				SG-SY on pile.	Ra ref.
33890	- Day beacon 133	30-17-01.413N 087-52-11.354W				SG-SY on pile.	Ra ref.
33895	- LIGHT 135	30-17-01.529N 087-52-35.521W	Fl G 4s	17	4	SG-SY on pile.	Ra ref.
33900	- Day beacon 137	30-17-01.728N 087-52-57.113W				SG-SY on pile.	Ra ref.
33905	- Day beacon 139 50 feet outside channel limit.	30-17-01.427N 087-53-23.458W				SG-SY on pile.	Ra ref.
33910	- Day beacon 141	30-17-01.802N 087-53-45.690W				SG-SY on pile.	Ra ref.
33915	- Day beacon 143 50 feet outside channel limit.	30-17-01.428N 087-54-06.809W				SG-SY on pile.	Ra ref.
33920	- Day beacon 145	30-17-01.844N 087-54-28.729W				SG-SY on pile.	Ra ref.
33925	- LIGHT 147	30-17-01.675N 087-54-55.206W	Q G	17	4	SG-SY on pile.	Ra ref.
33930	- Day beacon 149 50 feet outside channel limit.	30-16-45.961N 087-55-35.497W				SG-SY on pile.	Ra ref.
33935	- LIGHT 151	30-16-29.931N 087-56-16.887W	Fl G 4s	17	4	SG-SY on pile.	Ra ref.
33940	- Day beacon 153 50 feet outside channel limit.	30-16-14.691N 087-56-56.093W				SG-SY on pile.	Ra ref.
33945	- LIGHT 155	30-15-56.830N 087-57-42.383W	Fl G 4s	17	4	SG-SY on pile.	Ra ref.
33950	- LIGHT 157	30-15-32.061N 087-58-48.874W	Q G	17	4	SG-SY on pile.	Ra ref.
33955 6280	Mobile Channel Lighted Buoy 26	30-16-25.007N 088-02-06.029W	Fl (2)R 5s		3	Red with yellow triangle.	
33960 6275	Mobile Channel Lighted Buoy 25	30-16-27.229N 088-02-13.491W	Fl G 4s		3	Green with yellow triangle.	
	Pass Aux Herons						
33965	- LIGHT 2	30-17-01.838N 088-04-54.911W	Fl R 4s	17	4	TR-TY on pile.	Ra ref.
33970	- A RANGE FRONT LIGHT	30-17-37.978N 088-07-17.071W	Q R	17		KRW-I on pile.	Visible 2° each side of rangeline.
33975	- A RANGE FRONT LIGHT PASSING LIGHT	30-17-37.978N 088-07-17.072W	Q W	18	5	On same structure as Pass Aux Herons Range A Front Light.	
33980	- A RANGE REAR LIGHT 884 yards, 286.8° from front light.	30-17-45.578N 088-07-46.036W	Iso R 6s	35		KRW-I on pile structure.	Visible 2° each side of rangeline.
33985	- Day beacon 3	30-17-05.667N 088-05-22.279W				SG-SY on pile.	Ra ref.
33990	- Day beacon 4	30-17-14.990N 088-05-42.936W				TR-TY on pile.	Ra ref.
33995	- Day beacon 5	30-17-18.325N 088-06-10.105W				SG-SY on pile.	Ra ref.
34000	- Buoy 6	30-17-32.389N 088-06-45.425W				Red nun with yellow triangle.	

Light List corrected through LNM week: 01/18

(1) No.	(2) Name and Location	(3) Position	(4) Characteristic	(5) Height	(6) Range	(7) Structure	(8) Remarks
		INTRACOASTAL WATERWAY (Alabama) - Eighth District					
	SANTA ROSA SOUND TO DAUPHIN ISLAND (Chart 11378)						
	Pass Aux Herons						
34005	- Buoy 8	30-17-38.621N 088-06-57.823W				Red nun with yellow triangle.	
34010	- Buoy 9	30-17-31.839N 088-07-05.015W				Green can with yellow square.	
34015	- Buoy 10	30-17-35.093N 088-07-10.943W				Red nun with yellow triangle.	
34020	- Buoy 11	30-17-27.670N 088-07-19.350W				Green can with yellow square.	
34025	- Buoy 12	30-17-26.830N 088-07-33.453W				Red nun with yellow triangle.	
34030	- Buoy 13	30-17-23.294N 088-07-31.548W				Green can with yellow square.	
34035	- Buoy 14	30-17-10.514N 088-08-15.454W				Red nun with yellow triangle.	
34040	- Buoy 15	30-17-13.005N 088-07-58.696W				Green can with yellow square.	
34060	- C RANGE REAR PASSING LIGHT	30-15-29.624N 088-12-47.366W	Q W	14	5	On same structure as Pass Aux Herons Range C Rear Light.	
34065	- Buoy 17	30-17-06.430N 088-08-17.976W				Green can with yellow square.	
34070	- Buoy 18	30-17-03.766N 088-08-35.943W				Red nun with yellow triangle.	
34075	- Buoy 19	30-16-55.306N 088-08-48.417W				Green can with yellow square.	
34080	- Buoy 20	30-16-53.115N 088-09-05.200W				Red nun with yellow triangle.	
34085	BAYOU ALOE JUNCTION LIGHT	30-16-42.729N 088-09-18.001W	Fl (2+1)G 6s	17	3	JG-SY on pile.	Ra ref.
	Bayou Aloe						
34090	- Day beacon 1	30-16-30.263N 088-08-55.420W				SG on pile.	Ra ref.
34095	- LIGHT 2	30-16-17.233N 088-08-32.736W	Fl R 4s	17	3	TR on pile.	Ra ref.
34100	- Day beacon 3 60 feet outside channel limit.	30-16-09.188N 088-08-10.230W				SG on pile.	Ra ref.
34105	- LIGHT 5	30-15-57.833N 088-07-46.105W	Fl G 4s	17	4	SG on pile.	Ra ref.
34110	- Day beacon 6 60 feet outside channel limit.	30-15-55.885N 088-07-46.616W				TR on pile.	Ra ref.
34115	- Day beacon 7 60 feet outside channel limit.	30-15-46.204N 088-07-20.682W				SG on pile.	Ra ref.
34120	- Day beacon 8	30-15-44.861N 088-07-22.713W				TR on pile.	Ra ref.
34125	- LIGHT 9	30-15-34.264N 088-06-55.104W	Fl G 4s	17	4	SG on pile.	Ra ref.
34130	- Day beacon 10 35 feet outside channel limit.	30-15-32.829N 088-06-56.158W				TR on pile.	Ra ref.
	Dauphin Bay						
34135	- Day beacon 1	30-16-01.000N 088-07-53.000W				SG on pile.	Private aid.
34140	- Day beacon 2	30-16-00.000N 088-07-37.000W				TR on pile.	Private aid.
34145	- Day beacon 3	30-16-01.000N 088-07-19.000W				SG on pile.	Private aid.
34150	- Day beacon 4	30-16-00.000N 088-07-00.000W				TR on pile.	Private aid.
34155	- Day beacon 5	30-16-00.000N 088-06-57.000W				SG on pile.	Private aid.

Light List corrected through LNM week: 01/18

(1) No.	(2) Name and Location	(3) Position	(4) Characteristic	(5) Height	(6) Range	(7) Structure	(8) Remarks
\multicolumn{8}{c}{**INTRACOASTAL WATERWAY (Alabama) - Eighth District**}							

SANTA ROSA SOUND TO DAUPHIN ISLAND (Chart 11378)

Pass Aux Herons

Dauphin Bay

No.	Name and Location	Position	Characteristic	Height	Range	Structure	Remarks
34160	- day beacon 6	30-15-57.000N 088-06-56.000W				TR on pile.	Private aid.
34165	- Day beacon 7	30-15-55.000N 088-06-51.000W				SG on pile.	Private aid.
34170	- Day beacon 8	30-15-55.000N 088-06-31.000W				TR on pile.	Private aid.

Pass Aux Herons

No.	Name and Location	Position	Characteristic	Height	Range	Structure	Remarks
34175	- Buoy 22	30-16-39.252N 088-09-40.681W				Red nun with yellow triangle.	
34180	- Buoy 23	30-16-30.622N 088-09-55.821W				Green can with yellow square.	
34185	- Buoy 24	30-16-28.016N 088-10-13.297W				Red nun with yellow triangle.	
34190	DAUPHIN ISLAND WRECK LIGHT WR1	30-15-20.157N 088-10-20.130W	Q G	17	3	SG on pile.	Ra ref.
34195	- Buoy 25	30-16-18.619N 088-10-27.839W				Green can with yellow square.	
34200	- Buoy 26	30-16-17.338N 088-10-41.485W				Red nun with yellow triangle.	
34205	- Buoy 27	30-16-09.278N 088-10-52.063W				Green can with yellow square.	
34210	- *Lighted Buoy 28*	30-16-07.386N 088-11-10.128W	Q R		3	Red with yellow triangle.	
34215	- D RANGE FRONT LIGHT	30-16-07.725N 088-10-38.809W	Q W	15		KRW-I on dolphin.	Visible 2° each side of rangeline.
34220	- D RANGE FRONT LIGHT PASSING LIGHT	30-16-07.725N 088-10-38.809W	Fl W 4s	17	5	On same structure as Pass Aux Herons Range D Front Light.	
34225	- D RANGE REAR LIGHT 2,909 yards, 084.8° from front light.	30-16-15.585N 088-08-59.719W	Iso W 6s	65		KRW-I on piles.	Visible 2° each side of rangeline.
34230	- D RANGE REAR LIGHT PASSING LIGHT	30-16-15.585N 088-08-59.719W	Fl W 4s	67	5	On same structure as Pass Aux Herons Range D Rear Light.	
34235	- Buoy 29	30-16-01.916N 088-11-26.811W				Green can with yellow square.	
34237	*Mobile Oyster Company Special Lighted Buoy B*	30-15-08.770N 088-11-25.410W	Fl Y 2.5s			Marks perimeter of off-bottom aquaculture farm.	Private aid.
34237.01	*Mobile Oyster Company Special Lighted Buoy C*	30-15-08.130N 088-11-30.130W	Fl Y 2.5s			Marks perimeter of off-bottom aquaculture farm.	Private aid.
34237.02	MOBILE OYSTER COMPANY SPECIAL LIGHT D	30-15-06.040N 088-11-30.130W	Fl Y 2.5s			Marks perimeter of off-bottom aquaculture farm.	Private aid.
34237.03	MOBILE OYSTER COMPANY SPECIAL LIGHT A	30-15-06.700N 088-11-25.380W	Fl Y 2.5s			Marks perimeter of off-bottom aquaculture farm.	Private aid.
34240	- Buoy 30	30-16-04.596N 088-11-43.960W				Red nun with yellow triangle.	

DAUPHIN ISLAND TO DOG KEYS PASS (Chart 11374)

Pass Aux Herons

No.	Name and Location	Position	Characteristic	Height	Range	Structure	Remarks
34245	- Buoy 31	30-15-58.518N 088-12-09.603W				Green can with yellow square.	
34250	- Day beacon 32	30-16-01.360N 088-12-34.518W				TR-TY on pile.	Ra ref.
34255	- Day beacon 33	30-15-56.506N 088-12-34.380W				SG-SY on pile.	Ra ref.
34260	- Day beacon 34	30-15-57.143N 088-13-26.553W				TR-TY on pile.	Ra ref.

(1) No.	(2) Name and Location	(3) Position	(4) Characteristic	(5) Height	(6) Range	(7) Structure	(8) Remarks
		INTRACOASTAL WATERWAY (Alabama) - Eighth District					
	DAUPHIN ISLAND TO DOG KEYS PASS (Chart 11374)						
	Pass Aux Herons						
34265	- Day beacon 35	30-15-51.886N 088-13-27.273W				SG-SY on pile.	Ra ref.
34270	- Day beacon 36	30-15-52.692N 088-14-21.531W				TR-TY on pile.	Ra ref.
34275	- Day beacon 37	30-15-48.276N 088-14-21.418W				SG-SY on pile.	Ra ref.
34280	- Day beacon 37A	30-15-46.898N 088-14-49.381W				SG-SY on pile.	Ra ref.
34285	- Day beacon 38	30-15-48.583N 088-15-14.177W				TR-TY on pile.	Ra ref.
34290	- Day beacon 39	30-15-44.124N 088-15-14.175W				SG-SY on pile.	Ra ref.
34295	- LIGHT 40 90 feet outside channel limit.	30-15-44.266N 088-16-02.012W	Fl R 4s	17	5	TR-TY on piles.	Ra ref.
34300	- LIGHT 41	30-15-40.200N 088-16-01.131W	Fl G 4s	17	5	SG-SY on piles.	Ra ref.
34305	Gulf Intracoastal Waterway Mooring Buoy 103	30-15-56.540N 088-19-19.240W				White and blue band.	Maintained by U.S. Army Corps of Engineers. Ra ref. Aid maintained by U.S. Army Corps of Engineers.
34310	Gulf Intracoastal Waterway Mooring Buoy 102	30-15-55.480N 088-16-47.540W				White with blue band.	Maintained by U.S. Army Corps of Engineers. Ra ref. Aid maintained by U.S. Army Corps of Engineers.
		INTRACOASTAL WATERWAY (Mississippi) - Eighth District					
	DAUPHIN ISLAND TO DOG KEYS PASS (Chart 11374)						
	Bayou La Batre						
34315 7665	- LIGHT 5	30-15-16.571N 088-20-45.385W	Q G	17	3	SG-TY on pile.	Ra ref.
34320 7660	- LIGHT 3	30-14-51.823N 088-25-32.550W	Fl G 4s	17	4	SG-TY on pile.	Ra ref.
34325 8035	Pascagoula Channel Lighted Buoy 30	30-15-24.956N 088-30-30.218W	Q R		3	Red with yellow triangle.	
34330 8030	Pascagoula Channel Lighted Buoy 29	30-15-24.404N 088-30-36.284W	Q G		3	Green with yellow triangle.	
	Round Island South Channel						
34335	- Lighted Buoy 1	30-15-11.466N 088-34-44.658W	Fl G 2.5s		4	Green with yellow square.	
34340	- LIGHT 2	30-15-19.159N 088-36-14.590W	Fl R 4s	17	4	TR-TY on pile.	Ra ref.
34345	- LIGHT 3	30-15-06.617N 088-36-42.301W	Q G	17	3	SG-SY on pile.	Ra ref.
34350	- LIGHT 5	30-16-49.017N 088-38-08.993W	Fl G 2.5s	17	5	SG-SY on pile.	Ra ref.
34355	- Buoy 5A	30-16-49.245N 088-38-08.034W				Green can with yellow square.	
34360	BELLE FONTAINE LIGHT 6	30-17-05.515N 088-41-05.252W	Fl R 4s	17	4	TR-TY on pile.	Ra ref.
34365	BELLE FONTAINE LIGHT 8	30-17-13.980N 088-44-42.285W	Fl R 6s	17	5	TR-TY on pile.	Ra ref.
	DOG KEYS PASS TO WAVELAND (Chart 11372)						
	Mississippi Sound						
34370	SHIP ISLAND LIGHT 2	30-17-10.969N 088-52-00.018W	Fl R 2.5s	17	5	TR-TY on pile.	Ra ref.
34375	SHIP ISLAND LIGHT 4	30-17-00.937N 088-57-11.687W	Fl R 2.5s	17	4	TR-TY on pile.	Ra ref.

Light List corrected through LNM week: 01/18

(1) No.	(2) Name and Location	(3) Position	(4) Characteristic	(5) Height	(6) Range	(7) Structure	(8) Remarks
	INTRACOASTAL WATERWAY (Mississippi) - Eighth District						
	DOG KEYS PASS TO WAVELAND (Chart 11372)						
	Mississippi Sound						
	Gulfport Ship Channel						
34380 9825	- LIGHT 42	30-16-31.829N 089-01-05.614W	Iso R 6s	17	4	TR-SY on pile.	Ra ref.
34385 9820	- LIGHT 41	30-16-31.500N 089-01-13.828W	Fl G 2.5s	17	3	TR-SY on pile.	Ra ref.
34390 9835	- LIGHT 44	30-17-03.627N 089-01-32.419W	Fl R 2.5s	17	4	TR-TY on pile.	Ra ref.
34395 9830	- LIGHT 43	30-17-03.596N 089-01-40.858W	Iso G 6s	17	4	SG-TY on pile.	Ra ref.
	Mississippi Sound						
34400	CAT ISLAND LIGHT 2	30-16-51.400N 089-05-05.959W	Fl R 2.5s	17	3	TR-TY on pile.	Ra ref.
	Marianne Channel						
34403	- WRECK LIGHT WR2	30-16-41.782N 089-09-37.600W	Q R	17	3	TR-TY on pile.	Ra ref.
34405	- Lighted Buoy 1	30-16-37.537N 089-08-59.279W	Fl G 2.5s		4	Green with yellow square.	
34410	- LIGHT 3	30-16-15.000N 089-09-37.500W	Fl G 6s	17	4	SG-SY on pile.	Ra ref.
34415	- LIGHT 5	30-15-26.216N 089-10-54.124W	Fl G 4s	17	4	SG-SY on pile.	Ra ref.
34420	- LIGHT 7	30-14-43.431N 089-11-44.000W	Fl G 6s	17	4	SG-SY on pile.	Ra ref.
34425	- LIGHT 8	30-14-15.466N 089-12-30.545W	Fl R 4s	17	4	TR-TY on pile.	Ra ref.
34430	- Buoy 10	30-14-00.715N 089-12-59.046W				Red nun with yellow triangle.	
34435	- LIGHT 13	30-13-18.715N 089-13-48.147W	Fl G 4s	17	4	SG-SY on pile.	Ra ref.
34440	- Buoy 12	30-13-24.810N 089-13-53.538W				Red nun with yellow triangle.	
34445	- LIGHT 14	30-12-53.328N 089-14-46.229W	Fl R 4s	17	3	TR-TY on pile.	Ra ref.
34450	- Buoy 16	30-12-39.215N 089-15-08.901W				Red nun with yellow triangle.	
34455	- Buoy 17	30-12-35.852N 089-15-06.211W				Green can with yellow square.	
34460	- Buoy 18	30-12-23.448N 089-15-34.920W				Red nun with yellow triangle.	
34465	- Buoy 19	30-12-18.929N 089-15-32.593W				Green can with yellow square.	
34470	- Buoy 20	30-12-08.215N 089-16-03.153W				Red nun with yellow triangle.	
34475	- Buoy 21	30-12-02.972N 089-16-01.332W				Green can with yellow square.	
34480	- LIGHT 22	30-11-52.240N 089-16-31.824W	Fl R 4s	17	3	TR-TY on pile.	Ra ref.
34485	- Buoy 23	30-11-47.959N 089-16-28.127W				Green can with yellow square.	
34490	- LIGHT 24	30-11-24.969N 089-17-17.450W	Fl R 2.5s	17	4	TR-TY on pile.	Ra ref.
34495	- Buoy 25	30-11-19.715N 089-17-14.155W				Green can with yellow square.	
34500	- Buoy 26	30-11-00.072N 089-18-01.037W				Red nun with yellow triangle.	
	Pass Marianne						
34505	- Daybeacon 2	30-15-47.257N 089-12-13.960W				TR-TY on pile.	Ra ref.
34510	- LIGHT 4P	30-15-31.764N 089-12-59.466W	Fl R 2.5s	17	3	TR-TY on pile.	Ra ref.

(1) No.	(2) Name and Location	(3) Position	(4) Characteristic	(5) Height	(6) Range	(7) Structure	(8) Remarks
	INTRACOASTAL WATERWAY (Mississippi) - Eighth District						
	DOG KEYS PASS TO WAVELAND (Chart 11372)						
	Mississippi Sound						
	Pass Marianne						
34515	- Day beacon 5	30-14-43.970N 089-14-13.974W				SG-SY on pile.	Ra ref.
34520	- Day beacon 6	30-14-37.701N 089-14-40.129W				TR-TY on pile.	Ra ref.
34525	- Day beacon 7	30-14-28.419N 089-14-35.305W				SG-SY on pile.	Ra ref.
34530	- Day beacon 8	30-14-30.720N 089-14-42.166W				TR-TY on pile.	Ra ref.
34535	PASS MARIANNE WRECK LIGHT WR 8A	30-14-28.381N 089-14-44.042W	Q R	17	3	TR-TY on pile.	Ra ref.
34540	- Day beacon 9	30-14-18.713N 089-14-42.160W				SG-SY on pile.	Ra ref.
34545	- Day beacon 10	30-14-23.703N 089-14-55.196W				TR-TY on pile.	Ra ref.
34550	- Day beacon 11	30-14-09.279N 089-15-01.691W				SG-SY on pile.	Ra ref.
34555	- Day beacon 12	30-14-11.727N 089-15-45.146W				TR-TY on pile.	Ra ref.
34560	- Day beacon 13	30-13-58.710N 089-16-08.140W				SG-SY on pile.	Ra ref.
34565	- LIGHT 15P	30-13-46.712N 089-17-02.777W	Fl G 4s	17	5	SG-SY on pile.	Ra ref.
34570	- LIGHT 17P	30-12-16.698N 089-21-19.152W	Fl G 2.5s	17	4	SG-SY on pile.	Ra ref.
	Grand Island Channel						
34575	- LIGHT 1	30-10-47.059N 089-18-13.011W	Q G	17	4	SG-SY on pile.	Ra ref.
34580	- Day beacon 3	30-10-47.936N 089-19-10.473W				SG-SY on pile.	Ra ref.
34585	- LIGHT 5	30-10-46.875N 089-20-05.226W	Fl G 4s	17	4	SG-SY on pile.	Ra ref.
34590	- Day beacon 7	30-10-46.627N 089-21-07.274W				SG-SY on pile.	Ra ref.
	WAVELAND TO CATAHOULA BAY (Chart 11367)						
	Mississippi Sound						
	Grand Island Channel						
34595	- LIGHT 9	30-10-46.851N 089-21-53.663W	Fl G 4s	17	4	SG-SY on pile.	Ra ref.
34600	- Day beacon 11	30-10-46.974N 089-22-37.796W				SG-SY on pile.	Ra ref.
34605	- Day beacon 13	30-10-46.443N 089-23-24.395W				SG-SY on pile.	Ra ref.
34610	- LIGHT 15	30-10-45.130N 089-24-08.212W	Q G	17	4	SG-SY on pile.	Ra ref.
34615	ST JOSEPH ISLAND LIGHT 22	30-11-04.462N 089-25-33.624W	Fl R 4s	17	5	TR-TY on platform on piles.	Ra ref.
34620	St Joe Pass Day beacon 2	30-10-19.842N 089-27-10.869W				TR-TY on pile.	Ra ref.
34625	ST JOE PASS LIGHT 3	30-09-29.794N 089-28-22.440W	Fl G 4s	17	5	SG-SY on pile.	Ra ref.
	INTRACOASTAL WATERWAY (Louisiana) - Eighth District						
	WAVELAND TO CATAHOULA BAY (Chart 11367)						
	Lake Borgne						
34630	- Day beacon 5	30-09-20.714N 089-30-09.184W				SG-SY on pile.	Ra ref.
34635	- Day beacon 7	30-09-09.968N 089-31-05.464W				SG-SY on pile.	Ra ref.

INTRACOASTAL WATERWAY (Louisiana) - Eighth District

WAVELAND TO CATAHOULA BAY (Chart 11367)

Lake Borgne

(1) No.	(2) Name and Location	(3) Position	(4) Characteristic	(5) Height	(6) Range	(7) Structure	(8) Remarks
34640 10430	PEARL RIVER ENTRANCE CHANNEL LIGHT 1 30 feet outside channel limit.	30-09-20.881N 089-31-29.549W	Fl G 4s	17	4	SG-TY on pile.	Ra ref.
34645	- LIGHT 11	30-09-00.859N 089-31-48.461W	Fl G 4s	17	5	SG-SY on pile.	Ra ref.
34650	- Day beacon 12	30-09-07.800N 089-31-50.644W				TR-TY on pile.	Ra ref.
34655	- Day beacon 14	30-08-58.713N 089-32-40.190W				TR-TY on pile.	Ra ref.
34660	- LIGHT 15 180 feet outside channel limit.	30-08-44.688N 089-33-35.298W	Fl G 4s	17	4	SG-SY on pile.	
34665	- Day beacon 16	30-08-50.713N 089-33-34.192W				TR-TY on pile.	Ra ref.
34670	- Day beacon 18	30-08-42.713N 089-34-36.194W				TR-TY on pile.	Ra ref.
34675	- LIGHT 19	30-08-30.085N 089-35-40.811W	Q G	17	4	SG-SY on pile.	Ra ref.
34680	- Day beacon 20	30-08-37.000N 089-35-36.000W				TR-TY on pile.	Ra ref.
34685	- *Lighted Buoy 21*	30-08-39.604N 089-36-53.867W	Fl G 4s		4	Green can with yellow square.	
34690	- Buoy 23	30-08-42.889N 089-37-21.378W				Green can with yellow square.	
34695	- LIGHT 25	30-08-45.266N 089-37-45.959W	Fl G 6s	17	4	SG-SY on dolphin.	Ra ref.
34700	- LIGHT 26	30-08-51.567N 089-37-46.337W	Q R	17	4	TR-TY on pile.	Ra ref.

Rigolets - New Orleans

(1) No.	(2) Name and Location	(3) Position	(4) Characteristic	(5) Height	(6) Range	(7) Structure	(8) Remarks
34705	NEW ORLEANS CUT LIGHT 1	30-05-20.183N 089-44-29.764W	Fl G 4s	17	4	SG-SY on pile.	Ra ref.
34710 10820	CHEF MENTEUR PASS LIGHT 4	30-03-54.220N 089-47-19.230W	Fl R 2.5s	17	4	TR-TY on pile.	Ra ref.
34715 10825	CHEF MENTEUR PASS LIGHT 5	30-03-34.330N 089-47-44.384W	Fl G 2.5s	25	5	SG-SY on pile.	Ra ref.
34717	ORLEANS LEVEE DISTRICT ICWW SURGE BARRIER SECTOR GATE LIGHT 2	30-00-54.770N 089-54-00.770W	Fl R 2.5s			Flashing red light marks northeast gate wall when open. Fixed red light marks closed gate.	Private aid.
34717.01	ORLEANS LEVEE DISTRICT ICWW SURGE BARRIER SECTOR GATE LIGHT 1	30-00-52.200N 089-54-01.460W	Fl G 2.5s			Flashing green light marks southeast gate wall when open. Fixed red light marks closed gate.	Private aid.
34717.02	ORLEANS LEVEE DISTRICT ICWW SURGE BARRIER SECTOR GATE LIGHT 4	30-00-50.020N 089-54-11.960W	Fl R 2.5s			Flashing red light marks northwest gate wall when open. Fixed red light marks closed gate.	Private aid.
34717.03	ORLEANS LEVEE DISTRICT ICWW SURGE BARRIER SECTOR GATE LIGHT 3	30-00-49.130N 089-54-09.150W	Fl G 2.5s			Flashing green light marks southwest gate wall when open. Fixed red light marks closed gate.	Private aid.

Light List corrected through LNM week: 01/18

(1) No.	(2) Name and Location	(3) Position	(4) Characteristic	(5) Height	(6) Range	(7) Structure	(8) Remarks
		INTRACOASTAL WATERWAY (Louisiana) - Eighth District					
	WAVELAND TO CATAHOULA BAY (Chart 11367)						
	Rigolets - New Orleans						
34717.04	ORLEANS LEVEE DISTRICT ICWW SURGE BARRIER BYPASS GATE LIGHT 2A	30-00-51.310N 089-54-01.080W	Fl R 2.5s			Flashing red light marks northeast gate wall when bypass gate is open for navigation.	Private aid.
34717.05	ORLEANS LEVEE DISTRICT ICWW SURGE BARRIER BYPASS GATE LIGHT 1A	30-00-49.530N 089-53-59.410W	Fl G 2.5s			Flashing green light marks southeast gate wall when bypass gate is open for navigation.	Private aid.
34717.06	ORLEANS LEVEE DISTRICT ICWW SURGE BARRIER BYPASS GATE LIGHT 4A	30-00-48.530N 089-54-08.880W	Fl R 2.5s			Flashing red light marks northwest gate wall when bypass gate is open for navigation.	Private aid.
34717.07	ORLEANS LEVEE DISTRICT ICWW SURGE BARRIER BYPASS GATE LIGHT 3A	30-00-46.130N 089-54-07.660W	Fl G 2.5s			Flashing green light marks southwest gate wall when bypass gate is open for navigation.	Private aid.
34720	MICHOUD CANAL LIGHT 2	30-00-48.755N 089-54-19.180W	Fl R 2.5s	17	3	TR-TY on pile.	Ra ref.
	Mississippi River - Gulf Outlet						
34725 11875	- JUNCTION LIGHT MRGO	30-00-27.566N 089-55-18.004W	Fl (2+1)R 6s	30	3	JR-SY on skeleton tower on piles.	
34730 11880	- LIGHT 129 150 feet outside channel limit.	30-00-19.410N 089-55-53.972W	Fl G 4s	17	4	SG-SY on pile.	
34735 11885	MICHOUD DOCK LIGHTS (2)	30-00-24.000N 089-56-03.000W	Fl R 2.5s	6		On dock.	Private aid.
34740 11890	GRANT STREET DISCHARGE LIGHT	30-00-14.000N 089-56-59.000W	Fl R 2.5s	10		On dolphin.	Private aid.
34750 11900	AMID STATION DISCHARGE LIGHTS (2)	29-59-52.000N 090-00-35.000W	Fl R 2.5s			On dolphins.	Private aid.
34755 13840	INNER HARBOR NAVIGATION CANAL LIGHT 2	29-57-26.118N 090-01-35.250W	Q R		4	TR-SY on skeleton tower.	
34760 13835	INNER HARBOR NAVIGATION CANAL LIGHT 1	29-57-30.732N 090-01-48.254W	Fl G 2.5s		4	SG-TY on skeleton tower.	
	New Orleans - Port Arthur						
	Via Mississippi River and Harvey Canal						
34765 13850	GOVERNOR NICHOLLS LIGHT 94 LDB mile 94.3.	29-57-37.914N 090-03-23.070W	Fl R 4s		6	Skeleton tower. On same structure as Governor Nicholls Harbor Traffic Control Light.	Not operated when traffic control lights are in operation.
34770 13855	**Governor Nicholls Harbor Traffic Control Light 94** LDB mile 94.3.	29-57-37.902N 090-03-22.872W	Fl G 5s		16	On skeleton tower. 94	Operated by Vessel Traffic Safety New Orleans during periods of high water. Controls one way traffic around Algiers Point.
34775 13860	ALGIERS POINT LIGHT 95	29-57-18.883N 090-03-19.092W	Q G		5	SG-SY on skeleton tower on piles.	
34780 13865	NEW ORLEANS POLICE MOORING DOLPHIN LIGHT LDB mile 94.8.	29-56-58.600N 090-03-43.800W	Fl R 2.5s			On dolphin.	Private aid.
34785 13870	UPPER ALGIERS FERRY LANDING LIGHTS (2) RDB mile 94.8.	29-57-12.000N 090-03-21.000W	Fl G 2.5s			On dock.	HORN: 1 BLAST EV 20S (2S BL). OPERATED ONLY DURING LOW VISIBILITY. Private aid.

Light List corrected through LNM week: 01/18

(1) No.	(2) Name and Location	(3) Position	(4) Characteristic	(5) Height	(6) Range	(7) Structure	(8) Remarks
		INTRACOASTAL WATERWAY (Louisiana) - Eighth District					
	WAVELAND TO CATAHOULA BAY (Chart 11367)						
	New Orleans - Port Arthur						
	Via Mississippi River and Harvey Canal						
34790 13875	CANAL STREET FERRY LANDING LIGHTS (2) LDB mile 94.8.	29-56-58.000N 090-03-43.000W	Fl R 2.5s			On dock.	HORN: 1 BLAST EV 20S (2S BL). OPERATED ONLY DURING LOW VISIBILITY. Private aid.
34795 13880	**Gretna Harbor Traffic Control Light 97** RDB mile 96.6.	29-55-33.156N 090-03-29.982W	Fl R 5s (NIGHT) Fl G 5s (NIGHT)		16 16	On skeleton tower. 25	Operated by Vessel Traffic Safety Office New Orleans during periods of high water. Controls one way traffic around Algiers Point.
34800 13885	GRETNA LIGHT 97 RDB mile 96.6.	29-55-33.162N 090-03-30.078W	Fl G 4s		6	SG-SY on skeleton tower on same structure as Gretna Harbor Traffic Control Light.	Not operated when traffic control lights are in operation.
34805 13890	GRETNA WATER INTAKE LIGHT RDB mile 96.7.	29-55-27.000N 090-03-38.000W	Fl G 2.5s			On dolphin.	Private aid.
34808 13892	GRETNA FERRY BOAT RAMP LIGHT	29-55-07.871N 090-04-00.494W	Fl W 2.5s			Marks outermost upstream piling designating the riverward end of boat ramp.	Private aid.
34810 13895	GRETNA FERRY LANDING LIGHTS (2) RDB mile 97.2.	29-55-06.000N 090-04-02.000W	Fl G 2.5s			On dock.	HORN: 1 BLAST EV 20S (2S BL). OPERATED ONLY DURING LOW VISIBILITY. Private aid.
34815 13900	JACKSON AVENUE FERRY LANDING LIGHTS (2) LDB mile 97.2.	29-55-20.000N 090-04-15.000W	Fl R 2.5s			On dock.	HORN: 1 BLAST EV 20S (2S BL). OPERATED ONLY DURING LOW VISIBILITY. Private aid.
34820 13905	INTERNATIONAL MATEX DOCK LIGHTS (4) RDB mile 97.3.	29-55-00.000N 090-04-18.000W	Fl G 2.5s			(2) on floating dock, (2) on outermost upstream and downstream dolphins.	Private aid.
34825	HERO CUT OBSTRUCTION LIGHT A	29-50-02.224N 090-03-57.022W	Q W	17	5	NB on pile.	
	Via Mississippi River and Algiers Cutoff						
34830 13830	FORSTALL STREET DISCHARGE LIGHT LDB mile 92.2.	29-57-19.000N 090-01-25.000W	F R			On dolphins.	Private aid.
34835 13825	DELERY STREET DISCHARGE LIGHT LDB mile 91.6.	29-56-59.000N 090-00-43.000W	Q R			On pile cluster.	Private aid.
34840 13820	Quarantine Anchorage Upper Day beacon 91.6	29-56-36.900N 090-00-54.996W				NY on pile.	Ra ref.
34845 13815	Quarantine Anchorage Lower Day beacon 90.9	29-56-15.168N 090-00-19.242W				NY on pile.	Ra ref.
34850 13810	New Orleans General Anchorage Upper Day beacon 90.5	29-56-15.030N 090-00-19.020W				NY on pile.	Ra ref.
34855 13800	CHALMETTE NATIONAL PARK TOUR BOAT DOCK LIGHTS (2) LDB mile 90.3.	29-56-20.000N 089-59-38.000W	Fl R 2.5s			On dock.	Lights flash in unison. Private aid.
34860 13790	New Orleans General Anchorage Lower Day beacon 90.1	29-55-52.050N 089-59-40.614W				NY on pile.	Ra ref.
34865 13785	CHALMETTE OBSTRUCTION LIGHT LDB mile 89.9.	29-56-00.000N 089-59-12.000W	Q R			On multi-pile structure.	Private aid.

Light List corrected through LNM week: 01/18

(1) No.	(2) Name and Location	(3) Position	(4) Characteristic	(5) Height	(6) Range	(7) Structure	(8) Remarks
	**INTRACOASTAL WATERWAY (Louisiana) - Eighth District**

WAVELAND TO CATAHOULA BAY (Chart 11367)
New Orleans - Port Arthur
Via Mississippi River and Algiers Cutoff

(1) No.	(2) Name and Location	(3) Position	(4) Characteristic	(5) Height	(6) Range	(7) Structure	(8) Remarks
34870 13780	NORFOLK SOUTHERN CORPORATION LIGHT LDB mile 89.8	29-56-23.000N 089-59-42.000W	Fl R 2.5s			On wall.	Private aid.
34880 13770	KAISER UPPER LIGHT LDB mile 89.3.	29-55-48.000N 089-58-48.000W	F R			On multi-pile structure.	Private aid.
34885 13765	TENNECO COKE WHARF LIGHT LDB mile 89.1.	29-55-49.000N 089-58-44.000W	Fl R 2.5s			On dolphin.	Private aid.
34890 13760	MOBIL ST. BENARD MOORING DOLPHIN LIGHTS (4) LDB mile 89.1	29-55-42.000N 088-58-30.000W	Fl R 2.5s			On dolphins.	Private aid.
34895 13755	TENNECO DOCK LIGHTS (2) LDB mile 89.1.	29-55-45.000N 089-58-37.000W	F R				Private aid.
34900 13750	CHALMETTE ALGIERS WEST BANK MAINTENANCE LANDING LIGHTS (2) RDB mile 88.7.	29-55-20.100N 089-55-28.100W	Fl G 2.5s			On barge.	Private aid.
34905 13745	CHALMETTE-ALGIERS EAST BANK FERRY LANDING LIGHTS (2) LDB mile 88.7.	29-55-41.700N 089-58-15.500W	Fl R 2.5s			Dolphin and barge.	Private aid.
34910 13740	CHALMETTE-ALGIERS WEST BANK FERRY LANDING LIGHTS (2) RDB mile 88.7.	29-55-18.600N 089-58-24.300W	Fl G 2.5s			On barge.	Horn: 1 blast ev 20S (2S BL). Private aid.
34915 13735	HUMBLE DOCK LIGHTS (3) LDB mile 88.6.	29-55-31.000N 089-56-47.000W	Fl R 2.5s			On dolphins.	Private aid.
34920 13730	MERAUX INTAKE LIGHTS (7) LDB mile 88.5.	29-55-31.000N 089-56-42.000W	Fl R 2.5s				Private aid.
34925 13725	Mobil St. Bernard Intake Lighted Buoy	29-55-32.400N 089-57-54.000W	Fl R 4s			Red.	Private aid.
34930 13720	TENNECO DOCK LIGHTS (2) RDB mile 88.2.	29-55-33.000N 089-57-51.000W	Fl R 2.5s			On dolphin.	Private aid.

Algiers Alternate Route

(1) No.	(2) Name and Location	(3) Position	(4) Characteristic	(5) Height	(6) Range	(7) Structure	(8) Remarks
34935 13715	- JUNCTION LIGHT A RDB mile 88.2.	29-55-11.922N 089-58-03.168W	Fl (2+1)G 6s		4	JG-TY on skeleton tower on piles.	
34940	- JUNCTION LIGHT	29-49-17.940N 090-04-03.721W	Fl (2+1)R 6s	20	3	JR-TY on dolphin.	Higher intensity beam up Algiers Alternate Route and down Bayou Barataria.
34945	USACE WEST CLOSURE COMPLEX LIGHTS (2)	29-48-55.083N 090-04-13.844W	Q R	12		Marks ends of structure.	HORN: 1 BLAST EV 20S (2S BL). Private aid.
34950	Hole In The Wall Daybeacon 1	29-47-13.413N 090-03-47.161W				SG-SY on pile.	
34955	Hole In The Wall Daybeacon 3	29-46-59.249N 090-03-49.282W				SG-SY on pile.	Ra Ref
34957	TEN MILE EXCHANGE LIGHT 1	29-46-39.700N 090-04-01.710W	Fl G 2.5s			On pile cluster.	Private aid.
34957.01	TEN MILE EXCHANGE LIGHT 2	29-46-45.020N 090-04-05.330W	Fl R 2.5s			On pile cluster.	Private aid.
34957.02	TEN MILE EXCHANGE LIGHT 3	29-46-21.330N 090-04-24.190W	Fl G 2.5s			On pile cluster.	Private aid.
34957.03	TEN MILE EXCHANGE LIGHT 4	29-46-27.580N 090-04-27.000W	Fl R 2.5s			On pile cluster.	Private aid.
34957.04	TEN MILE EXCHANGE LIGHT 5	29-46-06.650N 090-04-51.020W	Fl G 2.5s			On pile cluster.	Private aid.
34957.05	TEN MILE EXCHANGE LIGHT 6	29-46-10.140N 090-04-50.560W	Fl R 2.5s			On pile cluster.	Private aid.

New Orleans - Port Arthur

(1) No.	(2) Name and Location	(3) Position	(4) Characteristic	(5) Height	(6) Range	(7) Structure	(8) Remarks
34960	Bayou Villars Daybeacon 2	29-44-20.965N 090-08-32.797W				TR on pile.	Ra Ref

Light List corrected through LNM week: 01/18

(1) No.	(2) Name and Location	(3) Position	(4) Characteristic	(5) Height	(6) Range	(7) Structure	(8) Remarks
		INTRACOASTAL WATERWAY (Louisiana) - Eighth District					
	WAVELAND TO CATAHOULA BAY (Chart 11367)						
	New Orleans - Port Arthur						
34965	Bayou Perot Entrance Crossing Day beacon 2	29-41-15.172N 090-11-15.344W				TR-TY on pile.	Ra ref.
34970	Bayou Perot Entrance Crossing Day beacon 4	29-40-53.591N 090-11-36.054W				TR-TY on pile.	Ra ref.
34975	BAYOU SEGNETTE PUMP STATION LIGHTS (3)	29-53-45.000N 090-09-32.000W	Fl W 4s			On dolphins. NW on upstream and downstream dolphins WORDED: DANGER WATER DISCHARGE.	Private aid.
	CATAHOULA BAY TO WAX LAKE OUTLET (Chart 11355)						
	New Orleans - Port Arthur						
34980	Delta Farms Buoy 1	29-36-29.626N 090-21-27.734W				Green can with yellow square.	
34985	Delta Farms Buoy 3	29-36-12.985N 090-21-38.991W				Green can with yellow square.	
34990	HARVEY CANAL NO. 2 HUMBLE PIPELINE LIGHTS (2)	29-35-15.000N 090-22-18.000W	F G	8		On pile bulkhead.	Private aid.
34992	TERREBONNE PARISH PUMP STATION DANGER LIGHT	29-34-58.250N 090-43-02.710W	Fl W 2.5s			Marks submerged pipe.	Private aid.
34995	TERREBONE PARISH WATER INTAKE LIGHTS (2)	29-34-30.000N 090-43-04.000W	Fl R 2.5s			On dolphins.	Private aid.
35000	USACE COPESAW CANAL METERING STATION LIGHT	29-34-14.000N 090-57-10.300W	Fl Y 2.5s			On pile.	Private aid.
35005	USACE MINORS CANAL METERING STATION LIGHT	29-31-50.000N 090-47-42.000W				On pile.	Private aid.
35010	USACE GICWW METERING STATION LIGHT	29-32-10.300N 090-47-50.450W	Fl Y 2.5s			On pile.	Private aid.
35013	LAFOURCHE-TERREBONNE S&W CONSERVATION DISTRICT DANGER LIGHT	29-34-19.129N 090-57-09.037W	Fl W 2.5s			Marks shoreline restoration breakwater.	Private aid.
35013.01	LAFOURCHE-TERREBONNE S&W CONSERVATION DISTRICT DANGER LIGHT	29-33-41.564N 090-55-54.218W	Fl W 2.5s			Marks shoreline restoration breakwater.	Private aid.
35013.02	LAFOURCHE-TERREBONNE S&W CONSERVATION DISTRICT DANGER LIGHT	29-33-34.257N 090-55-40.874W	Fl W 2.5s			Marks shoreline restoration breakwater.	Private aid.
35013.03	Lafourche-Terrebonne S&W Conservation District Danger Day beacons (10)	29-33-57.757N 090-56-25.736W				Marks shoreline restoration breakwater.	Private aid.
35013.04	Lafourche-Terrebonne S&W Conservation District Danger Day beacons (11)	29-34-16.982N 090-57-09.498W				Marks shoreline restoration breakwater.	Private aid.
35013.05	Lafourche-Terrebonne S&W Conservation District Danger Day beacons (22)	29-33-34.466N 090-55-44.429W				Marks shoreline restoration breakwater.	Private aid.
	Lake Cocodrie						
35015	- LIGHT 2	29-35-20.401N 090-57-53.268W	Fl R 4s	17	3	TR-TY on pile.	Ra ref.
35020	- Buoy 3	29-35-23.992N 090-58-02.094W				Green can with yellow square.	
35025	- Buoy 4	29-35-25.902N 090-57-57.185W				Red nun with yellow triangle.	
35030	- Buoy 5	29-36-07.265N 090-58-28.882W				Green can with yellow square.	
35035	- Buoy 6	29-36-07.723N 090-58-23.095W				Red nun with yellow triangle.	
35040	- Buoy 7	29-36-33.410N 090-58-46.640W				Green can with yellow square.	
35045	- Buoy 8	29-36-39.289N 090-58-42.472W				Red nun with yellow triangle.	
35050	- Buoy 9	29-36-45.560N 090-58-56.851W				Green can with yellow square.	

Light List corrected through LNM week: 01/18

(1) No.	(2) Name and Location	(3) Position	(4) Characteristic	(5) Height	(6) Range	(7) Structure	(8) Remarks

INTRACOASTAL WATERWAY (Louisiana) - Eighth District

CATAHOULA BAY TO WAX LAKE OUTLET (Chart 11355)
New Orleans - Port Arthur
Lake Cocodrie

(1)	(2)	(3)	(4)	(5)	(6)	(7)	(8)
35055	- LIGHT 10	29-36-48.162N 090-58-52.727W	Fl R 2.5s	17	4	TR on pile.	Ra ref.
35060	- Buoy 12	29-37-00.703N 090-59-11.589W					Red nun with yellow triangle.
35065	- Buoy 13	29-36-57.298N 090-59-14.375W					Green can with yellow square.
35070	- LIGHT 14	29-37-30.294N 091-00-11.623W	Fl R 2.5s	17	4	TR-TY on skeleton tower on piles.	

MORGAN CITY TO PORT ALLEN (Chart 11354)
Morgan City - Port Allen (Landside Route)
Lake Verret

(1)	(2)	(3)	(4)	(5)	(6)	(7)	(8)
35085	- LIGHT C	29-56-47.000N 091-11-30.000W	Fl W 4s	8		Pile structure.	Private aid.
35090	- LIGHT B	29-50-50.000N 091-06-05.000W	Fl W 4s	8		Pile structure.	Private aid.
35095	- LIGHT A	29-49-30.000N 091-05-55.000W	Fl W 4s	8		Pile structure.	Private aid.

New Orleans - Port Arthur
Morgan City-Port Allen Alternate Route

(1)	(2)	(3)	(4)	(5)	(6)	(7)	(8)
35100	DOW CHEMICAL BARGE DOCK LIGHT(2)	29-54-30.000N 091-13-30.000W	Fl R 2.5s	13		On mooring dolphins.	Private aid.
35102	LEJEUNE BOAT HOUSE LIGHT	29-46-02.810N 091-09-48.800W	Fl W 2.5s			Marks boat house structure.	Private aid.
35105	- Day beacon	29-44-09.035N 091-10-42.185W				NW on pile.	

CATAHOULA BAY TO WAX LAKE OUTLET (Chart 11355)
New Orleans - Port Arthur
Morgan City-Port Allen Alternate Route

(1)	(2)	(3)	(4)	(5)	(6)	(7)	(8)
35110	- Day beacon 10 120 feet outside channel limit.	29-43-59.949N 091-10-45.194W				TR-TY on pile.	Ra ref.
35115	- Day beacon 11 135 feet outside channel limit.	29-44-01.652N 091-10-39.390W				SG-SY on pile.	Ra ref.
35120	- Day beacon 12 165 feet outside channel limit.	29-43-46.636N 091-10-55.435W				TR-TY on pile.	Ra ref.
35125	- Day beacon 13 80 feet outside channel limit.	29-43-44.805N 091-10-50.408W				SG-GY on pile.	Ra ref.
35130	- Day beacon 14 90 feet outside channel limit.	29-43-37.448N 091-11-08.360W				TR-TY on pile.	Ra ref.
35135	- Day beacon 15 215 feet outside channel limit.	29-43-32.608N 091-11-07.114W				SG-SY on pile.	Ra ref.
35140	- Day beacon 16	29-43-32.506N 091-11-21.095W				TR-TY on pile.	Ra ref.
35145	- Day beacon 17 200 feet outside channel limit.	29-43-28.632N 091-11-19.202W				SG-SY on pile.	Ra ref.
35150 19185	Berwick Locks Buoy 1	29-42-50.101N 091-13-21.841W					Green can with yellow triangle.
35155 19180	CONRAD DRYDOCK LIGHTS	29-42-00.000N 091-13-00.000W	Fl R 2.5s	25		On drydock and dolphin.	Private aid.
35160	CONRAD DRYDOCK LIGHT	29-42-08.000N 091-12-59.000W	Fl R 2.5s	20		On dolphin.	Private aid.
35165 19165	BERWICK LIGHT	29-41-39.000N 091-13-03.000W	Fl W 6s	45		Red tapered tower.	Private aid.
35170 19155	BERWICK BAY RANGE FRONT A LIGHT	29-41-10.099N 091-12-37.364W	Q R	19		KRW on skeleton tower on piles.	Visible from 054.6° to 215.6°.

(1) No.	(2) Name and Location	(3) Position	(4) Characteristic	(5) Height	(6) Range	(7) Structure	(8) Remarks
	**INTRACOASTAL WATERWAY (Louisiana) - Eighth District**						

CATAHOULA BAY TO WAX LAKE OUTLET (Chart 11355)

New Orleans - Port Arthur

Morgan City-Port Allen Alternate Route

(1) No.	(2) Name and Location	(3) Position	(4) Characteristic	(5) Height	(6) Range	(7) Structure	(8) Remarks
35175 19160	BERWICK BAY RANGE REAR A LIGHT 139 yards, 160.6° from front light.	29-41-06.138N 091-12-35.823W	Iso R 6s	28		KRW on skeleton tower on piles.	Visible from 147.6° to 172.6°.
35180 19170	BERWICK BAY BRIDGE APPROACH DANGER RANGE FRONT LIGHT	29-41-46.704N 091-12-54.837W	Q Y	64		KGR-I on west side bridge abutment.	Visible downbound only. Range marks the western most boundary of the suggested downbound course for approaching the bridges. NOTE: Range is not to be steered on.
35185 19175	BERWICK BAY BRIDGE APPROACH DANGER RANGE REAR LIGHT	29-41-43.612N 091-12-53.194W	Iso Y 6s	86		KGR-I on west side bridge abutment.	Visible downbound only. NOTE: Range is not to be steered on.

Little Wax Bayou

(1) No.	(2) Name and Location	(3) Position	(4) Characteristic	(5) Height	(6) Range	(7) Structure	(8) Remarks
35190 19145	- JUNCTION LIGHT A	29-39-38.139N 091-14-32.559W	Fl (2+1)G 6s	30	5	JG-TY on dolphin.	
35195 19150	- LIGHT 1	29-39-24.390N 091-14-48.500W	Q G	17	4	SG-SY on pile.	Ra ref.
35200	- LIGHT 2	29-39-27.864N 091-14-55.547W	Fl R 2.5s	17	4	TR on pile.	Ra ref.
35205	- LIGHT 3	29-38-32.283N 091-18-07.537W	Fl G 2.5s	17	4	SG-NW on pile worded: VTS BERWICK CHECK POINT SIGN.	Ra ref.
35210	Wax Outlet East Approach Day beacon E	29-38-47.780N 091-23-11.454W				NG-NW on pile worded WARNING EXTREME CURRENT.	Ra ref.
35215	Wax Outlet Northeast Approach Day beacon NE	29-38-54.912N 091-23-19.374W				NG-NW on pile worded WARNING EXTREME CURRENT.	Ra ref.
35220	Wax Outlet Northwest Approach Day beacon NW	29-39-00.730N 091-23-46.057W				NG-NW on pile worded WARNING EXTREME CURRENT.	Ra ref.
35225	Wax Outlet West Approach Day beacon W	29-38-58.006N 091-23-58.064W				NG-NW on pile worded WARNING EXTREME CURRENT.	Ra ref.

WAX LAKE OUTLET TO FORKED ISLAND (Chart 11350)

New Orleans - Port Arthur

(1) No.	(2) Name and Location	(3) Position	(4) Characteristic	(5) Height	(6) Range	(7) Structure	(8) Remarks
35228	ST. MARY LEVEE DISTRICT FLOOD PROTECTION STRUCTURE LIGHT 1	29-46-59.700N 091-31-42.300W	Fl G 2.5s			Marks port side structure.	Private aid.
35228.01	ST. MARY LEVEE DISTRICT FLOOD PROTECTION STRUCTURE LIGHT 2	29-46-59.200N 091-31-42.000W	Fl R 2.5s			Marks starboard side structure.	Private aid.
35228.02	ST. MARY LEVEE DISTRICT FLOOD PROTECTION STRUCTURE LIGHT 3	29-47-00.300N 091-31-41.100W	Fl G 2.5s			Marks port side structure.	Private aid.
35228.03	ST. MARY LEVEE DISTRICT FLOOD PROTECTION STRUCTURE LIGHT 4	29-46-59.800N 091-31-40.900W	Fl R 2.5s			Marks starboard side structure.	Private aid.
35228.04	HANSON CANAL LIGHT 1	29-45-14.040N 091-29-48.430W	Fl G 2.5s			Marks port side of flood gate structure.	Private aid.
35228.05	HANSON CANAL LIGHT 2	29-45-13.980N 091-29-48.270W	Fl R 2.5s			Marks starboard side of flood gate structure.	Private aid.
35230	MUD LAKE LIGHT 9	29-45-08.175N 091-35-57.639W	Fl G 2.5s	17	3	SG on pile.	Ra ref.
35235	MUD LAKE LIGHT 11	29-45-25.769N 091-36-13.838W	Fl G 4s	17	4	SG-SY on pile.	Ra ref.

INTRACOASTAL WATERWAY (Louisiana) - Eighth District

WAX LAKE OUTLET TO FORKED ISLAND (Chart 11350)
New Orleans - Port Arthur

(1) No.	(2) Name and Location	(3) Position	(4) Characteristic	(5) Height	(6) Range	(7) Structure	(8) Remarks
35240	IVANHOE CANAL RIP-RAP OBSTRUCTION LIGHTS (2)	29-45-49.000N 091-44-26.000W	Q G	16		NW on structure.	Private aid.
35245	Weeks Bay P/L Marker C	29-48-36.686N 091-49-22.159W				NW on pile.	Private aid.
35250	Weeks Bay P/L Marker D	29-48-37.453N 091-49-18.634W				NW on pile.	Private aid.
35255	WEEKS ISLAND PIPELINE MARKER LIGHT	29-48-45.000N 091-49-25.500W	Fl Y 2.5s	14		On dolphin.	Private aid.
35260	WEEKS BAY PIPELINE LIGHT A	29-49-06.000N 091-49-36.000W	Fl Y 2.5s	10		NW on pile.	Private aid.
35265	WEEKS BAY PIPELINE LIGHT B	29-49-07.571N 091-49-30.467W	Fl Y 2.5s	10		NW on pile.	Private aid.
35270	WEEKS BAYOU LIGHT	29-49-13.700N 091-49-29.800W	Q W	10		On dolphin.	Private aid.
35274	VERMILLION RIVER ENTRANCE LIGHT 1	29-47-04.692N 092-08-38.633W	Fl G 2.5s	17	3	SG on pile.	
35278	VERMILLION RIVER LIGHT 2	29-47-05.339N 092-08-34.367W	Fl R 2.5s	17	3	TR on pile.	
35285	BROUSSARD LANDING DOCK LIGHT	29-46-52.000N 092-11-20.000W	Fl R 2.5s	14		On pile.	Private aid.

FORKED ISLAND TO ELLENDER (Chart 11348)
New Orleans - Port Arthur
Mermentau River Crossing

(1) No.	(2) Name and Location	(3) Position	(4) Characteristic	(5) Height	(6) Range	(7) Structure	(8) Remarks
35295 20950	- Buoy 1	29-58-17.998N 092-47-19.038W				Green can with yellow square.	
35300 20955	- Buoy 2A	29-58-24.653N 092-47-24.534W				Red nun with yellow triangle.	
35302 20954	- LIGHT 2	29-58-23.457N 092-47-14.524W	Fl R 2.5s	17	3	TR-TY on pile.	
35310 20965	- Buoy 4	29-58-23.751N 092-47-38.829W				Red nun with yellow triangle.	
35315 20970	- Buoy 5	29-58-16.440N 092-47-51.427W				Green can with yellow square.	
35320 20975	- Junction Buoy M	29-58-20.651N 092-48-04.118W				Red nun with green band and yellow triangle.	
35325 20980	- LIGHT 7	29-58-16.645N 092-48-10.590W	Fl G 2.5s	17	3	SG-SY on pile.	

Gibbstown

(1) No.	(2) Name and Location	(3) Position	(4) Characteristic	(5) Height	(6) Range	(7) Structure	(8) Remarks
35330	Mermentau-Gibbstown Buoy 1	29-55-44.775N 092-57-13.156W				Green with yellow square.	
35335	- Day beacon 2	29-56-06.428N 093-05-32.055W				TR-TY on pile.	
35340	- Day beacon 4	29-56-08.586N 093-06-04.317W				TR-TY on pile.	
35345	- Day beacon 6	29-56-11.217N 093-06-35.750W				TR-TY on pile.	

Sweet Lake

(1) No.	(2) Name and Location	(3) Position	(4) Characteristic	(5) Height	(6) Range	(7) Structure	(8) Remarks
35350	- Day beacon 2	29-56-05.564N 093-08-29.946W				TR-TY on pile.	
35355	- Day beacon 4	29-56-05.907N 093-08-52.122W				TR-TY on pile.	
35360	- Day beacon 6	29-56-06.192N 093-09-13.966W				TR-TY on pile.	Ra ref.

Devils Elbow

(1) No.	(2) Name and Location	(3) Position	(4) Characteristic	(5) Height	(6) Range	(7) Structure	(8) Remarks
35365 21830	- INDUSTRIAL CANAL RANGE FRONT LIGHT 5	30-06-27.801N 093-18-19.678W	Q G	20		KRW-I and SG on skeleton tower on piles.	Visible all around; higher intensity on rangeline. KRW-I for inbound traffic. SG for outbound traffic.

Light List corrected through LNM week: 01/18

(1) No.	(2) Name and Location	(3) Position	(4) Characteristic	(5) Height	(6) Range	(7) Structure	(8) Remarks
	INTRACOASTAL WATERWAY (Louisiana) - Eighth District						

FORKED ISLAND TO ELLENDER (Chart 11348)
New Orleans - Port Arthur
Devils Elbow

(1) No.	(2) Name and Location	(3) Position	(4) Characteristic	(5) Height	(6) Range	(7) Structure	(8) Remarks
35370 21835	- INDUSTRIAL CANAL RANGE REAR LIGHT 192 yards, 046.4° from front light.	30-06-31.843N 093-18-14.816W	F G	37		KRW-I on skeleton tower on piles.	Visible all around; higher intensity on rangeline. Ra ref.
35375 21800	- JUNCTION LIGHT	30-06-14.039N 093-18-27.324W	Fl (2+1)R 6s	20	3	JR-TR on skeleton tower.	
35380 21795	- LIGHT 3	30-06-16.399N 093-18-40.888W	Fl G 2.5s	17	3	SG-SY on pile.	
35385 21790	- LIGHT 2	30-05-47.623N 093-19-01.149W	Oc R 4s	17	3	TR-SY on pile.	
35390 21785	- LIGHT 1	30-05-48.804N 093-19-14.341W	Oc G 4s	17	3	SG-TY on pile.	
35395 21805	- RANGE FRONT LIGHT	30-05-14.763N 093-19-47.153W	Q W	20		KRW-I on pile.	Visible all around; higher intensity on rangeline.
35400 21810	- RANGE REAR LIGHT 103 yards, 226.9° from front light.	30-05-12.642N 093-19-49.672W	Iso W 6s	40		KRW-I on skeleton tower.	Visible all around; higher intensity on rangeline.

Calcasieu Channel

(1) No.	(2) Name and Location	(3) Position	(4) Characteristic	(5) Height	(6) Range	(7) Structure	(8) Remarks
35405 21780	- LIGHT 92	30-05-21.790N 093-19-24.920W	Fl R 2.5s	17	4	TR-SY on pile.	
35410 21775	- LIGHT 91	30-05-18.123N 093-19-34.478W	Fl G 2.5s	17	4	SG-SY on skeleton tower on piles.	

CATAHOULA BAY TO WAX LAKE OUTLET (Chart 11355)
New Orleans - Port Arthur

(1) No.	(2) Name and Location	(3) Position	(4) Characteristic	(5) Height	(6) Range	(7) Structure	(8) Remarks
35415	BLACK BAYOU CUTOFF CANAL LIGHT 1	30-03-24.620N 093-37-05.180W				SG on pile.	Private aid.
35420	BLACK BAYOU CANAL CUTOFF LIGHT 2	30-03-24.620N 093-37-06.630W	Fl R 4s			TR on pile.	Private aid.
35425	CALCASIEU-SABINE WEST LIGHT 2	30-03-31.961N 093-41-54.896W	Fl R 4s	17	4	TR-TY on pile.	

INTRACOASTAL WATERWAY (Louisiana-Texas) - Eighth District

ELLENDER TO GALVESTON BAY (Chart 11331)
New Orleans - Port Arthur
Sabine River

(1) No.	(2) Name and Location	(3) Position	(4) Characteristic	(5) Height	(6) Range	(7) Structure	(8) Remarks
35430 23210	- LIGHT 22	30-03-17.811N 093-43-07.540W	Fl R 4s	17	3	TR-TY on pile.	
35435 23205	- Day beacon 21	30-03-15.258N 093-43-17.086W				SG-TY on pile.	Ra ref.
35440 23200	- LIGHT 20	30-02-54.372N 093-43-27.260W	Fl R 2.5s	17	3	TR-SY on pile.	
35445 23180	ADAMS BAYOU LIGHT 2	30-02-55.205N 093-43-46.772W	Fl R 4s	17	3	TR-SY on pile.	
35450 23170	- OUTER Q RANGE FRONT LIGHT	30-02-22.394N 093-44-17.957W	Q W	25		KRW-I on skeleton tower on piles.	Visible all around; higher intensity on rangeline.
35455 23175	- OUTER Q RANGE REAR LIGHT 464 yards, 231.6° from front light.	30-02-13.842N 093-44-30.362W	Iso W 6s	49		KRW-I on skeleton tower on mud sills.	Visible all around; higher intensity on rangeline.
35460	BURTON CANAL ROCK WEIR OBSTRUCTION LIGHT	30-02-41.000N 093-43-36.000W	Fl W 2.5s			NW on pile worded DANGER ROCK WEIR.	Private aid.
35465 23165	- LIGHT 16	30-02-16.838N 093-44-09.400W	Q R	17	4	TR-SY on pile.	
35470 23160	DYNEGY MIDSTREAM DOCK LIGHTS(2)	30-02-09.000N 093-44-21.000W	Fl G 2.5s			On dolphins.	Private aid.
35475 23155	- LIGHT 15	30-02-02.258N 093-44-24.174W	Fl G 4s	17	4	SG-TY on pile.	
35480 23150	- Day beacon 13A	30-01-49.067N 093-44-24.648W				SG-TY on pile.	

Light List corrected through LNM week: 01/18

(1) No.	(2) Name and Location	(3) Position	(4) Characteristic	(5) Height	(6) Range	(7) Structure	(8) Remarks
	**INTRACOASTAL WATERWAY (Louisiana-Texas) - Eighth District**							

ELLENDER TO GALVESTON BAY (Chart 11331)
New Orleans - Port Arthur
Sabine River

(1) No.	(2) Name and Location	(3) Position	(4) Characteristic	(5) Height	(6) Range	(7) Structure	(8) Remarks
35485 23145	- LIGHT 13	30-01-38.960N 093-44-26.574W	Fl G 4s	17	4	SG-TY on pile.	
35490 23140	- LIGHT 11	30-01-21.578N 093-44-37.416W	Fl G 4s	17	4	SG-TY on pile.	
35495 23135	- Day beacon 10	30-01-13.405N 093-44-35.039W				TR-SY on pile.	
35500 23130	- LIGHT 8	30-01-04.832N 093-44-51.420W	Fl R 2.5s	17	4	TR-SY on skeleton tower on piles.	
35505 23115	- LIGHT 5	30-00-51.162N 093-45-36.518W	Fl G 4s	17	4	SG-TY on skeleton tower on piles.	
35510 23120	- P RANGE FRONT LIGHT	30-01-06.720N 093-45-15.876W	Q W	24		KRW-I on skeleton tower piles.	Visible 4° either side of rangeline.
35515 23125	- P RANGE REAR LIGHT 1,204 yards, 038.9° from front light.	30-01-34.543N 093-44-50.090W	Iso W 6s	47		KRW-I on skeleton tower on piles.	
35520 23110	- Day beacon 4	30-00-50.085N 093-45-23.894W				TR-SY on pile.	
35525.01 23105.01	*Lighted Buoy 2*	29-59-59.407N 093-46-14.851W	Fl R 4s		3	Red nun with yellow square.	
35530 23100	- LIGHT 1	29-59-51.077N 093-46-29.954W	Fl G 2.5s	17	4	SG-TY on pile.	Ra ref.

Sabine-Neches Canal

(1) No.	(2) Name and Location	(3) Position	(4) Characteristic	(5) Height	(6) Range	(7) Structure	(8) Remarks
35535 23085	- O RANGE FRONT LIGHT	29-59-30.974N 093-47-02.276W	Q R	20		KRW-I on skeleton tower.	For eastbound traffic.
35540 23090	- O RANGE REAR LIGHT 954 yards, 070.3° from front light.	29-59-40.570N 093-46-31.661W	Fl R 4s	54		KRW on skeleton tower on mud sills.	Passing light visible all around.
	**INTRACOASTAL WATERWAY (Texas) - Eighth District**							

ELLENDER TO GALVESTON BAY (Chart 11331)
New Orleans - Port Arthur
Sabine-Neches Canal

(1) No.	(2) Name and Location	(3) Position	(4) Characteristic	(5) Height	(6) Range	(7) Structure	(8) Remarks
35545 23080	- Buoy 80	29-59-08.722N 093-48-05.484W				Red nun with yellow square.	
35550 23075	- Buoy 79	29-59-12.709N 093-48-07.890W				Green can with yellow triangle.	
35555 23070	- Buoy 78	29-59-02.422N 093-48-25.344W				Red nun with yellow square.	
35560 23065	- Buoy 77	29-59-06.647N 093-48-27.556W				Green can with yellow triangle.	
35565 23060	- Buoy 76	29-58-54.009N 093-48-51.394W				Red nun with yellow square.	
35570 23055	- Buoy 75	29-58-57.979N 093-48-54.786W				Green can with yellow triangle.	
35575 23050	- LIGHT 74	29-58-44.130N 093-49-21.324W	Fl R 4s	17	4	TR-SY on pile.	
35580 23045	- LIGHT 73	29-58-49.867N 093-49-23.096W	Fl G 4s	17	4	SG-TY on pile.	Ra ref.
35585 23040	- Buoy 72	29-58-35.623N 093-49-51.175W				Red nun with yellow square.	
35590 23035	- Buoy 71	29-58-39.735N 093-49-53.000W				Green can with yellow triangle.	
35595 23030	- Buoy 70	29-58-28.839N 093-50-12.653W				Red nun with yellow square.	
35600 23025	- Buoy 69	29-58-32.871N 093-50-15.026W				Green can with yellow triangle.	
35605 23020	- Buoy 68	29-58-22.031N 093-50-33.350W				Red nun with yellow square.	
35610 23015	- Buoy 67	29-58-27.437N 093-50-36.611W				Green can with yellow triangle.	

Light List corrected through LNM week: 01/18

INTRACOASTAL WATERWAY (Texas) - Eighth District

ELLENDER TO GALVESTON BAY (Chart 11331)
New Orleans - Port Arthur
Sabine-Neches Canal

(1) No.	(2) Name and Location	(3) Position	(4) Characteristic	(5) Height	(6) Range	(7) Structure	(8) Remarks
35615 23005	- N RANGE FRONT LIGHT	29-58-02.223N 093-51-44.648W	Q G (NIGHT) Q W (DAY)	35 38		On skeleton tower on piles.	For westbound traffic.
35620 23010	- N RANGE REAR LIGHT 984 yards, 250.1° from front light.	29-57-52.310N 093-52-16.094W	Iso G 6s (NIGHT) Iso W 6s (DAY)	91 89		On skeleton tower on piles.	Range is not effective inland of Sabine-Neches Canal Buoys 75 and 76.
35625 23000	- LIGHT 66	29-58-04.708N 093-51-08.228W	Fl R 2.5s	17	4	TR-SY on pile.	
35630 22970	- M UPPER RANGE FRONT LIGHT	29-58-15.912N 093-51-10.204W	Q W	29		On skeleton tower.	For upbound traffic. Visible 2° each side of rangeline. Lighted throught 24 hours.
35635 22975	- M UPPER RANGE REAR LIGHT 745 yards, 020.1° from front light.	29-58-37.577N 093-51-01.130W	Iso W 6s	40		On skeleton tower on piles. On same structure as Neches River Outer Range R Rear Light.	
35640 22995	- LIGHT 65	29-57-57.250N 093-51-24.998W	Fl G 4s	17	4	SG-TY on pile.	
35645 22985	- Buoy 64A	29-57-33.927N 093-51-21.846W				Red nun with yellow square.	
35650 22980	- LIGHT 64	29-56-56.521N 093-51-39.189W	Fl R 4s	17	4	TR-SY on pile.	Ra ref.
35655 22955	- K RANGE FRONT LIGHT	29-56-04.480N 093-52-05.146W	Q W (NIGHT) Q W (DAY)	30 30			
35660 22960	- K RANGE FRONT PASSING LIGHT	29-56-04.480N 093-52-05.146W	Fl R 2.5s	15	3	On same structure as Neches Canal Range K Front Light.	
35665 22965	- K RANGE REAR LIGHT 1088 yards, 197.4° from front light.	29-55-34.101N 093-52-17.831W	Iso W 6s (NIGHT) Iso W 6s (DAY)	53 70			Visible only on rangeline. Lighted throughout 24 hours.
35670 22945	- L RANGE FRONT LIGHT	29-56-35.682N 093-51-46.591W	Q W	32		KRW-I on skeleton tower on piles.	
35675 22950	- L RANGE REAR LIGHT 957 yards, 037.6° from front light.	29-56-58.197N 093-51-26.690W	Iso W 6s	56		KRW on skeleton tower on piles.	
35680 22940	- LIGHT 62	29-55-43.904N 093-52-26.839W	Fl R 4s	17	4	TR-SY on pile.	
35685 22935	- LIGHT 60	29-54-55.621N 093-53-10.641W	Fl R 2.5s	17	4	TR-SY on pile.	
35690 22930	- LIGHT 58	29-54-36.408N 093-53-29.077W	Fl R 4s	17	3	TR-SY on pile.	Ra ref.
35695 22925	- LIGHT 56	29-54-06.059N 093-53-55.405W	Fl R 4s	17	4	TR-SY on pile.	
35700 22920	- LIGHT 54	29-53-27.573N 093-54-37.275W	Fl R 4s	17	4	TR-SY on pile.	
35705 22915	- LIGHT 52A	29-51-36.262N 093-56-12.650W	Fl R 2.5s	17	4	TR-SY on pile.	Ra ref.
35710 22905	- H RANGE FRONT LIGHT	29-52-05.832N 093-55-49.118W	Q R	42		KRW-I on skeleton tower on block.	For upbound traffic. Visible 2° each side of rangeline.
35715 22910	- H RANGE REAR LIGHT 326 yards, 040.0° from front light.	29-52-13.251N 093-55-41.974W	Iso R 6s	49		KRW on skeleton tower on concrete block.	

Light List corrected through LNM week: 01/18

(1) No.	(2) Name and Location	(3) Position	(4) Characteristic	(5) Height	(6) Range	(7) Structure	(8) Remarks
		INTRACOASTAL WATERWAY (Texas) - Eighth District					
	ELLENDER TO GALVESTON BAY (Chart 11331)						
	New Orleans - Port Arthur						
	Sabine-Neches Canal						
35720 22900	- LIGHT 52	29-50-45.168N 093-56-58.394W	Q R	17	4	TR-SY on pile.	
35725 22895	- LIGHT 51	29-50-48.687N 093-57-06.548W	Fl G 4s	17	4	SG-TY on pile.	
35730 22890	- LIGHT 50A	29-50-20.211N 093-57-06.188W	Fl R 4s	17	3	TR-SY on pile.	Ra ref.
35735 22885	- LIGHT 50	29-49-48.673N 093-57-12.315W	Fl R 2.5s	17	4	TR-SY on pile.	Ra ref.
35740 22870	PORT ARTHUR CANAL LIGHT 49	29-49-23.493N 093-57-45.195W	Fl G 4s	17	4	SG-SY on pile.	
35742	GT LOGISTICS BARGE DOCK LIGHTS (2)	29-51-40.610N 093-59-26.710W	Fl R 2.5s			Marks upstream and downstream dock pilings.	Private aid.
	Mc Faddin Wildlife Refuge						
35745	- Danger Day beacon A	29-44-40.440N 094-04-43.420W				NW on pile worded DANGER ROCK.	Marks rock groin. Private aid.
35750	- Danger Day beacon B	29-44-35.810N 094-04-50.080W				NW on pile worded DANGER ROCK.	Marks rock groin. Private aid.
35755	- Danger Day beacon C	29-44-18.170N 094-05-15.220W				NW on pile worded DANGER ROCK.	Marks rock groin. Private aid.
35760	- Danger Day beacon D	29-44-00.210N 094-05-39.560W				NW on pile worded DANGER ROCK.	Marks rock groin. Private aid.
	Sabine-Neches Canal						
35765	U.S. DEPT. OF ENERGY RAW WATER INTAKE LIGHTS (2)	29-40-58.000N 094-11-41.000W	Fl R 2.5s	13		On fenders.	Private aid.
	Port Arthur - Galveston						
	East Bay Bayou						
35770	- LIGHT 1	29-33-16.251N 094-27-53.389W	Fl G 4s	17	4	SG-SY on pile.	Ra ref.
35775	- Buoy 2	29-33-11.729N 094-28-02.242W				Red nun with yellow triangle.	
35780	- Buoy 3	29-33-09.579N 094-27-59.689W				Green can with yellow square.	
35785	- Buoy 5	29-32-59.127N 094-28-07.084W				Green can with yellow square.	
35790	- Buoy 6	29-32-50.786N 094-28-16.856W				Red nun with yellow triangle.	
35795	- Buoy 7	29-32-47.668N 094-28-15.540W				Green can with yellow square.	
35800	- LIGHT 8	29-32-40.111N 094-28-25.397W	Fl R 4s	17	3	TR-TY on pile.	
	Rollover Bay						
35805	- Buoy 1	29-31-29.698N 094-29-17.909W				Green can with yellow square.	
35810	- Buoy 2	29-31-32.846N 094-29-18.950W				Red nun with yellow triangle.	
35815	- RANGE FRONT LIGHT	29-31-35.390N 094-29-06.712W	Q G	17		KRW-I on pile.	Visible all around; higher intensity 14° each side of rangeline.
35820	- RANGE REAR LIGHT 450 yards, 067° from front light.	29-31-40.436N 094-28-52.881W	Iso G 6s	32		KRW-I on skeleton tower.	
35825.01	- LIGHT 3	29-31-23.387N 094-29-36.495W	Fl G 2.5s	17	3	SG-SY on pile.	Ra ref.
35830.01	- LIGHT 4	29-31-25.601N 094-29-37.325W	Fl R 2.5s	17	3	TR-TY on pile.	Ra ref.
35835	- Buoy 5	29-31-17.301N 094-29-53.004W				Green can with yellow square.	

Light List corrected through LNM week: 01/18

(1) No.	(2) Name and Location	(3) Position	(4) Characteristic	(5) Height	(6) Range	(7) Structure	(8) Remarks
	INTRACOASTAL WATERWAY (Texas) - Eighth District						
	ELLENDER TO GALVESTON BAY (Chart 11331)						
	Port Arthur - Galveston						
	Rollover Bay						
35840	- Buoy 6	29-31-19.673N 094-29-54.267W				Red nun with yellow triangle.	
35845	- Buoy 7	29-31-12.071N 094-30-06.841W				Green can with yellow square.	
35850	- Buoy 8	29-31-14.385N 094-30-08.462W				Red nun with yellow triangle.	
35855.01	- LIGHT 9	29-31-05.663N 094-30-24.901W	Fl G 2.5s	17	3	SG-SY on pile.	Ra ref.
35860.01	- LIGHT 10	29-31-08.467N 094-30-25.625W	Fl R 2.5s	17	3	TR-TY on pile.	Ra ref.
35865	- Buoy 11	29-31-00.666N 094-30-38.463W				Green can with yellow square.	
35870	- Buoy 12	29-31-03.281N 094-30-40.141W				Red nun with yellow triangle.	
35875	- LIGHT 14	29-31-00.246N 094-30-50.451W	Fl R 2.5s	17	3	TR-TY on pile.	Ra ref.
	Bolivar Peninsula						
35880	- Daybeacon 2	29-26-17.505N 094-42-12.856W				TR-TY on pile.	Ra ref.
35885	- Buoy 2A	29-26-05.087N 094-42-28.476W				Red nun with yellow triangle.	
35895	- LIGHT 4	29-25-51.198N 094-42-46.268W	Fl R 4s	17	3	TR-TY on pile.	
35910	- LIGHT 13A	29-22-40.985N 094-46-35.134W	Fl G 2.5s	17	5	SG-SY on pile.	
35915	- LIGHT 14	29-22-44.352N 094-46-39.292W	Fl R 2.5s	17	4	TR-TY on pile.	
35920	- LIGHT 15A	29-22-33.120N 094-46-43.887W	Q G	17	4	SG-SY on pile.	
35925	- LIGHT 16A	29-22-37.089N 094-40-47.915W	Q R	17	3	TR-TY on pile.	
35930	- Buoy 17	29-22-20.702N 094-46-57.173W				Green can with yellow square.	
35935	- Buoy 18	29-22-25.252N 094-47-00.916W				Red nun with yellow triangle.	
35940	- Lighted Buoy 19	29-22-10.778N 094-47-08.755W	Fl G 4s		3	Green with yellow square.	
35945	- Lighted Buoy 20	29-22-19.793N 094-47-09.542W	Q R		3	Red with yellow triangle.	
	GALVESTON BAY ENTRANCE (Chart 11324)						
	Galveston-Freeport						
	Galveston-Freeport Cutoff Channel						
35950	- Buoy 3	29-21-22.291N 094-48-25.283W				Green can with yellow square.	
35955	- Buoy 5	29-21-18.027N 094-48-32.072W				Green can with yellow square.	
35965	- LIGHT 7 75 feet outside channel limit.	29-21-09.893N 094-48-44.430W	Fl G 4s	17	4	SG-SY on pile.	Ra ref.
35970	- LIGHT 9 50 feet outside channel limit.	29-20-45.275N 094-49-16.272W	Fl G 4s	17	4	SG-SY on pile.	
35975	- Buoy 11	29-20-24.157N 094-49-47.513W				Green can with yellow square.	
35980	- Buoy 12	29-20-27.103N 094-49-51.275W				Red nun with yellow triangle.	
35985	- Buoy 11A	29-20-02.914N 094-50-16.624W				Green can with yellow square.	
35990	- Buoy 12A	29-20-06.333N 094-50-20.723W				Red nun with yellow triangle.	
35995	- LIGHT 13	29-19-39.849N 094-50-49.712W	Fl G 2.5s	17	4	SG-SY on pile.	Ra ref.

(1) No.	(2) Name and Location	(3) Position	(4) Characteristic	(5) Height	(6) Range	(7) Structure	(8) Remarks
	INTRACOASTAL WATERWAY (Texas) - Eighth District							

GALVESTON BAY ENTRANCE (Chart 11324)
Galveston-Freeport
Galveston-Freeport Cutoff Channel

(1) No.	(2) Name and Location	(3) Position	(4) Characteristic	(5) Height	(6) Range	(7) Structure	(8) Remarks
36000	- Buoy 13A	29-19-25.448N 094-51-11.027W				Green can with yellow square.	
36005	- LIGHT 14	29-19-42.849N 094-50-54.712W	Fl R 2.5s	17	5	TR-TY on pile.	Ra ref.
36010	- Buoy 14A	29-19-28.345N 094-51-14.709W				Red nun with yellow triangle.	
36015	- Buoy 15	29-19-01.369N 094-51-45.570W				Green can with yellow square.	
36020	- Buoy 16	29-19-04.561N 094-51-48.951W				Red nun with yellow triangle.	
36025	- LIGHT 17	29-18-39.104N 094-52-16.321W	Fl G 4s	17	5	SG-SY on pile.	Ra ref.
36030	- LIGHT 18	29-18-42.957N 094-52-20.508W	Fl R 4s	17	4	TR-TY on pile.	Ra ref.
36035	- Junction Buoy	29-18-32.567N 094-52-26.693W				Green can with red band and yellow square.	
36040	- Buoy 20	29-18-31.254N 094-52-36.343W				Red nun with yellow triangle.	
36045 36290	- Buoy 22	29-18-23.851N 094-52-45.714W				Red nun with yellow triangle.	

Galveston Channel

(1) No.	(2) Name and Location	(3) Position	(4) Characteristic	(5) Height	(6) Range	(7) Structure	(8) Remarks
36050	BOLIVAR POINT LIGHT 21	29-21-28.866N 094-46-44.709W	Fl G 4s	17	4	SG-SY on pile.	
36055 23900	Houston Ship Channel Entrance Lighted Buoy 18	29-21-05.030N 094-46-59.466W	Q R		3	Red with yellow square.	
36060 23825	Pelican Island Spit Shoal Lighted Buoy P	29-20-27.248N 094-46-20.704W	Fl (2+1)G 6s		4	Green with red bands.	
36065 23865	- Lighted Buoy 1 50 feet outside channel limit.	29-20-16.349N 094-46-11.203W	Fl G 4s		4	Green with yellow square.	
36070 23870	- LIGHT 2	29-20-14.811N 094-46-35.752W	Q R	17	3	TR-TY on pile.	Ra ref.
36075 23880	- LIGHT 3	29-19-47.349N 094-46-28.703W	Fl G 2.5s	17	4	SG-SY on pile.	Ra ref.
36080 23885	GRASSO MARINE DOCK LIGHTS (2)	29-19-24.000N 094-46-52.000W	Fl R 2.5s	15		On end of dock.	Private aid.
36085 23890	GALVESTON ISLAND MARINA LIGHT	29-19-03.500N 094-46-40.000W	Q R	6			Private aid.
36090	HOUSTON LIGHTING AND POWER SOUTH TOWER LIGHT	29-18-36.000N 094-49-27.000W	Q G	26		On dolphin.	Private aid.
36095	HOUSTON LIGHTING AND POWER NORTH TOWER LIGHT	29-18-39.000N 094-49-25.000W	Q R	26		On dolphin.	Private aid.

Galveston-Freeport

(1) No.	(2) Name and Location	(3) Position	(4) Characteristic	(5) Height	(6) Range	(7) Structure	(8) Remarks
36100.01	- LIGHT 1	29-18-37.442N 094-49-51.240W	Fl G 4s	17	3	SG-SY on pile.	Ra ref.
36105	- LIGHT 2 150 feet outside channel limit.	29-18-40.605N 094-49-51.639W	Fl R 4s	17	3	TR-TY on pile.	
36110	- LIGHT 3	29-18-32.711N 094-50-16.222W	Fl G 2.5s	17	3	SG-SY on pile.	
36115	- LIGHT 4	29-18-35.897N 094-50-16.123W	Fl R 2.5s	17	3	TR-TY on pile.	
36120	- LIGHT 5	29-18-27.083N 094-50-47.982W	Fl G 4s	17	3	SG-SY on pile.	
36125	- LIGHT 6	29-18-29.956N 094-50-48.897W	Fl R 4s	17	3	TR-TY on pile.	
36130.01	- LIGHT 7	29-18-25.108N 094-51-01.813W	Q G	17	3	SG-SY on pile.	Ra ref.

Light List corrected through LNM week: 01/18

(1) No.	(2) Name and Location	(3) Position	(4) Characteristic	(5) Height	(6) Range	(7) Structure	(8) Remarks
	**INTRACOASTAL WATERWAY (Texas) - Eighth District**

GALVESTON BAY ENTRANCE (Chart 11324)

Galveston-Freeport

(1) No.	(2) Name and Location	(3) Position	(4) Characteristic	(5) Height	(6) Range	(7) Structure	(8) Remarks
36135.01	- LIGHT 8	29-18-28.340N 094-51-01.542W	Q R	17	3	TR-TY on pile.	Ra ref.
36140 36305	- B&C RANGE FRONT LIGHT	29-18-32.157N 094-52-41.557W	Q R	17		KRW-I on pile structure. On same structure as Range C Front Light.	Visible all around; higher intensity on rangeline.
36145	- B RANGE REAR LIGHT 843.9 yards, 272.9° from front light.	29-18-33.430N 094-53-10.130W	Iso R 6s	35		KRW-I on skeleton tower.	
36150	- LIGHT 9	29-18-26.298N 094-51-21.095W	Fl G 6s	17	3	SG-SY on pile.	
36155	- LIGHT 10	29-18-29.354N 094-51-20.544W	Fl R 6s	17	3	TR-TY on pile.	

Pier 77 Channel

(1) No.	(2) Name and Location	(3) Position	(4) Characteristic	(5) Height	(6) Range	(7) Structure	(8) Remarks
36215	- Buoy 3	29-17-54.780N 094-51-21.120W				Green can.	Private aid.
36220	- Buoy 4	29-17-57.540N 091-51-26.640W				Red nun.	Private aid.
36225	- Buoy 7	29-17-53.400N 094-51-28.800W				Green can.	Private aid.
36230	- Buoy 9	29-17-53.640N 094-51-31.500W				Green can.	Private aid.
36235	- Buoy 10	29-17-56.340N 094-51-32.100W				Red nun.	Private aid.
36240	- Buoy 12	29-17-52.860N 094-51-32.880W				Red nun.	Private aid.
36245	- Buoy 13	29-17-49.260N 094-51-30.000W				Green can.	Private aid.
36250	- Buoy 14	29-17-48.900N 094-51-32.220W				Red nun.	Private aid.

Galveston-Freeport

(1) No.	(2) Name and Location	(3) Position	(4) Characteristic	(5) Height	(6) Range	(7) Structure	(8) Remarks
36255.01	- LIGHT 11	29-18-27.918N 094-51-45.804W	Fl G 2.5s	17	3	SG-SY on pile.	Ra ref.
36260.01	- LIGHT 12	29-18-30.554N 094-51-45.717W	Fl R 2.5s	17	3	TR-TY on pile.	Ra ref.
36265	- LIGHT 14	29-18-31.288N 094-52-00.478W	Fl R 4s	17	3	TR-TY on pile.	
36270	- LIGHT 15	29-18-29.159N 094-52-13.501W	Q G	17	3	SG-SY on pile.	
36275	- LIGHT 17	29-18-29.016N 094-52-22.841W	Fl G 2.5s	17	3	SG-SY on pile.	
36280	- LIGHT 19	29-18-26.592N 094-52-32.471W	Fl G 4s	17	3	SG-SY on pile.	
36285	- LIGHT 21	29-18-22.091N 094-52-39.634W	Fl G 6s	17	3	SG-SY on pile.	
36290 36045	- Cutoff Channel Buoy 22	29-18-23.851N 094-52-45.714W				Red nun with yellow triangle.	
36295	- Buoy 23	29-18-13.831N 094-52-49.758W				Green can with yellow square.	
36300	- Buoy 24	29-18-12.889N 094-52-55.744W				Red nun with yellow triangle.	
36305 36140	- B&C RANGE FRONT LIGHT	29-18-32.157N 094-52-41.557W	Q R	17		KRW-I on pile structure. On same structure as Range C Front Light.	Visible all around; higher intensity on rangeline.
36310	- C RANGE REAR LIGHT 835 yards, 029.3° from front light.	29-18-53.841N 094-52-27.650W	Iso R 6s	35		KRW-I on skeleton tower on piles.	
36315	- Buoy 25	29-17-58.769N 094-53-00.992W				Green can with yellow square.	
36320	- Buoy 26	29-18-02.168N 094-53-04.499W				Red nun with yellow triangle.	

(1) No.	(2) Name and Location	(3) Position	(4) Characteristic	(5) Height	(6) Range	(7) Structure	(8) Remarks
	INTRACOASTAL WATERWAY (Texas) - Eighth District						
	GALVESTON BAY TO CEDAR LAKES (Chart 11322)						
	Galveston-Freeport						
36325	- Buoy 27	29-17-34.781N 094-53-16.065W				Green can with yellow square.	
36330	- Buoy 28	29-17-37.076N 094-53-18.280W				Red nun with yellow triangle.	
	Offatts Bayou Entrance Channel						
36335	- Day beacon 1	29-17-23.743N 094-53-19.874W				SG on pile.	Ra ref.
36340	- Day beacon 2	29-17-21.792N 094-53-20.713W				TR on pile.	Ra ref.
36350	- Day beacon 3	29-17-15.988N 094-53-15.204W				SG on pile.	Ra ref.
36352	- Day beacon 4	29-17-16.994N 094-53-18.502W				TR on pile.	Ra ref.
36355	- Day beacon 5	29-17-09.155N 094-53-10.949W				SG on pile.	Ra ref.
36360	- Day beacon 6	29-17-09.553N 094-53-15.216W				TR on pile.	Ra ref.
36365	- Day beacon 7	29-16-58.681N 094-53-05.090W				SG on pile.	
36370	- Day beacon 8	29-16-54.940N 094-53-08.073W				TR on pile.	
36375	- Day beacon 9	29-16-52.043N 094-53-03.114W				SG on pile.	
36380	- Day beacon 10	29-16-49.594N 094-53-05.334W				TR on pile.	Ra ref.
36385	- Day beacon 11	29-16-44.944N 094-52-57.874W				SG on pile.	
36390	- Day beacon 12	29-16-42.684N 094-53-00.306W				TR on pile.	Ra ref.
	Galveston-Freeport						
36395	Galveston Airport Channel Day beacon 2	29-16-34.784N 094-52-54.166W				TR on pile.	
36400	Galveston Airport Channel Day beacon 4	29-16-25.678N 094-52-47.197W				TR on pile.	
	Offatts Bayou Entrance Channel						
36405	- Day beacon 14	29-16-42.235N 094-52-56.648W				TR on pile.	Ra ref.
36410	- Day beacon 16	29-16-41.399N 094-52-46.613W				TR on pile.	
36415	- Day beacon 18	29-16-43.280N 094-52-37.153W				TR on pile.	
36420	- Day beacon 20	29-16-44.864N 094-52-27.147W				TR on piles.	
36425	- Day beacon 22	29-16-44.674N 094-52-06.220W				TR on pile.	
36430	- Day beacon 24	29-16-49.451N 094-51-48.672W				TR on pile.	Ra ref.
36435	- Day beacon 26	29-16-56.468N 094-51-34.183W				TR on pile.	Ra ref.
36437	PELICAN REST MARINA NORTHWEST DANGER LIGHTS (2)	29-16-59.340N 094-51-25.790W	Fl W 2.5s			Marks floating dock structure.	Private aid.
36437.01	PELICAN REST MARINA SOUTHEAST DANGER LIGHTS (3)	29-16-58.950N 094-51-22.960W	Fl W 2.5s			Marks floating dock structure.	Private aid.
36437.02	PELICAN REST MARINA PILING LIGHTS (2)	29-17-00.870N 094-51-17.460W	Fl W 2.5s			Marks perimeter piles.	Private aid.
36438	- Day beacon 26A	29-16-53.571N 094-51-28.195W				TR on pile.	
36440	- Day beacon 28	29-16-53.747N 094-51-19.714W				TR on pile.	

Light List corrected through LNM week: 01/18

(1) No.	(2) Name and Location	(3) Position	(4) Characteristic	(5) Height	(6) Range	(7) Structure	(8) Remarks
	INTRACOASTAL WATERWAY (Texas) - Eighth District						
	GALVESTON BAY TO CEDAR LAKES (Chart 11322)						
	Galveston-Freeport						
36445	Offatts Bayou Day beacon 1	29-17-02.767N 094-50-32.368W				SG on pile.	Ra ref.
36450	Offatts Bayou Day beacon 2	29-16-58.627N 094-50-22.110W				TR on pile.	Ra ref.
	Tiki Island Channel						
36455	- Day beacon 1	29-17-33.180N 094-53-30.840W				SG on pile.	Private aid.
36460	- Day beacon 2	29-17-34.500N 094-53-29.880W				TR on pile.	Private aid.
36465	- Day beacon 3	29-17-35.640N 094-53-35.460W				SG on pile.	Private aid.
36470	- Day beacon 4	29-17-37.200N 094-53-34.380W				TR on pile.	Private aid.
36475	- Day beacon 5	29-17-41.640N 094-53-45.720W				SG on pile.	Private aid.
36480	- Day beacon 6	29-17-42.720N 094-53-45.240W				TR on pile.	Private aid.
36485	- Day beacon 7	29-17-45.840N 094-53-53.340W				SG on pile.	Private aid.
36490	- Day beacon 8	29-17-47.880N 094-53-55.080W				TR on pile.	Private aid.
36495	- Day beacon 9	29-17-51.360N 094-54-03.780W				SG on pile.	Private aid.
36500	- Day beacon 10	29-17-51.240N 094-54-01.620W				TR on pile.	Private aid.
36505	- Day beacon 11	29-17-54.000N 094-54-08.820W				SG on pile.	Private aid.
36510	- Day beacon 12	29-17-55.920N 094-54-09.420W				TR on pile.	Private aid.
	Galveston-Freeport						
36515	- D RANGE FRONT LIGHT	29-16-57.159N 094-53-42.063W	Q G	20		KRW-I on pile structure on same structure as Range E Front Light.	For westbound traffic. Visible all around; higher intensity on rangeline.
36520	- D RANGE REAR LIGHT 835 yards, 209.3° from front light.	29-16-35.434N 094-53-55.849W	Iso G 6s	40		KRW-I on skeleton tower.	
36525.01	- LIGHT 30	29-17-28.572N 094-53-24.575W	Fl R 2.5s	17	3	TR-TY on pile.	Ra ref.
36530	- Buoy 32	29-17-18.851N 094-53-33.416W				Red nun with yellow triangle.	
36535.01	- LIGHT 33	29-17-07.363N 094-53-38.735W	Fl G 2.5s	17	3	SG-SY on pile.	Ra ref.
36540.01	- LIGHT 34	29-17-11.898N 094-53-41.636W	Q R	17	3	TR-TY on pile.	Ra ref.
36545	- Buoy 35	29-17-02.512N 094-53-49.909W				Green can with yellow square.	
36550	- Buoy 36	29-17-07.877N 094-53-51.782W				Red nun with yellow triangle.	
36555	- Buoy 37	29-17-01.192N 094-54-01.518W				Green can with yellow square.	
36560	- Buoy 38	29-17-06.407N 094-54-01.996W				Red nun with yellow triangle.	
36565.01	- LIGHT 39	29-17-03.204N 094-54-13.484W	Fl G 2.5s	17	3	SG-SY on pile.	Ra ref.
36570.01	- LIGHT 40	29-17-07.274N 094-54-12.443W	Q R	17	3	TR-TY on pile.	Ra ref.
36585	- E RANGE FRONT LIGHT	29-16-57.206N 094-53-42.088W	Q W	15		KRW-I on pile structure; on same structure as Range D Front Light.	For eastbound traffic. Visible all around; higher intensity on rangeline.
36590	- E RANGE REAR LIGHT	29-16-50.227N 094-53-14.955W	Iso G 6s	38		KRW-I on skeleton tower.	

Light List corrected through LNM week: 01/18

(1) No.	(2) Name and Location	(3) Position	(4) Characteristic	(5) Height	(6) Range	(7) Structure	(8) Remarks
		INTRACOASTAL WATERWAY (Texas) - Eighth District					
	GALVESTON BAY TO CEDAR LAKES (Chart 11322)						
	Galveston-Freeport						
36595	- Buoy 41	29-17-07.623N 094-54-30.692W				Green can with yellow square.	
36600	- Buoy 42	29-17-11.411N 094-54-31.583W				Red nun with yellow triangle.	
36605	- Buoy 43	29-17-15.256N 094-54-59.514W				Green can with yellow square.	
36610	- Buoy 44	29-17-19.016N 094-54-58.692W				Red nun with yellow triangle.	
36615	- Buoy 45	29-17-19.630N 094-55-16.158W				Green can with yellow square.	
36620	- Buoy 46	29-17-21.593N 094-55-07.173W				Red nun with yellow triangle.	
36625	- LIGHT 47	29-17-19.490N 094-55-21.876W	Fl G 4s	17	4	SG-SY on pile.	
36630	- Buoy 48	29-17-23.461N 094-55-15.398W				Red nun with yellow triangle.	
36635	- Buoy 49	29-17-19.469N 094-55-30.151W				Green can with yellow square.	
36640.01	- LIGHT 50	29-17-22.407N 094-55-31.121W	Fl R 2.5s	17	3	TR-TY on pile.	Ra ref.
36645	- F RANGE FRONT LIGHT	29-17-24.922N 094-55-04.424W	Q W	15		KRW-I on pile structure.	For eastbound traffic.
36650	- F RANGE REAR LIGHT 935 yards, 079.9° from front light.	29-17-29.787N 094-54-33.217W	Iso W 6s	35		KRW-I on skeleton tower on piles.	
36655	- Buoy 51	29-17-17.446N 094-55-43.258W				Green can with yellow square.	
36660.01	- LIGHT 52	29-17-20.848N 094-55-43.029W	Fl R 4s	17	3	TR-TY on pile.	Ra ref.
36665	- Buoy 53	29-17-11.841N 094-56-19.950W				Green can with yellow square.	
36670	- Buoy 54	29-17-14.881N 094-56-20.314W				Red nun with yellow triangle.	
36675	- Buoy 55	29-17-08.782N 094-56-41.529W				Green can with yellow square.	
36680	- Buoy 56	29-17-11.665N 094-56-41.993W				Red nun with yellow triangle.	
36685	- Buoy 57	29-17-05.440N 094-57-03.466W				Green can with yellow square.	
36690	- Buoy 58	29-17-08.175N 094-57-03.719W				Red nun with yellow triangle.	
36695	- Buoy 59	29-17-01.421N 094-57-31.552W				Green can with yellow square.	
	Harborwalk Entrance East						
36700	- Buoy 1	29-17-05.960N 094-57-31.100W				Green can.	Private aid.
36705	- Buoy 2	29-17-06.190N 094-57-28.860W				Red nun.	Private aid.
36710	- Buoy 3	29-17-08.660N 094-57-31.460W				Green can.	Private aid.
36715	- Buoy 4	29-17-08.900N 094-57-29.220W				Red nun.	Private aid.
36720	- Buoy 5	29-17-11.420N 094-57-31.830W				Green can.	Private aid.
36725	- Buoy 6	29-17-11.650N 094-57-29.590W				Red nun.	Private aid.
36730	- Buoy 7	29-17-14.290N 094-57-32.000W				Green can.	Private aid.
36735	- Buoy 8	29-17-14.300N 094-57-29.750W				Red nun.	Private aid.
36740	- Buoy 9	29-17-17.070N 094-57-32.020W				Green can.	Private aid.
36745	- Buoy 10	29-17-17.070N 094-57-29.760W				Red nun.	Private aid.

Light List corrected through LNM week: 01/18

(1) No.	(2) Name and Location	(3) Position	(4) Characteristic	(5) Height	(6) Range	(7) Structure	(8) Remarks
	INTRACOASTAL WATERWAY (Texas) - Eighth District						
	GALVESTON BAY TO CEDAR LAKES (Chart 11322)						
	Galveston-Freeport						
	Harborwalk Entrance East						
36750	- Buoy 11	29-17-20.650N 094-57-32.190W				Green can.	Private aid.
36755	- Buoy 12	29-17-19.810N 094-57-29.770W				Red nun.	Private aid.
36760	- Buoy 14	29-17-22.230N 094-57-30.890W				Red nun.	Private aid.
	Galveston-Freeport						
36765	- Buoy 60	29-17-04.118N 094-57-32.313W				Red nun with yellow triangle.	
36770	- Buoy 61	29-16-58.248N 094-57-53.123W				Green can with yellow square.	
	Harborwalk Entrance West						
36775	- Buoy 1	29-17-02.390N 094-57-56.780W				Green can.	Private aid.
36780	- Buoy 2	29-17-02.590N 094-57-55.680W				Red nun.	Private aid.
36785	- Buoy 3	29-17-04.760N 094-57-57.350W				Green can.	Private aid.
36790	- Buoy 4	29-17-04.960N 094-57-56.240W				Red nun.	Private aid.
36795	- Buoy 5	29-17-07.130N 094-57-57.920W				Green can.	Private aid.
36800	- Buoy 6	29-17-07.690N 094-57-56.900W				Red nun.	Private aid.
36805	- Buoy 7	29-17-08.440N 094-57-59.230W				Green can.	Private aid.
	Galveston-Freeport						
36810	- Buoy 62	29-17-00.853N 094-57-54.723W				Red nun with yellow triangle.	
36815.01	- LIGHT 63	29-16-54.069N 094-58-17.428W				SG-SY on pile.	Ra ref.
36820	- G RANGE FRONT LIGHT	29-16-54.135N 094-58-28.078W	Q W	15		KRW-I on pile.	For westbound traffic. Visible 2° each side of rangeline.
36825	- G RANGE REAR LIGHT 892 yards, 258° from front light.	29-16-49.664N 094-58-57.855W	Iso W 6s	35		KRW-I on skeleton tower.	Visible 2° each side of rangeline.
36830	- Buoy 75	29-11-48.179N 095-03-50.753W				Green can with yellow square.	
	Delhide Cove						
36835	- Danger Day beacon A	29-13-50.200N 094-57-07.000W				NW on pile. Worded: DANGER BREAKWATER.	Marks Geotext tube Breakwater. Private aid.
36840	- Danger Day beacon B	29-13-50.400N 094-57-15.800W				NW on pile. Worded: DANGER BREAKWATER.	Marks Geotext tube Breakwater. Private aid.
36845	- Danger Day beacon C	29-13-47.900N 094-57-20.100W				NW on pile. Worded: DANGER BREAKWATER.	Marks Geotext tube Breakwater. Private aid.
36850	- Danger Day beacon D	29-13-44.400N 094-56-59.800W				NW on pile. Worded: DANGER BREAKWATER	Marks Geotext tube Breakwater. Private aid.
36855	- Danger Day beacon E	29-13-47.700N 094-57-09.900W				NW on pile. Worded: DANGER BREAKWATER.	Marks Geotext tube Breakwater. Private aid.
36860	- Danger Day beacon F	29-13-45.000N 094-57-20.300W				NW on pile. Worded: DANGER BREAKWATER.	Marks Geotext tube Breakwater. Private aid.

Light List corrected through LNM week: 01/18

(1) No.	(2) Name and Location	(3) Position	(4) Characteristic	(5) Height	(6) Range	(7) Structure	(8) Remarks
	INTRACOASTAL WATERWAY (Texas) - Eighth District						

GALVESTON BAY TO CEDAR LAKES (Chart 11322)

Delhide Cove

No.	Name and Location	Position	Characteristic	Height	Range	Structure	Remarks
36865	- Danger Day beacon G	29-13-39.300N 094-56-54.000W				NW on pile. Worded: DANGER BREAKWATER.	Markes Geotext tube Breakwater. Private aid.
36870	- Danger Day beacon H	29-13-35.900N 094-56-43.200W				NW on pile. Worded: DANGER BREAKWATER.	Marks Geotext tube Breakwater. Private aid.
36875	- Danger Day beacon I	29-13-26.100N 094-56-37.100W				NW on pile. Worded: DANGER BREAKWATER.	Marks Geotext tube Breakwater. Private aid.
36878	CITY OF GALVESTON ECHERT BAYOU OUTFALL DANGER LIGHT	29-13-18.370N 094-56-09.740W	Fl W 2.5s			Marks submerged wastewater outfall structure.	Private aid.

Galveston-Freeport

Jamaica Beach Village Channel

No.	Name and Location	Position	Characteristic	Height	Range	Structure	Remarks
36880	- LIGHT 1	29-12-29.000N 094-59-30.000W	Fl G 2.5s			SG on pile.	Private aid.
36885	- LIGHT 2	29-12-28.000N 094-59-31.000W	Fl R 2.5s			TR on pile.	Private aid.
36890	- Day beacon 3	29-12-20.000N 094-59-25.000W				SG on pile.	Private aid.
36895	- Day beacon 4	29-12-19.000N 094-59-31.000W				TR on pile.	Private aid.
36900	- Day beacon 5	29-12-12.000N 094-59-19.000W				SG on pile.	Private aid.
36905	- Day beacon 6	29-12-11.000N 094-59-20.000W				TR on pile.	Private aid.
36910	- Day beacon 7	29-12-05.000N 094-59-15.000W				SG on pile.	Private aid.
36915	- Day beacon 8	29-12-04.000N 094-59-16.000W				TR on pile.	Private aid.

Galveston-Freeport

No.	Name and Location	Position	Characteristic	Height	Range	Structure	Remarks
36920	WEST BAY (TEXAS) LIGHT 2	29-11-36.226N 095-04-19.605W	Fl R 2.5s	17	3	TR-TY on pile.	Ra ref.
36925	WEST BAY (TEXAS) LIGHT 3	29-11-33.720N 095-04-17.633W	Fl G 2.5s	17	3	SG-SY on pile.	Ra ref.
36930	West Bay (Texas) Buoy 4	29-11-24.466N 095-04-37.522W				Red nun with yellow triangle.	
36935	West Bay (Texas) Buoy 5	29-11-21.936N 095-04-35.681W				Green can with yellow square.	
36940	West Bay (Texas) Buoy 6	29-11-10.929N 095-04-56.407W				Red nun with yellow triangle.	
36945	West Bay (Texas) Buoy 7	29-11-08.953N 095-04-54.496W				Green can with yellow square.	
36950	West Bay (Texas) Buoy 8	29-11-03.430N 095-05-07.322W				Red nun with yellow triangle.	
36955	West Bay (Texas) Buoy 9	29-11-01.483N 095-05-05.015W				Green can with yellow square.	
36960	West Bay (Texas) Buoy 10	29-10-54.601N 095-05-20.843W				Red nun with yellow triangle.	
36965	West Bay (Texas) Buoy 11	29-10-48.949N 095-05-23.601W				Green can with yellow square	
36970	West Bay (Texas) Buoy 12	29-10-42.622N 095-05-38.459W				Red nun with yellow triangle.	
36975	West Bay (Texas) Buoy 13	29-10-37.114N 095-05-41.179W				Green can with yellow square.	
36980	West Bay (Texas) Buoy 14	29-10-35.511N 095-05-50.658W				Red nun with yellow triangle.	
36985	WEST BAY (TEXAS) LIGHT 15	29-10-32.766N 095-05-49.915W	Fl G 2.5s	17	3	SG-SY on pile.	
36990	West Bay (Texas) Buoy 16	29-10-33.080N 095-05-59.246W				Red nun with yellow triangle.	

Chocolate Bay

No.	Name and Location	Position	Characteristic	Height	Range	Structure	Remarks
36995	- Buoy 1	29-10-23.405N 095-06-38.570W				Green can with yellow square.	

Light List corrected through LNM week: 01/18

(1) No.	(2) Name and Location	(3) Position	(4) Characteristic	(5) Height	(6) Range	(7) Structure	(8) Remarks
\multicolumn{8}{c}{INTRACOASTAL WATERWAY (Texas) - Eighth District}							
\multicolumn{8}{l}{**GALVESTON BAY TO CEDAR LAKES (Chart 11322)**}							
\multicolumn{8}{l}{**Galveston-Freeport**}							
\multicolumn{8}{l}{**Chocolate Bay**}							
37000	- Buoy 1A	29-10-17.794N 095-06-54.587W				Green can with yellow square.	
37005	- A RANGE FRONT LIGHT	29-10-25.726N 095-06-44.466W	Q W	15		KRW-I on pile.	For eastbound traffic. Visible all around; higher intensity on rangeline.
37005.1	- A RANGE FRONT LIGHT PASSING LIGHT	29-10-25.726N 095-06-44.466W	Fl R 2.5s	10	3		On same structure as Chocolate Bay A Range Front Light.
37010	- A RANGE REAR LIGHT 703 yards, 055.4° from front light	29-10-39.735N 095-06-21.346W	Iso W 6s	32		KRW-I on skeleton tower on piles.	Visible all around; higher intensity on rangeline.
37015	- Buoy 3	29-10-10.719N 095-07-06.809W				Green can with yellow square.	
37020	- Buoy 4	29-10-12.896N 095-07-08.533W				Red nun with yellow triangle.	
37025	- Buoy 5	29-10-02.974N 095-07-19.523W				Green can with yellow square.	
37030	- Buoy 7	29-09-54.554N 095-07-32.923W				Green can with yellow square.	
37035	- Buoy 8	29-09-57.438N 095-07-35.083W				Red nun with yellow triangle.	
\multicolumn{8}{l}{**Chocolate Bayou Channel**}							
37040	- North Entrance Junction Buoy E	29-09-47.142N 095-07-52.905W				Red nun with green band.	
37045	Chocolate Bay Buoy 10	29-09-51.865N 095-07-46.361W				Red nun.	
37050	Chocolate Bayou West Channel Buoy 1	29-09-43.073N 095-08-08.634W				Green can.	
37055	- Buoy 1	29-09-50.555N 095-07-58.446W				Green can.	
37060	- Buoy 2	29-09-53.548N 095-07-55.514W				Red nun.	
37065	Chocolate Bayou West Channel Buoy 2	29-09-42.052N 095-08-06.110W				Red nun.	
37070	Chocolate Bayou Junction Buoy C	29-09-52.607N 095-08-04.509W				Green can with red band.	
37075	- Buoy 4	29-09-56.783N 095-08-01.456W				Red nun.	
37080	Chocolate Bayou West Channel Buoy 3	29-09-53.698N 095-08-07.204W				Green can.	
37085	- LIGHT 5	29-10-09.694N 095-08-12.381W	Fl G 2.5s	17	3	SG on pile.	Ra ref.
37090	- INNER RANGE A FRONT LIGHT	29-11-00.768N 095-08-24.799W	Q W	25		KRW on skeleton tower on pile.	Visible all around; higher intensity on rangeline.
37095	- INNER A RANGE REAR LIGHT 600 yards, 345.7° from front light.	29-11-18.029N 095-08-29.817W	Iso W 6s	36		KRW on skeleton tower on pile.	Visible all around; higher intensity on rangeline.
37100	- LIGHT 6	29-10-09.156N 095-08-09.090W	Fl R 2.5s	17	3	TR on pile.	Ra ref.
37105	- Buoy 7	29-10-21.968N 095-08-15.080W				Green can.	
37110	- Buoy 8	29-10-22.096N 095-08-12.164W				Red nun.	
37115	- LIGHT 9	29-10-38.256N 095-08-20.764W	Q G	17	3	SG on pile.	Ra ref.
37120	- OUTER RANGE FRONT LIGHT 745 yards, 142.8° from front light.	29-10-27.236N 095-08-06.671W	Q W	25		KRW on skeleton tower on piles.	Visible all around; higher intensity on rangeline.

Light List corrected through LNM week: 01/18

(1) No.	(2) Name and Location	(3) Position	(4) Characteristic	(5) Height	(6) Range	(7) Structure	(8) Remarks
	INTRACOASTAL WATERWAY (Texas) - Eighth District						
	GALVESTON BAY TO CEDAR LAKES (Chart 11322)						
	Galveston-Freeport						
	Chocolate Bayou Channel						
37125	- OUTER RANGE REAR LIGHT 745 yards, 142.8° from front light.	29-10-09.625N 095-07-51.424W	Iso W 6s	40		KRW on skeleton tower on piles.	Visible all around; higher intensity on rangeline.
37130	- LIGHT 10	29-10-39.981N 095-08-18.460W	Q R	17	3	TR on pile.	Ra ref.
37135	- LIGHT 12	29-10-49.649N 095-08-24.797W	Fl R 4s	17	3	TR on pile.	Ra ref.
37140	- LIGHT 13	29-10-47.348N 095-08-26.300W	Fl G 4s	17	3	SG on pile.	Ra ref.
37145	- LIGHT 15	29-11-03.351N 095-08-39.339W	Fl G 2.5s	17	3	SG on pile.	Ra ref.
37150	- LIGHT 16	29-11-04.350N 095-08-37.216W	Fl R 2.5s	17	3	TR on pile.	Ra ref.
37155	- LIGHT 17	29-11-19.078N 095-08-53.074W	Fl G 6s	17	3	SG on pile.	Ra ref.
37160	- LIGHT 18	29-11-20.572N 095-08-51.277W	Fl R 6s	17	3	TR on pile.	Ra ref.
37165	- Buoy 19	29-11-34.825N 095-09-07.910W				Green can.	
37170	- Buoy 20	29-11-36.184N 095-09-05.419W				Red nun.	
37175	- Buoy 21	29-11-44.038N 095-09-18.742W				Green can.	
37180	- Buoy 22	29-11-45.865N 095-09-16.747W				Red nun.	
37185	- Buoy 23	29-11-47.736N 095-09-25.392W				Green can.	
37190	- Buoy 24	29-11-49.865N 095-09-23.747W				Red nun.	
37195	- Buoy 25	29-11-50.340N 095-09-32.305W				Green can.	
37200	- Buoy 26	29-11-52.865N 095-09-30.747W				Red nun.	
37205	- Buoy 27	29-11-53.115N 095-09-49.138W				Green can.	
37210	- Buoy 28	29-11-55.359N 095-09-48.018W				Red nun.	
37215	- Day beacon 30	29-11-57.368N 095-10-03.561W				TR on pile.	
37220	- Buoy 31	29-11-56.339N 095-10-19.977W				Green can.	
37225	- Buoy 32	29-11-58.864N 095-10-19.749W				Red nun.	
37230	- Day beacon 34	29-12-04.719N 095-10-33.650W				TR on pile.	
37235	- Buoy 35	29-12-09.824N 095-10-53.365W				Green can.	
37240	- Buoy 36	29-12-11.529N 095-10-51.865W				Red nun.	
37245	- Buoy 37	29-12-20.778N 095-11-19.211W				Green can.	
37250	- Buoy 38	29-12-22.877N 095-11-18.172W				Red nun.	
37255	- LIGHT 39	29-12-31.490N 095-11-44.439W	Fl G 4s	17	4	SG on pile.	
37260	- LIGHT 40	29-12-34.252N 095-11-42.663W	Fl R 4s	17	3	TR on pile.	
37265	- Day beacon 42	29-12-53.060N 095-12-40.755W				TR on pile.	
37270	- Day beacon 43	29-13-00.720N 095-12-53.283W				SG on pile.	

INTRACOASTAL WATERWAY (Texas) - Eighth District

(1) No.	(2) Name and Location	(3) Position	(4) Characteristic	(5) Height	(6) Range	(7) Structure	(8) Remarks
	GALVESTON BAY TO CEDAR LAKES (Chart 11322)						
	Galveston-Freeport						
	Chocolate Bayou Channel						
37275	- Day beacon 44	29-13-27.406N 095-13-02.037W				TR on pile.	
37280	- Day beacon 45	29-13-33.923N 095-13-05.923W				SG on pile.	
	Chocolate Bay						
37285	- Buoy 9	29-09-47.435N 095-07-44.678W				Green can with yellow square.	
37290	- Buoy 11	29-09-38.505N 095-07-59.299W				Green can with yellow square.	
37295	- Buoy 13	29-09-29.648N 095-08-14.034W				Green can with yellow square.	
37300	- Junction Buoy W	29-09-34.267N 095-08-13.483W				Red nun with green band.	
37305	- Buoy 15	29-09-18.142N 095-08-32.970W				Green can with yellow square.	
37310	- Buoy 17	29-09-09.254N 095-08-48.027W				Green can with yellow square.	
37315	- Buoy 18	29-09-11.609N 095-08-49.996W				Red nun with yellow triangle.	
37320	- Buoy 19	29-09-01.469N 095-09-00.701W				Green can with yellow square.	
37325	- Buoy 21	29-08-52.640N 095-09-15.480W				Green can with yellow square.	
37330	- Buoy 22	29-08-54.887N 095-09-16.804W				Red nun with yellow triangle.	
37335	- Buoy 23	29-08-44.291N 095-09-29.525W				Green can with yellow square.	
37340	- B RANGE FRONT LIGHT	29-08-36.281N 095-09-45.326W	Q W	15		KRW-I on tower.	For westbound traffic. Visible all around; higher intensity on rangeline.
37345	- B RANGE REAR LIGHT 699 yards, 235.4° from front light.	29-08-24.487N 095-10-04.801W	Iso W 6s	30		KRW-I on skeleton tower on piles.	Visible all around; higher intensity on rangeline.
	Oyster Lake						
37350	- Day beacon 1	29-07-46.475N 095-10-32.336W				SG-SY on pile.	
37355	- Buoy 2	29-07-37.873N 095-10-46.339W				Red nun with yellow triangle.	
37360	- Day beacon 3	29-07-34.935N 095-10-44.720W				SG-SY on pile.	
37365	- Buoy 4	29-07-29.690N 095-10-55.483W				Red nun with yellow triangle.	
37370	- Day beacon 5	29-07-21.382N 095-10-59.735W				SG-SY on pile.	
37375	BRAZORIA WILDLIFE REFUGE WAVE BARRIER LIGHT	29-04-57.430N 095-12-24.580W	Fl R 2.5s			On wave barrier.	Private aid.
	Galveston-Freeport						
37380 26960	FREEPORT ENTRANCE LIGHT 12	28-56-39.607N 095-18-21.359W	Q R	17	4	TR-SY on pile.	Ra ref.
	Freeport - Port O`Connor						
	Brazos River Crossing						
37395	- LIGHT 2	28-53-48.575N 095-23-01.367W	Fl R 4s	17	4	TR-TY on tower on mud sill.	
37400	- LIGHT 4	28-53-48.550N 095-23-10.088W	Fl R 4s	20	4	TR-TY on tower on mud sill.	
	CLEAR LAKES TO ESPIRITU SANTO BAY (Chart 11319)						
	Freeport - Port O`Connor						
	Matagorda Bay						
37405	- LIGHT 2	28-36-33.253N 096-10-10.152W	Q R	17	5	TR-TY on pile.	Ra ref.

Light List corrected through LNM week: 01/18

(1) No.	(2) Name and Location	(3) Position	(4) Characteristic	(5) Height	(6) Range	(7) Structure	(8) Remarks
		INTRACOASTAL WATERWAY (Texas) - Eighth District					
	CLEAR LAKES TO ESPIRITU SANTO BAY (Chart 11319)						
	Freeport - Port O'Connor						
	Matagorda Bay						
37410	- LIGHT 3	28-35-41.737N 096-10-47.279W	Fl G 4s	17	4	SG-SY on pile.	Ra ref.
37415	- Buoy 5	28-35-29.989N 096-10-57.183W				Green can with yellow square.	
37420	- Buoy 6	28-35-31.311N 096-10-59.371W				Red nun with yellow triangle.	
37425	- Buoy 7	28-35-17.606N 096-11-06.435W				Green can with yellow square.	
37430	- Buoy 8	28-35-18.931N 096-11-08.624W				Red nun with yellow triangle.	
37435	- Buoy 9	28-35-05.223N 096-11-15.688W				Green can with yellow square.	
37440	- Buoy 10	28-35-06.548N 096-11-17.876W				Red nun with yellow triangle.	
37445	- LIGHT 11 90 feet outside channel limit.	28-34-52.346N 096-11-24.097W	Fl G 2.5s	17	3	SG-SY on pile.	
37450	- Buoy 12	28-34-54.164N 096-11-27.128W				Red nun with yellow triangle.	
37455	- Buoy 13	28-34-40.456N 096-11-34.190W				Green can with yellow square.	
37460	- Buoy 14	28-34-41.781N 096-11-36.379W				Red nun with yellow triangle.	
37465	- Buoy 15	28-34-28.072N 096-11-43.441W				Green can with yellow square.	
37470	- Buoy 16	28-34-29.397N 096-11-45.630W				Red nun with yellow triangle.	
37475	- Buoy 17	28-34-15.689N 096-11-52.693W				Green can with yellow square.	
37495	- LIGHT 19 90 feet outside channel limit.	28-34-02.813N 096-12-01.102W	Fl G 4s	17	4	SG-SY on pile.	
37500	- Buoy 21	28-33-50.922N 096-12-11.193W				Green can with yellow square.	
37505	- Buoy 23	28-33-38.539N 096-12-20.444W				Green can with yellow square.	
37510	- Buoy 25	28-33-26.156N 096-12-29.693W				Green can with yellow square.	
37540	- LIGHT 27 90 feet outside the channel limit.	28-33-13.279N 096-12-38.101W	Fl G 2.5s	17	3	SG-SY on pile.	
37545	- Buoy 29	28-33-01.389N 096-12-48.192W				Green can with yellow square.	
	Matagorda Bay - Alternate Route						
37550	- LIGHT 2	28-32-39.618N 096-13-28.818W	Fl R 4s	17	4	TR-TY on pile.	Ra ref.
37555	- Day beacon 2A	28-32-00.270N 096-14-39.440W				TR-TY on pile.	
37565	- LIGHT 4	28-31-22.832N 096-15-46.258W	Fl R 6s	17	4	TR-TY on pile.	
37570	- Day beacon 4A	28-30-41.860N 096-17-02.310W				TR-TY on pile.	
37580	- LIGHT 6	28-30-03.092N 096-18-13.746W	Q R	17	4	TR-TY on pile.	
37585	- Day beacon 6A	28-29-44.290N 096-19-13.440W				TR-TY on pile.	
37595	- LIGHT 8	28-29-25.446N 096-20-13.245W	Fl R 4s	17	4	TR-TY on pile.	
37600	- Day beacon 8A	28-29-07.991N 096-21-10.310W				TR-TY on pile.	Ra ref.
37605	- Buoy 9	28-28-41.957N 096-22-01.022W				Green can with yellow square.	
37610	- LIGHT 10	28-28-49.036N 096-22-09.054W	Fl R 2.5s	17	4	TR-TY on pile.	

Light List corrected through LNM week: 01/18

(1) No.	(2) Name and Location	(3) Position	(4) Characteristic	(5) Height	(6) Range	(7) Structure	(8) Remarks
	**INTRACOASTAL WATERWAY (Texas) - Eighth District**						

CLEAR LAKES TO ESPIRITU SANTO BAY (Chart 11319)
Freeport - Port O'Connor
Matagorda Bay - Alternate Route

No.	Name and Location	Position	Characteristic	Height	Range	Structure	Remarks
37615	- Buoy 11	28-28-30.711N 096-22-17.401W				Green can with yellow square.	
37620	- Buoy 12	28-28-23.745N 096-22-26.215W				Red nun with yellow triangle.	Ra ref.
37625	- LIGHT 13 25 feet outside channel limit.	28-28-04.456N 096-22-34.700W	Fl G 6s	17	4	SG-SY on pile.	
37630	- Buoy 13A	28-27-57.329N 096-22-39.923W				Green can with yellow square.	
37635.01	- Lighted Buoy 14	28-28-07.220N 096-22-37.944W	Fl R 6s		4		Red.
37640	- Buoy 15	28-27-34.721N 096-22-54.924W				Green can with yellow square.	
37645	- Buoy 16	28-27-36.392N 096-22-58.057W				Red nun with yellow triangle.	
37650	- Buoy 17	28-27-20.392N 096-23-04.330W				Green can with yellow square.	
37655	- Buoy 18	28-27-10.965N 096-23-15.076W				Red nun with yellow triangle.	
37660	- Buoy 20	28-26-58.993N 096-23-21.225W				Red nun with yellow triangle.	

Matagorda Bay

No.	Name and Location	Position	Characteristic	Height	Range	Structure	Remarks
37665	MATAGORDA BAY LIGHT 30	28-32-54.991N 096-13-02.190W	Q R	17	3	TR on pile.	
37670	HALFMOON REEF LIGHT	28-32-20.672N 096-15-30.867W	Fl W 4s	30	5	NR on skeleton tower on piles.	Ra ref.
37675	The Nature Conservancy Halfmoon Reef Lighted Danger Buoy	28-34-18.813N 096-14-08.396W	Fl W 2.5s			Marks reef perimeter.	Private aid.
37675.01	The Nature Conservancy Halfmoon Reef Lighted Danger Buoy	28-34-07.787N 096-14-18.338W	Fl W 2.5s			Marks reef perimeter.	Private aid.
37675.02	The Nature Conservancy Halfmoon Reef Lighted Danger Buoy	28-33-56.968N 096-14-28.968W	Fl W 2.5s			Marks reef perimeter.	Private aid.
37675.03	The Nature Conservancy Halfmoon Reef Lighted Danger Buoy	28-34-15.692N 096-13-59.352W	Fl W 2.5s			Marks reef perimeter.	Private aid.
37675.04	The Nature Conservancy Halfmoon Reef Lighted Danger Buoy	28-34-04.928N 096-14-09.614W	Fl W 2.5s			Marks reef perimeter.	Private aid.
37675.05	The Nature Conservancy Halfmoon Reef Lighted Danger Buoy	28-33-53.847N 096-14-19.472W	Fl W 2.5s			Marks reef perimeter.	Private aid.

MATAGORDA BAY (Chart 11317)
Palacios Channel

No.	Name and Location	Position	Characteristic	Height	Range	Structure	Remarks
37695	- Day beacon 6 90 feet outside channel limit.	28-30-21.569N 096-18-07.440W				TR on pile.	Ra ref.
37700	- LIGHT 8 60 feet outside channel limit.	28-30-47.542N 096-18-17.889W	Fl R 4s	17	3	TR on pile.	Ra ref.
37705	- Day beacon 10 90 feet outside channel limit.	28-31-27.377N 096-18-33.198W				TR on pile.	Ra ref.
37710	- Day beacon 12 90 feet outside channel limit.	28-32-00.280N 096-18-46.080W				TR on pile.	Ra ref.
37715	- LIGHT 13	28-32-11.027N 096-18-52.060W	Q G	17	4	SG on pile.	Ra ref.
37720	- LIGHT 14 90 feet outside channel limit.	28-32-21.050N 096-18-44.638W	Q R	17	4	TR on pile.	Ra ref.

Light List corrected through LNM week: 01/18

(1) No.	(2) Name and Location	(3) Position	(4) Characteristic	(5) Height	(6) Range	(7) Structure	(8) Remarks
	INTRACOASTAL WATERWAY (Texas) - Eighth District						
	MATAGORDA BAY (Chart 11317)						
	Palacios Channel						
37725	- Day beacon 16 90 feet outside channel limit.	28-32-57.312N 096-18-24.667W				TR on pile.	Ra ref.
37730	- LIGHT 18 60 feet outside channel limit.	28-33-33.572N 096-18-04.693W	Fl R 2.5s	17	3	TR on dolphin.	Ra ref.
37735	- Day beacon 20 90 feet outside channel limit.	28-34-09.832N 096-17-44.714W				TR on pile.	Ra ref.
37740	- LIGHT 22 90 feet outside channel limit.	28-34-46.091N 096-17-24.732W	Fl R 4s	17	4	TR on pile.	Ra ref.
37745	- Day beacon 24	28-35-22.349N 096-17-04.746W				TR on pile.	Ra ref.
37750	- LIGHT 26 90 feet outside channel limit.	28-35-58.606N 096-16-44.756W	Fl R 6s	17	4	TR on pile.	Ra ref.
37755	- Day beacon 28	28-36-34.862N 096-16-24.763W				TR on pile.	Ra ref.
37760	- LIGHT 30	28-37-11.117N 096-16-04.766W	Fl R 2.5s	17	3	TR on pile.	Ra ref.
37765	- LIGHT 32 90 feet outside channel limit.	28-37-37.824N 096-15-50.032W	Fl R 6s	17	4	TR on pile.	Ra ref.
37770	- LIGHT 34	28-38-04.531N 096-15-35.297W	Fl R 4s	17	3	TR on pile.	Ra ref.
37775	- LIGHT 36	28-38-31.237N 096-15-20.556W	Fl R 2.5s	17	4	TR on pile.	Ra ref.
37780	- LIGHT 38	28-38-57.942N 096-15-05.819W	Fl R 6s	17	4	TR on pile.	Ra ref.
37785	- LIGHT 40	28-39-24.647N 096-14-51.077W	Fl R 4s	17	4	TR on pile.	Ra ref.
37790	- LIGHT 42	28-39-51.351N 096-14-36.334W	Fl R 2.5s	17	3	TR on pile.	Ra ref.
37795	- LIGHT 44	28-40-18.055N 096-14-21.588W	Fl R 6s	17	4	TR on pile.	Ra ref.
37805	- LIGHT 46	28-40-51.226N 096-14-03.333W	Fl R 4s	17	3	TR on pile.	Ra ref.
37810	- LIGHT 48	28-41-11.462N 096-13-52.090W	Fl R 6s	17	4	TR on pile.	Ra ref.
37815	- LIGHT 49	28-41-46.645N 096-13-36.061W	Fl G 2.5s	17	4	SG on dolphin.	Ra ref.
37820	- LIGHT 50 60 feet outside channel limit.	28-41-43.981N 096-13-34.453W	Fl R 2.5s	17	3	TR on pile.	Ra ref.
	Freeport - Port O`Connor						
	Matagorda Bay						
37855	- Buoy 111	28-27-12.442N 096-22-01.925W				Green can with yellow square.	
37860	- Buoy 112	28-27-13.887N 096-22-10.542W				Red nun with yellow triangle.	
37865	- Buoy 113	28-27-07.082N 096-22-17.028W				Green can with yellow square.	
37880	- Buoy 115	28-27-01.566N 096-22-32.547W				Green can with yellow square.	
37885	- Buoy 117	28-26-55.832N 096-22-48.192W				Green can with yellow square.	
37890	- LIGHT 118	28-27-01.121N 096-22-50.378W	Fl R 2.5s	17	4	TR-TY on pile.	
37895	- Buoy 119	28-26-50.532N 096-23-03.584W				Green can with yellow square.	
37900	- Buoy 121	28-26-41.540N 096-23-27.670W				Green can with yellow square.	

Light List corrected through LNM week: 01/18

(1) No.	(2) Name and Location	(3) Position	(4) Characteristic	(5) Height	(6) Range	(7) Structure	(8) Remarks
		INTRACOASTAL WATERWAY (Texas) - Eighth District					
	MATAGORDA BAY (Chart 11317)						
	Freeport - Port O`Connor						
	Port O' Connor Channel						
37905	- LIGHT 1	28-26-37.262N 096-23-39.037W	Q G	20	5	SG-SY on skeleton tower.	Higher intensity beam up and down channel.
37910	- LIGHT 2	28-26-44.661N 096-23-42.358W	Q R	23	5	TR-TY on skeleton tower.	Higher intensity beam up and down channel.
37915	- Buoy 4	28-26-38.082N 096-23-52.094W				Red nun with yellow triangle.	
37920	- Buoy 5	28-26-31.222N 096-24-04.698W				Green can with yellow square.	
37925	- Buoy 6	28-26-33.691N 096-24-05.640W				Red nun with yellow triangle.	
37928	CARACOL MARINA DOLPHIN LIGHTS (5)	28-26-33.302N 096-24-08.354W	Fl W 2.5s			Marks marina dolphins.	Private aid.
37928.01	Caracol Marina Day beacon 1	28-26-32.702N 096-24-10.061W				SG on pile. Marks port side marina entry.	Private aid.
37928.02	Caracol Marina Day beacon 2	28-26-32.394N 096-24-10.969W				TR on pile. Marks starboard side marina entry.	Private aid.
	ESPIRITU SANTO BAY TO CARLOS BAY (Chart 11315)						
	Port O`Connor - Corpus Christi						
	Espiritu Santo Bay Ferry Channel						
37935	- Day beacon 3	28-24-25.868N 096-28-45.774W				SG on pile.	Ra ref.
37940	- Day beacon 5	28-24-18.696N 096-28-48.793W				SG on pile.	Ra ref.
37945	- Day beacon 7	28-24-10.697N 096-28-51.115W				SG on pile.	Ra ref.
37950	- Day beacon 9	28-24-02.012N 096-28-53.114W				SG on pile.	Ra ref.
37955	- Day beacon 11	28-23-29.483N 096-29-01.580W				SG on pile.	Ra ref.
37960	- Day beacon 13	28-22-53.214N 096-29-10.905W				SG on pile.	Ra ref.
37970.01	- Day beacon 17	28-21-40.724N 096-29-29.361W				SG on pile.	Ra ref.
37985	- Day beacon 23	28-20-33.518N 096-28-12.415W				SG on pile.	Ra ref.
37990.01	- Day beacon 24	28-20-17.518N 096-27-58.915W				TR on pile.	Ra ref.
37995	- Day beacon 25	28-20-19.515N 096-27-55.913W				SG on pile.	Ra ref.
38000	- Day beacon 27	28-20-11.518N 096-27-52.915W				SG on pile.	Ra ref.
	Port O' Connor Landcut						
38005	- Day beacon 2	28-24-21.622N 096-29-22.672W				TR-TY on pile.	Ra ref.
38010	- Day beacon 4	28-23-23.681N 096-31-33.378W				TR-TY on pile.	Ra ref.
38015	- Day beacon 4A	28-22-56.841N 096-32-32.753W				TR-TY on pile.	Ra ref.
38020	- Day beacon 6	28-22-37.853N 096-33-15.920W				TR-TY on pile.	Ra ref.
38025	- Day beacon 6A	28-22-09.250N 096-34-13.297W				TR-TY on pile.	Ra ref.
38030	- Day beacon 6B	28-21-34.320N 096-35-22.195W				TR-TY on pile.	Ra ref.
38035	- Day beacon 8	28-21-08.750N 096-36-11.276W				TR-TY on pile.	Ra ref.

(1) No.	(2) Name and Location	(3) Position	(4) Characteristic	(5) Height	(6) Range	(7) Structure	(8) Remarks
	INTRACOASTAL WATERWAY (Texas) - Eighth District						
	ESPIRITU SANTO BAY TO CARLOS BAY (Chart 11315)						
	Port O`Connor - Corpus Christi						
	Port O' Connor Landcut						
38040	- Day beacon 10	28-20-40.546N 096-37-05.053W				TR-TY on pile.	Ra ref.
38045	- Day beacon 10A	28-20-09.395N 096-38-02.274W				TR-TY on pile.	Ra ref.
38050	- Day beacon 12	28-19-45.881N 096-38-45.694W				TR-TY on pile.	Ra ref.
38055	- Day beacon 14	28-19-17.804N 096-39-40.162W				TR-TY on pile.	Ra ref.
38060	- Day beacon 15	28-18-53.365N 096-40-16.212W				SG-SY on pile.	Ra ref.
	Victoria East Entrance Channel *Channel aids located 20 to 70 feet outside channel limit.*						
38065	- Junction Buoy A	28-18-53.453N 096-40-22.433W				Red nun with green band and yellow triangle.	
38070	- Buoy 2E	28-18-56.305N 096-40-20.427W				Red nun.	
38075	- Buoy 4E	28-18-55.722N 096-40-28.555W				Red nun.	
38080	- Buoy 5E	28-18-55.438N 096-40-37.379W				Green can.	
38085	- Buoy 6E	28-19-00.080N 096-40-44.389W				Red nun.	
	Victoria Channel *Channel aids are located 20 to 70 feet outside channel limits.*						
38090	- Junction Buoy C	28-18-58.049N 096-40-45.175W				Green can with red band.	
38095	- Buoy 7	28-19-05.331N 096-40-53.211W				Green can.	
38100	- Buoy 8	28-19-06.125N 096-40-50.908W				Red nun.	
38105	- Buoy 9	28-19-16.505N 096-41-01.835W				Green can.	
38110	- Buoy 10	28-19-28.855N 096-41-09.728W				Red nun.	
38115	- LIGHT 11	28-19-39.006N 096-41-21.015W	Fl G 2.5s	17	3	SG on pile.	Ra ref.
38120	- Buoy 13	28-19-48.910N 096-41-28.766W				Green can.	
38125	- Buoy 14	28-19-58.296N 096-41-33.594W				Red nun.	
38130	- Buoy 15	28-20-06.800N 096-41-43.606W				Green can.	
38135	- LIGHT 16	28-20-17.449N 096-41-49.091W	Fl R 2.5s	17	3	TR on pile.	Ra ref.
38140	- Buoy 17	28-20-24.918N 096-41-58.422W				Green can.	
38145	- Buoy 18	28-20-34.518N 096-42-03.720W				Red nun.	
38150	- Buoy 19	28-20-42.775N 096-42-13.273W				Green can.	
38155	- LIGHT 21	28-20-52.714N 096-42-22.030W	Fl G 4s	17	4	SG on pile.	Ra ref.
38160	- LIGHT 22	28-21-06.436N 096-42-27.076W	Fl R 4s	17	3	TR on pile.	Ra ref.
38165	- Buoy 23	28-21-05.352N 096-42-29.277W				Green can.	
38170	- Buoy 25	28-21-17.650N 096-42-37.014W				Green can.	
38175	- Day beacon 27	28-21-29.564N 096-42-45.561W				SG on pile.	Ra ref.

Light List corrected through LNM week: 01/18

(1) No.	(2) Name and Location	(3) Position	(4) Characteristic	(5) Height	(6) Range	(7) Structure	(8) Remarks

INTRACOASTAL WATERWAY (Texas) - Eighth District

ESPIRITU SANTO BAY TO CARLOS BAY (Chart 11315)

Port O'Connor - Corpus Christi

Victoria Channel
Channel aids are located 20 to 70 feet outside channel limits.

No.	Name and Location	Position	Characteristic	Height	Range	Structure	Remarks
38180	- Buoy 29	28-21-42.245N 096-42-52.491W				Green can.	
38185	- LIGHT 30	28-21-47.402N 096-42-52.853W	Fl R 6s	17	4	TR on pile.	Ra ref.
38190	- Buoy 31	28-21-54.553N 096-43-00.231W				Green can.	
38195	- Day beacon 33	28-22-06.373N 096-43-08.864W				SG on pile.	Ra ref.
38200	- Buoy 35	28-22-19.138N 096-43-15.711W				Green can.	
38205	- Buoy 37	28-22-31.435N 096-43-23.451W				Green can.	
38210	- LIGHT 38	28-22-38.668N 096-43-25.121W	Fl R 4s	17	3	TR on pile.	Ra ref.
38215	- Buoy 39	28-22-43.732N 096-43-31.193W				Green can.	
38220	- Buoy 41	28-22-56.029N 096-43-38.934W				Green can.	
38225	- Buoy 42	28-23-07.876N 096-43-44.633W				Red nun.	
38230	- LIGHT 43	28-23-20.217N 096-43-55.371W	Fl G 2.5s	17	3	SG on pile.	Ra ref.
38235	- Buoy 44	28-23-21.426N 096-43-53.078W				Red nun.	
38240	- Buoy 46	28-23-34.693N 096-44-01.516W				Red nun.	
38245	- Buoy 47	28-23-43.450N 096-44-08.793W				Green can.	
38250	- Buoy 49	28-23-54.864N 096-44-15.982W				Green can.	
38255	- LIGHT 50	28-24-01.850N 096-44-17.428W	Fl R 4s	17	3	TR on pile.	Ra ref.
38260	- Buoy 51	28-24-06.277N 096-44-23.170W				Green can.	
38265	- Buoy 53	28-24-17.690N 096-44-30.358W				Green can.	
38270	- LIGHT 55	28-24-28.645N 096-44-38.537W	Fl G 4s	17	4	SG on pile.	Ra ref.
38275	- Buoy 56	28-24-29.874N 096-44-35.984W				Red nun.	
38280	- LIGHT 58	28-24-41.600N 096-44-42.537W	Fl R 6s	17	4	TR on pile.	Ra ref.

Seadrift Channel

No.	Name and Location	Position	Characteristic	Height	Range	Structure	Remarks
38285	Seadrift South Entrance Channel Day beacon 1S	28-23-15.174N 096-43-46.983W				SG on pile.	
38290	Seadrift South Entrance Channel Day beacon 2S	28-23-18.923N 096-43-43.647W				TR on pile.	
38295	- Junction Day beacon C	28-23-27.089N 096-43-41.413W				JG on pile.	
38300	- Buoy 4	28-23-28.727N 096-43-34.897W				Red nun.	
38305	- LIGHT 6 30 feet outside channel limit.	28-23-42.930N 096-43-05.832W	Fl R 4s	17	3	TR on pile.	Ra ref.
38310	- Day beacon 8	28-23-54.750N 096-42-41.604W				TR on pile.	Ra ref.
38315	CITY OF SEADRIFT BREAKWATER LIGHT	28-24-18.000N 096-42-43.000W	Fl R 2.5s	10		On concrete slab.	Private aid.
38320	Seadrift North Entrance Channel Day beacon 2N	28-23-28.528N 096-43-55.133W				TR on pile.	
38325	Seadrift North Entrance Channel Day beacon 3N	28-23-29.961N 096-43-53.419W				SG on pile.	

(1) No.	(2) Name and Location	(3) Position	(4) Characteristic	(5) Height	(6) Range	(7) Structure	(8) Remarks
	INTRACOASTAL WATERWAY (Texas) - Eighth District						
	ESPIRITU SANTO BAY TO CARLOS BAY (Chart 11315)						
	Port O`Connor - Corpus Christi						
	Victoria West Entrance Channel						
38330	- Buoy 2W	28-18-35.532N 096-40-49.053W				Red nun with yellow triangle.	
38335	- Buoy 1W	28-18-34.170N 096-40-51.988W				Green can.	
38340	- Buoy 3W	28-18-45.388N 096-40-47.632W				Green can.	
38345	- Buoy 4W	28-18-49.687N 096-40-45.264W				Red nun.	
38350	- Buoy 5W	28-18-57.807N 096-40-47.944W				Green can	
	San Antonio Bay						
38355.01	- Day beacon 1	28-18-46.399N 096-40-28.533W				SG on pile.	Ra ref.
38360	- LIGHT 2 90 feet outside channel limit.	28-18-46.836N 096-40-36.136W	Q R	17	4	TR-TY on pile.	Ra ref.
38365.01	- Day beacon 3	28-18-24.184N 096-41-00.751W				SG-SY on pile.	Ra ref.
38375.01	- Day beacon 4	28-18-14.876N 096-41-20.720W				TR-TY on pile.	Ra ref.
38385	- LIGHT 5 90 feet outside channel limit.	28-17-57.455N 096-41-37.889W	Fl G 2.5s	17	4	SG-SY on pile.	Ra ref.
38390	- Day beacon 6	28-18-00.104N 096-41-40.071W				TR-TY on pile.	
38395	- Buoy 7	28-17-46.072N 096-41-54.774W				Green can with yellow square.	
38400.01	- Day beacon 9	28-17-34.694N 096-42-10.405W				SG on pile.	Ra ref.
38410	- LIGHT 11 90 feet outside channel limit.	28-17-11.255N 096-42-42.301W	Fl G 4s	17	4	SG-SY on pile.	Ra ref.
38415.01	- Day beacon 12	28-17-13.822N 096-42-44.610W				TR on pile.	Ra ref.
38425.01	- Day beacon 13	28-16-48.947N 096-43-14.617W				SG on pile.	Ra ref.
38435	- LIGHT 15 90 feet outside channel limit.	28-16-24.955N 096-43-47.914W	Fl G 4s	17	4	SG-SY on pile.	Ra ref.
38440	- Day beacon 16	28-16-27.721N 096-43-50.218W				TR-TY on pile.	
38450.01	- Day beacon 17	28-16-01.487N 096-44-20.778W				SG on pile.	Ra ref.
38455	- PIPELINE LIGHT A	28-16-07.550N 096-44-18.130W	Fl Y 2.5s	12		NR on dolphin worded WARNING DO NOT ANCHOR OR DREDGE PIPELINE CROSSING.	Private aid.
38460	- PIPELINE LIGHT B	28-16-02.920N 096-44-13.920W	Fl Y 2.5s	12		NR on dolphin worded WARNING DO NOT ANCHOR OR DREDGE PIPELINE CROSSING.	Private aid.
38470	- LIGHT 19 90 feet outside channel limit.	28-15-38.746N 096-44-52.832W	Fl G 4s	17	4	SG-SY on pile.	Ra ref.
38475.01	- Day beacon 20	28-15-41.195N 096-44-55.758W				TR on pile.	Ra ref.
38485.01	- Day beacon 21	28-15-17.381N 096-45-22.838W				SG on pile.	Ra ref.

Light List corrected through LNM week: 01/18

(1) No.	(2) Name and Location	(3) Position	(4) Characteristic	(5) Height	(6) Range	(7) Structure	(8) Remarks
		INTRACOASTAL WATERWAY (Texas) - Eighth District					
	ESPIRITU SANTO BAY TO CARLOS BAY (Chart 11315)						
	Port O`Connor - Corpus Christi						
	San Antonio Bay						
38495	- LIGHT 23 90 feet outside channel limit.	28-14-52.528N 096-45-57.735W	Fl G 4s	17	4	SG-SY on pile.	Ra ref.
38500	- Day beacon 24	28-14-55.358N 096-46-00.406W				TR-TY on pile.	Ra ref.
38510.01	- Day beacon 25	28-14-22.154N 096-46-41.115W				SG on pile.	Ra ref.
38520	- LIGHT 27 90 feet outside channel limit.	28-14-06.411N 096-47-02.796W	Fl G 4s	17	4	SG-SY on pile.	Ra ref.
38530.01	- Day beacon 28	28-14-01.447N 096-47-15.265W				TR on pile.	Ra ref.
38540	- LIGHT 29 90 feet outside channel limit.	28-13-23.547N 096-48-02.610W	Fl G 2.5s	17	4	SG-SY on pile.	Ra ref.
38545.01	- Day beacon 30	28-13-17.226N 096-48-17.630W				TR on pile.	Ra ref.
38550.01	- Day beacon 31	28-13-06.002N 096-48-28.542W				SG on pile.	Ra ref.
38555.01	- Day beacon 32	28-13-02.434N 096-48-39.817W				TR on pile.	Ra ref.
38560.01	- Day beacon 33	28-12-49.832N 096-48-51.036W				SG on pile.	Ra ref.
38565	- LIGHT 34	28-12-43.072N 096-49-04.953W	Q R	17	4	TR-TY on pile.	Ra ref.
38570.01	- Day beacon 35	28-12-31.428N 096-49-10.332W				SG on pile.	Ra ref.
38575.01	- Day beacon 36	28-12-25.226N 096-49-20.021W				TR on pile.	Ra ref.
38580.01	- Day beacon 37	28-12-14.417N 096-49-24.675W				SG on pile.	Ra ref.
38585	- LIGHT 39	28-12-05.485N 096-49-32.654W	Q G	17	4	SG-SY on pile.	Ra ref.
38590.01	- Day beacon 40	28-11-45.748N 096-50-05.806W				TR on pile.	Ra ref.
	Sundown Bay						
38595	- Buoy 1	28-11-30.531N 096-50-22.082W				Green can with yellow square.	
38600	- Buoy 3	28-11-21.297N 096-50-35.212W				Green can with yellow square.	
38605	- Day beacon 4 150 feet outside channel limit.	28-11-23.880N 096-50-37.145W				TR-TY on pile.	Ra ref.
38610	- Buoy 5	28-11-12.063N 096-50-48.340W				Green can with yellow square.	
38615	- LIGHT 7	28-11-02.324N 096-51-01.017W	Fl G 4s	17	4	SG-SY on pile.	Ra ref.
38620	- Day beacon 8 150 feet outside channel limit.	28-11-05.155N 096-51-03.552W				TR-TY on pile.	Ra ref.
38625	- Buoy 9	28-10-53.594N 096-51-14.596W				Green can with yellow square.	
38630	- Buoy 11	28-10-44.358N 096-51-27.723W				Green can with yellow square.	
38635	- Day beacon 12 150 feet outside channel limit.	28-10-46.838N 096-51-29.366W				TR-TY on pile.	Ra ref.
38640	- Buoy 13	28-10-35.123N 096-51-40.849W				Green can with yellow square.	

Light List corrected through LNM week: 01/18

(1) No.	(2) Name and Location	(3) Position	(4) Characteristic	(5) Height	(6) Range	(7) Structure	(8) Remarks
		INTRACOASTAL WATERWAY (Texas) - Eighth District					

CARLOS BAY TO REDFISH BAY (Chart 11314)
Port O`Connor - Corpus Christi
Aransas Bay

(1) No.	(2) Name and Location	(3) Position	(4) Characteristic	(5) Height	(6) Range	(7) Structure	(8) Remarks
38645	- LIGHT 1 90 feet outside channel limit.	28-08-01.955N 096-54-40.251W	Fl G 2.5s	17	3	SG on pile.	Ra ref.
38650	- Buoy 2	28-07-53.739N 096-54-51.332W				Red nun with yellow triangle.	
38665	- Buoy 4	28-07-16.303N 096-55-23.716W				Red nun with yellow triangle.	
38670	- LIGHT 5	28-07-04.655N 096-55-29.488W	Fl G 4s	17	4	SG-SY on pile.	Ra ref.
38685	- Day beacon A	28-06-20.440N 096-54-44.282W				NR on pile.	
38687	- Day beacon 7	28-06-40.955N 096-55-49.767W				SG-SY on pile.	Ra ref.
38690	- Buoy 8	28-06-31.856N 096-56-01.326W				Red nun with yellow triangle.	
38700	- LIGHT 9 90 feet outside channel limit.	28-06-07.307N 096-56-18.732W	Fl G 2.5s	17	4	SG-SY on pile.	
38705.01	- Day beacon 10	28-06-05.096N 096-56-24.516W				TR-TY on pile.	Ra ref.
38710.01	- Day beacon 11	28-05-32.718N 096-56-48.080W				SG-SY on pile.	Ra ref.
38725	- LIGHT 13 90 feet outside channel limit	28-05-09.903N 096-57-08.096W	Fl G 4s	17	4	SG-SY on pile.	Ra ref.
38730.01	- Day beacon 14	28-05-11.745N 096-57-11.161W				TR-TY on pile.	Ra ref.
38735.01	- Day beacon 15	28-04-46.156N 096-57-28.498W				SG-SY on pile.	Ra ref.
38755	- LIGHT 17 90 feet outside channel limit.	28-04-12.256N 096-57-57.045W	Fl (2)G 5s	17	4	SG-SY on pile.	Ra ref.
38757	- Day beacon 18	28-04-14.247N 096-58-00.996W				TR-TY on pile.	Ra ref.
38760	- Day beacon C	28-03-25.885N 096-57-19.386W				NR on pile.	
38770	COPANO BAY APPROACH LIGHT 1	28-03-36.258N 097-00-49.309W	Fl G 2.5s	17	3	SG on pile.	Ra ref.
38775	COPANO BAY APPROACH LIGHT 2	28-04-58.895N 097-00-36.736W	Fl R 4s	17	3	TR on pile.	Ra ref.
38780	COPANO BAY APPROACH LIGHT 3	28-06-26.871N 097-00-40.089W	Fl G 4s	17	4	SG on dolphin.	
38785	Aransas County Shellfish Mkr C	28-06-19.000N 097-00-58.000W				NW on pile.	Private aid.

Fulton Channel

(1) No.	(2) Name and Location	(3) Position	(4) Characteristic	(5) Height	(6) Range	(7) Structure	(8) Remarks
38790	- Day beacon 1	28-03-31.108N 097-01-25.146W				SG on pile.	Ra ref.
38795	- LIGHT 2	28-03-34.594N 097-01-47.528W	Fl R 4s	17	3	TR on dolphin.	
38800	- Day beacon 3	28-03-32.842N 097-01-56.264W				SG on pile.	
38805	- LIGHT 4	28-03-34.803N 097-01-57.163W	Fl R 6s	17	4	TR on dolphin.	
38810	- Day beacon 5	28-03-34.858N 097-01-58.958W				SG on pile.	

Goose Island Breakwater

(1) No.	(2) Name and Location	(3) Position	(4) Characteristic	(5) Height	(6) Range	(7) Structure	(8) Remarks
38815	- Danger Day beacon A	28-07-38.700N 096-59-28.900W				NW on pile worded: DANGER BREAKWATER.	Private aid.
38820	- Danger Day beacon B	28-07-38.000N 096-59-39.500W				NW on pile worded: DANGER BREAKWATER.	Private aid.

Light List corrected through LNM week: 01/18

(1) No.	(2) Name and Location	(3) Position	(4) Characteristic	(5) Height	(6) Range	(7) Structure	(8) Remarks
	INTRACOASTAL WATERWAY (Texas) - Eighth District						
	CARLOS BAY TO REDFISH BAY (Chart 11314)						
	Port O`Connor - Corpus Christi						
	Goose Island Breakwater						
38825	- DANGER LIGHT C	28-07-38.700N 096-59-48.200W	Fl W 2.5s			NW on pile worded: DANGER BREAKWATER.	Private aid.
38830	- Danger Day beacon D	28-07-40.900N 096-59-56.200W				NW on pile worded: DANGER BREAKWATER.	Private aid.
38835	- DANGER LIGHT E	28-07-44.700N 097-00-02.200W	Fl W 2.5s			NW on pile worded: DANGER BREAKWATER.	Private aid.
38840	- Danger Day beacon F	28-07-49.500N 097-00-06.200W				NW on pile worded: DANGER BREAKWATER.	Private aid.
	Aransas Bay						
38845.01	- Day beacon 19	28-03-42.248N 096-58-22.289W				SG-SY on pile.	Ra ref.
38860	- LIGHT 21 90 feet outside channel limit.	28-03-14.549N 096-58-47.242W	Fl G 4s	17	4	SG-SY on pile.	Ra ref.
38865.01	- Day beacon 22	28-03-16.100N 096-58-51.560W				TR-TY on pile.	Ra ref.
38870.01	- Day beacon 23	28-02-49.177N 096-59-10.113W				SG-SY on pile.	Ra ref.
38875	- PIPELINE MARKER LIGHT A	28-02-40.000N 096-59-20.000W	Q W	10		On pile, worded WARNING DO NOT ANCHOR OR DREDGE-GAS PIPELINE CROSSING.	Private aid.
38880	- PIPELINE MARKER LIGHT B	28-02-35.000N 096-59-15.000W	Q W			On pile, worded WARNINGDO NOT ANCHOR OR DREDGE-GAS PIPELINE CROSSING.	Private aid.
38890.01	- Day beacon 26	28-02-08.096N 096-59-51.581W				TR-TY on pile.	Ra ref.
38895	- LIGHT 25 90 feet outside channel limit.	28-02-11.472N 096-59-44.293W	Fl G 2.5s	17	3	SG-SY on pile.	Ra ref.
38905.01	- Day beacon 27	28-01-40.642N 097-00-11.014W				SG-SY on pile.	Ra ref.
38920	- LIGHT 29 90 feet outside channel limit.	28-01-08.405N 097-00-41.397W	Fl G 4s	17	4	SG-SY on pile.	
38925	Nine Mile Point Dump Day beacon 1	28-01-08.318N 097-00-54.523W				SG on pile.	Ra ref.
38927	- Day beacon 30	28-01-21.150N 097-00-37.223W				TR-TY on pile.	Ra ref.
38930	Nine Mile Point Dump Day beacon 2	28-01-12.919N 097-00-50.236W				TR on pile.	
38935	NINE MILE POINT LIGHT NP	28-01-24.771N 097-01-13.733W	Fl W 6s	17	5	NR on pile.	Ra ref.
38940	Aransas County Navigaton District Little Bay Day beacons (3)	28-02-48.000N 097-01-57.000W				SG on pile.	Private aid.
38942	Aransas County Day beacon 1	28-03-04.200N 097-01-46.620W				SG on pile.	Private aid.
38942.01	Aransas County Day beacon 2	28-03-04.740N 097-01-46.740W				TR on pile.	Private aid.
38942.02	Aransas County Day beacon 3	28-03-03.540N 097-01-47.340W				SG on pile.	Private aid.
38942.03	Aransas County Day beacon 4	28-03-03.900N 097-01-47.760W				TR on pile.	Private aid.

Light List corrected through LNM week: 01/18

(1) No.	(2) Name and Location	(3) Position	(4) Characteristic	(5) Height	(6) Range	(7) Structure	(8) Remarks
	**INTRACOASTAL WATERWAY (Texas) - Eighth District**						
	CARLOS BAY TO REDFISH BAY (Chart 11314)						
	Port O`Connor - Corpus Christi						
	Krueger Channel						
38945	- LIGHT 1	28-01-43.000N 097-01-50.000W	Fl G 4s	20		On dolphin.	Private aid.
38950	- LIGHT 2	28-01-44.000N 097-01-45.000W	Fl R 4s	20		On dolphin.	Private aid.
38955	- Day beacon 3	28-01-46.200N 097-01-57.000W				SG on pile.	Private aid.
38960	- Day beacon 4	28-01-45.600N 097-01-51.000W				TR on pile.	Private aid.
38965	- Day beacon 5	28-01-50.400N 097-01-50.400W				SG on pile.	Private aid.
38970	- Day beacon 6	28-01-51.000N 097-01-51.000W				TR on pile.	Private aid.
38975	- Day beacon 7	28-01-52.800N 097-01-51.000W				SG on pile.	Private aid.
38980	- Day beacon 8	28-01-52.800N 097-01-51.000W				TR on pile.	Private aid.
	Rockport Channel						
38985	- LIGHT 1	28-00-52.481N 097-02-47.808W	Fl G 2.5s	17	3	SG on dolphin.	
38990	- Day beacon 3 Marks rock ledge.	28-00-59.907N 097-02-50.457W				SG on pile.	
38995	- Day beacon 5 Marks rock ledge.	28-01-07.593N 097-02-54.057W				SG on pile.	
39000	- LIGHT 6	28-01-11.201N 097-02-53.128W	Fl R 4s	17	3	TR on pile.	Ra ref.
39005	- Day beacon 7	28-01-11.109N 097-02-55.173W				SG on pile.	
39010	TEXAS MARITIME MUSEUM LIGHTHOUSE	28-01-34.980N 097-02-54.840W	Q W	43		White building with red roof.	Private aid.
	Rockport Smallboat Harbor Channel						
39015	ROCKPORT SMALLBOAT HARBOR JETTY LIGHT 1	28-00-05.030N 097-03-15.930W	Fl G 2.5s			SG on dolphin.	Private aid.
39020	ROCKPORT SMALLBOAT HARBOR JETTY LIGHT 2	28-00-05.960N 097-03-15.490W	Fl R 2.5s			TR on dolphin.	Private aid.
	Aransas Bay						
39030	- PIPELINE MARKER LIGHT C	28-00-50.000N 097-01-00.000W	Q W			On pile, worded WARNING DO NOT ANCHOR OR DREDGE-GAS PIPELINE CROSSING.	Private aid.
39035	- PIPELINE MARKER LIGHT D	28-00-40.000N 097-00-45.000W	Q W			On pile worded WARNINGDO NOT ANCHOR OR DREDGE-GAS PIPELINE CROSSING.	Private aid.
39040.01	- Day beacon 31	28-00-34.043N 097-01-11.222W				SG-SY on pile.	Ra ref.
39055	- LIGHT 33	28-00-05.574N 097-01-37.857W	Q G	17	4	SG-SY on pile.	Ra ref.
	Aransas-Corpus Christi Bay Cutoff Channel						
39060	- Junction Buoy	28-00-00.728N 097-01-49.101W				Red nun with green band and yellow triangle.	
39065.01	- Day beacon 2	28-00-02.701N 097-02-03.715W				TR-TY on pile.	Ra ref.
39080.01	- Day beacon 3	27-59-43.492N 097-03-00.994W				SG-SY on pile.	Ra ref.
39085.01	- Day beacon 4	27-59-47.112N 097-03-01.436W				TR-TY on pile.	Ra ref.

INTRACOASTAL WATERWAY (Texas) - Eighth District

CARLOS BAY TO REDFISH BAY (Chart 11314)
Port O'Connor - Corpus Christi
Aransas-Corpus Christi Bay Cutoff Channel

(1) No.	(2) Name and Location	(3) Position	(4) Characteristic	(5) Height	(6) Range	(7) Structure	(8) Remarks
39090	- LIGHT 5 105 feet outside channel limit.	27-59-34.065N 097-03-38.830W	Fl G 2.5s	17	3	SG-SY on pile.	Ra ref.
39095	- Buoy 8	27-59-33.746N 097-03-53.186W				Red nun with yellow triangle.	
39100.01	- Day beacon 7	27-59-30.672N 097-03-56.189W				SG-SY on pile.	Ra ref.
39105.01	- Day beacon 10	27-59-30.103N 097-04-05.857W				TR-TY on pile.	Ra ref.
39110	- Buoy 9	27-59-27.647N 097-04-06.917W				Green can with yellow square.	
39115	- LIGHT 12	27-59-24.566N 097-04-19.158W	Q R	17	4	TR-TY on pile.	Visible all around; higher intensity beam down channel into Aransas Bay. Ra ref.
39120	- LIGHT 13 60 feet outside channel limit.	27-58-04.125N 097-05-17.612W	Fl G 2.5s	17	3	SG-SY on pile.	
39130	- Day beacon 15	27-57-39.351N 097-05-34.698W				SG-SY on pile.	
39135	Mobil Channel Day beacon 1	27-57-00.570N 097-05-00.660W				NG on pile.	Private aid.
39140	Mobil Channel Day beacon 2	27-57-00.580N 097-05-00.650W				NR on pile.	Private aid.
39150	- LIGHT 16	27-57-14.896N 097-05-55.155W	Fl R 4s	17	3	TR-TY on pile.	
39155	- Day beacon 17	27-57-01.921N 097-06-00.937W				SG-SY on pile.	Ra ref.
39170	- Day beacon 19	27-56-23.885N 097-06-27.278W				SG-SY on pile.	
39180.01	- Day beacon 20	27-56-05.464N 097-06-43.255W				TR-TY on pile.	Ra ref.
39190	- Day beacon 21	27-55-44.747N 097-06-54.918W				SG-SY on pile.	
39195	- LIGHT 22	27-55-28.527N 097-07-09.568W	Q R	17	3	TR-TY on pile.	Ra ref.
39200	- Buoy 23	27-55-14.175N 097-07-15.639W				Green can with yellow square.	
39205	- Buoy 24	27-55-15.924N 097-07-16.169W				Red nun with yellow triangle.	
39210	- Buoy 25	27-54-33.132N 097-07-38.356W				Green can with yellow square.	
39215	- Buoy 26	27-54-33.481N 097-07-40.681W				Red nun with yellow triangle.	
39225 28290	ARANSAS CHANNEL LIGHT 23 50 feet outside channel limit.	27-53-51.523N 097-08-06.438W	Fl G 4s	17	4	SG-TY on pile.	
39230	- Buoy 27	27-53-25.204N 097-08-16.220W				Green can with yellow square.	
39235	- Buoy 28	27-53-26.879N 097-08-18.017W				Red nun with yellow triangle.	
39245	- LIGHT 29	27-52-58.458N 097-08-32.943W	Q G	17	3	SG-SY on pile.	
39250	- Buoy 30	27-52-59.679N 097-08-35.510W				Red nun with yellow triangle.	
39255	- Day beacon 31 50 feet outside channel limit.	27-52-43.266N 097-08-50.558W				SG-SY on pile.	
39265	- Day beacon 33 50 feet outside channel limit.	27-52-22.246N 097-09-19.513W				SG-SY on pile.	Ra ref.

Light List corrected through LNM week: 01/18

(1) No.	(2) Name and Location	(3) Position	(4) Characteristic	(5) Height	(6) Range	(7) Structure	(8) Remarks
	INTRACOASTAL WATERWAY (Texas) - Eighth District						
	CARLOS BAY TO REDFISH BAY (Chart 11314)						
	Port O`Connor - Corpus Christi						
	Aransas-Corpus Christi Bay Cutoff Channel						
39270	- LIGHT 34	27-52-15.105N 097-09-33.009W	Q R	17	3	TR-TY on pile.	
39275	- Day beacon 35	27-51-39.336N 097-09-54.321W				SG-SY on pile.	
39280	- PIPELINE LIGHT A	27-51-30.000N 097-10-03.000W	Fl R 4s	20		On piles.	Private aid.
39285	- Day beacon 37	27-51-07.414N 097-10-14.339W				SG-SY on pile.	
	San Jose Island Dock Channel						
39290	- Day beacon 1	27-57-21.000N 096-59-42.000W				SG on pile.	Ra ref. Private aid.
39295	- LIGHT 2	27-57-00.200N 096-59-00.700W	Fl R 6s			TR on pile.	Ra ref. Private aid.
39300	- Day beacon 3	27-57-14.000N 096-59-41.000W				SG on pile.	Ra ref. Private aid.
39305	- Day beacon 4	27-57-03.000N 096-59-07.000W				TR on pile.	Ra ref. Private aid.
39310	- Day beacon 5	27-57-14.000N 096-59-37.000W				SG on pile.	Ra ref. Private aid.
39315	- Day beacon 6	27-57-03.000N 096-59-07.000W				TR on pile.	Ra ref. Private aid.
39320	- Day beacon 7	27-57-03.000N 096-59-07.000W				SG on pile.	Ra ref. Private aid.
39325	- Day beacon 8	27-57-03.000N 096-59-07.000W				TR on pile.	Ra ref. Private aid.
39330	- Day beacon 9	27-57-03.000N 096-59-07.000W				SG on pile.	Ra ref. Private aid.
39335	- Day beacon 10	27-57-03.000N 096-59-07.000W				TR on pile.	Ra ref. Private aid.
39340	CITY BY THE SEA CHANNEL LIGHT 2	27-57-05.000N 097-06-03.000W	Fl R 2.5s	7		TR on pile.	Private aid.
39345	CITY BY THE SEA CHANNEL DAYBEACON 1	27-57-04.000N 097-06-03.000W				SG on pile.	Private aid.
	REDFISH BAY TO MIDDLE GROUND (Chart 11308)						
	Port O`Connor - Corpus Christi						
	Aransas-Corpus Christi Bay Cutoff Channel						
39355	- Day beacon 39	27-50-34.510N 097-10-35.240W				SG-SY on pile.	
39365	- Day beacon 41	27-50-00.869N 097-10-56.004W				SG-SY on pile.	
	CARLOS BAY TO REDFISH BAY (Chart 11314)						
	Port O`Connor - Corpus Christi						
	Aransas-Corpus Christi Bay Cutoff Channel						
39380.01	- LIGHT 43	27-49-34.189N 097-11-13.763W	Fl G 4s	17	3	SG-SY on pile.	Ra ref.
	REDFISH BAY TO MIDDLE GROUND (Chart 11308)						
	Port O`Connor - Corpus Christi						
	Corpus Christi Bay						
39385	- Buoy 44	27-48-55.683N 097-11-40.185W				Red nun with yellow triangle.	
39390	- WRECK LIGHT 46A Marks submerged pipe.	27-48-43.842N 097-11-47.587W	Q R	17	3	TR-TY on pile.	

Light List corrected through LNM week: 01/18

(1) No.	(2) Name and Location	(3) Position	(4) Characteristic	(5) Height	(6) Range	(7) Structure	(8) Remarks
	INTRACOASTAL WATERWAY (Texas) - Eighth District						

REDFISH BAY TO MIDDLE GROUND (Chart 11308)
Port O`Connor - Corpus Christi
Corpus Christi Bay

39395	- Day beacon 45 60 feet outside channel limit.	27-48-42.943N 097-11-44.184W				SG-SY on pile.	
39400	- Day beacon 48	27-48-26.593N 097-11-59.847W				TR-TY on pile.	Ra ref.
39405	- Day beacon 49	27-48-10.138N 097-12-05.992W				SG-SY on pile.	
39410	- Day beacon 50	27-47-52.033N 097-12-22.690W				TR-TY on pile.	Ra ref.
39415	- LIGHT 51	27-47-27.953N 097-12-30.858W	Fl G 2.5s	17	3	SG on pile.	Ra ref.
39420	- Day beacon 52	27-46-58.811N 097-12-39.623W				TR-TY on pile.	
39425	- Day beacon 55	27-46-26.738N 097-12-38.504W				SG-SY on pile.	
39430	- Day beacon 54	27-46-34.999N 097-12-46.489W				TR-TY on pile.	
39435	- Day beacon 57	27-46-07.108N 097-12-42.962W				SG-SY on pile.	
39440	- LIGHT 58	27-45-42.274N 097-12-49.577W	Fl R 4s	17	3	TR on pile.	Ra ref.
39445	- Day beacon 59	27-45-13.111N 097-12-48.962W				SG-SY on pile.	
39450	- Day beacon 60	27-44-44.882N 097-12-56.673W				TR-TY on pile.	Ra ref.
39455	- Day beacon 61	27-44-21.470N 097-12-55.394W				SG-SY on pile.	Ra ref.

CARLOS BAY TO REDFISH BAY (Chart 11314)
Port O`Connor - Corpus Christi
Aransas Bay Alternate Route

39470.01	- Day beacon 35	27-59-32.627N 097-02-07.990W				SG-SY on pile.	Ra ref.
39475.01	- Day beacon 38	27-59-12.529N 097-02-32.418W				TR-TY on pile.	Ra ref.
39480	- LIGHT 37 90 feet outside channel limit.	27-59-10.588N 097-02-28.310W	Fl G 2.5s	17	4	SG-SY on pile.	Ra ref.
39485	PI ENERGY PIPELINE LIGHT A	27-58-59.486N 097-02-43.296W	Fl Y 2.5s	12		On dolphin.	Private aid.
39490	PI ENERGY PIPELINE LIGHT B	27-58-55.149N 097-02-37.208W	Fl Y 2.5s	12		On dolphin.	Private aid.
39500.01	- Day beacon 39	27-58-49.349N 097-02-47.145W				SG-SY on pile.	Ra ref.
39515	- LIGHT 41	27-58-15.010N 097-03-16.892W	Q G	17	4	SG-SY on pile.	Ra ref.
39520.01	- Day beacon 42	27-58-16.750N 097-03-22.623W				TR-TY on pile.	Ra ref.
39530.01	- Day beacon 43	27-57-21.153N 097-03-26.358W				SG-SY on pile.	Ra ref.
39540.01	- Day beacon 44	27-57-21.867N 097-03-30.921W				TR-TY on pile.	Ra ref.
39560	- LIGHT 45	27-56-33.986N 097-03-33.412W	Q G	17	4	SG-SY on pile.	Ra ref.
39565.01	- Day beacon 46	27-56-33.780N 097-03-38.282W				TR-TY on pile.	Ra ref.
39575.01	- Day beacon 48	27-56-07.506N 097-03-36.281W				TR-TY on pile.	Ra ref.
39580.01	- Day beacon 47	27-55-56.111N 097-03-29.069W				SG-SY on pile.	Ra ref.

Light List corrected through LNM week: 01/18

(1) No.	(2) Name and Location	(3) Position	(4) Characteristic	(5) Height	(6) Range	(7) Structure	(8) Remarks
		INTRACOASTAL WATERWAY (Texas) - Eighth District					
	CARLOS BAY TO REDFISH BAY (Chart 11314)						
	Port O`Connor - Corpus Christi						
	Aransas Bay Alternate Route						
39595	- LIGHT 49 90 feet outside channel limit.	27-55-18.077N 097-03-23.531W	Fl G 2.5s	17	3	SG-SY on pile.	Ra ref.
39600.01	- Day beacon 50	27-55-17.436N 097-03-28.070W				TR-TY on pile.	Ra ref.
39620	- LIGHT 51	27-54-40.823N 097-03-10.064W	Q G	17	3	SG-SY on pile.	Ra ref.
39625.01	- Day beacon 52	27-54-39.906N 097-03-14.465W				TR-TY on pile.	Ra ref.
39645	- LIGHT 53	27-54-01.243N 097-02-59.415W	Fl G 6s	17	4	SG-SY on pile.	Ra ref.
39650.01	- Day beacon 54	27-53-59.317N 097-03-05.180W				TR-TY on pile.	Ra ref.
39665.01	- LIGHT 55	27-53-25.346N 097-02-50.654W	Fl G 4s	17	3	SG-SY on pile.	Ra ref.
39670	- Buoy 56	27-52-48.968N 097-02-53.131W				Red nun with yellow triangle.	
	Aransas Bay						
39680	SAN JOSE ISLAND BREAKWATER LIGHT 1	27-57-12.000N 096-59-27.000W	Q G	6		SG on pile.	Private aid.
39685	- Alternate Route Buoy 58	27-52-18.428N 097-02-55.197W				Red nun with yellow triangle.	
39690	- Alternate Route Danger Buoy A	27-51-45.312N 097-03-00.123W				White with orange stripe.	
	Aransas Bay Alternate Route						
39695	- Buoy 60	27-51-59.306N 097-03-03.594W				Red nun with yellow triangle.	
39700	- Lighted Buoy WR 59	27-51-49.408N 097-03-01.060W	Q G		3	Green can.	
39705	- Danger Buoy B	27-51-50.190N 097-02-58.326W				White with orange stripe.	
39710	- Buoy 62	27-51-15.121N 097-03-29.028W				Red nun with yellow triangle.	
39715	- Buoy 61	27-51-11.192N 097-03-18.881W				Green can with yellow square.	
39720	LYDIA ANN CHANNEL LIGHT	27-51-51.000N 097-03-21.000W	F W			Red and brown brick tower.	Private aid.
	REDFISH BAY TO MIDDLE GROUND (Chart 11308)						
	Corpus Christi - Port Isabel						
	Corpus Christi Baffin Bay						
	Lights 50 feet outside channel limits.						
39725	- LIGHT C	27-43-05.559N 097-13-07.298W	Mo (A) W	17	5	MR-I on dolphin.	Ra ref.
39730	- LIGHT 1	27-42-22.541N 097-13-09.748W	Fl G 2.5s	17	3	SG-I on pile.	Ra ref.
39740	- Day beacon 3	27-41-50.973N 097-13-18.463W				SG-SY on pile.	Ra ref.
39750	- LIGHT 5	27-41-25.121N 097-13-24.961W	Fl G 6s	17	4	SG-I on pile.	Ra ref.
39760	- Day beacon 6	27-41-18.226N 097-13-31.327W				TR-TY on pile.	Ra ref.
39765	- Day beacon 7	27-41-03.809N 097-13-31.139W				SG-SY on pile.	Ra ref.
39770	- Buoy 10	27-40-41.811N 097-13-39.206W				Red nun with yellow triangle.	
39775	- Buoy 9	27-40-38.704N 097-13-37.652W				Green can with yellow square.	
39780	- LIGHT 11	27-40-23.676N 097-13-40.923W	Fl G 4s	17	4	SG-SY on pile.	Ra ref.
39785	- Day beacon 12	27-40-24.622N 097-13-44.267W				TR-TY on pile.	Ra ref.

Light List corrected through LNM week: 01/18

(1) No.	(2) Name and Location	(3) Position	(4) Characteristic	(5) Height	(6) Range	(7) Structure	(8) Remarks
	INTRACOASTAL WATERWAY (Texas) - Eighth District							

REDFISH BAY TO MIDDLE GROUND (Chart 11308)

Corpus Christi - Port Isabel

Corpus Christi Baffin Bay

Lights 50 feet outside channel limits.

No.	Name and Location	Position	Characteristic	Height	Range	Structure	Remarks
39787	Naval Air Station Corpus Christi Marina Channel Day beacon 1	27-41-14.870N 097-14-35.590W				SG on pile.	Private aid.
39787.01	Naval Air Station Corpus Christi Marina Channel Day beacon 2	27-41-17.690N 097-14-44.550W				TR on pile.	Private aid.
39787.02	Naval Air Station Corpus Christi Marina Channel Day beacon 3	27-41-15.750N 097-14-46.760W				SG on pile.	Private aid.
39787.03	Naval Air Station Corpus Christi Marina Channel Day beacon 4	27-41-15.700N 097-14-55.190W				TR on pile.	Private aid.
39787.04	Naval Air Station Corpus Christi Marina Channel Day beacon 5	27-41-11.100N 097-14-58.130W				SG on pile.	Private aid.
39787.05	Naval Air Station Corpus Christi Marina Channel Day beacon 6	27-41-13.000N 097-15-00.910W				TR on pile.	Private aid.
39787.06	Naval Air Station Corpus Christi Marina Channel Day beacon 7	27-41-09.970N 097-15-03.830W				SG on pile.	Private aid.
39787.07	Naval Air Station Corpus Christi Marina Channel Day beacon 8	27-41-17.000N 097-15-21.480W				TR on pile.	Private aid.
39787.08	Naval Air Station Corpus Christi Marina Channel Day beacon 9	27-41-15.780N 097-15-22.350W				SG on pile.	Private aid.
39795	- Day beacon 13	27-39-55.497N 097-13-48.672W				SG-SY on pile.	Ra ref.
39805	- LIGHT 15	27-39-21.476N 097-13-56.833W	Fl G 2.5s	17	3	SG-SY on pile.	Ra ref.
39810	- Day beacon 16	27-39-22.214N 097-14-00.437W				TR-TY on pile.	Ra ref.
39820	- Day beacon 17	27-38-53.218N 097-14-04.556W				SG-SY on pile.	Ra ref.
39830	- LIGHT 19	27-38-25.581N 097-14-11.521W	Q G	17	3	SG-SY on pile.	Ra ref.
39835	- Day beacon 20	27-38-26.377N 097-14-14.739W				TR-TY on pile.	Ra ref.
39845	- Buoy 37	27-37-54.157N 097-14-28.267W				Green can with yellow square.	Ra ref.

Corpus Christi Baffin Bay

Packery Channel

No.	Name and Location	Position	Characteristic	Height	Range	Structure	Remarks
39855	- Day beacon 1	27-36-54.960N 097-12-22.080W				SG on pile.	Private aid.
39860	- Day beacon 2	27-36-56.700N 097-12-22.080W				TR on pile.	Private aid.
39865	- Day beacon 3	27-36-57.780N 097-12-44.880W				SG on pile.	Private aid.
39870	- Day beacon 4	27-37-01.200N 097-12-42.420W				TR on pile.	Private aid.
39875	- Day beacon 5	27-37-25.860N 097-12-56.100W				SG on pile.	Private aid.
39880	- Day beacon 6	27-37-36.000N 097-12-55.560W				TR on pile.	Private aid.
39885	- Day beacon 7	27-37-46.900N 097-13-05.170W				SG on pile.	Private aid.
39890	- Day beacon 8	27-37-48.720N 097-13-03.720W				TR on pile.	Private aid.
39895	- Day beacon 9	27-37-58.620N 097-13-13.980W				SG on pile.	Private aid.
39900	- Day beacon 10	27-38-00.120N 097-13-14.240W				TR on pile.	Private aid.

Light List corrected through LNM week: 01/18

(1) No.	(2) Name and Location	(3) Position	(4) Characteristic	(5) Height	(6) Range	(7) Structure	(8) Remarks
		INTRACOASTAL WATERWAY (Texas) - Eighth District					
	REDFISH BAY TO MIDDLE GROUND (Chart 11308)						
	Corpus Christi Baffin Bay						
	Packery Channel						
39905	- Day beacon 11	27-38-00.660N 097-13-18.240W				SG on pile.	Private aid.
39910	- Day beacon 12	27-38-01.500N 097-13-17.760W				TR on pile.	Private aid.
39915	- Day beacon 13	27-38-01.140N 097-13-21.960W				SG on pile.	Private aid.
39920	- Day beacon 14	27-38-01.500N 097-13-24.300W				TR on pile.	Private aid.
39925	- Day beacon 15	27-37-56.700N 097-13-27.480W				SG on pile.	Private aid.
39930	- Day beacon 16	27-37-55.800N 097-13-29.100W				TR on pile.	Private aid.
39935	- Day beacon 17	27-37-49.980N 097-13-30.600W				SG on pile.	Private aid.
39940	- Day beacon 18	27-37-51.840N 097-13-32.760W				TR on pile.	Private aid.
39945	- Day beacon 19	27-37-49.260N 097-13-33.620W				SG on pile.	Private aid.
39950	- Day beacon 20	27-37-49.860N 097-13-35.040W				TR on pile.	Private aid.
39955	- Day beacon 21	27-37-49.320N 097-13-37.620W				SG on pile.	Private aid.
39960	- Day beacon 22	27-37-51.120N 097-13-39.300W				TR on pile.	Private aid.
39965	- Day beacon 23	27-37-57.660N 097-13-56.640W				SG on pile.	Private aid.
39970	- Day beacon 24	27-38-00.360N 097-13-58.980W				TR on pile.	Private aid.
39975	- Day beacon 25	27-38-07.440N 097-14-19.560W				SG on pile.	Private aid.
39980	- Day beacon 26	27-38-09.000N 097-14-18.440W				TR on pile.	Private aid.
	Corpus Christi - Port Isabel						
	Padre Isles North Channel						
39985	- LIGHT 1	27-37-07.000N 097-14-05.000W	Fl G 2.5s	10		SG on pile.	Private aid.
39990	- Day beacon 2	27-37-07.000N 097-14-05.000W				TR on pile.	Private aid.
39995	- Day beacon 3	27-37-42.000N 097-14-29.000W				SG on pile.	Private aid.
40000	- Day beacon 4	27-37-41.000N 097-14-30.000W				TR on pile.	Private aid.
40005	- Day beacon 6	27-37-40.000N 097-14-26.000W				SG on pile.	Private aid.
40010	- Day beacon 5	27-37-39.000N 097-14-27.000W				TR on pile.	Private aid.
40015	- Day beacon 7	27-37-42.000N 097-14-23.000W				SG on pile.	Private aid.
40020	- Day beacon 8	27-37-36.000N 097-14-24.000W				TR on pile.	Private aid.
40025	- Day beacon 9	27-37-36.000N 097-14-18.000W				SG on pile.	Private aid.
40030	- Day beacon 10	27-37-37.000N 097-14-22.000W				TR on pile.	Private aid.
40035	- Day beacon 11	27-37-36.000N 097-14-18.000W				SG on pile.	Private aid.
40040	- Day beacon 12	27-37-36.000N 097-14-19.000W				TR on pile.	Private aid.
40045	- Day beacon 13	27-37-37.000N 097-14-16.000W				SG on pile.	Private aid.
40050	- Day beacon 15	27-37-38.000N 097-14-13.000W				SG on pile.	Private aid.
40055	- Day beacon 16	27-37-37.000N 097-14-12.000W				TR on pile.	Private aid.

Light List corrected through LNM week: 01/18

(1) No.	(2) Name and Location	(3) Position	(4) Characteristic	(5) Height	(6) Range	(7) Structure	(8) Remarks

INTRACOASTAL WATERWAY (Texas) - Eighth District

REDFISH BAY TO MIDDLE GROUND (Chart 11308)
Corpus Christi - Port Isabel
Padre Isles North Channel

(1) No.	(2) Name and Location	(3) Position	(4) Characteristic	(5) Height	(6) Range	(7) Structure	(8) Remarks
40060	- Day beacon 17	27-37-38.000N 097-14-11.000W				SG on pile.	Private aid.
40065	- Day beacon 18	27-37-37.000N 097-14-10.000W				TR on pile.	Private aid.
40070	- Day beacon 20	27-37-37.000N 097-14-09.000W				TR on pile.	Private aid.
40075	- Day beacon 21	27-37-39.000N 097-14-06.000W				SG on pile.	Private aid.
40080	- Day beacon 22	27-37-37.000N 097-14-07.000W				TR on pile.	Private aid.
40085	- Day beacon 24	27-37-37.000N 097-14-07.000W				TR on pile.	Private aid.

Corpus Christi Baffin Bay
Lights 50 feet outside channel limits.

(1) No.	(2) Name and Location	(3) Position	(4) Characteristic	(5) Height	(6) Range	(7) Structure	(8) Remarks
40090	- LIGHT 39	27-37-29.475N 097-14-39.989W	Fl G 2.5s	17	3	SG-SY on pile.	Ra ref.
40095	- Day beacon 40	27-37-32.017N 097-14-44.107W				TR-TY on pile.	Ra ref.
40105.01	- Day beacon 41	27-37-00.776N 097-14-55.219W				SG-SY on pile.	Ra ref.
40115	- LIGHT 43	27-36-35.762N 097-15-08.823W	Fl G 4s	17	4	SG-SY on pile.	Ra ref.
40120	- Day beacon 44	27-36-37.350N 097-15-12.005W				TR-TY on pile.	Ra ref.

Corpus Christi Baffin Bay
Lights 50 feet outside channel limit.

(1) No.	(2) Name and Location	(3) Position	(4) Characteristic	(5) Height	(6) Range	(7) Structure	(8) Remarks
40130.01	- Day beacon 45	27-36-11.788N 097-15-20.885W				SG-SY on pile.	Ra ref.

Corpus Christi - Port Isabel
Corpus Christi Baffin Bay
Lights 50 feet outside channel limits.

(1) No.	(2) Name and Location	(3) Position	(4) Characteristic	(5) Height	(6) Range	(7) Structure	(8) Remarks
40135	Tropic Isles Entrance Day beacon 1	27-37-28.320N 097-17-10.740W				SG on pile.	Private aid.
40140	Tropic Isles Entrance Light 2	27-37-29.160N 097-17-09.360W	Fl R 2.5s			TR on pile.	Private aid.

Padre Isles South Channel

(1) No.	(2) Name and Location	(3) Position	(4) Characteristic	(5) Height	(6) Range	(7) Structure	(8) Remarks
40145	- LIGHT 1	27-36-03.000N 097-15-19.000W	Fl G 2.5s	10		SG on pile.	Private aid.
40150	- Day beacon 2	27-36-01.000N 097-15-25.000W				TR on pile.	Private aid.
40155	- Day beacon 3	27-36-03.000N 097-15-21.000W				SG on pile.	Private aid.
40160	- Day beacon 5	27-36-02.000N 097-15-19.000W				SG on pile.	Private aid.
40165	- Day beacon 7	27-36-00.000N 097-15-03.000W				SG on pile.	Private aid.
40170	- Day beacon 8	27-35-59.000N 097-15-17.000W				TR on pile.	Private aid.
40175	- Day beacon 9	27-36-02.000N 097-15-13.000W				SG on pile.	Private aid.
40180	- Day beacon 10	27-35-59.000N 097-15-12.000W				TR on pile.	Private aid.
40185	- Day beacon 11	27-36-02.000N 097-15-12.000W				SG on pile.	Private aid.
40190	- Day beacon 13	27-36-03.000N 097-15-10.000W				SG on pile.	Private aid.
40195	- Day beacon 14	27-36-01.000N 097-15-10.000W				TR on pile.	Private aid.

Corpus Christi Baffin Bay
Lights 50 feet outside channel limits.

(1) No.	(2) Name and Location	(3) Position	(4) Characteristic	(5) Height	(6) Range	(7) Structure	(8) Remarks
40205	- LIGHT 47	27-35-43.915N 097-15-35.749W	Fl G 6s	17	4	SG-SY on pile.	Ra ref.

(1) No.	(2) Name and Location	(3) Position	(4) Characteristic	(5) Height	(6) Range	(7) Structure	(8) Remarks
	INTRACOASTAL WATERWAY (Texas) - Eighth District						
	REDFISH BAY TO MIDDLE GROUND (Chart 11308)						
	Corpus Christi - Port Isabel						
	Corpus Christi Baffin Bay						
	Lights 50 feet outside channel limits.						
40210	- Day beacon 48	27-35-44.797N 097-15-39.012W				TR-TY on pile.	Ra ref.
40445.01	- Day beacon 49	27-35-13.580N 097-15-52.570W				SG-SY on pile.	Ra ref.
40455	- LIGHT 51	27-34-48.206N 097-16-05.072W	Fl G 4s	17	4	SG-SY on pile.	Ra ref.
40460.01	- Day beacon 52	27-34-50.836N 097-16-07.526W				TR-TY on pile.	Ra ref.
	Corpus Christi Baffin Bay						
	Lights 50 feet outside channel limit.						
40470.01	- Day beacon 53	27-34-20.054N 097-16-20.986W				SG-SY on pile.	Ra ref.
	Corpus Christi - Port Isabel						
	Corpus Christi Baffin Bay						
	Lights 50 feet outside channel limits.						
40480	- LIGHT 55	27-33-54.531N 097-16-33.793W	Fl G 4s	17	4	SG-SY on pile.	Ra ref.
40485	- Day beacon 56	27-33-54.000N 097-16-37.000W				TR-TY on pile.	Ra ref.
40495.01	- Day beacon 57	27-33-29.740N 097-16-46.902W				SG-SY on pile.	Ra ref.
40505	- LIGHT 59	27-32-57.501N 097-17-03.679W	Fl G 4s	17	4	SG-SY on pile.	Ra ref.
40510.01	- Day beacon 60	27-32-58.096N 097-17-06.544W				TR-TY on pile.	Ra ref.
40520.01	- Day beacon 61	27-32-32.155N 097-17-17.236W				SG-SY on pile.	Ra ref.
40530	- LIGHT 63	27-32-03.762N 097-17-31.392W	Fl G 4s	17	4	SG-SY on pile.	Ra ref.
40535	- Day beacon 64	27-31-59.061N 097-17-37.836W				TR-TY on pile.	Ra ref.
40545.01	- Day beacon 65	27-31-33.724N 097-17-47.717W				SG-SY on pile.	Ra ref.
40555	- LIGHT 67	27-31-09.054N 097-18-00.228W	Fl G 4s	17	4	SG-SY on pile.	Ra ref.
	Corpus Christi Baffin Bay						
	Lights 50 feet outside channel limit.						
40560.01	- Day beacon 68	27-31-10.262N 097-18-03.196W				TR-TY on pile.	Ra ref.
40570.01	- Day beacon 69	27-30-44.905N 097-18-13.453W				SG-SY on pile.	Ra ref.
	Corpus Christi - Port Isabel						
	Corpus Christi Baffin Bay						
	Lights 50 feet outside channel limits.						
40580	- LIGHT 71	27-30-17.484N 097-18-27.565W	Fl G 4s	17	4	SG-SY on pile.	Ra ref.
40585	- Day beacon 72	27-30-18.961N 097-18-30.333W				TR-TY on pile.	Ra ref.
	Corpus Christi Baffin Bay						
	Lights 50 feet outside channel limit.						
40595.01	- Day beacon 73	27-29-49.255N 097-18-42.199W				SG-SY on pile.	Ra ref.
	Corpus Christi - Port Isabel						
	Corpus Christi Baffin Bay						
	Lights 50 feet outside channel limits.						
40605	- LIGHT 75	27-29-21.013N 097-18-57.163W	Fl G 4s	17	4	SG-SY on pile.	Ra ref.

(1) No.	(2) Name and Location	(3) Position	(4) Characteristic	(5) Height	(6) Range	(7) Structure	(8) Remarks
	**INTRACOASTAL WATERWAY (Texas) - Eighth District**						
	**REDFISH BAY TO MIDDLE GROUND (Chart 11308)**						
	Corpus Christi Baffin Bay *Lights 50 feet outside channel limit.*						
40610.01	- Day beacon 76	27-29-18.288N 097-19-01.591W				TR-TY on pile.	Ra ref.
40620.01	- Day beacon 77	27-28-54.857N 097-19-11.316W				SG-SY on pile.	Ra ref.
	Corpus Christi - Port Isabel **Padre Island National Seashore**						
40630	- Day beacon 1	27-28-36.000N 097-19-09.000W				SG on pile.	Private aid.
40635	- Day beacon 2	27-28-32.000N 097-19-10.000W				TR on pile.	Private aid.
40640	- Day beacon 4	27-28-28.000N 097-18-58.000W				TR on pile.	Private aid.
40645	- Day beacon 5	27-28-30.000N 097-18-52.000W				SG on pile.	Private aid.
40650	- Day beacon 6	27-28-25.000N 097-18-47.000W				TR on pile.	Private aid.
40655	- Day beacon 7	27-28-25.000N 097-18-39.000W				SG on pile.	Private aid.
40660	- Day beacon 8	27-28-23.000N 097-18-40.000W				TR on pile.	Private aid.
	Corpus Christi Baffin Bay *Lights 50 feet outside channel limit.*						
40665	- LIGHT 79	27-28-21.397N 097-19-28.265W	Fl G 4s	17	4	SG-SY on pile.	Ra ref.
40670	- Day beacon 80	27-28-22.824N 097-19-31.409W				TR-TY on pile.	Ra ref.
40680.01	- Day beacon 81	27-27-53.070N 097-19-42.589W				SG-SY on pile.	Ra ref.
40690	- LIGHT 83	27-27-27.450N 097-19-56.314W	Fl G 4s	17	4	SG-SY on pile.	Ra ref.
40695.01	- Day beacon 84	27-27-27.687N 097-20-00.765W				TR-TY on pile.	Ra ref.
40705.01	- Day beacon 85	27-26-58.655N 097-20-11.386W				SG-SY on pile.	Ra ref.
40715	- LIGHT 87	27-26-38.633N 097-20-21.776W	Fl G 4s	17	4	SG-SY on pile.	Ra ref.
40720	- Day beacon 88	27-26-39.566N 097-20-25.413W				TR-TY on pile.	Ra ref.
40730.01	- Day beacon 89	27-26-10.751N 097-20-36.514W				SG-SY on pile.	Ra ref.
40740	- LIGHT 91	27-25-44.703N 097-20-50.201W	Fl G 6s	17	4	SG-SY on pile.	Ra ref.
40745.01	- Day beacon 92	27-25-47.310N 097-20-52.297W				TR-TY on pile.	Ra ref.
40755.01	- Day beacon 93	27-25-12.497N 097-21-06.687W				SG-SY on pile.	Ra ref.
40765	- LIGHT 95	27-24-45.225N 097-21-21.345W	Fl G 4s	17	4	SG-SY on pile.	Ra ref.
40770	- Day beacon 96	27-24-46.440N 097-21-24.151W				TR-TY on pile.	Ra ref.
40780.01	- Day beacon 97	27-24-17.369N 097-21-36.243W				SG-SY on pile.	Ra ref.
40790	- LIGHT 99	27-23-50.706N 097-21-49.946W	Fl G 2.5s	17	3	SG-SY on pile.	Ra ref.
40795.01	- Day beacon 100	27-23-53.304N 097-21-52.648W				TR-TY on pile.	Ra ref.
40805.01	- Day beacon 101	27-23-24.782N 097-22-04.350W				SG-SY on pile.	Ra ref.
40815	- LIGHT 103	27-23-04.403N 097-22-13.884W	Q G	17	3	SG-SY on pile.	Ra ref.

(1) No.	(2) Name and Location	(3) Position	(4) Characteristic	(5) Height	(6) Range	(7) Structure	(8) Remarks
	**INTRACOASTAL WATERWAY (Texas) - Eighth District**						

REDFISH BAY TO MIDDLE GROUND (Chart 11308)

Corpus Christi Baffin Bay
Lights 50 feet outside channel limit.

No.	Name and Location	Position	Characteristic	Height	Range	Structure	Remarks
40820	- Day beacon 104	27-23-05.193N 097-22-17.581W				TR-TY on pile.	Ra ref.
40830.01	- Day beacon 105	27-22-36.990N 097-22-26.010W				SG-SY on pile.	Ra ref.
40840	- LIGHT 107	27-22-10.149N 097-22-38.291W	Fl G 2.5s	17	3	SG-SY on pile.	Ra ref.
40845.01	- Day beacon 108	27-22-12.289N 097-22-41.095W				TR-TY on pile.	Ra ref.
40855.01	- Day beacon 109	27-21-41.963N 097-22-50.381W				SG-SY on pile.	Ra ref.
40865	- LIGHT 111	27-21-15.274N 097-23-02.603W	Fl G 4s	17	4	SG-SY on pile.	Ra ref.
40870	- Day beacon 112	27-21-16.164N 097-23-04.907W				TR-TY on pile.	Ra ref.
40880.01	- Day beacon 113	27-20-52.314N 097-23-11.465W				SG-SY on pile.	Ra ref.
40890	- LIGHT 115	27-20-20.649N 097-23-26.272W	Fl G 4s	17	4	SG-SY on pile.	Ra ref.
40895	- Day beacon 116	27-20-21.250N 097-23-29.354W				TR-TY on pile.	Ra ref.
40910.01	- Day beacon 117	27-19-56.479N 097-23-36.819W				SG-SY on pile.	Ra ref.
40920	- LIGHT 119	27-19-22.645N 097-23-51.182W	Fl G 2.5s	17	3	SG-SY on pile.	Ra ref.
40925	- Day beacon 120	27-19-24.235N 097-23-54.036W				TR-TY on pile.	Ra ref.
40930.01	- Day beacon 121	27-19-10.524N 097-23-56.965W				SG-SY on pile.	Ra ref.
40935.01	- Day beacon 122	27-19-09.111N 097-24-00.582W				TR-TY on pile.	Ra ref.
40940.01	- Day beacon 123	27-18-54.045N 097-24-03.942W				SG-SY on pile.	Ra ref.
40945.01	- Day beacon 124	27-18-53.846N 097-24-07.174W				TR-TY on pile.	Ra ref.
40950	- LIGHT 125	27-18-40.742N 097-24-09.216W	Q G	17	3	SG-SY on pile.	Ra ref.
40965.01	- Day beacon 127	27-18-11.509N 097-24-16.293W				SG-SY on pile.	Ra ref.
40980	- LIGHT 129	27-17-46.926N 097-24-21.389W	Fl G 2.5s	17	3	SG-SY on pile.	Ra ref.
40985.01	- Day beacon 130	27-17-36.588N 097-24-27.096W				TR-TY on pile.	Ra ref.
40995.01	- Day beacon 131	27-17-19.235N 097-24-28.212W				SG-SY on pile.	Ra ref.
41005	- LIGHT 133	27-16-44.992N 097-24-34.923W	Fl G 4s	17	4	SG-SY on pile.	Ra ref.

Baffin Bay

No.	Name and Location	Position	Characteristic	Height	Range	Structure	Remarks
41010.01	- Junction Day beacon	27-16-28.709N 097-24-42.368W				JR-TY on pile.	
41015	- Day beacon 2	27-16-39.529N 097-24-46.336W				TR on pile.	
41020	- Day beacon 4	27-16-40.959N 097-25-05.456W				TR on pile.	
41025	- Day beacon 5	27-16-28.614N 097-25-12.819W				SG on pile.	
41030	- Day beacon 6	27-16-41.429N 097-25-37.694W				TR on pile.	
41035	- Day beacon 8	27-16-39.468N 097-26-31.248W				TR on pile.	

Light List corrected through LNM week: 01/18

(1) No.	(2) Name and Location	(3) Position	(4) Characteristic	(5) Height	(6) Range	(7) Structure	(8) Remarks

INTRACOASTAL WATERWAY (Texas) - Eighth District

REDFISH BAY TO MIDDLE GROUND (Chart 11308)
Corpus Christi Baffin Bay
Baffin Bay

No.	Name and Location	Position	Characteristic	Height	Range	Structure	Remarks
41040	- Day beacon 9	27-16-24.072N 097-27-09.003W				SG on pile.	
41045	- Day beacon 10	27-16-38.157N 097-27-20.959W				TR on pile.	
41050	- Day beacon 10A	27-16-23.978N 097-28-05.738W				TR on pile.	
41055	- Day beacon 12	27-16-09.465N 097-28-56.052W				TR on pile.	
41060	- Day beacon 11	27-16-06.882N 097-28-27.897W				SG on pile.	
41065	- Day beacon 14	27-15-54.000N 097-29-36.000W				TR on pile.	
41070	- Day beacon 16	27-15-46.100N 097-30-11.000W				TR on pile.	
41075	- Day beacon 18	27-15-34.289N 097-30-50.393W				TR on pile.	
41080	- Day beacon 20	27-15-36.925N 097-31-39.702W				TR on pile.	
41085	- Day beacon 22	27-15-39.534N 097-32-29.155W				TR on pile.	
41090	- Day beacon 24	27-15-41.712N 097-33-10.581W				TR on pile.	
41095	- Day beacon 26	27-15-45.240N 097-34-15.915W				TR on pile.	
41100	- Day beacon 28	27-15-47.118N 097-34-55.107W				TR on pile.	
41105	- Day beacon 30	27-15-48.987N 097-35-31.533W				TR on pile.	
41110	- Day beacon 32	27-16-09.087N 097-36-27.110W				TR on pile.	
41115	- Day beacon 34	27-16-20.520N 097-37-59.319W				TR on pile.	
41120	- Day beacon 36	27-16-34.926N 097-37-31.785W				TR on pile.	
41125	- Day beacon 38	27-16-47.655N 097-38-00.564W				TR on pile.	
41130	- Day beacon 40	27-16-55.855N 097-38-22.473W				TR on pile.	

Corpus Christi - Port Isabel
Baffin Bay Land Cut
Lights 50 feet outside channel limit, unless otherwise noted.

No.	Name and Location	Position	Characteristic	Height	Range	Structure	Remarks
41150.01	- Day beacon 1	27-15-55.931N 097-24-46.002W				SG-SY on pile.	Ra ref.
41160	- LIGHT 3	27-15-29.092N 097-24-51.168W	Fl G 6s	17	4	SG-SY on pile.	
41165	- Day beacon 4	27-15-30.919N 097-24-55.029W				TR-TY on pile.	Ra ref.
41175.01	- Day beacon 5	27-14-55.518N 097-24-59.491W				SG-SY on pile.	Ra ref.
41185	- LIGHT 7	27-14-25.927N 097-25-05.467W	Fl G 4s	17	4	SG-SY on pile.	
41190	- Day beacon 8	27-14-25.174N 097-25-08.504W				TR-TY on pile.	
41200.01	- Day beacon 9	27-13-54.873N 097-25-12.633W				SG-SY on pile.	Ra ref.
41210	- LIGHT 11 60 feet outside channel limit.	27-13-26.385N 097-25-18.319W	Fl G 4s	17	4	SG-SY on pile.	
41215	- Day beacon 12	27-13-26.952N 097-25-21.369W				TR-TY on pile.	
41225.01	- Day beacon 13	27-12-56.125N 097-25-24.340W				SG-SY on pile.	Ra ref.

Light List corrected through LNM week: 01/18

(1) No.	(2) Name and Location	(3) Position	(4) Characteristic	(5) Height	(6) Range	(7) Structure	(8) Remarks
	INTRACOASTAL WATERWAY (Texas) - Eighth District						
	REDFISH BAY TO MIDDLE GROUND (Chart 11308)						
	Corpus Christi - Port Isabel						
	Baffin Bay Land Cut						
	Lights 50 feet outside channel limit, unless otherwise noted.						
41235	- LIGHT 15	27-12-27.411N 097-25-31.004W	Fl G 4s	17	4	SG-SY on pile.	
41240	- Day beacon 16	27-12-27.854N 097-25-34.108W				TR-TY on pile.	Ra ref.
41250.01	- Day beacon 17	27-11-57.203N 097-25-37.078W				SG-SY on pile.	Ra ref.
41260	- LIGHT 19	27-11-25.431N 097-25-43.985W	Fl G 6s	17	4	SG-SY on pile.	
41265	- Day beacon 20	27-11-28.100N 097-25-47.000W				TR-TY on pile.	
41275.01	- Day beacon 21	27-10-52.731N 097-25-52.029W				SG-SY on pile.	Ra ref.
41285	- LIGHT 23	27-10-25.836N 097-25-56.912W	Fl G 4s	17	4	SG-SY on pile.	Ra ref.
41290	- Day beacon 24	27-10-26.067N 097-26-00.549W				TR-TY on pile.	
41295.01	- Day beacon 25	27-09-57.805N 097-26-03.808W				SG-SY on pile.	Ra ref.
	LAGUNA MADRE (Chart 11306)						
	Corpus Christi - Port Isabel						
	Baffin Bay Land Cut						
	Lights 50 feet outside channel limit, unless otherwise noted.						
41310	- LIGHT 27	27-09-28.178N 097-26-09.673W	Fl G 2.5s	17	3	SG-SY on pile.	Ra ref.
41315	- Day beacon 28	27-09-28.858N 097-26-13.400W				TR-TY on pile.	
	REDFISH BAY TO MIDDLE GROUND (Chart 11308)						
	Corpus Christi - Port Isabel						
	Baffin Bay Land Cut						
	Lights 50 feet outside channel limit, unless otherwise noted.						
41325.01	- Day beacon 29	27-09-02.333N 097-26-15.738W				SG-SY on pile.	Ra ref.
	LAGUNA MADRE (Chart 11306)						
	Corpus Christi - Port Isabel						
	Baffin Bay Land Cut						
	Lights 50 feet outside channel limit, unless otherwise noted.						
41335	- LIGHT 31	27-08-29.076N 097-26-22.314W	Q G	17	3	SG-SY on pile.	Ra ref.
41340	- Day beacon 32	27-08-29.100N 097-26-26.000W				TR-TY on pile.	
	REDFISH BAY TO MIDDLE GROUND (Chart 11308)						
	Corpus Christi - Port Isabel						
	Baffin Bay Land Cut						
	Lights 50 feet outside channel limit, unless otherwise noted.						
41350.01	- Day beacon 33	27-07-57.793N 097-26-24.773W				SG-SY on pile.	Ra ref.
	LAGUNA MADRE (Chart 11306)						
	Corpus Christi - Port Isabel						
	Baffin Bay Land Cut						
	Lights 50 feet outside channel limit, unless otherwise noted.						
41365	- LIGHT 34	27-07-24.346N 097-26-30.029W	Fl R 2.5s	17	3	TR-TY on pile.	Ra ref.
	Land Cut						
41370	- LIGHT 1	27-06-46.266N 097-26-28.950W	Fl G 4s	17	4	SG-SY on pile.	Ra ref.
41375	- LIGHT 2 50 feet outside channel limit.	27-05-54.489N 097-26-36.083W	Fl R 6s	17	4	TR-TY on pile.	Ra ref.

(1) No.	(2) Name and Location	(3) Position	(4) Characteristic	(5) Height	(6) Range	(7) Structure	(8) Remarks
\multicolumn{8}{c}{INTRACOASTAL WATERWAY (Texas) - Eighth District}

LAGUNA MADRE (Chart 11306)
Corpus Christi - Port Isabel
Land Cut

(1) No.	(2) Name and Location	(3) Position	(4) Characteristic	(5) Height	(6) Range	(7) Structure	(8) Remarks
41380	- Day beacon 3 80 feet outside channel limit.	27-04-57.507N 097-26-36.076W				SG-SY on pile.	
41385	- Day beacon 4 50 feet outside channel limit.	27-04-07.895N 097-26-42.167W				TR-TY on pile.	
41390	- LIGHT 5	27-03-20.069N 097-26-41.927W	Fl G 2.5s	17	3	SG-SY on pile.	Ra ref.
41395	- Day beacon 6	27-02-32.731N 097-26-48.419W				TR-TY on pile.	Ra ref.
41400	- LIGHT 7	27-01-32.313N 097-26-49.344W	Fl G 6s	17	4	SG-SY on pile.	Ra ref.
41405	- Day beacon 8	27-00-42.482N 097-26-55.239W				TR-TY on pile.	
41410	- Day beacon 9	26-59-48.527N 097-26-56.867W				SG-SY on pile.	Ra ref.
41415	- LIGHT 10	26-58-53.649N 097-27-06.639W	Fl R 2.5s	17	3	TR-TY on pile.	Ra ref.
41420	- Day beacon 11	26-58-02.224N 097-27-09.008W				SG-SY on pile.	Ra ref.
41425	- LIGHT 12	26-57-12.098N 097-27-18.138W	Fl R 4s	17	3	TR-TY on pile.	Ra ref.
41430	- Day beacon 13	26-56-23.283N 097-27-20.037W				SG-SY on pile.	
41435	- LIGHT 14	26-55-27.804N 097-27-29.646W	Fl R 2.5s	17	3	TR-TY on pile.	Ra ref.
41440	- Day beacon 15	26-54-36.875N 097-27-31.786W				SG-SY on pile.	
41445	- Day beacon 16	26-53-49.842N 097-27-41.155W				TR-TY on pile.	Ra ref.
41450	- LIGHT 17	26-52-55.660N 097-27-43.047W	Fl G 4s	17	4	SG-SY on pile.	Ra ref.
41455	- Day beacon 18	26-52-00.750N 097-27-52.466W				TR-TY on pile.	Ra ref.
41460	- LIGHT 19	26-51-10.839N 097-27-55.043W	Fl G 6s	17	4	SG-SY on pile.	Ra ref.
41465	- LIGHT 20	26-50-11.914N 097-28-05.015W	Fl R 6s	17	4	TR-TY on pile.	Ra ref.
41470	- LIGHT 21	26-49-26.967N 097-28-06.629W	Fl G 4s	17	4	SG-SY on pile.	
41475	- LIGHT 22 80 feet outside channel limit.	26-48-47.108N 097-28-14.129W	Fl R 2.5s	17	3	TR-TY on pile.	Higher intensity beam up and down channel.

Land Cut-Arroyo Colorado

(1) No.	(2) Name and Location	(3) Position	(4) Characteristic	(5) Height	(6) Range	(7) Structure	(8) Remarks
41480.01	- Day beacon 23	26-48-25.360N 097-28-14.010W				SG-SY on pile.	Ra ref.
41490	- LIGHT 25	26-48-05.579N 097-28-14.713W	Q G	17	3	SG-SY on pile.	Higher intensity beam up and down channel. Ra ref.
41495	- Day beacon 26	26-48-05.492N 097-28-18.200W				TR-TY on pile.	
41500.01	- Day beacon 27	26-47-37.650N 097-28-09.180W				SG-SY on pile.	Ra ref.
41520	- LIGHT 29	26-47-07.009N 097-28-01.500W	Fl G 4s	17	4	SG-SY on pile.	Ra ref.
41525	- Day beacon 30	26-47-06.180N 097-28-04.965W				TR-TY on pile.	
41530.01	- Day beacon 31	26-46-39.050N 097-27-55.580W				SG-SY on pile.	Ra ref.

Light List corrected through LNM week: 01/18

(1) No.	(2) Name and Location	(3) Position	(4) Characteristic	(5) Height	(6) Range	(7) Structure	(8) Remarks
	INTRACOASTAL WATERWAY (Texas) - Eighth District						
	LAGUNA MADRE (Chart 11306)						
	Land Cut-Arroyo Colorado						
41550	- LIGHT 32	26-46-13.900N 097-27-52.883W	Fl R 4s	17	4	TR-TY on pile.	
41555.01	- Day beacon 33	26-45-44.020N 097-27-42.920W				SG-SY on pile.	Ra ref.
41570	- Day beacon 34	26-45-21.225N 097-27-40.446W				TR-TY on pile.	
41575.01	- Day beacon 35	26-44-55.452N 097-27-31.667W				SG-SY on pile.	Ra ref.
41590	- LIGHT 37 55 feet outside channel limit.	26-44-29.695N 097-27-25.162W	Fl G 4s	17	4	SG-SY on pile.	
41595	- Day beacon 38	26-44-29.084N 097-27-28.457W				TR-TY on pile.	Ra ref.
41600.01	- Day beacon 39	26-44-03.630N 097-27-19.850W				SG-SY on pile.	Ra ref.
41610	- Day beacon 40	26-43-36.758N 097-27-16.425W				TR-TY on pile.	Ra ref.
41615.01	- Day beacon 41	26-43-09.660N 097-27-07.270W				SG-SY on pile.	Ra ref.
	LAGUNA MADRE (Chart 11303)						
	Land Cut-Arroyo Colorado						
41620.01	- Day beacon 43	26-42-41.430N 097-27-00.240W				SG-SY on pile.	Ra ref.
	LAGUNA MADRE (Chart 11306)						
	Land Cut-Arroyo Colorado						
41630	- LIGHT 44	26-42-38.454N 097-27-04.494W	Q R	17	4	TR-TY on pile.	Higher intensity beam up and down channel.
	LAGUNA MADRE (Chart 11303)						
	Land Cut-Arroyo Colorado						
41635.01	- Day beacon 45	26-42-18.600N 097-26-52.900W				SG-SY on pile.	Ra ref.
	LAGUNA MADRE (Chart 11306)						
	Land Cut-Arroyo Colorado						
41650	- Day beacon 46	26-41-56.343N 097-26-47.781W				TR-TY on pile.	Ra ref.
41655.01	- Day beacon 47	26-41-39.890N 097-26-38.820W				SG-SY on pile.	Ra ref.
41670	- LIGHT 49 45 feet outside channel limit.	26-41-10.035N 097-26-27.987W	Fl G 4s	17	4	SG-SY on pile.	
	LAGUNA MADRE (Chart 11303)						
	Land Cut-Arroyo Colorado						
41670.01	- Day beacon 53	26-40-11.930N 097-26-07.870W					Ra ref.
	LAGUNA MADRE (Chart 11306)						
	Land Cut-Arroyo Colorado						
41675	- Day beacon 48	26-41-14.573N 097-26-32.984W				TR-TY on pile.	Ra ref.
41680.01	- Day beacon 51	26-40-50.901N 097-26-21.298W				SG-SY on pile.	Ra ref.
41695	- Day beacon 52	26-40-32.803N 097-26-18.189W				TR-TY on pile.	Ra ref.
41720	- LIGHT 54	26-39-51.034N 097-26-03.398W	Fl R 4s	17	4	TR-TY on pile.	Ra ref.
41725.01	- Day beacon 55	26-39-31.350N 097-25-53.620W				SG-SY on pile.	Ra ref.
41735	- Day beacon 56	26-39-09.262N 097-25-48.610W				TR-TY on pile.	Ra ref.

Light List corrected through LNM week: 01/18

(1) No.	(2) Name and Location	(3) Position	(4) Characteristic	(5) Height	(6) Range	(7) Structure	(8) Remarks
	INTRACOASTAL WATERWAY (Texas) - Eighth District						
LAGUNA MADRE (Chart 11306)							
Land Cut-Arroyo Colorado							
41740.01	- Day beacon 57	26-38-52.070N 097-25-39.990W				SG-SY on pile.	Ra ref.
41750	- LIGHT 59	26-38-11.433N 097-25-24.921W	Fl G 4s	17	4	SG-SY on pile.	Ra ref.
41755	- Day beacon 58	26-38-27.491N 097-25-33.825W				TR-TY on pile.	Ra ref.
41770	- Day beacon 60	26-37-45.710N 097-25-19.043W				TR-TY on pile.	Ra ref.
41775.01	- Day beacon 61	26-37-25.270N 097-25-09.070W				SG-SY on pile.	Ra ref.
41790	- LIGHT 62 70 feet outside channel limit.	26-37-03.946N 097-25-04.264W	Fl R 4s	17	4	TR-TY on pile.	
41795.01	- Day beacon 63	26-36-44.700N 097-24-54.830W				SG-SY on pile.	Ra ref.
41805	- Day beacon 64	26-36-22.174N 097-24-49.487W				TR-TY on pile.	Ra ref.
41810.01	- Day beacon 65	26-36-03.890N 097-24-39.873W				SG-SY on pile.	Ra ref.
41820	- LIGHT 67	26-35-41.317N 097-24-31.513W	Q G	17	4	SG on pile.	Ra ref.
41825	- Day beacon 68	26-35-40.263N 097-24-35.158W				TR-TY on pile.	Ra ref.
41830.01	- Day beacon 69	26-35-15.140N 097-24-28.950W				SG-SY on pile.	Ra ref.
41845	- Day beacon 70	26-34-43.589N 097-24-29.334W				TR-TY on pile.	Ra ref.
41850.01	- Day beacon 71	26-34-25.480N 097-24-25.810W				SG-SY on pile.	Ra ref.
41870	- Day beacon 72 60 feet outside channel limit.	26-34-00.634N 097-24-26.759W				TR-TY on dolphin.	Ra ref.
41875 29410	PORT MANSFIELD CHANNEL JUNCTION LIGHT PM	26-33-33.128N 097-24-26.319W	Fl (2+1)R 6s	17	4	JR-TY on pile.	Ra ref.
41875.01	- Day beacon 73	26-33-51.170N 097-24-23.820W				SG-SY on pile.	Ra ref.
41880 29405	Port Mansfield Channel Day beacon 27	26-33-31.533N 097-24-21.154W				SG-SY on pile.	Ra ref.
41885	- Day beacon 75	26-33-12.353N 097-24-20.179W				SG-SY on pile.	
41890	- Day beacon 74	26-33-17.678N 097-24-24.183W				TR-TY on dolphin.	Ra ref.
41895.01	- Day beacon 77	26-32-48.040N 097-24-20.150W				SG-SY on pile.	Ra ref.
41905	- LIGHT 79	26-32-26.636N 097-24-17.574W	Q G	17	4	SG-SY on dolphin.	Higher intensity beam up and down channel. Ra ref.
41910	- Day beacon 80	26-32-25.519N 097-24-21.056W				TR-TY on pile.	Ra ref.
41915.01	- Day beacon 81	26-32-01.840N 097-24-08.240W				SG-SY on pile.	Ra ref.
41925	- Day beacon 83	26-31-36.771N 097-23-55.775W				SG-SY on pile.	Ra ref.
41930	- Day beacon 84	26-31-32.406N 097-23-57.478W				TR-TY on pile.	
41935.01	- Day beacon 85	26-31-08.870N 097-23-44.540W				SG-SY on pile.	Ra ref.
41945	- Day beacon 87	26-30-45.737N 097-23-33.648W				SG-SY on pile.	Ra ref.

Light List corrected through LNM week: 01/18

(1) No.	(2) Name and Location	(3) Position	(4) Characteristic	(5) Height	(6) Range	(7) Structure	(8) Remarks
	INTRACOASTAL WATERWAY (Texas) - Eighth District						
	LAGUNA MADRE (Chart 11306)						
	Land Cut-Arroyo Colorado						
41950	- LIGHT 88	26-30-45.478N 097-23-37.404W	Fl R 4s	17	4	TR-TY on pile.	
41955.01	- Day beacon 89	26-30-20.320N 097-23-22.850W				SG-SY on pile.	Ra ref.
41970	- Day beacon 91	26-29-54.939N 097-23-10.510W				SG-SY on pile.	Ra ref.
41975	- Day beacon 90	26-30-04.684N 097-23-19.442W				TR-TY on pile.	Ra ref.
41980.01	- Day beacon 93	26-29-35.960N 097-23-02.980W				SG-SY on pile.	Ra ref.
	LAGUNA MADRE (Chart 11303)						
	Land Cut-Arroyo Colorado						
41990	- LIGHT 95	26-29-22.953N 097-22-55.975W	Fl G 4s	17	4	SG-SY on pile.	Ra ref.
41995	- Day beacon 96	26-29-21.096N 097-22-59.862W				TR-TY on pile.	
	LAGUNA MADRE (Chart 11306)						
	Land Cut-Arroyo Colorado						
42000.01	- Day beacon 97	26-28-57.840N 097-22-45.750W				SG-SY on pile.	Ra ref.
	LAGUNA MADRE (Chart 11303)						
	Land Cut-Arroyo Colorado						
42010	- LIGHT 99	26-28-23.277N 097-22-29.641W	Fl G 2.5s	17	3	SG-SY on pile.	
42015	- Day beacon 98	26-28-36.178N 097-22-38.999W				TR on pile.	
	LAGUNA MADRE (Chart 11306)						
	Land Cut-Arroyo Colorado						
42020.01	- Day beacon 101	26-27-58.730N 097-22-19.420W				SG-SY on pile.	Ra ref.
	LAGUNA MADRE (Chart 11303)						
	Land Cut-Arroyo Colorado						
42030	- Day beacon 103	26-27-37.770N 097-22-09.375W				SG-SY on pile.	Ra ref.
42035	- LIGHT 104	26-27-36.239N 097-22-11.790W	Fl R 4s	17	3	TR-TY on pile.	Ra ref.
42050	- Day beacon 107	26-26-59.202N 097-21-52.338W				SG-SY on pile.	Ra ref.
42055	- Day beacon 106	26-27-10.846N 097-22-00.421W				TR on pile.	
	LAGUNA MADRE (Chart 11306)						
	Land Cut-Arroyo Colorado						
42060.01	- Day beacon 109	26-26-45.510N 097-21-45.970W				SG-SY on pile.	Ra ref.
	LAGUNA MADRE (Chart 11303)						
	Land Cut-Arroyo Colorado						
42065	- LIGHT 111	26-26-28.200N 097-21-38.290W	Fl G 4s	17	4	SG-SY on pile.	
42070	- Day beacon 112	26-26-27.251N 097-21-40.921W				TR on pile.	
	LAGUNA MADRE (Chart 11306)						
	Land Cut-Arroyo Colorado						
42075.01	- Day beacon 113	26-26-05.062N 097-21-28.054W				SG-SY on pile.	Ra ref.
	LAGUNA MADRE (Chart 11303)						
	Land Cut-Arroyo Colorado						
42085	- LIGHT 115	26-25-35.855N 097-21-14.902W	Fl G 2.5s	17	3	SG-SY on pile.	
42090	- Day beacon 114	26-25-43.653N 097-21-21.425W				TR on pile.	

(1) No.	(2) Name and Location	(3) Position	(4) Characteristic	(5) Height	(6) Range	(7) Structure	(8) Remarks
	INTRACOASTAL WATERWAY (Texas) - Eighth District						
	LAGUNA MADRE (Chart 11306)						
	Land Cut-Arroyo Colorado						
42095.01	- Day beacon 117	26-25-16.300N 097-21-06.160W				SG-SY on pile.	Ra ref.
	LAGUNA MADRE (Chart 11303)						
	Land Cut-Arroyo Colorado						
42105	- Day beacon 119	26-24-52.644N 097-20-55.872W				SG-SY on pile.	Ra ref.
42110	- LIGHT 120	26-24-51.610N 097-20-58.362W	Fl R 4s	17	3	TR-TY on pile.	
	LAGUNA MADRE (Chart 11306)						
	Land Cut-Arroyo Colorado						
42115.01	- Day beacon 121	26-24-29.050N 097-20-45.020W				SG-SY on pile.	Ra ref.
	LAGUNA MADRE (Chart 11303)						
	Land Cut-Arroyo Colorado						
42125	- LIGHT 123	26-24-10.765N 097-20-36.683W	Fl G 2.5s	17	3	SG-SY on pile.	Ra ref.
42130	- Day beacon 122	26-24-16.460N 097-20-42.446W				TR on pile.	
	LAGUNA MADRE (Chart 11306)						
	Land Cut-Arroyo Colorado						
42135.01	- Day beacon 125	26-23-38.460N 097-20-22.580W				SG-SY on pile.	Ra ref.
	LAGUNA MADRE (Chart 11303)						
	Land Cut-Arroyo Colorado						
42145	- LIGHT 127	26-23-30.137N 097-20-18.620W	Fl G 4s	17	4	SG-SY on pile.	Ra ref.
42150	- Day beacon 126	26-23-32.861N 097-20-22.963W				TR on pile.	
	LAGUNA MADRE (Chart 11306)						
	Land Cut-Arroyo Colorado						
42155.01	- Day beacon 129	26-23-11.840N 097-20-10.450W				SG-SY on pile.	Ra ref.
	LAGUNA MADRE (Chart 11303)						
	Land Cut-Arroyo Colorado						
42165	- Day beacon 131	26-22-50.396N 097-20-00.342W				SG-SY on pile.	Ra ref.
42170	- Day beacon 132	26-22-49.262N 097-20-03.482W				TR on pile.	
42175	- Buoy 133	26-22-36.748N 097-19-54.973W				Green can with yellow square.	
42180	- Buoy 135	26-22-12.834N 097-19-44.282W				Green can with yellow square.	
42185	- LIGHT 136	26-22-06.570N 097-19-43.860W	Q R	17	4	TR-TY on pile.	
	Arroyo Colorado Cutoff Channel						
42190	- North Entrance Buoy 2N	26-21-59.525N 097-19-41.760W				Red nun.	
42195	- Junction Buoy N	26-21-54.981N 097-19-38.503W				Red nun with green band and yellow triangle.	
42200	- North Entrance Buoy 3N	26-21-47.612N 097-19-42.212W				Green can.	
42205	- North Entrance Buoy 4N	26-21-48.217N 097-19-44.601W				Red nun.	
42210	- South Entrance Buoy 2S	26-21-34.096N 097-19-29.628W				Red nun with yellow triangle.	
42215	- South Entrance Buoy 1S	26-21-32.086N 097-19-30.703W				Green can.	
42220	- South Entrance Buoy 4S	26-21-38.981N 097-19-38.197W				Red nun.	

Light List corrected through LNM week: 01/18

(1) No.	(2) Name and Location	(3) Position	(4) Characteristic	(5) Height	(6) Range	(7) Structure	(8) Remarks
		INTRACOASTAL WATERWAY (Texas) - Eighth District					
	LAGUNA MADRE (Chart 11303)						
	Land Cut-Arroyo Colorado						
	Arroyo Colorado Cutoff Channel						
42225	- South Entrance Buoy 3S	26-21-36.609N 097-19-38.762W				Green can.	
42230	- Junction Buoy A	26-21-41.351N 097-19-47.202W				Green can with red band.	
42235	- Buoy 4	26-21-43.291N 097-19-51.582W				Red nun.	
42240	- Buoy 5	26-21-38.370N 097-20-01.399W				Green can.	
42245	- Buoy 6	26-21-36.369N 097-20-21.312W				Red nun.	
42250	- Buoy 7	26-21-34.615N 097-20-21.105W				Green can.	
42255	- Buoy 8	26-21-33.693N 097-20-34.784W				Red nun.	
42260	- Day beacon 10	26-20-52.898N 097-24-23.058W				TR on pile.	Ra ref.
42265	- Day beacon 11	26-20-39.088N 097-25-19.812W				SG on pile.	Ra ref.
42270	- Day beacon 12	26-20-17.968N 097-26-10.007W				TR on pile.	Ra ref.
42275	- Day beacon 13	26-19-27.928N 097-26-48.503W				SG on pile.	Ra ref.
42280	- Buoy 14	26-19-37.343N 097-27-20.710W				Red nun.	
42285	- Day beacon 14A	26-19-52.340N 097-27-27.245W				TR on pile.	Ra ref.
42290	- Day beacon 15	26-19-50.951N 097-28-21.565W				SG on pile.	Ra ref.
42295	- Day beacon 16	26-20-15.220N 097-29-11.808W				TR on pile.	Ra ref.
42300	- Day beacon 18	26-19-38.740N 097-31-03.548W				TR on pile.	Ra ref.
42305	- Day beacon 19	26-18-59.077N 097-31-36.051W				SG on pile.	Ra ref.
42310	- Day beacon 20	26-18-11.130N 097-31-34.554W				TR on pile.	Ra ref.
42315	- Day beacon 21	26-17-44.664N 097-32-16.173W				SG on pile.	Ra ref.
42320	- Day beacon 22	26-17-20.629N 097-33-04.941W				TR on pile.	Ra ref.
42325	- Day beacon 23	26-16-54.747N 097-33-43.425W				SG on pile.	Ra ref.
42330	- Day beacon 24	26-17-04.337N 097-34-34.635W				TR on pile.	Ra ref.
42335	- Day beacon 25	26-16-29.557N 097-34-54.018W				SG on pile.	Ra ref.
42340	- Day beacon 26	26-15-39.132N 097-34-59.457W				TR on pile.	Ra ref.
42345	- Day beacon 27	26-14-38.377N 097-35-02.073W				SG on pile.	Ra ref.
42350	- Day beacon 28	26-13-53.144N 097-35-06.217W				TR on pile.	Ra ref.
42355	- Day beacon 29	26-13-05.025N 097-35-24.667W				SG on pile.	Ra ref.
	Land Cut-Arroyo Colorado						
42360	- Buoy 137	26-21-52.780N 097-19-35.341W				Green can with yellow square.	

Light List corrected through LNM week: 01/18

(1) No.	(2) Name and Location	(3) Position	(4) Characteristic	(5) Height	(6) Range	(7) Structure	(8) Remarks
	INTRACOASTAL WATERWAY (Texas) - Eighth District						
	LAGUNA MADRE (Chart 11303)						
	Corpus Christi - Port Isabel						
	Harlingen-Port Isabel *Lights and daybeacons 50 feet outside channel limit, unless otherwise noted.*						
42365	- Buoy 1	26-21-34.725N 097-19-27.245W				Green can with yellow square.	
42370	- Buoy 3	26-21-20.800N 097-19-20.903W				Green can with yellow square.	
42375	- LIGHT 4	26-21-20.681N 097-19-23.041W	Q R	17	3	TR-TY on pile.	
	STOVER POINT TO PORT BROWNSVILLE (Chart 11302)						
	Corpus Christi - Port Isabel						
	Harlingen-Port Isabel *Lights and daybeacons 50 feet outside channel limits, unless otherwise noted.*						
42380.01	- Daybeacon 5	26-20-59.160N 097-19-10.440W				SG-SY on pile.	Ra ref.
	LAGUNA MADRE (Chart 11303)						
	Corpus Christi - Port Isabel						
	Harlingen-Port Isabel *Lights and daybeacons 50 feet outside channel limit, unless otherwise noted.*						
42390	- LIGHT 7	26-20-35.520N 097-18-59.965W	Fl G 2.5s	17	3	SG-SY on pile.	
42395	- Daybeacon 8 90 feet outside channel limit.	26-20-34.388N 097-19-03.073W				TR-TY on pile.	Ra ref.
	STOVER POINT TO PORT BROWNSVILLE (Chart 11302)						
	Corpus Christi - Port Isabel						
	Harlingen-Port Isabel *Lights and daybeacons 50 feet outside channel limits, unless otherwise noted.*						
42400.01	- Daybeacon 9	26-20-06.400N 097-18-46.440W				SG-SY on pile.	Ra ref.
	LAGUNA MADRE (Chart 11303)						
	Corpus Christi - Port Isabel						
	Harlingen-Port Isabel *Lights and daybeacons 50 feet outside channel limit, unless otherwise noted.*						
42415	- LIGHT 11	26-19-40.476N 097-18-34.724W	Fl G 4s	17	4	SG-SY on pile.	
42420	- Daybeacon 12 90 feet outside channel limit.	26-19-39.344N 097-18-37.831W				TR-TY on pile.	Ra ref.
	STOVER POINT TO PORT BROWNSVILLE (Chart 11302)						
	Corpus Christi - Port Isabel						
	Harlingen-Port Isabel *Lights and daybeacons 50 feet outside channel limits, unless otherwise noted.*						
42425.01	- Daybeacon 13	26-19-13.140N 097-18-22.680W				SG-SY on pile.	Ra ref.
	LAGUNA MADRE (Chart 11303)						
	Corpus Christi - Port Isabel						
	Harlingen-Port Isabel *Lights and daybeacons 50 feet outside channel limit, unless otherwise noted.*						
42440	- LIGHT 15	26-18-46.007N 097-18-10.473W	Fl G 4s	17	4	SG-I on pile.	
42445	- Daybeacon 16 90 feet outside channel limit.	26-18-44.875N 097-18-13.580W				TR-TY on pile.	Ra ref.
	STOVER POINT TO PORT BROWNSVILLE (Chart 11302)						
	Corpus Christi - Port Isabel						
	Harlingen-Port Isabel *Lights and daybeacons 50 feet outside channel limits, unless otherwise noted.*						
42450.01	- Daybeacon 17	26-18-17.100N 097-17-57.600W				SG-SY on pile.	Ra ref.

Light List corrected through LNM week: 01/18

(1) No.	(2) Name and Location	(3) Position	(4) Characteristic	(5) Height	(6) Range	(7) Structure	(8) Remarks
		INTRACOASTAL WATERWAY (Texas) - Eighth District					

LAGUNA MADRE (Chart 11303)
Corpus Christi - Port Isabel
Harlingen-Port Isabel
Lights and daybeacons 50 feet outside channel limit, unless otherwise noted.

42465	- LIGHT 19	26-17-50.274N 097-17-45.648W	Fl G 2.5s	17	3	SG-SY on pile.	Ra ref.
42470	- Day beacon 20 90 feet outside channel limit.	26-17-49.142N 097-17-48.755W				TR-TY on pile.	Ra ref.

STOVER POINT TO PORT BROWNSVILLE (Chart 11302)
Corpus Christi - Port Isabel
Harlingen-Port Isabel
Lights and daybeacons 50 feet outside channel limits, unless otherwise noted.

42475.01	- Day beacon 21	26-17-23.040N 097-17-33.420W				SG-SY on pile.	Ra ref.

LAGUNA MADRE (Chart 11303)
Corpus Christi - Port Isabel
Harlingen-Port Isabel
Lights and daybeacons 50 feet outside channel limit, unless otherwise noted.

42490	- LIGHT 23	26-16-55.677N 097-17-20.866W	Q G	17	3	SG on pile.	
42495	- Day beacon 24 90 feet outside channel limit.	26-16-54.382N 097-17-23.674W				TR-TY on pile.	Ra ref.

STOVER POINT TO PORT BROWNSVILLE (Chart 11302)
Corpus Christi - Port Isabel
Harlingen-Port Isabel
Lights and daybeacons 50 feet outside channel limits, unless otherwise noted.

42500.01	- Day beacon 25	26-16-25.320N 097-17-10.140W				SG-SY on pile.	Ra ref.

LAGUNA MADRE (Chart 11303)
Corpus Christi - Port Isabel
Harlingen-Port Isabel
Lights and daybeacons 50 feet outside channel limit, unless otherwise noted.

42515	- LIGHT 27	26-15-58.347N 097-17-00.247W	Fl G 2.5s	17	3	SG-SY on pile.	
42520	- Day beacon 28 90 feet outside channel limit.	26-15-57.453N 097-17-03.447W				TR-TY on pile.	Ra ref.

STOVER POINT TO PORT BROWNSVILLE (Chart 11302)
Corpus Christi - Port Isabel
Harlingen-Port Isabel
Lights and daybeacons 50 feet outside channel limits, unless otherwise noted.

42525.01	- Day beacon 29	26-15-26.124N 097-16-48.818W				SG-SY on pile.	Ra ref.

LAGUNA MADRE (Chart 11303)
Corpus Christi - Port Isabel
Harlingen-Port Isabel
Lights and daybeacons 50 feet outside channel limit, unless otherwise noted.

42540	- LIGHT 31	26-15-00.513N 097-16-39.427W	Fl G 4s	17	4	SG-SY on pile.	Ra ref.
42545	- Day beacon 32 90 feet outside channel limit.	26-14-59.619N 097-16-42.627W				TR-TY on pile.	Ra ref.

STOVER POINT TO PORT BROWNSVILLE (Chart 11302)
Corpus Christi - Port Isabel
Harlingen-Port Isabel
Lights and daybeacons 50 feet outside channel limits, unless otherwise noted.

42550.01	- Day beacon 33	26-14-38.470N 097-16-32.004W				SG-SY on pile.	Ra ref.
42555.01	- Day beacon 35	26-14-12.809N 097-16-22.775W				SG-SY on pile.	Ra ref.

(1) No.	(2) Name and Location	(3) Position	(4) Characteristic	(5) Height	(6) Range	(7) Structure	(8) Remarks
	INTRACOASTAL WATERWAY (Texas) - Eighth District						
	LAGUNA MADRE (Chart 11303)						
	Corpus Christi - Port Isabel						
	Harlingen-Port Isabel						
	Lights and daybeacons 50 feet outside channel limit, unless otherwise noted.						
42570	- LIGHT 37	26-13-47.363N 097-16-13.721W	Fl G 6s	17	4	SG-SY on pile.	
42575	- Day beacon 38 90 feet outside channel limit.	26-13-46.535N 097-16-16.817W				TR-TY on pile.	Ra ref.
	STOVER POINT TO PORT BROWNSVILLE (Chart 11302)						
	Corpus Christi - Port Isabel						
	Harlingen-Port Isabel						
	Lights and daybeacons 50 feet outside channel limits, unless otherwise noted.						
42580.01	- Day beacon 39	26-13-16.380N 097-16-03.000W				SG-SY on Pile.	Ra ref.
	LAGUNA MADRE (Chart 11303)						
	Corpus Christi - Port Isabel						
	Harlingen-Port Isabel						
	Lights and daybeacons 50 feet outside channel limit, unless otherwise noted.						
42595	- LIGHT 41	26-12-50.034N 097-15-53.318W	Fl G 4s	17	4	SG-SY on dolphin.	Ra ref.
42600	- Day beacon 42 90 feet outside channel limit.	26-12-49.140N 097-15-56.517W				TR-TY on pile.	Ra ref.
42605.01	- Day beacon 43	26-12-19.020N 097-15-42.720W				SG-SY on pile.	Ra ref.
42620	- LIGHT 45	26-11-51.660N 097-15-33.100W	Fl G 2.5s	17	3	SG-SY on pile.	Ra ref.
42625	- Day beacon 46 90 feet outside channel limit.	26-11-50.766N 097-15-36.298W				TR-TY on pile.	Ra ref.
	STOVER POINT TO PORT BROWNSVILLE (Chart 11302)						
	Corpus Christi - Port Isabel						
	Harlingen-Port Isabel						
	Lights and daybeacons 50 feet outside channel limits, unless otherwise noted.						
42630.01	- Day beacon 47	26-11-24.098N 097-15-23.220W				SG-SY on pile.	Ra ref.
42645	- LIGHT 49 60 feet outside channel limit.	26-10-53.740N 097-15-12.018W	Q G	17	3	SG-SY on pile.	
42650	- Day beacon 50 90 feet outside channel limit.	26-10-52.603N 097-15-15.119W				TR-TY on pile.	Ra ref.
42655.01	- Day beacon 51	26-10-27.889N 097-14-58.253W				SG-SY on pile.	Ra ref.
42670	- LIGHT 53	26-10-05.183N 097-14-44.545W	Fl G 2.5s	17	3	SG-SY on pile.	
42675	- Day beacon 54 90 feet outside channel limit.	26-10-03.811N 097-14-47.527W				TR-TY on pile.	Ra ref.
42680.01	- Day beacon 55	26-09-34.140N 097-14-28.440W				SG-SY on pile.	Ra ref.
42695	- LIGHT 57	26-09-09.556N 097-14-13.867W	Fl G 4s	17	4	SG-SY on dolphin.	Ra ref.
42700	- Day beacon 58 90 feet outside channel limit.	26-09-08.184N 097-14-16.849W				TR-TY on pile.	Ra ref.
42705.01	- Day beacon 59	26-08-40.653N 097-13-57.722W				SG-SY on pile.	Ra ref.
42720	- LIGHT 61	26-08-16.468N 097-13-43.771W	Fl G 6s	17	4	SG-SY on pile.	Ra ref.
42725	- Day beacon 62 90 feet outside channel limit.	26-08-15.096N 097-13-46.752W				TR-TY on pile.	Ra ref.

Light List corrected through LNM week: 01/18

(1) No.	(2) Name and Location	(3) Position	(4) Characteristic	(5) Height	(6) Range	(7) Structure	(8) Remarks
		INTRACOASTAL WATERWAY (Texas) - Eighth District					
	STOVER POINT TO PORT BROWNSVILLE (Chart 11302)						
	Corpus Christi - Port Isabel						
	Harlingen-Port Isabel						
	Lights and daybeacons 50 feet outside channel limits, unless otherwise noted.						
42730.01	- Day beacon 63	26-07-44.021N 097-13-26.496W				SG-SY on pile.	Ra ref.
42745	- LIGHT 65	26-07-20.741N 097-13-12.538W	Fl G 6s	17	4	SG-I on pile.	
42750	- Day beacon 66 90 feet outside channel limit.	26-07-19.315N 097-13-15.554W				TR-TY on pile.	Ra ref.
42755.01	- Day beacon 67	26-06-52.920N 097-12-57.093W				SG-SY on pile.	Ra ref.
42770	- LIGHT 69	26-06-26.850N 097-12-42.212W	Fl G 4s	17	4	SG-SY on pile.	Ra ref.
42775	- Day beacon 70 90 feet outside channel limit.	26-06-25.380N 097-12-45.345W				TR-TY on pile.	Ra ref.
42780.01	- Day beacon 71	26-05-58.660N 097-12-26.110W				SG-SY on pile.	Ra ref.
42795	- LIGHT 73 90 feet outside channel limit.	26-05-32.956N 097-12-11.888W	Fl G 2.5s	17	3	SG-SY on dolphin.	Ra ref.
42800	- Day beacon 74 90 feet outside channel limit.	26-05-31.585N 097-12-14.869W				TR-TY on pile.	Ra ref.
	Port Isabel Small Boat Harbor Channel						
42805	- Day beacon 1	26-05-20.134N 097-12-11.711W				SG on pile.	Ra ref.
42810	- LIGHT 2	26-05-22.265N 097-12-13.329W	Fl R 2.5s	17	3	TR on dolphin.	
42815	- Day beacon 4	26-05-16.776N 097-12-26.082W				TR on pile.	Ra ref.
42820	- Buoy 5	26-05-08.165N 097-12-43.782W				Green can.	
42825	- Day beacon 9	26-04-58.044N 097-13-02.455W				SG on pile.	Ra ref.
42830	- *Lighted Buoy 10*	26-04-58.885N 097-13-06.520W	Q R		3	Red nun.	
42835	- Day beacon 11	26-04-54.377N 097-13-05.345W				SG on pile.	Ra ref.
42840	- Buoy 14	26-04-51.435N 097-13-11.356W				Red nun.	
42845.01	- Buoy 15	26-04-46.188N 097-13-10.134W				Green can.	
	Harlingen-Port Isabel						
	Lights and daybeacons 50 feet outside channel limits, unless otherwise noted.						
42850	- Buoy 75	26-05-19.711N 097-12-03.900W				Green can with yellow square.	
42855	- Buoy 77	26-05-06.281N 097-11-57.402W				Green can with yellow square.	
	Queen Isabella Causeway						
42860	- NORTH EAST DANGER LIGHTS (4)	26-04-58.500N 097-11-50.600W	Fl W 2.5s			On pile structure.	Private aid.
42865	- NORTH WEST DANGER LIGHTS (5)	26-04-53.500N 097-12-01.600W	Fl W 2.5s			On pile structure.	Private aid.
42870	- SOUTH WEST DANGER LIGHTS (5)	26-04-52.400N 097-12-01.000W	Fl W 2.5s			On pile structure.	Private aid.
42875	- SOUTH EAST DANGER LIGHTS(4)	26-04-57.400N 097-11-50.000W	Fl W 2.5s			On pile structure.	Private aid.
	Harlingen-Port Isabel						
	Lights and daybeacons 50 feet outside channel limits, unless otherwise noted.						
42880	- Buoy 79	26-04-49.574N 097-11-47.433W				Green can with yellow square.	

Light List corrected through LNM week: 01/18

(1) No.	(2) Name and Location	(3) Position	(4) Characteristic	(5) Height	(6) Range	(7) Structure	(8) Remarks
\<td colspan="8">**INTRACOASTAL WATERWAY (Texas) - Eighth District**</td>							
\<td colspan="8">**STOVER POINT TO PORT BROWNSVILLE (Chart 11302)** **Corpus Christi - Port Isabel** **Harlingen-Port Isabel** *Lights and daybeacons 50 feet outside channel limits, unless otherwise noted.*</td>							
42885	- Buoy 80	26-04-47.601N 097-11-51.701W				Red nun with yellow triangle.	
42890	- Buoy 81	26-04-41.359N 097-11-45.253W				Green can with yellow square.	
42895	- Buoy 83	26-04-33.591N 097-11-48.037W				Green can with yellow square.	
42900	- Day beacon 84	26-04-32.623N 097-11-53.188W				TR-TY on pile.	Ra ref.
42905	- LIGHT 85 70 feet outside channel limit.	26-04-27.540N 097-11-49.879W	Q G	17	3	SG-SY on dolphin.	Ra ref.
42910	- Day beacon 86	26-04-25.825N 097-11-56.405W				TR-TY on pile.	Ra ref.
42915	Harlingen - Port Isabel Day beacon 87	26-04-18.238N 097-11-57.792W				SG-SY on pile.	Ra ref.
42920	QUEEN ISABELLA FISHING PIER WEST LIGHTS (2)	26-04-28.000N 097-10-49.000W	Q G	25		On end of pier.	Private aid.
42925	- Day beacon 88	26-04-20.407N 097-12-00.389W				TR-TY on pile.	Ra ref.
42930	- Day beacon A	26-04-13.025N 097-12-10.886W				JR-I on pile.	
42935	- Day beacon B	26-04-08.797N 097-12-16.869W				JR-I on pile.	Ra ref.
42940 29830	- LIGHT 90	26-03-39.189N 097-12-40.083W	Q R	17	3	TR-TY on dolphin.	Ra ref.
42945 29850	PORT ISABEL CHANNEL LIGHT 8	26-03-15.080N 097-12-36.340W	Fl R 2.5s	17	3	TR-SY on dolphin.	
42955 29825	PORT ISABEL CHANNEL LIGHT 6	26-03-03.647N 097-12-29.536W	Q R	17	3	TR on dolphin.	
42960 29840	PORT ISABEL CUTOFF CHANNEL LIGHT 3	26-03-01.758N 097-12-33.941W	Q G	17	3	SG-TY on pile.	
42965 29820	PORT ISABEL CHANNEL LEADING LIGHT	26-02-50.856N 097-12-25.636W	Iso W 6s	17	5	NB on pile.	
42970 29835	PORT ISABEL CUTOFF CHANNEL LIGHT 1	26-02-41.939N 097-12-30.695W	Fl G 4s	17	4	SG-TY on dolphin.	Ra ref.
\<td colspan="8">**Brownsville Channel**</td>							
42975 29855	- LIGHT 30	26-02-25.148N 097-12-39.788W	Fl R 4s	17	3	TR-TY on pile.	Ra ref.
42980 29860	- C RANGE FRONT LIGHT	26-02-16.482N 097-12-43.282W	Q G	25		KRW-I on skeleton tower on piles.	Visible all around; higher intensity on range line.
42985 29865	- C RANGE REAR LIGHT	26-02-37.482N 097-11-57.635W	Iso G 6s	65		KRW on skeleton tower on piles.	Visible 2° each side of rangeline.
42990 29870	- A RANGE FRONT LIGHT	26-01-50.708N 097-13-32.067W	Q W (NIGHT) Q W (NIGHT)	33 35		KRW-I on skeleton tower.	Visible all around; higher intensity 14° each side of rangeline.
42995 29875	- A RANGE REAR LIGHT 1,601 yards, 235.7° from front light.	26-01-24.321N 097-14-15.894W	Iso W 6s	60		KRW on skeleton tower.	Visible 2° each side of rangeline.
43000 29880	- LIGHT 31	26-02-01.835N 097-13-09.264W	Q G	17	3	SG-SY on pile.	Ra ref.
43005 29885	- LIGHT 32	26-02-06.093N 097-13-11.633W	Q R	17	3	TR-TY on pile.	Ra ref.
43010 29890	- LIGHT 34	26-01-53.815N 097-13-38.485W	Fl R 2.5s	17	3	TR-TY on pile.	Ra ref.
43015 29895	- LIGHT 35	26-01-22.470N 097-14-34.736W	Fl G 4s	17	4	SG-SY on pile.	Ra ref.

Light List corrected through LNM week: 01/18

(1) No.	(2) Name and Location	(3) Position	(4) Characteristic	(5) Height	(6) Range	(7) Structure	(8) Remarks
	INTRACOASTAL WATERWAY (Texas) - Eighth District						
	STOVER POINT TO PORT BROWNSVILLE (Chart 11302)						
	Brownsville Channel						
43020 29900	- E RANGE FRONT LIGHT	26-01-22.652N 097-14-45.601W	Q W	33		KRW-I on skeleton tower on piles.	For downbound traffic. Visible all around; higher intensity 1.5° each side of rangeline.
43025 29905	- E RANGE REAR LIGHT 1,368 yards, 057.0° from front light.	26-01-44.065N 097-14-07.353W	Iso W 6s	63		KRW on skeleton tower on piles.	Visible 2° each side of rangeline.
43030 29910	- LIGHT 36	26-01-10.015N 097-15-13.456W	Q R	17	3	TR-TY on pile.	Ra ref.
43035 29915	- LIGHT 37	26-01-05.313N 097-15-11.452W	Q G	17	3	SG-SY on pile.	Ra ref.
43040 29920	- LIGHT 39	26-00-55.408N 097-15-28.497W	Fl G 4s	17	4	SG-SY on pile.	Ra ref.
43045 29925	- B RANGE FRONT LIGHT	26-00-52.470N 097-15-45.759W	Q R	35		KRW-I on skeleton tower on piles.	Visible all around; higher intensity 5.5° each side of rangeline.
43050 29930	- B RANGE REAR LIGHT	26-00-27.963N 097-16-39.127W	Iso R 6s	75		KRW on skeleton tower on piles.	Visible 2° each side of rangeline.
43055 29935	- LIGHT 40	25-59-55.487N 097-17-26.731W	Fl R 4s	17	3	TR-TY on pile.	
43060 29940	- LIGHT 41	25-59-50.651N 097-17-23.806W	Fl G 4s	17	4	SG-SY on pile.	
43065 29945	- LIGHT 42	25-59-24.254N 097-18-24.281W	Fl R 2.5s	17	3	TR-TY on pile.	
43070 29960	- LIGHT 44	25-58-49.345N 097-19-26.229W	Fl R 4s	17	3	TR-TY on skeleton tower on piles.	
43072 29967	- G RANGE FRONT LIGHT PASSING LIGHT	25-58-43.925N 097-19-22.137W	Q G	27	3	On same structure as Brownsville Channel G Range Front Light.	Visible all around.
43075 29965	- G RANGE FRONT LIGHT	25-58-43.925N 097-19-22.137W	Q G	25		KRW-I on skeleton tower on piles.	Visible all around; higher intensity on rangeline.
43080 29970	- G RANGE REAR LIGHT	25-59-00.459N 097-18-35.022W	Iso G 6s	58		KRW on skeleton tower.	Visible 2° each side of rangeline.
43085 29975	- LIGHT 45	25-58-33.011N 097-19-44.843W	Q G	17	3	SG-SY on pile.	Ra ref.
43090 29980	- LIGHT 46	25-58-38.077N 097-19-46.521W	Q R	17	3	TR-TY on pile.	Ra ref.
43095 29950	- D RANGE FRONT LIGHT	25-58-28.313N 097-19-56.658W	Q W	35		KRW-I on skeleton tower.	Visible all around; higher intensity 1.5° each side of rangeline.
43100 29955	- D RANGE REAR LIGHT	25-58-03.763N 097-20-40.411W	Iso W 6s	67		KRW on skeleton tower.	
43105 29985	- LIGHT 48	25-58-25.077N 097-20-21.696W	Fl R 2.5s	17	3	TR-TY on dolphin.	
43110 29990	- F RANGE FRONT LIGHT	25-57-02.311N 097-24-11.346W	Fl G 2.5s (NIGHT) Fl W 2.5s (DAY)	45 47		KRW-I on skeleton tower.	Visible 2° each side of rangeline.
43115 29995	- F RANGE REAR LIGHT 3,870 yards, 249° from front light.	25-56-20.523N 097-26-10.086W	Oc G 4s (NIGHT) Oc W 4s (DAY)	98 95		KRW on skeleton tower.	Visible 2° each side of rangeline. Lighted throughout 24 hours.

INDEX

A

Entry	Page
Acadiana Navigation Channel	20295
Adams Bay	15730
Adams Bayou	23180, 35445
Algiers Alternate Route	34940
Alligator Harbor	2310
Amerada Pass Channel	18770
Amite River	11650
Anahuac Channel	25910
Apalachee Bay	1475
Apalachicola Bay	30210
Apalachicola River	30410
Apalachicola River Entrance	30285
Aransas Bay	39680
Aransas Bay	38645
Aransas Bay Alternate Route	39470.01
Aransas Channel	28210
Aransas Pass	28155
Aransas-Corpus Christi Bay Cutoff Channel	39060
Arlington Channel	7535
Arroyo Colorado Cutoff Channel	42190
Atchafalaya Bay	19250
Atchafalaya Channel	18520
Atchafalaya River	18876
Avery Canal	20470
Avoca Island Cutoff Channel	18970.01

B

Entry	Page
Back Bay of Biloxi	9260
Baffin Bay	41010.01
Baffin Bay Land Cut	41150.01
Baptiste Collette Bayou	12380
Barataria Bay	16025
Barataria Pass	15802
Barataria Waterway	16095
Bay Cove Marina to Casino Magic Marina	10300
Bayou Aloe	34090
Bayou Bonfouca Channel	11025
Bayou Caddy	10390
Bayou Casotte Channel	8390
Bayou Castine	11190
Bayou Chico	5295
Bayou Coden	7765
Bayou Decade	18325
Bayou Dupont Canal Weir	16510
Bayou Dupre	10785
Bayou Garcon	6030
Bayou Grand Caillou	17975
Bayou Grande	5415
Bayou La Batre	7670
Bayou La Batre	7665, 34315
Bayou Petit Caillou Flood Canal	17570
Bayou Portage Channel	10205
Bayou Rigaud	15915
Bayou Rosa	17250
Bayou Sale Channel	19750
Bayou Shaffer	19075
Bayou St John	5940.01
Bayou St. Denis	16595
Bayou Terre Aux Boeufs	12355
Bayou Yscloskey	10760
Bayport Ship Channel	24430
Baytown Goose Creek Channel	24880
Baytown Marina Channel	24820
Belle Isle 340-29 Channel	19285
Belle Isle 340-39 Channel	19350
Belle Isle Well 38	19375
Belle Pass	16975
Bernard Bayou	9445
Big Lake	9380
Biloxi Channel	8955
Biloxi East Channel	8639
Black Bay Channel	12075
Blakeley River	7143
Boggy Bayou	32050
Bolivar Peninsula	35880
Bolivar Roads Alternate Inbound Route	23940
Bon Secour River	6805, 33770
Boston Bayou Channel	20560
Brazos River Crossing	37395
Brazos Santiago Pass	29460
Breton Sound	11905
Broadwater Beach Hotel Marina Channel	9540
Brownsville Channel	29855, 42975

C

Entry	Page
Caillou Island Channel	17090
Calcasieu Channel	21200
Calcasieu River	21860
Caminada Bay	16610
Caminada Bay Channel	16619
Carrabelle Channel	2525
Carrabelle River	2595
Cat Island Channel	10145
Cat Island Pass	17685
Cedar Bayou Channel	24615
Chandeleur Sound	11670
Charenton Canal Access	19840.01
Chef Menteur Pass	10815
Chevron Sabine Facility Channel	22640
Chinaman Bayou	17375
Chocolate Bay	36995
Chocolate Bay Channel	27820
Chocolate Bayou Channel	37040
Choctawhatchee Bay	4540
Citgo Petroleum	21955
Clear Creek Channel	26360
Clooneys Loop	22170
Coon Island Channel	22025
Corpus Christi Baffin Bay	40130.01
Corpus Christi Baffin Bay	39725
Corpus Christi Bay	29165
Corpus Christi Bay	39385
Corpus Christi Channel	28305

D

Entry	Page
Dauphin Bay	34135
Dauphin Island Channel	7155
Davis Bayou Channel	8830
Dickinson Bayou Channel	26220
Dog Keys Pass	8595
Dog River Channel	7450
Double Bayou Channel	25845
Double Bayou Light 19	12860
Dupre Cut	16470

E

Entry	Page
East Atchafalaya Bay	18365
East Bay	30780
East Bay Bayou	35770
East Point Channel	30115
Eden Isles Channel	10960
Empire Waterway	15725
Escambia Bay	5665
Escatawpa River	8350
Espiritu Santo Bay - Barroom Bay Navigation	27980
Espiritu Santo Bay Ferry Channel	37935

F

Entry	Page
Fannin Bayou	4190
Fannin Bayou Channel A	4210
Fannin Bayou Channel B	4285
Five Mile Cut	24410
Fly Creek	7045
Fowl River	7255
Freeport Entrance	26910
Freshwater Bayou	20573
Fulton Channel	38790

G

Entry	Page
Galveston Bay	23760
Galveston Channel	23865, 36065
Galveston Channel	36050
Galveston Inner Bar	23845
Galveston Outer Bar	23830
Galveston-Freeport	36100.01
Galveston-Freeport Cutoff Channel	35950
Gibbstown	35330
Goose Bayou Weir	16560
Goose Island Breakwater	38815
Governor Nicholls Harbor Traffic Control Light 94	13855, 34770
Grand Canal Channel	32915
Grand Hotel Yacht Basin	7015
Grand Island Channel	34575
Grand Isle Turning Basin	15945.01
Grand Lagoon Boat Basin Channel	33200
Grand Lagoon Channel	4305

INDEX

Grand Lake	20919
Gretna Harbor Traffic Control Light 97	13880, 34795
Gulf County Canal	3180
Gulf Power Electrical Tower	3510
Gulfport Ship Channel	9585
Gulfport Small Boat Harbor	9975
Gulfport Yacht Basin Channel	10025

H

Harbor Towne Channel	3780
Harborwalk Entrance East	36700
Harborwalk Entrance West	36775
Harlingen-Port Isabel	42365
Head of Passes to New Orleans	12945
Hilton Hotel Marina Channel	26760
Holiday Harbor Marina Channel	33355
Horn Island Pass	7855
Houma Navigation Canal	17750
Houston Ship Channel	23900, 36055
Houston Yacht Club	26900
Huey P. Long Bridge	14035

I

Ideal Channel	26790
Indian Bayou	31945
Inner Harbor Navigation Canal	13835, 34760
Ivanhoe Canal	19960

J

Jackson River	30510
Jamaica Beach Village Channel	36880
Jarboe Bayou Channel	26600
Jourdan River Channel	10280
Jug Lake	18250
Junction Channel	1920

K

Krebs Lake Channel	8265
Krueger Channel	38945

L

La Grange Bayou	31575
La Quinta Channel	28920
Lacombe Bayou	11090
Laguna Madre Channel	29540
Lake Arthur	21075
Lake Borgne	10755
Lake Boudreaux	17475
Lake Cocodrie	35015
Lake Decade	18240
Lake Fausse Pointe Channel	19520
Lake Five	16055
Lake La Graisse	17440
Lake Maurepas	11610
Lake Pelto	17915
Lake Pontchartrain	11230
Lake Pontchartrain Causeway Cut No. 2	11280
Lake Pontchartrain Causeway Cut No.1	11239
Lake Salvador	16840
Lake Wimico	30545
Lakewood Yacht Club Channel	26475
Land Cut	41370
Land Cut-Arroyo Colorado	41480.01
Lavaca Bay	27915
Lavaca Bay Channel	27840
Lavaca River	27905
Lincoln Beach	11075
Little Lake	10460
Little Lake North Pass	10505
Little Sabine Bay	32985
Little Wax Bayou	35200
Lonesome Bayou	12515
Long Beach Harbor	10075
Long Point	31000
Louisiana Coastal Restoration Project	19820
Lower Atchafalaya River	19245, 15790

M

Marianne Channel	34403
Marina Del Sol Channel	26665
Mariners Village Marina	11200
Matagorda Bay - Alternate Route	37550
Matagorda Bay	27928
Matagorda Bay	37405
Matagorda Marine Education Channel	27940
Matagorda Ship Channel Entrance Light	1385, 27110
Matagorda Ship Channel	27120
Mc Faddin Wildlife Refuge	35745
Mermentau Channel	20675
Mermentau River	20990
Mermentau River Crossing	20950, 35295
Mexico Beach Canal Entrance	3265
Mid-Bay Marina Channel	31900
Mississippi Fishing Reef FR-MS-04	10360
Mississippi River - Gulf Outlet	11885, 34735
Mississippi River - Gulf Outlet	11705
Mississippi Sound	7632
Mobil State Lease 356-2 Channel	16280
Mobile Bar	6100
Mobile Bay	6080
Mobile Channel	6255
Mobile Channel	6240
Mobile Point Light	180, 6095
Mobile River	6705
Morgan City-Port Allen Alternate Route	35100
Mound Point	20060

N

Nautical Landing Channel	27770
Navy Cove Harbor Channel	6055
Navy Dive School	3605
Neches River	23295
New Canal	11185
New Orleans - Port Arthur	34960
New Orleans Harbor	13850, 34765
New Orleans to Baton Rouge	13955
North Bay	4130
North Shore Beach	11005
North Shore Channel	10890

O

Offatts Bayou Entrance Channel	36335
Old East Pass Harbor Channel	4590
Old Fort Bayou Channel	9160
Orange County Pier	23280
Ott Bayou Channel	9130
Oyster Bay Channel	1955
Oyster Lake	37350

P

Padre Island National Seashore	40630
Padre Isles North Channel	39985
Padre Isles South Channel	40145
Palacios Channel	37695
Panacea Channel	2160
Pascagoula Channel	7955
Pascagoula River	8295
Pass A Loutre	12540
Pass Aux Herons	33965
Pass Christian	10185
Pass Manchac South Channel	11575
Pass Marianne	34505
Pearl River	10550
Pearl River Entrance Channel	10430, 34640
Pend Oreille-Bay Batiste	15745

INDEX

Entry	Page
Pensacola Bay	4705
Pensacola Light	140, 4715
Pensacola Navy Homeport Channel	4875
Pensacola-Mobile	33090
Perdido Pass	5890
Peterson Builders Turning Basin Channel	29020
Petit Lac des Allemands	16910
Pier 77 Channel	36215
Plantation Channel	26835
Point Comfort Inner Channel	27660
Point Comfort Turning Basin	27625
Polynesian Isle Channel	5635
Port Arthur Canal	22780
Port Bienville	10575
Port Isabel Channel	29800
Port Isabel Cutoff Channel	29830, 42940
Port Isabel Small Boat Harbor Channel	42805
Port Lavaca Channel	27700
Port Lavaca Harbor of Refuge	27795
Port Louis Channel	11355
Port Mansfield Channel	29270
Port O' Connor Channel	37905
Port O' Connor Landcut	38005
Port St Joe North Channel	3130
Posten Bayou Channel	3820
Presnells Channel	2970
Pretty Bayou Channel	3880

Q

Entry	Page
Quarantine Bay Channel	11920
Queen Isabella Causeway	42860

R

Entry	Page
Rigolets - New Orleans	34705
Rincon Canal	29105
Robinson Bayou	3990
Rockport Channel	38985
Rockport Smallboat Harbor Channel	39015
Rollover Bay	35805
Round Island	8580
Round Island South Channel	34335

S

Entry	Page
S.L. 11107 Pipeline	12555
Sabine Bank Channel	22305
Sabine Pass	22445
Sabine Pass East Jetty Light	1105, 22440
Sabine River	23100, 35530
Sabine River	35460
Sabine-Neches Canal	22885, 35735
Sabine-Neches Canal	35742
San Antonio Bay	38355.01
San Bernard River	27040
San Jacinto Bay Barge Channel	25105
San Jacinto River	25560
San Jose Island Dock Channel	39290
Sandestin Beach Channel	31720
Santa Rosa Sound	32220
Santa Rosa Sound Entrance	32140
Scotts Canal Light 23	12885
Scurlock Channel	22770
Sea Ranch Marina Channel	29480
Seadrift Channel	38285
Section Base Channel	3650
Section Base Magazine Area	3625
Shell Point Channel	1840
Sherman Cove Marina	33135
Shoal Point Bayou Channel	30970
South Boater Cut	24265
South Fork Channel	6855
South Louisiana Electric Co Op	18270
South Padre Island	29510
South Pass	12575
South Shore Harbor Marina	11105
Southwest Pass - Vermilion Bay Channel	20115
Southwest Pass	12685
Southwest Pass Entrance Light	420, 12740
Spring Creek Channel	1975
St Andrew Bay	105, 3335
St Andrew Bay Entrance	3340
St George Island	2840
St Joseph Bay Entrance	3020
St Marks River	1485
St. George Sound	2430
St. Louis Bay	10270
Stone Quarry Channel	33535
Sulphur Point	3680, 31170
Sundown Bay	38595
Sunshine Bridge Approach	14835
Sweet Lake	35350
	95, 3030

T

Entry	Page
Tangipahoa River	11560
Tchefuncta River	11320
Tensaw River	7145
Terrebonne Bay	17015
Texas City Channel	26030
Texas City Connection Channel	26185
The Rigolets	10840
Theodore Ship Channel	7335
Tiger Pass	15430
Tiki Island Channel	36455
Timbalier - Terrebonne Bay	17155
Timbalier Bay	17240
Timbalier Island 2703 Well 1	17110
Timbalier Island 2703 Well 4	17135
Treasure Bay Casino Channel	9490
Treasure Island Marina Channel	4355
Trinity Bay	25990
Tule Lake Channel	28835
Turkey Point	2440
Two Mile Channel	2855

U

Entry	Page
U. S. Coast Guard Base	4655
U.S. Air Force Instrumentation Tower	20
University Beach	29180
Upper Mud Lake	20800

V

Entry	Page
Vermilion Bay Cutoff Channel	20190
Via Mississippi River and Harvey Canal	34825
Victoria Channel	38090
Victoria East Entrance Channel	38065
Victoria West Entrance Channel	38330
Viola Channel	28895

W

Entry	Page
Ward Cove	32030
Waterford Harbor Channel	26620
Watergate Marina Channel	26525
Weeks Bay	20435
Weeks Island Channel	20365
West Black Bay Channel	12345
West Grand Lagoon Channel	4370
West Pass	2950
West Pearl River	10740
Wetappo Creek	30615
Weyerhaeuser Water Intake	6785
Windmark Beach	3215
Wolf River	10255
Woodlawn Bayou Channel	3730

CROSS REFERENCE - INTERNATIONAL VS. U.S. LIGHT NUMBER

Inter.	-	U.S.	Inter.	-	U.S.	Inter.	-	U.S.	Inter.	-	U.S.
J3299.40		1475	J3409.00		4960	J3482.60		6450	J3548.60		34105
J3299.60		1480	J3409.30		4980	J3483.00		6475	J3548.80		34125
J3300.00		1485	J3409.31		4985	J3489.60		6510	J3550.00		34215
J3300.10		10	J3410		5295	J3490.00		6515	J3550.10		34225
J3305.00		1830	J3412.00		5325	J3493.50		7335	J3552.00		34295
J3306.00		30	J3413		5415	J3493.51		7340	J3553		7765
J3306.20		40	J3418.00		33050	J3494.00		6545	J3553.2		7780
J3306.30		35	J3419.00		33045	J3497.00		6555	J3553.4		7805
J3306.32		45	J3420		33040	J3498.00		6560	J3553.6		7815
J3306.34		25	J3438.00		6080	J3503.00		6570	J3555.40		7685
J3306.40		2290	J3438.10		180	J3504.00		6575	J3558		7895
J3310		2560	J3438.10		6090	J3504.20		6580	J3558.10		7900
J3311.00		2570	J3440.00		33950	J3504.30		6585	J3561		7960
J3350.00		2950	J3441.00		33945	J3504.50		6590	J3561.10		7970
J3351		2960	J3442.00		33935	J3505.00		6595	J3561.40		7980
J3352.00		2965	J3443.00		33925	J3506.00		6600	J3562		7990
J3368.00		3025	J3444.00		33895	J3507.00		6605	J3562.10		7995
J3368.10		95	J3445.00		33860	J3508.00		6610	J3564		8095
J3370.40		3165	J3446.00		33840	J3509.00		6615	J3564.10		8100
J3371.40		3340	J3447.00		33820	J3509.50		6620	J3566.00		8110
J3371.41		3345	J3448.00		33800	J3510.00		6640	J3566.10		8115
J3372.40		3440	J3449.00		33785	J3510.10		6650	J3566.5		8120
J3372.60		3450	J3449.60		6805	J3511.00		6630	J3567		8125
J3373.00		3470	J3450.00		33755	J3512.00		6635	J3567.2		8130
J3373.24		3485	J3451.00		33745	J3516.00		6660	J3567.3		8135
J3373.26		3550	J3458.00		6960	J3517.00		6665	J3567.4		8175
J3373.30		4325	J3459.00		6970	J3517.10		6675	J3568		8180
J3373.60		3600	J3460.00		6980	J3517.50		6685	J3568.2		8185
J3373.8		3650	J3460.4		7025	J3518.00		6695	J3568.3		8190
J3373.90		3655	J3460.42		7030	J3524.20		6705	J3568.4		8195
J3374.00		3660	J3461.00		7045	J3524.3		6710	J3569		8200
J3374.2		3665	J3462.00		6180	J3525		7560	J3569.4		8205
J3374.40		3670	J3462.10		6190	J3526.20		7600	J3570		8210
J3374.60		3675	J3464.00		6495	J3526.60		7610	J3570.2		8225
J3374.8		4135	J3467.50		6295	J3527.00		7615	J3571.22		8335
J3375.50		4550	J3468.00		6300	J3527.1		7620	J3571.24		8360
J3376.00		4555	J3472.00		6305	J3537		7260	J3571.26		8375
J3377.00		4585	J3473.00		6310	J3538		7280	J3571.28		8385
J3394.00		140	J3474.00		6315	J3539		7300	J3571.30		8390
J3396.00		4705	J3475.00		6320	J3541.50		7155	J3571.31		8400
J3396.10		4710	J3477.00		6325	J3541.60		7205	J3571.32		8405
J3400		4780	J3478.00		6330	J3542.00		7210	J3571.33		8410
J3400.10		4785	J3478.40		6335	J3542.20		7220	J3571.34		8530
J3404.00		4850	J3479.00		6340	J3543.00		33965	J3571.36		8525
J3404.10		4855	J3479.40		6430	J3544.00		33970	J3571.40		8420
J3406.00		4920	J3481.00		6435	J3544.10		33980	J3571.42		8425
J3406.10		4925	J3481.20		6440	J3548.30		34085	J3571.44		8430
J3408.00		5070	J3482.00		6445	J3548.40		34095	J3571.46		8435

CROSS REFERENCE - INTERNATIONAL VS. U.S. LIGHT NUMBER

Inter. - U.S.	Inter. - U.S.	Inter. - U.S.	Inter. - U.S.
J3571.47 8450	J3626.80 9940	J3738 12790	J3835.00 13190
J3571.48 8455	J3628.00 9870	J3740 12795	J3836.00 13195
J3571.49 8470	J3628.10 9875	J3742 12800	J3836.10 13200
J3571.5 8475	J3631.40 9990	J3750 12805	J3836.20 13205
J3571.6 8485	J3632 10025	J3752 12810	J3837.00 13210
J3571.7 8510	J3633 10055	J3754 12815	J3838.00 13215
J3571.71 8515	J3650.2 11690	J3758 12820	J3840.00 13220
J3571.73 8540	J3651.2 11680	J3762 12825	J3841.00 13225
J3571.74 8545	J3651.24 11675	J3763 12830	J3841.20 13230
J3574.00 8585	J3651.26 11670	J3764 12835	J3842.00 13235
J3576.00 8700	J3661.34 11705	J3765.40 12845	J3843.00 13240
J3576.60 8710	J3661.36 11710	J3766.00 12855	J3844.00 13245
J3576.80 8735	J3663.4 11715	J3770.00 12860	J3845 13255
J3577.00 8745	J3664 11720	J3772 12870	J3846.00 13260
J3577.11 8325	J3666.2 11730	J3774 12875	J3848.00 13265
J3577.20 8765	J3666.4 11735	J3775.00 12880	J3850.00 13270
J3577.40 8780	J3666.45 11740	J3778.00 12885	J3850.20 13275
J3577.60 8795	J3666.5 11745	J3779.00 12895	J3851.80 13295
J3577.80 8805	J3666.6 11750	J3780 12890	J3854.00 13305
J3577.84 8815	J3666.8 11755	J3782 12900	J3856.00 13310
J3578.00 8955	J3667 11760	J3783 12905	J3858.00 13315
J3580.00 8965	J3667.1 11765	J3784.00 12910	J3859.00 13330
J3582.00 8970	J3667.14 11770	J3784.10 12920	J3860.00 13335
J3586 8980	J3667.2 11775	J3790.00 12945	J3864 13350
J3588 8985	J3667.3 11780	J3794.00 12970	J3865.00 13355
J3590.00 8995	J3667.4 11790	J3794.10 12975	J3866.00 13370
J3608.00 9675	J3667.6 11795	J3796.00 13000	J3869.00 13450
J3608.10 9680	J3667.8 11800	J3797.00 13005	J3870.00 13460
J3610 10070	J3668.4 11855	J3797.20 13010	J3872.00 13465
J3616.00 34395	J3668.6 11860	J3799.00 13015	J3876.00 13475
J3618.00 34390	J3668.7 11870	J3800.00 13025	J3880.00 13480
J3618.20 9840	J3668.8 11880	J3804.00 13035	J3881.00 13485
J3618.30 9845	J3669.00 11875	J3804.20 13040	J3881.20 13490
J3618.40 9850	J3671.00 12510	J3805.00 13050	J3881.40 13495
J3618.50 9855	J3673.00 12540	J3806.00 13055	J3884.00 13520
J3618.60 9860	J3675.00 12550	J3809 13070	J3888.00 13550
J3618.70 9865	J3692.00 12605	J3810.00 13090	J3890.00 13560
J3618.80 9880	J3694.00 12610	J3814.00 13100	J3895.00 13580
J3618.90 9885	J3696.00 12620	J3816.00 13105	J3898.00 13590
J3619.30 9890	J3700.00 12635	J3818.00 13115	J3900.00 13600
J3624.00 9895	J3702.00 12645	J3820.00 13120	J3900.20 13605
J3624.20 9905	J3704.00 12650	J3822.00 13135	J3900.40 13610
J3624.40 9910	J3708.10 12660	J3823.00 13140	J3900.60 13615
J3624.60 9915	J3710 12665	J3824.00 13145	J3901.00 13620
J3626.00 9920	J3714.00 420	J3825.00 13150	J3901.80 13625
J3626.20 9925	J3716.00 12730	J3826.00 13155	J3902.00 13630
J3626.40 9930	J3734 12780	J3828.00 13160	J3904.00 13635
J3626.60 9935	J3736 12785	J3834.00 13180	J3905.00 13660

CROSS REFERENCE - INTERNATIONAL VS. U.S. LIGHT NUMBER

Inter.	U.S.	Inter.	U.S.	Inter.	U.S.	Inter.	U.S.
J3906.00	13665	J3914.46	14205	J3915.62	14700	J3916.65	15050
J3909.00	13680	J3914.48	14210	J3915.64	14715	J3916.66	15055
J3910.00	13690	J3914.50	14215	J3915.66	14720	J3916.68	15060
J3910.40	13695	J3914.52	14220	J3915.68	14725	J3916.70	15065
J3911.00	13715	J3914.54	14225	J3915.70	14730	J3916.72	15070
J3911.20	13720	J3914.60	14260	J3915.72	14735	J3916.74	15075
J3911.50	13730	J3914.64	14300	J3915.74	14740	J3916.75	15080
J3911.70	13735	J3914.66	14305	J3915.82	14760	J3916.78	15090
J3912.00	13745	J3914.72	14315	J3915.84	14770	J3916.79	15095
J3912.02	13750	J3914.74	14330	J3915.86	14775	J3916.82	15105
J3912.04	13740	J3914.76	14335	J3915.88	14780	J3916.84	15110
J3912.20	13755	J3914.78	14340	J3915.90	14785	J3916.88	15115
J3913.20	13770	J3914.80	14360	J3915.92	14800	J3916.90	15120
J3913.40	13785	J3914.82	14355	J3915.94	14805	J3916.92	15135
J3913.44	13805	J3914.88	14365	J3915.96	14820	J3916.93	15140
J3913.50	13825	J3914.90	14370	J3915.97	14825	J3916.96	15165
J3913.60	13830	J3914.94	14380	J3915.98	14830	J3917.00	15170
J3913.62	13840	J3914.96	14395	J3916.00	14855	J3917.01	15175
J3913.64	13835	J3914.98	14400	J3916.02	14860	J3917.02	15180
J3913.69	13855	J3915.00	14410	J3916.04	14865	J3917.04	15185
J3913.70	13865	J3915.02	14420	J3916.06	14880	J3917.06	15190
J3913.72	13870	J3915.04	14425	J3916.08	14885	J3917.08	15195
J3913.74	13875	J3915.06	14440	J3916.10	14890	J3917.10	15200
J3913.80	13885	J3915.07	14455	J3916.12	14895	J3917.11	15205
J3913.82	13890	J3915.10	14480	J3916.14	14900	J3917.13	15210
J3913.86	13900	J3915.12	14485	J3916.16	14905	J3917.14	15215
J3913.88	13905	J3915.16	14495	J3916.18	14910	J3917.18	15225
J3913.90	13910	J3915.22	14510	J3916.20	14925	J3917.20	15230
J3914.00	13955	J3915.24	14515	J3916.22	14915	J3917.22	15235
J3914.01	13965	J3915.26	14520	J3916.24	14920	J3917.24	15240
J3914.06	13975	J3915.28	14525	J3916.26	14930	J3917.30	15255
J3914.07	13985	J3915.32	14535	J3916.28	14935	J3917.32	15260
J3914.12	13980	J3915.34	14545	J3916.29	14940	J3917.34	15265
J3914.14	13995	J3915.36	14550	J3916.30	14945	J3917.36	15270
J3914.16	14000	J3915.38	14595	J3916.32	14950	J3917.38	15275
J3914.18	14005	J3915.40	14605	J3916.34	14955	J3917.40	15280
J3914.24	14065	J3915.42	14615	J3916.35	14960	J3917.41	15285
J3914.28	14100	J3915.44	14620	J3916.36	14965	J3917.43	15300
J3914.29	14115	J3915.46	14625	J3916.38	14970	J3917.44	15305
J3914.32	14120	J3915.48	14630	J3916.47	14990	J3917.46	15310
J3914.34	14130	J3915.50	14635	J3916.50	15000	J3917.48	15320
J3914.36	14140	J3915.52	14650	J3916.52	15005	J3917.52	15400
J3914.37	14145	J3915.53	14655	J3916.54	15010	J3917.58	15425
J3914.38	14150	J3915.54	14670	J3916.56	15015	J3931.00	15900
J3914.41	14185	J3915.56	14680	J3916.58	15020	J3932.00	16610
J3914.42	14190	J3915.57	14685	J3916.60	15025	J3940.00	505
J3914.43	14195	J3915.58	14690	J3916.61	15030	J3945.00	585
J3914.44	14200	J3915.60	14695	J3916.64	15045	J3945.20	580

CROSS REFERENCE - INTERNATIONAL VS. U.S. LIGHT NUMBER

Inter.	U.S.	Inter.	U.S.	Inter.	U.S.	Inter.	U.S.
J3950	17005	J3989.70	21580	J3992.35	21945	J4008.1	22540
J3950.40	16995	J3989.75	21595	J3992.375	21950	J4011	22575
J3951.00	17010	J3989.80	21600	J3992.45	21970	J4013.00	22610
J3954.00	16980	J3989.85	21605	J3992.50	21980	J4017.00	22630
J3954.10	16985	J3989.90	21610	J3992.55	21990	J4019.00	22635
J3966.00	17955	J3989.95	21615	J3992.60	21995	J4020.00	22780
J3967.40	17970	J3990.00	21625	J3992.65	22000	J4022	22785
J3968	17985	J3990.05	21630	J3992.73	22005	J4022.1	22790
J3968.20	17990	J3990.10	21635	J3992.74	22120	J4022.2	22810
J3968.40	17995	J3990.15	21640	J3992.76	22035	J4022.21	22820
J3977.20	18655	J3990.20	21645	J3992.77	22040	J4022.25	22825
J3977.30	18665	J3990.25	21650	J3992.78	22090	J4022.30	22830
J3977.40	18685	J3990.30	21655	J3992.80	22065	J4022.35	22835
J3978.2	18705	J3990.35	21660	J3992.82	22075	J4022.36	22840
J3978.24	18710	J3990.40	21665	J3992.84	22080	J4022.40	22845
J3978.40	18720	J3990.45	21670	J3992.86	22085	J4022.45	22850
J3978.6	18725	J3990.50	21675	J3992.90	22125	J4022.46	22855
J3978.70	18735	J3990.55	21680	J3992.95	22130	J4022.50	22860
J3978.72	18730	J3990.60	21685	J3993.00	22135	J4022.55	22865
J3978.74	18740	J3990.65	21690	J3993.05	22140	J4022.60	22870
J3978.76	18745	J3990.8	21695	J3993.10	22145	J4022.65	22875
J3978.78	18750	J3990.85	21700	J3993.15	22150	J4022.70	22885
J3978.8	18755	J3990.90	21730	J3993.20	22165	J4022.75	22895
J3978.82	18760	J3990.95	21755	J3993.25	22170	J4022.80	22900
J3979.00	18765	J3991.00	21760	J3993.30	22175	J4022.85	22905
J3979.02	18815	J3991.05	21740	J3993.35	22180	J4022.86	22910
J3979.04	18820	J3991.06	21750	J3993.45	22190	J4022.90	22915
J3979.06	18825	J3991.10	21765	J3993.5	22200	J4022.95	22920
J3979.08	18830	J3991.15	21770	J3993.55	22205	J4023.00	22925
J3979.20	18835	J3991.2	21775	J3993.60	22210	J4023.05	22930
J3988	21325	J3991.25	21780	J3993.63	22215	J4023.10	22935
J3988.10	21335	J3991.30	21805	J3993.65	22235	J4023.15	22940
J3988.5	21410	J3991.31	21810	J3993.67	22240	J4023.20	22955
J3988.60	21415	J3991.50	21855	J3993.68	22245	J4023.21	22965
J3989.00	21430	J3991.55	21800	J3993.70	22250	J4023.25	22945
J3989.05	21435	J3991.6	21860	J3993.75	22260	J4023.26	22950
J3989.1	21440	J3991.65	21865	J3993.80	22265	J4023.30	22970
J3989.25	21450	J3991.70	21870	J3993.85	22280	J4023.31	22975
J3989.3	21455	J3991.75	21875	J3993.90	22285	J4023.35	22980
J3989.35	21530	J3991.8	21880	J3993.95	22290	J4023.40	22995
J3989.36	21535	J3991.85	21885	J3994.00	22295	J4023.45	23005
J3989.40	21540	J3991.9	21905	J3996.00	1095	J4023.46	23010
J3989.41	21550	J3991.91	21910	J4000.00	1105	J4023.50	22990
J3989.45	21555	J3992.05	21915	J4002.00	22410	J4023.55	23000
J3989.50	21560	J3992.10	21920	J4002.10	22415	J4023.63	23300
J3989.55	21565	J3992.2	21925	J4006	22475	J4023.65	23305
J3989.60	21570	J3992.25	21935	J4006.1	22480	J4023.70	23315
J3989.65	21575	J3992.30	21940	J4008	22535	J4023.71	23325

CROSS REFERENCE - INTERNATIONAL VS. U.S. LIGHT NUMBER

Inter.	U.S.	Inter.	U.S.	Inter.	U.S.	Inter.	U.S.
J4023.8	23335	J4042.00	23880	J4101.00	26350	J4143.15	25305
J4023.9	23345	J4042.40	23885	J4103.00	24205	J4143.31	25400
J4023.95	23350	J4043.00	23890	J4104.00	24215	J4143.35	25405
J4024	23355	J4045.00	35965	J4104.10	24220	J4143.36	25415
J4024.05	23360	J4046.00	35970	J4114.00	24245	J4143.50	25465
J4024.1	23365	J4047.00	35995	J4116.00	24250	J4143.51	25475
J4024.11	23370	J4047.50	36005	J4117.00	24295	J4143.56	25485
J4024.15	23375	J4048.00	36025	J4118.00	24300	J4143.6	25455
J4024.20	23380	J4050.90	36145	J4121.00	24315	J4143.75	25505
J4024.25	23385	J4051.00	36140	J4122.00	24320	J4143.8	25515
J4024.30	23390	J4051.1	36310	J4124.00	24365	J4143.85	25525
J4024.35	23395	J4051.9	36520	J4126.00	24370	J4143.86	25530
J4024.4	23400	J4052.00	36515	J4129	24385	J4143.90	25535
J4024.45	23410	J4052.1	36590	J4130.00	24390	J4143.91	25540
J4024.50	23415	J4052.30	36615	J4132.00	24395	J4143.95	25545
J4024.55	23420	J4052.60	36645	J4132.10	24400	J4144.00	25550
J4024.70	23425	J4052.61	36650	J4132.40	24430	J4144.20	25695
J4024.75	23430	J4052.80	36820	J4132.41	24440	J4144.25	25700
J4024.76	23435	J4052.81	36825	J4133.00	24525	J4144.3	25715
J4024.8	23440	J4056	26030	J4134.00	24530	J4144.35	25720
J4024.81	23445	J4056.10	26035	J4138.00	24545	J4144.4	25725
J4024.85	23450	J4058	26045	J4139.00	24550	J4144.5	25740
J4024.90	23460	J4058.10	26055	J4141.00	24565	J4144.55	25750
J4025.05	23515	J4060	26095	J4142.00	24575	J4144.6	25755
J4025.10	23520	J4060.10	26105	J4142.05	24585	J4144.65	25760
J4025.2	23530	J4062.00	26110	J4142.06	24590	J4144.75	25775
J4025.25	23535	J4062.10	26115	J4142.10	24605	J4144.9	25790
J4025.3	23540	J4064.00	26140	J4142.11	24610	J4145	25800
J4025.35	23545	J4064.1	26145	J4142.25	24595	J4145.05	25810
J4025.4	23550	J4067	26175	J4142.35	24760	J4145.1	25815
J4025.45	23555	J4067.1	26180	J4142.36	24770	J4145.25	25825
J4025.50	23565	J4069	26170	J4142.40	24775	J4148.00	26355
J4025.55	23570	J4071.00	23905	J4142.41	24780	J4158	24645
J4025.60	23575	J4071.10	23910	J4142.45	25060	J4160	24670
J4025.65	23585	J4072.00	23915	J4142.46	25065	J4165	25845
J4025.80	23595	J4072.10	23920	J4142.50	25070	J4166	25855
J4025.85	23600	J4076.00	23970	J4142.51	25075	J4167	25865
J4025.90	23605	J4076.10	23975	J4142.55	24810	J4168	25905
J4026.2	23610	J4080.00	24055	J4142.65	25230	J4179.00	26940
J4032.00	23725	J4080.10	24060	J4142.66	25235	J4180.00	26965
J4034.00	23720	J4084.00	24025	J4142.70	25240	J4180.10	26975
J4036.00	23690	J4086.00	24040	J4142.71	25245	J4181.1	26980
J4036.10	23695	J4088.00	24070	J4142.85	25280	J4181.2	26985
J4037.00	23740	J4090.00	24075	J4142.9	25285	J4181.30	27005
J4037.10	23745	J4091.00	24090	J4143.00	25320	J4181.31	27010
J4040	23780	J4092.00	24095	J4143.01	25325	J4181.70	27020
J4040.10	23785	J4098.00	24120	J4143.05	25330	J4181.8	27030
J4041.00	23870	J4099.00	24125	J4143.06	25335	J4181.90	27035

CROSS REFERENCE - INTERNATIONAL VS. U.S. LIGHT NUMBER

Inter. - U.S.	Inter. - U.S.	Inter. - U.S.	Inter. - U.S.
J4192.00 27120	J4195.38 27435	J4213.25 28305	J4215.80 28860
J4192.10 27125	J4195.40 27440	J4213.26 28310	J4215.81 28865
J4193.00 27170	J4195.42 27445	J4213.30 28320	J4215.90 28875
J4193.10 27180	J4195.44 27450	J4213.45 28345	J4215.91 28880
J4193.24 27165	J4195.46 27455	J4213.47 28350	J4215.95 28885
J4193.32 27195	J4195.48 27460	J4213.49 28355	J4215.96 28890
J4193.36 27205	J4195.50 27465	J4213.61 28600	J4216.00 28895
J4193.40 27210	J4195.52 27470	J4213.65 28605	J4216.01 28900
J4193.50 27215	J4195.54 27475	J4213.70 28610	J4216.15 28910
J4193.70 27220	J4195.56 27480	J4213.75 28615	J4216.16 28915
J4193.80 27235	J4195.58 27490	J4213.80 28630	J4216.2 28210
J4194.00 27240	J4195.59 27495	J4213.85 28635	J4216.25 28215
J4194.05 27245	J4195.62 27510	J4213.9 28640	J4216.30 28245
J4194.15 27250	J4195.63 27520	J4213.95 28645	J4216.35 28260
J4194.20 27255	J4195.66 27500	J4214.00 28650	J4216.4 28280
J4194.40 27260	J4195.68 27505	J4214.05 28655	J4216.45 28290
J4194.50 27265	J4195.70 27530	J4214.10 28665	J4216.55 39620
J4194.55 27270	J4195.72 27535	J4214.18 28675	J4216.57 39680
J4194.60 27275	J4195.74 27540	J4214.2 28680	J4216.6 28925
J4194.80 27280	J4195.76 27545	J4214.25 28685	J4216.65 28930
J4194.82 27285	J4195.78 27550	J4214.3 28620	J4216.75 28945
J4194.84 27290	J4195.80 27555	J4214.31 28625	J4216.80 28955
J4194.86 27295	J4195.82 27560	J4214.35 28690	J4216.9 28960
J4194.88 27300	J4195.84 27565	J4214.40 28700	J4216.91 28965
J4194.90 27305	J4195.85 27580	J4214.41 28710	J4216.95 28970
J4194.92 27310	J4195.88 27585	J4214.45 28720	J4216.96 28975
J4194.94 27315	J4195.90 27595	J4214.50 28725	J4217 28980
J4194.96 27320	J4195.91 27600	J4214.55 28730	J4217.05 28985
J4194.98 27325	J4195.94 27615	J4214.6 28735	J4217.2 29000
J4195.00 27330	J4195.96 27620	J4214.65 28750	J4217.25 29050
J4195.02 27335	J4196.02 27660	J4214.70 28755	J4217.3 29055
J4195.03 27345	J4196.04 27665	J4214.75 28760	J4217.35 29065
J4195.06 27355	J4196.06 27670	J4214.80 28765	J4217.40 29070
J4195.08 27360	J4196.12 27675	J4214.85 28780	J4217.45 29075
J4195.10 27365	J4196.14 27680	J4214.9 28785	J4217.55 29080
J4195.12 27370	J4196.2 27685	J4215.03 28790	J4217.6 29085
J4195.14 27375	J4196.22 27690	J4215.05 28795	J4217.65 29090
J4195.16 27380	J4196.23 27695	J4215.10 28800	J4217.70 29100
J4195.18 27385	J4196.26 27915	J4215.15 28805	J4217.75 29165
J4195.2 27390	J4196.28 27920	J4215.2 28810	J4217.8 29170
J4195.22 27395	J4196.3 27925	J4215.25 28770	J4217.85 29175
J4195.24 27400	J4196.40 27715	J4215.26 28775	J4224 29300
J4195.26 27405	J4196.44 27765	J4215.3 29250	J4224.20 29305
J4195.28 27410	J4196.50 37905	J4215.35 29260	J4226.50 29465
J4195.30 27415	J4197.00 37910	J4215.55 28835	J4226.51 29470
J4195.32 27420	J4213.00 28145	J4215.56 28840	J4226.55 29550
J4195.34 27425	J4213.1 28150	J4215.75 28850	J4226.56 29560
J4195.36 27430	J4213.20 28205	J4215.76 28855	J4226.60 29565

CROSS REFERENCE - INTERNATIONAL VS. U.S. LIGHT NUMBER

Inter.	-	U.S.
J4226.65	. . . .	29580
J4226.75	. . . .	29600
J4226.80	. . . .	29605
J4226.85	. . . .	29855
J4226.90	. . . .	29860
J4226.91	. . . .	29865
J4226.95	. . . .	29870
J4226.96	. . . .	29875
J4227.00	. . . .	29890
J4227.05	. . . .	29895
J4227.10	. . . .	29900
J4227.11	. . . .	29905
J4227.15	. . . .	29920
J4227.20	. . . .	29925
J4227.21	. . . .	29930
J4227.25	. . . .	29935
J4227.3	. . . .	29940
J4227.35	. . . .	29945
J4227.4	. . . .	29965
J4227.41	. . . .	29970
J4227.45	. . . .	29960
J4227.50	. . . .	29950
J4227.51	. . . .	29955
J4227.55	. . . .	29985
J4227.70	. . . .	30000
J4227.80	. . . .	30005
J4227.90	. . . .	30015
J4227.95	. . . .	30020
J4228	. . . .	30025
J4228.05	. . . .	29990
J4228.06	. . . .	29995
J4228.10	. . . .	29815
J4228.15	. . . .	29825
J4228.2	. . . .	29835
J4228.25	. . . .	29840
J4228.35	. . . .	29850
J4228.40	. . . .	29830
J4228.45	. . . .	42905

U.S. AIDS TO NAVIGATION SYSTEM
on the Western River System

AS SEEN ENTERING FROM SEAWARD

PORT SIDE
OR RIGHT DESCENDING BANK

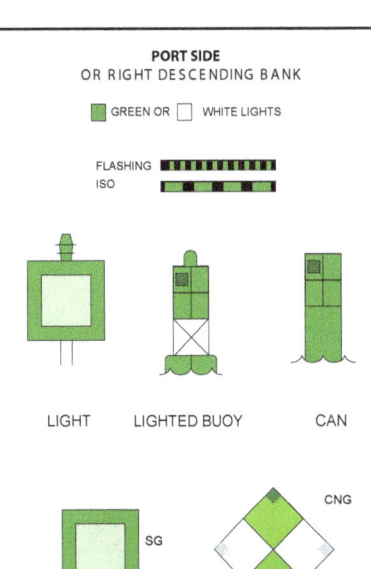

PREFERRED CHANNEL
MARK JUNCTIONS AND OBSTRUCTIONS
COMPOSITE GROUP FLASHING (2+1)

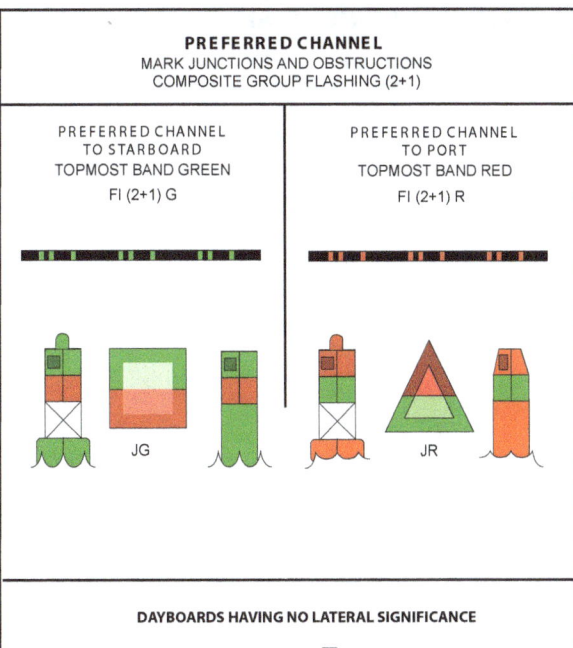

STARBOARD SIDE
OR LEFT DESCENDING BANK

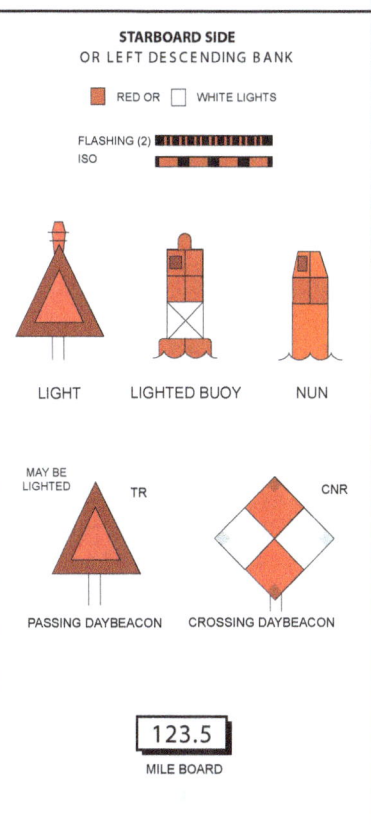

SPECIAL MARKS--MAY BE LETTERED

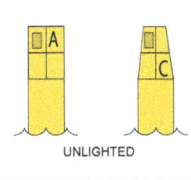  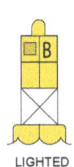

SHAPE: OPTIONAL--BUT SELECTED TO BE APPROPRIATE FOR THE POSITION OF THE MARK IN RELATION TO THE NAVIGABLE WATERWAY AND THE DIRECTION OF BUOYAGE.

MOORING BUOY
WHITE WITH BLUE BAND
MAY SHOW WHITE REFLECTOR OR LIGHT

TYPICAL INFORMATION AND REGULATORY MARKS
INFORMATION AND REGULATORY MARKERS
WHEN LIGHTED, INFORMATION AND REGULATORY MARKS MAY DISPLAY ANY LIGHT RHYTHM EXCEPT QUICK FLASHING, Mo(a) AND FLASHING (2)

NW ☐ WHITE LIGHT ONLY

 BOAT EXCLUSION AREA

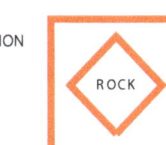 DANGER

 CONTROLLED AREA

EXPLANATION MAY BE PLACED OUTSIDE THE CROSSED DIAMOND SHAPE, SUCH AS DAM, RAPIDS, SWIM AREA, ETC.

THE NATURE OF DANGER MAY BE INDICATED INSIDE THE DIAMOND SHAPE, SUCH AS ROCK, WRECK, SHOAL, DAM, ETC.

TYPE OF CONTROL IS INDICATED IN THE CIRCLE, SUCH AS SLOW, NO WAKE, ANCHORING, ETC.

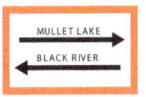 INFORMATION

FOR DISPLAYING INFORMATION SUCH AS DIRECTIONS, DISTANCES, LOCATIONS, ETC.

BUOY USED TO DISPLAY REGULATORY MARKERS

MAY SHOW WHITE LIGHT
MAY BE LETTERED

STATE WATERS

INLAND (STATE) WATERS OBSTRUCTION MARK
MAY SHOW WHITE REFLECTOR OR QUICK FLASHING WHITE LIGHT

BLACK-STRIPED WHITE BUOY

Used to indicate an obstruction to navigation, extends from the nearest shore to the buoy. This means "do not pass between the buoy and the nearest shore." This aid is replacing the red and white striped buoy within the USWMS, but cannot be used until all red and white striped buoys on a waterway have been replaced.

PLATE 4

U.S. AIDS TO NAVIGATION SYSTEM
on navigable waters except Western Rivers

LATERAL SYSTEM AS SEEN ENTERING FROM SEAWARD

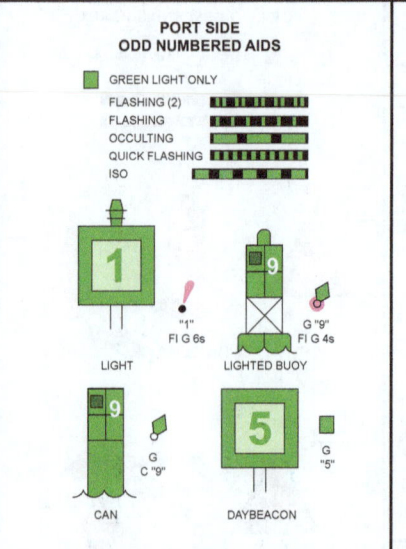
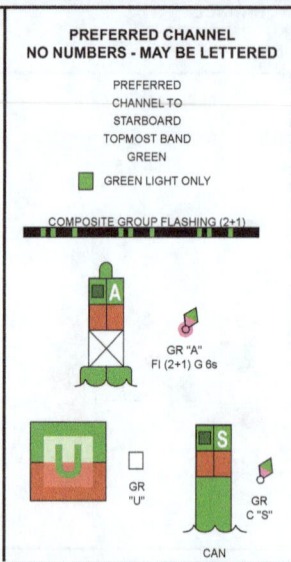
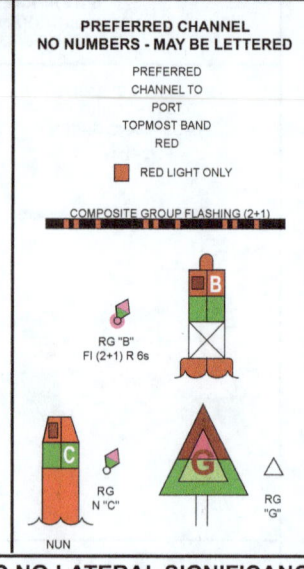
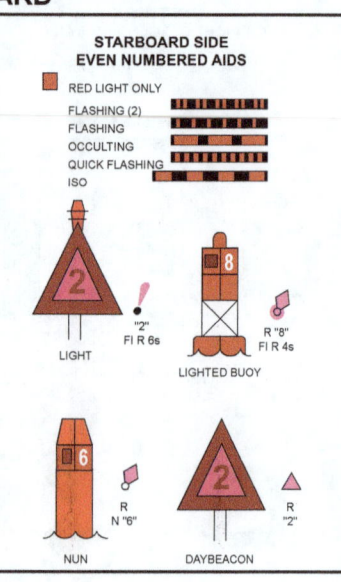

AIDS TO NAVIGATION HAVING NO LATERAL SIGNIFICANCE

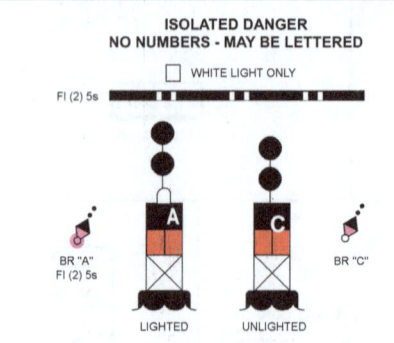

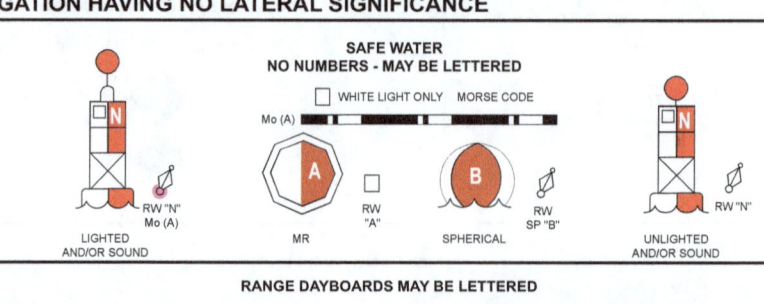
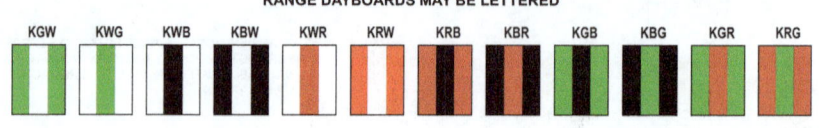
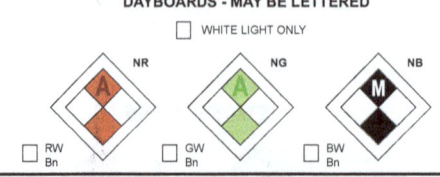
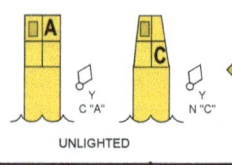

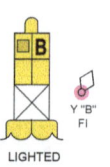
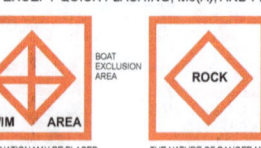

Aids to Navigation marking the Intracoastal Waterway (ICW) display unique yellow symbols to distinguish them from aids marking other waters. Yellow triangles 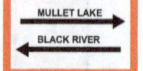 indicate aids should be passed by keeping them on the starboard (right) hand of the vessel. Yellow squares  indicate aids should be passed by keeping them on the port (left) hand of the vessel. A yellow horizontal band provides no lateral information, but simply identifies aids as marking the ICW.

PLATE 1

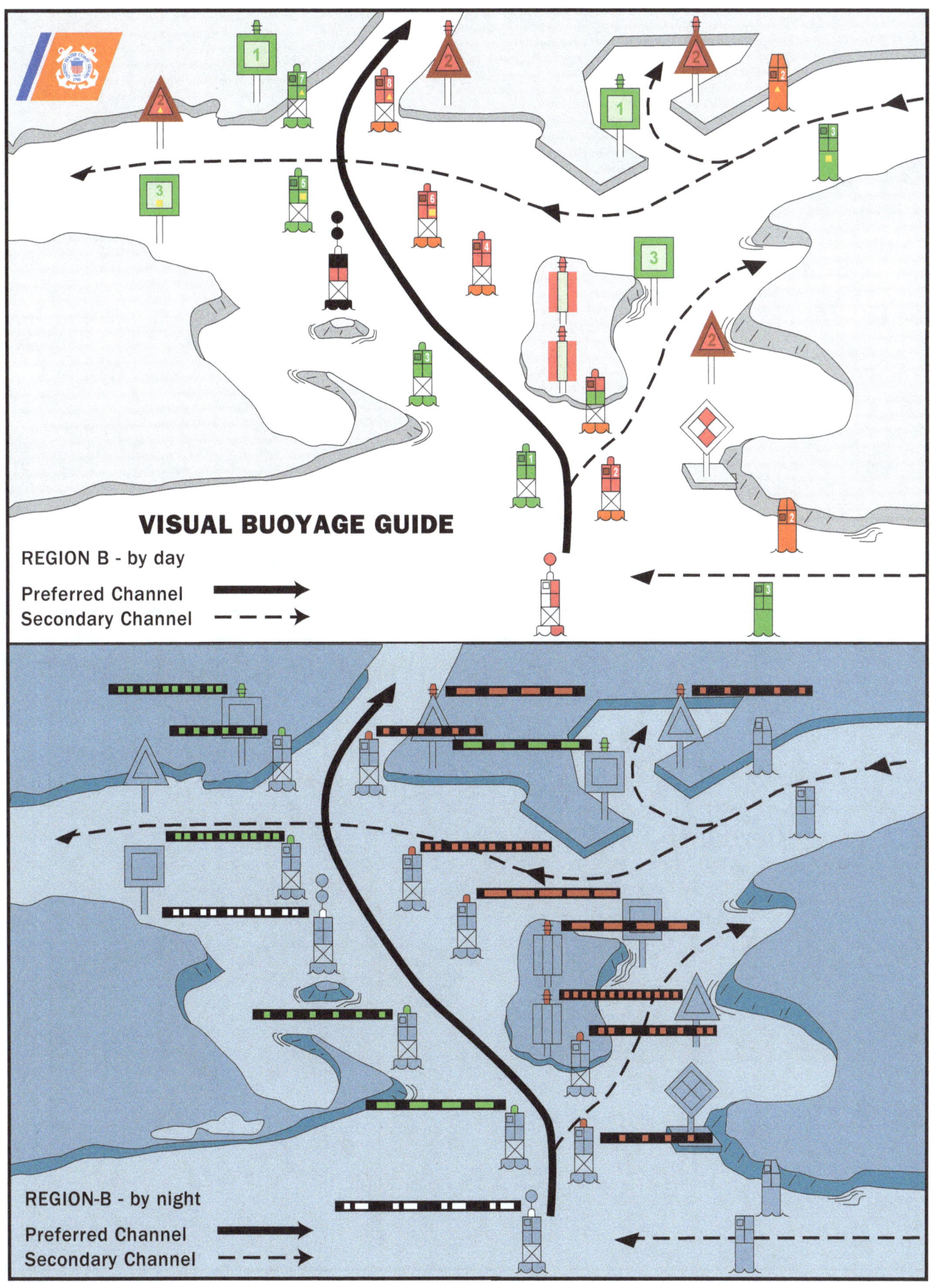

FICTITIOUS NAUTICAL CHART

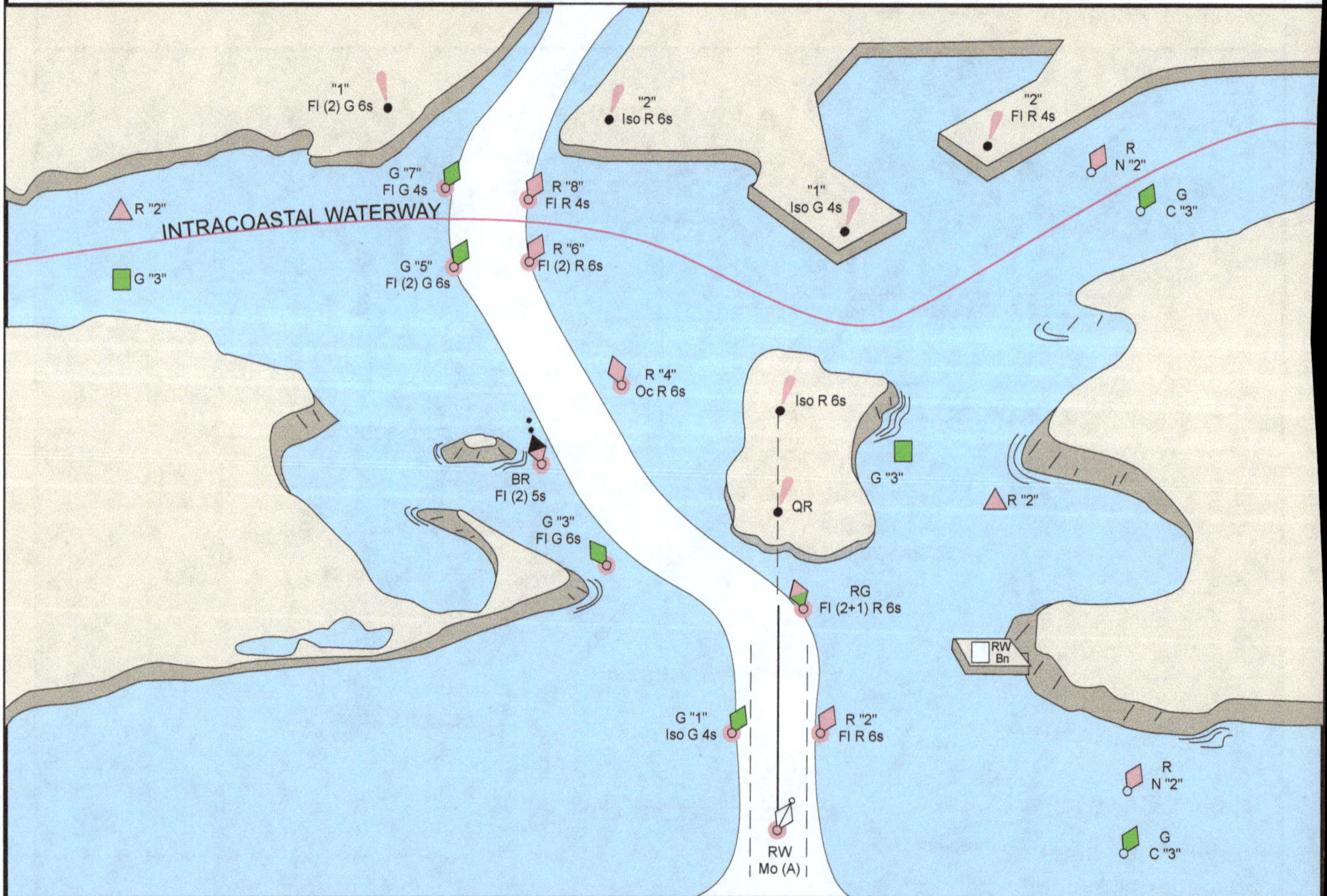

PLATE 3

www.ingramcontent.com/pod-product-compliance
Lightning Source LLC
Chambersburg PA
CBHW060303010526
44108CB00042B/2614